ADVANCED COURSE

ACCOUNTING

SYSTEMS AND PROCEDURES

David H. Weaver, Ph.D.
Vice President, Director of
Editorial Planning and Research
McGraw-Hill Book Company

James M. Smiley, Ph.D.
Professor of Accounting
and Information Sciences
Morehead State University
Morehead, Kentucky

Edward B. Brower, Ed.D.
Professor, Department of Vocational Education,
Business Education
Temple University
Philadelphia, Pennsylvania

Gregg Division
McGraw-Hill Book Company
New York Atlanta Dallas
St. Louis San Francisco
Auckland Bogotá Guatemala
Hamburg Johannesburg
Lisbon London Madrid
Mexico Montreal New Delhi
Panama Paris San Juan
São Paulo Singapore Sydney
Tokyo Toronto

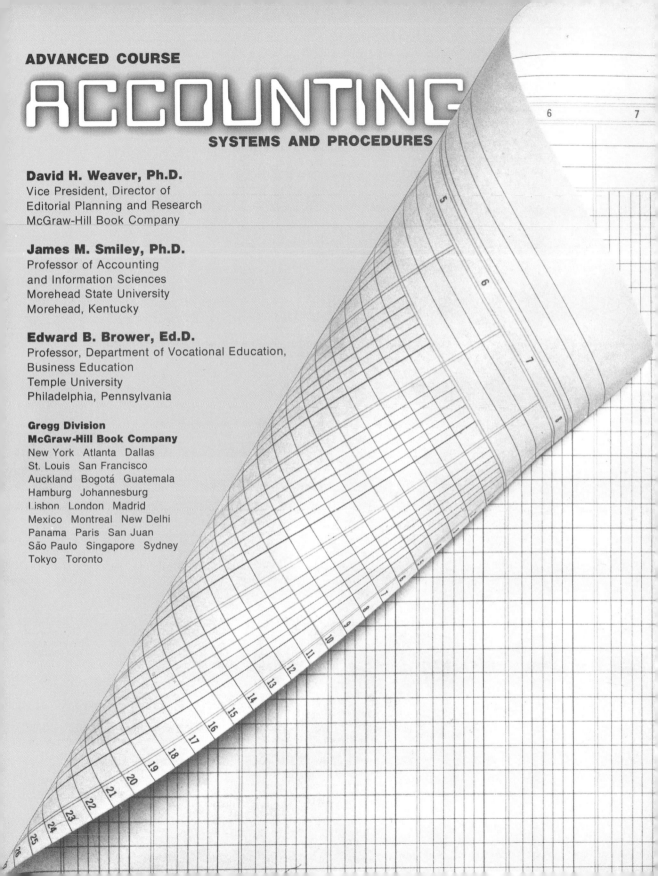

Sponsoring Editors:	Marie Orsini and Susan Schornstein
Editing Supervisor:	Gary Schwartz
Production Supervisor:	Steve Canaris
Design Supervisors:	Karen Tureck and Caryl Spinka
Photo Editor:	Mary Ann Drury
Cover Photographer:	Martin Bough, Corporate Studios Communciations, Inc.

Part Opening Photographs:
(*from left to right*)

Part 1
Courtesy Ford Motor Company
Ken Karp
Courtesy American Management Associations
Part 2
Michael Weisbrot
Courtesy Ron Tanner/Progressive Grocer
Donald Dietz/Stock, Boston

Library of Congress Cataloging in Publication Data

Weaver, David H., date
 Accounting: systems and procedures: advanced course.

 Includes index.
 1. Accounting. I. Brower, Edward B., date
II. Smiley, James M., date   . III. Title.
HF5635.W39   657   81-1217
ISBN 0-07-068931-8   AACR2

  3 4 5 6 7 8 9 0 DODO 8 9 8 7 6 5 4 3

ISBN 0-07-068931-8

Contents

Preface   v

Part 1
Introduction to Managerial Accounting   x

[Project 1, found in Working Papers and Chapter Problems, Part 1]

Chapter 1   Managerial Accounting for Merchandising Businesses   2
TOPIC 1   Elements of Managerial Accounting   3
TOPIC 2   Recording Sales Data by Departments   11
TOPIC 3   Recording Purchases Data by Departments   30
TOPIC 4   Gross Profits by Departments   49

Chapter 2   Summarizing and Analyzing the Results of Operations   57
TOPIC 1   Methods for Allocating Expenses to Departments   57
TOPIC 2   The Income Statement by Departments   72

Chapter 3   Accounting for Multistore Businesses   83
TOPIC 1   The Accounting Systems of Multistore Businesses   83
TOPIC 2   A Computer Application for a Multistore Business   115

Chapter 4   Accounting for Special Types of Sales   130
TOPIC 1   Installment Sales   130
TOPIC 2   COD Sales and Credit Card Sales   150

[Ray's Nursery Accounting Application]*

Chapter 5   Managerial Accounting for Manufacturing Businesses   167
TOPIC 1   The Manufacturing Process   167
TOPIC 2   Acquisition and Control of Materials   173
TOPIC 3   Factory Labor Costs   185
TOPIC 4   Factory Overhead Costs   193

Chapter 6   Process Cost Accounting   211
TOPIC 1   The Flow of Costs   211
TOPIC 2   Equivalent Units of Production   235
TOPIC 3   Cost of Production Reports   245

*Can be used anytime after Chapter 4.

Chapter 7 Job Order Cost Accounting 262
TOPIC 1 The Flow of Costs 262
TOPIC 2 Financial Statements for a Manufacturing Business 278

Chapter 8 The Voucher System 291
TOPIC 1 Understanding the Voucher System 291

Part 2
Introduction to Financial Accounting 310

Chapter 9 Controlling Current Assets 312
TOPIC 1 Accounting for Cash in Bank 312
TOPIC 2 Accounting for Imprest Cash Funds 329
TOPIC 3 Accounting for Marketable Securities 336
TOPIC 4 Accounting for Notes Receivable and Accrued Interest 344
TOPIC 5 Accounting for Accounts Receivable 355
TOPIC 6 Accounting for Merchandise Inventory and Prepaid Expenses 372

**Chapter 10 Accounting for Plant and Equipment,
Intangible Assets, and Natural Resources** 383
TOPIC 1 Cost and Depreciation of Plant and Equipment 383
TOPIC 2 Disposing of Plant and Equipment 394
TOPIC 3 Accounting for Intangible Assets and Natural Resources 405

Chapter 11 Accounting for Liabilities 413
TOPIC 1 The Nature of Liabilities 413
TOPIC 2 Accounting for Accounts Payable 416
TOPIC 3 Accounting for Accrued and Deferred Liabilities 421
TOPIC 4 Accounting for Long-Term Liabilities 430
TOPIC 5 General Accounting Subsystem for Single Proprietorship 444

Chapter 12 Accounting for Partnerships 461
TOPIC 1 The Partnership 461
TOPIC 2 Partnerships and the General Accounting Subsystem 469
TOPIC 3 Special Accounting Procedures 476

Chapter 13 Accounting for Corporations 483
TOPIC 1 The Corporation 483
TOPIC 2 Corporations and the General Accounting Subsystem 502

[Project 2, found in Working Papers and Chapter Problems, Part 2]

Chapter 14 Interpreting Financial Information 515
TOPIC 1 Comparison and Trend Analysis 515
TOPIC 2 Ratios That Measure Current Position 532
TOPIC 3 Ratios of Equity Position and Operating Results 544
TOPIC 4 Interpreting Changes in Financial Position 551
TOPIC 5 Interpreting Changes in Cash Flow 570

Index 587

Preface

Accounting: Systems and Procedures, Advanced Course, is an exciting new instructional program for the advanced accounting curriculum. This advanced course, while incorporating the equation and systems approach so successfully established in the first-year program, *Accounting: Systems and Procedures*, Fourth Edition, focuses on the important internal and external uses of accounting data. To accentuate this focus, the course is divided into two parts: *Managerial Accounting*, which covers internal uses and *Financial Accounting*, which emphasizes external uses.

To make the course responsive to current business practices, special efforts are made to integrate computer applications with the basic procedures of manual accounting systems.

Managerial Accounting and Financial Accounting

Managerial Accounting emphasizes the internal uses of accounting data by managers and others involved in making day-to-day business decisions and in controlling revenue, costs, and expenses. Topics discussed in managerial accounting include departmental accounting, accounting for multistore businesses, and accounting for manufacturing businesses.

Financial Accounting, on the other hand, is concerned with the organization and control of financial resources and the analysis of accounting data by management and external groups, such as stockholders, creditors, government agencies, unions, and the general public. Topics discussed in financial accounting include controlling financial resources, accounting for partnerships and corporations, and interpreting financial information.

Course Objectives

Accounting: Systems and Procedures, Advanced Course, has been developed to follow the first-year course in accounting. Preferably, the course should be taught as a capstone experience prior to the time the students enter the job market or continue their education at a postsecondary institution.

The instructional materials have been designed to enable students to have an opportunity to accomplish the following objectives.

• *Understanding both basic and advanced accounting concepts and principles that provide the theoretical basis for all accounting systems.* For instance, the student learns in the first year to record accounts payable using the gross amount method. The advanced course reviews the gross amount method and presents the net amount method. Then the two methods are compared. Likewise, the advanced course presents and compares alternative methods for computing the cost of merchandise. Thus, the student gains additional insight into the basic concepts and procedures, and also gains depth as a result of studying these advanced concepts and procedures.

• *Understanding work flow and the necessity for financial controls in a modern business.*

• *Analyzing accounting data for management's use.* For example, students learn that incurring liabilities may be viewed as a sound business practice when "trading on the equity." Similarly students learn that excess cash is "idle" and should be invested.

• *Using accounting data in making management decisions and developing the sound reasoning ability needed to formulate business decisions at various levels.* Decision making is emphasized throughout the course. Students are introduced to the types of decisions managers must make, such as developing a cash management plan, choosing a method for computing depreciation, or selecting ratios for interpreting financial information.

• *Expanding knowledge of business data processing procedures and practices and relating this knowledge to realistic business applications.*

• *Acquiring the capability to handle the accounting activities of a typical small, medium-sized, or large business office.*

• *Increasing vocational competency.* This contributes not only to success in initial entry-level jobs, but also to advancement in careers in accounting, computing, or related office occupations. Students gain a greater awareness of the environment in which accounting information is processed and, as a result, they gain a better understanding of each employee's role.

• *Understanding economic events in the business climate.*

• *Providing additional background for future study in accounting or accounting-related fields.* The analysis and decision-making approach used in *Accounting: Systems and Procedures, Advanced Course,* allows college-oriented students to sample accounting work—one meaningful input in making their career choices. Accurate career impressions are essential to good career planning.

• *Developing good work habits and business competencies and increasing the student's business vocabulary.*

Features of the Advanced Course

The same features that make the first-year program, *Accounting: Systems and Procedures*, Fourth Edition, such a dynamic teaching/learning program are included in the advanced course. Based on the premise that students need assistance in learning how to learn, a variety of instructional devices have been incorporated in the textbook to assist the students in learning accounting and to guide them in the development of good study habits.

Writing Style. The same writing style is used in the textbook to make it easy to read and to make the concepts and principles easy to understand. Illustrations, flowcharts, marginal notes, management cases, and the use of color—all known to be so effective—are continued in the advanced program. These items enhance the learning situation and provide the instructor with outstanding instructional materials.

Accounting Concepts and Principles. Basic accounting concepts and generally accepted accounting principles (GAAP) are identified and highlighted in the text. This helps students broaden their understanding of accounting and focuses their attention on essentials. The concepts and principles highlighted in this textbook include those endorsed by the Financial Accounting Standards Board (FASB) of the American Institute of Certified Public Accountants (AICPA).

Learning Units. Each topic in the textbook is divided into two or more learning units, consisting of a short reading section and followed by one or more reinforcement activities. The beginning of each learning unit is indicated by a lettered symbol, such as those shown in the margin. The end of the learning unit is indicated by an activity lettered to correspond to the learning unit symbol. Thus learning unit *A* will end with *Activity A* or *Activity A-1* and *A-2* if more than one activity is included. The activities often require responses about the accounting records discussed and illustrated in the learning unit. This type of application forces students to examine the illustrations carefully and thus make full use of them as a learning device.

The activities provide a good method of assessing student comprehension of a new concept or a new procedure immediately after it has been presented. If the students are having difficulty, the material can be retaught immediately.

Readability. Readability is enhanced by limiting concept density. Dividing each topic into small learning units enables the students to learn new concepts and procedures one at a time. In addition, the design of the textbook contains a new wide-open look with many relevant photographs.

Marginal Notes. Marginal notes identify key ideas, rules, and formulas. The brevity of the marginal notes aids students in learning these important aspects of accounting.

Marginal Illustrations. Numerous marginal illustrations serve a multitude of purposes. Two purposes are to provide references to illustrations previously presented and to highlight parts of larger illustrations.

Topic Problems. At the end of each topic, there is a section containing comprehensive problems relating to that topic. This section gives the student an opportunity to apply the material that has been presented in all the activities that make up the topic just studied.

The Language of Business. A vocabulary section is provided at the end of each chapter to help increase the student's grasp of modern business terminology.

Chapter Questions. This section, located at the end of each chapter, contains questions pertaining to the entire chapter. These questions help the students check their understanding of the content of the chapter just studied.

Chapter Problems. Additional problems for each chapter are provided in the workbooks. These problems cover the content of all the topics in a chapter.

Management Cases. Management cases are provided at the end of each chapter to give the students the opportunity to use their knowledge in making business decisions. Rarely is there just one correct solution to a business problem—there can be a variety of answers to the management cases. The solution is often a matter of how the student personally interprets the facts given.

Projects. Two projects have been included in the workbooks. One project is provided for each part. The projects are longer than topic and chapter problems but shorter than the accounting application (practice set). The projects enable students to integrate and apply the principles and concepts they have learned in that part of the course.

Performance Goals. Performance goals for each topic of each chapter are provided in the teacher's source book. Each performance goal is directed to the student to give a clear understanding of what should be accomplished in that topic.

The performance goals aid both the teacher and the student in evaluating the student's mastery of the subject matter throughout the course.

Correlated Materials

In addition to the many special features of the textbook, the advanced program provides an array of correlated materials that enhance the teaching and learning system. Most pertinent are the two workbooks, the accounting application (practice set), a teacher's facsimile of the workbooks, and a teacher's source book.

Working Papers and Chapter Problems. Workbooks correlated with each part of the textbook are available. Each workbook contains reading comprehension activities for every reading section, working papers for the activities and topic problems in the textbook, and chapter problems. *Working Papers and Chapter Problems, Part 1*, correlates with *Managerial Accounting;* and *Working Papers and Chapter Problems, Part 2*, accompanies *Financial Accounting.*

Teacher's Edition of Working Papers and Chapter Problems. The two teacher's editions of the workbooks are identical to the students' editions except that they contain solutions printed in bright red, which is easily distinguished from the student material. Each facsimile key is three-hole punched and bound with a soft cover. The pages are designed for easy separation from the cover so that the material may be placed in a binder or removed for making transparencies.

Source Book and Tests. The *Source Book and Tests* contains performance goals, teaching suggestions with a time schedule, transparency masters, solutions to the management cases and chapter questions, check figures, progress and comprehensive tests, and a test key.

Two types of prepared tests are provided in the sourcebook: chapter progress tests and comprehensive tests. Each progress test is correlated with the performance goals of a chapter. This test enables the teacher to decide how well the students have achieved the goals of that chapter. The comprehensive tests, on the other hand, are broader in scope and cover several chapters.

Accounting Application. Ray's Nursery accounting application (practice set) has been designed to correlate with Part 1 of the advanced program. Ray's Nursery was prepared with the help of Scott Peterson, Teacher of Business Education, Columbia Heights, Minnesota and Dr. Ralph Ruby, Jr., Associate Professor and Coordinator of Vocational Business Education, Arkansas State University, Jonesboro, Arkansas.

> **David H. Weaver**
> **James M. Smiley**
> **Edward B. Brower**

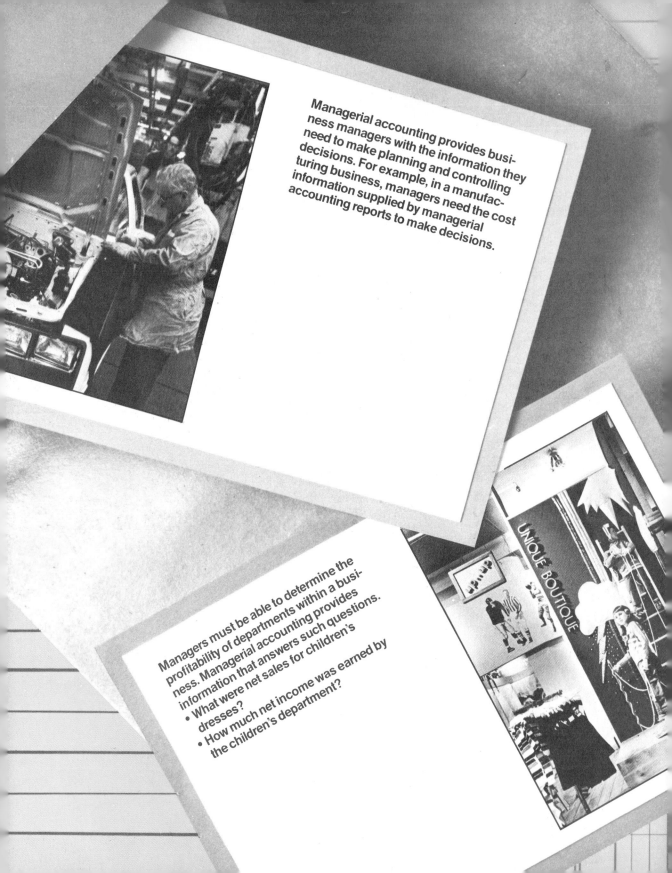

Managerial accounting provides business managers with the information they need to make planning and controlling decisions. For example, in a manufacturing business, managers need the cost information supplied by managerial accounting reports to make decisions.

Managers must be able to determine the profitability of departments within a business. Managerial accounting provides information that answers such questions.

- What were net sales for children's dresses?
- How much net income was earned by the children's department?

UNIQUE BOUTIQUE

Part 1

Introduction to Managerial Accounting

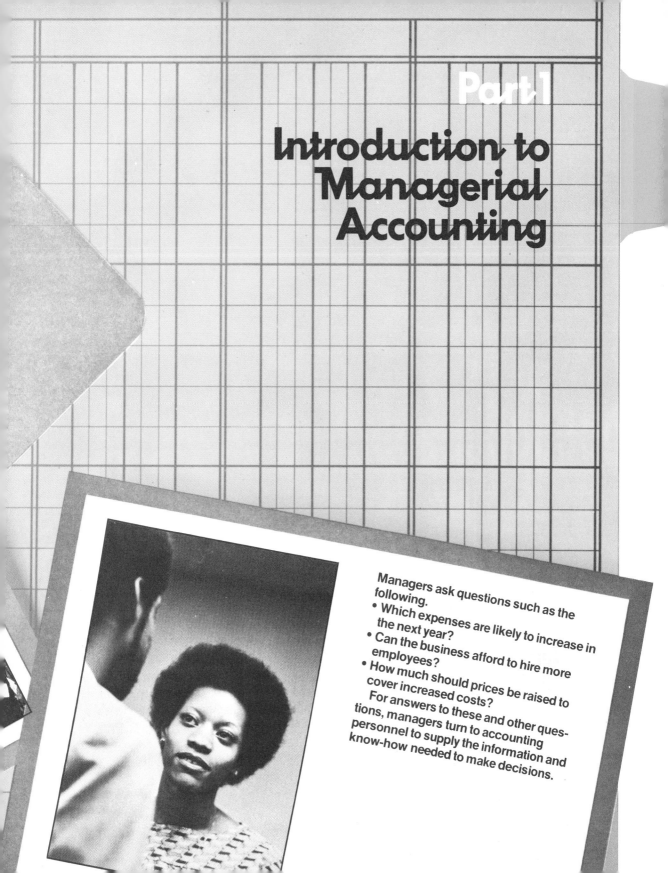

Managers ask questions such as the following.
- Which expenses are likely to increase in the next year?
- Can the business afford to hire more employees?
- How much should prices be raised to cover increased costs?

For answers to these and other questions, managers turn to accounting personnel to supply the information and know-how needed to make decisions.

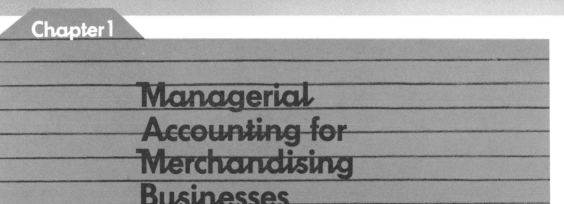

Managerial Accounting for Merchandising Businesses

Managerial accounting is helpful to a merchandising business. It provides detailed information about the business's operations. Management needs this kind of information in order to make wise decisions.

If you are using the *Working Papers and Chapter Problems*, you just completed Project 1. In the project, you processed financial data for a retail merchandising business. This firm sells four types of products: stereo equipment, tape recorders, transistor radios, and CB radios. At the end of the accounting period, you summarized the data and reported it in financial statements. These statements provide valuable information about the profitability and financial position of the business. However, they do not show many details about the operations of the business.

Think how much better the owner of this business could make decisions and manage his operations if he had more detailed information. For example, he should know the amount of sales, purchases, and merchandise inventory for each type of product. He should also know how much of the net income was earned by each type of product. Managerial accounting provides this kind of information.

We will discuss managerial accounting for merchandising businesses in this chapter and the next three chapters. Later chapters will deal with managerial accounting for manufacturing businesses. You will learn how accounting systems are set up to record managerial accounting data for both types of businesses. You will also become familiar with the major types of managerial accounting reports and

BEAUTIFUL SOUNDS
Income Statement
For the Month Ended
December 31, 19—

Revenue From Sales:		
Sales	30,708	25

The income statement shows the total amount of sales but not how much came from each type of product. The managerial accounting report provides this.

see how the information in these reports is used to make business decisions.

Although we will stress managerial accounting for merchandising businesses and manufacturing businesses, much of the material also applies to service businesses. For example, some service businesses offer several different types of services. The management of such businesses should have information about the amount of sales, expenses, and net income for each type of service. Keep in mind that managerial accounting can be helpful in all kinds of businesses.

BEAUTIFUL SOUNDS
Summary of Sales
by Type of Product
For the Month Ended
December 31, 19—

Stereo Equipment	*$14,680.25*
Tape Recorders	*3,200.00*
Transistor Radios	*4,407.90*
CB Radios	*8,420.10*
Total	*$30,708.25*

Topic 1
Elements of Managerial Accounting

A *What is one of the major functions of managerial accounting?* As you have already learned, one of the major functions of financial accounting is organizing and controlling the financial resources of a business. The financial resources are shown by the assets, liabilities, and owner's equity, which are reported on the balance sheet. On the other hand, managerial accounting deals mainly with revenues, cost of goods sold, and expenses, which are reported on the income statement.

From your previous accounting studies, you know that **revenues** are amounts received from the sale of merchandise or services. These amounts can be in the form of cash, accounts receivable, or other assets. Revenues increase owner's equity. The **cost of goods sold** is the total spent for the merchandise sold during an accounting period. The amounts paid for the merchandise sold decrease owner's equity. **Expenses** are amounts spent for the goods and services needed to operate a business. These amounts also decrease owner's equity. Revenues, cost of goods sold, and expenses are the three main elements of managerial accounting. These elements determine whether a business has a net income or a net loss from its operations.

Three Elements of Managerial Accounting:
• Revenues
• Cost of goods sold
• Expenses

Reporting Revenues, Cost of Goods Sold, and Expenses

A business's accounting system must be set up in such a way that it can meet the needs of managerial accounting. The system must therefore be able to report detailed information about revenues, cost of goods sold, and expenses. This is usually done by dividing the business into a number of sales departments. The accounting records show revenues, cost of goods sold, and expenses for each sales department as well as for the whole business.

Each department sells one type of merchandise or several similar types of merchandise. For example, the business presented in Project 1 could be divided into four sales departments—a department for stereo equipment, a department for tape recorders, a department for transistor radios, and a department for CB radios. (The organization of merchandising businesses is discussed later in this topic.)

An accounting system that gathers and records data for a number of departments as well as for the whole business is called a **managerial accounting system** or a **departmentalized accounting system.** A major advantage of this type of accounting system is that it can provide detailed information about a business's operations. This information is presented in a wide variety of reports.

Managerial Accounting Systems:
Gather and record data for both departments and the entire business.

Objectives of Managerial Accounting

Managerial accounting has a number of major objectives.
- To find the gross profit on sales for each sales department.
- To find the net income for each sales department.
- To help management reduce the cost of goods for the departments or keep the cost of goods within budgeted amounts.
- To help management reduce expenses for the department or keep the expenses within budgeted amounts.
- To help management make business decisions.
- To help management plan more efficient operations.

The information needed to carry out these objectives comes from a number of different sources. The gross profit on sales and the net income for each sales department are shown on the *income statement by departments.* (Remember that gross profit on sales is found by subtracting the cost of goods sold from the net sales. Net income is found by subtracting the total operating expenses from the gross profit on sales.) A budget by departments shows the estimated cost of goods and expenses for each department. Reports comparing budgeted amounts for the departments with actual cost of goods sold and expenses are usually prepared at regular intervals.

Other types of managerial accounting reports are a sales summary by departments, a purchases summary by departments, and an inventory report by departments. All these reports help management plan and control operations and make decisions. However, keep in mind that the income statement by departments is the most important managerial accounting report produced in a departmentalized business.

Managerial Accounting Reports

Examples
Income statement by departments
Budget by departments
Report comparing budgeted and actual amounts for departments
Sales summary by departments
Purchases summary by departments
Inventory report by departments

Organization of Merchandising Businesses

Merchandising businesses are organized in a number of different ways. A small merchandising business will usually be organized sim-

Courtesy Gino's Inc.

One type of retail business is the large chain store owned by a single company such as Sears, Roebuck; J. C. Penney; Montgomery Ward; and K Mart. Another type is a franchise chain store in which many of the stores have different owners but use the same name and sell the same products, such as Kentucky Fried Chicken and McDonalds.

ply. It often consists of one store that is divided into just a few departments. A large merchandising business will usually have a much more complex organization. It may consist of a chain of stores, or it may be a main store with one or more branches. Each of these stores may be divided into several departments.

Ownership. In some chains of stores, all the stores are owned by a single company. Examples of such chains are Woolworth's, A&P Food Stores, and Safeway Supermarkets. Other chains are *franchise* operations. Each franchise store in a chain uses the same name and sells the same products but has a different owner. Fast-food restaurants that serve hamburgers, fried chicken, pizzas, or steaks are the most common type of franchise operations. Other examples of franchise operations are ice cream stores, auto supply stores, paint stores, and motels.

Units of Operation. To obtain detailed information, a business must be divided into units of operation. A **unit of operation** is the smallest part of the business for which costs are recorded separately. For this reason, a unit of operation is often called a **cost center.**

A unit of operation may be a department in a store. It may also be one store in a chain of stores. Or it may be a branch of a downtown store that is located in a nearby shopping center. Having units of operation allows the business to determine how much net income is being earned by each part of its organization. The unit of operation discussed in Chapters 1 and 2 is the department within a store. The chain store and the branch store are discussed in Chapter 3.

Types of Departments. The departments within a store are usually classified as sales departments or supportive departments. A **sales department** is directly involved in selling merchandise or a service. A small merchandising business may set up a separate sales department for each type of product that it carries. For example, look at the floor plan shown here. This small retail sporting goods store sells three types of products: bicycles, golf equipment, and tennis equipment. The selling area of the store is therefore divided into three sales departments.

A larger merchandising business would probably have a single sporting goods department that would sell all three types of products and similar products. Other departments that a large merchandising business might have are an appliance department, a furniture department, a shoe department, and a children's clothing department.

A **supportive department** is not directly linked to selling merchandise or services to customers. The employees in a supportive department provide a service to the sales departments. These people perform such tasks as recording transactions, preparing payrolls, processing purchases of merchandise, and paying bills.

Examples of supportive departments in a large merchandising business are a finance or accounting department, a purchases department, an inventory department, and a personnel department. In a small merchandising business, supportive departments are usually limited to an administrative office and a stockroom. (See the floor plan of the small sporting goods store shown above.) The administrative office handles accounting activities, purchasing activities, and the hiring of new employees. The stockroom handles inventory control.

Advantages of Organization by Departments. There are several advantages to organizing by departments. Similar items of merchandise are placed in each sales department. This makes it easy for customers and salesclerks to locate needed merchandise. Management is able to obtain information about the results of operations in each sales department. For example, management can get the answers to the following types of questions. Which departments had a net income, and which departments had a net loss? What percentage of total store sales was made by each department? What percentage of expenses was incurred by each department? What percentage of total net income was earned by each department?

Floor plan of a store that is divided into departments.

Departments in a Small Business

Examples

Sales Departments:
  Bicycles
  Golf Equipment
  Tennis Equipment

Supportive Departments:
  Administrative Office
  Stockroom

Advantages of Organizing by Departments:
- Similar items of merchandise can be located in one place.
- Detailed information can be obtained about operations.
- Responsibility can be placed on the department manager.

A large merchandising business usually has department managers. Each manager is responsible for the performance of a department. If a department operates at a loss, its manager may be replaced by a new manager.

Activity A. Using a table similar to the one here, list the sales departments that you would expect to find in each of the following types of merchandising businesses.

Type of Business		Sales Departments
EXAMPLE:	*Shoe store*	Children's Shoes
		Men's Shoes
		Women's Shoes
		Miscellaneous (socks, shoe polish, and so on)

1. Grocery store   **3.** Electrical appliance store   **5.** Bookstore

2. Drugstore   **4.** Jewelry store   **6.** Furniture store

Managerial Accounting System

B *How does a managerial accounting system operate?* As you have learned, a managerial accounting system gathers and records data for departments as well as for the whole business. Like the accounting systems that you studied previously, a managerial accounting system is made up of four components. These components are the forms, equipment, procedures, and people needed to process data through the accounting cycle. However, the operations of a managerial accounting system are different from the operations of other accounting systems in several ways.

• The chart of accounts includes separate accounts for the sales, purchases, and merchandise inventory of each department.

• Forms such as source documents and journals are designed for recording data by departments.

• A wide variety of managerial accounting reports are produced. These reports are prepared in addition to the four basic financial statements—the income statement, the schedule of cost of goods sold, the balance sheet, and the statement of owner's equity.

Departmental accounts are the basis for a managerial accounting system. These accounts enable the system to produce detailed information about each unit of operation in the business.

In the next two topics of Chapter 1 and in Chapter 2, you will see how a managerial accounting system operates in a retail merchandising business, Olympic Sporting Goods. Olympic specializes in sports

Characteristics of Managerial Accounting Systems:
• Separate accounts for the sales, purchases, and inventory of each department.
• Forms designed to record data by departments.
• A wide variety of reports in addition to basic financial statements.

equipment. It is located in a large shopping center. Its evening hours are highly profitable since many customers shop there after work. A managerial accounting system was set up for this store because the owner, Ann Olson, and the store manager, Jim Costa, decided that they

OLYMPIC SPORTING GOODS
Income Statement
For the Month Ended April 30, 19—

Revenue From Sales:			
Sales	16,720 00		
Less: Sales Returns and Allowances	320 00		
Net Sales		16,400 00	
Cost of Goods Sold (*see schedule*)		8,000 00	
Gross Profit on Sales		8,400 00	
Operating Expenses:			
Advertising Expense	195 00		
Uncollectible Accounts Expense	50 00		
Cash Short and Over	7 00		
Delivery Expense	63 00		
Depreciation Expense—Equipment	125 00		
Insurance Expense	35 00		
Payroll Taxes Expense	456 00		
Rent Expense	650 00		
Salaries Expense	4,680 00		
Supplies Expense	60 00		
Utilities Expense	79 00		
Total Operating Expenses		6,400 00	
Net Income		2,000 00	

OLYMPIC SPORTING GOODS
Schedule of Cost of Goods Sold
For the Month Ended April 30, 19—

Merchandise Inventory, April 1		12,500 00	
Purchases	8,250 00		
Add: Transportation In	200 00		
Cost of Delivered Goods	8,450 00		
Less: Purchases Returns and Allowances . . $450.00			
Purchases Discount 120.00	570 00		
Net Purchases		7,880 00	
Cost of Goods Available for Sale		20,380 00	
Less: Merchandise Inventory, April 30		12,380 00	
Cost of Goods Sold		8,000 00	

were not getting all the information they needed to make intelligent business decisions. For example, look at the income statement and the schedule of cost of goods sold shown on page 8.

These statements list only the amounts for the whole business. They do not give any information about the sales, cost of goods sold, and expenses for each sales department. They also do not show the expenses involved in running the office. The owner and the manager of Olympic Sporting Goods want to have detailed information about each department from now on. They hired George Kline, a certified public accountant, to set up Olympic's accounting system, help the accounting clerk prepare reports, and give financial advice. He visits Olympic once a month to do these tasks.

When a managerial accounting system is set up, management must decide what types of reports it needs. For example, the owner and the manager of Olympic Sporting Goods will receive an income statement by departments at the end of each month. In addition, they want information about the sales of each department on a week-by-week basis. A weekly summary of sales for each department, like the one shown here, will therefore be prepared. This report will show the amount of sales made by each salesclerk as well as the total sales for the department. It will also provide a comparison of the sales of the current week and the previous week. The types of managerial accounting reports that are produced vary from business to business, according to the needs of management.

BICYCLES DEPARTMENT
Sales Summary
For the Week Ended
May 13, 19—

	Current Week	Previous Week
Mark Lopez. .	$ 390	$ 420
Joel McKay . .	250	210
Lois Myers . .	410	650
Total	$1,050	$1,280

Accounting Concept:
Departmental Accounts. Accounts are maintained by departments in order to provide information about each unit of operation.

Olympic Sporting Goods is a retail store that specializes in bicycles, golf equipment, and tennis equipment.

Activity B-1. Answer the following questions. Refer to the income statement and schedule of cost of goods sold shown on page 8.

1. What is the total of the operating expenses for the month of April?

2. What is the amount of the net purchases of merchandise for the month?

3. How much is paid for salaries during April?

4. What is the gross profit on sales for the month?

5. What is the advertising expense for April?

6. What is the cost of goods sold during the month?

Kip Peticolas / Fundamental Photographs

7. What is the net income?

8. Does the income statement show the gross profit on sales for each department in the store?

Activity B-2. Answer the following questions. Refer to the sales summary for the bicycles department shown on page 9.

1. What is the total amount of sales for the week ended May 13?

2. Do the department's sales increase or decrease from the previous week?

3. What is the total amount of sales for the department during the previous week?

4. Which salesclerk has the highest sales during the week ended May 13? What is the amount?

5. Which salesclerk has the lowest sales during that week? What is the amount?

6. Why do you think that management wants the sales summary to show information for both the current week and the previous week?

7. Why do you think that management wants to know the amount of sales made by each salesclerk?

8. If several sales summaries show that the sales of a department are dropping from week to week, what actions might management take to increase sales?

Topic 1   Problems

1-1. Select a supermarket, clothing store, sporting goods store, or other retail merchandising business that you have visited recently. Give the following information about the operations of the store you choose.

a. What is the method of serving customers? self-service? salesclerks provided to assist customers? a combination of both methods of serving customers?

b. What types of sales does the business have? cash sales? charge account sales? sales made with credit cards such as MasterCard and VISA? all three types of sales?

c. What types of source documents does the business use for its sales? cash register tapes for all sales? sales slips for all sales? cash register tapes for cash sales and sales slips for charge account and credit card sales?

d. Who receives the cash? a salesclerk? a cashier?

e. Where are cash receipts placed? in one cash register? in several cash registers? in a cash drawer in the counter? in a cash drawer in a forms register?

f. If there are several cash registers in the store, where are they located? in each department? in a central location?

g. Who do you think handles inventory activities in the store? (In a small store, these activities are usually handled by salesclerks. Large stores often have inventory clerks or stock clerks.)

h. Do you think that the store has efficient procedures for making sales? receiving cash? keeping needed merchandise on hand and placing it in easy-to-find locations? If not, what are the problems?

i. If there are problems with any of the store's procedures, what improvements would you suggest to the store's management?

1-2. Answer the following questions.

a. Why do you think that many merchandising businesses try to avoid keeping large inventories?

b. How would you explain the difference in the location of cash registers in a supermarket and in a large department store?

c. How would you explain why a department store might place expensive cameras in a locked counter but keep shirts on open shelves?

Topic 2
Recording Sales Data by Departments

A *Why must sales data be recorded for each sales department?* Sales data must be recorded for each sales department so that management can find out how much merchandise was sold by each department. This data is needed in order to determine the net income for each department. In this topic, we will discuss the procedures for originating, journalizing, and posting sales data by departments.

Processing Sales Data

Let's begin by reviewing the basic equipment, forms, and procedures involved in processing sales data and the controls needed to make sure that this data is handled properly. You will then learn how the equipment, forms, and procedures are used to record sales data by departments.

Equipment. Most retail merchandising businesses use cash registers to record data about cash sales. Cash registers may be mechanical devices or electronic devices. The newer electronic cash registers are sometimes connected to a computer located in another part of the business or in a data processing service center. These electronic cash registers are actually data terminals for a computer system. They allow the business to process sales data quickly and efficiently.

Some electronic cash registers also have a special optical scanner attached to them. Optical scanners simplify the recording of sales because they can read bar-coded data on merchandise tags or packages. The bar-coded data enables the cash register to record the price of each item automatically.

Two other types of equipment sometimes used in recording retail sales are forms registers and imprinting devices. Forms registers are metal devices that hold prenumbered sales slip forms. As the sales slips are written and given to customers, duplicate copies remain locked in the register. Some forms registers have cash drawers and are used instead of cash registers.

Cash
Sale

↓

Record on
Cash register

↓

Audit
Tape

↓

Prove audit
tape and
cash receipts

↓

Cash Proof

↓

Journalize

↓

Cash
Receipts
Journal

↓

Post

↓

General
Ledger

PROCESSING CASH
SALES IN RETAIL
BUSINESSES

Retail businesses may issue their own credit cards to charge account customers, or they may accept bank credit cards such as MasterCard and VISA. These businesses use imprinting devices to transfer data from the credit cards to sales slips.

Forms and Procedures. The forms and procedures used in recording sales vary from business to business. As we have just discussed, most retail merchandising businesses use a cash register to record cash sales. The register produces a printed receipt for the customer and also enters the data on a detailed audit tape locked inside the machine. At regular intervals, usually every day or every week, the audit tape is removed from the cash register and a cash proof is prepared. The cash proof is often used as the source document to journalize cash sales.

When a credit sale is made, it is necessary to prepare a record showing the customer's name and address as well as the amount of the sale so that the transaction can be charged to the customer's account. Thus retail merchandising businesses usually record data about a credit sale on a sales slip. This form consists of at least two copies. One copy is given to the customer. The other copy is used by the business as the source document for journalizing a credit sale. (Remember that the sales invoice is the source document for journalizing a credit sale in a wholesale merchandising business.)

Some retail businesses also record credit sales on their cash registers. The customer's name and address are entered on the sales slip. The form is then placed in a slot in the cash register. The register prints data, such as the amount of the sale, on the sales slip and also records the same data on the audit tape inside the machine. One of the advantages of this procedure is that the cash register can automatically compute the total credit sales each day as well as the total cash sales. Thus management can obtain sales data rapidly.

In a very small business, cash sales and credit sales might be entered in a combination journal. However, most merchandising businesses use special journals. Cash sales are entered in a cash receipts journal, and credit sales are entered in a sales journal. During the month, each credit sale in the sales journal is posted to the appropriate customer's account in the accounts receivable ledger. At the end of the month, the columns in the cash receipts journal and the sales journal are added. The totals of the columns are posted to the appropriate accounts in the general ledger.

The flowcharts shown here and on the next page summarize the basic procedures for recording cash sales and credit sales.

People. The number of people involved in handling sales activities and recording sales data varies from business to business. In a small business, this work may be done by salesclerks and an accounting clerk. A store manager or the owner usually supervises all operations. In a large business, there may be cashiers as well as salesclerks and data processing personnel as well as accounting personnel. Operations may be supervised by department managers as well as a store manager.

Controlling Sales. The control of sales is an important management activity. Management must set up procedures to make sure that customers are given good service and that sales data is processed with accuracy, honesty, efficiency, and speed. The procedures used for controlling sales vary, but many retail merchandising businesses base their controls on the following principles.

• Customers are helped to select merchandise whenever necessary. This must be done promptly and courteously.

• Each sale is recorded on a source document. This source document may be a prenumbered sales slip or an audit tape prepared by a cash register.

• Any sales taxes are computed and recorded on the source document when the sale is made.

• Merchandise is packaged for the customer. If the merchandise is to be delivered, the packaging should be adequate to prevent damage during shipment.

• Responsibility is divided. For example, the person who operates the cash register should not prepare the cash proof.

• When merchandise is sold on credit, the salesclerk or cashier follows the business's credit approval policy. In some businesses, all credit sales must be approved. In other businesses, only credit sales above a certain amount need to be approved.

• Each credit sale is recorded as an account receivable.

• Customers who buy on credit are billed for all merchandise they receive. This is usually done by sending monthly statements of account to the customers.

• Each account receivable is collected as soon as possible.

• Merchandise is reordered and restocked as needed.

• Provision is made for handling returns of merchandise and allowances granted for defective goods. A source document is prepared for each return or allowance. If returned merchandise is in good condition, it is placed back in stock. If it is damaged, it is repaired or returned to the manufacturer. Or the damaged merchandise may be sold to another customer at a reduced price.

Originating Sales Data by Departments

Departmentalized businesses must be able to identify the department or departments involved in each sale. This information is gathered when the original data about the sale is recorded.

PROCESSING CREDIT SALES IN RETAIL BUSINESSES

Departmental Codes for a Sporting Goods Store

Department	Code
Bicycles	1
Golf Equipment	2
Tennis Equipment	3

May 6

320.35	TCa	1
410.50	TCa	2
889.15	TCa	3
81.00	TTx	
1701.00	TCr	

Audit tape showing total cash sales (TCa) for each department, total sales tax (TTx), and total cash received (TCr).

Departmental Codes for a Supermarket

Department	Code
Dairy Products	DA
Groceries	GR
Meat	MT
Produce	PR

The Universal Product Code.

CASH PROOF

Date *December 10, 19—*

Register No. *II*

Department *Hardware*

Cash Sales	625 40

Cash Sales. There are several ways to identify the departments when a cash register is used for recording cash sales. A small store usually has a single cash register with special keys for the departments. Each department is assigned a different key to identify its sales.

Olympic Sporting Goods uses this procedure. The business's cash register is located in the front of the store and is used by all the salesclerks. The machine contains three special keys, each of which has a code number on it. (See the codes shown in the margin.) A salesclerk who is entering a sale of a bicycle on the cash register presses the special key marked *1* to identify the bicycles department. This code number is then printed next to the amount of the sale on the audit tape inside the register.

At the end of each week, the cash register is used to compute the total cash sales for each department. This information is recorded on the audit tape, as is shown here. The store manager proves cash and enters the totals for the departments on the cash proof form. This form is given to the accounting clerk for use in journalizing the cash sales and preparing the weekly sales summary for each department.

Large stores with several cash registers in one location usually follow a similar procedure for identifying the departments. For example, the cash registers in a supermarket might have special keys with codes for four departments—dairy products, groceries, meat, and produce. (See the codes shown here. Notice that this business uses letters rather than numbers in its departmental codes.) The codes appear on the receipt tapes given to the customers as well as on the audit tape. This practice makes it easier for the customers to check the items listed on their receipts.

When a business uses electronic cash registers with optical scanners, it is a much simpler procedure to identify the departments. The merchandise tag or package for each item has data printed in the Universal Product Code (UPC). This code consists of bars and numbers. When the cashier places the tag or package near the optical scanner, the scanner reads the code. The cash register then records the sales data and the department automatically.

The recording of sales data for departments is also easier when each department has its own cash register. In that case, there is no need to use special keys to identify amounts by departments. The heading of each cash proof shows which department made the cash sales listed on the form. See the cash proof shown here.

Credit Sales. If a departmentalized business has credit sales, it is also necessary to identify the department that makes each credit sale. Most businesses do this by having the salesclerks or cashiers enter codes for the departments on all sales slips. Look at the sales slip shown here. One of the salesclerks at Olympic Sporting Goods prepared this sales slip to record a credit sale of tennis equipment. Notice that the form has a special box for the department. The salesclerk has written 3, the code number of the tennis equipment department, in this box.

The accounting clerk sorts and totals the sales slips by departments. The data on these slips is used in preparing the weekly sales summary for each department. The sales slips are also the accounting clerk's source document for journalizing credit sales by departments.

Some businesses have special sales slips for each department with the department's code number preprinted on the forms. If a business records credit sales on the cash register, the machine can be used to print codes for the departments as well as sales amounts on the sales slips.

Activity A-1. Answer the following questions. Refer to the sales slip shown above.

1. What items is the customer buying?

2. What is the total price of the items before the sales tax is added?

3. How much is the sales tax?

4. What is the total amount that the customer owes?

5. Is this a cash sale or a credit sale?

6. What is the code number for the salesclerk who is making the sale?

7. What is the purpose of recording the salesclerk's number?

8. Which department is making the sale?

9. Why is it necessary to identify the department?

Activity A-2. List three stores where you have bought merchandise and received a sales slip. Do these stores use cash registers, forms registers, or imprinting devices in preparing sales slips? Name the device that each one uses, if any.

Journalizing Cash Sales by Departments

B *How are cash sales journalized by departments?* A business that is organized into departments must have a separate sales account for each sales department. For example, Olympic Sporting Goods has three sales accounts—one for bicycles, one for golf equipment, and one for tennis equipment. When the accounting clerk journalizes the store's cash sales, it is necessary to credit each of these accounts. Of course, the Cash account is debited.

As you have seen, the original data about the cash sales for each department may be recorded on the detailed audit tape inside the cash register. When the tape is removed from the machine, a cash proof is prepared to check the actual cash against the amounts listed on the

**Olympic Sporting Goods
Chart of Accounts**

Revenue
401   Sales—Bicycles
411   Sales—Golf Equipment
421   Sales—Tennis
        Equipment

CASH PROOF

Date _May 6, 19—_

Cash Sales:		
Dept. 1 — Bicycles	320	35
Dept. 2 — Golf Equipment	410	50
Dept. 3 — Tennis Equipment	889	15
Sales Tax	81	00
Total Cash Received	1,701	00

tape. Many businesses then use the cash proof form as the source document for the entries in the cash receipts journal. Olympic Sporting Goods follows this procedure. Its cash proof shows the total cash sales for each department and the sales tax collected on these sales.

If a business has several cash registers in a department, the accounting clerk must add the totals on all the cash proofs to find the overall total for the department. If sales slips were used instead of a cash register for recording the cash sales, the accounting clerk must first sort the slips by departments. Then the accounting clerk must add the totals on all the sales slips for cash sales to find the overall total for each department.

The entries for the cash sales of the departments can be made in a cash receipts journal with a single money column. If this is done, a separate line is needed to record each department's total and another line is needed for the sales tax, if any. The journal here shows how cash sales at Olympic Sporting Goods for the week ending May 6 would be recorded in a one-column cash receipts journal.

CASH RECEIPTS JOURNAL					Page *1*
DATE	ACCOUNT CREDITED	EXPLANATION	POST. REF.	AMOUNT	
19—					
May 1	Cash Balance	$5,679.43	—		
6	Sales—Bicycles	Cash sales for week	401	320	35
6	Sales—Golf Equipment	Cash sales for week	411	410	50
6	Sales—Tennis Equipment	Cash sales for week	421	889	15
6	Sales Tax Payable . .	Tax on cash sales .	216	81	00

A more efficient way of making such entries is to use a *cash receipts journal by departments*. This journal speeds up the recording process, saves space, and reduces the possibility of making errors. The cash receipts journal by departments has a separate Sales Credit column for each department. The daily or weekly cash sales for all the departments can be recorded on a single line. The amounts for the departments are accumulated in the Sales Credit columns during the month. Thus there is no need to post these entries individually. Posting is done by total at the end of the month.

Olympic Sporting Goods uses a cash receipts journal by departments. This journal is shown on the next page. In addition to the Sales Credit columns for the three departments, there are special columns for recording cash received on account from customers (Accounts Receivable Credit column) and the sales tax collected on cash sales (Sales Tax Payable Credit column). The General Ledger Credit column is used for items that cannot be recorded in any of the special columns.

						CASH RECEIPTS JOURNAL BY DEPARTMENTS						Page 1

DATE	ACCOUNT CREDITED	EXPLANATION	POST. REF.	GENERAL LEDGER CREDIT	ACCOUNTS RECEIVABLE CREDIT	BICYCLES	GOLF EQUIPMENT	TENNIS EQUIPMENT	SALES TAX PAYABLE CREDIT	NET CASH DEBIT
19—										
May 1	Cash Balance .	$5,679.43 . .	—							
2	Joan Wise . .	On account .	√		160 00					160 00
5	Peter Thomas .	On account .	√		34 50					34 50
6	Sales	Cash sales for week .	—			320 35	410 50	889 15	81 00	1,701 00
9	Marie D'Amico	On account .	√		98 60					98 60
13	Sales	Cash sales for week .	—			298 70	502 30	775 00	78 80	1,654 80
15	Equipment . .	Sold store fixtures . .	122	500 00						500 00
16	Ann Olson, Capital . . .	Additional investment	301	4,000 00						4,000 00
31	Harold Rose .	On account .	√		125 00					125 00

Look at the entry for May 6. Notice how the weekly cash sales for each department and the sales tax are distributed to the proper columns. Also notice that the amounts recorded in the three Sales Credit columns and the Sales Tax Payable Credit column equal the amount recorded in the Net Cash Debit column. Remember that equal debits and credits must always be recorded in an entry.

Activity B-1. Answer the following questions. Refer to the cash receipts journal by departments shown above.

1. On May 2, $160 is received from Joan Wise. What is the nature of this transaction?
2. What is the amount of cash sales recorded on May 13 for the tennis equipment department?
3. How much sales tax is recorded on May 13?

4. What is the amount of the debit to Cash journalized on May 13?
5. Which column is used for recording the credit to the Equipment account on May 15?
6. What has caused the $4,000 debit to Cash on May 16?

Activity B-2. Record the following transactions in the cash receipts journal by departments used at the Mod Shoe Store. This business is divided into three departments—children's shoes, men's shoes, and women's shoes. Before you start, make a memorandum entry for the cash balance of $4,267.80 on July 1.

July 3 Received $50 from Neil Linski on account.

July 8 Received $41 from Penny Nolan on account.

July 15 Recorded the cash proof showing the following cash sales: children's shoes, $290; men's shoes, $320; and women's shoes, $400. The sales tax was $50.50.

18 Received $37 from Scott Ellis on account.

23 Received $130 from the sale of a used cash register.

July 27 Received $62 from Brenda Fox on account.

31 Recorded the cash proof showing the following cash sales: children's shoes, $320; men's shoes, $410; and women's shoes, $500. The sales tax was $61.50.

NOTE: Save the cash receipts journal for further use in Activity D-2.

Journalizing Credit Sales by Departments

Sales Journal:
A sales journal has a separate column for each sales department.

C *How are credit sales journalized by departments?* In the sales journal, a separate column is set up for each sales department. This makes it possible to journalize credit sales by departments. Remember that the same procedure was followed for the cash receipts journal.

The *sales journal by departments* used at Olympic Sporting Goods is shown on the next page. This journal has three Sales Credit columns, one for each of the business's three departments. In addition, it includes special columns for recording the amounts to be collected from the customers (Accounts Receivable Debit column) and the sales tax owed on the credit sales (Sales Tax Payable Credit column).

The sales slips provide the data needed to journalize the credit sales each day. The accounting clerk checks the accuracy of each sales slip and then enters it in the sales journal by departments. The code number in the Department box of the sales slip shows which department made the sale.

Look at the first entry in the sales journal by departments shown on the next page. This credit sale was made by the tennis equipment department. The total of the sale ($32.03) is recorded in the Accounts Receivable Debit column. The price of the merchandise ($30.50) is recorded in the Sales Credit—Tennis Equipment column. The sales tax ($1.53) is recorded in the Sales Tax Payable Credit column.

Activity C. Record the following transactions in the sales journal by departments used at the Wayne Office Center. This business is organized into three departments—office equipment, office supplies, and repairs on equipment.

July 3 Sold electric typewriter for $290 plus $14.50 sales tax to Louis Garcia; Sales Slip 2017.

Sales slip

OLYMPIC SPORTING GOODS
Lincoln Shopping Center
Elmont, Illinois 60639

Date *May 1,* 19 —

M *s. Donna Kelly*

Address *103 Park Drive, Elmont, IL 60639*

Dept.	Clerk	COD	Charge	On Acct.	Ship	Paid Out
3	10		✓			

QUAN.	DESCRIPTION	PRICE	AMOUNT
1	T-35 Tennis Racket		24 00
1	T-82 Equipment Tote Bag		6 50
		Subtotal	30 50
		Tax	1 53
		Total	32 03

All claims and returned goods must be accompanied by this bill.

No. **1001**   Rec'd by _____

SALES JOURNAL BY DEPARTMENTS

DATE		ACCOUNT DEBITED	SALE NO.	POST. REF.	ACCOUNTS RECEIVABLE DEBIT	SALES CREDIT			SALES TAX PAYABLE CREDIT
						BICYCLES	GOLF EQUIPMENT	TENNIS EQUIPMENT	
19—									
May	1	Donna Kelly	1001	√	32 03			30 50	1 53
	1	Paul Janowski	1002	√	115 50		110 00		5 50
	2	Frank Montez.	1003	√	231 00		220 00		11 00
	2	Jean Miller.	1004	√	63 00			60 00	3 00
	2	Ellen Davis	1005	√	173 25	165 00			8 25
	31	John Carter	1098	√	28 35		27 00		1 35

July 8 Repaired three calculators for $43.15 plus $2.16 sales tax for Artex Inc.; Sales Slip 2018.	July 21 Sold electronic accounting machine for $1,200 plus $60 sales tax to Lake Motel; Sales Slip 2021.
12 Sold business forms for $67.10 plus $3.36 sales tax to Cox & Ames; Sales Slip 2019.	25 Sold business forms for $148 plus $7.40 sales tax to Artex Inc.; Sales Slip 2022.
16 Sold electronic desk calculator for $215 plus $10.75 sales tax to United Bank; Sales Slip 2020.	30 Repaired two typewriters for $35.40 plus $1.77 sales tax for United Bank; Sales Slip 2023.

NOTE: Save the sales journal for further use in Activity D-2.

Posting From the Cash Receipts Journal by Departments and Sales Journal by Departments

D *How are amounts posted from the cash receipts journal by departments and the sales journal by departments?* The procedure followed in posting from these journals is the same as the procedure followed in posting from any multicolumn special journal. Individual entries are posted to the subsidiary ledger accounts on a daily basis. The column totals are posted to the general ledger accounts at the end of each month.

Let's discuss the posting of the sales journal by departments first. Since Olympic Sporting Goods uses balance ledger forms for its subsidiary ledger accounts, the sales journal is posted before the cash receipts journal. (Remember that it is a good practice to post the debits to the customers' accounts before the credits.)

Sales Journal by Departments. Each amount in the Accounts Receivable Debit column of this journal is posted to the debit side of

Proof of Sales Journal by Departments

Accounts Receivable
  Debit $12,715.50

Sales Credit:
  Bicycles . . . . $ 3,290.00
  Golf Equipment 5,205.00
  Tennis Equipment . . .   3,615.00
Sales Tax Payable
  Credit 605.50
    Total Credits $12,715.50

the appropriate customer's account in the accounts receivable ledger. At the end of the month, all the money columns of the sales journal by departments are pencil-footed and the totals are proved. The total of the debit column should equal the totals of the credit columns. After the totals are proved, they are entered in ink and the journal is ruled. The column totals are posted as follows.

• The total of the Accounts Receivable Debit column is posted to the debit side of the Accounts Receivable account in the general ledger. This total represents the sum of the debits posted individually to the accounts receivable ledger during the month.

• The total of the Sales Credit column for each department is posted to the credit side of the sales account for that department in the general ledger. For example, the total of the Sales Credit—Bicycles column is posted to the Sales—Bicycles account.

• The total of the Sales Tax Payable Credit column is posted to the credit side of the Sales Tax Payable account in the general ledger. (After the cash receipts journal is posted, this liability account shows the total sales tax that has been collected on cash sales and will be collected on credit sales. The sales tax must be sent to the proper tax agency at regular intervals.)

SALES JOURNAL BY DEPARTMENTS — Page 1

DATE		ACCOUNT DEBITED	SALE NO.	POST. REF.	ACCOUNTS RECEIVABLE DEBIT	SALES CREDIT			SALES TAX PAYABLE CREDIT
						BICYCLES	GOLF EQUIPMENT	TENNIS EQUIPMENT	
19—									
May	1	Donna Kelly	1001	√	32 03			30 50	1 53
	31	John Carter	1098	√	28 35		27 00		1 35
	31	Totals			12,715 50	3,290 00	5,205 00	3,615 00	605 50
					(111)	(401)	(411)	(421)	(216)

Accounts Receivable   111
12,715.50

Sales—Bicycles   401
                  3,290.00

Sales—Golf Equipment   411
                      5,205.00

Sales—Tennis Equipment   421
                        3,615.00

Sales Tax Payable   216
                     605.50

Cash Receipts Journal by Departments. During the month, the amounts in the General Ledger Credit column and the Accounts Receivable Credit column are posted individually. Each amount in the General Ledger Credit column is posted to the credit side of the appropriate account in the general ledger. Each amount in the Accounts Receivable Credit column is posted to the credit side of the appropriate customer's account in the accounts receivable ledger. At the end of the month, all the money columns of the cash receipts journal by departments are pencil-footed and the totals are proved. Then the totals are entered in ink, and the journal is ruled. The column totals are posted as follows. (Note that the total of the General Ledger Credit column is not posted.)

● The total of the Accounts Receivable Credit column is posted to the credit side of the Accounts Receivable account in the general ledger. This total represents the sum of the credits posted individually to the accounts receivable ledger during the month.

● The total of the Sales Credit column for each department is posted to the credit side of the sales account for that department in the general ledger.

● The total of the Sales Tax Payable Credit column is posted to the credit side of the Sales Tax Payable account in the general ledger.

● The total of the Net Cash Debit column is posted to the debit side of the Cash account in the general ledger.

Proof of Cash Receipts Journal by Departments

Net Cash Debit	$16,973.50
General Ledger	
Credit	$ 4,500.00
Accounts Receivable	
Credit	6,100.00
Sales Credit:	
Bicycles	1,330.00
Golf Equipment	1,425.00
Tennis Equipment . . .	3,315.00
Sales Tax Payable	
Credit	303.50
Total Credits	$16,973.50

CASH RECEIPTS JOURNAL BY DEPARTMENTS — Page 1

DATE	ACCOUNT CREDITED	EXPLANATION	POST. REF.	GENERAL LEDGER CREDIT	ACCOUNTS RECEIVABLE CREDIT	SALES CREDIT BICYCLES	SALES CREDIT GOLF EQUIPMENT	SALES CREDIT TENNIS EQUIPMENT	SALES TAX PAYABLE CREDIT	NET CASH DEBIT
19— May 1	Cash Balance .	$5,679.43 . .	—							
31	Harold Rose .	On account .	√		125 00					125 00
31	Totals			4,500 00	6,100 00	1,330 00	1,425 00	3,315 00	303 50	16,973 50
				(—)	(111)	(401)	(411)	(421)	(216)	(101)

Accounts Receivable 111	**Sales—Bicycles 401**	**Sales—Golf Equipment 411**
6,100.00	1,330.00	1,425.00
Sales—Tennis Equipment 421	**Sales Tax Payable 216**	**Cash 101**
3,315.00	303.50	16,973.50

Accounting Concept:
Departmental Journals. A cash receipts journal by departments and a sales journal by departments permit the efficient journalizing and posting of sales data for each unit of operation.

Activity D-1. Answer the following questions. Refer to the sales journal by departments and its proof shown on page 20 and the cash receipts journal by departments and its proof shown on page 21.

1. What amount is posted to the Cash account as a debit from the cash receipts journal?

2. What amount is posted to the Accounts Receivable account as a debit from the sales journal? What amount is posted to this account as a credit from the cash receipts journal?

3. On the proof of the sales journal, what is the total of the debit column? the credit columns?

4. On the proof of the cash receipts journal, what is the total of the debit column? the credit columns?

5. What amount is posted to the Sales—Golf Equipment account from the sales journal? from the cash receipts journal?

Activity D-2. Foot and prove the cash receipts journal by departments that you prepared in Activity B-2 and the sales journal by departments that you prepared in Activity C. Enter the totals, and rule the journals.

Activity D-3. Answer the following questions. Refer to the journals that you totaled and ruled in Activity D-2.

1. Which entries in the sales journal are posted individually? To which ledger are they posted?

2. To which ledger are the totals of the sales journal posted?

3. Which entries in the cash receipts journal are posted individually?

To which ledgers are they posted?

4. To which ledger are the totals of the cash receipts journal posted?

5. Which column total in the cash receipts journal is not posted?

Olympic Sporting Goods
Chart of Accounts

Revenue
401   Sales—Bicycles
402   Sales Returns and Allowances—Bicycles
411   Sales—Golf Equipment
412   Sales Returns and Allowances—Golf Equipment
421   Sales—Tennis Equipment
422   Sales Returns and Allowances—Tennis Equipment

Journalizing Sales Returns and Allowances by Departments

E *How are sales returns and allowances handled in a departmentalized business?* Under certain conditions, most businesses permit the return of merchandise and give allowances for damaged goods. When a business is organized into departments, its sales returns and allowances are usually handled in the following way.

• A separate sales returns and allowances account is used for each department.

• The source document for each return or allowance identifies the department that sold the merchandise.

• All sales returns and allowances for credit sales are recorded in a sales returns and allowances journal by departments.

Olympic Sporting Goods uses these procedures. The business permits sales returns and allowances on both cash sales and credit sales.

Returns and Allowances on Cash Sales. Customers who buy for cash usually want to receive a cash refund when they return merchandise or obtain an allowance. At Olympic Sporting Goods, the money for this type of return or allowance is taken from the cash register. The amount is recorded on the cash register as a paid-out item. In addition, a paid-out slip is prepared to show details about the refund. At the end of each week, the accounting clerk sorts and totals the paid-out slips by department. Since the Cash account must be credited, the necessary entries are made in the cash payments journal. The sales returns and allowances account for each department is debited for the price of the returned merchandise from that department during the week. The amount of sales tax paid out on the returns for all departments is debited to the Sales Tax Payable account.

During the week ended June 10, Olympic Sporting Goods had returns on cash sales for only one department, bicycles. See below.

This sales slip is used as a paid-out slip. It shows the details about a cash refund.

CASH PAYMENTS JOURNAL									Page 2
DATE	ACCOUNT DEBITED	EXPLANATION	CHECK NO.	POST. REF.	GENERAL LEDGER DEBIT	ACCOUNTS PAYABLE DEBIT	PURCHASES DISCOUNT CREDIT	NET CASH CREDIT	
19— June 10	Sales Ret. & Allow.— Bicycles	Returns for week . .	—	402	12 95			12 95	
10	Sales Tax Payable . .	Tax on returns . . .	—	216	65			65	

Returns and Allowances on Credit Sales. A credit memorandum is prepared for each return or allowance on a credit sale. One copy of this form is given to the customer as evidence that his or her account is being reduced. Another copy of the credit memorandum is used by the accounting clerk to journalize the transaction.

Entries for returns and allowances on credit sales can be made in the general journal. However, some businesses use a special journal for recording such entries. Olympic Sporting Goods follows this practice. The *sales returns and allowances journal by departments* that the store uses is shown on page 24.

Notice that this journal has a separate Sales Returns and Allowances Debit column for each of the three departments. There are also special columns for recording the decrease in the amounts to be collected from customers (Accounts Receivable Credit column) and the decrease in the sales tax owed (Sales Tax Payable Debit column).

Look at the first entry in the sales returns and allowances journal by departments. This return is for goods sold by the tennis equipment

This credit memorandum provides a record of a return on a credit sale.

SALES RETURNS AND ALLOWANCES JOURNAL BY DEPARTMENTS								Page 1	
DATE	ACCOUNT CREDITED	CREDIT MEMO NO.	POST. REF.	ACCOUNTS RECEIVABLE CREDIT	SALES RETURNS AND ALLOWANCES DEBIT			SALES TAX PAYABLE DEBIT	
					BICYCLES	GOLF EQUIPMENT	TENNIS EQUIPMENT		
19—									
May 2	Donna Kelly	66	√	6 83			6 50	33	
3	Frank Montez.	67	√	21 00		20 00		1 00	
6	Eric Shuster	68	√	10 50			10 00	50	
31	Susan Roberts	84	√	15 75	15 00			75	

department. The total of the return ($6.83) is recorded in the Accounts Receivable Credit column. The price of the merchandise ($6.50) is recorded in the Sales Returns and Allowances Debit—Tennis Equipment column. The sales tax ($0.33) is recorded in the Sales Tax Payable Debit column.

Posting From the Sales Returns and Allowances Journal by Departments

Proof of Sales Returns and Allowances Journal by Departments

Sales Returns and Allowances Debit:	
Bicycles	$ 70.00
Golf Equipment	175.00
Tennis Equipment	160.00
Sales Tax Payable Debit . .	20.25
Total Debits	$425.25
Accounts Receivable Credit	$425.25

The posting procedure for the sales returns and allowances journal by departments is similar to the posting procedure for the cash receipts journal by departments and the sales journal by departments. During the month, each amount in the Accounts Receivable Credit column is posted to the credit side of the appropriate customer's account in the accounts receivable ledger. At the end of the month, the money columns of the journal are pencil-footed and a proof is prepared. Then the totals are entered in ink, the journal is ruled, and the totals are posted.
• The total of the Accounts Receivable Credit column is posted to the credit side of the Accounts Receivable account in the general ledger. This amount is the sum of the individual postings to the accounts receivable ledger from this column during the month.
• The total of the Sales Returns and Allowances Debit column for each department is posted to the debit side of the sales returns and allowances account for that department in the general ledger.
• The total of the Sales Tax Payable Debit column is posted to the debit side of the Sales Tax Payable account in the general ledger. The debit to this account reduces the liability for sales tax previously recorded for credit sales.

Determining Net Sales by Departments

After the data about sales returns and allowances is posted at the end of the month, it is possible to find the net sales for each department.

SALES RETURNS AND ALLOWANCES JOURNAL BY DEPARTMENTS									Page 1
DATE	ACCOUNT CREDITED	CREDIT MEMO NO.	POST. REF.	ACCOUNTS RECEIVABLE CREDIT	SALES RETURNS AND ALLOWANCES DEBIT				SALES TAX PAYABLE DEBIT
					BICYCLES	GOLF EQUIPMENT	TENNIS EQUIPMENT		
19— May 2	Donna Kelly	66	√	6 83			6 50		33
31	Susan Roberts	84	√	15 75	15 00				75
31	Totals			425 25	70 00	175 00	160 00		20 25
				(111)	(402)	(412)	(422)		(216)

Accounts Receivable 111	Sales Ret. & Allow.— Bicycles 402	Sales Ret. & Allow.— Golf Equipment 412
425.25	70.00	175.00

Sales Ret. & Allow.— Tennis Equipment 422	Sales Tax Payable 216
160.00	20.25

- The sales account for each department shows the total sales for that department during the month. The data about the cash sales came from the cash receipts journal. The data about the credit sales came from the sales journal.
- The sales returns and allowances account for each department shows the total sales returns and allowances for that department during the month. The data about returns and allowances on cash sales came from the cash payments journal. The data about returns and allowances on credit sales came from the sales returns and allowances journal.

The amount of net sales for each department is computed by subtracting the sales returns and allowances from the sales. If a business has a monthly accounting period, this information is reported on the income statement by departments. Otherwise, it is reported on a monthly sales summary.

		Departments		
	Total	Bicycles	Golf Equipment	Tennis Equipment
Sales	$18,180	$4,620	$6,630	$6,930
Less: Sales Returns and Allowances............	405	70	175	160
Net Sales	$17,775	$4,550	$6,455	$6,770

Accounting Concept:

Special Journals. Special journals are set up to increase accuracy, efficiency, and speed in journalizing and posting. Each special journal is designed to record only one type of transaction. Thus the journal entries are simplified, and posting can be done by total.

Activity E-1. Answer the following questions. Refer to the sales returns and allowances journal by departments shown on pages 24 and 25.

1. What amount is credited to Donna Kelly's account? Which sales department is involved in the return?

2. What is the price of the merchandise returned by Frank Montez? What is the amount of the sales tax on this return? Which sales department is involved in the return?

3. Does this sales returns and allowances journal include entries for returns on cash sales?

4. What amount is posted to the sales returns and allowances ac-

count for each department at the end of the month?

5. What amount is posted to the Accounts Receivable account at the end of the month? Why is this account credited for returns?

6. What amount is posted to the Sales Tax Payable account at the end of the month? Why is this account debited when there are returns?

7. What are the advantages of using a special journal for sales returns and allowances?

Activity E-2. Record the following transactions in the sales returns and allowances journal by departments used at the Home Decorating Center. This business is organized into three departments—furniture, lamps, and rugs.

July 5 Wendy Wong returned a brass lamp bought for $65 plus $3.25 sales tax; Credit Memo 102.

8 Alan Gold returned a walnut coffee table bought for $110 plus $5.50 sales tax; Credit Memo 103.

19 George Pappas returned a shag area rug bought for

$82 plus $4.10 sales tax; Credit Memo 104.

July 24 Diane Carr returned a pine bookcase bought for $135 plus $6.75 sales tax; Credit Memo 105.

28 Nancy Dahl returned a crystal lamp bought for $49 plus $2.45 sales tax; Credit Memo 106.

Foot and prove the sales returns and allowances journal by departments. Then enter the totals, and rule the journal.

Activity E-3. Answer the following questions about the net sales data for Olympic Sporting Goods. This data is shown on page 25.

1. Which department has the highest net sales during the month? What is the amount?

2. Which department has the lowest net sales during the month? What is the amount?

3. How were the net sales found?

4. Which department has the most sales returns and allowances during the month? What is the amount?

5. What is the total amount of sales for the business during the month? What is the total of the net sales?

Other Methods of Recording Sales Data by Departments

F *When a business has a large number of sales, how is the recording of sales data by departments handled?* Businesses that have a large number of sales generally use either a time-saving manual method or an automated method to record this data. Some of the procedures involved in these methods differ from the conventional journalizing and posting procedures that we have been discussing. However, the basic principles of managerial accounting are followed no matter what method is used to process the data.

Time-Saving Manual Methods. Journalizing batch totals and direct posting are two common methods of reducing the amount of time and work needed to record sales data manually. The procedure for *journalizing batch totals* eliminates the individual journal entries for credit sales. The sales slips for the credit sales made each day or week are sorted and totaled by department. Only the daily or weekly total of the batch of sales slips for each department is recorded in the sales journal.

The posting of the credit sales to the customers' accounts in the accounts receivable ledger is done from the sales slips. This procedure is called **direct posting** because the necessary data is taken directly from the source documents rather than from journal entries.

Other time-saving manual methods that some businesses use are journalless accounting and ledgerless accounting. In **journalless accounting,** the sales journal is replaced by a binder containing the daily or weekly batches of sales slips. At the end of the month, the batch totals are added and the overall total for each department is posted to the general ledger.

In **ledgerless accounting,** the accounts receivable ledger is replaced by an accounts receivable file. This file contains a folder for each credit customer. Copies of the unpaid sales slips for the customer are kept in the folder. When a payment is received, the sales slips covered by the payment are removed from the folder.

Automated Methods. There are many different automated methods for handling sales data. We have already discussed one common automated method. This method involves the use of electronic cash registers with optical scanners. These registers collect data for a computer system. Most of the data is read and recorded automatically from bar-coded merchandise tags or package labels. However, some items, such as the account number of each customer involved in a credit sale, must be entered manually by the cashier.

All this data is listed on a cassette tape inside the register. At the end of the day or the week, the cassette tape is sent to the business's data

Time-Saving Manual Methods of Recording Sales Data:
• Journalizing batch totals
• Direct posting
• Journalless accounting
• Ledgerless accounting

processing center. There the computer system processes the tape and prints the departmental journals and sales summaries. (Remember that the bar-coded data identifies the departments.) The computer system also updates the customers' accounts, which are usually stored on magnetic tape or magnetic disks.

Another common automated method involves printing data on sales slips in optical type. At the end of each day or week, the sales slips are sent to the business's data processing center. There, an optical scanner reads the sales data into the computer system for processing. A code number in optical type identifies the unit of operation that made each sale. (For the form shown in the margin, the unit of operation is a service station that belongs to a nationwide chain. The same procedure can be used in a business that is divided into departments.)

OPTICAL TYPE. The form shown above has sales data printed in optical type.

Activity F. Answer the following questions about time-saving manual methods and automated methods for recording sales data.

1. What manual methods can businesses use to speed up the recording of their sales data?
2. How does the journalizing of batch totals differ from the regular journalizing procedure?
3. What is direct posting?
4. What replaces the sales journal in the journalless method?
5. What replaces the accounts receivable ledger in the ledgerless method?

6. What are two ways of providing sales data for use by a computer system?
7. Look at the source document for the credit sale made by the service station. What is the amount of the sale? What is the dealer number? What other items are printed in optical type?

Topic 2 Problems

1-3. The Plaza Photo Mart is a retail store that has departments for cameras, film, and projectors. The business makes most of its sales for cash but provides charge accounts to a few customers. Photography is an active hobby for these customers, and they buy equipment and film often.

a. Open the following accounts, and enter the April 1 balances. General ledger: Cash, $3,826.40; Accounts Receivable, $275.50; Sales Tax Payable; Sales—Cameras; Sales—Film; Sales—Projectors; Sales Returns and Allowances—Cameras; Sales Returns and Allowances—Film; and Sales Returns and Allowances—Projectors. Accounts receivable ledger:

Janet Anton, $42.70; Paul Marsh, $57.30; and Gail Niska, $175.50.
b. During the first two weeks of April, the business had the following transactions involving cash receipts, sales, and sales returns and allowances. Record each transaction in the appropriate journal. The business has a cash receipts journal by departments, a sales journal by depart-

ments, and a sales returns and allowances journal by departments. Before you start work, make a memorandum entry for

the April 1 cash balance in the cash receipts journal.
c. Post the individual entries from the journals.

April 1 Sold film for $24 plus $1.20 sales tax to Paul Marsh on credit; Sales Slip 872.
   3 Sold a slide projector for $89 plus $4.45 sales tax to Janet Anton on credit; Sales Slip 873.
   4 Paul Marsh returned two rolls of film bought for $6 plus $0.30 sales tax; Credit Memo 38.
   5 Received $42.70 from Janet Anton on account.
   6 Recorded the cash proof showing the following cash sales: cameras,

$600; film, $375; and projectors, $225. The sales tax was $60.
April 8 Received $57.30 from Paul Marsh on account.
   10 Sold film for $18 plus $0.90 sales tax to Janet Anton on credit; Sales Slip 874.
   12 Received $100 from Gail Niska on account.
   13 Recorded the cash proof showing the following cash sales: cameras, $580; film, $320; and projectors, $200. The sales tax was $55.

1-4. Do the following work for the Plaza Photo Mart during the last two weeks of April.
a. Record these transactions.
b. Post the individual entries from the journals.
c. Foot and prove the journals.

Then enter the totals, and rule the journals.
d. Post the totals from the journals.

April 15 Sold two cameras for $130 plus $6.50 sales tax to Gail Niska on credit; Sales Slip 875.
   17 Sold film for $12 plus $0.60 sales tax to Janet Anton on credit; Sales Slip 876.
   19 Gail Niska returned a camera bought for $55 plus $2.75 sales tax; Credit Memo 39.
   20 Recorded the cash proof showing the following cash sales: cameras, $610; film, $400; and projectors, $160. The sales tax was $58.50.
   24 Paul Marsh bought a

movie projector for $220 plus $11 sales tax on credit; Sales Slip 877.
April 25 Granted an allowance of $10 plus $0.50 sales tax to Paul Marsh for scratches on the projector; Credit Memo 40.
   26 Received $75.50 from Gail Niska on account.
   27 Recorded the cash proof. Cash sales: cameras, $550; film, $380; and projectors, $120. The sales tax was $52.50.
   29 Sold film for $19 plus $0.95 sales tax to Gail Niska on credit; Sales Slip 878.

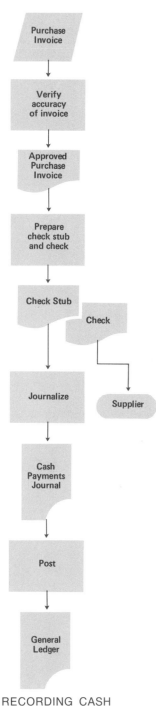

RECORDING CASH
PURCHASES

April 30 Recorded the cash proof showing the following cash sales: cameras, $230; film, $140; and projectors, $85. The sales tax was $22.75.

1-5. Prepare a sales summary for the Plaza Photo Mart for the month ended April 30. This summary should report the sales, sales returns and allowances, and net sales for each department and for the business as a whole.

NOTE: Save the sales summary for further use in Topic Problem 1-10.

Topic 3
Recording Purchases Data by Departments

A *Why does management need to know the amount of merchandise purchased for each department?* This information is needed so that management can determine the cost of goods sold for each department. The report summarizing this information is the *schedule of cost of goods sold by departments.* Look at the schedule shown here. Beginning merchandise inventory and the net purchases are added to find the cost of goods available for the shirts and blouses department. The ending inventory is then subtracted to determine cost of goods sold.

This topic presents the procedures commonly used in accounting for purchases and merchandise inventory in businesses that keep departmental records.

UPS & DOWNS Shirts and Blouses Department Schedule of Cost of Goods Sold by Departments For the Month Ended August 31, 19—			
Merchandise Inventory, August 1			4,200 00
Purchases		2,970 00	
Add: Transportation In		80 00	
Cost of Delivered Goods		3,050 00	
Less: Purchases Ret. and Allow.	$200.00		
Purchases Discount	50.00	250 00	
Net Purchases			2,800 00
Cost of Goods Available for Sale			7,000 00
Less: Merchandise Inventory, August 31			4,000 00
Cost of Goods Sold			3,000 00

Processing Purchases Data

In your previous studies, you learned about the basic forms and procedures needed to process data about purchases of merchandise. You also learned about the basic controls that should be used to ensure accuracy, honesty, efficiency, and speed in processing the data. Let's review these forms, procedures, and controls before we discuss the handling of purchases in departmentalized businesses.

Forms and Procedures. Purchasing activities begin when a business identifies the need for new merchandise. If the business keeps its inventory records manually, the information about items to be ordered usually comes from inventory cards. If the business uses a computer system to keep its inventory records, this information is usually produced automatically by the system.

The next purchasing activity in many businesses is preparing a purchase requisition for each type of merchandise that is needed. This form asks the person or department in charge of purchasing to order the items. An appropriate supplier is then selected, and a purchase order is issued. The purchase order lists the merchandise that is wanted and authorizes the supplier to deliver the items at specified prices. The form used for the purchase order consists of several copies. One copy is sent to the supplier, and the other copies are kept by the business for various uses such as checking the merchandise when it arrives from the supplier.

For each purchase order sent to a supplier, the business receives a purchase invoice from the supplier. This form serves as a bill for the merchandise. The invoice must be verified carefully to make sure that all items and amounts are correct.

In a very small business, both cash purchases and credit purchases might be entered in a combination journal. However, most merchandising businesses use special journals. Cash purchases are entered in the cash payments journal, and credit purchases are entered in the purchases journal. The check stub provides the necessary data for journalizing a cash purchase. The purchase invoice is the source document for journalizing a credit purchase.

During the month, each credit purchase recorded in the purchases journal is posted to the appropriate creditor's account in the accounts payable ledger. At the end of the month, the total of the purchases journal is posted to the appropriate accounts in the general ledger. If the cash payments journal does not have a special column for merchandise purchases, these amounts must be posted individually to the Purchases account in the general ledger during the month.

The flowcharts shown here and on page 30 summarize the basic procedures for recording the purchase of merchandise. Keep in mind that the details of the procedures vary from one business to another and may be based on manual, mechanical, or automated operations.

People. The number of people involved in buying, receiving, checking, and storing merchandise and in recording the purchases varies from business to business. In a small business, this work may be done

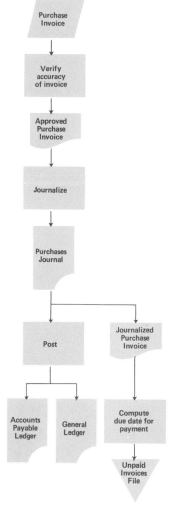

RECORDING CREDIT
PURCHASES

by the owner or store manager, the salesclerks, and the accounting clerk. In a large business, many other people are involved. These people may include purchasing agents, purchasing clerks, receiving clerks, inventory clerks, and data processing personnel.

Controlling Purchases. The basic procedures involved in controlling purchases of merchandise are as follows.
- Merchandise to be ordered is identified.
- Purchasing activity is started by authorized personnel.
- Prenumbered forms are used.
- Responsibility is divided among employees.
- Merchandise is purchased from approved suppliers.
- Shipments are accepted only for the approved quantities and quality
- Accuracy of quantities, quality, terms, prices, and computations on the invoices is verified before payment is approved.
- Quantities of merchandise in stock are verified with the inventory records.
- Data from completed purchase transactions is recorded.
- Refunds or credits are obtained for all purchases returns and allowances.
- All invoices are paid in time to take cash discounts.

Originating Purchases Data by Departments

Each purchase invoice must be examined to find out which sales department should be charged for the cost of the merchandise. In some cases, an invoice is for the merchandise of only one sales department. In other cases, merchandise for two or more departments is listed on a single invoice. All the items must then be analyzed, and the amount to be charged to each department must be noted on the invoice.

SPORTS EQUIPMENT INC.
101 Drake Avenue • Summit, New Jersey 07901

To: Olympic Sporting Goods
Lincoln Shopping Center
Elmont, IL 60639

Invoice No. **J221**
Date: 5/1/--
Terms: 2/10, n/30
Order No. 343

QUANTITY	STOCK NO.	DESCRIPTION	UNIT PRICE	AMOUNT
5	4789	Star golf clubs, sets of irons	54.00	270.00
12	5241	Star tennis rackets	20.00	240.00
20	5668	Martin racket covers	3.50	70.00
		TOTAL		580.00

Golf Equipment Dept. $270
Tennis Equipment Dept. $310

Journalizing Purchases by Departments

To find the cost of goods sold for each department, it is necessary that a business keep separate purchases accounts for each department. For example, Olympic Sporting Goods has three purchases accounts: one for bicycles, one for golf equipment, and one for tennis equipment. Before purchases are journalized, the departments involved must be identified so that the correct accounts can be used. This is done by examining each purchase invoice, as discussed in the last section.

Purchases for Cash. As you have already learned, a purchase of merchandise for cash is recorded in the cash payments journal because the transaction involves a credit to the Cash account. The check stub is the source document for this entry. In a departmentalized business, the data on the check stub must include the name of the department that is to be charged for the purchase. The accounting clerk can then debit the purchases account of the correct department. For example, look at the following journal entry. It was made by the accounting clerk at Olympic Sporting Goods to record a purchase for the bicycles department. The check stub that provided the data for this entry is shown here.

If a business has a large number of cash purchases, special columns may be included in the cash payments journal to speed up the recording of purchases by departments. However, merchandising businesses such as Olympic Sporting Goods usually do not make many cash purchases and therefore have no need for a cash payments journal by departments.

Olympic Sporting Goods Chart of Accounts

Costs and Expenses
501 Purchases—Bicycles
511 Purchases—Golf Equipment
521 Purchases—Tennis Equipment

Balance Brought Forward	6,582 50
No. *1021*	
Date *June 1,* 19—	
Pay To *Ace Sports Equipment*	
For *Invoice 698— cash purchase for bicycles department.*	
Total	6,582 50
Amount This Check	430 00
Balance Carried Forward	6,152 50

			CASH PAYMENTS JOURNAL						Page 2	
DATE	ACCOUNT DEBITED	EXPLANATION	CHECK NO.	POST. REF.	GENERAL LEDGER DEBIT	ACCOUNTS PAYABLE DEBIT	PURCHASES DISCOUNT CREDIT	NET CASH CREDIT
19—								
June 1	Purchases—Bicycles	Ace Sports Equipment	1021	501	430 00			430 00

Purchases on Credit. Merchandising businesses make most of their purchases on credit. In a business that has several sales departments, a *purchases journal by departments* provides an efficient way to record purchases on credit. The purchases journal by departments used by Olympic Sporting Goods is shown on pages 34 and 35. Notice that this journal has columns for entering all the business's purchases on credit, both merchandise items and nonmerchandise items. The Purchases Debit columns for the business's three sales departments are used for merchandise purchases. All other purchases on credit, such as

PURCHASES JOURNAL

DATE		ACCOUNT CREDITED	INVOICE		TERMS	POST. REF.	ACCOUNTS PAYABLE CREDIT
			NO.	DATE			
19—							
May	3	Champion Sports Company ..	873	4/30	2/10, n/30	√	678 00
	5	Sports Equipment Inc.	J221	5/1	2/10, n/30	√	580 00
	6	Kelso Corporation	3652	5/2	1/10, n/30	√	730 00
	10	Central Supply Company ..	79-B	5/8	n/EOM	√	93 00
	30	Sports Equipment Inc.	J318	5/26	2/10, n/30	√	1,370 00

purchases of supplies and equipment, are recorded in the General Ledger Debit column. Of course, the Accounts Payable Credit column is used to record the amounts owed to creditors.

Look at the first entry in the purchases journal by departments. On May 3, an invoice for a credit purchase of merchandise was recorded. The debit amount ($678) appears in the Purchases Debit—Bicycles column because the merchandise was bought for the bicycles department. On May 10, an invoice for a credit purchase of office supplies was recorded. The debit amount ($93) appears in the General Ledger Debit column because nonmerchandise items are involved.

CHAMPION SPORTS COMPANY
650 Briggs Avenue
Jacksonville, Florida 33207

SOLD TO: Olympic Sporting Goods
Lincoln Shopping Center
Elmont, IL 60639

INVOICE NO. **873**

DATE 4/30/--
ORDER NO. 341

TERMS 2/10, n/30

QUANTITY	STOCK NO.	DESCRIPTION	UNIT PRICE	AMOUNT
10	1239	Silver Streak Bicycles, 5-Speed	50.00	500.00
4	1582	Road Runner Bicycles, 5-Speed	44.50	178.00
			TOTAL	678.00

BY DEPARTMENTS   Page *1*

PURCHASES DEBIT			GENERAL LEDGER DEBIT		
BICYCLES	GOLF EQUIPMENT	TENNIS EQUIPMENT	ACCOUNT TITLE	POST. REF.	AMOUNT
678 00					
	270 00	310 00			
	730 00				
			Office Supplies .	*141*	93 00
		1,370 00			

Activity A-1. Answer the following questions. Refer to the purchases journal by departments shown above.

1. For which department is merchandise purchased from the Champion Sports Company?

2. What is the amount of Invoice 3652?

3. Does the purchase from the Central Supply Company involve merchandise? If not, what items are being bought?

4. Which accounts are debited and credited in the entry of May 5?

5. Can a purchase of merchandise for cash be recorded in the purchases journal? If not, what journal would be used for this type of transaction?

6. Which source document provides the information needed to journalize a credit purchase?

Activity A-2. Record the following transactions in the purchases journal by departments used at the Do-It-Yourself Shop. This business is divided into three departments: floor tiles, paint, and wallpaper.

June 4 Bought paint for $310 from Spectrum Paint Company; Invoice 347, dated June 1; terms 1/10, n/30.

15 Bought floor tiles for $3,130 from Superior Flooring Inc.; Invoice 1225, dated June 12; terms 2/10, n/30.

June 19 Bought wallpaper for $2,189 from Lopez Corporation; Invoice A564, dated June 17; terms 1/10, n/30.

22 Bought office supplies for $132 from Taylor Supply Company; Invoice 7329, dated June 20; terms n/30.

June 25 Bought floor tiles for $860 from Durable Tile Corporation; Invoice 9813, dated June 23; terms 1/10, n/30.

June 30 Bought paint for $1,600 from Brown & Davis Inc.; Invoice H265, dated June 27; terms 2/10, n/30.

NOTE: Save the purchases journal for further use in Activity B-2.

Posting From the Purchases Journal by Departments

B *How are amounts posted from the purchases journal by departments?* As you have seen, the various money columns in the purchases journal by departments make it easier to record purchases data for all the departments of a business. Another advantage of this type of journal is that much of the posting can be done by total at the end of each month.

During the month, the amounts in the Accounts Payable Credit column of the purchases journal by departments are posted individually to the creditors' accounts in the accounts payable ledger. The amounts in the General Ledger Debit column are posted individually to accounts in the general ledger.

At the end of the month, the money columns of the purchases journal by departments are pencil-footed and the totals are proved. The totals of the debit columns should equal the total of the credit column. After the totals are proved, they are entered in ink and the journal is

Proof of Purchases Journal by Departments

Purchases Debit:	
Bicycles	$1,000
Golf Equipment	2,100
Tennis Equipment	4,200
General Ledger Debit . . .	2,699
Total Debits	$9,999
Accounts Payable Credit . . .	$9,999

PURCHASES JOURNAL

DATE		ACCOUNT CREDITED	INVOICE		TERMS	POST. REF.	ACCOUNTS PAYABLE CREDIT
			NO.	DATE			
19— May	3	Champion Sports Company . .	873	4/30	2/10, n/30	✓	678 00
	10	Central Supply Company . .	79-B	5/8	n/EOM	✓	93 00
	30	Sports Equipment Inc.	J318	5/26	2/10, n/30	✓	1,370 00
	31	Totals					9,999 00
							(211)

ruled. Then all the column totals are posted except the total of the General Ledger Debit column. The following procedure is used to post the column totals.

• The total of the Accounts Payable Credit column is posted to the credit side of the Accounts Payable account in the general ledger. This total represents the sum of the credits posted individually to the accounts payable ledger from this column during the month.

• The total of the Purchases Debit column for each department is posted to the debit side of the purchases account for that department in the general ledger.

Notice that a dash is placed under the total of the General Ledger Debit column in the journal shown here. The dash indicates that the amount is not posted.

Accounts Payable 211		Purchases — Bicycles 501		Purchases — Golf Equipment 511
	9,999	1,000		2,100

Purchases — Tennis Equipment 521		Office Supplies 141
4,200		93

BY DEPARTMENTS   Page 1

PURCHASES DEBIT			GENERAL LEDGER DEBIT		
BICYCLES	GOLF EQUIPMENT	TENNIS EQUIPMENT	ACCOUNT TITLE	POST. REF.	AMOUNT
678 00					
			Office Supplies .	141	93 00
		1,370 00			
1,000 00	2,100 00	4,200 00			2,699 00
(501)	(511)	(521)			(—)

Accounting Concept:
Departmental Journal. A purchases journal by departments permits the efficient journalizing and posting of purchases data for each unit of operation in a business.

Activity B-1. Answer the following questions. Refer to the purchases journal by departments and its proof shown on pages 36 and 37.

1. On the proof of the purchases journal, what is the total of the debit columns? What is the total of the credit column?

2. From which columns of the purchases journal are amounts posted individually during the month?

3. What amount is posted to the Accounts Payable account from the purchases journal on May 31?

4. What amount is posted to the Purchases—Tennis Equipment account from the purchases journal on May 31?

5. What are some of the advantages of the type of purchases journal used by Olympic Sporting Goods?

Activity B-2. Foot and prove the purchases journal by departments that you prepared in Activity A-2. Then enter the totals, and rule the journal.

Activity B-3. Answer the following questions. Refer to the journal that you totaled and ruled in Activity B-2.

1. What amount will be posted to the Accounts Payable account in the general ledger? Will this account be debited or credited?

2. What amounts will be posted to the Purchases—Floor Tiles, Purchases—Paint, and Purchases—Wallpaper accounts in the general ledger? Will these accounts be debited or credited?

3. Will the total of the General Ledger Debit column be posted?

Journalizing Purchases Returns and Allowances by Departments

C *How are purchases returns and allowances handled in a departmentalized business?* When merchandise is received, the purchaser must examine the items to make sure that they are the ones ordered and that they are in good condition. If the seller has sent the wrong items or the items have been damaged in shipment, the purchaser generally returns the merchandise and asks for a credit. However, in some cases, the seller offers an allowance if the purchaser agrees to keep the merchandise. In a business with departmental records, a separate account is usually set up for recording the purchases returns and allowances of each department.

When the seller accepts returned merchandise or grants an allowance, a credit memorandum is prepared and sent to the purchaser. This provides proof that the purchaser's account is being reduced for the amount of the return or allowance. In a departmentalized business,

Olympic Sporting Goods Chart of Accounts

Costs and Expenses

501	Purchases—Bicycles
502	Purchases Returns and Allowances—Bicycles
511	Purchases—Golf Equipment
512	Purchases Returns and Allowances—Golf Equipment
521	Purchases—Tennis Equipment
522	Purchases Returns and Allowances—Tennis Equipment

CHAMPION SPORTS COMPANY

650 Briggs Avenue
Jacksonville, Florida 33207

TO: Olympic Sporting Goods
Lincoln Shopping Center
Elmont, IL 60639

Credit Memorandum No. **76**
Date: 5/8/--
Invoice No. 873

We have credited your account as follows:

QUANTITY	STOCK NO.	DESCRIPTION	UNIT PRICE	AMOUNT
1	1239	Silver Streak Bicycle,5-Speed, returned in damaged condition.	50.00	50.00

it is necessary to find out which department was originally charged for the merchandise so that the return or allowance can be recorded correctly. This information is usually noted on the credit memorandum.

Entries for the returns and allowances on credit purchases can be made in the general journal. However, if a business has many purchases returns and allowances, a special journal is often used to speed up the recording of these transactions. Olympic Sporting Goods maintains the *purchases returns and allowances journal by departments* shown here.

PURCHASES RETURNS AND ALLOWANCES JOURNAL BY DEPARTMENTS

Page 1

DATE	ACCOUNT DEBITED	CREDIT MEMO NO.	POST. REF.	ACCOUNTS PAYABLE DEBIT	PURCHASES RETURNS AND ALLOWANCES CREDIT			GENERAL LEDGER CREDIT		
					BICYCLES	GOLF EQUIPMENT	TENNIS EQUIPMENT	ACCOUNT TITLE	POST. REF.	AMOUNT
19—										
May 11	Champion Sports Company	76	√	50 00	50 00					
12	Kelso Corporation	108	√	120 00			120 00			
15	Central Supply Company	12-B	√	11 00				Office Supplies . .	141	11 00
29	Star Athletics Inc.	249		75 00		75 00				

Notice that this journal provides a separate Purchases Returns and Allowances Credit column for each of the business's three sales departments. There is also a General Ledger Credit column for entering returns and allowances on purchases of nonmerchandise items such as supplies and equipment. The decreases in the amounts owed to the creditors are recorded in the Accounts Payable Debit column.

On May 11, Olympic Sporting Goods received a credit memorandum for returned merchandise that was originally purchased for the bicycles department. The total of the credit memorandum ($50) was therefore entered in the Accounts Payable Debit and in the Purchases Returns and Allowances Credit—Bicycles columns.

Proof of Purchases Returns and Allowances Journal by Departments

Accounts Payable Debit . $656

Purchases Ret. and Allow.
  Credit:
  Bicycles . . . . $ 50
  Golf Equipment 125
  Tennis Equipment . . . 250
General Ledger Credit . . 231
    Total Credits $656

Posting From the Purchases Returns and Allowances Journal by Departments

The posting procedure for the purchases returns and allowances journal by departments is simple. During the month, the amounts in the Accounts Payable Debit column are posted individually to the creditors' accounts in the accounts payable ledger. The amounts in the General Ledger Credit column are also posted individually. These amounts are posted to the appropriate accounts in the general ledger. At the end of the month, the journal is proved, totaled, and ruled. Then all the totals, except the total of the General Ledger Credit column, are posted as follows.

• The total of the Accounts Payable Debit column is posted to the debit side of the Accounts Payable account in the general ledger. This amount is the sum of the individual postings to the accounts payable ledger from this column during the month.

• The total of the Purchases Returns and Allowances Credit column for each department is posted to the credit side of the purchases returns and allowances account for that department in the general ledger.

PURCHASES RETURNS AND ALLOWANCES JOURNAL BY DEPARTMENTS Page 1

DATE	ACCOUNT DEBITED	CREDIT MEMO NO.	POST. REF.	ACCOUNTS PAYABLE DEBIT	PURCHASES RETURNS AND ALLOWANCES CREDIT			GENERAL LEDGER CREDIT		
					BICYCLES	GOLF EQUIPMENT	TENNIS EQUIPMENT	ACCOUNT TITLE	POST. REF.	AMOUNT
19—										
May 11	Champion Sports Company	76	√	50 00	50 00					
15	Central Supply Company	12-B	√	11 00				Office Supplies . .	141	11 00
29	Star Athletics Inc.	249	√	75 00		75 00				
31	Totals			656 00	50 00	125 00	250 00			231 00
				(211)	(502)	(512)	(522)			(—)

Accounts Payable 211	
	656

Purch. Ret. & Allow.— Bicycles 502	
	50

Purch. Ret. & Allow.— Golf Equipment 512	
	125

Purch. Ret. & Allow.— Tennis Equipment 522	
	250

Office Supplies 141	
	11

Activity C-1. Answer the following questions. Refer to the credit memorandum on page 39 and the purchases returns and allowances journal by departments on pages 39 and 40.

1. Which company issued Credit Memorandum 76 to Olympic Sporting Goods? What is the amount? Which department is involved?

2. Which accounts are debited and credited on May 12 to record the return of merchandise?

3. Does the return recorded on May 15 involve merchandise? If not, which items are involved?

4. What amount is posted to the Accounts Payable account in the general ledger on May 31? Why is this account debited for returns and allowances on credit purchases?

5. What amount is posted to the Purchases Returns and Allowances—Golf Equipment account on May 31?

6. Which department has the largest amount of purchases returns and allowances during May?

Activity C-2. Record the following transactions in the purchases returns and allowances journal by departments used at the House of Fashion. This business is organized into three departments: children's wear, men's wear, and women's wear.

Aug. 5 Received Credit Memorandum 95 for $420 from Popovich Inc. for the return of men's suits.

12 Received Credit Memorandum G-37 for $263 from Casual Styles for the return of women's slacks.

16 Received Credit Memorandum 14 for $50 from Apex Supplies for the return of store supplies.

21 Received Credit Memorandum 68A for $257 from Anderson Clothes as an allowance on children's jeans that are damaged.

Aug. 29 Received Credit Memorandum 346 for $110 from Star Fashions for the return of women's skirts.

31 Received Credit Memorandum 102 for $25 from Popovich Inc. as an allowance on men's slacks that are damaged.

Foot and prove the purchases returns and allowances journal. Then enter the totals, and rule the journal.

Determining Purchase Discounts and Transportation Charges by Departments

D *Are purchase discounts and transportation charges usually recorded in departmental accounts?* No, most departmentalized businesses use a single account for all purchase discounts and a single account for all transportation charges.

Purchase Discounts. As you learned in your previous studies, it is a sound business practice to take advantage of purchase discounts by

Olympic Sporting Goods Chart of Accounts

Costs and Expenses
531 Transportation In
532 Purchases Discount

Purchases Discount	
	532
	May 31 94

The balance of this account is the total amount of purchase discounts for the business during the month. An examination of the purchase invoices paid during May shows that the following amounts belong to the three departments.

Bicycles	$21
Golf Equipment	32
Tennis Equipment . .	41
	$94

Transportation In	
	531
May 31 100	

The balance of this account is the total amount of transportation charges for the business during the month. An examination of the transportation bills shows that the three departments incurred the following amounts during May.

Bicycles	$ 15
Golf Equipment	35
Tennis Equipment . .	50
	$100

paying invoices within the discount period. Purchase discounts are important because they reduce the cost of purchases.

In a departmentalized business, it is necessary to determine the amount of the purchase discounts that belongs to each sales department. However, it is often too difficult and time-consuming to record purchase discounts by departments as the invoices are paid during the accounting period. Remember that some invoices list merchandise for several departments. In such cases, the accounting clerk would have to analyze the invoices and divide up the discounts according to the amount of merchandise purchased for each department. This procedure would delay the recording of cash payments. Thus it is more efficient to use a single account for purchase discounts.

At the end of the accounting period, the amount of the purchase discounts that each department should receive is determined. In small businesses such as Olympic Sporting Goods, this can be done by examining all the invoices for the period. However, in a business that makes a large number of purchases, this method may not be practical. The accountant therefore works out a way to *allocate* (assign) part of the total purchase discounts for the period to each department. For example, each department might receive a percentage of the total purchase discounts that is equal to its percentage of the business's total purchases. Thus if a department had 30 percent of the total purchases during an accounting period, it would be given 30 percent of the total purchase discounts. (More information about allocating amounts is presented in the next chapter.)

Transportation Charges. Sometimes a business must pay transportation charges on the merchandise it buys. These charges increase the cost of purchases.

The amount shown on a bill for transportation charges may cover freight for the purchases of several departments. Thus recording transportation charges by departments as the bills are paid during an accounting period involves the same type of problems that we discussed in regard to purchase discounts. For this reason, departmentalized businesses generally use a single account for transportation charges. At the end of the accounting period, the amount of transportation charges that each department should bear is determined. This is done by examining the bills or by allocating part of the total to each department.

Determining Net Purchases by Departments

The data about departmental purchases, transportation charges, purchases returns and allowances, and purchase discounts is used to determine the net purchases for each department and for the business as a whole. These amounts are reported on the schedule of cost of goods sold. Some managerial accounting systems also produce a purchases summary with information about net purchases. In a large business, this summary might go to all the people who supervise purchasing activities, such as merchandise managers and purchasing agents.

OLYMPIC SPORTING GOODS
Purchases Summary
For the Month Ended May 31, 19—

| | | | Departments | |
| | | | Golf | Tennis |
	Total	Bicycles	Equipment	Equipment
Purchases..........................	$7,300	$1,000	$2,100	$4,200
Add: Transportation In.....................	100	15	35	50
Cost of Delivered Goods...................	$7,400	$1,015	$2,135	$4,250
Less: Purchases Ret. and Allow..............	425	50	125	250
Purchases Discount...................	94	21	32	41
Net Purchases........................	$6,881	$ 944	$1,978	$3,959

Other Methods of Recording Purchases Data by Departments

The journalizing and posting procedures for purchases that we have been discussing are used by many businesses. Like Olympic Sporting Goods, these businesses are usually fairly small and make a limited number of purchases each month. Larger businesses, which have many more purchases, normally use a time-saving manual method or an automated method of recording purchases data.

Time-Saving Manual Methods. As you learned previously, journalizing batch totals and posting directly from source documents can reduce the amount of time and work needed to record transactions manually. If these methods are used for recording credit purchases in a departmentalized business, the accounting clerk sorts and totals the purchase invoices by departments. Then the batch total for each department is entered in the purchases journal. The accounting clerk uses the invoices to post the individual purchases to the creditors' accounts in the accounts payable ledger.

Journalless accounting and ledgerless accounting simplify the handling of purchases data because no formal purchases journal is kept. Instead, daily or weekly batches of invoices are placed in a binder. At the end of the month, the batch totals are added and the overall total for each department is posted to the general ledger.

Businesses that use ledgerless accounting for purchases keep an accounts payable file rather than an accounts payable ledger. The file has folders for all the creditors. Copies of the unpaid purchase invoices are placed in these folders. When an invoice is paid, the copy is removed from the file. Credit memorandums are also placed in the accounts payable file.

Automated Methods. When a computer system is used to record purchases, the procedures vary somewhat from business to business. However, in most businesses with a computer system, the accounts payable are kept on magnetic tape or magnetic disks. As purchase invoices are received, a clerk checks each one and enters a code number identifying the department that ordered the merchandise. The data from the invoices is then recorded on input media such as punched cards or magnetic tape. The computer system reads the data on the input media, processes it, prints the departmental purchases journal, and updates the accounts payable. The system also produces a purchases summary and a schedule of accounts payable at regular intervals. (Of course, data about purchases returns and allowances and payments to creditors is also processed by the system so that the accounts payable will always show the current balances.)

Activity D. Answer the following questions about the net purchases data for Olympic Sporting Goods. This data is shown on page 43.

1. What is the total amount of purchases for the business? What is the amount of net purchases for the business?

2. Which department has the lowest net purchases?

3. Which department has the highest net purchases?

4. Which department has the smallest amount of purchases returns and allowances? What is the amount?

5. What is the total amount of purchase discounts for the business?

6. How is the cost of delivered goods computed?

7. Why are purchases returns and allowances and purchase discounts subtracted from the cost of delivered goods to find net purchases?

Computing Merchandise Inventory by Departments

E *Are departmental accounts used for merchandise inventory?* Yes, businesses that have several sales departments usually set up a separate merchandise inventory account for each department. For example, the general ledger of Olympic Sporting Goods contains three merchandise inventory accounts.

At the close of the accounting period, the amount of merchandise inventory for each department must be computed. This information is needed to adjust the merchandise inventory accounts and to prepare the end-of-period financial statements. Some businesses also compute

Olympic Sporting Goods Chart of Accounts

Assets

131 Merchandise Inventory—Bicycles
132 Merchandise Inventory—Golf Equipment
133 Merchandise Inventory—Tennis Equipment

departmental inventory amounts during the accounting period so that they can produce inventory reports or interim financial statements.

As you learned in your previous studies, there are two procedures for computing inventory amounts: the perpetual inventory procedure and the periodic inventory procedure. Let's review these procedures and see how they are used in departmentalized businesses.

Perpetual Inventory Procedure. In the **perpetual inventory procedure,** continuous records are kept for all items in stock. If a business has a manual inventory system, these records usually consist of inventory cards in a card file or inventory sheets in a loose-leaf binder. The cards or sheets are updated whenever merchandise is received or sold. The changes in inventory are added or subtracted so that the record for each item always shows the current balance on hand.

In a perpetual inventory, continuous records are kept for all items.

An inventory card used by Olympic Sporting Goods is illustrated here. The department to which the merchandise belongs (the tennis equipment department) is identified by the letter T in the stock number code. (The letter B is used for the bicycles department and the letter G for the golf equipment department.) Other businesses may use different coding systems to identify their sales departments. They may also use different forms for their inventory cards and include additional information, such as the selling price of each item, on the inventory card.

The amount of inventory for each department can be computed from the inventory cards whenever it is needed for reports or financial statements.

INVENTORY CARD

No. T-14
Item Ward Pro-Am Tennis Racket
Location: Aisle 5   Bin 3
Maximum 25   Minimum 10

Date	Quant. Rec'd	Unit Cost	Quant. Sold	Balance
3/20	24	20.00		24
3/27			2	22
4/4			6	16
4/12			2	14
4/18			3	11
4/23			2	9
4/28	10	22.50		19
5/2			5	14
5/8			2	12
5/15			1	11
5/26			2	9

Periodic Inventory Procedure. When the **periodic inventory procedure** is used, continuous inventory records are not kept. Instead, an actual count of all the merchandise on hand is made at regular intervals. This information is usually recorded on inventory sheets. The sheets are totaled to find the amount of inventory for each department and for the business as a whole.

In a periodic inventory, merchandise on hand is counted and recorded at regular intervals.

The counting of items is called a **physical inventory.** All businesses, including those that use a perpetual inventory procedure, must take a physical inventory at least once a year to obtain an accurate record of the merchandise on hand. Clerical errors in making entries on the inventory cards and loss of items due to theft are usually not found until the results of the physical inventory are compared with the information on the inventory cards.

In a physical inventory, items are physically counted.

One of the inventory sheets prepared during a physical inventory at Olympic Sporting Goods is shown on the next page. It lists merchandise from the golf equipment department. As each item is counted, the stock number, quantity, unit of count, description, and unit price are recorded on the inventory sheet. (The unit price is taken from a code on the price tag.) The extension for each item is computed by multiplying the unit price by the quantity. The total of the sheet is determined by adding the extensions.

INVENTORY SHEET

Department *Golf Equipment*

Date *May 31, 19—*   Sheet No. *4*

Counted By *J. Lee*		Recorded By *L. Cox*		Figured By *R. Moro*	
STOCK NO.	QUANTITY	UNIT OF COUNT	DESCRIPTION	UNIT PRICE	EXTENSION
G-153	34	doz	*Mercury Golf Balls*	3 50	119 00
G-154	12	doz	*Super-Star Golf Balls*	4 90	58 80
G-211	8	ea.	*Curtis Golf Bags*	59 00	472 00
				TOTAL	2,365 00

When all the inventory sheets are completed, the totals are written on a summary sheet and added to find the amount of inventory for the golf equipment department. The same process is followed for the other two departments of Olympic Sporting Goods.

Automated Inventory

When a business has many items in stock and makes a large number of sales each day, it is not practical to keep perpetual inventory records manually. However, with the development of modern computer systems, such a business can maintain an up-to-date perpetual inventory on thousands of items.

The inventory records are usually kept on magnetic tape or magnetic disks. The data about items received from suppliers and items sold to customers is fed into the computer system each day. For example, if a department store or supermarket uses electronic cash registers with optical scanning devices, the registers can be used to gather data about the items sold. The optical scanning devices read the stock numbers that appear on the price tags or on package labels. This data is used to update the inventory records automatically.

The computer system not only saves time and work but also helps management to control inventory effectively. Complete information about the merchandise on hand can be produced often. In some businesses, the computer system prints inventory reports on a daily or weekly basis. The system may also be programmed to prepare purchase

```
●                                                                              ●
●              Downing Company                                                 ●
●                 86 Broadway                                                  ●
●             Atlanta, Georgia 30310        Purchase Order No.  783            ●
●                                         Date    2/25/--                      ●
●     To   LANSING DESK CO                Terms  2/10 N/30                      ●
●          137 WALNUT ST                  Deliver to DOWNING WAREHOUSE         ●
●          NEWARK NJ 07102                         765 PARR ST                 ●
●                                                  ATLANTA GA 30312            ●
●                                         Ship Via TRUCK                       ●
●                                                                              ●
●                                            FOB  ATLANTA                      ●
●     Please furnish the following material.                                   ●
```

QUANTITY	STOCK NO.	DESCRIPTION	UNIT PRICE	EXTENSION
4	68	DESK SECRETARIAL PLASTIC	112 50	450 00
6	77	DESK CLERICAL FORMICA	84 00	504 00
10	134	CHAIR ARMREST FABRIC	40 50	405 00
			TOTAL	1359 00

Robert Lang

Purchasing Agent

This purchase order was prepared by a computer system.

orders automatically when items reach their minimum inventory levels.

The use of the computer for controlling inventory is discussed in more detail in Chapter 3.

Activity E-1. Answer the following questions. Refer to the inventory card on page 45.

1. What is the purpose of the inventory card?

2. The inventory card provides information about which item?

3. What is the stock number of the item?

4. What are the maximum and minimum quantities for the item?

5. What is the unit cost of the merchandise received on April 28?

6. How many units of the item are on hand on March 27? on April 18? on May 2?

7. Does the balance of the item ever fall below the minimum quantity? If so, on what dates?

Activity E-2. Answer the following questions. Refer to the inventory sheet on page 46.

1. The merchandise for what sales department is listed on the inventory sheet?

2. How many people were involved in preparing the inventory sheet? Why do you think that several people were assigned to this task?

3. How many Stock No. G-211 golf bags are on hand? What is the unit cost? What is the total cost?

4. When was the inventory sheet prepared?

5. What is the total cost of all the items listed on the inventory sheet?

Topic 3 Problems

1-6. The Plaza Photo Mart purchases cameras, film, and projectors for its three departments. Most of these purchases are made on credit from two suppliers. However, small amounts of merchandise are sometimes bought for cash from other suppliers.

a. Open the following accounts, and enter the April 1 balances. General ledger: Cash, $3,826.40; Accounts Payable; Purchases—Cameras; Purchases—Film; Purchases—Projectors; Transportation In; Purchases Returns and Allowances—Cameras; Purchases Returns and Allowances—Film; Purchases Returns and Allowances—Projectors; and Purchases Discount. Accounts payable ledger: Galaxy Products and Osaka Corporation.

b. During the first two weeks of April, the business had the following transactions involving purchases, purchases returns, and cash payments. Record each transaction in the appropriate journal. The business has a purchases journal by departments, a purchases returns and allowances journal by departments, and a multicolumn cash payments journal.

c. Post the individual entries from the journals.

April	3	Bought film for $100 from Osaka Corporation; Invoice 3216, dated April 1; terms 2/10, n/30.
	5	Bought cameras for $520 from Galaxy Products; Invoice 741, dated April 3; terms 1/10, n/60.
	8	Received Credit Memorandum 29 for $70 from Galaxy Products for the return of a damaged camera bought on Invoice 741.
	9	Issued Check 502 for $98 to Osaka Corporation to pay Invoice 3216, less discount.
	10	Bought cameras and film

for $360 ($200 for cameras and $160 for film) from Osaka Corporation; Invoice 3298, dated April 8; terms 2/10, n/30.

April 11 Issued Check 503 for $445.50 to Galaxy Products to pay Invoice 741, less return and discount.

13 Bought projectors for $250 from Galaxy Products; Invoice 788, dated April 11; terms 1/10, n/60.

13 Issued Check 504 for $22 to Fleet Trucking for transportation of purchases from Galaxy Products.

1-7. Do the following work for the Plaza Photo Mart during the last two weeks of April.

a. Record these transactions.
b. Post the individual entries from the journals.
c. Foot and prove the journals.

Then enter the totals, and rule the journals.
d. Post the totals from the journals.

April 15 Issued Check 505 for $48 to Rex Industries for film purchased for cash.

April 16 Issued Check 506 for $352.80 to Osaka Corporation to pay Invoice 3298, less discount.

April 18 Bought cameras and projectors for $580 ($260 for cameras and $320 for projectors) from Galaxy Products; Invoice 825, dated April 16; terms 1/10, n/60.

19 Issued Check 507 for $247.50 to Galaxy Products to pay Invoice 788, less discount.

22 Received Credit Memorandum 35 for $140 from Galaxy Products for the return of a damaged projector purchased on Invoice 825.

24 Issued Check 508 for $435.60 to Galaxy Products to pay Invoice 825, less return and discount.

April 26 Bought film for $275 from Osaka Corporation; Invoice 3350, dated April 24; terms 2/10, n/30.

28 Received Credit Memorandum 106 for $35 from Osaka Corporation for the return of damaged film purchased on Invoice 3350.

29 Bought cameras for $630 from Galaxy Products; Invoice 848, dated April 26; terms 1/10, n/60.

29 Issued Check 509 for $18 to Ace Express for transportation of purchases from Osaka Corporation.

30 Received Credit Memorandum 39 for $110 from Galaxy Products for return of damaged cameras purchased on Invoice 848.

1-8. Prepare a purchases summary for the Plaza Photo Mart for the month ended April 30. This summary should report the purchases, transportation in, cost of delivered goods, purchases returns and allowances, purchase discounts, and net purchases for each department and for the business as a whole.

An examination of the transportation bills and purchase invoices for the month shows that the balances of the Transportation In account and the Purchases Discount account should be divided on the purchases summary as follows.

Transportation In: cameras, $20; film, $12; projectors, $8

Purchases Discount: cameras, $11.10; film, $5.20; projectors, $4.30

NOTE: Save the purchases summary for use in Topic Problem 1-9.

Topic 4
Gross Profit by Departments

A *Why does management need to know how profitable each sales department is?* This information helps management to judge how well the various parts of the business are operating. In a company that has a managerial accounting system, each sales department is considered a *profit center* because it earns revenue and is expected to produce a profit.

Olympic Sporting Goods Chart of Accounts

Assets
131 Merchandise Inventory—Bicycles
132 Merchandise Inventory—Golf Equipment
133 Merchandise Inventory—Tennis Equipment

Revenue
401 Sales—Bicycles
402 Sales Returns and Allowances—Bicycles
411 Sales—Golf Equipment
412 Sales Returns and Allowances—Golf Equipment
421 Sales—Tennis Equipment
422 Sales Returns and Allowances—Tennis Equipment

Costs and Expenses
501 Purchases—Bicycles
502 Purchases Returns and Allowances—Bicycles
511 Purchases—Golf Equipment
512 Purchases Returns and Allowances—Golf Equipment
521 Purchases—Tennis Equipment
522 Purchases Returns and Allowances—Tennis Equipment
531 Transportation In
532 Purchases Discount

The procedures for processing departmental sales, purchases, and merchandise inventory were covered in Topics 2 and 3. This topic shows how the data that results from these procedures is used to compute the gross profit on sales for each sales department and for the business as a whole.

Preparing a Statement of Gross Profit by Departments

As you learned in your previous studies, the gross profit on sales is determined by subtracting the cost of goods sold from the net sales. The amount of the gross profit on sales is reported on the income statement. However, it may also be presented on a *statement of gross profit by departments.* The information on this statement is important to management because the gross profit on sales earned by each department must be used to cover operating expenses and to provide net income for the business.

The data needed to prepare the statement of gross profit by departments is taken from the worksheet and from the schedule of cost of goods sold by departments. (See the illustrations on the next page and on page 52.) The steps for completing the statement are as follows.

STEP 1. *Revenue From Sales.* Enter the amount of sales and sales returns and allowances for each department. This data is shown in the Income Statement section of the worksheet. Compute the net sales for each department by subtracting the amount of sales returns and allowances from the amount of sales. Then compute the total amount of sales for the business by adding the individual amounts for the departments. Use the same procedure to compute the total sales returns and allowances and the total net sales.

STEP 2. *Cost of Goods Sold.* Enter the amount of cost of goods sold for each department and for the business as a whole. This data is shown on the schedule of cost of goods sold by departments.

STEP 3. *Gross Profit on Sales.* Compute the amount of gross profit on sales for each department and for the business as a whole by subtracting the cost of goods sold from the net sales.

The schedule of cost of goods sold by departments and the statement of gross profit by departments provide management with valuable information about departmental operations. In addition to reporting the cost of goods sold and the gross profit on sales for each department, these financial statements show data about departmental sales, purchases, and merchandise inventory.

Accounting Concept:
Departmental Gross Profit. The departmental gross profit on sales is the amount that each sales department contributes to the business to cover operating expenses and to provide net income.

Accounting Concept:

Profit Center. Each sales department is expected to produce a profit and is therefore often referred to as a profit center. Knowing the amount of profit for each department helps management to judge how well the department is operating.

Activity A-1. Answer the following questions. Refer to the chart of accounts shown on page 50 and the partial worksheet shown below.

1. How many accounts does the business use for merchandise inventory?

2. Are departmental accounts kept for sales and sales returns and allowances?

3. How many accounts does the business use for purchases? for transportation in? for purchases returns and allowances? for purchase discounts?

4. The worksheet shows decreases in which merchandise inventory accounts? What are the amounts of the decreases?

5. What balance is recorded on the worksheet for Sales—Bicycles? for Purchases—Bicycles?

OLYMPIC SPORTING GOODS
Worksheet
For the Month Ended May 31, 19—

ACCOUNT TITLE	ADJUSTMENTS DEBIT	ADJUSTMENTS CREDIT	INCOME STATEMENT DEBIT	INCOME STATEMENT CREDIT
Merchandise Inventory—Bicycles		(a) 875		
Merchandise Inventory—Golf Equipment		(b) 1,500		
Merchandise Inventory—Tennis Equipment	(c) 600			
Sales—Bicycles				4,620
Sales Ret. & Allow.—Bicycles			70	
Sales—Golf Equipment				6,630
Sales Ret. & Allow.—Golf Equipment			175	
Sales—Tennis Equipment				6,930
Sales Ret. & Allow.—Tennis Equipment			160	
Purchases—Bicycles			1,000	
Purchases Ret. & Allow.—Bicycles				50
Purchases—Golf Equipment			2,100	
Purchases Ret. & Allow.—Golf Equipment				125
Purchases—Tennis Equipment			4,200	
Purchases Ret. & Allow.—Tennis Equipment . . .				250
Transportation In			100	
Purchases Discount				94
Income Summary	(a) 875 (b) 1,500	(c) 600		

Activity A-2. Answer the following questions. Refer to the schedule of cost of goods sold by departments and the statement of gross profit by departments shown on page 52.

1. What is the total amount of purchases for the tennis equipment department? What is the net amount of purchases for that department?

2. Why is there a difference between the total amount of purchases and the net amount of purchases for each department?

3. What is the cost of goods sold for the golf equipment department?

4. What is the cost of goods sold for the whole business?

5. Which department has the highest net sales? Does it also have the highest gross profit on sales?

6. What is the gross profit on sales for the bicycles department?

7. What is the gross profit on sales for the whole business?

8. How is gross profit on sales computed?

OLYMPIC SPORTING GOODS
Schedule of Cost of Goods Sold by Departments
For the Month Ended May 31, 19—

	TOTAL	BICYCLES	GOLF EQUIPMENT	TENNIS EQUIPMENT
Merchandise Inventory, May 1	16,100 00	5,100 00	6,200 00	4,800 00
Purchases	7,300 00	1,000 00	2,100 00	4,200 00
Add: Transportation In .	100 00	15 00	35 00	50 00
Cost of Delivered Goods	7,400 00	1,015 00	2,135 00	4,250 00
Less: Purchases Ret. and Allow.	425 00	50 00	125 00	250 00
Purchases Discount	94 00	21 00	32 00	41 00
Net Purchases	6,881 00	944 00	1,978 00	3,959 00
Cost of Goods Available for Sale	22,981 00	6,044 00	8,178 00	8,759 00
Less: Merchandise Inventory, May 31 . . .	14,325 00	4,225 00	4,700 00	5,400 00
Cost of Goods Sold	8,656 00	1,819 00	3,478 00	3,359 00

OLYMPIC SPORTING GOODS
Statement of Gross Profit by Departments
For the Month Ended May 31, 19—

	TOTAL	BICYCLES	GOLF EQUIPMENT	TENNIS EQUIPMENT
Revenue From Sales: Sales	18,180 00	4,620 00	6,630 00	6,930 00
Less: Sales Returns and Allowances . . .	405 00	70 00	175 00	160 00
Net Sales	17,775 00	4,550 00	6,455 00	6,770 00
Cost of Goods Sold (see schedule)	8,656 00	1,819 00	3,478 00	3,359 00
Gross Profit on Sales . . .	9,119 00	2,731 00	2,977 00	3,411 00

Preparing an Income Statement for a Departmentalized Business

B *Can the information from the statement of gross profit by departments be used to prepare an income statement?* Yes, it is easy to prepare an income statement from the statement of gross profit. Look at the income statement shown below. The Total column of the statement of gross profit by departments is expanded by listing the operating expenses for the business. Then the total of the operating expenses is subtracted from the total gross profit to find the net income.

Notice that percentages appear below the departmental gross profit amounts. The percentages are computed by dividing the gross profit for each department by the total gross profit for the business. The percentage for the bicycles department was found as follows.

$$\$2,731 \div \$9,119 = 0.2994 = 30\%$$

OLYMPIC SPORTING GOODS
Income Statement
For the Month Ended May 31, 19—

	TOTAL	BICYCLES	GOLF EQUIPMENT	TENNIS EQUIPMENT
Revenue From Sales:				
Sales.	18,180 00	4,620 00	6,630 00	6,930 00
Less: Sales Returns				
and Allowances . . .	405 00	70 00	175 00	160 00
Net Sales	17,775 00	4,550 00	6,455 00	6,770 00
Cost of Goods Sold	8,656 00	1,819 00	3,478 00	3,359 00
Gross Profit on Sales. . .	9,119 00	2,731 00	2,977 00	3,411 00
	100%	30% *	33% *	37% *
Operating Expenses:				
Advertising Expense .	195 00			
Uncollectible Accounts				
Expense.	50 00			
Cash Short and Over .	10 00			
Delivery Expense. . . .	45 00			
Depreciation Expense	125 00			
Insurance Expense . . .	35 00			
Payroll Taxes Expense	367 00			
Rent Expense	650 00			
Salaries Expense	4,375 00			
Supplies Expense	70 00			
Utilities Expense	75 00			
Total Operating				
Expenses	5,997 00			
Net Income	3,122 00			

* This is the percent of departmental gross profit to total gross profit.

Bicycles:

$$\frac{\text{Departmental Gross Profit}}{\text{Total Gross Profit}} = \frac{\$2,731}{\$9,119} = 30\%$$

Golf Equipment:

$$\frac{\text{Departmental Gross Profit}}{\text{Total Gross Profit}} = \frac{\$2,977}{\$9,119} = 33\%$$

Tennis Equipment:

$$\frac{\text{Departmental Gross Profit}}{\text{Total Gross Profit}} = \frac{\$3,411}{\$9,119} = 37\%$$

These percentages make it easier to judge the profitability of the various departments. They provide a measure of the contribution that each department is making to the total gross profit for the business. By examining the percentages for a number of accounting periods, management can see the trend of profitability for each department.

Activity B. The gross profit amounts shown here are taken from two monthly income statements prepared for the Ryan Hardware Store.

1. Compute the percent of gross profit for each department for May and for June.

2. Study the departmental gross profit percents for each month. Which departments showed an increase in June? Which departments showed a decrease in June?

Department	Gross Profit for Month Ended May 31	Gross Profit for Month Ended June 30
Lumber	$12,000	$13,000
Paint	5,000	6,500
Roofing Materials	7,000	6,000
Supplies	2,000	2,000
Tools	3,000	3,500
Total	$29,000	$31,000

Topic 4   Problems

1-9. Prepare a schedule of cost of goods sold by departments for the Plaza Photo Mart. This schedule should cover the month ended April 30. Obtain the necessary data from the purchases summary that you completed in Topic Problem 1-8. The changes in the departmental merchandise inventories are as follows.

Department	Beginning Inventory	Ending Inventory
Cameras	$1,680	$2,000
Film	700	300
Projectors	1,200	1,050

1-10. Prepare a statement of gross profit by departments for the Plaza Photo Mart. This statement should cover the month ended April 30. Obtain the sales data from the sales summary that you completed in Topic Problem 1-5. Obtain the cost of goods sold from the schedule that you prepared in Topic Problem 1-9.

After you finish the statement of gross profit, compute the percent of gross profit for each department.

The Language of Business

Here are some basic terms that make up the language of business. Do you understand the meaning of each? Can you define each term in an original sentence?

revenues
cost of goods sold
expenses
managerial accounting
  system
income statement by
  departments
franchise operation

unit of operation
cost center
sales department
supportive department
cash receipts journal
  by departments
sales journal by
  departments

sales returns and
  allowances journal
  by departments
purchases journal by
  departments
purchases returns and
  allowances journal
  by departments

perpetual inventory
  procedure
physical inventory
profit center
statement of gross
  profit by
  departments

Chapter 1   Questions

1. What is a managerial accounting system?
2. What are the major objectives of managerial accounting?
3. What is a sales department? A supportive department?
4. What are the advantages of organizing a business by departments?
5. What types of departmental accounts are used in a managerial accounting system?
6. What principles should be followed for controlling sales?

7. What principles should be followed for controlling purchases?
8. Why do departmental journals make it easier to record transactions in a managerial accounting system?
9. Why is it important for management to know the gross profit for each department?
10. How is the percent of gross profit computed? Why is it helpful for management to study a department's percent of gross profit for several accounting periods?

Chapter 1   Problems

Problems for Chapter 1 are given in the *Working Papers and Chapter Problems* for Part 1. If you are using the workbook, do the problems in the space provided there. Complete your assigned topic problems before answering the chapter problems.

Chapter 1   Management Cases

Responsibility Accounting. The term *responsibility accounting* is sometimes used to describe an accounting system that provides financial information about each unit of an organization: a department, a branch store, or a chain store. Because this type of system reports the costs and profits for each unit, the efficiency of individual units can be determined. Responsibility for the financial results of each unit's operations can therefore be placed on the people who are running the unit.

Responsibility accounting gives management the information needed to control a business effectively and make decisions. Management can spot the weak areas of the organization and the people who are performing poorly. It can also spot the strong areas and the people who are doing a good job in running their operations.

Case 1M-1. The Jennings Department Store has ten sales departments. Each one is headed by a department manager who has a great deal of authority to select new merchandise, set prices, hire personnel, develop advertising plans, decide when to run sales, and so on. The department managers are paid a salary and receive no commissions. Salary increases are given to all the managers each year. The increases are usually about 9 percent of the present salaries. (The amount of the increase is intended to help the managers keep pace with inflation.)

During the past three years, the total amount of sales for the business has risen but the net income has fallen. Tom Jennings, the owner of the business, wants to find ways to improve the situation.

a. What factors might have caused the net income to fall even though the total amount of sales was rising? On what financial statements will Mr. Jennings find this information?

b. Mr. Jennings is thinking about changing his policy of yearly salary increases for all department managers. Instead, he is considering the idea of giving end-of-year bonuses to the managers whose departments show a higher gross profit on sales. The amount of the bonus would be tied to the size of the increase in profitability. The managers whose departments show no increase or have a smaller gross profit than the year before would receive no bonus. Do you agree with this idea? Why or why not?

c. Mr. Jennings is also thinking of starting a policy of transferring a department manager to a lower-level job and appointing a new manager if a department shows a decrease in profitability for two years in a row. Do you agree with this idea? Why or why not?

Case 1M-2. Alice Chang recently became the manager of a department that sells radios and television sets at the Top Value Appliance Store. She is disturbed about the inventory practices of the department and believes that they are hurting the efficiency and profitability of operations.

A perpetual inventory system is used. A set of inventory cards are kept by the stock clerk. The master set of inventory cards is kept in the accounting department to ensure proper internal control. However, when the stock clerk is busy unpacking new merchandise, the salesclerks often remove items they need from the stockroom and do not update the inventory cards. As a result, the department is constantly running out of stock on popular items. Since the inventory cards often do not show how low the quantity of such items is, the stock clerk is not able to reorder them on time.

A physical inventory is taken twice a year. However, the department has no established procedures for these inventories. There are no special forms for recording the count of the items. Any lined paper that happens to be available is used. Also, the counting and recording are done by salesclerks during business hours. They are often interrupted to help customers, and they lose track of their count for the items on a table or shelf. Each salesclerk works alone, counting, recording, and computing totals.

When the physical inventory is completed, the stock clerk compares the information on the inventory lists with the information on the inventory cards. There are many differences, but the stock clerk does not know whether the missing items were lost, stolen, or sold.

a. In what ways can these poor inventory practices hurt the efficiency and profitability of the department's operations?

b. What procedures would you suggest that Ms. Chang set up to improve the handling and recording of inventory?

Summarizing and Analyzing the Results of Operations

It is possible to determine net income or net loss for each sales department. If separate accounts are not kept for the expenses of each department, there are ways for allocating the expenses to the various departments. The total expenses for each department are then subtracted from the department's gross profit on sales to find the department's net income. (Of course, if the total amount of expenses is greater than the gross profit on sales, the department has incurred a net loss.)

In Chapter 1, you learned about the procedures for gathering data about the sales, purchases, and merchandise inventory of each department. You also learned how this data is used to prepare the statement of gross profit by departments. This chapter discusses methods for allocating expenses to departments. Having data about departmental expenses makes it possible to prepare an income statement by departments. The preparation of this type of income statement is covered later in the chapter. The chapter also discusses how business managers interpret the information shown on the income statement by departments and use it to make decisions.

Topic 1
Methods for Allocating Expenses to Departments

A *How are expense amounts allocated to specific departments?* Remember that **operating expenses** are the amounts spent for the goods and services needed to operate a business. **Allocating** these

Expenses are allocated by assigning shares of a business's expenses to its departments.

amounts simply means assigning shares of the expenses to the business's departments. For example, each department is charged with a share of the total rent expense.

There are a number of methods for allocating expenses. This topic explains several widely used methods.

Common Methods of Allocating Expenses to Departments:
- By net sales
- By equipment used
- By space occupied
- By salaries paid

- Allocating expenses by the amount of net sales in each department.
- Allocating expenses by the cost of the equipment that each department uses.
- Allocating expenses by the amount of space that each department occupies.
- Allocating expenses by the amount of salaries paid to the employees working in each department.

Each of these methods is suitable for allocating certain kinds of expenses, and most businesses use more than one method. For example, look at the worksheet shown on page 70. Notice that Olympic Sporting Goods uses all the methods listed above. (The worksheet for allocating expenses to departments is discussed later in the chapter.)

Types of Operating Expenses

Operating expenses may be classified as either direct or indirect expenses. A **direct expense** is one that is directly related to the selling of merchandise. Examples of direct expenses are the amounts spent for salaries of salesclerks, store supplies, and deliveries to customers. These expenses can usually be identified with specific sales departments. An **indirect expense** is one that is not directly related to the selling of merchandise. However, indirect expenses are necessary in the operation of a business. Examples of indirect expenses are the amounts spent for rent, utilities, and insurance. These expenses benefit the entire business and not a specific sales department. Expenses involved in the operation of a supportive department, such as the administrative office, are also classified as indirect expenses.

It is not always clear whether an expense item is a direct or indirect expense. For example, advertising can be either a direct expense or an indirect expense. If the purpose of the advertising is to publicize the name of the business, then the advertising can be viewed as an indirect expense because the entire business benefits. However, if the purpose of the advertising is to sell the products of a specific department, the advertising is a direct expense of that department.

Accounting Concept:
Departmental Net Income or Net Loss. To determine the net income or net loss for each sales department, it is necessary to collect data about departmental revenues and cost of goods sold and to allocate expenses among the departments. The data about revenues, cost of

goods sold, and expenses is summarized on the income statement by departments.

Accounting Concept:
Allocation Methods. Suitable methods must be selected for allocating expenses to the departments. Different methods may be needed for various kinds of expense items.

Activity A. Some operating expenses for a department store are listed here. Indicate whether each expense is a direct expense or an indirect expense. Use an "X" in the correct column.

	Direct Expense	Indirect Expense
EXAMPLE: Salaries paid to employees.	*X*	

1. Rent for the store building.
2. Utilities, such as electricity.
3. Office supplies, such as stationery.
4. Advertisements for the merchandise of one department.
5. Store supplies, such as wrapping paper.
6. Deliveries of merchandise to customers.

7. Insurance against fire damage.
8. Advertisements to publicize the name and location of the store.
9. Depreciation of the store equipment.
10. Uncollectible accounts owed by charge account customers.

Allocation by Net Sales Method

B *What kinds of operating expenses can be allocated to departments on the basis of departmental net sales?* These expenses include advertising expense, uncollectible accounts expense, cash short and over, delivery expense, and supplies expense.

Advertising Expense. The Advertising Expense account at Olympic Sporting Goods had a balance of $195 on May 31. An examination of the advertising bills for May showed that $120 was spent for radio commercials and $75 was spent for newspaper advertisements.

The advertising expense can be allocated according to the net sales of each department. For example, the bicycles department had 26 percent of the store's total net sales. Thus the bicycles department would be charged with 26 percent of the amount spent for advertising. This method is simple to apply. Also, it can be used when it is difficult to determine which department benefits directly from specific advertisements.

There is also another method, called the **time/space method,** that is often used to allocate advertising expense to the sales departments

Computing the Percent of Net Sales for a Department:

$$\frac{\text{Net Sales for Dept.}}{\text{Total Net Sales for Store}} = \text{Dept. Percent of Net Sales}$$

$$\frac{\$4,550}{\$17,775} = 0.255 = 26\%$$

Methods of Allocating Advertising Expense to Departments:
• By net sales
• By time or space used

within a store. This method involves assigning the advertising expense according to the time or space used. All the advertisements are analyzed to find the proportion of radio or television time or newspaper space devoted to the products of individual departments. Olympic Sporting Goods uses this procedure.

Radio. The business ran a series of short commercials on a local radio station during May. The total time involved in the commercials was 15 minutes. The $120 spent for this advertising is allocated on the basis of the number of minutes devoted to the products of each of the three sales departments. An examination of the radio commercials results in the following distribution.

Department	Number of Minutes for Each Department	Percent of Radio Time Devoted to Each Department		Total Spent for Radio Commercials		Amount Allocated to Each Department
Bicycles	3	20%	×	$120	=	$ 24
Golf Equipment	6	40	×	120	=	48
Tennis Equipment	6	40	×	120	=	48
	15	100%				$120

Computing the Percent of Radio Advertising Time for a Department:

$$\frac{\text{Radio Time for Dept.}}{\text{Total Time for Store}} = \frac{\text{Dept. Percent of Radio Time}}{}$$

$$\frac{3 \text{ min}}{15 \text{ min}} = 0.20 = 20\%$$

Each department's percent of radio time is found by dividing the number of minutes used to advertise the department's products by the total number of minutes that the business bought (15 minutes). For example, the bicycles department used 3 minutes of the total 15 minutes during May. Thus the percent of radio time for the bicycles department is computed as follows: $3 \div 15 = 0.20 = 20\%$. The amount allocated to each department is found by multiplying the total spent on radio commercials ($120) by the percent for the department. Thus the amount assigned to the bicycles department for radio advertising is computed in this way: $120 \times 20\% = \$24$.

Newspaper. Olympic Sporting Goods also had several advertisements in a local newspaper during May. The $75 spent for this advertising is allocated on the basis of the percent of newspaper space devoted to each sales department. The newspaper advertisements are measured to find the number of square inches (or square millimeters) used for the products of each department. Analysis of the May newspaper advertisements leads to the distribution shown at the top of the next page.

The analysis of the newspaper advertisements showed that 35 percent of the space was used for the bicycles department, 35 percent for the golf equipment department, and 30 percent for the tennis equipment department. The amount allocated to each department is found by multiplying the total spent on newspaper advertisements ($75)

Department	Percent of Newspaper Space Devoted to Each Department		Total Spent for Newspaper Advertisements		Amount Allocated to Each Department
Bicycles	35%	×	$75	=	$26.25
Golf Equipment	35	×	75	=	26.25
Tennis Equipment	30	×	75	=	22.50
	100%				$75.00

by the percent of space used for each department. Thus the amount assigned to the bicycles department is computed as follows: $75 × 35% = $26.25.

The share of the total advertising expense charged to each sales department is determined by adding the amounts for the department's radio advertising and newspaper advertising as shown below.

Department	Amount Allocated for Radio Commercials		Amount Allocated for Newspaper Advertisements		Advertising Expense for Each Department
Bicycles	$ 24	+	$26.25	=	$ 50.25
Golf Equipment	48	+	26.25	=	74.25
Tennis Equipment	48	+	22.50	=	70.50
	$120		$75.00		$195.00

Similar applications of the time/space method can be used to allocate amounts spent for television commercials, billboard advertisements, and magazine advertisements.

The advertisements discussed above are related to specific departments and are therefore classified as a direct expense. However, if a store runs advertisements that are intended to promote its name and publicize its location, business hours, and other general information, these advertisements are an indirect expense. The amounts spent for such advertisements benefit all the departments and would therefore be allocated on the basis of the net sales that each department had.

Uncollectible Accounts Expense. When management decides to make sales on credit, it is almost certain that some customers will not pay their accounts. The accounts receivable that cannot be collected are referred to as **uncollectible accounts.** The amount of uncollectible accounts is an indirect expense for the business because it results from the granting of credit by management.

After the uncollectible accounts expense is determined, management must decide how to allocate it to the sales departments. One

Uncollectible accounts expenses result from uncollectible accounts receivable.

logical way to allocate this expense is to use the net sales of the departments as the basis for determining the departmental shares. For example, Olympic Sporting Goods had an uncollectible accounts expense of $50 for the month of May. This amount was divided among the departments as shown here.

Department	Amount of Net Sales for Each Department	Percent of Net Sales for Each Department		Total Uncollectible Accounts Expense		Uncollectible Accounts Expense for Each Department
Bicycles	$ 4,550	26%	×	$50	=	$13
Golf Equipment	6,455	36	×	50	=	18
Tennis Equipment	6,770	38	×	50	=	19
	$17,775	100%				$50

Each department's percent of net sales is found by dividing the amount of net sales for the department by the total net sales for the business. During May, the bicycles department had net sales of $4,550 and the business had total net sales of $17,775. Thus the percent of net sales for the bicycles department is computed as follows: $4,550 ÷ $17,775 = 25.6\%$, or 26%.

Cash Short. As we discussed in Chapter 1, the three sales departments at Olympic Sporting Goods use the same cash register. Therefore, shortages in cash must be allocated to the departments. This is done on the basis of the net sales of each department.

A debit balance in the Cash Short and Over account represents a cash shortage and is a direct expense. Olympic Sporting Goods had a debit balance of $10 in the Cash Short and Over account on May 31. This amount was divided as follows.

Department	Amount of Net Sales for Each Department	Percent of Net Sales for Each Department		Total Cash Short and Over		Cash Short and Over for Each Department
Bicycles	$ 4,550	26%	×	$10	=	$ 2.60
Golf Equipment	6,455	36	×	10	=	3.60
Tennis Equipment	6,770	38	×	10	=	3.80
	$17,775	100%				$10.00

Delivery expenses are amounts spent to send merchandise to customers.

Delivery Expense. The management of Olympic Sporting Goods decided to allocate delivery expense on the basis of the net sales of each department. The total amount of delivery expense for May was $45.

The computation of each department's share of this amount is shown here. Delivery expense is a direct expense.

Department	Amount of Net Sales for Each Department	Percent of Net Sales for Each Department		Total Delivery Expense		Delivery Expense for Each Department
Bicycles	$ 4,550	26%	×	$45	=	$11.70
Golf Equipment	6,455	36	×	45	=	16.20
Tennis Equipment	6,770	38	×	45	=	17.10
	$17,775	100%				$45.00

Supplies Expense. During the month of May, Olympic Sporting Goods used store supplies that cost $50 and office supplies that cost $20. The store supplies are a direct expense. They are divided among the departments on the basis of the net sales of each department.

The $20 of office supplies that were used are an indirect expense. They are charged to the administrative office, which is a supportive department.

Stores supplies expenses are amounts spent for supplies needed in the operation of the sales departments.

Office supplies expenses are amounts spent for supplies needed in the operations of the office.

Department	Amount of Net Sales for Each Department	Percent of Net Sales for Each Department		Total Store Supplies Expense		Store Supplies Expense for Each Department
Bicycles	$ 4,550	26%	×	$50	=	$13
Golf Equipment	6,455	36	×	50	=	18
Tennis Equipment	6,770	38	×	50	=	19
	$17,775	100%				$50

Activity B. The Northside Supermarket recently spent $290 on advertising: $200 for radio commercials and $90 for newspaper advertisements. An analysis of the radio commercials and the newspaper advertisements revealed the following percent breakdown by departments.

Department	Percent of Radio Time	Percent of Newspaper Space
Baked Goods	10%	10%
Canned Goods	20	15
Dairy Products	15	10
Frozen Foods	5	10
Meats	30	30
Produce	10	15
Seafood	5	5
Snack Foods	5	5

1. Using the breakdown for radio time, allocate the $200 for radio commercials to the departments.
2. Using the breakdown for newspaper space, allocate the $90 for newspaper advertisements to the departments.
3. Determine the total advertising expense for each department of the Northside Supermarket.

Allocation by Equipment Used Method

C *What kinds of operating expenses can be allocated to departments on the basis of the equipment they use?* Depreciation expense and insurance expense are often allocated according to the cost of the equipment used by each department.

Depreciation expenses are amounts that result from allocating the cost of plant and equipment over its expected useful life.

Depreciation Expense. Each sales department at Olympic Sporting Goods uses certain store equipment, such as shelves, counters, and display racks. These items are part of the business's plant and equipment (fixed assets). All plant and equipment except land has a limited useful life. Eventually the items wear out or become inadequate for the business's needs. **Depreciation** is the process of allocating the cost of plant and equipment over its expected useful life. The amount of depreciation charged off during each accounting period is considered an expense.

The total monthly depreciation expense for the store equipment owned by Olympic Sporting Goods is $100. This expense is allocated to the sales departments according to the cost of the equipment used by each one. The monthly amounts assigned to the departments are shown here.

Department	Store Equipment Depreciation Expense for Each Department	Office Equipment Depreciation Expense for Each Department
Bicycles	$ 20	—
Golf Equipment	40	—
Tennis Equipment	40	—
Office	—	$25
	$100	$25

In addition to store equipment, Olympic Sporting Goods also owns office equipment—a typewriter, an electronic calculator, and so on. The total monthly depreciation expense for the office equipment is $25. The whole amount is assigned to the administrative office, a supportive department.

Since store equipment is associated with sales departments, the depreciation of store equipment is a direct expense of the business. The depreciation of office equipment represents an indirect expense.

Insurance Expense. According to its insurance records, Olympic Sporting Goods has a monthly cost of $35 for insuring its merchandise inventory and the equipment used in the store and the office. The $35 is an indirect expense.

The management of Olympic Sporting Goods believes that the main purpose of the insurance is to protect the merchandise and the store equipment. Therefore, none of the insurance expense is allocated to the administrative office. Instead, the total insurance expense is distributed to the sales departments in proportion to the cost of the merchandise and equipment in each department. The amount of merchandise and equipment that each department has is determined by a physical inventory.

Insurance expenses are amounts spent to buy protection against losses resulting from fire, theft, and other causes.

Department	Cost of Merchandise and Equipment in Each Department	Percent of Merchandise and Equipment in Each Department		Total Insurance Expense		Insurance Expense for Each Department
Bicycles	$ 8,000	20%	×	$35	=	$ 7.00
Golf Equipment	18,000	45	×	35	=	15.75
Tennis Equipment	14,000	35	×	35	=	12.25
	$40,000	100%				$35.00

The merchandise and store equipment owned by Olympic Sporting Goods has a total cost of $40,000. Each department's percent is found by dividing the cost of the merchandise and equipment in the department by the total cost for the business. The bicycles department has merchandise and equipment that cost $8,000. Thus its percent of merchandise and equipment is computed as follows: $8,000 ÷ $40,000 = 20%.

Activity C. The monthly insurance expense for a clothing store called the Jeans Scene is $75. The total cost of the merchandise and store equipment in each sales department is used as the basis for allocating the insurance expense. The total costs for the three sales departments are shown here.

Computing the Percent of Merchandise and Equipment for a Department:

$$\frac{\text{Cost of Merch. and Equip. in Dept.}}{\text{Total Cost of Merch. and Equip. for store}} = \frac{\text{Dept. Percent of Merch. and Equip.}}{}$$

$$\frac{\$\ 8,000}{\$40,000} = 0.20 = 20\%$$

Department	Cost of Merchandise and Equipment
Jeans	$35,000
Shirts	18,000
Sweaters	5,000
	$58,000

1. Compute the percent of the merchandise and equipment in each sales department.

2. Compute the amount of insurance expense to be allocated to each sales department.

Allocation by Space Occupied Method

D *What kinds of operating expenses can be allocated on the basis of the amount of the floor space in each department?* Both rent expense and utilities expense are usually assigned to the departments according to their floor space.

Rent expenses are amounts spent for the use of a building, land, or other items.

Rent Expense. Each month Olympic Sporting Goods pays $650 in rent for the store. This expense is an indirect expense. It is divided among the three sales departments and the administrative office on the basis of the amount of floor space occupied by each department and by the office.

The total floor space in the store is 4,500 square feet. The breakdown of floor space for the various units of the business is shown below. The amount for each sales department includes both the floor space that it uses in its selling area and the floor space it uses in the stockroom.

The allocation of the monthly rent expense to the three departments and the office was made in the following way.

Computing the Percent of Floor Space for a Department:

$$\frac{\text{Space in Bicycles Dept.}}{\text{Total Space in Store}} = \frac{\text{Dept. Percent of Space}}{}$$

$$\frac{900 \text{ sq ft}}{4{,}500 \text{ sq ft}} = 0.20 = 20\%$$

Department	Floor Space (Square Feet) in Each Department	Percent of Floor Space in Each Department		Total Rent Expense		Rent Expense for Each Department
Bicycles	900	20%	×	$650	=	$130.00
Golf Equipment	1,800	40	×	650	=	260.00
Tennis Equipment	1,575	35	×	650	=	227.50
Office	225	5	×	650	=	32.50
	4,500	100%				$650.00

Utilities expenses are amounts spent for electricity, heating fuel, and water.

Utilities Expense. The amounts that Olympic Sporting Goods spends for electricity and heating are recorded in the Utilities Expense account. This account had a balance of $75 on May 31. The $75 is allocated to the sales departments and the administrative office on the basis of the floor space that each one occupies, as shown here. Utilities expense is an indirect expense.

Department	Floor Space (Square Feet) in Each Department	Percent of Floor Space in Each Department		Total Utilities Expense		Utilities Expense for Each Department
Bicycles	900	20%	×	$75	=	$15.00
Golf Equipment	1,800	40	×	75	=	30.00
Tennis Equipment	1,575	35	×	75	=	26.25
Office	225	5	×	75	=	3.75
	4,500	100%				$75.00

Activity D. The management of the Family Clothing Center allocates rent expense to the sales departments and the administrative office on the basis of the amount of floor space that each occupies. The total monthly rent is $800. The breakdown of floor space for the various departments of the business is shown here.

Department	Floor Space (Square Feet)
Accessories	400
Children's Clothing	1,000
Men's Clothing	1,000
Women's Clothing	1,600
Shoes	400
Office	100
	4,500

1. Compute the percent of floor space for each sales department and for the administrative office.

2. Compute the amount of rent expense to be allocated to each unit.

Allocation by Salaries Method

E *What kinds of operating expenses can be allocated on the basis of the amount of salaries paid by each department?* Salaries expense and payroll taxes expense are two expenses that can be allocated to departments in this way.

Salaries Expense. The total salaries expense for Olympic Sporting Goods in May was $4,375. The share of this expense to be charged to each department is the payroll for the employees in that department.

Salaries expenses are the gross earnings of employees.

The payroll journal shows the amount earned by each employee in each department. These amounts must be added to compute the payroll for each department. (The gross earnings are used for this computation, not the net pay.)

The allocation of salaries expense shown here assumes that the salesclerks sell merchandise in only the department to which they are assigned. This is not always the case. A salesclerk will sometimes sell merchandise from another department. However, in most situations, the method used here is reasonably accurate.

Department	Salaries Expense for Each Department
Bicycles	$ 800
Golf Equipment	900
Tennis Equipment	975
Office	1,700
	$4,375

Salaries paid to salesclerks are a direct expense, whereas salaries paid to office personnel are an indirect expense.

Payroll taxes expenses are taxes paid by a business on its payroll, such as federal and state unemployment taxes and the employer's share of FICA tax.

Payroll Taxes Expense. Olympic Sporting Goods had a total payroll taxes expense of $367 for the month of May. This expense includes the employer's share of FICA tax, the federal unemployment tax, and the state unemployment tax. After the payroll records are examined, the total payroll taxes expense is allocated to the departments as shown here.

Department	Payroll Taxes Expense for Each Department
Bicycles	$ 67.10
Golf Equipment	75.50
Tennis Equipment	81.80
Office	142.60
	$367.00

In a larger business than Olympic Sporting Goods, it is usually not practical to examine the payroll records to see which employees in which departments are subject to each payroll tax. Thus since payroll taxes are determined by the amount of the payroll, this expense is allocated on the basis of the salaries expense for each department. The amount of the total payroll taxes expense for the business is multiplied by each department's percentage of the total salaries expense to find the share of the payroll taxes to be assigned to each department. Payroll taxes expense is classified as an indirect expense.

Activity E. The monthly payroll for Stacy's Farm and Garden Center during June was $15,185. This is the total gross earnings for all employees in the three sales departments and the office. The payroll journal shows the following information about the monthly salaries of the employees in each unit.

Equipment and Tools Department	Fertilizer and Pesticides Department	Plants and Seed Department	Administrative Office
6 employees earned $650 each	5 employees earned $500 each	3 employees earned $540 each	2 employees earned $525 each
3 employees earned $525 each	2 employees earned $700 each	2 employees earned $710 each	
1 employee earned $500		2 employees earned $610 each	

Using the information provided, compute the amount of salaries expense to be allocated to each sales department and to the office.

Worksheet for Allocating Expenses to Departments

F *What is the purpose of the worksheet for allocating expenses?* The **worksheet for allocating expenses to departments** is used to distribute the business's expenses to each of the sales departments and to any supportive departments. The steps involved in preparing the worksheet are as follows. (Refer to the worksheet on page 70 as you read each step.)

1 The direct expenses are usually entered first. Then the indirect expenses are recorded. The name and balance of each expense account are listed on the worksheet.

2 The method to be used to allocate each expense is written in the Allocation Method column. As you have seen, different methods are used for different kinds of expenses. The accountant and management decide which methods are most suitable.

3 Each expense is distributed to the proper departments by the method shown in the Allocation Method column.

4 After all expenses have been distributed, the column for each department is totaled. The Account Balance column is also totaled.

5 The total of the Office column is distributed among the sales departments. The percent of departmental net sales to total net sales is used as the basis for distributing the expenses of the office to the sales departments. This distribution completes the allocation of expenses to the departments.

6 The columns for the sales departments are totaled again to determine the overall amount of operating expenses to be charged to each department.

When the worksheet for allocating expenses to departments is completed, management is able to analyze and compare the operating expenses for all the departments. For example, the expenses of the tennis equipment department can be compared to the expenses of the other two sales departments.

An examination of the worksheet shows that the tennis equipment department had the highest total expenses in May. However, this total is very close to the total for the golf equipment department. The bicycles department had much lower total expenses than the tennis equipment department. One reason for the difference is that the tennis equipment department has a larger payroll. Another reason is that the tennis equipment department occupies more floor space than the bicycles department and must therefore absorb more of the rent and utilities expenses.

The total expenses for each department can now be matched with the departmental gross profit amounts, and the net income or net loss for each department can be determined.

OLYMPIC SPORTING GOODS
Worksheet for Allocating Expenses to Departments
For the Month Ended May 31, 19—

EXPENSES (1)	ACCOUNT BALANCE	ALLOCATION METHOD (2)	OFFICE	BICYCLES	GOLF EQUIPMENT	TENNIS EQUIPMENT
Direct Expenses:						
Advertising Expense	195 00	Time/Space		50 25	74 25	70 50
Cash Short and Over	10 00	Net Sales		2 60	3 60	3 80
Delivery Expense	45 00	Net Sales		11 70	16 20	17 10
Depreciation Expense—Store		Equipment		20 00	40 00	40 00
Equipment	100 00					
Sales Salaries Expense	2,675 00	Salaries		800 00	900 00	975 00
Store Supplies Expense	50 00	Net Sales		13 00	18 00	19 00
Indirect Expenses:						
Uncollectible Accounts Expense . .	50 00	Net Sales		13 00	18 00	19 00
Depreciation Expense—Office		Equipment	25 00			
Equipment	25 00					
Insurance Expense	35 00	Merchandise/				
		Equipment		7 00	15 75	12 25
Office Salaries Expense	1,700 00	Salaries	1,700 00			
Office Supplies Expense	20 00	Office	20 00			
Payroll Taxes Expense	367 00	Salaries	142 60	67 10	75 50	81 80
Rent Expense	650 00	Floor Space	32 50	130 00	260 00	227 50
Utilities Expense	75 00	Floor Space	3 75	15 00	30 00	26 25
Totals	5,997 00	(4)	1,923 85	1,129 65	1,451 30	1,492 20
Allocation of Expenses for Office . .		Net Sales	(1,923 85)	500 20	692 59	731 06
Total Expenses Charged to						
Sales Depts.		(5)	(6)	1,629 85	2,143 89	2,223 26

Activity F. Answer the following questions. Refer to the worksheet for allocating expenses to departments, which is shown above.

1. How much advertising expense is charged to the bicycles department? to the tennis equipment department?

2. What is the largest expense for each sales department?

3. What method is being used to allocate store supplies expense? rent expense? payroll taxes expense?

4. What is the largest expense for the office?

5. What is the total of the operating expenses for the office?

6. What method is being used to allocate the office expenses to the sales departments?

7. What is the total of the operating expenses for the tennis equipment department after the office expenses are allocated?

Topic 1   Problems

2-1. The total uncollectible accounts expense for the Wilderness Recreation Shop during April was $175. The management of the business decided to allocate this expense on the basis of each department's net sales. Information about the net sales amounts for the month follows.

Department	Net Sales
Camping Equipment	$15,000
Canoes	10,000
Fishing Tackle	12,000
Motorboats	20,000
Sailboats	18,000
	$75,000

a. Compute the percent of net sales for each department.

b. Compute the amount of uncollectible accounts expense to be allocated to each department.

2-2. What method of allocating expenses to departments would you use for each of the following operating expenses?

a. Sales Salaries Expense
b. Cash Short and Over
c. Advertising Expense
d. Utilities Expense
e. Uncollectible Accounts Expense
f. Rent Expense
g. Store Supplies Expense
h. Depreciation Expense

2-3. The Style-N-Comfort Shoe Center has three sales departments: children's shoes, men's shoes, and women's shoes. There is also a supportive department, the administrative office. Prepare a worksheet for allocating expenses to the departments of this business. The worksheet should cover the month ended March 31. The operating expenses, their account balances, and the allocation methods to be used are listed here.

Operating Expense	Account Balance	Allocation Method
Direct Expenses:		
Advertising Expense	$ 100	Net Sales
Delivery Expense	110	Net Sales
Sales Salaries Expense	4,850	Departmental Salaries
Indirect Expenses:		
Uncollectible Accounts Expense	70	Net Sales
Office Salaries Expense	1,800	Departmental Salaries
Rent Expense	700	Floor Space
Utilities Expense	150	Floor Space

The percent of net sales and percent of floor space for the departments are as follows. The salary amounts are given on the top of page 72.

Department	Percent of Net Sales	Percent of Floor Space
Children's Shoes	25%	20%
Men's Shoes	35	35
Women's Shoes	40	40
Office	—	5

MONTHLY SALES SALARIES BY DEPARTMENTS

Children's Shoes	Men's Shoes	Women's Shoes
1 employee earned $500	1 employee earned $900	1 employee earned $960
1 employee earned $250*	1 employee earned $600	1 employee earned $740
	1 employee earned $200*	1 employee earned $700

*A part-time employee.

NOTE: Save the worksheet for further use in Topic Problem 2-4.

Topic 2
The Income Statement by Departments

A *Why is the income statement by departments an important source of information for management?* The income statement by departments reports the results of operations for each department and for the business as a whole during a period of time. For example, the income statement by departments shown on page 73 presents the revenues, cost of goods sold, expenses, and net income for Olympic Sporting Goods during the month of May. Financial information is provided for the administrative office as well as the sales departments. This information allows management to analyze the operations of each unit of the business.

Preparing the Income Statement by Departments

In Chapter 1, you learned how to prepare the statement of gross profit by departments. The Revenue From Sales section, Cost of Goods Sold section, and Gross Profit on Sales section of the income statement by departments are completed in the same way as they were on the statement of gross profit by departments.

Refer to the income statement by departments on page 73. The data needed to compute the net sales and the cost of goods sold comes from the business's regular worksheet (page 51). The details of the cost of goods sold do not appear on the income statement by departments. They are presented on a separate schedule of cost of goods sold by departments (page 52). The gross profit on sales is computed by subtracting the cost of goods sold from the net sales.

The Operating Expenses section is prepared from the data on the worksheet for allocating expenses to departments (page 70). The net income for the whole business is computed by subtracting the total operating expenses from the total gross profit on sales. The net income for each sales department is computed by subtracting the total departmental expenses from the departmental gross profit on sales.

OLYMPIC SPORTING GOODS
Income Statement by Departments
For the Month Ended May 31, 19—

	TOTAL	OFFICE	BICYCLES	GOLF EQUIPMENT	TENNIS EQUIPMENT
Revenue From Sales:					
Sales	18,180 00		4,620 00	6,630 00	6,930 00
Less: Sales Returns					
and Allowances .	405 00		70 00	175 00	160 00
Net Sales	17,775 00		4,550 00	6,455 00	6,770 00
Cost of Goods Sold					
(see schedule)	8,656 00		1,819 00	3,478 00	3,359 00
Gross Profit on Sales .	9,119 00		2,731 00	2,977 00	3,411 00
Operating Expenses:					
Direct Expenses:					
Advertising					
Expense	195 00		50 25	74 25	70 50
Cash Short					
and Over	10 00		2 60	3 60	3 80
Delivery Expense	45 00		11 70	16 20	17 10
Depreciation					
Expense—Store					
Equipment . . .	100 00		20 00	40 00	40 00
Sales Salaries					
Expense	2,675 00		800 00	900 00	975 00
Store Supplies					
Expense	50 00		13 00	18 00	19 00
Total Direct					
Expenses . . .	3,075 00		897 55	1,052 05	1,125 40
Indirect Expenses:					
Uncollectible					
Accounts					
Expense	50 00		13 00	18 00	19 00
Depreciation					
Expense—Office					
Equipment . . .	25 00	25 00			
Insurance Expense	35 00		7 00	15 75	12 25
Office Salaries					
Expense	1,700 00	1,700 00			
Office Supplies					
Expense	20 00	20 00			
Payroll Taxes					
Expense	367 00	142 60	67 10	75 50	81 80
Rent Expense . . .	650 00	32 50	130 00	260 00	227 50
Utilities Expense .	75 00	3 75	15 00	30 00	26 25
Total Indirect					
Expenses . . .	2,922 00	1,923 85	232 10	399 25	366 80
Total Operating					
Expenses	5,997 00	1,923 85	1,129 65	1,451 30	1,492 20
Allocation of					
Expenses for Office .		(1,923 85)	500 20	692 59	731 06
Total Departmental					
Expenses			1,629 85	2,143 89	2,223 26
Net Income	3,122 00		1,101 15	833 11	1,187 74

Interpreting the Income Statement by Departments

Net Income for Departments	
Bicycles	$1,101.15
Golf Equipment	833.11
Tennis Equipment	1,187.74

The first step in interpreting the income statement by departments is usually to compare the net income amounts for the various sales departments. When the owner and the manager of Olympic Sporting Goods do this with the income statement shown on page 76, they find that the tennis equipment department earned the highest net income ($1,187.74) in May and the golf equipment department produced the lowest net income ($833.11). The net income for the bicycles department ($1,101.15) was close to that of the tennis equipment department.

Being able to interpret financial information is an important skill.

Martin Bough/Studios, Inc.

The owner and the manager of Olympic Sporting Goods feel that the result of the golf equipment department's operations during May was disappointing. They decide to study the situation further by comparing the net sales amounts. They find that the net sales amount for the golf equipment department ($6,455) is similar to the net sales amount for the tennis equipment department ($6,770). The bicycles department had much lower net sales ($4,550). On the basis of these figures, it appears that the golf equipment department should have earned more net income than the bicycles department and almost as much net income as the tennis equipment department.

The next step that the owner and the manager of the store take is to compare the cost of goods sold amounts. They determine that the golf

Net Sales for Departments	
Bicycles	$4,550
Golf Equipment	6,455
Tennis Equipment	6,770

equipment department had the highest cost of goods sold ($3,478). This reduced the department's profitability. Although the golf equipment department had net sales of $6,455, its gross profit was only $2,977. The bicycles department, which had net sales of $4,550, earned a gross profit of $2,731.

Finally, the owner and the manager of the store examine the operating expenses. They find that the total of the departmental expenses for the golf equipment department ($2,143.89) is close to that for the tennis equipment department ($2,223.26). The bicycles department has a much lower total for departmental expenses ($1,629.85).

Since many of the operating expenses are allocated on the basis of net sales, the level of the operating expenses for the golf equipment department reflects the amount of its net sales to a great extent. The level of the operating expenses also reflects the fact that this department occupies more floor space than any other department.

The major factor lowering the net income of the golf equipment department seems to be its cost of goods sold. The owner and the manager of Olympic Sporting Goods plan to look into this matter carefully. For example, they want to find out why the golf equipment department had a large decrease ($1,500) in its merchandise inventory during May. (See the schedule of cost of goods sold by departments on page 52.)

Costs of Goods Sold for Departments	
Bicycles	$1,819
Golf Equipment	3,478
Tennis Equipment . .	3,359

Gross Profit on Sales for Departments	
Bicycles	$2,731
Golf Equipment	2,977
Tennis Equipment . .	3,411

Accounting Concept:

Income Statement by Departments. The income statement by departments reports financial information about the operations of a departmentalized business during a period of time. This statement shows how each sales department's net income was earned or how its net loss was incurred.

Activity A. Answer the following questions. Refer to the income statement by departments shown on page 73.

1. What is the total net income for the business?

2. Which department has the highest net sales?

3. Which department has the highest net income?

4. Which department has the lowest cost of goods sold?

5. What amount of gross profit has the bicycles department earned?

6. What is the amount of direct expenses for the tennis equipment department?

7. How much advertising expense is assigned to the golf equipment department?

8. How much of the total operating expenses for the office is allocated to the bicycles department?

9. What is the amount of the total departmental expenses for the tennis equipment department?

10. What document supplies the data that appears in the Revenue From Sales section?

11. What document supplies the

data that appears in the Operating Expenses section?

12. Why do you think that the bicycles department has been able to earn almost as much net income as the tennis equipment department even though its net sales are $2,200 less than the net sales of the tennis equipment department?

Interpreting a Series of Income Statements

B *Does management ever use a series of income statements to make business decisions?* Yes, a series of income statements can be used to compare the results of operations for a number of months or years. Management can then see what trends are developing. Several common ways of comparing the information from a series of income statements are discussed in this section.

Sometimes the revenues, costs, expenses, and net income from two or more income statements are presented in a single financial report. This report is called a *comparative income statement.*

Comparing Net Income. The comparative income statement illustrated here for Olympic Sporting Goods covers a five-month period. This statement shows the following net income amounts for the business from January through May.

Net income increased during the first three months but dropped sharply in April. (It went from $5,100 in March to $2,000 in April.) Net income rose again in May but did not reach the levels of the first three months.

OLYMPIC SPORTING GOODS Comparative Income Statement For the Five Months Ended May 31, 19—					
	JANUARY	FEBRUARY	MARCH	APRIL	MAY
Net Sales	16,100 00	17,360 00	19,600 00	16,400 00	17,775 00
Cost of Goods Sold (see schedule)	7,000 00	7,400 00	8,500 00	8,000 00	8,656 00
Gross Profit on Sales .	9,100 00	9,960 00	11,100 00	8,400 00	9,119 00
Operating Expenses: Direct Expenses: Advertising Expense	100 00	130 00	195 00	195 00	195 00
Total Operating Expenses	5,100 00	5,800 00	6,000 00	6,400 00	5,997 00
Net Income	4,000 00	4,160 00	5,100 00	2,000 00	3,122 00

	January	February	March	April	May
Net Income	$4,000	$4,160	$5,100	$2,000	$3,122

Usually, April and May are very busy months at Olympic Sporting Goods. However, because several local businesses have laid off employees, many people do not have money to spend on new sports equipment. The owner and the manager of the store have therefore decided to do two things. They will increase their advertising in a nearby suburban area that is not affected by unemployment. They will also control expenses very carefully.

Comparing Net Sales. Changes in sales patterns can easily be identified by comparing each department's net sales from month to month. The following table shows each department's share of the total net sales at Olympic Sporting Goods during the five-month period from January to May.

$$\frac{\text{Net Sales for a Dept.}}{\text{Total Net Sales for Store}} = \frac{\text{Dept. Percent of Net Sales}}{}$$

Department	Percent of Net Sales for Each Department				
	January	February	March	April	May
Bicycles	21%	22%	22%	24%	26%
Golf Equipment	40	39	38	37	36
Tennis Equipment	39	39	40	39	38
	100%	100%	100%	100%	100%

Computing the percent of net sales for the Bicycles Department in May:

$$\frac{\$\ 4,550}{\$17,775} = 0.255 = 26\%$$

The net sales for the golf equipment department decreased steadily, going from 40 percent in January to 36 percent in May. However, the bicycles department figures showed an improvement. Its net sales increased from 21 percent of total net sales in January to 26 percent in May. The net sales for the tennis equipment department moved up and down and then ended the five-month period 1 percent below the level of January.

The poor sales trend for the golf equipment department shows that the operations of this department must be examined carefully. Remember that the income statement for May also indicated that there may be operations problems in the golf equipment department.

Comparing Expenses. The trend of each expense item can be analyzed over several periods. For example, the following table on top of page 78 shows the trend of the advertising expense at Olympic Sporting Goods from January to May. The percents were computed by dividing the total advertising expense for each month by the total net sales for that month. For example, $100 \div $16,100 = 0.6\%$.

$$\frac{\text{Expense Item}}{\text{Net Sales}} = \frac{\text{Percent of Expense Item to Net Sales}}{}$$

Month	Advertising Expense		Net Sales		Percent of Advertising Expense to Net Sales
January	$100	÷	$16,100	=	0.6%
February	130	÷	17,360	=	0.7
March	195	÷	19,600	=	1.0
April	195	÷	16,400	=	1.2
May	195	÷	17,775	=	1.1

Both the amount of the advertising expense and the percent of this expense to net sales increased between January and May. The amount rose from $100 in January to $195 in March and then remained at the same level. The percent rose from 0.6 in January to 1.2 in April and then dropped slightly in May.

$$\frac{\text{Net Sales for a Dept.}}{\text{No. of Salesclerks in Dept.}} = \frac{\text{Average Sales}}{\text{for Salesclerks}}$$

Comparing Salesclerk Productivity. The productivity of the salesclerks working in a department can easily be measured. The amount of the department's net sales is divided by the number of salesclerks in the department during the period. This shows the average sales revenue produced by each salesclerk. By comparing such amounts for several periods, management can see the trend of productivity within the department.

Month	Net Sales of Tennis Equipment Department		Number of Salesclerks in Department		Average Sales for Each Salesclerk
January	$4,400	÷	4	=	$1,100
February	4,800	÷	4	=	1,200
March	5,000	÷	4	=	1,250
April	5,900	÷	4	=	1,475
May	6,770	÷	5	=	1,354

The productivity of the four salesclerks in the tennis equipment department of Olympic Sporting Goods increased from January to April. In May, a fifth salesclerk was hired and the average sales for each salesclerk decreased. This is not surprising since new salesclerks usually need training and some experience before they can perform effectively.

It is also useful to compare the productivity of the salesclerks in one department to the productivity of the salesclerks in the other departments.

Comparing Expenses for Supportive Departments. The trend of expenses involved in operating a supportive department can be examined over several periods. For example, the following table shows a substantial increase in total expenses for the administrative office at Olympic Sporting Goods from January to May.

	January	February	March	April	May
Total Expenses for Office*	$1,300	$1,412	$1,805	$1,910	$1,924

*All these amounts are rounded to the nearest whole dollar.

Since office salaries make up the largest part of the total office expenses, the payroll register was studied to find the reasons for the upward trend in office expenses. The payroll register showed the following information. The manager of the store received a salary increase in February. A full-time accounting clerk was hired in March to replace a part-time accounting clerk who worked in the office previously. The new accounting clerk did a lot of overtime work in April and May.

Activity B. The Norris Marina sells boats in addition to renting space at its docks and providing a repair service. The business has been running an advertising campaign for its boats during the past five months. The monthly amounts spent for advertising and the monthly net sales for the boats are shown here.

1. Compute the percent of advertising expense to the net sales for each month.
2. Did the percent of advertising expense increase during the five months?
3. Study the trend of the advertising expense and the trend of the net sales. Would you suggest that the marina continue its advertising campaign in future months? Why or why not?

Month	Advertising Expense	Net Sales
March	$100	$20,000
April	125	22,000
May	150	26,000
June	180	27,000
July	180	28,000

Topic 2 Problems

2-4. Prepare an income statement by departments for the Style-N-Comfort Shoe Center. Data about the sales, sales returns and allowances, and cost of goods sold for the three sales departments is given on page 80. Obtain the data about the operating expenses from the worksheet for allocating expenses that you prepared in Topic Problem 2-3. The income statement by departments should cover the month ended March 31. Be sure to compute the totals for the business. For example, add the departmental sales amounts to find the total sales.

	Children's Shoes	Men's Shoes	Women's Shoes
Sales	$4,400	$6,200	$6,900
Sales Returns and Allowances	150	250	100
Cost of Goods Sold	1,300	1,800	2,100

2-5. The management of the Style-N-Comfort Shoe Center wishes to make an analysis of the operations of the department that sells children's shoes. Prepare an analysis sheet like the one shown here. The amounts needed to complete the analysis sheet are given on the income statement that you prepared in Topic Problem 2-4. Compute the percents. (Do this work in your workbook or on a sheet of paper if you are not using the workbook.)

INCOME STATEMENT ANALYSIS SHEET

	Total for Store	Percent of Total Net Sales*	Amount for Children's Department	Percent of Dept. Net Sales**
Net Sales	$	100	$	100
Cost of Goods Sold				
Gross Profit on Sales	$		$	
Total Direct Expenses				
Total Indirect Expenses				
Total Operating Expenses	$		$	
Allocation of Expenses for Office				
Total Departmental Expenses				
Net Income	$		$	

* To find these percents, divide each total amount for the store by the total net sales.
** To find these percents, divide each departmental amount by the departmental net sales.

2-6. Examine the analysis sheet that you prepared in Topic Problem 2-5. Using the information from this sheet, answer the following questions.

a. Has the department for children's shoes produced a higher or lower percent of gross profit on sales than the store as a whole?

b. Does the department for children's shoes have a higher or lower percent of total operating expenses than the store as a whole?

c. Has the department for children's shoes produced a higher or lower percent of net income than the store as a whole?

d. Does it appear that the department for children's shoes is being operated efficiently and profitably in comparison to the store as a whole? Explain your answer.

The Language of Business

Here are some basic terms that make up the language of business. Do you understand the meaning of each? Can you define each term and use it in an original sentence?

allocating expenses
direct expense
indirect expense
advertising expense
delivery expense
store supplies expense

office supplies expense
depreciation expense
insurance expense
rent expense
utilities expense
salaries expense

payroll taxes expense
uncollectible
  accounts expense
worksheet for
  allocating expenses
  to departments

income statement by
  departments
comparative income
  statement

Chapter 2   Questions

1. What are four common methods of allocating expenses to departments?
2. What is a direct expense? What is an indirect expense?
3. What two methods can be used to allocate advertising expense to sales departments?
4. How is store supplies expense allocated? How is office supplies expense allocated?
5. Explain how utilities expense is allocated.
6. Explain how to prepare the worksheet for allocating expenses to departments.

7. Why is it necessary for a business to allocate expenses to its departments?
8. How can an income statement by departments help management to evaluate the operations of a business?
9. What is the purpose of a comparative income statement?
10. Why is it useful to compare financial data, such as net sales and net income, for several periods?

Chapter 2   Problems

Problems for Chapter 2 are given in the *Working Papers and Chapter Problems* for Part 1. If you are using the workbook, do the problems in the space provided there. Complete your assigned topic problems before answering the chapter problems.

Chapter 2   Management Cases

The Bottom Line. Business managers often use the term *the bottom line.* They are referring to the last line of the income statement—the line that shows the net income or net loss. The bottom line plays a major role in many business decisions. For example, in a departmentalized business, the net income or net loss of each sales department over several periods will usually determine whether the unit is expanded, kept at its present size, or closed. Management wants to use the business's space and financial resources for the departments that have the best profit potential.

Of course, there are other factors that must be considered besides the bottom line when making decisions about the future of a sales department. One important factor is the relationship of the department to the other departments in the business. Some departments produce little or no profit themselves but attract many customers to a store. Once these customers are in the store, they buy goods in several departments. Thus one unprofitable department may be responsible for building up the amount of sales in a number of profitable departments.

While some unprofitable departments make a strong contribution to the overall profitability of a business, other unprofitable departments do not. These departments are simply a drain on the resources of the business and should be closed.

Case 2M-1. The Madison Shop is a large store that sells men's clothing. The store has departments for coats, suits, sportswear, shirts and ties, and shoes. Of these five departments, all are operating profitably except the shoe department, which has had small losses in 10 of the last 12 months. Although the losses are small, management is disturbed because a trend of unprofitability has clearly developed in this department.

The shoe department has a good location near the front of the store, but its appearance is old-fashioned and unappealing. A manager and two salesclerks work in the department. The manager feels that the department's problems are caused by the opening of two attractive, modern shoe stores in the area during the past year. He also feels that the business does not run enough advertising for the shoe department.

The Madison Shop's slogan is "One-stop shopping for the busy man." Many of the customers seem to like the convenience of being able to buy all their clothes in one place. When they visit the store, they usually buy items in several departments, including the shoe department.

The general manager of the Madison Shop is considering the following three plans for dealing with the unprofitability of the shoe department.

Plan 1: Close the shoe department. Give its selling space to the sportswear department, which is highly profitable, has a growing sales volume, and needs space for expansion.

Plan 2: Keep the shoe department open. Leave it in its present good selling location. However, buy new equipment, and redecorate the department so that it has an eye-catching, modern look. Run a major advertising campaign for the department.

Plan 3: Keep the shoe department open, but move it to a smaller area at the back of the store. Give the extra space to the sportswear department for expansion. Use the old equipment for the shoe department, and maintain its advertising at the present level. Reduce the staff of the department by transferring one of its salesclerks to the sportswear department.

a. Does the shoe department seem to have any importance to the business besides its ability to produce a profit?

b. What are the advantages and disadvantages of each of the plans that the general manager is considering?

c. Which plan would you select if you were the general manager? Why?

d. Can you think of any other ways to improve the profitability of the shoe department?

Case 2M-2. Quality Photographic Products sells cameras, projectors, film, and accessories such as camera cases and lenses. The business occupies a large store that is located on a highway several miles from town. The staff consists of four full-time salesclerks and two part-time salesclerks. The owner manages operations.

All the departments earn a good rate of gross profit. However, when the expenses are subtracted, the net income is usually very small. Prices cannot be raised because of competition from other stores that sell the same type of products.

Several months ago, the business's accountant told the owner that the total expenses are too great in relation to the amount of sales. The owner therefore tried to reduce expenses by stopping all advertising. This did not help the situation. Although expenses went down, the sales revenue also decreased.

The accountant has now suggested that the owner move the business to a smaller, less costly store in a downtown area and reduce the number of salesclerks. However, the owner wants to stay and start a film developing department.

One of the salesclerks who currently works in the store would be placed in the new department. The actual developing would be done by a photographic laboratory in town. This laboratory would pick up the film and deliver the finished pictures to the store. Thus there would be no need for the store to buy equipment. Despite this, the owner does not expect that the new department will earn much profit from its own operations.

a. Do you think that it was wise for the owner to stop the store's advertising in an effort to reduce expenses? Why or why not?

b. How could the accountant's suggestions improve the business's net income?

c. How could the owner's plan for starting a film developing department improve the business's net income even though the new department would not be very profitable?

d. If you were the owner of the store, would you follow the accountant's suggestions or would you start the new department? Why?

Accounting for Multistore Businesses

A **multistore business** is a business that has two or more stores. It may be a downtown store with several branch stores in nearby suburban shopping centers. It may also be a chain of stores scattered over a large area. Some examples of well-known chains of department stores and variety stores are listed in the margin. Many supermarkets and drugstores are also parts of large chains.

In a managerial accounting system, each branch store or chain store is considered a separate unit of operation. It is both a cost center and a profit center. The accounting system therefore gathers data about the revenues, cost of goods sold, and expenses of each store. This makes it possible to determine the profitability of the individual stores in a multistore business.

The first topic of this chapter discusses two types of managerial accounting systems that are used in multistore businesses. The second topic provides a description of the computerized merchandising and accounting procedures used in a chain of department stores.

Examples of Large Chains of Stores

J.C. Penney
K Mart
Montgomery Ward
Sears, Roebuck
Woolworth's and Woolco

Topic 1
The Accounting Systems of Multistore Businesses

 What are the accounting systems of a multistore business? Managerial accounting systems for multistore businesses are similar to

Accounting Subsystems:
- Cash Receipts
- Cash Payments
- Purchases on Credit
- Sales on Credit
- Payroll
- General Accounting

the accounting systems for single-store businesses that have several sales departments. There are subsystems for cash receipts, cash payments, purchases on credit, sales on credit, payroll, and general accounting. These subsystems are set up in such a way that financial data is recorded for each unit of operation. In the case of a multistore business, separate ledger accounts are usually kept for the assets, liabilities, revenues, cost of goods sold, and expenses of each branch store or chain store. Because separate accounts are used, financial reports and statements are prepared for the individual stores as well as for the business as a whole.

Having an accounting system that can provide timely, accurate information about each store is very important for a multistore business. For example, in a large chain of stores, each store has its own manager, but the top management of the business may be located in an administrative office hundreds or thousands of miles away from the stores. These people must rely on financial reports and statements for the information they need to judge the efficiency of operations and to make decisions.

Types of Accounting Systems

A centralized accounting system is an accounting system in which the financial records for all the stores are kept in a single location.

The accounting systems of multistore businesses are either centralized or decentralized. An accounting system is said to be **centralized** if the financial records for all the stores are kept in a single administrative office or data processing center and if most of the accounting work is done there. An accounting system is said to be **decentralized** if each store keeps its own financial records and does most of its own accounting work.

A decentralized accounting system is an accounting system in which each store keeps its own financial records.

In this topic, a branch store organization is used to describe a centralized accounting system. A chain store organization is used to describe a decentralized accounting system. Keep in mind, however, that each kind of multistore business can use either a centralized accounting system or a decentralized accounting system.

A Centralized Accounting System

Blue Ridge Gift Shops is an example of a multistore business that uses a centralized accounting system. The firm has a main store in a busy Southern city and two branch stores in that city's bus terminal and airport. Its owners are Judy and Don Miller. The Millers employ managers at all their stores but make financial and personnel decisions themselves. All financial records are kept in an administrative office at the main store. The staff of this office does the accounting work for the three stores: journalizing and posting transactions, paying invoices, preparing the payroll, and so on. At regular intervals, the staff of the administrative office also prepares a number of financial reports and statements for each store and for the business as a whole.

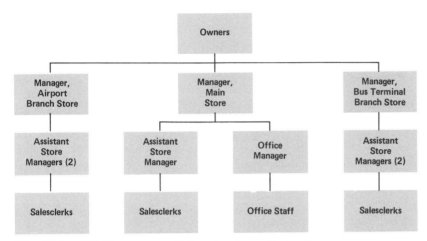

Blue Ridge Gift Shops, a multistore business that sells candy, gifts, greeting cards, magazines, newspapers, and paperback books, uses a centralized accounting system.

The data needed to record transactions for the branch stores comes from source documents that are sent to the administrative office at the main store.

Sales and Cash Receipts. All sales at the Blue Ridge Gift Shops are made for cash. Each store uses a cash register to record the sales and to safeguard the cash until a bank deposit is made. Because the stores take in a lot of money, the managers prove cash and deposit it several times during the day. Each manager has a supply of prenumbered deposit tickets for the business's checking account. The deposits for the branch stores are made at nearby branches of the bank that is used by the main store.

The manager of each branch store prepares a daily cash receipts summary. For example, the cash receipts summary for the airport branch on September 14 is shown on page 86. Notice that this form lists the amount of cash sales for each department, the total cash sales for the branch, the cash overage, the total cash receipts, and the total bank deposits. The manager of the airport branch sends this summary to the main store along with the cash proofs, the audit tape from the cash register, and duplicate copies of the deposit tickets.

BLUE RIDGE GIFT SHOPS—AIRPORT BRANCH
Cash Receipts Summary
September 14, 19—

Department	Amount
Candy	$ 475
Gifts	790
Greeting Cards	110
Magazines and Newspapers	535
Paperback Books	580
Total Cash Sales	$2,490
Cash Overage	9
Total Cash Receipts	$2,499
Bank Deposits	
Deposit Ticket 1087	$ 875
Deposit Ticket 1088	1,100
Deposit Ticket 1089	524
Total Cash Deposited	$2,499

The staff of the administrative office at the main store uses the data from the cash receipts summary to journalize the branch's sales, cash short or over, and cash receipts. It also uses the data to enter the branch's bank deposits in the business's checkbook.

Purchases and Cash Payments. All purchases of merchandise at the Blue Ridge Gift Shops are made on credit. The merchandise for the branch stores is shipped directly to these stores by the suppliers. Whenever new merchandise arrives at one of the stores, a clerk checks it and prepares a receiving report. This report allows the staff of the administrative office at the main store to verify each purchase invoice.

Some of the suppliers mail the invoices for a branch store's merchandise to the main store. Other suppliers place the invoices in the cartons when the goods are shipped to the branch stores.

The manager of each branch store prepares a weekly cash payments request listing the amounts owed to the suppliers who billed the branch store. This form is sent to the main store along with the purchase invoices and the receiving reports. A cash payments request for the airport branch is shown on the next page.

The staff of the administrative office at the main store verifies all the invoices and journalizes the merchandise purchases for the branch stores. When the due dates for the invoices arrive, the staff of this office issues the checks to the suppliers and journalizes the payments.

BLUE RIDGE GIFT SHOPS—AIRPORT BRANCH
Cash Payments Request
For the Week Ended September 14, 19—

Company	Items Received	Amount
Atlantic News Inc.	Newspapers	$ 700
Delta Distributors	Candy	525
Fairmont Products	Gifts	1,000
Industrial Cleaning Inc.	Cleaning service	75
Metro Distributors	Magazines and books	2,200
Universal Cards	Greeting cards	250
Total Cash Payments Requested		$4,750

Bills for the expenses of each branch store are handled in the same way. Some of these bills are mailed to the main store by the firms that provide the services or goods. Other bills go to the branch stores and are then sent to the main store with the weekly cash payments request. (For example, the cash payments request for the airport branch lists a bill for cleaning service.) The staff of the administrative office verifies all the bills, issues the checks, and journalizes the payments.

Payroll. At the Blue Ridge Gift Shops, most of the employees are paid on the hourly-rate plan. Time clocks are located in each store, and the employees use these devices to record their arrival and departure times on time cards. At the end of each week, the managers of the branch stores total the time cards and compute the gross earnings. Then they prepare a payroll summary and send this form along with the time cards to the administrative office at the main store. The payroll summary for the airport branch is shown on page 88. (Because this branch operates seven days a week and 24 hours a day, there are two assistant managers in addition to the manager. These three people are paid according to the salary plan.)

The staff of the administrative office prepares and records the payroll for all the stores. The checks for the employees of the branch stores are delivered to the managers on payday. All the necessary records of employee earnings and deductions are kept at the main store.

General Accounting. Blue Ridge Gift Shops has a yearly accounting period. The staff of the administrative office at the main store prepares all the financial statements and makes the adjusting and closing entries. (The preparation of financial statements for multistore businesses is discussed later in this topic.)

The staff of the administrative office also prepares three monthly financial reports that provide information about the operations of each

BLUE RIDGE GIFT SHOPS—AIRPORT BRANCH
Payroll Summary
For the Week Ended September 14, 19—

Employee Number	Position	Hourly Rate	Hours Worked	Gross Earnings
1	Manager	—	44	$ 240
2	Asst. Manager	—	42	185
3	Asst. Manager	—	42	185
4	Salesclerk	$3.50	40	140
5	Salesclerk	3.40	40	136
6	Salesclerk	3.40	35	119
7	Salesclerk	3.50	38	133
8	Salesclerk	3.40	40	136
9	Salesclerk	3.40	40	136
		Total Gross Earnings		**$1,410**

EXPENSE REPORT

PURCHASES REPORT

SALES REPORT

STORE 1	STORE 2	STORE 3

Financial reports supply information needed by management to control the operations of a multi-store business.

store: a sales report, a purchases report, and an expense report. These reports go to the managers of the stores and the owners of the business.

Some of the procedures and forms used in multistore businesses that have centralized accounting systems vary according to the needs of each firm. However, the accounting system of Blue Ridge Gift Shops is a good illustration of the basic procedures that are followed.

Activity A. Answer the following questions about the source documents prepared by the airport branch of the Blue Ridge Gift Shops to report its transactions. Refer to the cash receipts summary on page 86, the cash payments request on page 87, and the payroll summary shown above.

1. What types of information are shown on the cash receipts summary?

2. Which department has the highest cash sales on September 14?

3. What is the amount of cash sales for magazines and newspapers?

4. What is the total amount of cash sales for the airport branch on September 14?

5. How many bank deposits are made by the airport branch on September 14?

6. What is the total amount of cash receipts for the airport branch on September 14? Is all of this cash being deposited?

7. How much must be paid to Delta Distributors? Industrial Cleaning Inc.? Universal Cards?

8. What is the total amount of cash payments requested by the airport branch for the week ended September 14?

9. What is the total gross earnings for the employees of the airport branch for the week ended September 14?

10. How many employees work at the airport branch?

A Decentralized Accounting System

B *How does a decentralized accounting system operate?* Best Auto Products is a multistore business that uses a decentralized accounting system. Best Auto is owned and managed by John Kovacs. He and his top managers, administrators, and house staff work in the home office. The firm has a chain of 15 stores, all located on busy highways near shopping centers in the Southwest. Each store keeps a complete set of financial records and prepares its own financial statements on a monthly basis. These financial statements are sent to the accounting staff at the home office (headquarters) of the firm, which uses the information to prepare financial statements for the business.

ORGANIZATION OF HOME OFFICE

ORGANIZATION OF EACH CHAIN STORE

Best Auto Products, a multistore business that operates a chain of fifteen stores which sell a wide variety of auto parts and accessories, uses a decentralized accounting system.

The chart of accounts, financial records, and accounting procedures for each store were set up by the accounting staff of the home office when the store started its operations. The home office also opened a checking account for each store at a local bank so that the store can deposit its cash and issue checks.

The accounting activities for each store are performed by a *full-charge bookkeeper* who works at the store. The bookkeeper journalizes and posts transactions, prepares checks to pay bills, reconciles the monthly bank statement, prepares the payroll, proves the journals and ledgers, and prepares the monthly financial statements. Every three months an accountant from the home office visits each store to verify the accuracy of its financial records and make sure that correct procedures are being used. This accountant is known as an *auditor.*

Each store has special journals and subsidiary ledgers in addition to the general journal and the general ledger. The subsystems, procedures, and controls that are used are very similar to those you learned about in your previous studies. However, multistore businesses like Best Auto Products also have some special accounting procedures.

Accounts Used by the Home Office

Besides having a chart of accounts and a set of financial records for each store, a multistore business with a decentralized accounting system has a chart of accounts and a set of financial records for the home office. The partial chart of accounts shown in the margin is for the home office of Best Auto Products. Notice that the home office has a number of accounts that differ from the accounts of a single-store business. These accounts are explained here. Later sections of this topic show how these accounts are used.

Asset Accounts. The general ledger of the home office contains an asset account for each of the 15 stores in the chain. These accounts are called *Store 1—Investment, Store 2—Investment,* and so on. The balance of the asset account for a store shows the investment of the home office in that store.

When each store in the chain was opened, the home office gave it certain assets, such as cash, merchandise inventory, and equipment. The asset account for the store was debited to record this beginning investment. As various types of transactions take place between the home office and the store, the amount of the investment changes. For example, if the home office sends more merchandise to the store, the investment increases. The asset account for the store is debited to reflect this increase. The net income or net loss from the store's operations also changes the amount of the investment. At the end of each accounting period, the asset account for the store is debited to record the increase in investment resulting from a net income or credited to record the decrease in investment resulting from a net loss.

Revenue Accounts. When the individual stores in the chain close their financial records at the end of each accounting period, their net

**Best Auto Products
Home Office
Chart of Accounts**

Assets
101   Cash
111   Accounts Receivable
113   Merchandise Inventory
114   Supplies on Hand
131   Equipment
141   Store 1—Investment

155   Store 15—Investment

Owner's Equity
301   John Kovacs, Capital
302   John Kovacs, Drawing
399   Income Summary

Revenue
401   Sales
402   Sales Returns and Allowances
403   Sales Discount
411   Net Income From Store 1

425   Net Income From Store 15

Costs and Expenses
501   Purchases
502   Transportation In
503   Purchases Returns and Allowances
504   Purchases Discount
511   Shipments to Store 1

525   Shipments to Store 15

income or net loss must be entered in the financial records of the home office. The general ledger of the home office has a series of temporary owner's equity accounts that are used for this purpose. These accounts are called *Net Income From Store 1*, *Net Income From Store 2*, and so on. They are credited to record the net income earned by each store or debited to record the net loss.

Cost of Goods Sold Accounts. The home office of Best Auto Products buys certain types of merchandise for all the stores in the chain. This merchandise is kept in the warehouse of the home office until it is needed by the individual stores. The warehouse staff then ships the merchandise to the stores. The general ledger of the home office has a series of temporary owner's equity accounts that are used to record the cost of the merchandise transferred from the home office to the stores. These accounts are called *Shipments to Store 1*, *Shipments to Store 2*, and so on. They are credited whenever a shipment is made to a store.

Accounts Used by Each Chain Store

The chart of accounts for a store that belongs to a chain is very similar to the chart of accounts for a single-store business. However, there are a few differences. The accounts that differ are explained here. Later sections of this topic show how these accounts are used.

Owner's Equity Account. The general ledger of each chain store contains a permanent owner's equity account called *Home Office*. This account takes the place of a capital account. Only the general ledger of the home office has a capital account. (Refer to the chart of accounts for the home office on page 90.) The Home Office account in the general ledger of each store shows the amount of the business's total capital that is invested in the store.

When a store is opened, its Home Office account is credited to record the beginning investment that the home office makes in the store. After the store is operating, the Home Office account is credited to record increases in investment and debited to record decreases in investment. These changes in investment result from transactions between the home office and the store and also from the net income or net loss of the store.

The Home Office account links the general ledger of each chain store to the general ledger of the home office. The balance of a store's Home Office account is always the same as the balance of the asset account for that store in the general ledger of the home office. However, one account has a debit balance, and the other account has a credit balance. The illustration in the margin shows the relationship between these two accounts.

**Best Auto Products
Store 1
Chart of Accounts**

Owner's Equity
311 Home Office
399 Income Summary

Costs and Expenses
501 Purchases
502 Transportation In
503 Purchases Returns and
      Allowances
504 Purchases Discount
510 Shipments From Home
      Office
531 Operating Expenses

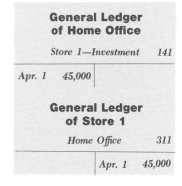

**General Ledger
of Home Office**

Store 1—Investment   141

| *Apr. 1* | *45,000* | |

**General Ledger
of Store 1**

Home Office   311

| | *Apr. 1* | *45,000* |

Cost of Goods Sold Account. Each chain store must record the cost of the merchandise that the home office buys for the store and ships to it. A temporary owner's equity account called *Shipments From Home Office* is used for such transactions. This account is debited whenever the store receives merchandise from the home office.

The Shipments From Home Office account in the general ledger of each store is related to an account in the general ledger of the home office. For example, at the end of each accounting period, the Shipments From Home Office account in the general ledger of Store 1 will have the same balance as the Shipments to Store 1 account in the general ledger of the home office. However, one account has a debit balance and the other account has a credit balance.

Internal Transactions

Internal transactions take place between units of the same business and do not involve outside parties.

In a multistore business like Best Auto Products, certain types of transactions take place between the home office and the stores. These transactions are called **internal transactions** because they involve units of the same business rather than outside parties, such as creditors, customers, or government agencies. Some examples of internal transactions are listed here. These transactions are common in many multistore businesses.

Examples of Internal Transactions.

• The home office invests assets such as cash, merchandise inventory, and equipment in a new store.
• The home office sends additional merchandise to the store after it is operating.
• The home office sends additional cash to the store after it is operating.
• The store sends cash to the home office.

At Best Auto Products, the two types of internal transactions that occur most often are transfers of cash from the stores to the home office and transfers of merchandise from the home office to the stores. Each of these transactions requires two entries: an entry in the financial records of the home office and an entry in the financial records of the store involved in the transaction.

Transfers of Cash. The accounting staff of the home office watches the cash balance of each chain store carefully. Whenever a store builds up more cash than it needs for its operations, the store manager is told to send some of the cash to the home office. Cash from the stores is used to pay the expenses of the home office, to buy more merchandise for the stores, and to open new stores. Effective management of the business's cash is an important task for the controller and the accounting staff of the home office.

The transfer of cash from a store to the home office decreases the investment of the home office in that store. On April 5, Store 1 sends a check for $10,000 to the home office of Best Auto Products. This transaction is entered in the financial records of Store 1 by debiting the Home Office account and crediting the Cash account. When the check is received at the home office, the transaction is entered in its financial records by debiting the Cash account and crediting the Store 1—Investment account. After these entries are journalized and posted, the accounts appear as follows.

**Best Auto Products
Store 1
Chart of Accounts**

Owner's Equity
311   Home Office

**Best Auto Products
Home Office
Chart of Accounts**

Assets
141   Store 1—Investment

General Ledger of Store 1

	Cash		101		Home Office		311
Apr. 1	18,000	Apr. 5	10,000	Apr. 5	10,000	Apr. 1	45,000

General Ledger of Home Office

	Cash		101		Store 1—Investment		141
Apr. 1	12,000			Apr. 1	45,000	Apr. 5	10,000
5	10,000						

Notice that the balance of the owner's equity account Home Office in the general ledger of Store 1 has decreased to $35,000. The balance of the asset account Store 1—Investment in the general ledger of the home office has also decreased to $35,000. Thus the balances of these two accounts remain equal. Both accounts show the current investment of the home office in Store 1.

Transfers of Merchandise. Multistore businesses with decentralized accounting systems can handle purchases of merchandise in several ways. Here are three of the most common methods.

• The home office orders all merchandise for the stores, pays for it, and has it delivered to a central warehouse. The warehouse ships the items to the individual stores as the stores need them.

• The home office orders all merchandise for the stores but has it sent directly to the stores and billed to the stores.

• Each store orders and pays for the merchandise it needs. However, the stores may be required to make their purchases from certain suppliers that are approved by the home office.

Best Auto Products uses a combination of two of these methods. The home office buys merchandise that is needed often by all the stores in the chain and keeps the items on hand in the business's warehouse. Each store orders this merchandise from the warehouse when its stock runs low. Other items, which are not needed often or are carried only by certain stores, are purchased by each store. These items are shipped directly to the store by the suppliers.

One of the benefits of a multistore business is that it can buy many types of merchandise at favorable prices and on favorable terms because it is able to order large quantities. The purchasing procedures of Best Auto Products are designed to take advantage of this situation. However, by allowing individual stores to buy items that are not needed often by the whole chain, the home office avoids building up a big stock of slow-moving items in the warehouse.

The home office makes its purchases on credit. Each of these transactions is recorded by debiting the home office's Purchases account and crediting its Accounts Payable account as well as the creditor's account. When some of the merchandise is sent to a store, the home office makes another entry. For example, on April 8 the warehouse ships goods that were bought for $2,000. These goods go to Store 1. This transaction is entered in the financial records of the home office by debiting the Store 1—Investment account and crediting the Shipments to Store 1 account. For the home office, the effect of the transaction is to increase its investment in Store 1 and to decrease its cost for merchandise purchases.

When the goods arrive at Store 1, the transaction is entered in the store's financial records by debiting the Shipments From Home Office account and crediting the Home Office account. For Store 1, the effect of this transaction is to increase its cost for merchandise purchases and to increase the investment of the home office in the store.

After the transfer of merchandise from the home office to Store 1 is journalized and posted in the two sets of financial records, the accounts appear as shown on the next page.

Notice that the balance of the Store 1—Investment account in the general ledger of the home office and the balance of the Home Office account in the general ledger of Store 1 are still equal. Each one now has a balance of $37,000.

The balances of the Shipments to Store 1 account and the Shipments From Home Office account are also equal. However, one account has a credit balance and the other account has a debit balance. The credit balance of Shipments to Store 1 represents a reduction in the cost of the purchases charged to the home office. The debit balance of Shipments From Home Office represents an addition to the cost of the purchases charged to Store 1.

**Best Auto Products
Home Office
Chart of Accounts**

Costs and Expenses
511   Shipments to Store 1

**Best Auto Products
Store 1
Chart of Accounts**

Costs and Expenses
510   Shipments From Home
         Office

General Ledger of Home Office

Store 1—Investment			141		Shipments to Store 1		511
Apr. 1	45,000	Apr. 5	10,000			Apr. 8	2,000
8	2,000						

General Ledger of Store 1

Home Office			311		Shipments From Home Office		510
Apr. 5	10,000	Apr. 1	45,000	Apr. 8	2,000		
		8	2,000				

Keep in mind that only an internal transaction must be entered in the financial records of both the home office and the store involved in the transaction. Transactions with outside parties such as customers and creditors are handled just as they would be in a single-store business. For example, the daily cash sales of Store 1 are entered in the store's financial records by debiting its Cash account and crediting its Sales account. No entry is made in the financial records of the home office for this transaction.

Activity B. Answer the following questions about the organization of Best Auto Products, its accounts, and its entries for internal transactions. Refer to the organization charts on page 89, the charts of accounts on pages 90 and 91, and the ledger accounts shown above and on page 93.

1. Who is in charge of the accounting staff at the home office?
2. Who is in charge of the warehouse staff at the home office?
3. What types of employees work in each chain store?
4. Who performs the accounting activities in each chain store?
5. What type of account is the Store 1—Investment account in the general ledger of the home office?
6. Does Store 1 have a capital account? If not, what account takes the place of the capital account in the general ledger of the store?
7. What accounts does Store 1 debit and credit when it sends cash to the home office?
8. What accounts does the home office debit and credit when it receives cash from Store 1?
9. What accounts does the home office debit and credit when it ships merchandise to Store 1?
10. What accounts does Store 1 debit and credit when it receives merchandise from the home office?
11. The balance of the Store 1—Investment account in the general ledger of the home office is equal to the balance of what account in the general ledger of Store 1?
12. The balance of the Shipments From Home Office account in the general ledger of Store 1 is equal to the balance of what account in the general ledger of the home office?

Financial Statements for Multistore Businesses

C *How are financial statements prepared in a multistore business?* If a multistore business has a centralized accounting system, the financial statements for the individual stores and for the business as a whole are prepared at the main store or the home office. This is the procedure followed at Blue Ridge Gift Shops, the firm that is discussed on pages 84 to 88. If a multistore business has a decentralized accounting system, each store prepares its own financial statements. These statements are sent to the accounting staff of the main store or the home office, which uses the information to prepare financial statements for the business as a whole.

This section describes how financial statements are prepared at Best Auto Products, a firm that has a decentralized accounting system. Keep in mind that the same types of financial statements are prepared by firms with centralized accounting systems. No matter where the accounting work is done, the accounting system of a multistore business must be designed to provide management with detailed information about the operations and financial position of the individual stores.

Financial Statements for Each Store

Each of the 15 stores owned by Best Auto Products issues the following financial statements on a monthly basis: an income statement, a schedule of cost of goods sold, and a balance sheet. These financial statements are prepared by the accounting clerks who work at the stores and are sent to the accounting staff of the home office.

The procedures used to prepare the financial statements for the individual stores in the chain are the same as the procedures used in other merchandising businesses. After a physical inventory is taken and the journals and ledgers are proved, the adjustments are determined and a worksheet is completed. The data needed to prepare the financial statements comes from the worksheet.

Before sending the financial statements to the home office, the accounting clerk of each store makes a copy so that the information will be available at the store. The store manager studies this information carefully and uses it in making decisions.

The Income Statement. An income statement for one of the stores owned by Best Auto Products is shown on the next page. This income statement reports the results of operations for Store 1 during the month of April. The information on the income statement is supplemented by a schedule of cost of goods sold, which is also shown below the income statement.

Notice that the income statement for this chain store is the same as

BEST AUTO PRODUCTS—STORE 1
Income Statement
For the Month Ended April 30, 19—

Revenue From Sales:			
Sales...........................	12,500 00		
Less: Sales Returns and Allowances	260 00		
Net Sales		12,240 00	
Cost of Goods Sold (see schedule)		8,250 00	
Gross Profit on Sales................		3,990 00	
Operating Expenses.................		2,400 00	
Net Income		1,590 00	

BEST AUTO PRODUCTS—STORE 1
Schedule of Cost of Goods Sold
For the Month Ended April 30, 19—

Merchandise Inventory, April 1			14,500 00
Purchases......................	4,000 00		
Add: Transportation In	95 00		
Cost of Delivered Goods	4,095 00		
Less: Purchases Returns and			
Allowances $275.00			
Purchases Discount 70.00	345 00		
Net Purchases...................		3,750 00	
Add: Shipments From Home Office		3,000 00	
Cost of Goods Available for Sale..........		21,250 00	
Less: Merchandise Inventory, April 30		13,000 00	
Cost of Goods Sold.................		8,250 00	

the income statement for a single-store business. But the schedule of cost of goods sold differs in one way. The balance of the Shipments From Home Office account is listed. This amount ($3,000) is added to the beginning inventory ($14,500) and the net purchases ($3,750) to find the cost of goods available for sale during the period ($21,250).

A single amount is shown for operating expenses on the income statement because the store has a subsidiary ledger that contains the individual expense accounts. The amount reported on the income statement is the balance of the Operating Expenses controlling account in the general ledger. This procedure is followed by some single-store businesses as well as some multistore businesses such as Best Auto

General Ledger of Store 1

Shipments From
Home Office   510

Apr. 8	2,000	
25	1,000	

SCHEDULE OF
ACCOUNTS PAYABLE

SCHEDULE OF
ACCOUNTS RECEIVABLE

SCHEDULE OF
OPERATING EXPENSES

ACCOUNT	BALANCE

These schedules, prepared from the subsidiary ledgers, provide information for the store manager to control operations.

Products. Detailed information about the expenses is given on a schedule of operating expenses, which is prepared each month when the subsidiary ledger is proved.

The Balance Sheet. The balance sheet shown here was prepared for Store 1 of Best Auto Products. It reports the store's financial position as of April 30.

BEST AUTO PRODUCTS—STORE 1 Balance Sheet April 30, 19—		
ASSETS		
Cash	11,490 00	
Accounts Receivable	2,850 00	
Merchandise Inventory	13,000 00	
Supplies on Hand	250 00	
Equipment	15,100 00	
Total Assets		42,690 00
LIABILITIES		
Accounts Payable		3,100 00
OWNER'S EQUITY		
Home Office, Before Transfer of Net Income . .	38,000 00	
Net Income	1,590 00	
Home Office, April 30		39,590 00
Total Liabilities and Owner's Equity		42,690 00

Notice that the only difference between the balance sheet for a chain store and the balance sheet for a single-store business is the way the Owner's Equity section is handled. The Home Office account is listed instead of a capital account. Remember that the general ledger of a chain store does not have a capital account. The Home Office account shows the portion of the business's total capital that is invested in the store.

Activity C. Answer the following questions about the financial statements for Store 1 of Best Auto Products. Refer to the illustrations shown above and on page 97.

1. What is the amount of net sales for the store?

2. What is the amount of net purchases for the goods bought directly from suppliers?

3. What is the cost of the goods that the store received from the home office?

4. What is the cost of the goods available for sale during the month?

5. Does the inventory increase or decrease?

6. What is the cost of goods sold for the month?

7. How much net income does the store earn for the month?

8. What is the amount of merchandise inventory on April 30?

9. How much cash does the store have on April 30?

10. What is the balance of the Home Office account on April 30?

Financial Statements for the Home Office

D *What is done with the financial statements for the individual stores when they are received at the home office?* The accounting staff of the home office checks these financial statements and then enters the net income of each store in the home office's records. The information about the net income earned by the stores is needed to prepare financial statements for the home office. The accounting staff of the home office also gives copies of the financial statements from the stores to the top management of the business. These people analyze the statements so that they can assess the efficiency of each store's operations and the soundness of its financial position.

Recording the Net Income of Each Store. At the end of the accounting period, the net income of each store must be entered in the financial records of the home office. For example, after the income statement for April is received from Store 1 and checked, the following entry is journalized and posted at the home office. The accounts used are the asset account Store 1—Investment and the revenue account Net Income From Store 1.

> **Best Auto Products Home Office Chart of Accounts**
>
> **Assets**
> 141   Store 1—Investment
>
> **Revenue**
> 411   Net Income From Store 1

Financial Records of Home Office

GENERAL JOURNAL   Page 8

DATE		ACCOUNT TITLE AND EXPLANATION	POST. REF.	DEBIT	CREDIT
19—					
Apr.	30	Store 1—Investment	141	1,590 00	
		Net Income From Store 1	411		1,590 00
		Record net income of store.			

Store 1—Investment		141		Net Income From Store 1	411
Apr. 1	45,000	Apr. 5	10,000		
8	2,000			Apr. 30	1,590
25	1,000				
30	1,590				

Remember that the Store 1—Investment account shows the investment of the home office in this store. Net income increases the investment. The Store 1—Investment account is therefore debited for $1,590, the amount of net income earned by Store 1 during April. The Net Income From Store 1 account is credited for the amount because the store's net income increases the revenues of the home office.

The same procedure is used to record the net income for all the stores owned by Best Auto Products. Then the financial statements for the home office can be prepared. The data needed for these statements comes from the worksheet, which is completed after a physical inventory is taken, financial records are proved, and adjustments are made.

The Income Statement. The home office of Best Auto Products makes sales to local auto service centers. These businesses buy parts and accessories from the warehouse. Thus the home office earns a net income from its own operations as well as receiving the net income of the stores. The income statement of the home office for the month of April follows along with the schedule of cost of goods sold.

Notice that the schedule of cost of goods sold lists the balance of the Shipments to Store 1 account. This amount ($3,000) is subtracted from the total of the beginning inventory and the net purchases ($116,000 + $10,075 = $126,075) to find the cost of goods available for sale during the period ($123,075).

The income statement lists the net income for the home office ($2,225) and the net income for Store 1 ($1,590). These two amounts are added to find the total net income ($3,815).

In actual practice, the shipments to each store in the chain would appear on the schedule of cost of goods sold for the home office and the net income for each store would appear on the income statement for

**General Ledger
of Home Office**

Shipments to Store 1		511
Apr. 8	2,000	
25	1,000	

BEST AUTO PRODUCTS—HOME OFFICE
Income Statement
For the Month Ended April 30, 19—

Revenue From Sales:		
Sales.	26,000 00	
Less: Sales Returns and Allowances	600 00	
Net Sales		25,400 00
Cost of Goods Sold (see schedule)		13,075 00
Gross Profit on Sales.		12,325 00
Operating Expenses.		10,100 00
Net Income From Home Office.		2,225 00
Add: Net Income From Store 1		1,590 00
Total Net Income		3,815 00

BEST AUTO PRODUCTS—HOME OFFICE
Schedule of Cost of Goods Sold
For the Month Ended April 30, 19—

Merchandise Inventory, April 1			116,000	00
Purchases	10,550	00		
Add: Transportation In	175	00		
Cost of Delivered Goods.	10,725	00		
Less: Purchases Returns and Allowances . . $500.00				
Purchases Discount 150.00	650	00		
Net Purchases.			10,075	00
			126,075	00
Less: Shipments to Store 1			3,000	00
Cost of Goods Available for Sale			123,075	00
Less: Merchandise Inventory, April 30.			110,000	00
Cost of Goods Sold			13,075	00

Large chain operations carry many different types of goods. Department stores often use a centralized accounting system to record sales data in the home-office computer.

the home office. However, for the sake of simplicity, the financial statements presented here include the amounts for only one of the 15 stores.

The Balance Sheet. The balance sheet shown here reports the assets, liabilities, and owner's equity of the home office as of April 30. The statement of owner's equity, which is also shown here, supplements the balance sheet by reporting the changes in owner's equity that took place during April. Remember that the general ledger of the home office contains the owner's capital account.

BEST AUTO PRODUCTS—HOME OFFICE
Balance Sheet
April 30, 19—

ASSETS				
Cash	20,000	00		
Accounts Receivable	3,750	00		
Merchandise Inventory	110,000	00		
Supplies on Hand	1,000	00		
Equipment	30,000	00		
Store 1—Investment	39,590	00		
Total Assets			204,340	00
LIABILITIES				
Accounts Payable			21,050	00
OWNER'S EQUITY				
John Kovacs, Capital			183,290	00
Total Liabilities and Owner's Equity			204,340	00

BEST AUTO PRODUCTS—HOME OFFICE
Statement of Owner's Equity
For the Month Ended April 30, 19—

Capital, April 1			181,475	00
Net Income From Home Office for the Month	2,225	00		
Net Income From Store 1 for the Month	1,590	00		
Total Net Income for the Month	3,815	00		
Less: Withdrawals	2,000	00		
Increase in Capital			1,815	00
Capital, April 30			183,290	00

Notice that the Assets section of the balance sheet lists the Store 1—Investment account, which represents the home office's investment in Store 1. The statement of owner's equity lists the net income from Store 1 as well as the net income from the home office. Both of these amounts are used in computing the increase in the owner's equity.

In actual practice, the asset account for each store in the chain would appear on the balance sheet for the home office and the net income for each store would appear on the statement of owner's equity. However, for the sake of simplicity, the financial statements again present the amounts for only one of the 15 stores owned by Best Auto Products.

Activity D. Answer the following questions about the entry to record the net income of Store 1 and about the financial statements prepared for the home office of Best Auto Products. Refer to the illustrations on pages 99 to 102.

1. What accounts are debited and credited when the net income of Store 1 is entered in the financial records of the home office?

2. What is the cost of the goods that the home office shipped to Store 1? Is this amount added to or subtracted from the beginning inventory and the net purchases for the home office?

3. What is the amount of the gross profit on sales?

4. What is the amount of the operating expenses?

5. How much net income does the home office earn for the month? What is the total net income?

6. In what section of the balance sheet does the Store 1—Investment account appear?

7. What is the amount of the home office's investment in Store 1?

8. What is the largest asset?

9. What is the balance of the capital account on April 1?

10. What is the balance of the capital account on April 30? What factors are causing a change in the balance?

Closing Entries for Multistore Businesses

E *What procedures does a multistore business follow to close the temporary accounts at the end of the accounting period?* If the business has a decentralized accounting system, each store must journalize and post closing entries in its own financial records. A series of closing entries is also made in the financial records of the home office.

Closing Entries for Each Store. The closing entries that were journalized for Store 1 of Best Auto Products at the end of April are shown on page 104. (The adjusting entry for merchandise inventory appears on the same journal page.) Notice that the closing entries for this chain store are very similar to those that would be made in a

single-store business. However, there are two differences. The closing
entry for the temporary accounts with debit balances includes the

Financial Records of Store 1

GENERAL JOURNAL

Page 4

DATE		ACCOUNT TITLE AND EXPLANATION	POST. REF.	DEBIT	CREDIT
19—					
Apr. 30		Income Summary	399	1,500 00	
		Merchandise Inventory	113		1,500 00
		Adjust inventory.			
	30	Sales	401	12,500 00	
		Purchases Returns and Allowances .	503	275 00	
		Purchases Discount	504	70 00	
		Income Summary	399		12,845 00
		Close accounts with credit balances.			
	30	Income Summary	399	9,755 00	
		Sales Returns and Allowances . . .	402		260 00
		Purchases	501		4,000 00
		Transportation In	502		95 00
		Shipments From Home Office	510		3,000 00
		Operating Expenses	531		2,400 00
		Close accounts with debit balances.			
	30	Income Summary	399	1,590 00	
		Home Office	311		1,590 00
		Transfer net income.			

Income Summary			399		Home Office			311
Apr. 30	1,500	Apr. 30	12,845	Apr. 5	10,000	Apr. 1	45,000
30	9,755					8	2,000
30	1,590					25	1,000
						30	1,590

General Ledger of Home Office					General Ledger of Store 1			
Store 1—Investment			141		Home Office			311
Apr. 1	45,000	Apr. 5	10,000	Apr. 5	10,000	Apr. 1	45,000
8	2,000					8	2,000
25	1,000					25	1,000
30	1,590					30	1,590
39,590	49,590					39,590	49,590

Shipments From Home Office account. The last closing entry transfers the store's net income to the Home Office account rather than to a capital account. (The posting of this entry is also shown on page 104.)

After Store 1 closes its temporary accounts, the balance of the Home Office account in its general ledger is again equal to the balance of the Store 1—Investment account in the general ledger of the home office. Remember that the home office recorded the net income of $1,590 in the Store 1—Investment account when it received the store's income statement for April. Now both the Store 1—Investment account and the Home Office account have balances of $39,590. Thus the relationship between the two general ledgers is maintained. (Look at the ledger accounts at the bottom of page 104.)

Closing Entries for the Home Office. The closing entries for the home office are also very similar to the closing entries for a single-store business. However, there is a difference in the first closing entry. Look at the closing entries in the general journal shown on page 106. These entries were made by the home office of Best Auto Products at the end of April. (The adjusting entry for merchandise inventory again appears on the journal page.) Notice that the closing entry for the temporary accounts with credit balances includes the Net Income From Store 1 account and the Shipments to Store 1 account. (In actual practice, the accounts for the net income of all 15 stores in the chain and the accounts for the shipments to these stores would be closed at the same time. For the sake of simplicity, the accounts for only one store are presented.)

The third closing entry transfers the net income of the home office to the capital account. Notice that the amount of this entry ($3,815) is the same as the total net income for the month shown on the income statement of the home office (see page 100). After the posting of the fourth closing entry, the balance of the capital account ($183,290) matches the ending balance listed on the statement of owner's equity (see page 102 and the accounts on page 106).

Activity E-1. Answer the following questions about the closing entries for Store 1 of Best Auto Products. Refer to the illustrations on page 104.

1. How is the Shipments From Home Office account closed?

2. What does the $1,590 in the last closing entry represent?

3. What accounts are debited and credited in the last closing entry?

4. What is the balance of the Home Office account after the closing entries are posted?

5. The balance of the Home Office account in the general ledger of Store 1 is equal to the balance of what account in the general ledger of the home office?

Financial Records of Home Office

GENERAL JOURNAL   Page 9

DATE		ACCOUNT TITLE AND EXPLANATION	POST. REF.	DEBIT	CREDIT
19—					
Apr.	30	Income Summary	399	6,000 00	
		Merchandise Inventory	113		6,000 00
		Adjust inventory.			
	30	Sales	401	26,000 00	
		Net Income From Store 1	411	1,590 00	
		Purchases Returns and Allowances .	503	500 00	
		Purchases Discount	504	150 00	
		Shipments to Store 1	511	3,000 00	
		Income Summary	399		31,240 00
		Close accounts with credit balances.			
	30	Income Summary	399	21,425 00	
		Sales Returns and Allowances . . .	402		600 00
		Purchases	501		10,550 00
		Transportation In	502		175 00
		Operating Expenses	531		10,100 00
		Close accounts with debit balances.			
	30	Income Summary	399	3,815 00	
		John Kovacs, Capital	301		3,815 00
		Transfer net income to capital.			
	30	John Kovacs, Capital	301	2,000 00	
		John Kovacs, Drawing	302		2,000 00
		Transfer withdrawals to capital.			

Income Summary			399		John Kovacs, Capital		301
Apr. 30	6,000	Apr. 30	31,240			Apr. 1	181,475
30	21,425					30	3,815
30	3,815						

John Kovacs, Drawing			302		John Kovacs, Capital			301
Apr. 10	1,000	Apr. 30	2,000	Apr. 30	2,000	Apr. 1	181,475
28	1,000					30	3,815

Activity E-2. Answer the following questions about the closing entries for the home office of Best Auto Products. Refer to the illustrations shown above.

1. How is the Net Income From Store 1 account closed?

2. How is the Shipments to Store 1 account closed?

3. What is the purpose of the third closing entry? What accounts are debited and credited?

4. What is the purpose of the fourth closing entry? What accounts are debited and credited?

5. What is the balance of the capital account after the closing entries are posted?

Combined Financial Statements

F *What are combined financial statements?* A multistore business may prepare financial statements that show information for the business as a whole. These statements are called **combined financial statements** because they combine the amounts for all the stores and for the home office. A **combined income statement** reports the revenues, cost of goods sold, and expenses for the business as a whole. A **combined balance sheet** reports the assets, liabilities, and owner's equity for the business as a whole.

The accounting staff at the home office of Best Auto Products prepares combined financial statements. These statements are very useful when the business must provide financial information to outsiders such as a bank, a new supplier, or a real estate company from which the firm wants to rent a new store.

The Combined Income Statement. A special worksheet is used to gather the data and compute the amounts needed for the combined income statement. Look at the worksheet shown on page 108.

The worksheet is prepared as follows.

- All the items that appear on the income statement of the home office and the income statement of Store 1 are listed on the worksheet.
- The amounts from the income statement of the home office are recorded in the first money column. The amounts from the income statement of Store 1 are recorded in the second money column.
- The balances of related accounts for the home office and Store 1 are eliminated (canceled). These accounts are used for internal transactions, and they should not be reported on the combined income statement. The $3,000 credit balance of the Shipments to Store 1 account is canceled by recording a debit of $3,000 in the Eliminations section of the worksheet. Similarly, the $3,000 debit balance of the Shipments From Home Office account is canceled by recording a credit of $3,000 in the Eliminations section. (The eliminations are not journalized and posted. They are made only on the worksheet.)
- The two amounts for each item, which are listed in the Home Office column and the Store 1 column, are added together. The total is the amount that will be shown for the item on the combined income statement. For example, the home office had sales of $26,000 and Store 1 had sales of $12,500. The amount of sales reported on the combined income statement will be $38,500 ($26,000 + $12,500). The totals for all items are entered under Combined Amounts on the worksheet.

A combined income statement is used to report totals of revenues, costs, and expenses for all units of a business.

BEST AUTO PRODUCTS
Worksheet for Combined Income Statement
For the Month Ended April 30, 19—

	HOME OFFICE	STORE 1	ELIMINATIONS DEBIT	ELIMINATIONS CREDIT	COMBINED AMOUNTS
Revenue From Sales:					
Sales...................	26,000	12,500			38,500
Less: Sales Ret. and Allow.	600	260			860
Net Sales	25,400	12,240			37,640
Cost of Goods Sold:					
Merchandise Inventory, April 1	116,000	14,500			130,500
Purchases	10,550	4,000			14,550
Add: Transportation In	175	95			270
Cost of Delivered Goods	10,725	4,095			14,820
Less: Purchases Ret. and Allow.........	500	275			775
Purchases Discount..............	150	70			220
Net Purchases	10,075	3,750			13,825
Less: Shipments to Store 1	3,000		(a) 3,000		
Add: Shipments From Home Office		3,000		(a) 3,000	
Cost of Goods Available for Sale	123,075	21,250			144,325
Less: Merchandise Inventory, April 30	110,000	13,000			123,000
Cost of Goods Sold	13,075	8,250			21,325
Gross Profit on Sales...........	12,325	3,990			16,315
Operating Expenses..........	10,100	2,400			12,500
Net Income	2,225	1,590	3,000	3,000	3,815

(a) To eliminate related accounts for shipments of merchandise from the home office to Store 1.

After the worksheet is completed, the combined income statement can be prepared along with the combined schedule of cost of goods sold. See the illustration on page 109.

BEST AUTO PRODUCTS
Combined Income Statement
For the Month Ended April 30, 19—

Revenue From Sales:		
Sales.....................	38,500 00	
Less: Sales Returns and Allowances	860 00	
Net Sales		37,640 00
Cost of Goods Sold (see schedule)		21,325 00
Gross Profit on Sales...........		16,315 00
Operating Expenses..........		12,500 00
Net Income		3,815 00

BEST AUTO PRODUCTS
Combined Schedule of Cost of Goods Sold
For the Month Ended April 30, 19—

Merchandise Inventory, April 1		130,500 00
Purchases.	14,550 00	
Add: Transportation In	270 00	
Cost of Delivered Goods	14,820 00	
Less: Purchases Returns and		
Allowances $775.00		
Purchases Discount 220.00	995 00	
Net Purchases.		13,825 00
Cost of Goods Available for Sale.		144,325 00
Less: Merchandise Inventory, April 30		123,000 00
Cost of Goods Sold.		21,325 00

The Combined Balance Sheet. The combined balance sheet is prepared in the same way as the combined income statement. A special worksheet, such as the one shown here, is used to gather the necessary data and compute the combined amounts.

BEST AUTO PRODUCTS
Worksheet for Combined Balance Sheet
April 30, 19—

	HOME OFFICE	STORE 1	ELIMINATIONS DEBIT	ELIMINATIONS CREDIT	COMBINED AMOUNTS
Assets:					
Cash	20,000	11,490			31,490
Accounts Receivable	3,750	2,850			6,600
Merchandise Inventory	110,000	13,000			123,000
Supplies on Hand	1,000	250			1,250
Equipment	30,000	15,100			45,100
Store 1—Investment.	39,590			(a) 39,590	
Total	204,340	42,690			207,440
Liabilities and Owner's Equity:					
Accounts Payable	21,050	3,100			24,150
John Kovacs, Capital	183,290				183,290
Home Office			39,590 (a) 39,590		
Total	204,340	42,690	39,590	39,590	207,440

(a) To eliminate related accounts for Store 1 and the home office.

The procedure for preparing the worksheet for the combined balance sheet is as follows.

A combined balance sheet is used to report totals of assets, liabilities, and owner's equity for all units of a business.

• All the items that appear on the balance sheet of the home office and the balance sheet of Store 1 are listed on the worksheet.

• The amounts from the balance sheet of the home office are recorded in the first money column. The amounts from the balance sheet of Store 1 are recorded in the second money column.

• The balances of related accounts for the home office and Store 1 are eliminated. The $39,590 debit balance of the Store 1—Investment account is canceled by recording a credit of $39,590 in the Eliminations section of the worksheet. The $39,590 credit balance of the Home Office account is canceled by recording a debit of $39,590 in the Eliminations section. (Again, no entries are journalized and posted for the eliminations. These two accounts remain open in the ledgers, and they keep their balances.)

• The two amounts for each item, which are listed in the Home Office column and the Store 1 column, are added together to find the total needed for the combined balance sheet. For example, the home office has $20,000 in cash and Store 1 has $11,490 in cash. The amount of cash reported on the combined balance sheet will be $31,490 ($20,000 + $11,490). The totals for all the items are entered in the Combined Amounts column of the worksheet.

After the worksheet is completed, a combined balance sheet can be prepared along with a combined statement of owner's equity.

In actual practice, the combined financial statements for Best Auto

BEST AUTO PRODUCTS
Combined Balance Sheet
April 30, 19—

ASSETS

Cash	31,490 00	
Accounts Receivable	6,600 00	
Merchandise Inventory	123,000 00	
Supplies on Hand	1,250 00	
Equipment	45,100 00	
Total Assets		207,440 00

LIABILITIES

Accounts Payable		24,150 00

OWNER'S EQUITY

John Kovacs, Capital		183,290 00
Total Liabilities and Owner's Equity		207,440 00

BEST AUTO PRODUCTS
Combined Statement of Owner's Equity
For the Month Ended April 30, 19—

Capital, April 1		181,475 00
Net Income for the Month	3,815 00	
Less: Withdrawals	2,000 00	
Increase in Capital		1,815 00
Capital, April 30		183,290 00

Products would include the amounts for the home office and for all 15 stores in the chain. However, for the sake of simplicity, only the amounts for the home office and Store 1 are used in the statements presented in this section.

Accounting Concept:
Combined Statements. Combined financial statements summarize financial data for all the units of a business. A total amount is shown for each item listed on these statements.

Activity F-1. Answer the following questions about the worksheets for the combined financial statements that were prepared at Best Auto Products. Refer to the illustrations on pages 108 and 109.

1. Which accounts are eliminated on the worksheet for the combined income statement?
2. Which accounts are eliminated on the worksheet for the combined balance sheet?
3. How is an account eliminated?
4. Which money column on each worksheet provides the figures that are used on the combined financial statements?
5. How is each amount in the Combined Amounts column computed?

Activity F-2. Answer the following questions about the combined financial statements that were prepared at Best Auto Products. Refer to the illustrations on pages 108 to 111.

1. What amount of gross profit on sales is reported?
2. Are the Shipments to Store 1 account and the Shipments From Home Office account listed on the combined income statement? Why or why not?
3. What amount is shown for the cost of goods sold?
4. How much are the operating expenses?
5. Are the net income for the home office and the net income for Store 1 listed separately on the combined income statement?
6. What is the total asset amount?
7. How much is owed for accounts payable?

8. Are the Store 1—Investment account and the Home Office account listed on the combined balance sheet? Why or why not?

Topic 1 Problems

3-1. Super-Value Drugstores is a multistore business with a centralized accounting system. The business consists of a main store and three branch stores. All financial records for the branch stores are kept at the main store. Assume that you are working on the accounting staff of the main store. One of your duties is to check the accuracy of source documents prepared by the branch stores. On June 1, you receive the following cash receipts summary for the branch store located in the suburb of Delmar. (This is the source document for journalizing the branch's cash sales, sales returns, cash short and over, and cash receipts.) You also receive the audit tape from the cash register and duplicate copies of the deposit tickets for the bank deposits made by the branch.

```
          295.10  TCa 1
          230.50  TCa 2
  June 1  480.20  TCa 3
          145.00  TCa 4
         1150.80  TL
           30.00  TPd
         1120.80  TL
```

AUDIT TAPE FROM
CASH REGISTER

No. 1201	No. 1202
Total: $609.30	Total: $511.50

DEPOSIT TICKETS.
These amounts were
verified by the bank
teller.

SUPER-VALUE DRUGSTORES—DELMAR BRANCH
Cash Receipts Summary
June 1, 19—

Department	Amount
Drugs—Nonprescription	$ 295.10
Drugs—Prescription	230.50
Other Health Care Products	480.20
Perfumes and Cosmetics	145.00
Total Cash Sales	$1,150.20
Less: Cash Paid Out for Sales Returns	30.00
Total Cash Receipts	$1,180.20
Bank Deposits	
Deposit Ticket 1201	$ 609.30
Deposit Ticket 1202	511.00
Total Cash Deposited	$1,120.30

a. Check the amounts on the cash receipts summary. If there are any errors, give the correct amounts. Use the data on the audit tape and the copies of the deposit tickets to help you with this task.

b. Ellen Rossi, the accounting supervisor at the main store, is worried because there have recently been a lot of errors in the source documents from the Delmar branch. She has asked you to notify her whenever you find errors. She plans to discuss the situation with the manager of the branch. Write an interoffice memorandum to Ms. Rossi. Explain the types of errors that you saw on the cash receipts summary for June 1.

3-2. The World of Music is a multistore business with a decentralized accounting system. The business operates a chain of stores that sell stereo records and tapes. Assume that you are working on the accounting staff of the home office. During the first week of November, you receive the financial statements that were sent to the home office by Store 1. These statements report data for the month of October. The statements are shown on page 114.

The accuracy of the computations on the statements has been checked by another member of the staff. Now the controller asks you to perform the following tasks.

a. Make an entry in the general journal to record the net income of Store 1.

b. Prepare the October financial statements for the home office: a schedule of cost of goods sold, an income statement, a statement of owner's equity, and a balance sheet. The worksheet for the home office shows the following adjusted account balances. The Merchandise Inventory account was adjusted for a decrease of $5,000. Thus its balance on October 1 was $75,000. The journal entry that you made in Part **a** of this problem was posted, and the amounts are reflected in the balances shown in the table on page 114. The balance of the capital account on October 1 was the same as the balance shown on the table.

3-3. The World of Music issues combined financial statements. The controller has given you the task of preparing the worksheet for the combined income statement and the worksheet for the combined balance sheet. Obtain the necessary data from the October financial statements for the home office that you completed in Topic Problem 3-2 and from the October financial statements for Store 1 that are shown in Topic Problem 3-2. (Be sure to use $18,400 as the balance of the Home Office account.) Remember that certain related accounts must be eliminated.

3-4. The combined financial statements used at the World of Music are a combined schedule of cost of goods sold, a combined income statement, a combined statement of owner's equity, and a combined balance sheet. The controller wants you to prepare these statements for October. Obtain the necessary data from the worksheets that you completed in Topic Problem 3-3. (When you prepare the combined statement of owner's equity, use $114,675 as the capital on October 1 and $2,400 for the withdrawals.)

WORLD OF MUSIC—STORE 1
Income Statement
For the Month Ended October 31, 19—

Revenue From Sales:		
Sales	24,000 00	
Less: Sales Returns and Allowances . . .	400 00	
Net Sales		23,600 00
Cost of Goods Sold (see schedule)		11,200 00
Gross Profit on Sales. . .		12,400 00
Operating Expenses. . . .		9,000 00
Net Income		3,400 00

WORLD OF MUSIC—STORE 1
Balance Sheet
October 31, 19—

ASSETS			
Cash	7,200 00		
Accounts Receivable . . .	1,000 00		
Merchandise Inventory .	10,000 00		
Supplies on Hand	200 00		
Equipment	4,000 00		
Total Assets			22,400 00
LIABILITIES			
Accounts Payable			4,000 00
OWNER'S EQUITY			
Home Office, Before Transfer of Net Income	15,000 00		
Net Income	3,400 00		
Home Office, October 31			18,400 00
Total Liabilities and Owner's Equity . . .			22,400 00

WORLD OF MUSIC—STORE 1
Schedule of Cost of Goods Sold
For the Month Ended October 31, 19—

Merchandise Inventory, October 1		11,400 00	
Purchases	6,000 00		
Add: Transportation In .	150 00		
Cost of Delivered Goods	6,150 00		
Less: Purchases Ret. and Allow. . . $250.00			
Purchases Discount . . 100.00	350 00		
Net Purchases		5,800 00	
Add: Shipments From Home Office		4,000 00	
Cost of Goods Available for Sale		21,200 00	
Less: Merchandise Inventory, October 31		10,000 00	
Cost of Goods Sold		11,200 00	

Adjusted Account Balances
Home Office
October 31, 19—

Account	Balance
Cash	$ 18,000
Accounts Receivable	4,000
Merchandise Inventory	70,000
Supplies on Hand	800
Equipment	25,000
Store 1—Investment	18,400
Accounts Payable	12,000
Ann Riley, Capital	114,675
Ann Riley, Drawing	2,400
Sales	40,000
Sales Returns and Allowances	1,200
Net Income From Store 1	3,400
Purchases	14,000
Transportation In	700
Purchases Returns and Allowances . .	200
Purchases Discount	225
Shipments to Store 1	4,000
Operating Expenses	15,000

Topic 2
A Computer Application For a Multistore Business

A *How do large multistore businesses process their accounting data quickly and efficiently?* Large multistore businesses have a huge number of transactions. For example, each store in a chain may make thousands of sales a day. Because there is so much data to record, large multistore businesses use *computers* in much of their accounting work. Computers allow these businesses to process a great deal of accounting data quickly and efficiently. Computers also help such businesses to control their inventories and identify merchandise that must be ordered.

In this topic, we discuss the computerized accounting and merchandising procedures used at a chain of stores, Pacific Department Stores. This chain consists of 27 stores scattered over several states.

Computers process accounting data quickly and easily.

The Accounting System

Pacific Department Stores is a large chain store that uses a computerized centralized accounting system. It is owned by its stockholders and managed by individual store managers. Its top managers, administrators, data processing center, and warehouse are located at its home office. The ledger accounts for the stores are kept on magnetic disks at the data processing center of the home office. Each store in the chain sends data about its transactions to this center. The data is processed by the business's computer system, which updates the accounts receivable, the accounts payable, and the general ledger accounts. The computer system also prints journals and reports, prepares checks for creditors, prepares statements of account for customers with charge accounts, prepares payroll records and checks for all employees, and reconciles the bank statements. At the end of each month, the computer system uses the data in the ledger accounts to prepare financial statements for the individual stores and for the business as a whole.

The staff of the data processing center includes a data processing manager, systems analysts, computer programmers, computer operators, and data-entry clerks. Although most of the financial records are produced at the data processing center, the business also has a large accounting department at the home office. The staff of the accounting department consists of a vice president—finance, a controller, accountants, and accounting clerks.

The members of the accounting staff analyze, plan, and control the financial operations of the business. Much of the information needed

Division of Work in a Computerized Accounting System

Data Processing Center
- Prepares journals and reports.
- Keeps ledger accounts and inventory records.
- Prepares checks for creditors.
- Prepares statements of account for charge account customers.
- Prepares payroll records and checks.
- Prepares bank reconciliations.
- Prepares financial statements.

Accounting Department
- Sets up accounting procedures.
- Analyzes, plans, and controls financial operations.
- Performs manual accounting tasks such as checking the accuracy of purchase invoices and bills.

A computer system for a large business consists of many pieces of equipment. This equipment includes a central processing unit, magnetic tape units, magnetic disk units, and a printer.

Liamute E. Druskis

for these tasks comes from the computer-prepared reports and financial statements. The members of the accounting staff also perform certain accounting activities that are not done by the computer system. For example, the accounting clerks check the accuracy of purchase invoices and bills.

The accounting procedures for the business are set up by the accounting staff. These people work closely with the data processing manager and the systems analysts to develop any new procedures that are needed and to improve current procedures. They also develop new reports that will help management.

Merchandising Procedures

Purchasing merchandise and controlling inventories are important activities in a multistore business. Management must select merchandise that meets the needs of the customers in each store. The merchandise must be ordered on time and in large enough quantities to serve all the customers who will want the items. Otherwise, customers will go to competing stores and sales will be lost. However, management must be careful not to tie up the business's money in big inventories of slow-moving items.

At Pacific Department Stores, certain types of merchandise, such as television sets and radios, are purchased by the home office for all the stores in the chain. These items are shipped to the stores from the warehouse of the home office whenever the stores need the goods. Other types of merchandise, such as clothing and furniture, are purchased by each store according to local needs and fashion trends. The suppliers send these items directly to the individual stores.

The data processing center at the home office keeps inventory records for the warehouse and for all the stores in the chain. The necessary information is on magnetic disks. As goods are received or sold, this information is updated. The computer system also prints weekly inventory reports. These reports are used by the people at the home office and the stores who are involved in purchasing and inventory control activities.

Processing Sales and Cash Receipts

At Pacific Department Stores, sales are made for cash and on credit. Each store takes in large amounts of cash every day from cash sales. However, the chain also has thousands of charge account customers who buy on credit. The sales data for all the stores is processed by the computer system at the home office on a daily basis. This data is gathered by electronic cash registers and data collectors at the stores.

Procedures at the Stores. Each store in the chain uses electronic cash registers to record its sales and sales returns. The cashiers who operate the registers enter a code number for each transaction by pressing certain keys on the keyboard. This code number identifies the type of transaction: cash sale, credit sale, return on a cash sale, or return on a credit sale. After the code number is entered, most of the data about a sales transaction can be recorded automatically. (Sales returns must be entered manually.)

Each **electronic cash register** has a **tag reader** connected to it. The tag reader looks like a pencil with a light on one end. This device is an optical scanner that can read coded data and transmit it to the cash register. The cashier passes the tag reader over the tag attached to each merchandise item that a customer is buying. The tag contains bar-coded data about the item: inventory classification number, style number, size, color, sales department number, and price. (A **bar code** is a series of lines of different thicknesses that represent numbers.)

As the tag reader transmits the data about the items involved in a sale, the electronic cash register automatically records this data. Then the register automatically computes and records the total price of the goods, the sales tax, and the total amount owed by the customer.

If the sale is being made on credit, the cashier must enter the customer's account number manually. This number is shown on the plastic credit card issued to each charge account customer by the business. (The cashier must also prepare a sales slip and obtain credit approval when a customer is charging goods.)

The electronic cash register produces a printed customer receipt for each cash sale. Detailed data about all transactions recorded on the register is listed on an audit tape inside the machine. The same data is also automatically recorded on a cassette or magnetic tape. This cassette tape is in a unit called a **data collector.** The unit is located in another part of the store away from the sales areas.

At the end of each day, the audit tape is removed from the electronic cash register, a cash proof is prepared, and the cash receipts are deposited in the store's bank account. During the evening, after the store is closed, the data from the cassette tape in the data collector is transmitted to the home office over telephone lines. This procedure is followed for all the cash registers in the stores.

Procedures at the Home Office. Every evening, the data processing center of the home office receives data about cash sales, credit sales, and sales returns from all the stores in the chain. As noted previously, the data is transmitted to the home office over telephone lines. The data processing center has equipment that records this data on magnetic tape.

In the morning, the computer system processes the data for each store. The system performs a number of activities. It updates the accounts receivable ledger accounts, the general ledger accounts, and the inventory records. It also prints journals for the store. These journals show cash sales by departments, credit sales by departments, and sales returns by departments. The store manager and the accounting staff of the home office receive copies of the journals.

Remember that the accounts receivable ledger accounts, the general ledger accounts, and the inventory records are kept on magnetic disks. After these files are updated, the balances reflect the transactions that took place the previous day. The balances of the accounts receivable ledger accounts reflect the sales to charge account customers and the returns made by such customers. The balances of the general ledger accounts reflect the totals for sales, sales returns, cash received from cash sales, and accounts receivable from credit sales. The balances of the inventory accounts reflect the quantities on hand.

In addition to processing data about cash sales, credit sales, and sales returns, the computer system processes data about cash received on account. Every month, the data processing center of the home office prepares statements of account for the customers who have charge accounts. The computer system uses the data in the accounts receivable file to print the statements.

The customers are directed to send their checks to the home office along with part of the statement of account. This part of the statement serves as a remittance slip. It shows the customer's name, address,

STATEMENT OF ACCOUNT

PACIFIC DEPARTMENT STORES

27 Valley Drive   Los Angeles, California 91008

NANCY GOMEZ
897 WALTON AVENUE
WHITTIER, CA 90605

ACCOUNT NO. 015924
DATE 2/28/--
BALANCE DUE $252.30

Please detach this part of the statement
and enclose it with your check. Enter the
amount of your payment here ——▶

AMOUNT OF PAYMENT $ _____

DATE	REFERENCE	CHARGES	REMITTANCES AND RETURNS	BALANCE
2/1	BALANCE FORWARDED			120.35
2/10	20246	53.10		173.45
2/12	PAYMENT		120.35	53.10
2/21	38351	209.80		262.90
2/23	1079 RETURN		10.60CR	252.30
			BALANCE DUE	252.30

account number, and balance. The customer enters the amount of the payment.

All cash received on account is handled by the accounts receivable section of the accounting department at the home office. The accounting clerks who work in this section verify the accuracy of the amounts on each check and remittance slip. Then the checks are deposited in the bank, and the remittance slips are taken to the data processing center. The data from the remittance slips is recorded on magnetic tape.

Every day, the computer system processes the data about cash received on account. The system updates the accounts receivable ledger and the general ledger accounts. It also prints a detailed listing of the remittances. After the files are updated, the accounts receivable ledger reflects the payments made by charge account customers. The general ledger accounts reflect the increase in cash and the decrease in the total accounts receivable resulting from customer remittances.

Processing Purchases and Cash Payments

At Pacific Department Stores, all merchandise is purchased on credit. The business deals with thousands of suppliers. As noted previously, the home office buys certain types of goods for the stores and stocks these goods in its warehouse. Each store in the chain buys other types of goods directly from the suppliers. The computer system at the home office records all purchases, issues checks to the suppliers, and records the payments. The computer system also records transfers of goods from the warehouse to the stores and keeps inventory records for the warehouse and for the stores.

Procedures at the Stores. Each store prepares purchase orders for the goods that it buys directly from the suppliers. A prenumbered purchase order form that has several copies is used. One copy of each purchase order is given to a data-entry clerk in the administrative office of the store. The clerk records data about the orders on a cassette tape. A machine called a *key-to-cassette device* is used for this work. The machine has a keyboard that is similar to the keyboard of a typewriter.

Each day, the data on the cassette tape is transmitted to the home office over telephone lines. This data is needed by the home office because the inventory records show the quantity of each item that is on order as well as the quantity on hand.

When goods arrive at the store, a receiving clerk checks the shipment and prepares a receiving report. This report is actually a copy of the purchase order. It has spaces for filling in information about the quantities received and the condition of the goods.

If the goods are acceptable, a stock control clerk attaches a bar-coded tag to each item. The tag shows the store's inventory classification number for the item, the selling price, and other important information. The stock control clerk uses a device called a *tag printer* to prepare the tags. After all the tags are attached, the goods are taken to the sales area or the stockroom of the appropriate department.

The completed receiving reports are given to the data-entry clerk in the administrative office of the store. This clerk uses the key-to-cassette device to record data about the goods received by the store. The data on the cassette tape is transmitted to the home office over telephone lines on a daily basis. This allows the home office to update the inventory records it keeps for the store.

When purchase invoices arrive from the suppliers, the office personnel at the store check the quantities and the prices. (The receiving reports are used to verify the quantities.) The office personnel also enter code numbers on the invoices to identify the store and the department involved in each purchase. Then the invoices are sent to the accounting staff of the home office.

Procedures at the Home Office. Each day, the data about goods ordered and goods received is transmitted to the home office by all the stores in the chain. This data is recorded on magnetic tape at the data processing center. The computer system can then update the inventory records for the stores. Remember that the inventory records are also updated each day to reflect the quantities sold. In this way, the business is able to keep a perpetual inventory system for a huge number of items.

The accounts payable section of the accounting department at the home office handles the purchase invoices for the goods bought by the stores. The accounting clerks who work in this section verify the extensions and totals on the invoices. They also compute the date on which each invoice should be paid. The purchase invoices are then taken to the data processing center.

The data from the invoices is recorded on magnetic tape and processed by the computer system. The system performs several procedures with this data. It updates the accounts payable and the general ledger accounts that are affected by the purchases. It prints a purchases journal by departments for each store. It sorts the transactions by payment date and transfers the data to an unpaid invoices file. This file is kept on magnetic disks.

Each day, the computer system examines the data in the unpaid invoices file. It prints checks for the invoices due for payment on that day. If there is a cash discount, the system computes the discount and the net amount to be paid. It also updates the accounts payable and the

PACIFIC DEPARTMENT STORES			CHECK DATE 2/15/--		CHECK NO. 2419
	VENDOR			VENDOR NO. 07642	
APEX FURNITURE COMPANY					
INVOICE DATE	INVOICE NO.	INVOICE TOTAL	DISCOUNT	NET AMOUNT	
2/8/--	8262-P	6,000.00	120.00	5,880.00	
TOTAL PAYMENT				5,880.00	

DETACH BEFORE DEPOSITING

PACIFIC DEPARTMENT STORES   90-4160
                                                                   1221
27 Valley Drive   Los Angeles, California 91008

                                        NO.   2419
                                        DATE   2/15/--

                                        $ 5,880 | 00

PAY EXACTLY   5,880 DOLLARS AND 00 CENTS
TO THE ORDER OF   APEX FURNITURE COMPANY
                   1682 MASON STREET
                   SPOKANE, WA 99201

UNITED WESTERN BANK
LOS ANGELES, CALIFORNIA 91008

⑆1221⑆4160⑆ 0337⑈5602⑈

general ledger accounts that are affected by the payments. A listing of the checks issued is printed during the computer processing. This listing is called a **check register.**

```
2/15/--                     CHECK REGISTER                        PAGE 1

UNITED WESTERN BANK   ACCOUNT NO. 0337-5602

CHECK        VENDOR NAME          VENDOR   INVOICE   INVOICE   PURCHASE      NET
 NO.         AND ADDRESS            NO.      NO.      TOTAL    DISCOUNT    AMOUNT

2419    APEX FURNITURE COMPANY    07642   8262-P   6,000.00    120.00   5,880.00
        1682 MASON STREET
        SPOKANE, WA 99201

TOTAL PAYMENT ON CHECK                                                  5,880.00

2420    FASHION SPORTSWEAR INC.   03881    53771   1,750.00            1,750.00
        451 CORTEZ AVENUE                  53780   1,110.00            1,110.00
        SAN DIEGO, CA 92101

TOTAL PAYMENT ON CHECK                                                  2,860.00
```

In addition to recording the purchases data for the stores, the computer system processes the purchases made by the home office and records all transfers of goods to the stores.

Activity A. Answer the following questions about the procedures, equipment, and forms involved in processing sales, cash receipts, purchases, and cash payments at Pacific Department Stores. Refer to the text, illustrations, and marginal notes on pages 116 to 121.

1. Does the business have a centralized or a decentralized accounting system? Where are most of the financial records for the stores prepared?

2. What types of employees work at the data processing center of the home office?

3. What types of employees work on the accounting staff of the home office?

4. What devices are used to gather data about the sales made by each store in the chain?

5. What is a tag reader?

6. What is a bar code?

7. What data is recorded on each tag attached to a merchandise item?

8. How is sales data transmitted from each store to the data processing center at the home office?

9. Look at the statement of account prepared by the computer system (page 118). What is the customer's name? What is the customer's account number? How much did the customer owe at the end of the month?

10. Look at the check prepared by the computer system (page 121). What invoice is being paid? What is the invoice total? What is the amount of the discount? What is the amount of the payment?

11. Look at the check register prepared by the computer system (page 121). What bank are the checks drawn on? What is the bank account number? To which supplier (vendor) has Check 2419 been issued? What is the amount of Check 2420?

Reports for Management

B *What types of reports can a computerized accounting system produce to help management make decisions?* One of the advantages of a computerized accounting system is that it can quickly produce many different types of reports. For example, the data processing center at the home office of Pacific Department Stores prepares the weekly and monthly reports listed in the margin. These reports provide the managers of the business with much of the information they need to make decisions and control operations.

Weekly Reports. A weekly sales analysis report and a weekly inventory analysis report are prepared for each store in the chain. Copies of these reports go to the management of the stores and the management of the home office. The two reports contain detailed sales and inventory information for each item that a store carries. These reports also include total sales and total inventory amounts for each department and for the store as a whole.

Part of a sales analysis report and an inventory analysis report for Store 1 are shown on the next page. Notice that the sales analysis

**Management Reports
Produced by
a Computerized
Accounting System**

Weekly Reports
Inventory analysis report
Sales analysis report

Monthly Reports
Budget analysis report
Cash flow report
Expense report
Merchandise transfer summary
Payroll summary
Purchases summary
Sales summary
Sales staff productivity report
Schedule of accounts payable by age
Schedule of accounts receivable by age

report shows the units sold and the amount of sales for the week, the month to date, and the year to date. This allows management to see how well each item is selling now and how well it has done over longer periods of time. The inventory analysis report follows a similar pattern. It shows all inventory transactions for the month to date and the year to date. Notice that the inventory analysis report also lists the units that are on order, the unit prices, the balances on hand, and the total prices.

WEEK ENDED 2/14/--		SALES ANALYSIS REPORT--STORE 1						PAGE 1
DEPT. NO.	INVENTORY CLASSIFICATION NO.	DESCRIPTION	----CURRENT WEEK--- UNITS SOLD	AMOUNT	---MONTH TO DATE--- UNITS SOLD	AMOUNT	----YEAR TO DATE---- UNITS SOLD	AMOUNT
1	1011	KENMORE DENIM JACKET	6	239.70	12	479.40	23	918.85
1	1012	STYLECRAFT CORDUROY JACKET	2	139.90	5	349.75	10	699.50
1	1013	SAXON POLYESTER JACKET	10	299.50	21	628.95	39	1,168.09
TOTAL SALES FOR DEPT. 1				4,566.70		8,814.65		18,794.65

WEEK ENDED 2/14/--		INVENTORY ANALYSIS REPORT--STORE 1										PAGE 1
DEPT. NO.	INVENTORY CLASSIFICATION NO.	DESCRIPTION	-----MONTH TO DATE---- UNITS RECD.	UNITS SOLD	------YEAR TO DATE------ UNITS RECD.	UNITS SOLD	UNITS ON ORDER	---UNIT PRICE--- COST	SELLING	BALANCE ON HAND	----TOTAL PRICE---- COST	SELLING
1	1011	KENMORE DENIM JACKET	12		50	23	100	24.00	39.95	27	648.00	1,078.65
1	1012	STYLECRAFT CORDUROY JACKET	5			10		42.00	69.95	40	1,680.00	2,798.00
1	1013	SAXON POLYESTER JACKET	21			39	150	18.00	29.95	51	918.00	1,527.45
TOTAL INVENTORY FOR DEPT. 1											21,746.85	36,244.75

The store manager and the assistant store manager use the sales analysis report to see how successfully each department is operating. They use the inventory analysis report to see how efficiently purchasing and inventory control procedures are being carried out. The merchandise manager and the department managers use the two reports to identify goods that are selling rapidly and goods that are selling slowly. The goods that are selling rapidly are reordered promptly to prevent the store from running out of stock on these items. The goods that are selling slowly may be reduced in price, or they may receive more advertising to build sales. If prospects for an item are poor, the remaining stock may be closed out at low prices to make room for new items that may sell better.

The management of the home office uses the sales analysis report and the inventory analysis report to gain information about the week-to-week operations of each store in the chain. These people also use the sales analysis report to compare the sales of the various stores.

Monthly Reports. The monthly reports present a wide range of information about the operations of the individual stores and the operations of the business as a whole. These reports cover cash flow, expenses, merchandise transfers to the stores, payroll, purchases, sales, productivity of the sales staff, accounts payable, and accounts receivable. There is also a report that compares budgeted amounts for sales, cost of goods, and expenses with the actual amounts.

These reports help management to identify problems in certain stores that must be corrected. For example, expenses in one store may be too high in relation to sales. The productivity of the sales staff may be too low in another store.

The monthly reports also help management to plan for the future. For example, the computer system ages the accounts payable as well as the accounts receivable. The totals for the various time periods shown on the schedule of accounts payable by age provide a basis for estimating how much cash the home office will need to pay invoices. The managers of the accounting staff can then make sure that sufficient funds are on hand in the bank account of the home office during each period.

The number and types of reports prepared in a computerized accounting system vary in each business according to the needs of its management.

Financial Statements

Computers can be used to prepare financial statements.

In addition to producing many reports, the computer system at the home office of Pacific Department Stores prepares monthly financial statements for the individual stores and for the business as a whole. The data for the financial statements comes from the general ledger accounts, which are kept on magnetic disks.

As you have seen, the general ledger accounts are updated automatically during the daily processing of transactions by the computer system. The necessary amounts are recorded in the accounts when sales, cash receipts, purchases, cash payments, and payroll are processed. At the end of each month, the computer system is used to prepare a trial balance. The accounting staff of the home office checks the trial balance before the financial statements are produced.

The computer system prepares an income statement, a schedule of cost of goods sold, and a balance sheet for each store in the chain. An income statement for one of the stores is shown on the next page. This income statement reports the results of operations at Store 1 for the month ended February 28. Notice that the percent of each item to net sales is given as well as the amount for each item. This helps the management of the home office to judge the performance of each store and make comparisons among the stores.

The computer system also produces combined financial statements that present information for the business as a whole. The system automatically combines the amounts for all the stores in the chain.

```
MONTH ENDED 2/28/--          INCOME STATEMENT--STORE 1

                             -----AMOUNT-----    PERCENT
REVENUE FROM SALES
   SALES                       260,310
   LESS SALES RETURNS           11,060
   NET SALES                                249,250   100.0
COST OF GOODS SOLD (SEE SCHEDULE)           167,825    67.3
GROSS PROFIT ON SALES                        81,425    32.7
OPERATING EXPENSES
   ADVERTISING EXPENSE           3,200                  1.3
   UNCOLLECTIBLE ACCOUNTS EXPENSE  300                  0.1
   CASH SHORT AND OVER              75                  0.0
   DELIVERY EXPENSE              2,275                  0.9
   DEPRECIATION EXPENSE          2,925                  1.2
   INSURANCE EXPENSE             1,300                  0.5
   MAINTENANCE AND REPAIRS EXPENSE 1,025               0.4
   MISCELLANEOUS EXPENSE           525                  0.2
   PAYROLL TAXES EXPENSE         2,400                  1.0
   RENT EXPENSE                  6,075                  2.4
   SALARIES EXPENSE             31,350                 12.6
   SUPPLIES EXPENSE             2,675                  1.1
   TELEPHONE EXPENSE            1,100                  0.4
   UTILITIES EXPENSE            2,700                  1.1
      TOTAL OPERATING EXPENSES              57,925     23.2
   NET INCOME                               23,500      9.4
```

Activity B-1. Answer the following questions. Refer to the sales analysis report on page 123.

1. What period of time does the report cover? Which store is the report for?

2. What is the classification number for Saxon polyester jackets?

3. How many units of Item 1011 were sold during the current week? during the month to date? during the year to date?

4. Which item had the largest amount of sales during the current week?

5. What is the amount of sales for Item 1011 during the current week? during the month to date? during the year to date?

6. What department sells Items 1011, 1012, and 1013?

7. What is the total amount of sales for the department during the current week? during the month to date? during the year to date?

8. Why do you think that it is helpful to management for the sales analysis report to show information about the month to date and the year to date as well as the current week?

Activity B-2. Answer the following questions about the inventory analysis report shown on page 123.

1. How many units of Item 1011 were received during the year to date? sold during the year to date?

2. What is the balance on hand for Item 1013?

3. What is the unit cost for Item 1012? the unit selling price?

4. What is the total cost for Item 1011? What is the total selling price for this item?

5. How many units of Item 1013 are on order?
6. What is the total cost of the inventory for Department 1?
7. Why do you think that it is helpful to management for the inventory analysis report to show how many units of an item are on order?

Activity B-3. Answer the following questions about the income statement shown on page 125.

1. What period of time is covered by the income statement?
2. What is the amount of net sales shown on the income statement?
3. How much gross profit on sales does the store earn?
4. What is the largest expense?
5. How much is spent for advertising?

6. What is the amount of the total operating expenses?
7. How much net income does the store earn?
8. What is the percent of each of the following items to net sales: cost of goods sold? gross profit on sales? total operating expenses? net income?

Topic 2   Problems

3-5. The financial records produced by a computer system provide a great deal of information about the operations of a business. The accounting staff is often asked to help management analyze such information. Sometimes this task involves preparing special reports for management.

The Dalton Company operates a chain of seven department stores. Assume that you work on the accounting staff at the home office. The vice president for store operations wants your help in comparing the profitability of the individual stores in the chain during the past month. Your first step is to look at the income statements for the stores, which were prepared by the business's computer system. These statements show the following information about the net income of each store for the month ended March 31.

	Amount of Net Income	Percent of Net Income to Net Sales
Store 1	$16,782	15.6%
Store 2	21,325	18.9
Store 3	11,561	10.7
Store 4	15,970	16.8
Store 5	20,795	19.4
Store 6	19,877	21.7
Store 7	12,438	9.5

a. Prepare a report that ranks the stores according to the amount of net income each one earned. List the store with the highest net income first. Then list the store with the next highest net income and so on. The column heads and the first line of the report are given in the table at the top of page 127.

Rank	Store	Amount of Net Income
1	Store 2	$21,325

b. Prepare a report that ranks the stores by the percent of net

income to net sales. List the store with the highest percent of net income first. Then list the store with the next highest percent of net income and so on.

3-6. Answer the following questions about the profitability of the stores owned by the Dalton Company. Refer to the reports that you prepared in Topic Problem 3-5.

a. Which store earns the highest amount of net income?
b. Which store has the highest percent of net income to net sales?
c. Which store earns the lowest amount of net income?
d. Which store has the lowest percent of net income to net sales?
e. The percent of net income to net sales is often used to judge the efficiency of operations. On

this basis, what two stores in the chain seem to have the most efficient operations? (Look for the stores with a high percent of net income to net sales.)
f. At the Dalton Company, management expects the net income for each store to be at least 15 percent of net sales. Did any of the stores fall below this level during March? If so, which stores?

The Language of Business

Here are some basic terms that make up the language of business. Do you understand the meaning

of each? Can you define each term and use it in an original sentence?

multistore business
accounting subsystems
centralized accounting
  system

decentralized
  accounting system
internal transactions
combined balance sheet

combined income
  statement
computer
electronic cash register

tag reader
bar code
data collector
tag printer

Chapter 3   Questions

1. What are the two types of accounting systems used by multistore businesses?
2. What is the difference between a centralized accounting system and a decentralized accounting system?
3. Give some examples of internal transactions.
4. Describe the relationship between the following accounts in a multistore business like Best Auto

Products: The Store 1 account in the general ledger of the home office and the Home Office account in the general ledger of Store 1.
5. What is a combined income statement used for? What is a combined balance sheet used for?
6. How can an electronic cash register with a tag reader be used to gather data for a computer?
7. When a business has a computerized accounting

system, what types of accounting work are done by the data processing center? by the accounting department?

8. What types of jobs are there in the data processing center? What types of jobs are there in the accounting department?

9. What types of information are provided by the weekly sales analysis reports prepared at Pacific Department Stores? How can this information be used by management?

10. What types of information are provided by the weekly inventory analysis reports prepared at Pacific Department Stores? How can this information be used by management?

Chapter 3   Problems

Problems for Chapter 3 are given in the *Working Papers and Chapter Problems* for Part 1. If you are using the workbook, do the problems in the space provided there. Complete your assigned topic problems before answering the chapter problems.

Chapter 3   Management Cases

Computers and Accounting. Many businesses now use computers to help perform their accounting work. One of the advantages of a computerized accounting system is its ability to process large amounts of data quickly. However, the most important benefit of such a system is its ability to produce a wide range of financial information about the operations of a business.

Computers change the way financial records are prepared, but they do not change the need to understand the principles of accounting. In a large business, many different people must work with computer-prepared financial reports and statements: members of the accounting staff, managers, office employees, store employees, and so on. To use these reports and statements effectively, it is necessary to understand the information they contain. It is also necessary to be able to interpret the information.

Case 3M-1. The Homecraft Company operates a chain of home decorating stores. Each store sells paint, wallpaper, floor tiles, carpeting, and lighting fixtures. Store 1 has always produced the highest sales revenue of all the stores in the chain. Alan Carr, the manager of Store 1, works hard to increase sales from month to month. He believes in doing a great deal of advertising, including expensive television commercials. He also cuts prices far below those of competing stores in order to build up sales.

Janet Gold recently became vice president for store operations at the home office. When Mrs. Gold received the April income statement for Store 1 from the business's data processing center, she became concerned. She found that the net income earned by Store 1 was very low: $900. This is only 1 percent of the store's net sales.

Mrs. Gold called the manager of Store 1 and asked why the profitability of his store was so poor in April. Mr. Carr told her that the weather was bad in his area and sales did not increase as much as they usually do. Mrs. Gold asked him about the cost of goods sold and the operating expenses for the store. He explained that he really doesn't understand these items. When he receives the monthly income statement, he pays attention to the revenue from sales. He feels that the store will earn a high net income in the future if he can continue to build up sales through advertising and low prices.

After speaking to Mr. Carr, Mrs. Gold looked at the income statements of Store 1 for January through March. Some of the information from these income statements and from the income statement for April is given at the top of page 128. The percent of each item to net sales is also shown.

When Mrs. Gold compared the financial information about Store 1 with similar information for the other stores in the chain, she found that Store 1 has the lowest percent of gross profit on sales and the highest percent of operating expenses. Store 1 also has the most salesclerks. It employs 12 salesclerks. Store 2, which had net sales of $80,000 during April, employs 8 salesclerks.

	January		February		March		April	
Net Sales	$81,000	100%	$86,000	100%	$89,000	100%	$90,000	100%
Cost of Goods Sold	47,790	59	51,600	60	53,400	60	54,900	61
Gross Profit on Sales	$33,210	41	$34,400	40	$35,600	40	$35,100	39
Operating Expenses	26,730	33	30,100	35	32,040	36	34,200	38
Net Income	$ 6,480	8	$ 4,300	5	$ 3,560	4	$ 900	1

a. Is Mr. Carr doing a good job of managing Store 1? Why or why not? (Study the results of operations for January through April.)

b. What do you think of Mr. Carr's idea that the store will earn a high net income in the future if he can continue to build up sales? Do increases in sales always lead to increases in net income?

c. How productive does the sales staff of Store 1 seem to be in comparison to the sales staff of Store 2? (Divide the net sales of Store 1 for April by the number of salesclerks the store employs. This will give you the average amount of sales for each salesclerk. Then divide the net sales for Store 2 by the number of salesclerks it has.)

d. If you were Mrs. Gold, would you allow Mr. Carr to continue running Store 1 in the same way he has been running it up to now? Why or why not?

e. What steps can be taken to improve the profitability of Store 1?

Case 3M-2. The ABC Corporation operates a large chain of hardware stores. Every month, the home office gives a bonus to the manager of the store that produces the highest amount of net income. During June, stores 10 and 32 earned the same net income. The controller has suggested that the bonus for that month should go to the manager whose store had the most efficient operations.

	Store 10	Store 32
Net Sales	$75,000	$60,000
Cost of Goods Sold	38,250	28,800
Gross Profit on Sales	$36,750	$31,200
Operating Expenses	24,750	19,200
Net Income	$12,000	$12,000

a. Determine the profitability of each store in terms of the percent of net income to net sales. (Find this percent by dividing each store's amount of net income by the amount of its net sales.)

b. Determine the productivity of the sales staff in each store. Store 10 employs 6 salesclerks. Store 32 employs 5 salesclerks. (Compute the average amount of sales for each salesclerk. Divide each store's net sales by the number of salesclerks it has.)

c. Which store do you think had the most efficient operations during June? Explain your answer.

d. Do you think that the business should continue to award the monthly bonus on the basis of the highest amount of net income? Would it be more fair to give the bonus on the basis of the efficiency of operations? Why or why not?

Accounting for Special Types of Sales

Examples of Special Types of Sales

Installment Sales
COD Sales
Credit Card Sales

Some merchandising businesses have special types of sales. Three of the most common of these special types of sales are installment sales, COD sales, and credit card sales.

The procedures and records needed to process installment sales are discussed in the first topic of this chapter. The procedures and records for processing COD sales and credit card sales are presented in the second topic.

Topic 1
Installment Sales

Types of Sales on Credit:
• Charge Account Sales
• Installment Sales
• COD Sales
• Credit Card Sales

A *How is credit in a merchandising business provided?* The management of each merchandising business must select suitable credit policies. As you have already learned, many retail stores, such as clothing stores and department stores, provide credit in the form of charge accounts. Some stores require that customers with charge accounts pay for their purchases in 25 or 30 days. Other stores allow more time if the customer is willing to pay interest on the amount owed.

Retail firms that specialize in expensive items, such as cars, motorcycles, boats, furniture, and large appliances, often make their credit sales in a different way. Instead of offering charge accounts, they sell on the installment plan. One of the most important features of an **installment sale** is that it permits the customer to make a series of payments over a period of time. This period is usually much longer than the period allowed a charge account customer. It may be as much as a year or several years.

Some businesses have both charge account sales and installment sales. Other businesses provide only one form of credit to their customers.

Features of Installment Sales

Installment sales have several features that make them different from other types of sales.

• *A customer who buys on the installment plan is usually asked to pay part of the price before receiving the goods.* This amount is called a **down payment.** After receiving the goods, the customer makes a series of equal payments at regular intervals over a period of time. These payments are called **installments.**

Installments are a series of payments that a customer makes for goods bought on the installment plan.

• *Installments are usually paid monthly.* The total period of time allowed for the installments is determined by the policies of each business, the price of the goods, the credit rating of the customer, and other factors. As noted before, the total period is often a year or several years. For example, the installments on a car usually extend over two, three, or four years.

• *The amount that the customer pays for goods bought on the installment plan is higher than the cash selling price of the goods.* This is because the business adds a **finance charge,** or *carrying charge*, to the cash selling price. The finance charge covers the cost of providing credit to the customer. Other charges such as an insurance charge may also be added. Each monthly installment includes part of the cash selling price and part of the finance charge and any other charges.

A finance charge is an amount that is added to the price of goods to cover the cost of providing credit.

• *The customer must sign an* **installment contract.** (This type of legal paper is also called a *conditional sales contract.*) The contract gives the terms of the installment sale. It describes the goods and lists the cash selling price, the amount of the down payment, the amount to be financed, the amount and percentage rate of the finance charge, the amount of any other charges, and the total amount to be paid. The contract also lists the amount of each monthly installment and the number of installments. An example of an installment contract is shown on page 132.

• *Ownership of goods sold on the installment plan usually remains with the seller until the customer pays the total amount owed.* This allows the seller to **repossess** (take back) the goods if the customer fails to pay some of the installments.

Seller's Name: _Bay Electronics_
Boston, MA 02116

Contract # _578_

RETAIL INSTALLMENT CONTRACT AND SECURITY AGREEMENT

The undersigned (herein called Purchaser, whether one or more) purchases from _Bay Electronics_ (seller) and grants to _Bay Electronics_ a security interest in, subject to the terms and conditions hereof, the following described property.

PURCHASER'S NAME _Gail Ryan_
PURCHASER'S ADDRESS _232 Mason St._
CITY _Boston_ STATE _MA_ ZIP _02111_

QUANTITY	DESCRIPTION	AMOUNT	
1	Apex color TV set	500	00
	21" #861-M		
	Description of Trade-in:		
	Sales Tax	25	00
	Total	525	00

1. CASH PRICE $ _500.00_
2. LESS: CASH DOWN PAYMENT $ _50.00_
3. TRADE-IN
4. TOTAL DOWN PAYMENT $ _50.00_
5. UNPAID BALANCE OF CASH PRICE $ _450.00_
6. OTHER CHARGES:
   Sales tax $ _25.00_
   Insurance _5.00_
7. AMOUNT FINANCED $ _480.00_
8. FINANCE CHARGE $ _48.12_
9. TOTAL OF PAYMENTS $ _528.12_
10. DEFERRED PAYMENT PRICE (1+6+8) $ _578.12_
11. ANNUAL PERCENTAGE RATE _18_ %

Insurance Agreement

The purchase of insurance coverage is voluntary and not required for credit. _Credit life_ insurance coverage is available at a cost of $ _5.00_ for the term of credit.

I desire insurance coverage
Signed _Gail Ryan_ Date _8/1/—_

I do not desire insurance coverage

Signed_____ Date_____

Purchaser hereby agrees to pay to _Bay Electronics_ at their offices shown above the "TOTAL OF PAYMENTS" shown above in _12_ monthly installments of $ _44.01_ (final payment to be $ _44.01_) the first installment being payable _Sept. 1,_ 19 _—_, and all subsequent installments on the same day of each consecutive month until paid in full. The finance charge applies from _8/1/—_

Signed _Gail Ryan_

Notice to Buyer: You are entitled to a copy of the contract you sign. You have the right to pay in advance the unpaid balance of this contract and obtain a partial refund of the finance charge based on the "Actuarial Method." [Any other method of computation may be so identified, for example, "Rule of 78's," "Sum of the Digits," etc.]

NOTE: The interest rate shown here is the true annual interest rate. It was computed on the declining balance of the amount owed.

Advantages and Disadvantages of Installment Sales

Advantages of Installment Sales for a Business:
- Can sell expensive goods to large numbers of people.
- Can take back goods if customer fails to pay.

Installment sales have both advantages and disadvantages for a business. One of the major advantages is that the installment plan makes it possible to sell expensive goods to large numbers of people. Many people cannot afford to pay cash for these goods. They also cannot afford to buy the goods on a charge account and pay for them in a short period of time.

Another major advantage of the installment plan is that it gives a business some protection against losses from customers who do not pay for their purchases. The installment plan permits the seller to repossess the goods if a customer does not make all the necessary payments.

One important disadvantage of the installment plan is that a business must wait a long period of time to receive the full amount owed by each customer. To overcome this disadvantage and get cash quickly, some businesses sell their installment contracts to a finance company. Other businesses arrange to have banks provide credit for customers who want to buy on the installment plan. (The financing of installment sales is discussed later in this topic.)

Another important disadvantage of the installment plan is the risk involved. Although the business has the right to repossess its goods if a customer fails to make all the payments, there is still a possibility of losses. For example, the customer may leave town with the goods. Also, the goods a business is able to repossess may be in poor condition. The business may therefore need to spend money for repairs before reselling the goods.

The installment plan also has advantages and disadvantages for the customers. They can buy the goods they need or want and pay while they are using the goods. They do not have to save for months or years before obtaining the goods. On the other hand, the customers must pay finance charges in addition to the price of the goods.

Disadvantages of Installment Sales for a Business:
- Must wait a long time to receive full price of goods.
- Can lose money if customer moves with the goods before making all payments.
- Repossessed goods may be in poor condition.

Activity A. Answer the following questions about installment sales. Refer to the text and illustrations on pages 130 to 133.

1. What is an installment sale?
2. What is a down payment? What are installments?
3. What is an installment contract? What information does this contract show?
4. What happens to goods when the customer does not pay the installments?
5. What is a finance charge?
6. What are some advantages of installment sales for a business?
7. What are some disadvantages of installment sales for a business?

Accounting for Installment Sales

B *How does a business record its installment sales?* The procedures for recording installment sales are very similar to the procedures for recording charge account sales. Remember that charge account sales increase a business's accounts receivable and increase its revenues. Installment sales have the same effect. However, separate records are kept for the accounts receivable and the revenues from installment sales.

The chart given on page 134 shows the entries that are made for cash sales, charge account sales, and installment sales at Bay Electronics. Bay Electronics is a retail store located in an Eastern city. It specializes in electronic equipment. It is owned by Anthony Rocco and has an expert sales staff.

Bay Electronics Chart of Accounts

Assets
101 Cash
111 Accounts Receivable
112 Installment Accounts Receivable

Liabilities
216 Sales Tax Payable
221 Insurance Payable

Revenue
401 Sales
402 Installment Sales
491 Finance Charges

The amount of each charge account sale is debited to the Accounts Receivable account in the general ledger and the customer's account in the accounts receivable ledger. The price of the goods is credited to the Sales account. The amount of the sales tax is credited to the Sales Tax Payable account. However, notice that installment sales are handled differently. The business uses an Installment Accounts Receivable account and an installment accounts receivable ledger to record the amounts that customers owe for these sales. The revenues from such sales are credited to two accounts: the Installment Sales account and the Finance Charges account. The sales tax is credited to the Sales Tax Payable account. If the customer wants insurance, the price of the coverage is credited to the Insurance Payable account.

Type of Sale	Account(s) Debited	Account(s) Credited
Cash sale	Cash	Sales
		Sales Tax Payable*
Charge account sale	Accounts Receivable (also customer's account in accounts receivable ledger)	Sales
		Sales Tax Payable*
Installment sale	Installment Accounts Receivable (also customer's account in installment accounts receivable ledger)	Installment Sales
		Finance Charges
		Sales Tax Payable*
		Insurance Payable

*This account is used if sales tax must be paid.

The **installment accounts receivable ledger** is a subsidiary ledger. It contains the individual accounts for all customers who buy goods on the installment plan. The balances of the accounts in the installment accounts receivable ledger are summarized in a controlling account in the general ledger. This account is called *Installment Accounts Receivable.*

It is important for a business to have separate records of the accounts receivable from charge account sales and the accounts receivable from installment sales. This allows the accounting system to produce information that management needs to control both types of accounts receivable. It also provides management with information that is needed to assess the business's credit policies.

The revenues from goods sold on the installment plan are recorded in an account called *Installment Sales.* The revenues from the finance charges on installment sales are recorded in an account called *Finance Charges.* Some firms enter cash sales, charge account sales, and installment sales in the Sales account. However, the use of a separate account for installment sales allows management to see exactly how much these sales are contributing to the total revenues of the business.

Kip Peticolas/Fundamental Photographs

Bay Electronics, a retail store specializing in electronic equipment such as television sets, video tape recorders, stereos, cassette players, stereo records, and tapes offers a generous installment plan to customers who want to buy on credit.

Some customers who buy goods on the installment plan want to obtain insurance for the goods. The business that sells the goods may offer such insurance. In most cases, the business does not provide the insurance coverage itself. Instead, it arranges to have an insurance company do this. If a customer decides to take the insurance, an insurance charge is included in the total of the installment sale. The amount of this charge is a liability until the business pays the insurance company. An account called *Insurance Payable* is therefore credited when the sale is recorded.

Accounting Principle:
Reporting Receivables. The generally accepted accounting principle is that accounts receivable should be reported on the balance sheet as the total amount billed and that the allowance for accounts estimated to be uncollectible should be subtracted from that amount.

Activity B. Answer the following questions about the recording of sales transactions at Bay Electronics. Refer to the text and illustrations on pages 133 to 135.

1. What types of sales does the business have?

2. What accounts are debited and credited to record a charge account sale?

3. What accounts are debited and

credited to record an installment sale?

4. What is the installment accounts receivable ledger?

5. What kind of account is Installment Accounts Receivable? What is the relationship of this account to the installment accounts receivable ledger?

6. Why are separate records kept for the accounts receivable from charge account sales and the accounts receivable from installment sales?

7. What kind of account is the Installment Sales account? the Finance Charges account?

Journalizing Installment Sales and Down Payments

C *What journal is used to record installment sales? What journal is used to record the down payments on these sales?* Sales of merchandise on the installment plan are entered in the sales journal. Down payments are entered in the cash receipts journal.

On August 1, Bay Electronics sold a color television set on the installment plan to Gail Ryan. The total amount that the customer must pay is $578.12. This amount includes the cash selling price of the item ($500), the sales tax ($25), an insurance charge ($5), and a finance charge ($48.12). A sales slip and an installment contract were prepared for the sale. The customer signed the contract and received a copy. She also received a copy of the sales slip shown on the next page. The installment contract is shown on page 132.

The sales journal at the bottom of the next page shows the entry made to record the installment sale to Gail Ryan. The data for this entry came from the sales slip.

Notice that the sales journal used by Bay Electronics has special columns for recording the amounts of charge account sales and the amounts of installment sales. Both types of sales on credit are entered in the same journal.

Look at the entry for the installment sale to Gail Ryan. The amount in the Installment Accounts Receivable Debit column ($578.12) is the total amount owed by the customer. The amount in the Finance Charges Credit column ($48.12) is the finance charge on the sale. The amount in the Insurance Payable Credit column ($5) is the insurance charge. The amount in the Sales Tax Payable Credit column ($25) is the tax that must be paid on the sale. The amount in the Installment Sales Credit column ($500) is the cash selling price of the goods.

The entries for installment sales are posted individually to the installment accounts receivable ledger. At the end of the month, the sales journal is totaled, proved, and ruled. The column totals are posted to the proper accounts in the general ledger.

When Gail Ryan bought the color television set from Bay Electronics, she was asked to make a down payment. The amount of the down

BAY ELECTRONICS
825 South Bay Street
Boston, Massachusetts 02116

SOLD TO *Gail Ryan*

ADDRESS *232 Mason Street*

Boston, MA 02111

DELIVER TO *Same*

☐ CASH SALE

☐ CHARGE ACCOUNT SALE

☑ INSTALLMENT SALE

SALES CLERK *P. Jacobs*

CREDIT APPROVAL *AR*

QUAN.	DESCRIPTION	UNIT PRICE	AMOUNT
1	*Apex Color TV set 21" #861-M*	500 00	500 00

OTHER CHARGES:

INSTALLATION *free*

DELIVERY *free*

INSURANCE *$ 5.00*

FINANCE *48.12*

TOTAL *$53.12*

TOTAL PRICE	500 00
SALES TAX	25 00
OTHER CHARGES	53 12
AMOUNT OWED	578 12

INSTALLMENT SALES ONLY	CONTRACT NO. 578	DOWN PAYMENT $50.00	RECEIVED BY PJ

OFFICE COPY

No. **4308**

		SALES JOURNAL								Page *16*
DATE	SALE NO.	ACCOUNT DEBITED	POST. REF.	ACCOUNTS RECEIVABLE DEBIT	INSTALL. ACCTS. REC. DEBIT	SALES TAX PAYABLE CREDIT	INSURANCE PAYABLE CREDIT	FINANCE CHARGES CREDIT	SALES CREDIT	INSTALL. SALES CREDIT
19—										
Aug. 1	4308	*Gail Ryan . . . . .*	√		578 12	25 00	5 00	48 12		500 00
1	4309	*Frank Santelli . . .*	√	57 75		2 75			55 00	
31		*Totals . . . .*		1,770 00	3,820 00	261 00	52 00	317 80	1,681 50	3,225 70
				(111)	(112)	(216)	(221)	(491)	(401)	(402)

payment ($50) is listed on the sales slip. After recording the installment sale in the sales journal, the accounting clerk entered the down payment in the cash receipts journal. This entry is shown here.

	CASH RECEIPTS JOURNAL								Page 23
DATE	ACCOUNT CREDITED	EXPLANATION	POST. REF.	GENERAL LEDGER CREDIT	ACCOUNTS RECEIVABLE CREDIT	INSTALL. ACCTS. REC. CREDIT	SALES CREDIT	SALES TAX PAYABLE CREDIT	NET CASH DEBIT
19—									
Aug. 1	Cash Balance	$16,850	—						
1	Gail Ryan	Down payment	√			50 00			50 00
1	Howard Scott	On account	√		108 00				108 00
2	Donna Hanson	Installment	√			38 60			38 60
6	Sales	Cash sales for week	—				2,625 00	131 25	2,756 25
31	Totals			578 00	1,100 00	2,410 00	13,290 00	664 50	18,042 50
				(—)	(111)	(112)	(401)	(216)	(101)

Notice that the business's cash receipts journal has several special columns. The down payment from Gail Ryan is entered in the Installment Accounts Receivable Credit and the Net Cash Debit columns.

The cash receipts journal is also used for recording cash sales, cash on account from customers who have charge accounts, cash from monthly installments, and other types of cash receipts. (The journalizing of cash received from installments is discussed in the next segment of this topic.)

The entries for down payments and installments are posted individually to the installment accounts receivable ledger. At the end of the month, the cash receipts journal is totaled, proved, and ruled. The column totals are posted to the proper accounts in the general ledger.

Journalizing Cash Received From Installments

When goods are sold on the installment plan, many businesses give the customer a booklet with payment slips. There is a payment slip for each installment. The payment slip shows the due date and the amount of the installment. At the proper time, the customer removes each payment slip and sends it to the business with a check for the installment. Bay Electronics provides booklets of payment slips. The advantage of this procedure is that the business does not have to prepare monthly statements of account for installment plan customers.

On September 1, Bay Electronics received a check for $44.01 from Gail Ryan. This was the first installment on the color television set.

The payment slip that came with the check identified the payment. The accounting clerk at Bay Electronics made the following entry in the cash receipts journal to record the receipt of the installment.

				CASH RECEIPTS JOURNAL					Page 24
DATE	ACCOUNT CREDITED	EXPLANATION	POST. REF.	GENERAL LEDGER CREDIT	ACCOUNTS RECEIVABLE CREDIT	INSTALL. ACCTS. REC. CREDIT	SALES CREDIT	SALES TAX PAYABLE CREDIT	NET CASH DEBIT
19— Sept.									
1	Gail Ryan . . .	Installment . .	√			44 01			44 01

The entry for an installment is made in the same way as the entry for a down payment. The amount is recorded in the Installment Accounts Receivable Credit column and the Net Cash Debit column of the cash receipts journal.

Activity C. Answer the following questions about the installment sale to Gail Ryan and the journal entries for the sale, the down payment, and the first installment. Refer to the illustrations on pages 137 to 139.

1. Which journal is used to record the sale? What source document provides the data?

2. According to the source document, what is the cash selling price of the television set? the sales tax? the insurance charge? the finance charge?

3. What is the total amount that the customer must pay?

4. Which accounts and amounts are involved in the journal entry for the sale?

5. Which journal is used to record the down payment and the installment?

6. What is the amount of the down payment?

7. What is the amount of the first installment? When is it received from the customer?

8. Which accounts are debited and credited to record the down payment and the installment?

Posting to the Installment Accounts Receivable Ledger

D *What types of entries are posted to the installment accounts receivable ledger?* All entries for installment sales are posted to the installment accounts receivable ledger. These entries appear in the Installment Accounts Receivable Debit column of the sales journal. All entries for cash received from down payments and installments are also posted to the installment accounts receivable ledger. These entries appear in the Installment Account Receivable Credit column of the cash receipts journal.

After an installment sale is made, the accounting clerk at Bay Electronics opens an account for the customer in the installment accounts receivable ledger. The account for Gail Ryan is shown here.

Year *19*— Months	J	F	M	A	M	J	J	A	S √	O	N	D
Year Months	J	F	M	A	M	J	J	A	S	O	N	D

Contract No. *578*

Name   *Gail Ryan*
Home Address *232 Mason Street*   Home Telephone *(617) 555-2175*
        Boston, MA 02111
Occupation   *Office manager*
Business Address *Metro Real Estate Agency*   Business Telephone *(617) 555-4144*
        1220 Drake Avenue, Boston, MA 02116
Bank *Security National Bank*
    1200 Drake Avenue, Boston, MA 02116

TERMS OF Total *$578.12*   Down Payment *$50.00*   No. of Installments *12*
CONTRACT Installments Begin *Sept. 1, 19—*   Amount *$44.01*   per *month*

DATE		EXPLANATION	POST. REF.	CHARGES	PAYMENTS	BALANCE
19—						
Aug.	*1*	*Sales Slip 4308*	*S16*	*578 12*		*578 12*
	1	*Down payment*	*CR23*		*50 00*	*528 12*
Sept.	*1*	. . . .	*CR24*		*44 01*	*484 11*

INSTALLMENT ACCOUNTS RECEIVABLE LEDGER

Notice that the upper part of the account lists information about the customer and about the terms of the sale. This information comes from the installment contract and from a credit application form that the customer completed. Most businesses require that the customer fill in a credit application form before they approve an installment sale. The data on the credit application form is used to check the customer's credit rating.

The total of the installment sale ($578.12) was posted from the sales journal. This amount appears in the Charges column and the Balance column of the account. The down payment ($50) was posted from the cash receipts journal. This amount appears in the Payments column of the account. The accounting clerk computed the new balance and recorded it in the Balance column ($578.12 − $50 = $528.12). The

---

BAY ELECTRONICS
CREDIT APPLICATION

☐ Charge Account

☑ Installment Credit

Name _Gail Ryan_

Home Address _232 Mason Street_ Home Telephone _(617) 555-2175_
Boston, MA 02111

☐ House ☑ Apartment ☐ Own ☑ Rent How many years at present address? _4_

Occupation _Office Manager_

Business Address _Metro Real Estate Agency_ Business Telephone _(617) 555-4144_
1220 Drake Avenue, Boston, MA 02116

How many years at present job? _5_

Bank(s): ☑ Checking Account _Security National Bank_
1200 Drake Avenue, Boston, MA 02116

☑ Savings Account _same as above_

Do you have charge accounts at other stores? ☑ Yes ☐ No

Store(s) _Regal Clothing Center_
Marshall's Shoe Store

Answer additional questions on reverse side of this form.

---

same procedure was followed in posting the first installment ($44.01) from the cash receipts journal.

At the top of the ledger account are boxes for the months. After posting the first installment, the accounting clerk placed a check mark in the box for September. When future installments are posted, the accounting clerk will continue to check off the months.

Controlling Installment Accounts Receivable

The accounts in the installment accounts receivable ledger must be examined regularly to see whether all the customers are paying their monthly installments. The check marks at the top of the ledger accounts make it easy to gather this information. Any customers who have failed to pay during a month can be identified quickly.

The accounting clerk prepares a report listing the customers who have not paid their installments. Management contacts these customers to ask for payment. If the customers do not send in the installments, the goods they bought will eventually be repossessed.

REPORT OF
PAST-DUE INSTALLMENTS

CUSTOMER	DUE DATE	AMOUNT

The accounting staff must supply information that management needs to control installment accounts receivable.

The balance in the installment accounts receivable
ledger must equal the balance of the Installment Accounts Receivable account.

Every month, the accounting clerk must also add the balances of the accounts in the installment accounts receivable ledger. The total is checked against the balance of the Installment Accounts Receivable account in the general ledger. The two amounts should be equal.

Reporting Installment Sales and Installment Accounts Receivable

The income statement shows the total installment sales and the total finance charges for the accounting period. The installment sales appear in the Revenue From Sales section. The finance charges appear in the Other Revenue section.

BAY ELECTRONICS
Income Statement
For the Month Ended August 31, 19—

Revenue From Sales:			
Sales.......................	14,971 50		
Installment Sales	3,225 70		
Total Sales		18,197 20	
Less: Sales Returns and Allowances		626 00	
Net Sales		17,571 20	
Net Income From Operations............		1,522 00	
Other Revenue:			
Finance Charges		317 80	
Net Income		1,839 80	

Installment accounts receivable are an asset for the business. They represent money that is owed to the business and will be received in the future. The total of the installment accounts receivable appears on

BAY ELECTRONICS
Balance Sheet
August 31, 19—

ASSETS			
Current Assets:			
Cash	17,600 00		
Petty Cash	75 00		
Change Fund	200 00		
Accounts Receivable	2,870 00		
Installment Accounts Receivable	12,910 00		

the balance sheet as shown in the illustration at the bottom of page 142. Notice that this amount is listed just below the total of the accounts receivable from charge account sales.

Installment accounts receivable are classified as a current asset even though some of the accounts may not be fully paid for several years. This is because cash is received from these customers each month.

Activity D. Answer the following questions about the installment accounts receivable and the financial statements for Bay Electronics. Refer to the text and illustrations on pages 140 to 142.

1. What documents provide the information that is recorded in the upper part of each account in the installment accounts receivable ledger?

2. What is the number of Gail Ryan's installment contract?

3. How many installments must Gail Ryan pay?

4. What types of entries are posted to Gail Ryan's account on August 1?

5. What is the balance of Gail Ryan's account on September 1?

6. What is the purpose of the boxes for the months at the top of the ledger account?

7. On which financial statement do installment sales and finance charges appear?

8. What is the balance of the Installment Accounts Receivable account on August 31?

9. On which financial statement is the Installment Accounts Receivable account listed?

Recording Repossessions

E *How does a business record the repossession of merchandise?* Most installment contracts specify that a business can take back its merchandise if the customer fails to pay an installment. Ownership remains with the business until the item is fully paid for. If the merchandise is in good condition when it is repossessed, the business will sell it as used merchandise to another customer. If the merchandise is in poor condition, the business may have to discard it or may have to repair the merchandise before reselling it. The types of accounting entries that are made for repossessed merchandise depend on the *resale value* of each item.

When merchandise is repossessed, the customer is no longer legally responsible for the balance owed on the installment contract. The debt is wiped out because the business has taken back the goods.

Resale Value Covers Unpaid Balance. Sometimes repossessed merchandise has a resale value that will cover the unpaid balance of the installment contract. For example, on September 10, Bay Electronics repossessed stereo equipment from Roy West. The unpaid balance

**Bay Electronics
Chart of Accounts**

Assets
111   Accounts Receivable
112   Installment Accounts
         Receivable

Costs and Expenses
501   Purchases
505   Repossessed Merchandise Purchases
515   Loss on Repossessed Merchandise

of his installment contract is $150. The resale value of the merchandise is $180. The accounting clerk makes the following entry in the general journal to record the repossession from Roy West.

DATE		ACCOUNT TITLE AND EXPLANATION	POST. REF.	DEBIT	CREDIT
GENERAL JOURNAL					Page 9
19—					
Sept.	10	Repossessed Merchandise Purchases .	505	150 00	
		Installment Accounts Receivable/			
		Roy West	112/√		150 00
		Record repossessed merchandise.			

General Ledger

Repossessed Merchandise Purchases	505
Sept. 10 150	

Installment Accounts Receivable		112
Sept. 1 12,910	Sept. 10	150

Installment Accounts Receivable Ledger

Roy West		
Sept. 1 150	Sept. 10	150

Notice that a cost account called *Repossessed Merchandise Purchases* is debited for the unpaid amount ($150). The Installment Accounts Receivable account and the customer's account are credited for the same amount. When the entry is posted, the balance of the Installment Accounts Receivable account in the general ledger is reduced by $150. The balance of the customer's account in the installment accounts receivable ledger is reduced to zero.

If repossessed merchandise is sold for more than the customer owes, the business must give the additional amount to the customer. For example, Bay Electronics will send a check for $30 to Roy West if it sells the repossessed stereo equipment for $180.

Resale Value Does Not Cover Unpaid Balance. The resale value of repossessed merchandise may not be high enough to cover the unpaid balance of the installment contract. For example, on September 15, Bay Electronics repossessed a video tape recorder from Ann Cole. The unpaid balance of her installment contract is $300. However, the resale value of the merchandise is only $200. The business will therefore have a loss of $100. The general journal entry to record the repossession from Ann Cole is shown on page 145.

Notice that two accounts are debited in this entry. The Repossessed Merchandise Purchases account is debited for the resale value of the

GENERAL JOURNAL				Page 9
DATE	ACCOUNT TITLE AND EXPLANATION	POST. REF.	DEBIT	CREDIT
19— Sept.				
15	Repossessed Merchandise Purchases .	505	200 00	
	Loss on Repossessed Merchandise . .	515	100 00	
	Installment Accounts Receivable/			
	Ann Cole	112/√		300 00
	Record repossessed merchandise and loss.			

General Ledger

Repossessed Merchandise Purchases 505

Sept. 10	150		
15	200		

Loss on Repossessed Merchandise 515

Sept. 15	100		

Installment Accounts Receivable 112

Sept. 1	12,910	Sept. 10	150
		15	300

Installment Accounts Receivable Ledger

Ann Cole

Sept. 1	300	Sept. 15	300

item ($200). An expense account called *Loss on Repossessed Merchandise* is debited for the amount of the loss ($100). The Installment Accounts Receivable account and the customer's account are credited for the unpaid balance of the installment contract ($300). When the entry is posted, the balance of the Installment Accounts Receivable account in the general ledger is reduced by $300. The balance of the customer's account in the installment accounts receivable ledger is reduced to zero.

There Is No Resale Value. If repossessed merchandise is badly damaged, it may have no resale value. In this case, the unpaid balance of the installment contract is a loss to the business. For example, on September 26, Bay Electronics repossessed a color television set from John Shaw. The unpaid balance of his installment contract is $425. The television set was badly damaged and cannot be repaired. The following entry is made in the general journal to record the loss on the merchandise repossessed from John Shaw.

		GENERAL JOURNAL			Page 9
DATE		**ACCOUNT TITLE AND EXPLANATION**	**POST. REF.**	**DEBIT**	**CREDIT**
19— Sept.	26	Loss on Repossessed Merchandise .. Installment Accounts Receivable/ John Shaw............. Record loss on repossessed merchandise.	515 112/√	425 00	425 00

General Ledger

Loss on Repossessed Merchandise		515
Sept. 15	100	
26	425	

Installment Accounts Receivable			112	
Sept. 1	12,910	Sept. 10	150	
		15	300	
		26	425	

Installment Accounts Receivable Ledger

John Shaw			
Sept. 1	425	Sept. 26	425

The Loss on Repossessed Merchandise account is debited for the unpaid balance of the installment contract ($425). The Installment Accounts Receivable account and the customer's account are credited for this amount. When the entry is posted, the balance of the Installment Accounts Receivable account in the general ledger is reduced by $425. The balance of the customer's account in the installment accounts receivable ledger is reduced to zero.

The same type of entry is made when a customer leaves town with the merchandise before paying all the installments. If the business cannot locate the customer and repossess the merchandise, the unpaid balance of the installment contract must be recorded as a loss. However, an account called *Allowance for Doubtful Accounts* is debited rather than the Loss on Repossessed Merchandise account.

Selling Repossessed Merchandise

After Bay Electronics repossesses merchandise, it makes any repairs that may be necessary and places the items in stock. These items are labeled as used merchandise. They are sold to customers who are willing to buy used merchandise because of the lower prices.

Bay Electronics has two merchandise inventory accounts. One account is for new merchandise, and the other account is for repossessed

Bay Electronics Chart of Accounts

Assets
114 Inventory—New Merchandise
115 Inventory—Repossessed Merchandise

Revenue
401 Sales
402 Installment Sales
403 Repossessed Merchandise Sales

merchandise. There is also a separate revenue account for recording sales of repossessed merchandise. This account is called **Repossessed Merchandise Sales.** It is credited for all sales of repossessed merchandise. For example, on September 29, the accounting clerk at Bay Electronics made the following entry for a cash sale of repossessed merchandise.

						CASH RECEIPTS JOURNAL					Page 25
DATE	ACCOUNT CREDITED	EXPLANATION	POST. REF.	GENERAL LEDGER CREDIT	ACCOUNTS RECEIVABLE CREDIT	INSTALL. ACCTS. REC. CREDIT	SALES CREDIT	SALES TAX PAYABLE CREDIT	NET CASH DEBIT
19— Sept. 29	Repossessed Merch. Sales	Cash sale . .	403	200 00						200 00

Some businesses are not able to sell repossessed merchandise to their own customers. Instead, they sell the items to other businesses that deal in used merchandise.

Financing Installment Sales

Installment sales can be financed in several different ways.
• *Some businesses, such as Bay Electronics, provide installment credit themselves.* The customer signs a contract with the firm and makes all payments to the firm.
• *Some businesses arrange to have a bank or finance company give installment credit to their customers.* Each customer signs a contract with the bank or finance company and pays the installments to that organization. When this method is used, the business that sells the merchandise receives the full price from the bank or finance company soon after the contract is signed. The business therefore treats the transaction as a cash sale. This method is often used by businesses that deal in very expensive items such as cars and boats. As an alternative, the customers may be asked to obtain installment credit for themselves from a bank.
• *Some businesses provide installment credit but sell the contracts to a finance company later on.* The finance company pays the business the amount that each customer owes minus a fee. Then the finance company collects the installments from the customer.

The method of financing installment sales that management selects depends on a number of factors. One important factor is the financial resources of the business. Some firms cannot afford to provide installment credit themselves. They need to get the full price of each item when the sale is made so that they can use the money to pay expenses and buy more merchandise. Another important factor is the size of the business's accounting staff. Installment sales require a lot of accounting work because there are many payments from customers that must be recorded.

Activity E. Answer the following questions about the procedures for recording repossessed merchandise at Bay Electronics. Refer to the text and illustrations on pages 143 to 147.

1. What is the resale value of the merchandise that was repossessed from Roy West? Does the amount cover the unpaid balance of his installment contract?

2. Which accounts are debited and credited to record the repossession from Roy West? What amount is used in the entry?

3. What is the balance of Roy West's account after the entry for the repossession has been posted?

4. What is the business's loss on the merchandise repossessed from Ann Cole?

5. What accounts and amounts are involved in the entry to record the repossession from Ann Cole?

6. Is there a resale value for the merchandise repossessed from John Shaw?

7. What is the unpaid balance of John Shaw's installment contract?

8. Which account is debited to record the repossession from John Shaw? Which accounts are credited? What amount is used in the entry?

9. How many merchandise inventory accounts does Bay Electronics have? What type of inventory is recorded in each account?

10. How does the business record a cash sale of repossessed merchandise?

Topic 1 Problems

4-1. The Economy Furniture Center is a retail store that sells rugs, lamps, and lighting fixtures as well as furniture. The business has cash sales and sales on credit. Some sales on credit involve charge accounts. Other sales on credit are made on the installment plan.

a. Record the following transactions. Use a sales journal and a cash receipts journal. (Before you start, make a memorandum entry in the cash receipts journal for the

cash balance of $18,240 on April 1.)

b. Foot and prove the journals. Then enter the totals and rule.

April 1 Sold merchandise for $65 plus $3.25 sales tax on credit to Gary Burke; Sales Slip 4628. (This is a charge account sale.)

2 Sold merchandise for $700 plus $35 sales tax plus $5 insurance charge

plus $67.13 finance charge on credit to John Ruiz; Sales Slip 4629. The customer made a down payment of $70. (This is an installment sale.)

April 3 Received a monthly in-

April 5 stallment of $62.80 from Rita Hess.

April 5 Sold merchandise for $200 plus $10 sales tax on credit to Paul Dunn; Sales Slip 4630.

6 Recorded the cash proof showing weekly cash sales of $3,130 and sales tax of $156.50.

8 Received a monthly installment of $46.75 from Eric Lund.

10 Sold merchandise for $820 plus $41 sales tax plus $6 insurance charge plus $78.66 finance charge on credit to Lynn Calli; Sales Slip 4631. The customer made a down payment of $82.

12 Received $105 from Neil Wade on account.

13 Recorded the cash proof showing weekly cash sales of $3,620 and sales tax of $181.

15 Received a monthly installment of $57.35 from Dale Owens.

17 Sold merchandise for

$650 plus $32.50 sales tax plus $5 insurance plus $62.37 finance charge on credit to Carl Metz; Sales Slip 4632. The customer made a down payment of $65.

April 20 Recorded the cash proof showing weekly cash sales of $2,715 and sales tax of $135.75.

23 Received $88.20 from Lee Hall on account.

25 Sold merchandise for $110 plus $5.50 sales tax on credit to Gary Burke; Sales Slip 4633.

26 Received a monthly installment of $41.60 from Doris Alba.

27 Recorded the cash proof showing weekly cash sales of $4,100 and sales tax of $205.

29 Received $68.25 from Gary Burke on account.

30 Recorded the cash proof showing cash sales of $940 and sales tax of $47.

4-2. The Arden Appliance Mart is a retail store that sells many different types of appliances. Sales are made for cash and on credit. The business provides credit in the form of charge accounts and the installment plan.

a. Record the following transactions. Use a sales journal, a cash receipts journal, and a general journal. (Before you start, make a memorandum entry in the cash receipts journal for the cash balance of $14,700 on July 1.)

b. Foot and prove the sales journal and the cash receipts journal. Then enter the totals and rule.

July 1 Sold merchandise for $550 plus $27.50 sales tax plus $4 insurance charge plus $52.76 finance charge on credit to Maria Torres; Sales Slip 8270. The customer made a down payment of $55. (This is an installment sale.)

July 2 Received $112.60 from Frank Nye on account.

3 Sold merchandise for $150 plus $7.50 sales tax on credit to Jay Stein; Sales Slip 8271. (This is a charge account sale.)

4 Received a monthly installment of $39.20 from Iris Massi.

6 Recorded the cash proof showing weekly cash sales of $2,500 and sales tax of $125.

8 Repossessed merchandise from Joan Ellis. The resale value is $200. The unpaid balance of the installment contract is also $200.

9 Sold merchandise for $860 plus $43 sales tax plus $5 insurance charge plus $82.36 finance charge on credit to John McNab; Sales Slip 8272. The customer made a down payment of $86.

11 Received a monthly installment of $67.85 from Karen Case.

13 Recorded the cash proof showing weekly cash sales of $2,850 and sales tax of $142.50.

15 Sold merchandise for $730 plus $36.50 sales tax plus $5 insurance charge plus $69.99 finance charge on credit to Ruth Sims; Sales Slip 8273. The customer made a down payment of $73.

July 16 Received $105 from Roy Duval on account.

18 Repossessed merchandise from Don Kemp. There is no resale value because the merchandise is badly damaged. The unpaid balance of the installment contract is $332.

20 Recorded the cash proof showing weekly cash sales of $3,260 and sales tax of $163.

23 Received a monthly installment of $48.30 from Mark Chan.

24 Sold merchandise for $240 plus $12 sales tax on credit to Ann Walsh; Sales Slip 8274.

27 Recorded the cash proof showing weekly cash sales of $2,645 and sales tax of $132.25.

29 Repossessed merchandise from Earl Evans. The resale value is $250. The unpaid balance of the installment contract is $400.

31 Recorded the cash proof showing cash sales of $1,012 and sales tax of $50.60.

Topic 2
COD Sales and Credit Card Sales

A *What are COD sales?* In COD sales, the customers pay cash at the time the goods are delivered to their homes. The letters **COD** stand for **cash on delivery** or *collect on delivery*.

Whether or not a business makes COD sales depends on the nature of its operations. For example, COD sales are most common in mail-order businesses, such as Sears, Montgomery Ward, and J.C. Penney. Like installment sales, COD sales are intended to increase revenues by making it convenient for customers to buy.

Accounting for COD Sales

The accounting entries for COD sales vary from business to business. The types of entries that are recorded usually depend on how the goods are delivered.

Some businesses make COD sales to local customers and deliver the goods in their own trucks. This procedure is followed by certain department stores and other kinds of retail stores. Some businesses make COD sales to out-of-town customers and use a transportation service to deliver the goods. This procedure is generally followed by businesses that have mail-order transactions. The goods may be shipped by parcel post, which is run by the United States Postal Service. They may also be shipped by a private transportation service, such as a trucking company, a railroad, or an air freight company.

The chart here shows the entries that are made for COD sales at Trail Blazers, a firm that operates a retail store and also has a mail-order business, for which it provides a catalog. It is located in a western city near recreational areas. It is owned by two partners: Janet Hoppman who manages the retail store and Linda Brown who manages the mail-order operation. Notice that different types of entries are recorded for COD sales to local customers and COD sales to out-of-town customers. A COD sale to a local customer is treated as a special kind of cash sale. A COD sale to an out-of-town customer is treated as a special kind of credit sale.

Methods of Shipping COD Goods to Out-of-Town Customers:
- Parcel post
- Trucking company
- Railroad
- Air freight company

Type of Transaction	Time of Entry	Account(s) Debited	Account(s) Credited
COD sale in which goods are delivered to a local customer by the seller	After cash is collected from customer	Cash	Sales Tax Payable COD Sales
COD sale in which goods are delivered to an out-of-town customer by a transportation service	When goods are shipped to customer	COD Receivables	Sales Tax Payable* COD Sales Transportation on Sales
	After cash is collected from customer	Cash	COD Receivables

*There is a sales tax if the customer lives in the state in which the business is located and that state has a tax on sales. However, no sales tax is owed if the customer lives in a different state.

**Trail Blazers
Chart of Accounts**

Assets
110   COD Receivables

Liabilities
216   Sales Tax Payable

Revenue
401   Sales
402   COD Sales
404   Sales Returns and
        Allowances
405   Transportation on Sales

A single entry is made for a COD sale to a local customer. This entry is recorded after the cash is collected. A COD sale to an out-of-town customer is handled in a different way. Two entries are made. The first entry is recorded when the goods are sent to the customer. The second entry is recorded after the cash is collected.

The management of Trail Blazers wants to have a separate record of the revenues that the business receives from COD sales. The amounts of all these sales are therefore credited to an account called *COD Sales*. Some businesses enter their COD sales in the Sales account along with cash sales and charge account sales.

An asset account called *COD Receivables* is used in the two entries for a COD sale to an out-of-town customer. This account is debited at the time the goods are shipped and credited at the time the cash is received. The balance of the COD Receivables account shows the total amount to be collected for COD goods that are in transit to out-of-town customers.

Businesses must pay a fee when they have a transportation company deliver goods. This fee is usually passed along to out-of-town customers by adding a *shipping charge* to the price of the goods. Shipping charges are recorded in a revenue account called *Transportation on Sales*.

Recording COD Sales Delivered by the Seller

Trail Blazers provides free delivery to customers who live within 50 miles of its retail store. This service is often used by customers who order goods over the telephone in response to advertisements that the business runs in local newspapers. The goods are sold on a COD basis. Deliveries are made daily by the business's truck. The truck driver collects the cash from the customers.

A special sales slip is prepared for each COD sale. This sales slip consists of several copies. Copy 1 is kept by the order department. Copy 2 is sent along with the goods to the shipping department. A clerk in that department packs the goods and uses the top part of Copy 2 as an address label for the package. Copy 3 is sent to the accounting depart-

					CASH RECEIPTS
DATE		ACCOUNT CREDITED	EXPLANATION	POST. REF.	GENERAL LEDGER CREDIT
19— June	1	Cash Balance	$21,300	—	
	1	COD Sales	Collections on COD sales	—	

ment where it is placed in a binder for unpaid COD sales slips. Copies 4 and 5 are given to the truck driver.

When the truck driver delivers COD goods, the customer pays the amount owed. The driver then writes "Paid" on Copy 4 of the sales slip and gives it to the customer as a receipt. The driver keeps Copy 5 but asks the customer to sign it. This provides proof that the goods were delivered to the customer.

At the end of the day, the driver hands in all cash collected from COD sales and the signed copies of the sales slips. An accounting clerk counts the cash and makes a bank deposit. Another accounting clerk adds the amounts of the sales slips and compares the total owed by the customers with the total cash collected. The two totals should be the same. The clerk also compares the signed sales slips with the copies in the binder of unpaid COD sales slips. The clerk makes sure that no amounts were changed on the signed sales slips. Then the clerk places the signed copies in a file of paid COD sales slips. The copies from the binder are discarded.

The cash collected from COD sales is recorded in the cash receipts journal as shown below. The data for the entry comes from a calculator tape. This tape is prepared when the amounts on the sales slips are added.

The COD Sales account is credited for the total of the goods involved in the COD sales ($400). The Sales Tax Payable account is credited for the total tax on these sales ($12). The Cash account is debited for the total cash received from COD sales ($412).

Activity A. Answer the following questions about COD sales. Refer to the text, marginal notes, and illustrations on pages 150 to 153.

1. What is a COD sale?
2. What are four methods of shipping COD goods to out-of-town customers?
3. What is a shipping charge?
4. What type of account is COD Receivables? What does the balance of this account show?

5. How many journal entries are made for a COD sale if the seller delivers the goods to a local customer? Is this transaction recorded before the goods are delivered? If not, when is the transaction recorded?
6. Look at the COD sales slip on

			TRAIL BLAZERS	COD SALE 492

9773 Avon Street
Denver, Colorado 80202

DELIVER TO *Gary Swanson.*
ADDRESS *347 Rodeo Drive. – Apt 7*
Denver, CO 80223

DATE OF ORDER	ORDER TAKEN BY		
5/30/–	*J. Willenski*		

QUAN	DESCRIPTION	UNIT PRICE	AMOUNT
1 pr.	Hiking Boots – 10B #327	48 00	48 00
1	Sleeping Bag #681	42 00	42 00

	TOTAL PRICE	90 00
	SALES TAX	2 70
	SHIPPING CHARGE	
	TOTAL OWED	92 70

DATE OF DELIVERY	GOODS RECEIVED BY
6/11–	*Gary Swanson*
	DRIVER'S COPY

Collections on
COD Sales
June 1, 19–

0.00 T
92.70
56.65
72.10
87.55
103.00
412.00 T

Total of goods, $400
Total sales tax, $12

JOURNAL   Page *12*

ACCOUNTS RECEIVABLE CREDIT	COD RECEIVABLES CREDIT	SALES CREDIT	COD SALES CREDIT	SALES TAX PAYABLE CREDIT	NET CASH DEBIT
			400 00	12 00	412 00

page 153. How much does the customer owe? What is the date of the sale? What is the date of the delivery? Why is the customer asked to sign the sales slip?

7. How much cash does Trail Blazers collect from COD sales on June 1?

8. What journal is used to record cash collected from COD sales? What accounts and amounts are involved in the entry on June 1? What is the source of the data for the entry?

Recording COD Sales Delivered by a Transportation Service

B *How are COD sales recorded if the seller has a transportation service deliver the goods to out-of-town customers?* When shipments of COD goods are handled in this way, many businesses record COD sales in the sales journal. The entry is made at the time the goods are shipped. Because the goods leave the seller's possession and may be in transit for a week or more, these businesses want to have a financial record of their COD sales to out-of-town customers. After the money collected from the customers is received from the transportation service, a second entry is made. This entry is recorded in the cash receipts journal.

Trail Blazers uses parcel post to send COD goods to out-of-town customers. Every morning, the business's delivery truck takes packages of these goods to the post office. A special COD tag is attached to each package. This tag shows the customer's name and address and the amount that is to be collected.

A sales slip is prepared for each COD sale to an out-of-town customer. (The form used is the same as the one illustrated on page 153.) A clerk in the warehouse weighs each package, computes the shipping charge, and enters it on the sales slip. This clerk also computes and enters the total amount that the customer owes. One copy of the sales slip is placed in the package to provide the customer with a detailed record of the sale. Another copy of the sales slip goes to the accounting department.

CASH RECEIPTS

DATE	ACCOUNT CREDITED	EXPLANATION	POST. REF.	GENERAL LEDGER CREDIT
19—				
June 2	*COD Receivables*	*Collections on COD sales*.	—	

At the end of each day, a clerk in the accounting department adds the amounts on all the sales slips for COD goods that were shipped to out-of-town customers. The calculator tape that contains the totals is used to make an entry in the sales journal. The entry was made at Trail Blazers on June 2 to record COD sales shipped to out-of-town customers.

The COD Receivables account is debited for the total amount owed by the customers ($872). The Transportation on Sales account is credited for the total of the shipping charges ($43). The Sales Tax Payable account is credited for the total tax on the taxable sales ($11). (Some of the sales are not subject to sales tax. These sales were made to customers who live outside the state where the business is located.) The COD Sales account is credited for the total price of the goods ($818).

**Trail Blazers
Chart of Accounts**

Assets
110   COD Receivables

Liabilities
216   Sales Tax Payable

Revenue
401   Sales
402   COD Sales
404   Sales Returns and
        Allowances
405   Transportation on Sales

SALES JOURNAL Page 8

DATE	SALE NO.	ACCOUNT DEBITED	TERMS	POST. REF.	ACCOUNTS RECEIVABLE DEBIT	COD RECEIVABLES DEBIT	TRANS. ON SALES CREDIT	SALES TAX PAYABLE CREDIT	SALES CREDIT	COD SALES CREDIT
19— June 2	530– 541	COD Receivables		—		872 00	43 00	11 00		818 00

The postal service employees who make the deliveries collect the amounts owed by the customers. The postal service then sends a money order to the business to cover these amounts. When the money order arrives, an entry is made in the cash receipts journal. For example, the following entry was made at Trail Blazers on June 2. This entry shows the cash collected from out-of-town customers for COD goods that were shipped previously.

The COD Receivables account is credited for the total amount collected ($586). The Cash account is debited for the same amount.

Notice that the COD Receivables account increases when COD goods are shipped to out-of-town customers and decreases when the money is received for these goods. At the end of the accounting period, the balance of the COD Receivables account is reported on the balance sheet.

JOURNAL Page 12

ACCOUNTS RECEIVABLE CREDIT	COD RECEIVABLES CREDIT	SALES CREDIT	COD SALES CREDIT	SALES TAX PAYABLE CREDIT	NET CASH DEBIT
	586 00				586 00

This account appears in the Current Assets section because it represents amounts that are owed to the business and should be received in a short time. The total of the COD sales for each accounting period is shown on the income statement.

Recording Payments for Deliveries of COD Goods

As noted before, the seller must pay the transportation service for delivering goods. When the goods are sold on a COD basis to out-of-town customers, the seller usually adds a shipping charge to the price of the goods. This charge covers the cost of the delivery. The total collected from the customer includes the shipping charge.

The amount of the shipping charge is credited to the Transportation on Sales account at the time the COD sale is recorded in the sales journal. When the business issues a check to the transportation service for the deliveries, this account is debited. The Cash account is credited. For example, look at the following entry in the cash payments journal. This entry was made at Trail Blazers on June 2 to record the amount paid to the postal service for the COD goods shipped that day. (The postal service requires payment before the deliveries are made. Some transportation services bill the business after the goods are delivered.)

		CASH PAYMENTS JOURNAL						Page 10
DATE	ACCOUNT DEBITED	EXPLANATION	CHECK NO.	POST. REF.	GENERAL LEDGER DEBIT	ACCOUNTS PAYABLE DEBIT	PURCHASES DISCOUNT CREDIT	NET CASH CREDIT
19— June 2	Transportation on Sales	COD shipments . . .	1031	405	43 00			43 00

Recording Returns on COD Sales

Sometimes customers cannot pay for COD goods or decide not to accept the goods when they arrive. The goods are then returned to the seller. If the business did not record the COD sale when the goods were shipped, no entry is needed for the return. However, if the sale was recorded in the sales journal, an entry must be made for the return.

Trail Blazers receives a return of COD goods on June 3. The goods were shipped to an out-of-town customer on May 15. The sale was recorded in the sales journal at that time. When the returned goods arrive, they are put back in stock. The general journal entry shown on page 157 is made for the return.

GENERAL JOURNAL				Page 6
DATE	ACCOUNT TITLE AND EXPLANATION	POST. REF.	DEBIT	CREDIT
19—				
June 3	Sales Returns and Allowances	404	63 00	
	Sales Tax Payable	216	1 89	
	Transportation Expense on Returned			
	COD Goods	520	4 00	
	COD Receivables	110		68 89
	Record return of COD goods sold on Sales Slip 446.			

The Sales Returns and Allowances account is debited for the price of the goods ($63). The Sales Tax Payable account is debited for the tax on the sale ($1.89). The Transportation Expense on Returned COD Goods account is debited for the amount spent to ship the goods to the customer ($4). The COD Receivables account is credited for the total of the sale ($68.89).

Trail Blazers paid the postal service when the goods were sent to the customer. The total billed to the customer included a shipping charge. This charge would have covered the cost of delivering the goods. How-ever, since the customer did not pay the amount owed, the shipping charge becomes an expense to the business. For that reason, an account called *Transportation Expense on Returned COD Goods* is used to record the shipping charge.

The business has to pay a second fee to the postal service when the returned goods arrive. This fee is charged for shipping the goods back to Trail Blazers. The amount of the second fee ($4) is also debited to the Transportation Expense on Returned COD Goods account. The entry is made in the cash payments journal.

Trail Blazers Chart of Accounts

Costs and Expenses
520 Transportation Expense on Returned COD Goods

CASH PAYMENTS JOURNAL								Page 10
DATE	ACCOUNT DEBITED	EXPLANATION	CHECK NO.	POST. REF.	GENERAL LEDGER DEBIT	ACCOUNTS PAYABLE DEBIT	PURCHASES DISCOUNT CREDIT	NET CASH CREDIT
19—								
June 3	Transp. Exp. on Ret'd COD Goods	Postage	1040	520	4 00			4 00

Activity B. Answer the following questions about COD sales to out-of-town customers. Refer to the text and illustrations on pages 154 to 157.

1. Which journal is used to record COD sales to out-of-town customers? When is the entry made?

2. Which accounts are debited and credited for COD sales to out-of-town customers?

3. Which journal is used to record the amount collected from COD sales to out-of-town customers? Which account is debited? Which account is credited?

4. On what financial statement does the COD Receivables account appear?

5. How does a business record a check issued to pay a transportation service for delivering COD goods?

6. Is a return of COD goods journalized if the sale was not recorded when the goods were shipped? if the sale was recorded at that time?

7. What type of transaction has Trail Blazers entered in the general journal on June 3? What accounts and amounts are involved in the entry?

8. What type of transaction has Trail Blazers entered in the cash payments journal on June 3? What accounts are debited and credited?

CREDIT CARDS

Company Card

Bank Card

Travel and
Entertainment Card

Processing Credit Card Sales

C *How do businesses process credit card sales?* Credit card sales are processed in several different ways according to the kind of credit card that is used. There are many different credit cards in use. However, most credit cards fall into one of the following categories.

• *Company Cards.* Some businesses provide credit cards to their own charge account customers. These cards are usually referred to as **company cards** because they are intended for use in one business. Companies that operate chains of department stores, gasoline stations, and car rental agencies often issue such credit cards. The sales that are made with these cards are really charge account sales. The business is giving credit to its customers and receives payments from them when the amounts are due.

• *Bank Cards.* The most widely used credit cards in the United States are VISA and MasterCard. These cards are called **bank cards** because they are issued by banks and other financial institutions. Many stores, restaurants, hotels, and other retail businesses accept such credit cards. The bank cards are popular because they allow people to buy on credit at a great number of businesses. The customers are actually receiving credit from the bank, not from the retailers. The bank pays the retailers and gets its money from the customers later on.

• *Travel and Entertainment Cards.* American Express, Diner's Club, and Carte Blanche are usually referred to as **travel and entertainment cards.** This is because they are used most often in businesses such as restaurants, hotels, and motels. However, many stores also accept these cards. The businesses collect their money from the credit card company. The customers pay the credit card company.

In this section, we will discuss sales made with bank credit cards. A sale that involves a bank credit card is treated as a special type of cash sale.

The most widely used credit cards are VISA and MasterCard, which are issued by banks. These cards are accepted by large numbers of retail businesses throughout the world. The retailer is paid by the bank after making the sales. The bank collects from the customers later on. This arrangement has benefits for both the retailer and the customers. The retailer does not have to provide charge accounts. However, the customers can buy on credit.

On July 1, Trail Blazers starts accepting a bank credit card in its store. The business continues to make regular cash sales, COD sales, and charge account sales. However, management feels that revenues will increase if customers are allowed to use the bank credit card. Many people prefer to buy goods with this type of credit card rather than paying cash right away or having charge accounts in a lot of stores.

The credit card that Trail Blazers accepts is issued by several banks in town, including the one where the firm has its checking account. These banks are part of a nationwide group of banks that handle the same credit card.

Preparing Source Documents. Many businesses prepare two sales slips for each credit card sale. Trail Blazers follows this practice. First, the salesclerk records the transaction on the sales slip that the business uses for its regular cash sales. Then the salesclerk prepares a special credit card sales slip. This form is preprinted with the name of the credit card.

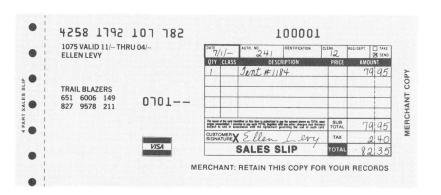

After filling in the credit card sales slip, the salesclerk places it and the customer's plastic credit card in an imprinting device. This device prints data on the sales slip. For example, it prints the customer's name and credit card number and the business's name and identification number. Some of this data is transferred from the credit card. The rest of the data comes from metal type in the imprinting device. When the sales slip is removed from the imprinting device, the customer is asked to sign the form.

Both the regular sales slip and the credit card sales slip consist of several copies. The customer receives one copy of each form. Other copies go to the business's accounting department. An accounting clerk verifies the accuracy of the amounts on the sales slips. Then a copy of the regular sales slip and a copy of the credit card sales slip are filed. Another copy of the credit card sales slip is kept in the accounting department until the bank deposit is prepared. (The processing of this copy is discussed later.)

Checking the Customer's Credit. Businesses usually require that their salesclerks get approval for credit card sales. At Trail Blazers, the customer's credit must be checked if the total price of the goods is $25 or more. The credit card system has an office that provides the necessary information. Before completing a sale, the salesclerk telephones this office. The salesclerk gives the customer's credit card number and the amount of the sale.

Trail Blazers
Credit Card Sales
July 1, 19—

```
   0.00 T
  82.35
  57.60
  36.95
 102.12
  40.28
 319.30 T
```

A clerk in the credit office uses a computer terminal to examine the customer's account. The clerk makes sure that the credit card was not stolen, that the sale is within the customer's credit limit, and so on. If the transaction is approved, the salesclerk enters a credit authorization code on the credit card sales slip.

Obtaining Payment From the Bank. One of the advantages of making sales with a bank credit card is that the business can obtain payment quickly. When a bank deposit is prepared at Trail Blazers, an accounting clerk adds the totals of all the credit card sales slips on a calculator. The accounting clerk then lists the overall total on a special deposit form. This form is provided by the bank.

The accounting clerk must also compute the amount that the bank will deduct for handling the business's credit card sales. Banks charge

CASH RECEIPTS

DATE		ACCOUNT CREDITED	EXPLANATION	POST. REF.	GENERAL LEDGER CREDIT
19—					
July	1	Cash Balance.................	$22,540......................	—	
	1	Sales	Cash sales for day.............	—	
	1	Credit Card Sales	Credit card sales for day	—	

a fee for this service. The fee is called a **discount.** It is a percentage of the business's credit card sales. For example, the bank that Trail Blazers deals with deducts 2 percent of the credit card sales as a fee. On July 1, this fee is $6.39 ($319.30 × 0.02). The accounting clerk lists the fee and the net amount of the credit card sales on the deposit form. The net amount is the amount that the business will actually receive from the bank. This amount is computed by subtracting the fee from the overall total of the credit card sales ($319.30 − $6.39 = $312.91).

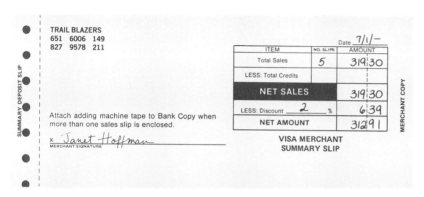

After the deposit form for the credit card sales is completed, the accounting clerk attaches the calculator tape and a copy of each sales slip. These items are taken to the bank along with a deposit ticket and the currency, coins, and checks that will also be deposited. When the bank records the deposit, it adds the net amount of the credit card sales to the balance of the business's checking account.

Recording Credit Card Sales

The total of the credit card sales slips included in the bank deposit must be journalized. Because bank credit card sales are treated as cash sales, the cash receipts journal is used. The following entry is made for credit card sales at Trail Blazers on July 1.

JOURNAL   Page *14*

ACCOUNTS RECEIVABLE CREDIT	COD RECEIVABLES CREDIT	SALES CREDIT	COD SALES CREDIT	CREDIT CARD SALES CREDIT	SALES TAX PAYABLE CREDIT	CREDIT CARD FEE EXPENSE DEBIT	NET CASH DEBIT
		775 00			23 25		798 25
				310 00	9 30	6 39	312 91

**Trail Blazers
Chart of Accounts**

Revenue
401 Sales
402 COD Sales
403 Credit Card Sales
404 Sales Returns and
      Allowances

Costs and Expenses
513 Credit Card Fee Ex-
      pense
520 Transportation Expense
      on Returned COD Goods

A revenue account called **Credit Card Sales** is credited for the total price of the goods ($310). The Sales Tax Payable account is credited for the total amount of sales tax ($9.30). An expense account called **Credit Card Fee Expense** is debited for the amount that the bank will deduct for handling the credit card sales ($6.39). The Cash account is debited for the total cash that the business will receive from the credit card sales ($312.91).

Notice that the business has set up a separate revenue account for credit card sales. Some firms use the Sales account for these sales as well as for regular cash sales. However, the management of Trail Blazers wants to have a separate record of credit card sales. This will allow management to see the amount that credit card sales contribute to the revenues of the business. The total credit card sales for each accounting period will appear on the income statement. The total amount of the credit card fee expense will also be shown on the income statement. It will be listed in the Operating Expenses section.

To make it easy to journalize and post credit card sales, the business had its cash receipts journal redesigned. This journal now has special money columns for credit card sales and credit card fee expense. The daily amounts in each of these columns will be posted as a total at the end of the month.

Activity C. Answer the following questions about credit card sales. Refer to the text and illustrations on pages 158 to 162.

1. What is a company credit card? Name two company cards.
2. What is a bank credit card? Name two popular bank credit cards.
3. What is a travel and entertainment credit card? Name three popular credit cards of this type.
4. Does a business record the sales made with a bank credit card as charge account sales or cash sales?
5. What types of source documents does Trail Blazers prepare for credit card sales?
6. What is the total of the credit card sale that Trail Blazers made to Ellen Levy on July 1?
7. How does Trail Blazers get paid for its credit card sales?
8. What accounts have been debited and credited to record the credit card sales that Trail Blazers had on July 1? What journal is used for this entry?

Topic 2 Problems

4-3. Circle Sporting Goods operates a retail store and a mail-order business. Most sales in the store are made for cash. However, steady customers are allowed to open charge accounts if they wish. The mail-order sales are made on a COD basis.

a. Record the following transactions. Use a sales journal, a cash receipts journal, a cash payments journal, and a general journal. (Before you start, make a memorandum entry in the cash receipts journal for the cash balance of $12,868 on June 1.)

b. Foot and prove the special journals. Then enter the totals, and rule the journals.

June **1** Sold merchandise for $80 plus $4 sales tax on credit to Ruth Moro; Sales Slip 610.

2 Issued Check 231 for $79 to All-States Parcel Service for deliveries to out-of-town COD customers during the last two weeks of May.

4 Sold merchandise for $465 plus $11.30 sales tax plus $37 shipping charges on a COD basis; Sales Slips 611 to 626. The merchandise was shipped to out-of-town customers.

6 Recorded the cash proof showing weekly cash sales of $2,100 and sales tax of $105.

8 Received a check for $842 from All-States Parcel Service to cover cash collected from out-of-town COD customers. The amount is for merchandise shipped during the last two weeks of May.

11 Sold merchandise for $392 plus $9.60 sales tax plus $31 shipping charges on a COD basis; Sales Slips 627 to 640. The merchandise was shipped to out-of-town customers.

13 Recorded the cash proof showing weekly cash sales of $2,850 and sales tax of $142.50.

15 Sold merchandise for $112 plus $5.60 sales tax on credit to Paul Hertz; Sales Slip 641.

June **16** Sold merchandise for $543 plus $14.10 sales tax plus $48 shipping charges on a COD basis; Sales Slips 642 to 658. The merchandise was shipped to out-of-town customers.

18 Issued Check 232 for $68 to All-States Parcel Service for deliveries to out-of-town customers during the first two weeks of June.

20 Recorded the cash proof showing weekly cash sales of $2,420 and sales tax of $121.

22 Received a check for $945.90 from All-States Parcel Service to cover cash collected from out-of-town COD customers. The amount is for merchandise shipped during the first two weeks of June.

24 Received a return of a COD sale for $46 plus $2.30 sales tax plus $4 shipping charge; Sales Slip 645. The merchandise was shipped to an out-of-town customer on June 16.

25 Sold merchandise for $418 plus $10.50 sales tax plus $33 shipping charges on a COD basis; Sales Slips 659 to 671. The merchandise was shipped to out-of-town customers.

June 27 Recorded the cash proof showing weekly cash sales of $3,110 and sales tax of $155.50.

29 Received $84 from Ruth Moro on account.

29 Received a return of a COD sale for $34 plus $1.70 sales tax plus $3 shipping charge; Sales Slip 669. The merchandise was shipped to an out-of-town customer on June 25.

June 30 Recorded the cash proof showing cash sales of $940 and sales tax of $47.

4-4. The Belmont Jewelry Store sells for cash, provides charge accounts, and allows customers to use a bank credit card.

a. Record the following transactions in a cash receipts journal. (Before you start, make a memorandum entry in the cash receipts journal for the cash balance of $8,542 on April 1.)

b. Foot and prove the cash receipts journal.

April 2 Received $120 from Joan Danko on account.

3 Received $2,000 from Mark Egan, the owner, as an additional investment.

6 Recorded the cash proof showing weekly cash sales of $852 and sales tax of $42.60.

6 Recorded weekly credit card sales of $427, sales tax of $21.35, and credit card fee expense of $8.97.

April 8 Received $139 from Glen Watts on account.

13 Recorded the cash proof showing weekly cash sales of $781 and sales tax of $39.05.

13 Recorded weekly credit card sales of $394, sales tax of $19.70, and credit card fee expense of $8.27.

15 Received $245 from Mary O'Dell on account.

15 Received $89 from Alan Fong on account.

The Language of Business

Here are some basic terms that make up the language of business. Do you understand the meaning of each? Can you define each term and use it in an original sentence?

charge account sale
installment sale
down payment
installment
finance charge
installment accounts receivable ledger
resale value
installment contract
repossess
Installment Accounts Receivable account
Insurance Payable account
Loss on Repossessed Merchandise account

Allowance for Doubtful Accounts account
Repossessed Merchandise Sale account
COD sales
COD Sales account
COD Receivables account
shipping charge
Transportation on Sales account
Transportation Expense on Returned COD Goods account
Credit Card Sales account
Credit Card Fee Expense account

Chapter 4   Questions

1. What are the basic features of an installment sale?

2. Why would a business sell on the installment plan rather than just offering credit in the form of charge accounts?

3. How is an installment sale recorded?

4. Why do businesses like Bay Electronics keep a separate revenue account for installment sales?

5. What is resale value? How do the accounting entries for repossessed merchandise vary according to the amount of the resale value?

6. What methods can be used to finance installment sales?

7. How does a COD sale differ from other types of sales?

8. How is a COD sale recorded if the goods are delivered to a local customer? How is a COD sale recorded if the goods are shipped to an out-of-town customer?

9. How does a sale made with a bank credit card differ from a regular cash sale?

10. What procedures does a business use to process its bank credit card sales?

Chapter 4   Problems

Problems for Chapter 4 are given in the *Working Papers and Chapter Problems* for Part 1. If you are using the workbook, do the problems in the space provided there. Complete your assigned topic problems before answering the chapter problems.

Chapter 4   Management Cases

Credit Policies. In some types of businesses, such as supermarkets, it is customary to make all sales for cash. Other types of businesses, such as department stores, normally provide credit as well as selling for cash. It is usually necessary for a business that handles expensive goods like appliances and furniture to offer credit to customers. However, credit can also be helpful in businesses that sell less costly items. Providing credit can increase revenues by making it easier for customers to shop.

The management of each business must select a suitable credit policy. Many factors must be considered in making such decisions. The financial resources of the business, the kinds of products it sells, the needs of the customers, and the policies of competing businesses are some of the factors that must be taken into account.

Every credit policy has advantages and disadvantages. For example, bank credit cards make it possible for businesses to sell for cash but give their customers the convenience of buying on credit. These businesses can avoid tying up money in accounts receivable. They can also avoid all the work involved in keeping records of the accounts receivable and issuing monthly statements to the customers. Despite this, some stores prefer to provide charge accounts. One reason is that there is a bank fee for handling credit card sales. Another reason is that people who have charge accounts often become steady customers. They develop a loyal relationship with the store that is providing the charge account.

Case 4M-1. The Sand and Surf Shop is located in a resort town. It sells casual clothes to vacationers and local residents. The business is small. Dennis Doyle, the owner, started it a year ago with a limited amount of capital. Mr. Doyle purchases the goods, sells, and keeps the financial records. He employs two salesclerks to help him with the selling.

Up to now, the business has made all sales for cash. However, Mr. Doyle feels that a change in this policy may increase revenues. He is thinking of accepting personal checks from vacationers and offering charge accounts to local residents. Several competing stores in town accept bank credit cards. Mr. Doyle is reluctant to do this. He does not want to pay a fee to the bank for handling the credit card sales.

a. Do you think that it is a good idea for Mr. Doyle to accept personal checks from vacationers? Why or why not?

b. Do you think that vacationers might prefer to buy at a store that accepts credit cards? Why or why not?

c. What advantages and disadvantages would charge accounts have for this business?

d. What policy would you suggest that Mr. Doyle follow? Should he continue to make all sales for cash? Should he accept personal checks? Should he offer charge accounts? Should he accept bank credit cards? Explain your answer.

Case 4M-2. The Stewart Appliance Center specializes in household appliances such as refrigerators, freezers, stoves, washers, and dryers. Most sales are made on credit. The business offers charge accounts and the installment plan. Other appliance stores in town follow a similar policy.

The business is successful and earns a fairly high rate of profit. However, it sometimes does not have enough cash to meet its needs. This usually happens when the business must pay for new goods. The business must then make a loan from the bank. To avoid this situation, Brenda Stewart, the owner, is thinking of adopting a policy of selling for cash only. However, to continue to attract customers, she would cut prices and advertise the business as a discount store.

a. Why do you think that this business runs short of cash even though it is successful?

b. What are the possible advantages and disadvantages of cutting prices and selling for cash only?

c. Are there ways that the business might obtain cash quickly but still offer customers the convenience of buying on credit? Explain your answer.

d. What type of credit policy would you select for this business? Why?

Chapter 5

Managerial Accounting for Manufacturing Businesses

A **manufacturing business** produces or assembles goods. These goods may be sold to wholesalers, to retailers, or directly to consumers. Some examples of well-known manufacturing businesses are listed here. Keep in mind that there are many different kinds of manufacturing businesses.

This chapter presents an overview of the manufacturing process. It also discusses the procedures used to gather and report information about manufacturing costs. The management of a manufacturing business needs this information to control operations, measure efficiency, and make decisions. Having accurate, complete, and timely financial information is just as important in manufacturing businesses as it is in merchandising businesses.

Topic 1
The Manufacturing Process

A *What does the manufacturing process involve?* The **manufacturing process** involves the use of labor to change raw materials into finished products. When making furniture, for example, workers apply their skills to change pieces of wood into products such as tables. It is essential for management to know all the costs involved in the manufacturing process. This data is needed to set selling prices that will earn a profit for the business. Because managerial accounting for manufacturing businesses is so concerned with costs, it is often referred to as *cost accounting.*

Cost accounting is another term used to mean managerial accounting for manufacturing businesses.

Elements of Cost Accounting

Elements of Cost Accounting:
- Direct materials
- Direct labor
- Factory overhead

There are three major costs associated with the manufacture of a product. These costs are for direct materials, direct labor, and factory overhead.

Direct Materials. The materials from which goods are made are called **direct materials** or *raw materials*. In a business that manufactures automobiles, direct materials would include steel, aluminum, glass, chrome, and plastic. The amounts of money spent to acquire such items are the costs of direct materials.

Goods that are finished products in one business may be direct materials in another business. For example, although sheets of steel are finished products in a steel manufacturing company, they are direct materials in an automobile manufacturing company.

Direct Labor. The work of people who change direct materials into finished products is referred to as **direct labor.** For example, in a furniture manufacturing company, the employees who cut, sand, stain, and varnish the wood for tables are performing direct labor. The wages paid to these employees are the costs of direct labor.

Factory Overhead. There are other costs involved in making goods besides the costs of direct materials and direct labor. These other costs are called **factory overhead.** (Sometimes they are also referred to as *manufacturing overhead, indirect manufacturing costs,* and *factory burden.*) Included in factory overhead are indirect materials and manufacturing supplies, indirect labor, and the costs of operating the factory.

Indirect materials are materials that are used in small amounts in making a product. They are not a major part of the product. For example, the pieces of wood used in making a table are direct materials. However, the glue used in assembling the parts of the table and the varnish used in finishing the table are indirect materials. Certain supplies are also used in the manufacturing process. These **manufacturing supplies** are needed to make a product, but, unlike indirect materials, they do not become a part of the product. Sandpaper, oil for lubricating cutting machines, and brushes for applying varnish are examples of manufacturing supplies in a furniture factory.

Indirect labor is work in a factory that is not closely associated with making products. For example, the jobs of factory supervisors, maintenance employees, and employees who receive and issue materials are considered indirect labor. The activities of these people are necessary to the smooth flow of the manufacturing process. However, these people are not directly involved in changing raw materials into finished products.

The types of costs incurred in operating a factory can vary from business to business. However, these costs often include rent for the factory building, heat, electricity, repairs on equipment, insurance on equipment, depreciation on equipment, and payroll taxes on factory wages.

Any manufacturing costs other than those of direct materials and direct labor are factory overhead costs.

Direct materials and direct labor are referred to as the **prime costs** of manufacturing. They are usually the main costs incurred in making goods. Direct labor and factory overhead are called the **conversion costs.** They are the costs involved in changing raw materials into finished products.

Accounting Concept:

Cost of Goods Manufactured. Direct materials, direct labor, and factory overhead are the three elements that determine the cost of the goods that a business manufactures.

Activity A-1. Define the following terms. Refer to the text and notes on pages 168 to 169.

1. Direct materials   **4.** Indirect materials
2. Direct labor   **5.** Manufacturing supplies
3. Factory overhead   **6.** Indirect labor

Activity A-2. Select two products with which you are familiar (such as a pair of shoes, a pair of jeans, a bicycle, a television, or a pencil). Make a list of the direct materials and indirect materials that you think are involved in manufacturing each product.

Cost Accounting Systems

B *What is the purpose of a cost accounting system?* A cost accounting system is used to determine the unit cost of each product that a business manufactures. Such a system gathers and reports information about the costs for direct materials, direct labor, and factory overhead.

Like any accounting system, a cost accounting system consists of forms, equipment, procedures, and people. This chapter and later chapters discuss the forms, equipment, and procedures that are associated with cost accounting. However, keep in mind that people are the most important part of an accounting system.

The people who operate cost accounting systems are usually referred to as cost accountants and cost clerks. **Cost accountants** set up the necessary cost accounting procedures, make sure that the procedures are carried out properly, and interpret the cost information produced

Cost accountants are employees who set up cost accounting procedures, supervise the procedures, and interpret the cost information.

Cost clerks are employees who record and classify cost data.

Types of Cost Accounting Systems:
- Process cost systems
- Job order cost systems

by the system. **Cost clerks** perform a variety of tasks. Most of these tasks involve recording and classifying cost data.

There are two major types of cost accounting systems: process cost systems and job order cost systems.

Process Cost Systems. Some factories **mass-produce** goods. They make very large quantities of a single product or several similar products. They are products usually in great demand by consumers. Automobiles, radios, pens and pencils, paint, canned foods, television sets, and steel are manufactured in this way. Process cost accounting is generally used by such businesses.

In these businesses, the manufacturing work for a product is divided into a series of operations. This is done to make the manufacturing process more efficient. Each operation is usually carried out in a separate department. For example, in a factory that makes radios, one department might assemble the electronic components that go inside the radios. Another department might mold the plastic parts that are used on the outside of the radios. The same operations are performed for every unit of the product.

In a process cost system, cost data is gathered for operations or departments and not for individual units of the product. An average unit cost is computed at the end of the period.

With a **process cost system,** cost data is gathered for each operation or each department and not for individual units of the product. At the end of the accounting period, an average unit cost is computed for the units worked on during the period.

Job Order Cost Systems. Certain kinds of goods are usually made in small quantities and may vary from unit to unit. Generally these products are in less demand by consumers—because they are expensive or because fewer are needed—than mass-produced goods. Airplanes, mobile homes, and expensive furniture are examples of such goods. Businesses that manufacture products of this nature generally use job order cost accounting.

In a job order cost system, cost records are kept for each unit of a product or for a small group of units.

With a **job order cost system,** cost records are kept for each unit of a product or for a small group of units. When a job is finished, the unit cost is determined from these records.

Process cost systems and job order cost systems are described in more detail in Chapters 6 and 7.

Accounts in Manufacturing Businesses

A manufacturing business needs certain accounts that are not used in other types of businesses. For example, a manufacturing business must have three inventory accounts: a Materials account, a Work-in-Process account, and a Finished Goods account. These three accounts are current assets. They appear on the balance sheet.

The *Materials account* shows the cost of the materials and supplies that have been acquired for use in making goods. The *Work-in-Process account* shows the cost of the direct materials, direct labor, and factory overhead for goods that are being manufactured. The *Finished Goods account* shows the cost of the goods that have been completed.

These accounts and other accounts are necessary to gather financial data in a cost accounting system. You will see how such accounts are used as you study cost accounting.

Inventory Accounts for a Manufacturing Business:
- Materials
- Work-in-Process
- Finished Goods

Organization of Manufacturing Businesses

Some manufacturing businesses consist of a single factory. However, many manufacturing businesses are large and have a number of factories located in different areas. The operations of the factories are directed by a home office, which also handles administration, sales, and financial affairs for the company. Each factory is headed by a manager, who works in the factory and supervises its day-to-day activities. The factory managers report to an executive at the home office. An organization chart for the home office of a manufacturing business is shown here.

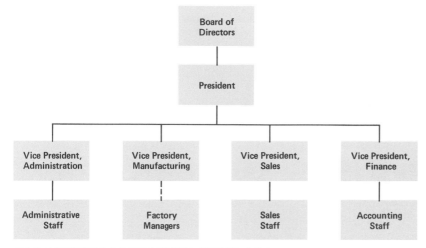

ORGANIZATION OF THE HOME OFFICE OF A MANUFACTURING BUSINESS

Factories are usually organized into departments. The individual departments vary from factory to factory, depending on the nature of the operations performed. However, the departments in a factory can be classified as production departments and service departments.

Types of Departments in a Factory:
- Production departments
- Service departments

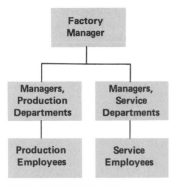

ORGANIZATION OF
A FACTORY

**Examples of Production
Departments:**
• Cutting
• Milling
• Assembling
• Finishing

**Examples of Service
Departments:**
• General Office
• Cost Accounting
• Materials Purchasing
• Receiving and Shipping
• Stores (Materials Inventory)
• Maintenance
• Quality Control

A **production department** is involved in changing raw materials into finished goods. Each production department carries out one operation or a group of related operations. A **service department** in a factory does not take part in the manufacturing process. However, it performs activities that are necessary to the functioning of the factory.

An organization chart for a factory is given here along with examples of production and service departments. (The examples of production departments are for a factory that makes wooden tables.) Notice that one of the service departments is called the **stores department.** This department is responsible for keeping the materials inventory and issuing materials as they are needed by the production departments.

Activity B. Answer the following questions about cost accounting systems and the organization of manufacturing businesses. Refer to the text and illustrations on pages 169 to 172.

1. What purpose does a cost accounting system serve?
2. What kinds of activities do cost accountants perform?
3. What kinds of activities do cost clerks perform?
4. What is a process cost system?
5. What is a job order cost system?

6. What kinds of inventory accounts does a manufacturing business have?
7. How does a production department differ from a service department?
8. What are some examples of service departments?

Topic 1   Problems

5-1. A number of manufacturing costs are listed here. Identify each cost as direct materials (DM), direct labor (DL), or factory overhead (FO). Remember that factory overhead includes indirect materials, manufacturing supplies, indirect labor, and the cost of operating a factory.

a. Rent for the factory building
b. Wages of supervisors
c. Steel for a truck
d. Electricity
e. Cloth for a shirt
f. Wages of assembly-line workers

g. Thread for sewing a shirt
h. Oil for lubricating a machine
i. Wages of receiving clerks
j. Glass for a truck
k. Insurance on equipment
l. Buttons for a shirt

5-2. Indicate what type of cost accounting system each of the following manufacturing businesses would probably have. Use *P* for process cost system and *J* for job order cost system.

a. A manufacturer of canned soft drinks
b. A manufacturer of large boats
c. A manufacturer of washing machines
d. A manufacturer of razor blades

e. A manufacturer of automobile tires
f. A manufacturer of custom-made clothing

5-3. List the production departments that you would expect to find in each of the following manufacturing businesses.

a. A manufacturer of wooden chairs

b. A manufacturer of shoes

c. A manufacturer of canned vegetables

Topic 2
Acquisition and Control of Materials

A *Why is it important to have efficient procedures for purchasing, storing, and issuing materials?* The necessary materials must be on hand to maintain a steady flow of production in a factory. When orders are received from customers, the factory must be able to make the goods promptly. Otherwise, sales may be lost. Slowdowns in production caused by a lack of materials may also increase costs and decrease profits.

This topic discusses perpetual inventory procedures for purchasing, storing, and issuing materials. Keep in mind that such procedures can vary from business to business. However, no matter what types of procedures are used, they should include controls to ensure accuracy, honesty, efficiency, and speed.

Purchasing Materials

In most manufacturing businesses, the purchasing department must perform the following activities.

- Gather information about possible sources of materials.
- Compare prices and terms submitted by suppliers.
- Select suitable suppliers.
- Place orders for needed materials.
- Contact suppliers to deal with problems such as late deliveries.

The purchasing department should carry out its activities in such a way that it meets the following three goals.

- Make sure that the correct types and quantities of materials are available for use in factory operations.
- Buy materials as economically as possible in order to hold down costs.
- Avoid tying up the business's money in excess inventory, that is, in amounts of materials that are much larger than necessary.

In a well-run business, there are procedures for identifying the materials that should be ordered. These procedures are usually built into the inventory system. For example, management may set a *reorder point* and a *reorder quantity* for each item that the business keeps in its

A purchase requisition is a form used to notify the purchasing department of materials that must be ordered.

materials inventory. This data is shown in the perpetual inventory records maintained by the stores department. As soon as the balance on hand for an item reaches or falls below the reorder point, the stores department notifies the purchasing department. The form used for this purpose is the **purchase requisition.**

STORES LEDGER CARD

Material No. *B-125*
Description *Wooden billets*

Reorder Point *15,000*
Reorder Quantity *20,000*

DATE		REFERENCE	RECEIVED			ISSUED			BALANCE		
			UNITS	PRICE	AMOUNT	UNITS	PRICE	AMOUNT	UNITS	PRICE	AMOUNT
19— Apr.	1	Balance							18,000	2 00	36,000 00
	5	MR961				4,000	2 00	8,000 00	14,000	2 00	28,000 00
	10	MR979				5,000	2 00	10,000 00	9,000	2 00	18,000 00

WESTERN MANUFACTURING COMPANY   PURCHASE REQUISITION
No. **503**

Date of Request *April 5, 19–*
Date Wanted *May 1, 19–*

Requested by   Ship to
Stores Department   *Receiving Department*

Quantity	Material No.	Description
20,000	*B-125*	*Wooden billets*

Requested by *J. Palma*
Approved by *R. Robinson*

COPY 1 — PURCHASING DEPARTMENT

The inventory records provide a signal to reorder materials. The type of material shown here is used by the Western Manufacturing Company to make baseball bats. A wooden billet is a round-shaped piece of wood.

The purchase requisition consists of at least two copies. One copy is sent to the purchasing department. Another copy is filed in the stores department. Purchase requisitions are usually prenumbered to protect against misuse of the forms.

In most cases management determines reorder points and reorder quantities on the basis of past experience. However, sometimes a factory needs unusually large amounts of certain materials. This generally happens when customer demand for one of the business's products is much greater than normal. Many manufacturing businesses have a procedure that helps them to avoid shortages of materials in such situations. This procedure involves the use of a form called a **bill of materials.**

When a factory receives orders for goods, the management staff must perform a number of planning activities. For example, a staff member must enter the necessary work in the production schedule. The same staff member or another staff member must analyze each order to see what materials will be used in making the goods. This staff member then prepares a bill of materials and sends it to the stores department. The bill of materials provides the stores department with advance information about the types and quantities of materials that will be needed to complete the order.

WESTERN MANUFACTURING COMPANY		BILL OF MATERIALS

Job No. _157_   To Be Started _May 21, 19—_
Product _Model 26 baseball bat_   Customer _Davis Sporting Goods Stores_
Quantity _5,000_

The following materials will be needed for this job.

Quantity	Material No.	Description
5,000	B-125	Wooden billets
100 rolls	J-57	Tape for handles
5,000	X-31	Decals ("Western Slugger")
20 cans	C-100	Stain

Prepared by _A. Martinez_
Date _April 8, 19—_

COPY 1 — STORES DEPARTMENT

As each bill of materials is received, the stores department checks to see whether sufficient quantities are on hand or have been requested. If not, the stores department prepares a purchase requisition for the necessary materials. In this way, the materials can be obtained before production of the goods begins. (Notice that the bill of materials shows the starting date for production.)

The reorder points and reorder quantities in the perpetual inventory records allow the business to identify the materials that must be ordered to meet normal needs. The bill of materials makes it possible to determine if additional quantities are required.

The purchasing department must check and approve each purchase requisition received from the stores department. The purchasing department must then choose a supplier and issue a *purchase order* for the materials. An approved supplier must be used, and the purchase order must be signed by an authorized person.

WESTERN MANUFACTURING COMPANY Lone Star Industrial Park Dallas, Texas 75207	PURCHASE ORDER No. 2120

To Delta Wood Products
4654 South Mill Road
Atlanta, GA 30336

This number must appear on all packages and forms.

Date April 6, 19--

Ship to Receiving Dept.	Date Wanted May 1, 19--	Ship Via Truck	FOB Dallas	Terms 2/10, n/30

Quantity	Stock No.	Description	Unit Price	Amount
20,000	87369	Wooden billets	2.00	40,000.00

By *P. Hoffman*
Purchasing Agent

COPY 1 — SUPPLIER

The purchase order specifies the materials that are needed, the quantities, the prices, the terms of payment, the date by which delivery should be made, and the method of shipment. A prenumbered multicopy form is used for the purchase order. The original is sent to the supplier, and one copy is kept in the purchasing department. Other copies go to the receiving department and the stores department.

Activity A. Answer the following questions about the procedures for purchasing materials. Refer to the text and illustrations on pages 173 to 176.

1. What is the reorder point shown on the perpetual inventory record for Material B-125?

2. What purpose does the purchase requisition serve?

3. Which department issued Purchase Requisition 503?

4. What quantity of the item has been requested on the purchase requisition?

5. When was the purchase requisition issued?

6. Who approved the purchase requisition?

7. What purpose does the bill of materials serve?

8. What types of materials are needed for Job 157?

9. When is Job 157 to be started?

10. What purpose does the purchase order serve?

11. To what supplier has Purchase Order 2120 been issued?

12. How are the materials to be shipped?

13. What unit price is listed on the purchase order?

14. By what date must the materials be delivered?

15. Who signs the purchase order?

Storing Materials

B *How are materials handled when they arrive from the supplier?* The receiving department unpacks, counts, and inspects the materials. This department must make sure that the supplier shipped the correct materials and that the materials are in good condition. A copy of the purchase order is used in checking the materials.

The receiving department prepares a form called a **receiving report** to provide information about each shipment of materials that arrives at the factory. This form shows the quantity of materials received. If any materials are rejected, the quantity rejected and the reason are also shown. Several copies of the receiving report must be made. One copy is sent to the purchasing department, which will need the data to verify the supplier's invoice. Another copy goes to the stores department along with the materials.

WESTERN MANUFACTURING COMPANY			RECEIVING REPORT	
Received From	Delta Wood Products 4654 South Mill Road Atlanta, GA 30336		No. **1404**	

Date Received April 29, 19–		Purchase Order No. 2120	Inspected by M. Wolinski	
Quantity Received	Quantity Accepted	Quantity Rejected	Description	
20,000	19,900	100	Wooden billets	

Reason for Rejection
Cracks in wood

COPY 1 — PURCHASING DEPARTMENT

In some businesses, copies of the purchase order are used for the receiving report. Other businesses have special prenumbered forms for the receiving report.

After the receiving department completes its examination of a shipment, the materials are taken to the stores department. This department plays an important role in factory operations. It must perform the following activities.

- Store materials that will be needed in the manufacturing process.
- Keep perpetual inventory records for all materials.
- Issue materials to the production departments when these departments require the materials.
- Notify the purchasing department when additional materials must be ordered.

Perpetual Inventory Records:
- Inventory tags
- Stores ledger cards

Materials are a valuable asset. They should be handled and stored carefully to protect against loss, theft, and damage. It is also essential that accurate, up-to-date records be maintained for the materials inventory. The way to keep up the perpetual inventory records is to continuously record the balances of all items in the materials inventory. Manufacturing businesses usually have two kinds of perpetual inventory records: inventory tags and stores ledger cards.

Each type of material in the stores department is identified by an **inventory tag** or **bin tag.** This tag shows quantities received, quantities issued, and the balance on hand as well as other inventory data.

Materials are normally stored in bins or on racks. There is an assigned location for each type of material. The inventory tag is attached to the proper bin or rack. Whenever any units are placed in storage or removed, the inventory tag is updated.

The **stores ledger** is the second kind of perpetual inventory record for materials. This ledger usually consists of cards in a file. There is an individual card for each type of material that the stores department has in its inventory.

INVENTORY TAG

Material No. B-125
Description Wooden billets
Location Aisle 3, Racks 1-30
Reorder Point 15,000 Reorder Quantity 20,000

Date	Quantity Received	Quantity Issued	Balance
19— 4/1			18,000
4/5		4,000	14,000
4/10		5,000	9,000
4/18		2,000	7,000
4/29	19,900		26,900

STORES LEDGER CARD

Material No. B-125
Description Wooden billets

Reorder Point 15,000
Reorder Quantity 20,000

DATE		REFERENCE	RECEIVED			ISSUED			BALANCE		
			UNITS	PRICE	AMOUNT	UNITS	PRICE	AMOUNT	UNITS	PRICE	AMOUNT
19— Apr.	1	Balance							18,000	2 00	36,000 00
	5	MR961				4,000	2 00	8,000 00	14,000	2 00	28,000 00
	10	MR979				5,000	2 00	10,000 00	9,000	2 00	18,000 00
	18	MR986				2,000	2 00	4,000 00	7,000	2 00	14,000 00
	29	RR1404	19,900	2 00	39,800 00				26,900	2 00	53,800 00

A stores ledger card shows quantity, unit price, and total dollar amount for every inventory transaction.

Western Manufacturing Company Chart of Accounts

Assets
121 Materials

Like the inventory tag, a stores ledger card is updated to show the current balance on hand whenever units are received or issued. However, the stores ledger card provides more information than the inventory tag. Besides showing quantities, the stores ledger card lists a unit price and a total dollar amount for each inventory transaction.

Look at the entry of April 29 on the stores ledger card illustrated above. The receiving report was the source document for this entry. (The same form also provided the data for the April 29 entry on the inventory tag.) The stores clerk computes the dollar amounts shown in the Received section and the Balance section of the stores ledger card. This is done by multiplying the number of units by the unit price.

The stores ledger is a subsidiary ledger for materials. The Materials account in the general ledger serves as the controlling account for this subsidiary ledger. The total dollar amount of the balances in the stores ledger must therefore equal the balance of the Materials account.

Activity B. Answer the following questions about the procedures for receiving and storing materials. Refer to the text and illustrations on pages 177 to 178.

1. What purpose does the receiving report serve?

2. What type of material did Western Manufacturing Company receive on April 29?

3. What quantity arrived on April 29? What quantity did the receiving department accept?

4. What is the reason for rejecting some units?

5. Who inspected the items that arrived on April 29?

6. Which departments get copies of the receiving report?

7. What kinds of perpetual inventory records are kept for materials?

8. What is the location of the billets in the stores department?

9. How many billets were in stock on April 1? on April 18? on April 29?

10. How many billets were issued on April 10?

11. What is the unit price of the billets received on April 29?

12. What source document was used for the April 29 entry on the stores ledger card?

13. What is the total dollar amount for the billets that are in stock on April 29?

Issuing Materials

C *How does a production department obtain materials from the stores department?* In a well-run business, the stores department does not issue any materials unless it receives a written request signed by an authorized person. When a production department needs materials, it sends a form called a **materials requisition** to the stores department. This form shows exactly what materials are required. It is approved by a production manager or supervisor before it goes to the stores department.

WESTERN MANUFACTURING COMPANY

MATERIALS REQUISITION

No. **998**

Deliver to _Milling Department_   Date _April 30, 19—_

Charge: Job No. _143_

Account _Work in Process_   _$8,000_

Account _____

Quantity	Material No.	Description	Unit Price	Amount
4,000	B-125	Wooden billets	2.00	8,000.00

Approved by _J. H. Hartman_   Delivered by _L. Stevens_   Received by _J. O'Keefe_

COPY 2 — STORES DEPARTMENT

INVENTORY TAG

Material No. B-125
Description Wooden billets
Location Aisle 3, Racks 1-30
Reorder Point 15,000   Reorder Quantity 20,000

Date	Quantity Received	Quantity Issued	Balance
19— 4/1			18,000
4/5		4,000	14,000
4/10		5,000	9,000
4/18		2,000	7,000
4/29	19,900		26,900
4/30		4,000	22,900

A prenumbered form is used for the materials requisition. Many businesses have a form that consists of three copies. The stores department receives Copy 1 (the original) and Copy 2. The production department keeps Copy 3.

When the stores department receives a materials requisition, a stores clerk removes the necessary items from stock and updates the inventory tag. The clerk also enters the unit cost and the total dollar amount for the items on the materials requisition. (The unit cost is taken from the stores ledger.)

The materials are sent to the production department along with Copy 2 of the requisition. The person who delivers the materials and the person who receives the materials must sign Copy 2. This copy is then returned to the stores department and filed. It serves as proof that the production department actually received the items listed on the requisition.

After the materials are issued, Copy 1 of the requisition is used in updating the stores ledger card. Then the stores department sends Copy 1 to the accounting department. (The accounting department needs the information for a journal entry. This entry is explained on page 182.)

STORES LEDGER CARD

Material No. B-125
Description Wooden billets
Reorder Point 15,000
Reorder Quantity 20,000

DATE		REFERENCE	RECEIVED			ISSUED			BALANCE		
			UNITS	PRICE	AMOUNT	UNITS	PRICE	AMOUNT	UNITS	PRICE	AMOUNT
19— Apr.	1	Balance							18,000	2 00	36,000 00
	29	RR 1404	19,900	2 00	39,800 00				26,900	2 00	53,800 00
	30	MR 998				4,000	2 00	8,000 00	22,900	2 00	45,800 00

Verifying the Materials Inventory

Although the stores department keeps perpetual inventory records, an actual count of the materials must be made at least once a year. This **physical inventory** is taken to verify the inventory balances and to discourage mishandling of materials. A physical inventory provides a check on the accuracy of the inventory records. It also provides a check on the effectiveness of the controls used by the stores department.

In addition to making a count of all the materials at the end of the accounting period, some businesses verify parts of the inventory at random intervals. This practice makes it difficult for employees to cover up mishandling of materials.

The procedures for taking a physical inventory can vary from business to business. However, many businesses use the following procedures. Special inventory tags are attached to the bins or racks. These tags are different in color from the regular inventory tags. As the materials are counted, the amounts are entered on the special inventory tags. When this process is completed for all items, the tags are removed. The data is then listed on inventory sheets. The special inventory tags are numbered to ensure that all tags are collected and reported on the inventory sheets.

The balances determined in the physical inventory must be compared with the balances on the regular inventory tags and the stores ledger cards. If necessary, adjustments are made to correct the perpetual inventory records. A large number of adjustments would show that there is a need for better recordkeeping and for tighter controls over the materials.

PHYSICAL INVENTORY TAG   No. 16

Material No. B-125
Description Wooden billets
Location Aisle 3, Racks 1-30
Balance 21,000   Date 12/28/—
Counted by J.S.   Checked by N.P.
Unit Price $2   Total Amount $42,000
Computed by W.B.   Date 12/31/—

Date	Received After Count	Issued After Count	Balance
19— 12/30		5,000	16,000

Activity C-1. Answer the following questions about the procedures for issuing materials. Refer to the text and illustrations on pages 179 and 180.

1. What purpose does the materials requisition serve?
2. What is the number of the materials requisition prepared on April 30?
3. Which production department sent the materials requisition to the stores department?
4. What quantity was requested?
5. Who approved the materials requisition?
6. What was the unit price for the materials? What was the total dollar amount?
7. Who received the materials?

Activity C-2. Answer the following questions about the procedures for verifying the materials inventory. Refer to the text and illustration on pages 180 and 181.

1. Why is it necessary to verify the materials inventory at least once a year?
2. What is the number of the physical inventory tag?
3. What type of material is the tag for?
4. When was the count made?
5. What was the balance on hand at the time of the count?
6. Were any items received or issued after the count? If so, what is the final balance?
7. What is the total dollar amount on December 31?
8. Why does this business have one employee make the count and another employee check the count?

Accounting for Materials

D *How do businesses record transactions involving materials?* When materials are purchased, the cost is debited to the Materials account. For example, the following entry is made at Western Manufacturing Company for materials that were purchased on credit from Delta Wood Products.

		GENERAL JOURNAL			Page 5
DATE		**ACCOUNT TITLE AND EXPLANATION**	**POST. REF.**	**DEBIT**	**CREDIT**
19— May	5	Materials	121	39,800 00	
		Accounts Payable/Delta Wood Products	211/√		39,800 00
		Purchased materials on credit.			

This entry is shown in the general journal. However, many manufacturing businesses record purchases of materials in a special journal called a **voucher register.** The voucher register is discussed further in Chapter 8.

When the production departments obtain materials from the stores department, these items leave the materials inventory and are used in making goods. The cost of such materials must be transferred from the Materials account. This is done by crediting the Materials account.

During the week ended May 7 the stores department at Western Manufacturing Company issued materials costing $9,400. The production departments will use items costing $8,100 as direct materials and items costing $1,300 as indirect materials and supplies. The entry shown on the next page is made to record the transfer of these items. The source document is a summary of the materials issued, as prepared by the accounting department.

Notice that the *Work-in-Process* account is debited for the cost of the direct materials. An account called *Factory Overhead* is debited for the cost of the indirect materials and supplies. The Materials account is credited for the total cost of the items issued to the production departments.

Some businesses have a special journal called a **materials requisitions journal.** The accounting department records each requisition in this journal after the materials are issued. When a materials requisitions journal is used, there is no need to make the general journal entry shown above.

WESTERN MANUFACTURING COMPANY
Summary of Materials Issued
For the Week Ended May 7, 19—

Materials Requisition No.	Job No.	Distribution of Costs Work-in-Process	Factory Overhead	Total Costs
1001	144	$1,100	$ 200	$1,300
1002	147	2,000	100	2,100
1003	145	1,500		1,500
1004	146	1,300	600	1,900
1005	144	1,200		1,200
1006	146	1,000	400	1,400
		$8,100	$1,300	$9,400

	GENERAL JOURNAL			Page 5

DATE	ACCOUNT TITLE AND EXPLANATION	POST. REF.	DEBIT	CREDIT
19— May				
7	Work-in-Process	122	8,100 00	
	Factory Overhead	501	1,300 00	
	Materials.	121		9,400 00
	Issued materials for production work.			

Materials		121
May 1	Bal. 200,000	May 7	9,400 ←
5	39,800		

Work-in-Process		122
May 7	8,100	Direct Materials

Factory Overhead		501
May 7	1,300	Indirect Materials

Activity D. Answer the following questions about the accounting entries for materials. Refer to the text and illustrations on pages 182 and 183.

1. How does a business record purchases of materials on credit?
2. What account is debited for the direct materials issued to the production departments?
3. What was the cost of the direct materials issued during the week ended May 7?
4. What account is debited for the indirect materials and supplies issued to the production departments?

5. What was the cost of the indirect materials and supplies issued during the week ended May 7?
6. What account is credited for the materials and supplies issued to the production departments?
7. What was the cost of all the materials and supplies issued during the week ended May 7?

Topic 2   Problems

5-4. The Colonial Furniture Company makes reproductions of antique furniture. Assume that you are working in the stores department. One of your duties is to keep the stores ledger.

a. Prepare a stores ledger card for Material X-35, a brass drawer handle. The reorder point is 300. The reorder quantity is 400. On July 1 the balance on hand is 300. The unit price is $1.50. Compute and record the total amount.

b. During July the following quantities of Material X-35 were received and issued. Record the data on the stores ledger card. The references for the source documents are shown in parentheses. Be sure to complete the Balance section of the stores ledger card after you enter each inventory transaction.

July	3	Received 400 units at a cost of $1.50 each (RR 1648).
	7	Issued 100 units at a cost of $1.50 each (MR 806).
	10	Issued 225 units at a cost of $1.50 each (MR 818).
	13	Issued 60 units at a cost of $1.50 each (MR 829).
	15	Issued 175 units at a cost of $1.50 each (MR 832).
July	26	Received 400 units at a cost of $2 each (RR 1677).
	27	Issued 140 units at a cost of $1.50 each (MR 851).
	29	Issued 50 units at a cost of $2 each (MR 857).
	30	Issued 90 units at a cost of $2 each (MR 859).

NOTE: Save your working papers for further use in Topic Problem 5-5.

5-5. Do the following work for the Colonial Furniture Company.

a. Examine the stores ledger card that you prepared in Topic Problem 5-4. Is it necessary to reorder Material X-35? If so, what quantity should be ordered?

b. If you think that Material X-35 must be reordered, complete a purchase requisition. Use July 31 as the date of the requisition and August 15 as the date the items are wanted.

5-6. The Valdez Clothing Corporation makes shirts and blouses. During the week ended January 14, the stores department of this business issued the following direct and indirect materials.

Materials Requisition 567:
  Job 43; direct materials, $2,910; indirect materials, $375.

Materials Requisition 568:
  Job 44; direct materials, $3,240; indirect materials, $410.

Materials Requisition 569:
  Job 45; direct materials, $2,120; indirect materials, $300.

Materials Requisition 570:
  Job 46; direct materials, $4,400; indirect materials, $625.

Assume that you are working in the accounting department. The cost accountant asks you to perform the following tasks.

a. Prepare a summary of the materials issued during the week ended January 14. Use the form shown on page 183 as a model.

b. Make a general journal entry to transfer the cost of the materials issued.

Topic 3
Factory Labor Costs

A *What types of information must a manufacturing business obtain about its labor costs?* A manufacturing business must determine the labor costs for each job or operation and for each department. It must also determine the costs incurred for direct labor and for indirect labor. The accounting staff needs this information to compute the cost of each product that the business makes. Management must have such information to judge the efficiency of each department.

This topic provides an overview of factory payroll procedures. It also discusses the methods for gathering and recording information about factory labor costs.

Payroll Procedures in a Factory

Many factories use different pay plans for different kinds of employees. Production department employees are usually paid according to the **hourly-rate plan** or the **piece-rate plan.** They receive a fixed amount for each hour worked or each item produced. Service department employees, such as maintenance workers, are also paid according to the hourly-rate plan in many factories. However, the **salary plan** is normally used for managers and supervisors. Employees on the salary plan are paid a fixed amount for each week or month. Examples of how to compute gross earnings with the hourly-rate plan, the piece-rate plan, and the salary plan are shown in the margin.

The length of the payroll period varies from factory to factory. Some factories have a monthly payroll period. Others have a biweekly (two-week) period. Still others have a weekly period.

The payroll procedures used in a factory are similar to the payroll procedures that you learned about in your previous studies. The following activities are usually performed.

- During each payroll period, records are kept of the hours that employees work. Most factories use **time cards** and **time clocks** for this purpose. The cards are placed in racks near the time clock. Whenever employees arrive at work or leave work, they insert their time cards in the time clock. This device prints the time on each card. At the end of the week, the time cards are collected. A clerk then computes the total regular and overtime hours worked. In some factories another type of time record, called a time ticket, is also used. (The time ticket is discussed on page 187.)
- At the end of each payroll period, the earnings and deductions are computed. Then the total deductions are subtracted from the **gross earnings** (total earnings) to find the **net pay** (take-home pay) for each

Hourly-Rate Plan:

Gross
Earnings = Hours × Rate
$200   =   40   × $5

Piece-Rate Plan:

Gross
Earnings = Items × Rate
$220   = 2,200 × $0.10

Salary Plan:

Gross
Earnings = Salary
$250   = $250

Name Donald Lee				Employee No. 12		
Department Milling						
Regular Hourly Rate $5.00						
Week Ending May 7, 19--						

Days	Regular				Other		Hours
	In	Out	In	Out	In	Out	
Mon.	8 00	12 00	12 58	5 00			8
Tues.	7 59	12 01	1 01	4 59			8
Wed.	8 04	11 56	12 57	5 01			8
Thurs.	7 53	12 06	1 00	5 07			8
Fri.	8 00	11 59	12 58	4 00	5 30	9 30	11
Sat.							
Sun.							

		Hours	Rate	Earnings
Extra Hours Approved	Regular	40	$5.00	$200.00
C. Keller	Overtime	3	7.50	22.50
Supervisor	Total Hours	43	Gross Earnings	$222.50

TIME CARD

Examples of Employee Payroll Deductions

Deductions Required by Law
Federal income tax
Social security (FICA) tax
State income tax (in some states)
City income tax (in some cities)

Voluntary Deductions
Life insurance
Medical insurance
Hospitalization insurance
Pension plan
Savings bonds
Charity donations

Deductions Required by Union Agreements
Union initiation fees
Union dues

Examples of Employer's Payroll Taxes

Employer's social security (FICA) tax
Federal unemployment (FUTA) tax
State unemployment tax

employee. Some typical examples of employee deductions are given in the margin.

• A **payroll journal** is prepared. This record contains detailed information about the earnings and deductions of all employees for the payroll period. After the payroll journal is completed and proved, the amounts are transferred to **employee earnings records.** An individual earnings record is kept for every employee. It shows the employee's earnings and deductions for each payroll period and for the year to date. (Some businesses use a payroll register instead of a payroll journal.)

• The employer's payroll taxes are computed. Examples of common payroll taxes are given in the margin.

• Payments are prepared for the employees. Some factories pay in cash. However, most factories use **voucher payroll checks.** This type of payroll check has a statement of earnings and deductions attached to it.

• The time records and the payroll journal are analyzed to determine the labor costs for the payroll period. A report is prepared showing the amounts for each job or operation, for each department, for direct labor, and for indirect labor. (This report is discussed on page 188.)

• Accounting entries are made to record the payroll and the payroll taxes and to distribute the labor costs to the proper accounts. (These entries are discussed on pages 189 to 191.)

In a small factory the activities described in this section might be performed manually by the payroll clerks and the cost clerks. However, in a large factory, most of the work would be done with the help of computers.

Determining Factory Labor Costs

The payroll journal shows the earnings and deductions for all employees in the factory. This data is usually grouped by departments. The amounts for each department are added separately. The total amount of gross earnings for a department is its labor cost for the payroll period. The payroll journal is shown at the top of the next page.

When a business has a job order cost accounting system, it is also necessary to determine the labor cost for each job that is in production. A job consists of a number of units of a product that are being made together. For example, Job 157 at Western Manufacturing Company will involve 5,000 baseball bats. These bats were ordered by a chain of sporting goods stores.

Special time records called **time tickets** are used to gather data about the hours an employee spends on each job or operation. Time

PAYROLL JOURNAL

For the Week Beginning *May 1*   19 —   and Ending *May 7*   19 —   Paid   19

	EMPLOYEE DATA				EARNINGS			DEDUCTIONS			NET PAY	
NO.	NAME	MARITAL STATUS	EXEMP.	HOURS	REGULAR	OVERTIME	TOTAL	INCOME TAX	FICA TAX	TOTAL	AMOUNT	CK. NO.
	Milling Department											
12	Donald Lee	M	4	43	200 00	22 50	222 50	17 90	13 46	31 36	191 14	
16	George Martins	S	1	45	160 00	30 00	190 00	27 20	11 50	38 70	151 30	
11	Robert Sadowski	M	3	40	215 00		215 00	18 70	13 01	31 71	183 29	
	Totals for Milling Department				2,550 00	260 00	2,810 00	393 40	170 01	563 41	2,246 59	
	Sanding Department											
15	Eileen Hogan	M	2	42	180 00	13 50	193 50	17 70	11 71	29 41	164 09	
	Totals for Sanding Department				2,510 00	40 00	2,650 00	371 00	160 33	531 33	2,118 67	
	Totals for Factory . . .				9,270 00	550 00	9,820 00	1,374 80	594 11	1,968 91	7,851 09	

tickets are prepared on a daily basis. There is an individual time ticket for every production employee.

The time ticket shows when an employee starts and stops work on each job. This data is recorded by the employee or by a production supervisor. At the end of the day all the time tickets are collected. A cost clerk then checks and enters the hours and the amounts.

The time tickets are analyzed at the end of the payroll period. The labor cost incurred for production work on each job is computed. This is done by adding all amounts for a job that appear on the time tickets.

A report called an **analysis of labor costs,** shown on page 188, shows the labor costs for each job and each department during a weekly payroll period at Western Manufacturing Company. The necessary data came from the time tickets and the payroll journal. A cost clerk summarized the data and classified it according to whether the costs were for direct labor or indirect labor.

Copies of the analysis of labor costs go to management. This report helps management to evaluate and control labor costs. The accounting department keeps a copy and uses it to journalize the labor costs.

Name Donald Lee				Employee No. 12		
Department Milling				Regular Hourly Rate $5.00		
Date May 7, 19--				Overtime Rate $7.50		
Job No.	Time Started	Time Stopped	Regular Hours	Overtime Hours	Amount	
145	8:00	11:59	4		$20.00	
146	12:58	4:00	3		15.00	
147	5:30	9:30	1	3	27.50	
		Totals	8	3	$62.50	
Approval C. Keller				Supervisor		

TIME TICKET

Accounting Concept:

Gross Earnings. To employees, gross earnings represent the total value of their services. To the employer, gross earnings are a major cost (labor) of operating a business.

WESTERN MANUFACTURING COMPANY
Analysis of Labor Costs
For the Week Ended May 7, 19—

Distribution of Direct Labor Cost by Job:

| | Milling Dept. | | Sanding Dept. | | Finishing Dept. | | Total |
Job No.	Hours	Amount	Hours	Amount	Hours	Amount	Cost
143	80	$ 575	85	$ 450	84	$ 470	$1,495
144	100	520	50	470	100	460	1,450
145	60	505	100	430	63	520	1,455
146	90	450	55	530	90	400	1,380
147	70	350	85	370	70	590	1,310
Totals	400	$2,400	375	$2,250	407	$2,440	$7,090

Distribution of Direct and Indirect Labor Costs by Department:

Department	Direct Labor Cost	Indirect Labor Cost	Total Cost
Milling	$2,400	$ 410	$2,810
Sanding	2,250	400	2,650
Finishing	2,440	405	2,845
Factory Office		600	600
Cost Accounting		525	525
Stores		390	390
Totals	$7,090	$2,730	$9,820

Summary:

Direct Labor Cost	$7,090
Indirect Labor Cost	2,730
Total	$9,820

Activity A-1. Answer the following questions about the payroll procedures used in factories. Refer to the text and illustrations on pages 185 to 188.

1. What types of pay plans are often used in factories?

2. What is the purpose of the time card?

3. What device is used to print data on the time card?

4. How many hours did Donald Lee work during the week ended May 7?

5. What is the amount of gross earnings for Donald Lee?

6. In which department did Donald Lee work?

7. What types of information does the payroll journal contain?

8. What two methods of paying the payroll are commonly used in factories?

Activity A-2. Answer the following questions about the procedures for determining factory labor costs. Refer to the text and illustrations on pages 186 to 188.

1. What is the purpose of the time ticket?

2. How many hours did Donald Lee devote to Job 145 on May 7?

3. What other jobs did Donald Lee work on during that day?

4. What is Donald Lee's regular hourly wage rate?

5. What is the cost of the labor that Donald Lee performed on Job 145?

6. What records provide the data needed for preparing the analysis of labor costs?

7. Which jobs are reported on the analysis of labor costs for the week ended May 7?

8. How many hours did the milling department spend on Job 144?

9. How many hours did the finishing department spend on Job 147?

10. What is the total direct labor cost for Job 145?

11. Which department has the highest direct labor cost?

12. Which department has the highest indirect labor cost?

13. What is the labor cost for the stores department? Does this department perform direct or indirect labor?

14. What is the direct labor cost for all production departments?

15. What is the total labor cost for the factory?

Accounting for Factory Labor Costs

B *How are factory labor costs recorded?* The cost of direct labor is debited to the Work-in-Process account. The cost of indirect labor is debited to the Factory Overhead account. At Western Manufacturing Company, the entry to distribute labor costs is made after the weekly payroll is recorded. For example, on May 7 the payroll and the labor costs are journalized as shown on page 190. The necessary data is taken from the payroll journal and the analysis of labor costs.

The total amount of the payroll is debited to a temporary account called *Factory Payroll*. The Employee Income Taxes Payable account is credited for the total amount withheld for federal income taxes. The FICA Taxes Payable account is credited for the total amount withheld for social security taxes. The Factory Wages and Salaries Payable account is credited for the total amount that must be paid to the employees (the total net pay).

When the labor costs are distributed, the Factory Payroll account is credited. The effect of this entry is shown on page 190.

The employer's liabilities for payroll taxes must also be recorded. As noted previously, payroll taxes are part of factory overhead. The total of these taxes is therefore debited to the Factory Overhead account. The FICA Taxes Payable account is credited for the employer's share of

Western Manufacturing Company
Chart of Accounts

Assets
122   Work-in-Process

Liabilities
221   Employee Income Taxes Payable
222   FICA Taxes Payable
223   Federal Unemployment Taxes Payable
224   State Unemployment Taxes Payable
225   Factory Wages and Salaries Payable

Factory Costs
501   Factory Overhead
502   Factory Payroll

PAYROLL JOURNAL

For the Week Beginning __May 1__ 19 __ and Ending __May 7__ 19 __ Paid __ 19 __

EMPLOYEE DATA				HOURS	EARNINGS			DEDUCTIONS			NET PAY	
NO.	NAME	MARITAL STATUS	EXEMP.		REGULAR	OVERTIME	TOTAL	INCOME TAX	FICA TAX	TOTAL	AMOUNT	CK. NO.
	Totals for Factory . . .				9,270 00	550 00	9,820 00	1,374 80	594 11	1,968 91	7,851 09	
							(502)	(221)	(222)		(225)	

WESTERN MANUFACTURING COMPANY
Analysis of Labor Costs
For the Week Ended May 7, 19—

Summary:

Direct Labor Cost	$7,090
Indirect Labor Cost	2,730
Total	$9,820

GENERAL JOURNAL   Page 5

DATE		ACCOUNT TITLE AND EXPLANATION	POST. REF.	DEBIT	CREDIT
19— May					
	7	Work-in-Process	122	7,090 00	
		Factory Overhead	501	2,730 00	
		Factory Payroll	502		9,820 00
		Distribution of labor costs.			

Work-in-Process   122

Direct Labor   May 7 8,100.00
                   7 7,090.00

Factory Payroll   502

May 7 9,820.00 | May 7 9,820.00

Factory Overhead   501

May 7 1,300.00
   7 2,730.00

Indirect Labor

social security taxes. The Federal Unemployment Taxes Payable account and the State Unemployment Taxes Payable account are credited for the amounts of the unemployment taxes.

Some manufacturing businesses use the general journal to record payroll and payroll taxes. Western Manufacturing Company follows this procedure. However, many manufacturing businesses use a voucher register for such entries. (The voucher register is discussed in Chapter 8.)

Accounting Concept:
Control—Labor Costs. Procedures must be established to ensure accuracy, honesty, efficiency, and speed in recording and controlling labor costs.

				GENERAL JOURNAL									Page 5	
DATE			ACCOUNT TITLE AND EXPLANATION		POST. REF.		DEBIT			CREDIT				
19—														
May														
	7	Factory Overhead		501	908	35							
		FICA Taxes Payable		222			594	11			
		Federal Unemployment Taxes									
		Payable		223			49	10			
		State Unemployment Taxes									
		Payable		224			265	14			
		Employer's taxes on May 7									
		payroll.									

FICA Taxes Payable 222		Factory Overhead 501	
	May 7 594.11	May 7 1,300.00	
	7 594.11	7 2,730.00	
		7 908.35	

Federal Unemployment Taxes Payable 223	
	May 7 49.10

State Unemployment Taxes Payable 224	
	May 7 265.14

Total Employer's
Payroll Taxes   908.35

Activity B. Answer the following questions about the procedures for recording payroll, labor costs, and payroll taxes. Refer to the text and illustrations on pages 189 to191.

1. How did Western Manufacturing Company record payroll on May 7?
2. What account is used to record direct labor costs? Is this account debited or credited?
3. What account is used to record indirect labor costs? Is this account debited or credited?
4. During the payroll period ended May 7, what amount did Western Manufacturing Company incur for direct labor costs? for indirect labor costs?
5. What source documents provide the data needed to journalize the payroll and the labor costs?
6. What accounts and amounts are involved in recording the employer's payroll taxes on May 7?

Topic 3   Problems

5-7. The Jensen Manufacturing Company makes neckties and scarves. Assume that you are working in the accounting department. One of your duties is to process records of labor costs and analyze the data.

Complete the following time tickets. The production supervisors have filled in the hours worked by the employees. Compute the cost of

Name Angela Cruz   Employee No. 5
Department Cutting   Regular Hourly Rate $5.50
Date June 5, 19--   Overtime Rate $8.25

Job No.	Time Started	Time Stopped	Regular Hours	Overtime Hours	Amount
277	7:55	10:01	2		
278	10:02	12:32	2½		
279	1:29	3:04	1½		
280	3:05	5:01	2		
		Totals	8		

Approval S. Montgomery
Supervisor

Name Richard Miles   Employee No. 11
Department Sewing   Regular Hourly Rate $5.20
Date June 5, 19--   Overtime Rate $7.80

Job No.	Time Started	Time Stopped	Regular Hours	Overtime Hours	Amount
275	8:02	10:31	2½		
276	10:31	12:05	1½		
277	1:01	5:58	4	1	
		Totals	8	1	

Approval J. R. Schmidt
Supervisor

Name Doris Green   Employee No. 14
Department Sewing   Regular Hourly Rate $5.20
Date June 5, 19--   Overtime Rate $7.80

Job No.	Time Started	Time Stopped	Regular Hours	Overtime Hours	Amount
275	7:57	9:45	1¾		
276	9:46	11:59	2¼		
278	12:55	6:31	4	1½	
		Totals	8	1½	

Approval J. R. Schmidt
Supervisor

Name Frank Casey   Employee No. 17
Department Pressing   Regular Hourly Rate $4.80
Date June 5, 19--   Overtime Rate $7.20

Job No.	Time Started	Time Stopped	Regular Hours	Overtime Hours	Amount
Absent for personal business during day shift					
277	6:05	7:44	1¾		
278	7:45	10:00	2¼		
		Totals	4		

Approval R. Mackenzie
Supervisor

the labor involved in each job and the total labor cost for each ticket. (Do this task in your workbook.)

5-8. Jobs 277 and 278 were started and finished on June 5 at the Jensen Manufacturing Company. Prepare an analysis of the direct labor costs for these jobs. Obtain the necessary data from the time tickets that you completed in Topic Problem 5-7. Use the following format for your report. (However, do the work in your workbook.)

JENSEN MANUFACTURING COMPANY
Analysis of Direct Labor Costs for Completed Jobs
June 5, 19—

Job No.	Cutting Dept. Hours	Amount	Sewing Dept. Hours	Amount	Pressing Dept. Hours	Amount	Total Cost
277		$		$		$	$
278							
Totals		$		$		$	$

5-9. The Ellsworth Corporation makes shoes and boots. Assume that you are a member of the accounting staff. The cost accountant asks you to perform the following work.

a. Make entries in the general journal to record the factory payroll and the labor costs for the week ended January 21. The payroll journal shows $1,156.40 withheld for federal income taxes, $495.60 withheld for FICA taxes, and $6,608 owed for wages and salaries. The analysis of labor costs shows that $6,340 was incurred for direct labor and $1,920 was incurred for indirect labor.

b. Compute the employer's payroll taxes. Then make an entry in the general journal to record these taxes. The total taxable amount of wages and salaries is $8,260. The tax rates are as follows: employer's share of FICA taxes, 6.05 percent; federal unemployment taxes, 0.5 percent; and state unemployment taxes, 2.7 percent.

Topic 4
Factory Overhead Costs

A *Why is it necessary to assign part of the total factory overhead to each product?* The cost of a product is determined by three elements: direct materials, direct labor, and factory overhead. Without information about overhead, it is not possible to find the cost of the goods a business makes. Management must know the cost of goods to be able to set selling prices accurately.

This topic discusses procedures for computing and recording factory overhead.

Computing Applied Factory Overhead

Factory Overhead:
- Indirect materials
- Manufacturing supplies
- Indirect labor
- Costs of operating the factory

Remember that factory overhead consists of indirect materials, manufacturing supplies, indirect labor, and the costs of operating the factory. The types of indirect materials and manufacturing supplies used in a business depend on the nature of the business's products. Examples of indirect labor and factory operating costs that are common in many manufacturing businesses are given here.

Types of Overhead Costs

Indirect Materials and Manufacturing Supplies
(These items vary according to the goods a business produces. The following examples are for a furniture factory.)
- Glue.
- Varnish.
- Sandpaper.
- Nails.
- Lubricants for machines.
- Brushes for applying varnish.
- Factory office supplies.

Costs of Operating the Factory
- Rent for factory building and equipment.
- Utilities (heat, electricity, and water).
- Telephone service.
- Fire insurance.

- Payroll taxes for factory employees.
- Repairs.
- Depreciation of factory building and equipment.*
- Property taxes for factory building.
- Damaged goods.

Indirect Labor
- Factory managers.
- Factory supervisors.
- Factory office employees.
- Cost accounting employees.
- Timekeeping and payroll employees.
- Purchasing employees.
- Stores employees.
- Receiving employees.
- Shipping employees.
- Maintenance employees.
- Quality control employees.

*Depreciation is incurred if the business owns rather than rents the factory building and equipment.

Factory overhead items are often classified as variable or fixed. In most factories the number of units produced changes from period to period. The amounts of some overhead items, such as manufacturing supplies and electricity, increase or decrease according to the level of production. These overhead items are called **variable overhead**

costs. The amounts of other overhead items, such as rent and fire insurance, remain the same no matter how many units are produced. These overhead items are called **fixed overhead costs.**

Because many overhead items are variable, it is not possible to know the real costs of factory overhead until the end of an accounting period. However, as noted before, it is necessary to assign overhead to goods completed during the accounting period. For this reason the cost accounting staff must estimate the total factory overhead and set an overhead rate at the beginning of each accounting period. The overhead rate is used to compute the amount of overhead to be charged to each product manufactured during an accounting period.

The real costs of factory overhead are referred to as **actual factory overhead.** The estimated costs are referred to as **applied factory overhead.**

Estimating total factory overhead for an accounting period requires skill and judgment. The cost accounting staff must consider actual overhead from previous periods, the expected level of production in the new period, and the effect of inflation on overhead costs.

After the applied factory overhead is determined, the overhead rate for the accounting period is set. There are a number of methods for setting overhead rates. Each method is based on a different factor. The most common methods use the following factors: estimated direct labor cost, estimated direct labor hours, estimated machine hours, estimated direct materials cost, and estimated units of production. The cost accounting staff must select a method that relates well to the operations of the factory. For example, some factories use a great deal of labor and not much machinery to produce goods. Farming also falls into this category. Usually more people (labor) than machinery are used. In such situations, there may be a close relationship between overhead cost and direct labor cost.

Five common methods of setting overhead rates are explained here and on the following pages. The use of these rates to assign applied factory overhead to completed goods is also shown.

Common Methods of Setting Overhead Rates:
- Direct labor method
- Direct labor hours method
- Machine hours method
- Direct materials cost method
- Units of production method

Direct Labor Cost Method. This is the most popular method of setting overhead rates. At the beginning of each accounting period estimates are made of the total factory overhead and the total direct labor cost for the period. Then the estimated factory overhead is divided by the estimated direct labor cost to find the overhead rate.

Assume that the estimated factory overhead for a business is $80,000 and the estimated direct labor cost is $100,000. The overhead rate will be 80 percent. This means that for every dollar spent on direct labor, an overhead cost of 80 cents will be incurred.

Direct labor is the work of employees who change direct materials into finished products.

$$\frac{\text{Estimated Factory Overhead}}{\text{Estimated Direct Labor Cost}} = \frac{\text{Overhead Rate (Percent of}}{\text{Direct Labor Cost)}}$$

$$\frac{\$80,000}{\$100,000} = 80\% \text{ of Direct Labor Cost}$$

As products are completed, factory overhead is charged at the rate of 80 percent of the direct labor cost for these products. Suppose that the records kept by the cost accounting staff show that a job involved a direct labor cost of $2,000. (Remember that a job consists of a group of units that are being made together.) The amount of overhead for the job is $1,600. This amount is computed by multiplying the direct labor cost by the overhead rate ($2,000 × 0.80 = $1,600).

Direct Labor Hours Method. This is another method that relates overhead to direct labor. Estimates are made of the total factory overhead and the total direct labor hours for the new accounting period. Then the estimated factory overhead is divided by the estimated direct labor hours to find the overhead rate.

Assume that the cost accounting staff has estimated $80,000 for factory overhead and 8,000 for direct labor hours. The overhead rate will be $10 for each hour of direct labor.

$$\frac{\text{Estimated Factory Overhead}}{\text{Estimated Direct Labor Hours}} = \frac{\text{Overhead Rate (Amount per}}{\text{Direct Labor Hour)}}$$

$$\frac{\$80,000}{8,000} = \$10 \text{ per Direct Labor Hour}$$

When a job is finished, the number of direct labor hours is obtained from the time records. This number is multiplied by the overhead rate to determine the amount of factory overhead for the job. Suppose that a job involves 120 hours of direct labor. With an overhead rate of $10 an hour, the overhead cost that should be charged to the job is $1,200 (120 × $10 = $1,200).

Machine Hours Method. In some businesses most of the production work is done by machines. These businesses may therefore use machine hours as the basis for computing overhead. Estimates are made of the total factory overhead and the total machine hours for the new accounting period. Then the estimated factory overhead is divided by the estimated machine hours to find the overhead rate.

Assume that the estimated factory overhead is $80,000 and the estimated machine hours are 10,000. The overhead rate will be $8 for each hour that the machines operate.

$$\frac{\text{Estimated Factory Overhead}}{\text{Estimated Machine Hours}} = \begin{array}{c}\text{Overhead Rate (Amount per}\\ \text{Machine Hour)}\end{array}$$

$$\frac{\$80,000}{10,000} = \$8 \text{ per Machine Hour}$$

When this method is used, it is necessary to keep records of the number of machine hours involved in each job. The number of machine hours is multiplied by the overhead rate to compute the amount of factory overhead. Suppose that a job requires 100 machine hours and the overhead rate is $8 an hour. The overhead cost for the job would be $800 ($100 \times \$8 = \$800$).

Direct Materials Cost Method. Remember that direct labor and direct materials are the prime costs incurred in making a product. The overhead rate can be based on the cost of direct materials as well as on the cost of direct labor. Estimates are made of the total factory overhead and the total cost of direct materials for the new accounting period. Then the estimated factory overhead is divided by the estimated direct materials cost to find the overhead rate.

Assume that the estimated factory overhead for a business is $80,000 and the estimated direct materials cost is $200,000. The overhead rate will be 40 percent of the direct materials cost for completed products.

$$\frac{\text{Estimated Factory Overhead}}{\text{Estimated Direct Materials Cost}} = \begin{array}{c}\text{Overhead Rate (Percent of}\\ \text{Direct Materials Cost)}\end{array}$$

$$\frac{\$80,000}{\$200,000} = 40\% \text{ of Direct Materials Cost}$$

When a job is finished, the amount spent for direct materials is obtained from the cost records. This amount is multiplied by the overhead rate to determine the amount of factory overhead. Suppose that direct materials costing $6,000 were used for a job. If the overhead rate is 40 percent, the amount of factory overhead to be charged to the job is $2,400 ($6,000 \times 0.40 = \$2,400$).

Units of Production Method. With this method, an equal amount of factory overhead is assigned to each unit that a business produces during an accounting period. At the start of each period, estimates are made of the total factory overhead and the total number of units that will be manufactured. Then the estimated factory overhead is divided by the estimated number of units to find the overhead rate.

Assume that the estimated factory overhead is $80,000 and the estimated number of units is 16,000. The overhead rate will be $5 for each unit.

$$\frac{\text{Estimated Factory Overhead}}{\text{Estimated Units of Production}} = \text{Overhead Rate (Amount per Unit)}$$

$$\frac{\$80,000}{16,000} = \$5 \text{ per Unit}$$

If a job consists of 300 units, the amount of factory overhead for the job would be $1,500 (300 × $5 = $1,500).

Some businesses have a single overhead rate for the whole factory. Other businesses have different rates for the various production departments. Often different methods are used to set the departmental rates. For example, the overhead rate for a milling department might be determined by the machine hours method. However, the overhead rate for a finishing department might be determined by the direct labor cost method.

Accounting Concept:
Control—Flow of Work. Procedures must be established to ensure accuracy, honesty, efficiency, and speed in recording and controlling factory overhead costs.

Activity A. The following estimates were made for the next accounting period at the Montez Manufacturing Company.

Factory overhead	$ 60,000	Direct labor hours	$ 15,000
Direct labor cost	120,000	Machine hours	12,000
Direct materials cost	100,000	Units of production	20,000

Compute the overhead rate according to each of the following methods.

1. Direct labor cost method
2. Direct labor hours method
3. Machine hours method

4. Direct materials cost method
5. Units of production method

Accounting for Actual and Applied Factory Overhead

B *How are actual factory overhead costs recorded?* Most manufacturing businesses set up a subsidiary ledger called the **factory overhead ledger.** This ledger contains accounts for the various types of overhead items that a factory has, such as insurance, rent, and utilities. The Factory Overhead account in the general ledger serves as a

controlling account for the factory overhead subsidiary ledger. Whenever an actual factory overhead cost is incurred, the amount is debited
to the Factory Overhead account and the proper subsidiary ledger account.

On May 10 Western Manufacturing Company received a bill for electricity used in the factory during April. The following general journal
entry was made to record the payment of this bill. Notice that two
account titles are shown in the debit part of the entry. The debit of
$410 must be posted to the Factory Overhead account in the general
ledger and the Utilities account in the factory overhead ledger. The
credit of $410 is posted to the Cash account in the general ledger.

**Factory Overhead
Subsidiary Ledger**

Insurance

Rent

Utilities

The factory overhead
subsidiary ledger con-
tains accounts for indi-
vidual overhead items.

		GENERAL JOURNAL				Page 5
DATE		ACCOUNT TITLE AND EXPLANATION	POST. REF.	DEBIT	CREDIT	
19— May						
	10	Factory Overhead/Utilities	501/√	410 00		
		Cash	101		410 00	
		Paid for electricity used in fac-				
		tory during April, Check 1210.				

General Ledger

Factory Overhead	501
May 7 1,300.00	
7 2,730.00	
7 908.35	
10 410.00	

Cash	101
May 10 410.00	

**Factory Overhead
Subsidiary Ledger**

Utilities	501
May 10 410.00	

Many manufacturing businesses use a voucher register rather than
the general journal to record the actual factory overhead costs they
incur.

At Western Manufacturing Company, the Factory Overhead account
is used to record applied factory overhead as well as actual factory
overhead. For example, the applied factory overhead for the month of
May was $5,600. This amount is debited to the Work-in-Process ac-
count and credited to the Factory Overhead account as shown on page
200.

Notice that the factory overhead ledger is not involved in recording
applied overhead. The accounts in this subsidiary ledger are used only
for the recording of actual overhead items.

The data about applied factory overhead comes from the cost records
that are kept for all jobs. Whenever a job is finished, a cost clerk uses

General Ledger

Factory Overhead 501

Actual Overhead	Applied Overhead

GENERAL JOURNAL				Page 6
DATE	**ACCOUNT TITLE AND EXPLANATION**	**POST. REF.**	**DEBIT**	**CREDIT**
19—				
May 31	Work-in-Process	122	5,600 00	
	Factory Overhead	501		5,600 00
	Applied factory overhead for May.			

General Ledger

Work-in-Process		122
May 7	8,100.00	
7	7,090.00	
31	5,600.00	

Factory Overhead				501
May 7	1,300.00	May 31	5,600.00
7	2,730.00		
7	908.35		
10	410.00		

the overhead rate to compute the amount of overhead that should be assigned to the job. The clerk then enters this amount in the cost record for the job. At the end of each month the amounts of applied factory overhead for the completed jobs are added. The total is journalized as shown above.

Some businesses do not record applied factory overhead in the Factory Overhead account. Instead, they set up a special account called *Applied Factory Overhead*. When this method is used, only actual overhead costs are recorded in the Factory Overhead account.

Activity B. Answer the following questions about the procedures for recording actual and applied factory overhead. Refer to the text and illustrations on pages 198 to 200.

1. What type of transaction was entered in the general journal of the Western Manufacturing Company on May 10? Does this transaction involve actual or applied factory overhead?

2. What general ledger account is debited for actual factory overhead?

3. What kind of account is the Utilities account? Was it debited or credited to record the May 10 transaction?

4. What was the purpose of the general journal entry made on May 31?

5. Which accounts are debited and credited to record applied factory overhead?

6. What amount of applied factory overhead did the Western Manufacturing Company have for the month of May?

7. Is the factory overhead ledger used in recording applied factory overhead?

8. Suppose that a business pays $1,500 in cash for monthly rent on the factory building. Is this actual overhead or applied overhead? What accounts would be debited and credited to record the transaction?

Comparing Actual and Applied Factory Overhead

C *Is the amount of actual factory overhead usually equal to the amount of applied factory overhead?* When these two amounts are compared at the end of a year, they will almost always differ. Skilled cost accountants are able to estimate factory overhead with great accuracy. However, they cannot determine the exact amount of overhead before the costs are incurred.

Actual factory overhead almost always differs from applied factory overhead.

If the Factory Overhead account has a debit balance at the end of the year, overhead has been **underapplied.** This means that too little factory overhead has been charged to completed goods. If the Factory Overhead account has a credit balance, overhead has been **overapplied.** This means that too much overhead has been charged to completed goods.

When the financial records are closed at the end of the year, the balance of the Factory Overhead account must be reduced to zero. At Western Manufacturing Company this is done by transferring the balance to the Income Summary account.

Sometimes there is a big difference between actual overhead and applied overhead. When this happens the cost accounting staff must reassess its methods for estimating factory overhead and setting the overhead rate.

Allocating Actual Factory Overhead Costs to Departments

Manufacturing businesses must have procedures for allocating actual factory overhead costs to their production and service departments. Each department must be assigned a share of the overhead items that relate to its operations. The procedures used to allocate factory overhead costs to departments are very similar to the procedures for allocating expenses to departments in a merchandising business. (These procedures are described in Chapter 2.)

There are a number of methods for allocating factory overhead costs to departments. Different methods are often chosen for different types of overhead costs. Some common allocation methods are listed on page 202.

A special worksheet may be used as an aid in allocating factory overhead costs to departments. For example, the worksheet on page 202 was prepared at Western Manufacturing Company on May 31.

The first three columns of the worksheet show the various overhead items that the factory has, the total amount for each item, and the allocation method for each item. (The totals are taken from the factory overhead subsidiary ledger.) The remaining columns of the worksheet show the amounts allocated to the departments. After all items have

WESTERN MANUFACTURING COMPANY
Worksheet for Allocating Factory Overhead Costs to Departments
For the Month Ended May 31, 19—

OVERHEAD ITEM	TOTAL	ALLOCATION METHOD	MILLING DEPARTMENT	SANDING DEPARTMENT	FINISHING DEPARTMENT	FACTORY OFFICE	COST ACCOUNTING DEPARTMENT	STORES DEPARTMENT
Rent	1,500 00	Floor Space . . .	450 00	300 00	375 00	90 00	60 00	225 00
Utilities	410 00	Metered Usage .	133 00	86 00	94 50	21 60	15 40	59 50

Examples of Methods Used to Allocate Factory Overhead Costs to Departments

Type of Overhead Cost	Basis for Allocation
Cleaning service.	Floor space occupied by each department.
Depreciation of factory building.	Floor space occupied by each department.
Depreciation of factory machines.	Cost of machines in each department.
Fire insurance premiums.	Valuation of insured items in each department.
Materials handling and storage.	Number of requisitions issued by each department or quantity of materials used by each department.
Payroll taxes for factory employees.	Payroll for covered employees in each department.
Property taxes for factory building.	Valuation of space occupied by each department.
Rent for factory building.	Floor space occupied by each department.
Repairs.	Actual cost of repairs made in each department.
Salaries of supervisors.	Estimate of time spent by supervisors in each department.
Supplies.	Usage by each department (often based on estimates).
Timekeeping and payroll preparation.	Number of employees in each department.
Utilities.	Actual metered usaged in each department.

COMPARISON OF BUDGETED AND
ACTUAL OVERHEAD COSTS
FOR DEPARTMENTS

SUMMARY OF OVERHEAD COSTS
FOR DEPARTMENTS

ITEM	DEPT.	DEPT.	DEPT.	DEPT.	DEPT.	DEPT.

The cost accounting staff provides owners and managers with reports about the overhead costs for all the departments of the factory.

been allocated, the total overhead cost for each department is determined. This is done by adding the amounts in each department's column.

The information from the completed worksheet is reported to management. It allows management to keep a close watch on actual factory overhead costs from month to month.

Because the service departments do not make any goods, their overhead costs must eventually be distributed to the production departments of the factory. Another worksheet is prepared to allocate the overhead costs of the service departments to the production departments.

Activity C-1. During July, $4,320 in applied factory overhead was recorded for the sewing department of the Dayton Dress Company. The actual factory overhead costs of this department for July are listed here.

Actual Factory Overhead Costs

Indirect labor	$1,100
Indirect materials	760
Rent	400
Depreciation of machines . .	390
Payroll taxes	550
Insurance	600
Utilities	340
Repairs for machines	70

1. What was the total of the actual factory overhead costs for the month?

2. Was factory overhead underapplied or overapplied for the month?

Activity C-2. Several factory overhead items are listed here. Indicate what method might be used for allocating each of these items to the departments of the factory. Refer to the illustration on page 202.

Depreciation of building	Rent
Repairs	Supplies
Materials handling and storage	Timekeeping and payroll preparation
Depreciation of machines	
Utilities	

Completing the Manufacturing Process

D *What happens to goods when the manufacturing process is completed?* The goods are removed from the production area and taken to the factory warehouse. They become part of the inventory of finished goods. If orders for the goods are already on hand, the warehouse staff ships them to the customers right away. Otherwise finished goods remain stored in the warehouse until they are sold.

While goods are in production, their costs are accumulated in the Work-in-Process account. (Remember that the Work-in-Process account is debited for direct materials, direct labor, and applied factory overhead.) When goods are completed, their costs must be transferred to the Finished Goods account. This is done by debiting the Finished Goods account and crediting the Work-in-Process account.

During May goods costing $16,200 were completed at Western Manufacturing Company. These goods left the work-in-process inventory and were placed in the finished goods inventory. On May 31 the general journal entry shown at the top of page 204 was made to transfer the total cost.

Western Manufacturing Company
Chart of Accounts

Assets
122 Work-in-Process
123 Finished Goods

The Work-in-Process account is debited for direct materials, direct labor, and applied factory overhead.

DATE	ACCOUNT TITLE AND EXPLANATION	POST. REF.	DEBIT	CREDIT
19— May				
31	Finished Goods	123	16,200 00	
	Work-in-Process	122		16,200 00
	Transfer cost of goods completed in May.			

GENERAL JOURNAL — Page 6

General Ledger

Finished Goods		123
May 1	Bal. 22,500	
31	16,200	

Work-in-Process		122
May 7	8,100	May 31 16,200
7	7,090	
31	5,600	

Management must have procedures for controlling the finished goods inventory. For example, many businesses keep a **finished goods ledger.** This subsidiary ledger provides a continuous record of all the items in the finished goods inventory.

The Flow of Costs

The flow of costs matches the activities in a manufacturing business.

The flow of costs in a manufacturing business matches the flow of activities. Before production starts on a job, materials are bought. During production, the costs of direct materials, direct labor, and applied factory overhead become work-in-process costs. When production is

The Flow of Costs in a Manufacturing Business

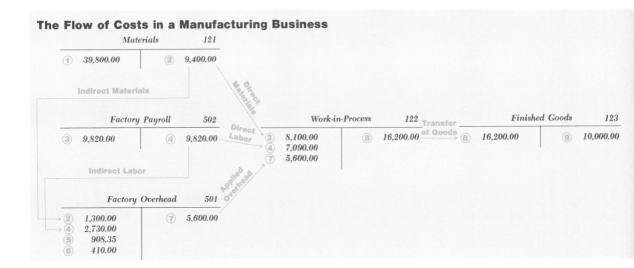

completed, the work-in-process costs become finished goods costs. Finally, when sales are made, the finished goods costs become part of the cost of goods sold.

The chart shown on page 204 and 205 shows the flow of costs at Western Manufacturing Company during May.

Automated Cost Accounting Procedures

Cost accounting systems require numerous detailed records. Preparing such records is a time-consuming task. For this reason many manufacturing businesses use computers in their cost accounting work. Computers make it possible for the cost accounting staff to process large amounts of information, prepare all the necessary records, and provide management with a wide range of useful reports.

The following are examples of cost accounting procedures that are often performed with the help of computers.
- Keeping records of the materials inventory.
- Computing the factory payroll and preparing the payroll records.
- Keeping records of labor costs for each job and each department.
- Keeping records of factory overhead costs.
- Allocating factory overhead costs to departments.
- Keeping records of the finished goods inventory.

Accounting Concept:
Flow of Costs. In a manufacturing business, the costs of direct materials, direct labor, and applied factory overhead become work-in-process costs. The work-in-process costs then become finished goods costs. Finally, the finished goods costs become part of the cost of goods sold.

Explanation of Entries
1 Purchased materials for $39,800.
2 Issued materials costing $9,400 to use in production ($8,100 was for direct materials and $1,300 was for indirect materials).
3 Recorded the factory payroll of $9,820.
4 Distributed the labor costs for the factory payroll of $9,820 ($7,090 was for direct labor and $2,730 was for indirect labor).
5 Recorded payroll taxes of $908.35.
6 Paid $410 for electricity used in the factory.
7 Recorded applied factory overhead of $5,600 for goods completed.
8 Recorded the transfer of goods costing $16,200 from the production area to the warehouse. These goods were completed during the month.
9 Sold finished goods costing $10,000.

A factory worker uses an optical scanning device to record cost accounting data.

Activity D. Answer the following questions about the flow of costs at Western Manufacturing Company. Refer to the illustration on pages 204 and 205.

1. Why was the Materials account debited for $39,800?

2. Why was the Materials account credited for $9,400?

3. What types of costs are debited to the Work-in-Process account?

4. Which account is debited for the cost of indirect materials?

5. Which account is debited for the cost of indirect labor?

6. Why was the Factory Overhead account credited for $5,600?

7. What accounts were debited and credited when goods were completed and taken to the warehouse?

8. Why was the Factory Overhead account debited for $410?

9. Do the entries on the debit side of the Factory Overhead account represent actual overhead or applied overhead?

10. Why was the Finished Goods account credited for $10,000?

Topic 4 Problems

5-10. The Seven Seas Boat Company produces custom-made sailboats. Assume that you work in the cost accounting department. The head of the department has assigned the following tasks to you.

a. Compute the overhead rate for the new year. The business uses the direct labor cost method to set its overhead rate. The esti-mated factory overhead for the year is $140,000. The estimated direct labor cost for the year is $200,000.

Jobs Completed in January	
Job No.	Direct Labor Cost
101	$3,000
102	2,100
103	1,500
104	3,600
105	2,300

b. Compute the amount of applied factory overhead for each of the five jobs completed during January. Use the overhead rate that you computed in Part **a.** Also compute the total applied factory overhead for the month. (Add the overhead amounts for all the completed jobs.)

c. Make an entry in the general journal to record the total applied factory overhead for the month. (Use January 31 as the date for this entry.)

5-11. The Wagner Toy Company is a small manufacturing business that specializes in model cars and model airplanes. Assume that you are responsible for keeping the cost accounting records. During March the business had the following transactions involving actual factory overhead costs.

March 1 Issued Check 546 for $970 to pay rent on the factory building.

     10 Issued Check 547 for $640 to pay for electricity used in the factory.

March 16 Issued Check 548 for $250 to pay the fire insurance premium.

     28 Issued Check 549 for $80 to pay for repairs to factory machines.

a. Make entries in the general journal to record the transactions listed above. Then post the journal entries to the proper accounts in the general ledger and the factory overhead subsidiary ledger.

b. Make an entry in the general journal to record the applied factory overhead for March. The amount is $1,890. (Use March 31 as the date of the entry.) Post the entry to the proper ledger accounts.

c. Pencil-foot the Factory Overhead account in the general ledger. Was overhead underapplied or overapplied during March?

5-12. The Well-Built Furniture Company produces garden furniture. Assume that you are working in the cost accounting department. On June 30 you are given the following data.

Jobs Completed in June	
Job No.	Cost of Goods
720	$3,540
722	4,270
723	6,900
724	5,430

a. Compute the total cost for all goods completed in June.

b. Make an entry in the general journal to transfer the total cost of the completed goods to the Finished Goods account. (Use June 30 as the date for this entry.)

The Language of Business

Here are some basic terms that make up the language of business. Do you understand the meaning of each? Can you define each term and use it in an original sentence?

manufacturing
  business
manufacturing process
cost accounting
direct materials
direct labor
factory overhead
indirect materials
manufacturing
  supplies
indirect labor
cost accountants
prime costs
cost clerks

mass-producing goods
process cost system
job order cost system
Materials account
Work-in-Process
  account
Finished Goods
  account
production department
service department
stores department
reorder point
reorder quantity
purchase requisition

bill of materials
purchase order
physical inventory
perpetual inventory
  records
receiving report
inventory tag
stores ledger
materials requisition
perpetual inventory
  procedure
hourly-rate plans
piece-rate plan
salary plan

time ticket
analysis of labor costs
variable overhead costs
fixed overhead costs
actual factory
  overhead
applied factory
  overhead
overhead rate
factory overhead
  ledger
underapplied overhead
overapplied overhead
finished goods ledger

Chapter 5 Questions

1. What is a manufacturing business? Give three examples of well-known manufacturing businesses.
2. Why is cost accounting important to the management of a manufacturing business?
3. Explain the three major costs involved in making a product.
4. What are the two types of cost accounting systems? Describe each type of system.
5. What kinds of inventories does a manufacturing business have?
6. The following forms are often used in connection with materials: purchase requisition, bill of materials, purchase order, receiving report, stores ledger card, inventory tag, and materials requisition. What is the purpose of each form?
7. What is the difference between actual factory overhead and applied factory overhead?

8. What is the factory overhead ledger? How does it relate to the Factory Overhead account in the general ledger?
9. The following forms and records are often used in factory payroll procedures: time card, time ticket, payroll journal, employee earnings records, and labor cost analysis. What is the purpose of each form or record?
10. Give three examples of each of the following factory overhead costs: indirect materials, indirect labor, and the costs of operating a factory.
11. Why is it necessary to estimate factory overhead before the costs are incurred?
12. Describe five methods of computing the factory overhead rate.
13. Describe the flow of costs in a manufacturing business.

Chapter 5 Problems

Problems for Chapter 5 are given in the *Working Papers and Chapter Problems* for Part 1. If you are using the workbook, do the problems in the space provided there. Complete your assigned topic problems before answering the chapter problems.

Chapter 5 Management Cases

Internal Control. Well-designed cost accounting systems supply management with accurate, complete, and timely information about manufacturing costs. This information is needed to judge the efficiency of operations and to make decisions. Well-designed cost accounting systems also provide for internal control. They have procedures to safeguard assets such as raw materials against theft and waste. These procedures also ensure that the time of factory employees is used properly. Mishandling of materials and misuse of time harm employees as well as management. They decrease a business's ability to operate successfully and to provide steady jobs.

Case 5M-1. Wheeler Music Products manufactures musical instruments, such as guitars and drums. Many of these instruments are custom-made for rock bands. The business also manufactures amplification systems for the bands. Gary Wheeler started the business ten years ago in his garage. Since then the business has grown a great deal and has moved into a factory building.

Working conditions at Wheeler Music Products are very informal and relaxed. Paperwork is kept to a minimum. The factory is divided into departments. However, employees in one department often borrow supplies, tools, and the services of employees in other departments without preparing any records. No time tickets are used to keep track of the hours spent on individual jobs. Employees can work overtime whenever they wish without getting a supervisor's approval.

There are no stores ledger cards. The stores department is open to all employees, and materials are removed whenever necessary. No materials requisitions are prepared. The only control on the materials inventory is a physical count, which is taken once a year.

The stores department determines the need to order more materials by checking all the bins and shelves at the end of each week. If the stock of an item seems to be low, more materials are ordered.

Recently Mr. Wheeler hired a cost accountant. After studying operations, the cost accountant found a number of serious problems. Profits are poor even though sales are constantly increasing. Production work is often interrupted by shortages of materials. Total labor costs are very high.

The cost accountant thinks that the business should keep detailed records. She also thinks that the business should have better procedures for controlling materials and for controlling the hours spent on each job. Mr. Wheeler is reluctant to follow this advice. He believes that all the paperwork will slow down production. He also believes that tight controls will upset his employees because this would suggest that he doubts their honesty.

a. Under the present system, does Mr. Wheeler have accurate information about the costs involved in each job? Explain your answer.

b. Can Mr. Wheeler be sure that he is selling all his goods at a profit? Why or why not?

c. What procedures and forms could the business use to control the materials inventory and make sure that items are reordered on time?

d. What procedures and forms could the business use to control labor costs?

e. How would you answer Mr. Wheeler's objection that more paperwork will slow down production?

f. Do you think that there is any way to avoid upsetting the employees if the new procedures are adopted? How would you handle the situation?

g. If you were Mr. Wheeler, would you accept the cost accountant's suggestions or keep the present system? Why or why not?

Case 5M-2. Atlantic Manufacturing Company produces microwave ovens and other kitchen appliances. The stores department has tight control over the materials inventory and keeps detailed records. However, the business seems to be losing materials. The cost accountant has been looking for the source of the problem.

A study of the receiving operation showed that the following procedures are used. Because there is no receiving clerk, shipments are accepted by a number of different employees. When materials arrive, any clerk or secretary in the factory office who happens to be available takes care of the shipment. This employee signs the shipper's release form and then tells the purchasing agent that the materials are on hand.

The purchasing agent arranges to have the materials moved to the stores department. Any maintenance or production employees who have some spare time are asked to perform this task. When the factory is very busy, the materials may stay in the receiving area for a day before they are moved.

No attempt is made to count the materials and check their quality until they are brought to the stores department. Often the stores clerks find that the quantity received is less than the quantity shown on the purchase order. However, no one knows whether the supplier failed to ship the correct quantity or whether an employee at Atlantic stole the missing items.

The cost accountant has suggested to management that a receiving clerk be hired and that new receiving procedures be set up.

a. What weaknesses do you see in the present procedures for receiving materials?

b. Do you agree with the idea of hiring a receiving clerk? Why or why not?

c. What procedures and forms do you think that this business should use for receiving materials?

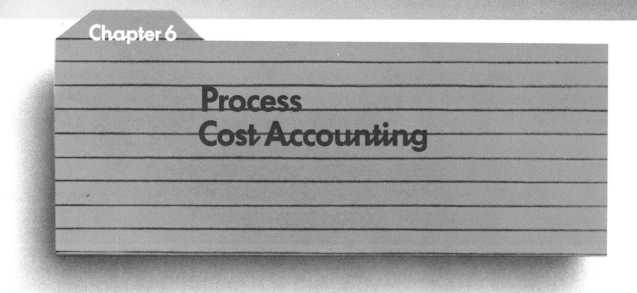

Chapter 6

Process Cost Accounting

The two major manufacturing cost accounting systems are process cost accounting systems and job order cost accounting systems. A process cost accounting system will be presented in this chapter. A job order cost accounting system will be discussed in Chapter 7.

Topic 1
The Flow of Costs

A *How are costs collected in a process cost accounting system?* A **process cost accounting system** collects cost data for each operation or for each department. Costs are not collected for individual units or individual products. Process cost accounting systems are generally used by businesses that manufacture only one product or a few products that are very similar. The products are frequently manufactured on an assembly line. Automobiles, clothing, and furniture are usually produced in this manner. These businesses divide the labor necessary to produce their products into different processes. Usually each process is handled by a separate department.

The Boyd Chair Company uses a process cost accounting system. The company produces wooden chairs by processing the raw lumber through three production departments. The milling department cuts, shapes, and sands the raw wood. The assembling department fits the

In a process cost accounting system, cost data is gathered for operations or departments.

Manufacturing Businesses Using Process Cost Accounting:
• Steel
• Pipe
• Paper products
• Automobiles
• Textiles
• Plastic products

Mining Businesses That Use Process Cost Accounting:
• Coal
• Oil

Public Utilities That Use Process Cost Accounting:
• Electric power

"Antique" telephones are being produced here on an assembly line. The manufacturer may use a process cost accounting system.

$$\text{Unit Cost} = \frac{\text{Materials} + \text{Labor} + \text{Factory Overhead}}{\text{Total Units Processed}}$$

Boyd Chair Company Chart of Accounts

Assets
121 Materials
122 Work-in-Process— Milling Department
123 Work-in-Process— Assembling Department
124 Work-in-Process— Finishing Department
125 Finished Goods

Revenue
401 Sales

Liabilities
211 Accounts Payable

Factory Costs
501 Factory Overhead
502 Factory Payroll
511 Cost of Goods Sold

milled pieces together. The finishing department applies the lacquer finish. Each department serves as a processing center for making the chair. Each chair should take approximately the same amount of material and the same amount of time to mill, assemble, and finish.

Computing Unit Costs

In process cost accounting, costs are collected for all products (units) worked on during an accounting period. Costs are then assigned to each product. At the end of the accounting period, the costs of all materials, labor, and factory overhead for a department are totaled. The total is then divided by the number of units processed by that department. The result is the **unit cost.** This method of accumulating costs is called **average costing.**

The Flow of Work and Accumulation of Costs

The flow of work and the accumulation of manufacturing costs are illustrated in the flowchart on page 213. It shows the flow of a single material (wood) from the stores department through three production departments to finished chairs in the warehouse.

The flowchart also shows that the sale of finished goods increases both the cost of goods sold and sales. The movement of wood through each department has an affect on the Materials account, the Factory Payroll account, and the Factory Overhead account. Note that in a process cost accounting system there is a separate Work-in-Process account for each production department. The following pages relate how the accounts are affected as the units move through the departments. Manufacturing other products may require the combination of several materials. For example, some chairs require wood, metal, fabric, and plastic coverings. However, the flow of work and the accumulation of costs would similarly affect several accounts.

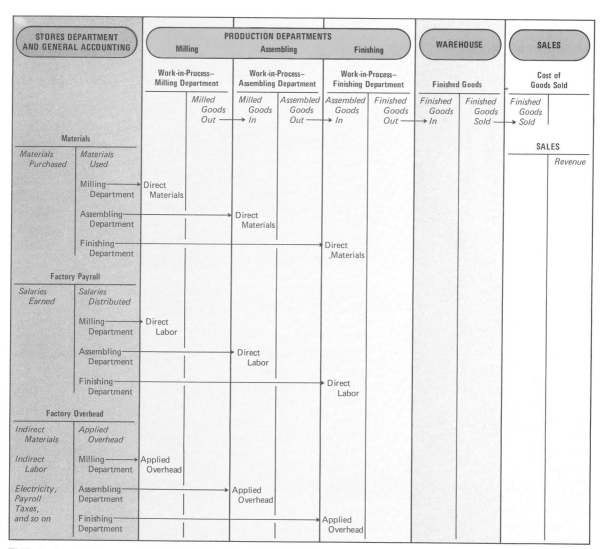

THE FLOW OF COSTS IN MANUFACTURING CHAIRS

Accounting Concept:
Process Cost Accounting System. Manufacturing costs are collected by operation or by department.

Accounting Concept:
Flow of Work. A successful business will establish procedures to ensure an adequate and steady flow of work through the business.

One of the first steps in the flow of costs in the textile business is purchasing cotton, a raw material. Each time cotton is purchased, it must be accounted for.

The cotton is processed to make yarn. The costs of the yarn includes the direct materials and direct labor used as well as the applied overhead.

Courtesy of Cotton Incorporated

Courtesy of American Textile Manufacturers Institute, Inc.

Courtesy of American Textile Manufacturers Institute, Inc.

Courtesy of Cotton Incorporated

The yarn, in turn, is used to prepare a fabric. Here a technician uses a computer system to develop a pattern for the fabric. The costs include the yarn, direct materials, direct labor, and applied overhead incurred in weaving the fabric.

The fabric is combined with other materials and processed to make finished goods, in this case, a cotton jacket and cotton shirt. To ensure success, a manufacturing business must have procedures to control the flow of work and the accumulation of costs.

Activity A-1. Listed on page 216 are manufacturing businesses that may use a process cost accounting system. For each type of business, name a company you are familiar with that manufactures that kind of product.

Type of Business	Name of Company
EXAMPLE: automobiles	**Ford Motor Company**
1. tissues	**7.** lawn mowers
2. stereos	**8.** tennis rackets
3. bath towels	**9.** bicycles
4. oil	**10.** soft drinks
5. electric power	**11.** chairs
6. steel	**12.** televisions

Activity A-2. Answer the following questions about the flow of costs in manufacturing chairs. Refer to the chart on page 213.

1. What is the stores department?
2. How many production departments are involved in the manufacturing of chairs? Name these departments.
3. How many Work-in-Process accounts are shown on the chart? Name the accounts.
4. When is the Materials account debited? credited?
5. When is the Factory Payroll account debited? credited?
6. When is the Factory Overhead account debited? credited?
7. What types of costs are debited to the Work-in-Process—Milling Department account? When is this account credited?
8. What types of costs are debited to the Work-in-Process—Assembling Department account? When is this account credited?
9. What types of costs are debited to the Work-in-Process—Finishing Department account? When is this account credited?
10. What account is debited for the cost of the completed chairs? What account is credited?

Raw Materials Cost

B *What is the source document for recording purchases of raw materials?* In order to begin manufacturing a product, a manufacturer must purchase raw materials. When the materials are purchased, the purchase invoices are the source documents for the journal entries. The Materials account is debited and the Accounts Payable account is credited.

The Boyd Chair Company purchased rough-cut lumber from Southern Lumber Supplies at a net cost of $40,000. The entry is recorded as shown on page 217. The materials received are also entered on the *stores ledger card.*

If a business uses only a few types of materials, only one Materials account is used. However, a business that has an inventory of many types of materials may keep a materials controlling account in the general ledger and a separate materials subsidiary ledger. In this case,

	GENERAL JOURNAL			Page 1
DATE	ACCOUNT TITLE AND EXPLANATION	POST. REF.	DEBIT	CREDIT
19— July 1	Materials . . . . Accounts Payable/Southern Lumber Supplies . . . . Purchase lumber on credit.	121 211/√	40,000 00	40,000 00

Entry for purchase invoice for $40,000 of lumber. Lumber received is also entered on stores ledger card.

Materials	121		Accounts Payable	211
19— July 1 J1 40,000			19— July 1 J1 40,000	

the materials subsidiary ledger consists of a separate stores ledger card for each type of material, as explained in Chapter 5. Each time raw materials are purchased, the stores ledger cards must be increased. When the raw materials are used, the stores ledger cards are decreased.

Milling Department Costs

The Boyd Chair Company manufactured 5,000 chairs during July. The procedures that were followed to record moving the materials and costs from the stores department into production are given here. As you read the procedures, you should refer to the chart on page 213.

Direct and Indirect Materials. Materials requisition forms are issued when the milling department needs materials. On July 2 a materials requisition form was issued for $11,000 of materials. The form is shown at the top of page 218. The saw blades for $1,000 were indirect materials. The other items ($10,000) were direct materials.

The Work-in-Process—Milling Department account is increased for the cost of direct materials. The Work-in-Process—Milling Department account is an asset inventory account. Thus the account must be debited for $10,000 to show the increase. The Factory Overhead account is increased by $1,000, the cost of the indirect materials. The Factory Overhead account is a cost account. Thus it also must be debited. The asset Materials account is credited to reduce the account for the total amount of materials issued ($10,000 + $1,000 = $11,000).

BOYD CHAIR COMPANY

MATERIALS REQUISITION
No. **107**

Deliver to Milling Department

Date July 2, 19--

Charge: Job No. M14, Standard Chair

Account 122 $10,000

Account 501   1,000

Quantity	Material No.	Description	Unit Price	Amount
5,000	940	Seat	0.50	2,500
10,000	941	Legs, Front	0.20	2,000
10,000	942	Legs, Rear	0.30	3,000
5,000	943	Brace, Top	0.35	1,750
5,000	944	Brace, Middle	0.15	750
25	84K6	Saw Blades	40.00	1,000
				Total 11,000

Approved by J. M.   Delivered by R C   Received by Tom M.

COPY 2 — STORES DEPARTMENT

The materials requisition form provides the data for this transaction. The transaction is recorded in the **materials requisition journal,** a special journal used to record the materials charged to production. The entries are posted from the materials requisition journal to the general ledger.

				WORK-IN-PROCESS—MILLING DEPARTMENT DEBIT 122	WORK-IN-PROCESS—ASSEMBLING DEPARTMENT DEBIT 123	WORK-IN-PROCESS—FINISHING DEPARTMENT DEBIT 124	FACTORY OVERHEAD DEBIT 501	MATERIALS CREDIT 121
DATE		REQ. NO.	DEPARTMENT					
19— July	2	107	Milling...	10,000 00			1,000 00	11,000 00

MATERIALS REQUISITION JOURNAL   Page *1*

Entry for direct and indirect materials requisitioned by milling department.

Materials 121		Work-in-Process—Milling Department 122	Factory Overhead 501
19— July 1 J1 40,000	19— July 2 MR1 11,000	19— July 2 MR1 10,000	19— July 2 MR1 1,000

Direct and Indirect Labor. The analysis of labor costs sheet is used to separate the total labor costs between direct and indirect labor. The sheet is the source document for recording the distribution of labor costs in the general journal.

BOYD CHAIR COMPANY
Analysis of Labor Costs
For the Month Ended July 31, 19—

Department	Direct Labor Cost	Indirect Labor Cost	Total Cost
Milling	$ 5,000	$2,000	$7,000
Assembling	4,500	1,500	6,000
Finishing	3,500	1,500	5,000
Totals	$13,000	$5,000	$18,000

The cost of direct labor for the milling department ($5,000) is recorded as an increase to the Work-in-Process—Milling Department account. Indirect labor costs ($2,000) are recorded as an increase to the Factory Overhead account. The total labor costs (direct and indirect) are credited to the Factory Payroll account. The general journal here shows the entry to distribute the total milling department labor costs of $7,000 for July.

GENERAL JOURNAL Page 2

DATE	ACCOUNT TITLE AND EXPLANATION	POST. REF.	DEBIT	CREDIT
19—				
July 31	Work-in-Process—Milling Department	122	5,000 00	
	Factory Overhead	501	2,000 00	
	Factory Payroll	502		7,000 00
	Distribute direct and indirect labor.			

Entry for direct and indirect labor costs for the milling department.

Work-in-Process—Milling Department 122		Factory Overhead 501		Factory Payroll 502	
19—		19—		19—	19—
July 2 MR1 10,000		July 2 MR1 1,000		July 31 J1 *18,000	July 31 J2 7,000
31 J2 5,000		31 J2 2,000			

* Note: This debit is part of the entry to record the payment of the factory payroll.

Factory Overhead Costs. The factory overhead costs must be applied to the products as they pass through each production department. The costs are usually applied by first estimating the yearly amount of factory overhead. Then a certain part of the yearly amount is applied to each job every month. One way is to estimate factory overhead costs as a percent of the direct labor costs. The percentage rate used for estimating factory overhead during the year is called the **predetermined overhead rate.**

Each month a certain amount of the yearly rate is applied. The Boyd Chair Company estimates its overhead rate as a percent of the direct labor charged to a processing department. The predetermined factory overhead rate for the milling department is estimated to be 80 percent of direct labor costs. Thus estimated factory overhead applied in July to the milling department is $4,000 ($5,000 × 80 percent = $4,000).

Estimated Factory Overhead	=	Predetermined Overhead Rate	×	Direct Labor Costs
$4,000	=	80%	×	$5,000

The entry for the factory overhead applied is recorded in the general journal. The Work-in-Process—Milling Department account (an asset) is increased. Thus the account is debited for $4,000. The Factory Overhead account (a cost account) is decreased by a credit for $4,000.

GENERAL JOURNAL Page 2

DATE	ACCOUNT TITLE AND EXPLANATION	POST. REF.	DEBIT	CREDIT
19—				
July 31	Work-in-Process—Milling Department	122	4,000 00	
	Factory Overhead	501		4,000 00
	Record overhead applied.			

Work-in-Process—Milling Department	122		Factory Overhead	501
19—			19—	19—
July 2 MRI 10,000			July 2 MRI 1,000	July 31 J2 4,000
31 J2 5,000			31 J2 2,000	
31 J2 4,000				

Entry for applied factory overhead to milling department.

Work in Process. As the milling department completes its work, the pieces are sent to the assembling department. This transfer of units from one department to the next must be recorded in the accounting records. The entry in the general journal contains a debit to the Work-in-Process—Assembling Department account to increase the account for the units received by the assembly department. The entry contains a credit to the Work-in-Process—Milling Department account to decrease the account for the units transferred to the assembly department from the milling department. Both accounts are assets.

The general journal entry shown here records the transfer of $19,000 from the milling department to the assembling department. This amount represents the total cost of the direct materials, direct labor, and applied factory overhead used to process the 5,000 chairs in the milling department.

	GENERAL JOURNAL			Page 2
DATE	ACCOUNT TITLE AND EXPLANATION	POST. REF.	DEBIT	CREDIT
19— July 31	Work-in-Process—Assembling Department . . . . Work-in-Process—Milling Department . . . . Record transfer of 5,000 unassembled chairs.	123 122	19,000 00	19,000 00

Entry to transfer costs for 5,000 unassembled chairs from the milling department to the assembling department.

Work-in-Process— Milling Department		122		Work-in-Process— Assembling Department		123
19— July 2 MR1 31 J2 31 J2	10,000 5,000 4,000	19— July 31 J2	19,000	19— July 31 J2	19,000	
	19,000		19,000			

The unit cost of each milled but unassembled chair at this point is $3.80. This unit cost is found by dividing the total milling costs by the number of units produced ($19,000 ÷ 5,000 = $3.80).

The chart on page 222 shows the flow of costs through the milling department.

$$\$3.80 = \frac{\$10,000 + \$5,000 + \$4,000}{5,000}$$

STORES DEPARTMENT AND GENERAL ACCOUNTING	PRODUCTION DEPARTMENTS			WAREHOUSE	SALES
	Milling	Assembling	Finishing		

Work-in-Process-- Milling Department

	Milled Goods Out 19,000

Work-in-Process-- Assembling Department

Milled Goods In → 19,000

Materials

Materials Purchased 40,000	Materials Used
	Milling Department 11,000

Direct Materials 10,000

Factory Payroll

Salaries Earned 18,000	Salaries Distributed
	Milling Department 7,000

Direct Labor 5,000

Factory Overhead

Indirect Materials 1,000	Applied Overhead
Indirect Labor 2,000	Milling Department 4,000

Applied Overhead 4,000

19,000	19,000	19,000

THE FLOW OF COSTS IN MANUFACTURING CHAIRS

Activity B-1. Explain each of the following terms. You may want to refer to Chapter 5 for help in understanding the meanings of the terms.

1. Analysis of Labor Costs Sheet
2. Estimated Factory Overhead
3. Materials Requisition Form
4. Materials Requisition Journal
5. Predetermined Overhead Rate
6. Stores Ledger Card

Activity B-2. Answer the following questions about the purchase of raw materials and the manufacturing costs for the milling department. Refer to the text and illustrations on pages 216 to 222.

1. Which account is debited on July 1 for the purchase of lumber on credit? Which account is credited?

2. Where is the entry recorded for the purchase of lumber on credit?

3. What is the number of the materials requisition form listing the materials needed by the milling department? What is the amount of the direct materials requested? What was the amount of the indirect materials requested?

4. Where is Materials Requisition 107 recorded? Which account(s) is (are) debited? credited?

5. What are the total labor costs for the milling department for the month ended July 31?

6. Of the total labor costs, how much is direct and indirect labor?

7. Which journal is used to record the milling department payroll? Which accounts are debited? credited?

8. Which journal is used to record the factory overhead applied to the milling department? Which account is debited? credited?

9. How many unassembled chairs are transferred from milling to assembling in July?

10. Which general journal entry records the transfer of unassembled chairs from the milling department to the assembling department?

11. What is the total cost of the unassembled chairs transferred from the milling department to the assembling department?

12. What is the unit cost of the unassembled chairs transferred from the milling department? How is this computed?

Assembling Department Costs

C *Are the costs for the assembling department recorded in the same way as the costs for the milling department?* Yes, the costs in each production department are recorded in a similar way. The costs for the direct and indirect materials, direct and indirect labor, and factory overhead costs must be recorded. Then an entry is made to record the goods completed and transferred to another department.

During July pieces for 5,000 chairs were processed in the milling department. The pieces were sent to the assembling department to be fitted into unfinished chairs. The cost of the milled goods is $19,000, which is recorded as a debit in the Work-in-Process—Assembling Department account.

Direct and Indirect Materials. No additional direct materials were used in the assembling department. Thus there is no entry needed. Indirect materials (sandpaper and special cloths to clean the sanded chairs) costing $2,000 were used. The materials requisition form is used to request these materials from stores. The transaction is recorded in the materials requisition journal.

Indirect materials (sandpaper and cloths) requisitioned during month: $2,000

			WORK-IN-PROCESS—MILLING DEPARTMENT DEBIT 122	WORK-IN-PROCESS—ASSEMBLING DEPARTMENT DEBIT 123	WORK-IN-PROCESS—FINISHING DEPARTMENT DEBIT 124	FACTORY OVERHEAD DEBIT 501	MATERIALS CREDIT 121
DATE	REQ. NO.	DEPARTMENT					
19— July 2	107	Milling...	10,000 00			1,000 00	11,000 00
2	108	Assembling				2,000 00	2,000 00

MATERIALS REQUISITION JOURNAL   Page *1*

Entry for indirect materials requisitioned by assembling department.

	Materials		121		Factory Overhead		501
19—	19—			19—		19—	
July 1 J1 40,000	July 2 MR1	11,000		July 2 MR1	1,000	July 31 J2	4,000
	2 MR1	2,000		31 J2	2,000		
				2 MR1	2,000		

Direct and Indirect Labor. Direct and indirect factory payroll costs for the assembling department are recorded from the analysis of labor costs sheet. The costs are recorded in the same way shown for the milling department labor costs. The total labor costs for the assembling department was $6,000. Direct labor was $4,500, and indirect labor was $1,500. The entry to record these labor costs contains a debit to the Work-in-Process—Assembling Department account for $4,500 and a debit to the Factory Overhead account for $1,500. The Factory Payroll account is credited for $6,000. The entry is recorded in the general journal. (See journal entry on page 225.)

Factory Overhead Costs. The applied factory overhead costs are recorded in the same manner as they were for the milling department. Again, assume a predetermined factory overhead rate of 80 percent of the direct labor costs is used. Thus the estimated factory overhead applied in July is $3,600 ($4,500 × 80 percent = $3,600). The entry in the general journal records the applied factory overhead for the assembling department. (See journal entry on page 225.)

Estimated Factory Overhead	=	Predetermined Overhead Rate	×	Direct Labor Costs
$3,600	=	80%		× $4,500

BOYD CHAIR COMPANY
Analysis of Labor Costs
For the Month Ended July 31, 19—

Department	Direct Labor Cost	Indirect Labor Cost	Total Cost
Milling	$ 5,000	$2,000	$7,000
Assembling	4,500	1,500	6,000
Finishing	3,500	1,500	5,000
Totals	$13,000	$5,000	$18,000

Work in Process. The assembling department sends the completed chairs to the finishing department to be stained and lacquered. The transfer of units between departments must also be recorded.

The entire 5,000 chairs were assembled during July. The total cost of these chairs to this point is $27,100. This represents the total cost of the milled goods ($19,000), the direct labor in the assembling department ($4,500), and the applied factory overhead ($3,600). Remember there were no direct materials used in the assembling department. The general journal entry to record the transfer contains a debit of $27,100 to increase the Work-in-Process—Finishing Department account and a credit to decrease the Work-in-Process—Assembling Department account. Both accounts are assets.

		GENERAL JOURNAL			Page 3
DATE		ACCOUNT TITLE AND EXPLANATION	POST. REF.	DEBIT	CREDIT
19—					
July	31	Work-in-Process—Assembling			
		Department	123	4,500 00	
		Factory Overhead	501	1,500 00	
		Factory Payroll	502		6,000 00
		Distribute direct and indirect labor.			
	31	Work-in-Process—Assembling			
		Department	123	3,600 00	
		Factory Overhead	501		3,600 00
		Record overhead applied.			
	31	Work-in-Process—Finishing			
		Department	124	27,100 00	
		Work-in-Process—Assembling			
		Department	123		27,100 00
		Record transfer of 5,000 unfinished chairs.			

Entry for direct and indirect labor costs for the assembling department.

Entry for applied factory overhead to assembling department.

Entry to transfer costs for 5,000 unfinished chairs from the assembling department to the finishing department.

Work-in-Process—Assembling Department			123
19—		19—	
July 31 J2	19,000	July 31 J3	27,100
31 J3	4,500		
31	3,600		
	27,100		27,100

Work-in-Process—Finishing Department			124
19—			
July 31 J3	27,100		

Factory Overhead			501
19—		19—	
July 2 MR1	1,000	July 31 J2	4,000
31 J2	2,000	31 J3	3,600
2 MR1	2,000		
31 J3	1,500		

Factory Payroll			502
19—		19—	
July 31 J1	18,000	July 31 J2	7,000
		31 J3	6,000

$5.42 = \dfrac{\$19,000 + \$4,500 + \$3,600}{5,000}$

The unit cost of each assembled but unfinished chair is found by dividing the total milling and assembling costs ($27,100) by the number of assembled chairs (5,000). The unit cost here is $27,100 ÷ 5,000 = $5.42. The chart shown here shows the flow of costs through the assembling department.

STORES DEPARTMENT AND GENERAL ACCOUNTING		PRODUCTION DEPARTMENTS			WAREHOUSE	SALES
		Milling	Assembling	Finishing		
		Work-in-Process--Milling Department	Work-in-Process--Assembling Department	Work-in-Process--Finishing Department		
		Milled Goods Out 19,000—	Milled Goods In →19,000 / Assembled Goods Out 27,100—	Assembled Goods In →27,100		
Materials						
Materials Purchased 40,000	Materials Used					
	Milling Department 11,000	Direct Materials 10,000				
	Assembling Department 2,000					
Factory Payroll						
Salaries Earned 18,000	Salaries Distributed					
	Milling Department 7,000	Direct Labor 5,000				
	Assembling Department 6,000		Direct Labor 4,500			
Factory Overhead						
Indirect Materials	Applied Overhead					
1,000 + 2,000	Milling Department 4,000	Applied Overhead 4,000				
Indirect Labor 2,000 + 1,500	Assembling Department 3,600		Applied Overhead 3,600			
		19,000 19,000	27,100	27,100		

THE FLOW OF COSTS IN MANUFACTURING CHAIRS

Activity C. Answer the following questions about the manufacturing costs of the assembling department. Refer to the text and illustrations on pages 223 to 226.

1. Why is no cost recorded for direct materials used by the assembling department in July?

2. What is the cost of indirect materials used by the assembling department in July?

3. Where is the entry recorded that shows the cost of materials used by the assembling department?
4. Which account is debited for the materials used? Which account is credited?
5. What is the total labor cost for the assembling department for the month ended July 31? How much is the direct labor? the indirect labor?
6. What is the estimated factory overhead for the assembling

department for July? Which general journal entry is made to record the estimated factory overhead?
7. What is the total of the manufacturing costs debited to the Work-in-Process—Assembling Department account in July?
8. What entry is made to transfer the cost of the assembled chairs to the next department?
9. What is the unit cost of the chairs after they leave the assembling department?

Finishing Department Costs

D *Are the costs for the finishing department recorded in the same manner as the costs for the milling department and the assembling department?* Yes, because the finishing department is a production department. Thus the costs are recorded in the same way.

The cost of the 5,000 chairs assembled and transferred to the finishing department in July was $27,100. This amount is shown on the debit side of the Work-in-Process—Finishing Department account. The way that the costs for the work done in the finishing department are recorded is described here.

Direct and Indirect Materials. The finishing department adds metal "feet" to the legs of the chairs. These feet (direct materials) are requested on a materials requisition form. The cost is $1,000. Indirect materials (stain, lacquer, and miscellaneous items) costing $1,000 are also used. The materials requisition form is recorded in the materials requisition journal by debiting the Work-in-Process—Finishing Department account for the direct materials ($1,000) and debiting the

Direct materials (metal feet) requisitioned during month: $1,000 (Requisition 109).

Indirect materials (stain, lacquer, etc.) requisitioned during month: $1,000 (Requisition 109).

			WORK-IN-PROCESS—MILLING DEPARTMENT DEBIT 122	WORK-IN-PROCESS—ASSEMBLING DEPARTMENT DEBIT 123	WORK-IN-PROCESS—FINISHING DEPARTMENT DEBIT 124	FACTORY OVERHEAD DEBIT 501	MATERIALS CREDIT 121
MATERIALS REQUISITION JOURNAL							**Page 1**
DATE	REQ. NO.	DEPARTMENT					
19—							
July 2	107	Milling...	10,000 00			1,000 00	11,000 00
2	108	Assembling				2,000 00	2,000 00
2	109	Finishing .			1,000 00	1,000 00	2,000 00

Entry for direct and indirect materials requisitioned by finishing department.

	Materials		121		Work-in-Process—Finishing Department		124		Factory Overhead		501

	Materials 121
19— July 1 J1 40,000	19— July 2 MR1 11,100 2 MR1 2,000 2 MR1 2,000

	Work-in-Process—Finishing Department 124
19— July 31 J3 27,100 2 MR1 1,000	

	Factory Overhead 501
19— July 2 MR1 1,000 31 J2 2,000 2 MR1 2,000 31 J3 1,500 2 MR1 1,000	19— July 31 J2 4,000 31 J3 3,600

Factory Overhead account for the indirect materials ($1,000). The Materials account is credited for the total materials used ($2,000).

Direct and Indirect Labor. Total labor costs are also separated into direct labor and indirect labor for the finishing department. The analysis of labor costs sheet shows total labor of $5,000. Direct labor is $3,500, and the indirect labor is $1,500. The transaction is recorded in the general journal. The Work-in-Process—Finishing Department account is debited for $3,500, the amount of direct labor. The Factory Overhead account is debited for $1,500, the amount of the indirect labor. The Factory Payroll account is credited for $5,000. (See journal entry on page 229.)

BOYD CHAIR COMPANY
Analysis of Labor Costs
For the Month Ended July 31, 19—

Department	Direct Labor Cost	Indirect Labor Cost	Total Cost
Milling	$ 5,000	$2,000	$ 7,000
Assembling	4,500	1,500	6,000
Finishing	3,500	1,500	5,000
Totals	$13,000	$5,000	$18,000

Factory Overhead Costs. The applied factory overhead costs for the finishing department are recorded at the same rate as for the other departments. Thus the predetermined factory overhead applied is $2,800 ($3,500 × 80 percent = $2,800). The general journal entry to record this amount for July includes a debit to the Work-in-Process—Finishing Department account for $2,800. The Factory Overhead account is credited for $2,800. (See journal entry on page 229.)

Estimated Factory Overhead	=	Predetermined Overhead Rate	×	Direct Labor Costs
$2,800	=	80%	×	$3,500

Work in Process. The manufacturing process is completed in the finishing department. The completed chairs are transferred to the warehouse and stored until they are sold and shipped to customers. The entry to record the transfer of the completed chairs from the finishing department to the warehouse during July is shown here. The total cost of the finished chairs is $34,400. This cost is found by adding the direct materials, direct labor costs, and applied factory overhead costs for the finishing department to the costs transferred from the assembling department. The Work-in-Process—Finishing Department account is credited for the total costs. The Finished Goods account, an asset, is debited to show the increase in finished goods.

		GENERAL JOURNAL			Page 4	
DATE		ACCOUNT TITLE AND EXPLANATION	POST. REF.	DEBIT	CREDIT	
19—						
July	31	Work-in-Process—Finishing Department	124	3,500 00		Entry for direct and indirect labor costs for the finishing department.
		Factory Overhead	501	1,500 00		
		Factory Payroll	502		5,000 00	
		Distribute direct and indirect labor.				
	31	Work-in-Process—Finishing Department	124	2,800 00		Entry for applied factory overhead to finishing department.
		Factory Overhead	501		2,800 00	
		Record overhead applied.				
	31	Finished Goods	125	34,400 00		Entry to transfer costs for 5,000 finished chairs from the finishing department to the warehouse.
		Work-in-Process—Finishing Department	124		34,400 00	
		Record transfer of 5,000 finished chairs.				

Work-in-Process—Finishing Department 124

19—			19—		
July 31 J3	27,100		July 31 J4	34,400	
2 MR1	1,000				
31 J4	3,500				
31 J4	2,800				

Finished Goods 125

19—		
July 31 J4	34,400	

Factory Overhead 501

19—			19—		
July 2 MR1	1,000		July 31 J2	4,000	
31 J2	2,000				
2 MR1	2,000		31 J3	3,600	
31 J3	1,500		31 J4	2,800	
2 MR1	1,000				
31 J4	1,500				

Factory Payroll 502

19—			19—		
July 31 J1	18,000		July 31 J2	7,000	
			31 J3	6,000	
			31 J4	5,000	

$$\$6.88 = \frac{\$34,400}{5,000}$$

The unit cost of each finished product is found by dividing the total manufacturing costs by the number of units produced. The unit cost of

THE FLOW OF COSTS IN MANUFACTURING CHAIRS

the chairs transferred from the finishing department during July is
$6.88 ($34,400 ÷ 5,000 = $6.88).

  The chart on page 230 shows the flow of costs from the stores department to finished goods. Note that gross profit on sales ($13,100) is also
shown as the difference between sales revenue and finished goods sold
($47,500 − $34,400 = $13,100).

Activity D. Answer the following questions about the manufacturing
costs for the finishing department. Refer to the text and illustrations
on pages 227 to 230.

1. What is the cost of the 5,000
chairs transferred to the finishing
department in July?

2. What is the cost of direct materials added to the chairs in the finishing department?

3. What is the cost of indirect materials used by the finishing department?

4. Which entry is made to record
the materials used by the finishing
department? Which journal is used
to record this entry?

5. What is the total cost of labor
used in the finishing department in
July?

6. How much of the total labor cost
is for direct labor? for indirect
labor?

7. Which report summarizes the
monthly labor costs by departments?

8. How much factory overhead is
applied to the chairs in the finishing department?

9. Which entry is made to record
the factory overhead?

10. What is the total cost of the
5,000 chairs after they are processed through the finishing department? What is the unit cost?

11. Which general journal entry is
made to transfer the cost of the
completed chairs from the finishing
department?

12. What happens to the chairs
after they leave the finishing department?

Selling the Finished Goods

E *Which entries are made to record the costs after the finished goods
leave the production department?* The costs of the finished goods
in the warehouse are shown in the Finished Goods account. When the
goods are sold, the costs are transferred from the Finished Goods account to the Cost of Goods Sold account.

  The finished chairs are kept in the warehouse until they are sold.
The cost of the completed chairs, shown in the Finished Goods account, is $34,400.

  When several products are produced, an inventory card is usually
kept for each product. These cards are used to maintain a perpetual
inventory of the finished products.

  When the goods are sold, two entries must be made. One entry records the sale. The second entry records an increase in the cost of
goods sold and a decrease in finished goods.

Recording the Sale. The entry to record the sale increases the asset received (Cash or Accounts Receivable) and increases owner's equity (revenue). If all the chairs are sold for $47,500 on credit on July 31, the following entry would be made.

		SALES JOURNAL			Page 1	
DATE	INVOICE NO.	ACCOUNT DEBITED	TERMS	POST. REF.	AMOUNT	
19— July 31	101	Nationwide Furniture Company	2/10, n/30	√	47,500	00

Entry for sale of 5,000
chairs on credit.

Recording the Cost of Goods Sold. Another entry is needed to record the decrease in finished goods ($34,400) and the increase in costs. The Finished Goods account, an asset, is credited to show the decrease. The Cost of Goods Sold account, a cost, is debited for $34,400 to show the decrease in owner's equity caused by the cost of the chairs.

		GENERAL JOURNAL			Page 5		
DATE		ACCOUNT TITLE AND EXPLANATION	POST. REF.	DEBIT		CREDIT	
19— July	31	Cost of Goods Sold............ Finished Goods .... Sold 5,000 chairs to Nationwide Furniture Co.	511 125	34,400	00	34,400	00

Entry for decrease in
cost of finished goods.

Accounts Receivable		111
19— July 31 S1	47,500	

Finished Goods			125
19— July 31 J4	34,400	19— July 31 J5	34,400

Sales		401
	19— July 31 S1	47,500

Cost of Goods Sold		511
19— July 31 J5	34,400	

Gross Profit on Sales. The two entries to record the sale of finished goods both affect owner's equity. The credit sale increases revenue and increases owner's equity by $47,500. The decrease in finished goods decreases owner's equity by $34,400. Thus manufacturing and selling the 5,000 chairs produces a gross profit on sales of $13,100 ($47,500 − $34,400 = $13,100).

Activity E. Answer the following questions on finished goods. Refer to the text and illustrations on pages 231 to 233.

1. Which company is buying the 5,000 finished chairs?

2. What is the total sales price of the chairs? the unit sales price?

3. Which entry is made to record the sale of the chairs? Which journal is used?

4. Which entry is made to transfer the cost of the 5,000 chairs from the Finished Goods account?

5. What kind of account is the Cost of Goods Sold account?

6. What effect does the cost of goods sold have on owner's equity?

Topic 1   Problems

6-1. For each transaction here, indicate in which journal the entry should be recorded and the account to be debited and credited.

SILVERMAN'S MANUFACTURING COMPANY

Transaction	Journal	Account(s) Debited	Account(s) Credited
EXAMPLE: Purchased raw materials on credit.	General Journal	Materials	Accounts Payable

a. Requisitioned direct materials for use in cutting department.
b. Recorded distribution of direct and indirect labor for cutting department.
c. Requisitioned indirect materials for use in sanding department.
d. Recorded factory overhead applied to finishing department
e. Transferred units from cutting department to sanding department.
f. Ordered indirect materials for the finishing department.
g. Recorded distribution of direct and indirect labor costs for sanding department.
h. Transferred units from the sanding department to the finishing department.
i. Recorded distribution of direct and indirect labor costs for the finishing department.
j. Transferred units from the finishing department to the warehouse.
k. Sold units on credit.
l. Recorded the decrease in finished goods.

6-2. You have been hired as a cost clerk by Ferrell Electronics. Your duties include recording and posting transactions involving the two assembling departments that make small calculators. The journals used are the materials requisition journal and the general journal. The ledger accounts used are listed here.

Accounts

Assets
111   Accounts Receivable
121   Materials
122   Work-in-Process—Assembling
       Department 1
123   Work-in-Process—Assembling
       Department 2
124   Finished Goods

Liabilities
211   Accounts Payable

Revenue
401   Sales

Factory Costs
501   Factory Overhead
502   Factory Payroll
511   Cost of Goods Sold

Other Information

FERRELL ELECTRONICS
Analysis of Labor Costs
For the Month Ended November 30, 19—

Department	Direct Labor Cost	Indirect Labor Cost	Total
Assembling Department 1	$ 7,200	$1,500	$ 8,700
Assembling Department 2	5,800	1,100	6,900
Total	$13,000	$2,600	$15,600

Materials are started in production in Assembly Department 1 and are then transferred to Assembly Department 2 as they are completed. However, the transfer of manufacturing costs of the calculators from one department to another are recorded only at the end of the month.

a. Record the following transactions for November in the appropriate journal.

b. Post the November transactions to the proper accounts. Pencil-foot the work-in-process accounts.

c. What were the total manufacturing costs for Assembling Department 1? for Assembling Department 2?

d. What was the unit cost of the products transferred to the Finished Goods account from Assembling Department 2?

Nov.   2 Bought materials for $60,000 on credit from Texas Supply Inc.
       5 Requisitioned the following materials by Assembling Department 1 on Materials Requisition 203: Direct Materials,

$20,000; Indirect Materials, $3,000.

Nov. 5 Requisitioned the following materials by Assembling Department 2 on Materials Requisition 204: Direct Materials, $10,000; Indirect Materials, $2,500.

30 Recorded distribution of factory payroll for Assembling Department 1: Direct Labor, $7,200; Indirect Labor, $1,500.

30 Recorded applied overhead for Assembling Department 1. Overhead rate is 80 percent of direct labor cost.

30 Recorded the transfer of

costs for 1,000 unfinished calculators from Assembling Department 1 to Assembling Department 2.

Nov. 30 Recorded distribution of factory payroll for Assembling Department 2: Direct Labor, $5,800; Indirect Labor, $1,100.

30 Recorded applied factory overhead for Assembling Department 2. Overhead rate is 80 percent of direct labor cost.

30 Recorded the transfer of costs for the 1,000 calculators from Assembling Department 2 to the warehouse.

6-3. On December 12 Ferrell Electronics sold the 1,000 calculators produced in Topic Problem 6-2 to Jax Discount Stores on credit. The total sales price on Invoice F2317 was $68,000. Use the working papers from Topic Problem 6-2 to do the following.
a. Record the sale of the calculators.   **c.** Compute the unit sales price.
b. Record the decrease in finished goods.

Topic 2
Equivalent Units of Production

A *Do production departments have beginning and ending work-in-process inventories?* Yes, usually there are partially completed items in inventory at the beginning and at the end of the accounting period. Our discussion of a process cost system in Topic 1 assumed that there was no beginning inventory in any of the work-in-process accounts. We also assumed that all units of materials put into production during the accounting period were completely processed. Thus there were no ending inventories in the milling department, assembling department, or finishing department.

In most cases, however, not all units are completed during an accounting period. Units that are not completed at the end of an accounting period become the **ending work-in-process inventory** for that department. In process cost accounting the ending inventory must be used to find the department's total processing costs.

Ending Work-in-Process Inventory

In Topic 1 the milling department completely processed 5,000 units during July. In August the milling department also began processing 5,000 units. But it completed only 4,600 units. Also, the remaining 400 units were only 25 percent completed. The 400 partially completed units are the ending inventory for the milling department.

Milling Department—August	Units
Units Started in Production	5,000 (Started)
Units Transferred to Assembling Department	4,600 (Completed and transferred)
Work in Process at End of Period	400 (Remaining in process)
Stage of Completion	25% (Stage of completion of units remaining in process)

The processing costs of the milling department must now be divided between the 4,600 completed units and the ending inventory of 400 partially completed units. To do this, the accountant must determine a number called the equivalent units of production. The **equivalent units of production (EUP)** is the number of whole units that would have been produced if there had not been a beginning inventory or an ending inventory. The EUP is found by multiplying the actual number of completed units transferred and the partially completed units in ending inventory by their percentages of completion. The EUP for the milling department at the end of August is found as follows.

Milling Department—August	Actual Units	×	Percent Completed	=	Equivalent Units of Production
a. Units Completed and Transferred	4,600	×	100%	=	4,600
b. Units Partially Completed in Ending Inventory	400	×	25	=	100
c. Total for Accounting Period	5,000				4,700

This example shows that completely processing 4,700 units (C) is equal to completely processing 4,600 units (A) and partially processing

400 units (B). The average number of completed units processed by the milling department during August was 4,700.

The stage of completion may be different for materials, labor, and applied factory overhead. Some businesses, for example, may take all the materials needed to process the products at one time. In the Boyd Chair Company, only the materials to be worked on are transferred from the stores department to the milling department. For example, the 400 units in the ending inventory that are 25 percent completed represent the braces for 400 chairs. The milling department has not received the materials for the seats and legs, which represent 75 percent of the costs. In our illustration the percent completed will be the same for materials, labor, and applied factory overhead.

Activity A-1. Answer the following questions about the milling department and the computation of EUP. Refer to the text and illustrations on pages 235 to 237.

1. How many units are completed in the milling department in July?
2. How many units are started in the milling department in August?
3. How many of these units are completed and transferred during August?
4. How many units are in the August ending work-in-process inventory of the milling department?
5. What is the stage of completion of the units in the August ending inventory?
6. What is the August EUP for the milling department?

Activity A-2. Listed here is data about the monthly EUP production in a manufacturing department. Compute the EUP for each item.

1. Units completed and transferred, 7,000; units in ending inventory (partially processed), 600 units, 20 percent completed.
2. Units completed and transferred, 10,500; units in ending inventory (partially completed), 2,000 units, 30 percent completed.
3. Units completed and transferred, 21,000; units in ending inventory (partially completed), 15,000 units, 60 percent completed.

Allocating Processing Costs

B *How are the processing costs allocated to units?* Once the EUP is known, the total processing costs for the milling department can be allocated. The costs are allocated between (1) the units that are completed and transferred to the assembling department and (2) the units that are only partially completed and still in the milling department.

Let's see how the total processing costs would be allocated when there is an ending work-in-process inventory. Refer to the illustration shown at the top of page 238.

Processing Costs Are Allocated to:
- Units completed and transferred
- Units partially completed and still in department

1. Unit Cost per EUP =

$$\frac{\text{Total Processing Costs}}{\text{EUP}}$$

$$\$3.80 = \frac{\$17,860}{4,700}$$

2. Total Costs for Completed Units =

EUP for Completed Units ×
Unit Cost per EUP
$17,480 = 4,600 × $3.80

3. Total Costs for Partially Completed Units =

EUP for Partially Completed Units ×
Unit Cost per EUP
$380 = 100 × $3.80

4. Total Processing Costs =

Total Costs for Completed Units +
Total Costs for Partially Completed Units
$17,860 = $17,480 + $380

Work-in-Process—
Milling Department

August 31, 19—	
Direct	
Materials	*9,400*
Direct Labor	*4,700*
Applied	
Overhead	*3,760*
Total	
Processing	
Costs	*17,860*

In August the total processing costs for the milling department are $17,860. (This included direct materials of $9,400, direct labor of $4,700, and applied factory overhead of $3,760.) These costs would be allocated using the following steps.

STEP 1. *Compute the unit cost per EUP.* Divide the total processing costs by the equivalent units of production. The EUP for the milling department was 4,700. Thus the unit cost is $3.80 per EUP.

STEP 2. *Compute the total costs for the completed units.* Multiply the unit cost per EUP by the EUP for completed units. The milling department completed 4,600 units at a cost of $3.80 each. Thus processing costs of $17,480 are applied to the completed units.

STEP 3. *Compute the total costs for the partially completed units.* Multiply the unit cost per EUP by the EUP for partially completed units. The milling department had 100 EUP for partially completed units. Therefore, processing costs of $380 are applied to the partially completed units in the ending Work-in-Process Inventory.

STEP 4. *Verify the total processing costs.* Add the total costs for the completed units and the total costs for the partially completed units. The total must equal the total processing costs. The total processing costs for the milling department are $17,860.

Activity B-1. Answer the following questions about the processing costs for the milling department. Refer to the text and illustrations on pages 237 and 238.

1. What are the total processing costs for the milling department in August?

2. How much of the total processing costs is for direct materials? direct labor? factory overhead?

3. What is the processing cost for each EUP?

4. How is the unit cost per EUP computed?

5. What are the total processing costs for the 4,600 completed units?

6. How is this total computed?

7. How many EUP units are in the ending work-in-process inventory for August?

8. What is the total cost for the partially completed units in the ending inventory?

9. How is the cost of the partially completed ending inventory computed?

10. What is the total cost of the 4,600 completed units and the 100 EUP included in the ending inventory?

11. What are the total processing costs for the milling department in August?

12. Does your answer to question 11 equal your answer to question 10? Should it or shouldn't it? Explain.

Activity B-2. The steps for allocating processing costs are listed on page 239. Arrange the steps in the correct order. Number the steps from 1 to 4 to indicate the correct order.

Compute the total costs for the partially completed units.
Compute the total costs for the completed units.

Verify the total processing costs.
Compute the unit cost for each EUP.

Beginning Work-in-Process Inventory

C *Is the EUP also computed for a beginning inventory?* Yes, the equivalent units of production are also computed when there is a beginning inventory in a processing department. The ending inventory for one accounting period becomes the beginning inventory for the next period. In the previous example the milling department had an August ending inventory of 400 units that were 25 percent completed and 75 percent partially completed. Thus the beginning inventory for the next period is 400 units.

Assume that during September, the next accounting period, the milling department completed the 400 units in the beginning inventory and started 6,000 additional units. It completed and transferred 5,400 units to the assembling department. There were 1,000 units 50 percent completed in the ending inventory.

Milling Department—September	Actual Units
Units in Beginning Inventory	400
Units Started in Production From Stores Department	6,000
Total Units in Production	6,400
Units Transferred to Assembling Department	5,400
Work in Process at End of Period	1,000
Stage of Completion	50%

Computing the EUP

The EUP for the milling department would be computed as shown in the following steps.

STEP 1. *Compute the EUP for the units that were in the beginning inventory and were completed.* Multiply the beginning inventory (400) by the percent it took to complete them. In the example the items were 25 percent completed. Thus it took another 75 percent to finish the units. The EUP for completing the units in the beginning inventory is 300.

STEP 2. *Compute the number of units that were started and completed during period.* Subtract the beginning inventory units (400) from the number of units completed and transferred to the assembling depart-

1. Units Started and Completed During Period =
Total Units Completed −
Units in Beginning Inventory
5,000 = 5,400 − 400

2. EUP for Completed Units in Beginning Inventory =
Actual Units in Beginning Inventory ×
Percent Needed to Complete
300 = 400 × 75%

3. EUP for Units Started and
Completed During Account-
ing Period =
Actual Units Started and
Completed During Period ×
Percent Needed to Complete
5,000 = 5,000 × 100%

4. EUP for Units Completed
During Accounting Period =
EUP for Units Started and
Completed During Period +
EUP for Completing Units in
Beginning Inventory
5,300 = 5,000 + 300

5. EUP for Units Partially
Completed in Ending
Inventory =
Actual Units in Ending Inven-
tory ×
Percent Completed
500 = 1,000 × 50%

6. Total EUP for Accounting
Period =
EUP for Units Completed During Accounting Period +
EUP for Units Partially Completed in Ending Inventory
5,800 = 5,300 + 500

ment (5,400) during the accounting period to find the units that were
started and completed in the milling department during this period. In
this step we determine that 5,000 (5,400 − 400) units are started and
completed during the period.

STEP 3. *Compute the EUP for the units that were started and completed.* Multiply the units started and completed by 100 percent, the
percent it took to complete them. The EUP for items started and completed is the same as the number completed. The EUP for starting and
completing the units is 5,000.

STEP 4. *Compute EUP for units completed during accounting period.*
Add the EUP units started and completed to the units completed from
the beginning inventory. Actual units completed are 5,400. The EUP
for the units completed during the accounting period is 5,300.

In addition to the 400 units in the beginning inventory, the milling
department has an ending inventory of 1,000 units. These 1,000 units
are 50 percent completed. The EUP for the milling department with
both beginning and ending inventories is computed by doing the additional steps shown here.

STEP 5. *Compute the EUP for the partially completed units in the
ending inventory.* Multiply the number of units (1,000) in the ending
inventory by their percent of completion. The EUP for 1,000 units 50
percent completed is 500.

STEP 6. *Compute the EUP for the accounting period.* Add the EUP for
the units completed (5,300) and the EUP for the ending inventory
(500). The EUP for the milling department with a beginning and ending inventory is 5,800 units. The total actual units for the period is
6,400.

Knowing the EUP makes it possible for the production supervisor to
prepare a production report. How to prepare this report is explained in
the next topic.

Milling Department—September	Actual Units	×	Percent Completed	=	EUP
Units Completed From Beginning Inventory	400	×	75%	=	300
Units Started and Completed During the Period (5,400 − 400)	5,000	×	100%	−	5.000
Total Units Completed During the Period	5,400				5,300
Units Partially Completed in Ending Inventory	1,000	×	50%	=	500
Total for Accounting Period	6,400				5,800

Activity C-1. Answer the following questions about the milling department with beginning and ending work-in-process inventories. Refer to the text and illustrations on pages 239 and 240.

1. How many units are in the September 1 inventory for the milling department?

2. How many additional units is the milling department starting in production in September?

3. How many units have been completed during September and transferred to the assembling department?

4. How many units are in the September ending inventory for the milling department?

5. What percent of completion are the units in the September ending inventory?

6. How many units were actually started and completed in September?

7. What is the EUP for the beginning inventory of 400 units completed in September?

8. What is the EUP for units started and completed in September?

9. What is the EUP for all units completed during September?

10. What is the EUP for the units in the ending inventory?

11. What is the total EUP for September?

Activity C-2. Listed here are some of the steps for computing the EUP when there are beginning and ending inventories. Fill in the missing steps.

STEP 1. Compute the EUP for the units that were in the beginning inventory and were completed.

STEP 2. _____

STEP 3. Compute the EUP for the units that were started and completed.

STEP 4. _____

STEP 5. _____

STEP 6. _____

Topic 2   Problems

6-4. This topic described how the Boyd Chair Company processes materials for chairs through the milling department. Apply this knowledge to solve the following problems concerning the assembling department.

The milling department transferred 4,600 units to the assembling department during August. The assembling department completed 4,400 units during August. The remaining units were only 50 percent completed.

a. Compute the August EUP for the assembling department. Follow the form on page 242 as you do your computations.

b. What happens to the 4,400 units that are processed and completed

in the assembling department during August?

c. Which account is debited for the cost of the units transferred to the next department? Which account is credited?

Assembling Department—August	Actual Units	×	Percent Completed	=	EUP
Units Completed and Transferred	____		____		____
Units Partially Completed in Ending Inventory	____		____		____
Total for Accounting Period	____		____		____

NOTE: Save your working papers for further use in Topic Problems 6-6 and 6-10.

6-5. During August the assembling department transferred the 4,400 completed units to the finishing department. The finishing department processed and completed 4,000 of these units. The units remaining in the ending inventory were 75 percent completed.

a. Compute the August EUP for the finishing department. Follow the form shown below as you do your computations.

b. What happened to the 4,000 units that were processed and completed in the finishing department during August?

c. Which account is debited for the cost of the units transferred out of the finishing department? Which account is credited?

Finishing Department—August	Actual Units	×	Percent Completed	=	EUP
Units Completed and Transferred	____		____		____
Units Partially Completed in Ending Inventory	____		____		____
Total for Accounting Period	____		____		____

NOTE: Save your working papers for further use in Topic Problem 6-7 and Chapter Problem 6-A.

6-6. On August 31 the Work-in-Process account for the assembling department had a balance of $25,580. This balance included the following amounts.

$17,480 for processing the 4,600 units transferred from the milling department.

$4,500 for direct labor.
$3,600 for applied factory overhead.

Refer to Topic Problem 6-4 and do the following.

a. Allocate the $25,580 costs to the units completed and transferred to the finishing department and to the units remaining in the ending inventory. To do these computations follow the form on page 243.

b. How many of the 4,600 units were completed and transferred to the next department?

c. How many units were in the ending inventory on August 31? What was the percent of completion of these units?

STEP 1. Processing costs transferred from milling department.

	Actual Units	Unit Cost
$17,480 ÷	4,600	= $_____

STEP 2. Processing costs added in
assembling department.

	EUP Units	Unit Cost
$ 8,100 ÷	4,500	= $_____

STEP 3. Total processing costs.

$_____ $_____

STEP 4. Units completed and transferred to the finishing
department.

	Unit Cost	Processing Costs
4,400 ×	$5.60	= $_____

Ending Inventory

STEP 5. Units transferred from
milling department.

	Actual Units	Unit Cost	Processing Costs
	200	× $3.80	= $_____

STEP 6. Units added in assembling
department.

	EUP Units	Unit Cost	Processing Costs
	100	× $1.80	= $_____

STEP 7. Total processing costs
for units remaining in ending
inventory.

Processing Costs
$_____

STEP 8. Total Processing Costs
(Step 4 + Step 7).

$_____

NOTE: Save your working papers for further use with Topic Problem
6-10.

6-7. On August 31 the Work-in-Process account for the finishing department had a balance of $34,530. This balance included the follow-
ing amounts.

$24,640 for processing the 4,400
  units transferred from the assembling department.
$2,150 for direct materials.

$4,300 for direct labor.
$3,440 for applied factory over-
  head.

Refer to Topic Problem 6-5 and do the following.

a. Allocate the $34,530 costs to
the units completed and transferred to the warehouse and to
the units remaining in the ending
inventory. To do these computations follow the steps of the form
at the top of page 244.

b. How many of the 4,400 units
are completed and transferred to
the warehouse?

c. How many units are in the
ending inventory on August 31?
What percent of these units are
completed?

STEP 1. Processing costs transferred from assembling department.

	Actual Units		Unit Cost
$24,640	÷ 4,400	=	$ _____

STEP 2. Processing costs added in finishing department.

	EUP Units		Unit Cost
$ 9,890	÷ 4,300	=	$ _____

STEP 3. Total processing costs.

$ _____ $ _____

STEP 4. Units completed and transferred to warehouse.

	Unit Cost		Processing Costs
4,000	× $7.90	=	$ _____

Ending Inventory

STEP 5. Units transferred from assembling department.

Actual Units	Unit Cost		Processing Costs
400	× $5.60	=	$ _____

STEP 6. Units added in finishing department.

EUP Units	Unit Cost		Processing Costs
300	× $2.30	=	$ _____

STEP 7. Total processing costs for units remaining in ending inventory.

Processing Costs

$ _____

STEP 8. Total Processing Costs (Step 4 + Step 7).

$ _____

NOTE: Save your working papers for use with Chapter Problem 6-A.

6-8. Complete the chart shown below on EUP for the assembling department for the month ended September 30. After completing the chart, answer the following questions.

a. How many units are in the beginning inventory? What percent is complete on September 1?
b. How many units are started and completed during September?
c. How many units are left in the ending inventory? What percent of these units is completed?
d. What is the total EUP for the accounting period?

EUP—Assembling Department	Actual Units	×	Percent Completed	=	EUP
Units Completed From Beginning Inventory	200	×	50%	=	_____
Units Started and Completed During September	4,900	×	100%	=	_____
Total Units Completed During September	_____				_____
Units Partially Completed in Ending Inventory	500	×	40%	=	_____
Total for Accounting Period (September)	_____				_____

NOTE: Save your working papers for use with Topic Problem 6-12.

6-9. Complete the chart shown below on EUP for the finishing department for the month ended September 30. Answer the following questions after completing the chart.

a. How many units are on the beginning inventory? What percent is complete in September 1?
b. How many units are started and completed during September?

c. How many units are left in the ending inventory? What percent of these units is completed?
d. What is the total EUP for the accounting period?

EUP—Finishing Department	Actual Units	×	Percent Completed	=	EUP
Units Completed From Beginning Inventory	400	×	25%	=	_____
Units Started and Completed During September	4,900	×	100%	=	_____
Total Units Completed During September	_____				_____
Units Partially Completed in Ending Inventory	200	×	50%	=	_____
Total for Accounting Period (September)	_____				_____

NOTE: Save your working papers for further use with Chapter Problem 6-B.

Topic 3
Cost of Production Reports

A *How are departmental costs reported in process cost accounting?* At regular intervals the department supervisor or manager prepares a cost of production report. The **cost of production report** summarizes both the units processed and the costs for a production department. Thus the cost of production report includes a quantity schedule and a cost schedule.

The **quantity schedule** shows the number of units of materials or products charged to the department and what happened to these units. The quantity schedule also shows the beginning work-in-process inventory, the number of units transferred to the next department or to finished goods, and the ending inventory.

The **cost schedule** lists the manufacturing costs for a department. The cost schedule includes the total cost of direct materials, direct labor, and factory overhead recorded in the Work-in-Process account for that department. It also explains how the costs are divided between the units transferred to the next department and the ending inventory.

The cost of production report for the milling department for July is shown on pages 246 and 247. This report covers the accounting period

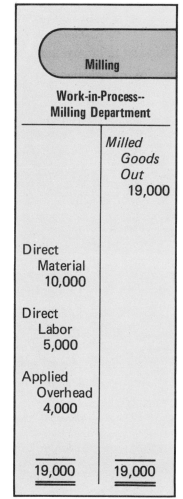

Milling

Work-in-Process--
Milling Department

	Milled Goods Out 19,000
Direct Material 10,000	
Direct Labor 5,000	
Applied Overhead 4,000	
19,000	19,000

THE FLOW OF COSTS
IN MANUFACTURING
CHAIRS

described in Topic 1. (Refer to the chart on page 245 on the flow of costs in manufacturing chairs.)

MILLING DEPARTMENT
Cost of Production Report
For the Month Ended July 31, 19—

Quantity Schedule	Actual Units		Percent Completed		EUP Units
Units to Be Accounted for:					
(a) Units in Beginning Work-in-Process Inventory	-0-				
(b) Units Transferred In From Prior Department.	5,000				
Total to Be Accounted for	5,000				
Units Accounted for:					
(c) Units Transferred to Next Department:					
Units Completed From Beginning Inventory.	-0-	×	-0-	=	-0-
Units Started and Completed	5,000	×	100%	=	5,000
Total Units Transferred	5,000				5,000
(d) Units in Ending Work-in-Process Inventory	-0-	×	-0-	=	-0-
Total Accounted for	5,000				5,000

Cost Schedule	Total Costs		EUP Units		Unit Cost
Costs to Be Accounted for:					
(e) Beginning Work-in-Process Inventory . . .	-0-				
(f) Cost of Goods From Prior Department. .	-0-	=	-0-	×	-0-
(g) Processing Costs:					
Direct Materials.	$10,000	÷	5,000	=	$2.00
Direct Labor	5,000	÷	5,000	=	1.00
Factory Overhead	4,000	÷	5,000	=	0.80
Total Processing Costs	$19,000				$3.80
Total Costs to Be Accounted for	$19,000				$3.80
Costs Accounted for:					
(h) Transferred to Next Department:					
Work Done Last Period on Beginning Inventory	-0-				
Work Done This Period on Beginning Inventory	-0-	=	-0-	×	-0-
Total Beginning Inventory	-0-				
Units Started and Completed	$19,000	=	5,000	×	$3.80
Total Transferred to Next Department . .	$19,000				$3.80

MILLING DEPARTMENT
Cost of Production Report (Continued)
For the Month Ended July 31, 19—

Cost Schedule	Total Costs		EUP Units		Unit Cost
(i) Ending Work-in-Process Inventory:					
Costs in Prior Department	-0-	=	-0-*	×	-0-
Costs in Current Department:					
Direct Materials	-0-	=	-0-	×	-0-
Direct Labor	-0-	=	-0-	×	-0-
Factory Overhead	-0-	=	-0-	×	-0-
Total Ending Work-in-Process	-0-				-0-
Total Costs Accounted for	**$19,000**				

*This will be Actual Units.

Quantity Schedule. The milling department did not have a beginning or ending work-in-process inventory for July, and so all 5,000 units started in production were completed and transferred to the assembly department. Refer to the cost of production report on page 246. The letters here correspond to those in parentheses in the report.

a. There was no beginning inventory.

b. Direct materials for 5,000 units were received from the stores department.

c. All items were completed and transferred to the assembling department. Thus the 5,000 units were 100 percent completed.

d. There were no items partially completed—no ending inventory.

	Actual Units	EUP Units
Units to Be Accounted for:	5,000	
Units Accounted for:	5,000	5,000

Cost Schedule. The cost schedule shows how the total costs of $19,000 are accounted for by the milling department. Refer to the cost of production report on page 246. The letters here correspond to those in parentheses in the report.

e. There was no beginning inventory to account for in July.

f. The milling department is the first production department. Thus there is no cost of goods from prior production departments. The materials from the stores department are shown as direct materials under processing costs. (The assembling department would show the cost of goods received from the milling department. Direct materials used by the assembling department would be shown under processing costs.)

g. The processing costs come from the Work-in-Process—Milling Department account in the general ledger. The amount of the direct materials is posted from the materials requisition journal. Direct labor and the factory overhead are posted from the general journal.

	Total Costs	Unit Cost
Costs to Be Accounted for:	$19,000	$3.80
Costs Accounted for:	19,000	3.80

The general journal, materials requisition journal, and general ledger account shown below and on pages 249 to 250 show the entries that affect the Work-in-Process—Milling Department account. The entries for August and September shown in the ledger are discussed later in this topic.

The processing costs show direct materials of $10,000, direct labor of $5,000, and factory overhead applied of $4,000. These amounts are divided by the number of EUP units processed in July (5,000) to find the unit cost of each item. The unit cost for direct materials is $2.00. Direct labor is $1, and factory overhead is $0.80.

The total unit cost ($3.80) is computed by adding the unit costs for direct materials, direct labor, and factory overhead.

The total costs and the unit cost are used to complete the next section of the cost schedule.

h. There was no beginning inventory in the milling department on July 1. Thus "-0-" is entered in the total cost column pertaining to work done in the previous period on beginning inventory. -0- is also entered in each column for work done this period on beginning inventory. The total production costs of $19,000 are started, completed, and transferred to the next department—the assembling department. All work is done in this accounting period, which means there is no ending inventory in the milling department.

i. The ending inventory section is left blank because there is no ending inventory. Thus the schedule shows that all the costs ($19,000) are accounted for. Note that the Work-in-Process—Milling Department account shows a zero balance for July 31.

Processing Costs	Total Costs	Unit Cost
Direct Materials	$10,000	$2.00
Direct Labor	5,000	1.00
Factory Overhead	4,000	0.80
Total	$19,000	$3.80

		GENERAL JOURNAL			Page 2
DATE		ACCOUNT TITLE AND EXPLANATION	POST. REF.	DEBIT	CREDIT
19— July	31	Work-in-Process—Milling Department	122	5,000 00	
		Factory Overhead	501	2,000 00	
		Factory Payroll	502		7,000 00
		Distribute direct and indirect labor.			
	31	Work-in-Process—Milling Department	122	4,000 00	
		Factory Overhead	501		4,000 00
		Record overhead applied.			
	31	Work-in-Process—Assembling Department	123	19,000 00	
		Work-in-Process—Milling Department	122		19,000 00
		Record transfer of 5,000 unassembled chairs.			

GENERAL JOURNAL				Page 2
DATE	ACCOUNT TITLE AND EXPLANATION	POST. REF.	DEBIT	CREDIT
Aug. 31	Work-in-Process—Milling Department	122	4,700 00	
	Factory Overhead	501	2,000 00	
	Factory Payroll	502		6,700 00
	Distribute direct and indirect labor.			
31	Work-in-Process—Milling Department	122	3,760 00	
	Factory Overhead	501		3,760 00
	Record overhead applied.			
31	Work-in-Process—Assembling Department	123	17,480 00	
	Work-in-Process—Milling Department	122		17,480 00
	Record transfer of 4,600 unassembled chairs.			
Sept. 30	Work-in-Process—Milling Department	122	5,800 00	
	Factory Overhead	501	2,200 00	
	Factory Payroll	502		8,000 00
	Distribute direct and indirect labor.			
30	Work-in-Process—Milling Department	122	4,640 00	
	Factory Overhead	501		4,640 00
	Record overhead applied.			
30	Work-in-Process—Assembling Department	123	20,520 00	
	Work-in-Process—Milling Department	122		20,520 00
	Record transfer of 5,400 unassembled chairs.			

MATERIALS REQUISITION JOURNAL							Page 1
DATE	REQ. NO.	DEPARTMENT	WORK-IN-PROCESS— MILLING DEPARTMENT DEBIT 122	WORK-IN-PROCESS— ASSEMBLING DEPARTMENT DEBIT 123	WORK-IN-PROCESS— FINISHING DEPARTMENT DEBIT 124	FACTORY OVERHEAD DEBIT 501	MATERIALS CREDIT 121
19— July 2	107	Milling. . . .	10,000 00			1,000 00	11,000 00
Aug. 1	120	Milling. . . .	9,400 00				9,400 00
Sept. 1	135	Milling. . . .	11,600 00				11,600 00

						BALANCE	
DATE	EXPLANATION	POST. REF.	DEBIT	CREDIT		DEBIT	CREDIT

Work-in-Process—Milling Department **Account No. 122**

DATE		EXPLANATION	POST. REF.	DEBIT	CREDIT	BALANCE DEBIT	BALANCE CREDIT
19—							
July	2	*Direct materials*	*MR1*	*10,000 00*		*10,000 00*	
	31	*Direct labor*	*J2*	*5,000 00*		*15,000 00*	
	31	*Factory overhead applied*	*J2*	*4,000 00*		*19,000 00*	①
	31	*Transfer 5,000 units*	*J2*		*19,000 00*	*-0-*	②
Aug.	31	*Direct materials*	*MR2*	*9,400 00*		*9,400 00*	
	31	*Direct labor*	*J6*	*4,700 00*		*14,100 00*	
	31	*Factory overhead applied*	*J6*	*3,760 00*		*17,860 00*	③
	31	*Transfer 4,600 units*	*J6*		*17,480 00*	*380 00*	④
Sept.	30	*Direct materials*	*MR3*	*11,600 00*		*11,980 00*	
	30	*Direct labor*	*J11*	*5,800 00*		*17,780 00*	
	30	*Applied factory overhead*	*J11*	*4,640 00*		*22,420 00*	⑤
	30	*Transfer 5,400 units*	*J11*		*20,520 00*	*1,900 00*	⑥

	Actual Units	EUP Units
Units to Be Accounted for:	6,400	
Units Accounted for:	6,400	5,800

Note the following amounts on the schedule.
1 Total costs to be accounted for in July.
2 Ending balance for July.
3 Total costs to be accounted for in August.
4 Ending balance for August.
5 Total costs to be accounted for in September.
6 Ending balance for September.

Accounting Concept:
Cost of Production Report. The cost of direct materials, direct labor, and factory overhead is summarized for each production department on the cost of production report.

Activity A-1. Answer the following questions about the July cost of production report for the milling department. Refer to the text and illustrations on pages 245 to 250.

1. What are the two parts of the cost of production report?
2. How many units are to be accounted for?
3. How much of the amount of processing costs is to be accounted for?
4. How many units are included in the July beginning work-in-process inventory?
5. How many units are transferred from the prior (stores) department to the milling department?

6. How many units are started and completed?
7. What is the July EUP?
8. What is the unit processing cost for direct materials? direct labor? factory overhead?
9. What is the total unit cost?
10. What are the total processing costs for the milling department? the unit processing cost?
11. What is the cost of the units completed and transferred to the next department?

Activity A-2. Answer the following questions about the milling department. Refer to the materials requisition journal, general journal, and
Work-in-Process account shown on pages 248 to 250.

1. What is the total amount of materials requisitioned by the milling department in July?

2. What is the amount for the direct materials? for the indirect materials?

3. Which account is debited for the direct materials? for the indirect materials?

4. What is the total factory payroll for the milling department in July?

5. How much of the total factory payroll is for direct labor? for indirect labor?

6. Which account is debited for the direct labor? the indirect labor?

7. How much factory overhead is applied to the milling department in July?

8. Which account is debited for the $19,000 of goods transferred from the milling department?

9. What is the balance in the Work-in-Process—Milling Department account on July 31?

Ending Work-in-Process Inventory

B *How is EUP computed for the ending inventory?* In August the milling department had an ending work-in-process inventory of 400 units, which were 25 percent completed. The equivalent units of production must be computed to allocate (distribute) the costs.

MILLING DEPARTMENT
Cost of Production Report
For the Month Ended August 31, 19—

Quantity Schedule	Actual Units		Percent Completed		EUP Units
Units to Be Accounted for:					
(a) Units in Beginning Work-in-Process Inventory	-0-				
(b) Units Transferred in From Prior Department.	5,000				
Total to Be Accounted for	5,000				
Units Accounted For:					
(c) Units Transferred to Next Department:					
Units Completed From Beginning Inventory	-0-	×	-0-	=	-0-
Units Started and Completed	4,600	×	100%	=	4,600
Total Units Transferred	4,600				4,600
(d) Units in Ending Work-in-Process Inventory	400	×	25%	=	100
Total Accounted for	5,000				4,700

MILLING DEPARTMENT
Cost of Production Report (Continued)
For the Month Ended August 31, 19—

Cost Schedule	Total Costs		EUP Units		Unit Cost
Costs to Be Accounted for:					
(e) Beginning Work-in-Process Inventory ...	-0-				
(f) Cost of Goods From Prior Department ..	-0-	=	-0-	×	-0-
(g) Processing Costs:					
Direct Materials................	$ 9,400	÷	4,700	=	$2.00
Direct Labor	4,700	÷	4,700	=	1.00
Factory Overhead	3,760	÷	4,700	=	0.80
Total Processing Costs	$17,860	÷	4,700	=	$3.80
Total Costs to Be Accounted for	$17,860				$3.80
Costs Accounted for:					
(h) Transferred to Next Department:					
Work Done Last Period on Beginning Inventory	-0-				
Work Done This Period on Beginning Inventory	-0-	=	-0-	×	-0-
Total Beginning Inventory	-0-				
Units Started and Completed	$17,480	=	4,600	×	$3.80
Total Transferred to Next Department...	$17,480				$3.80
(i) Ending Work-in-Process Inventory:					
Costs in Prior Department	-0-	=	-0-*	×	-0-
Costs in Current Department:					
Direct Materials...............	$ 200	=	100	×	$2.00
Direct Labor	100	=	100	×	1.00
Factory Overhead..............	80	=	100	×	0.80
Total Ending Work-in-Process	$ 380				$3.80
Total Costs Accounted for...............	$17,860				

*This will be Actual Units.

Quantity Schedule. The August report is different from the July report. The July report has no ending inventory. The Quantity schedule for August lists the actual number of units, the percent completed, and EUP units for the ending work-in-process inventory. Also, the cost schedule shows costs allocated to the ending work in process.

As you study this report, refer to the discussion in Topic 2 describing how to compute the EUP. The letters here correspond to those in parentheses in the report.

a. Since there is no ending inventory in July, there is no beginning inventory for August.

b. Direct materials to start 5,000 chairs are received from the stores department.

c. All chairs transferred to the assembly department are started during this period. None was started last period, and so there is no beginning inventory to report. The milling department started, completed, and transferred 4,600 chairs. The EUP units are 4,600 (4,600 × 100 percent = 4,600 completed).

d. The ending inventory consisted of 400 units that were 25 percent completed. The EUP units for the ending inventory are 100 (400 × 25 percent = 100 completed).

The total EUP units for the month of August are 4,700. The processing costs must be divided between the 4,600 units started, completed, and transferred and the 400 units in the ending inventory that are 25 percent completed.

Cost Schedule. The cost schedule shows how the total costs of $17,860 are accounted for by the milling department. These costs were discussed in Topic 2. The letters here correspond to those in parentheses in the report.

e. There is no beginning inventory in August.

f. Since the milling department is the first production department, there is no cost of goods from prior departments. The cost of the material from the stores department is shown as direct materials under processing costs.

g. The processing costs show the total costs of direct materials ($9,400), direct labor ($4,700), and factory overhead applied ($3,760). These amounts are obtained from the Work-in-Process account in the general ledger. The cost for each item is divided by the total EUP units (4,700) to find the unit cost of each item. The total unit cost ($3.80) is computed by adding the unit costs for each item.

h. There was no beginning inventory on August 1. Thus "-0-" is entered in the Total Cost column pertaining to work done last period on beginning inventory. -0- is also entered in each column for work done this period on beginning inventory. The total production costs ($17,480) for the 4,600 units started, completed, and transferred to the assembling department are computed as follows. Multiply the unit cost ($3.80) by the number of units transferred (4,600). The unit cost was obtained in (g) in the report.

i. The milling department is the first production department, and so there are no costs in a prior department to account for. The ending inventory consists of 400 units that are 25 percent completed. The EUP units are 100. The total cost for each item is computed by multiplying the unit cost for each item by the EUP units. For example, the unit cost for materials ($2) multiplied by the EUP units (100) gives a

	Actual Units	EUP Units
Units to Be Accounted for:	5,000	
Units Accounted for:	5,000	4,700

	Total Costs	Unit Cost
Costs to Be Accounted for:	$17,860	$3.80
Costs Accounted for:	17,860	3.80

total cost of $200. The unit cost for each item was obtained from (g) in the report on page 252. The ending work-in-process shown on the cost schedule is $380. This amount agrees with the Work-in-Process account in the general ledger, which has a balance of $380 on August 31.

Activity B. Answer the following questions. Refer to the cost of production report for the milling department for August on pages 251 and 252.

1. How many units of direct materials are transferred to the milling department from the prior department?

2. How many units must be accounted for by the milling department?

3. How many units are transferred to the next department?

4. How many units are in the ending inventory?

5. What percent of processing is completed on the ending inventory?

6. What are the total costs to be accounted for in August?

7. What is the EUP for the milling department?

8. What is the total cost for direct materials? direct labor? factory overhead?

9. What is the unit processing cost for direct materials? direct labor? factory overhead?

10. What is the total unit processing cost?

11. How much of the processing costs are transferred to the next department?

12. How much of the processing costs are allocated to the ending inventory?

13. What are the total costs accounted for in August?

Beginning Work-in-Process Inventory

C *How is the cost of production report prepared when there is a beginning inventory?* The September cost of production report differs from the August report. The September report shows a beginning inventory.

Quantity Schedule. Refer to the discussion of the September production in Topic 2. The letters here correspond to those in parentheses in the September cost of production report.

a. The beginning inventory consists of 400 units, the August ending inventory.

b. Direct materials to start 6,000 chairs are received from the stores department.

MILLING DEPARTMENT
Cost of Production Report
For the Month Ended September 30, 19—

Quantity Schedule	Actual Units		Percent Completed		EUP Units
Units to Be Accounted for:					
(a) Units in Beginning Work-in-Process Inventory	400				
(b) Units Transferred in From Prior Department.	6,000				
Total to Be Accounted for	6,400				
Units Accounted for:					
(c) Units Transferred to Next Department:					
Units Completed From Beginning Inventory	400	×	75%	=	300
Units Started and Completed	5,000	×	100%	=	5,000
Total Units Transferred	5,400				5,300
(d) Units in Ending Work-in-Process Inventory	1,000	×	50%	=	500
Total Accounted for	6,400				5,800

Cost Schedule	Total Costs		EUP Units		Unit Cost
Costs to Be Accounted for:					
(e) Beginning Work-in-Process Inventory . . .	$ 380				
(f) Cost of Goods From Prior Department . .	-0-	=	-0-	×	-0-
(g) Processing Costs:					
Direct Materials.	$11,600	÷	5,800	=	$2.00
Direct Labor	5,800	÷	5,800	=	1.00
Factory Overhead	4,640	÷	5,800	=	0.80
Total Processing Costs	$22,040	÷	5,800	=	$3.80
Total Costs to Be Accounted for	$22,420				$3.80
Costs Accounted for:					
(h) Transferred to Next Department:					
Work Done Last Period on Beginning Inventory	$ 380				
Work Done This Period on Beginning Inventory	1,140	=	300	×	$3.80
Total Beginning Inventory	$ 1,520				
Units Started and Completed	$19,000	=	5,000	×	$3.80
Total Transferred to Next Department. . .	$20,520				$3.80

MILLING DEPARTMENT
Cost of Production Report (Continued)
For the Month Ended September 30, 19—

Cost Schedule	Total Costs		EUP Units		Unit Cost
(i) **Ending Work-in-Process Inventory:**					
Costs in Prior Department	-0-	=	-0- *	×	-0-
Costs in Current Department:					
Direct Materials	$ 1,000	=	500	×	$2.00
Direct Labor	500	=	500	×	1.00
Factory Overhead	400	=	500	×	0.80
Total Ending Work-in-Process	$ 1,900				$3.80
Total Costs Accounted for	$22,420				

*This will be Actual Units.

	Total Costs	Unit Cost
Costs to Be Accounted for:	$22,420	$3.80
Costs Accounted for:	$22,420	$3.80

c. The units accounted for represent work done this accounting period. The units in the beginning inventory are only 25 percent completed. This work was done in the previous period. Thus 75 percent of the work needed to complete and transfer the units is to be done during this period. As a result, the beginning inventory consists of 300 EUP units. The total units started and completed is 5,000. The EUP units transferred is 5,300 units (5,000 + 300 = 5,300).

d. The ending inventory consists of 1,000 units, which are 50 percent completed. The ending inventory of 500 EUP units plus the 5,300 EUP units transferred make a total of 5,800 EUP units accounted for. The total actual units accounted for is 6,400.

Cost Schedule. The costs must be allocated to three phases of work: work needed to finish the beginning inventory (which is 25 percent completed), work needed to start and finish the units transferred from the stores department, and work started on the ending inventory (which is 50 percent completed). The letters here correspond to those in parentheses in the report.

e. The cost of the beginning inventory is $380. This amount is shown as the ending inventory on the August 31 report. The amount is also shown in the general ledger account on page 250.

f. Cost of goods from the stores department is shown as direct materials under processing costs.

g. The unit processing costs are computed by dividing the total costs by the total EUP units produced.

h. The cost of the units transferred to the assembling department is composed of three items: the costs incurred last period on the beginning inventory, the costs incurred this period on the beginning inventory, and the costs of the units started and completed this period. The costs from the last period ($380) are obtained from the August report. The work done this period on the beginning inventory is computed by multiplying 300 EUP by the unit cost of $3.80. The costs for the units started and completed are computed by multiplying the unit cost ($3.80) by the EUP (5,000). The total transferred to the next department is $20,520 ($19,000 + $1,520 = $20,520).

i. There were no costs transferred from a prior production department. Thus "-0-" is shown on the Costs in Prior Department line. The costs in the current department are obtained by multiplying the unit cost for each item by the 500 EUP in the ending work-in-process inventory. Total costs accounted for is $22,420 ($20,520 + $1,900). The second and third production departments—assembling and finishing—may have costs in a prior department to account for. When this happens, the costs in the prior department are computed by multiplying the number of actual units in the ending work-in-process inventory by the unit processing cost for the prior department.

The Report Balances. The Total Costs to Be Accounted for figure is $22,420, which equals the Total Costs Accounted for figure. These amounts also agree with the Work-in-Process—Milling Department account in the general ledger shown on page 250. The Total Costs column (beginning inventory plus current processing costs) has a balance of $22,420. After the amount transferred to the assembly department ($20,520) is recorded, the ending balance in the account is $1,900. This is the amount of the ending inventory.

By-Products and Joint Products

In this chapter you have learned about the processing of a single product—chairs—through three production departments. However, in many manufacturing businesses more than one product is produced from the same raw materials or processes.

Assume that the Boyd Chair Company has large amounts of scrap wood left over each month in the milling department. These scraps are too valuable to throw away. Ways to use the scraps productively are devised. They may be sold to another business for further processing, or the Boyd Chair Company may use them to make something else—for example, wooden pegs. The wooden pegs could be used to fasten together the parts of the more expensive chairs.

The Boyd Chair Company, therefore, would be involved with the production of a major product (chairs) and a minor product (wooden pegs). The wooden pegs would be a by-product of the manufacturing of chairs. A **by-product** is a minor product that is produced from the scraps of a major product. A by-product has a relatively small value.

Other companies produce more than one major product of considerable value from the same raw materials or processes. Products produced in this manner are referred to as **joint products.** A refinery of petroleum is an example of a business that produces joint products. A refinery can make several major products from the processing of petroleum: gasoline, heating oil, kerosene, some medicines, and various lubricants. The accounting for by-products and joint products is not covered in this text; it involves special accounting procedures which are covered in higher-level accounting courses.

Activity C. Answer the following questions. Refer to the cost of production report for the milling department for September on pages 255 to 256.

1. How many units are in the beginning inventory?

2. How many units of direct materials are transferred in from the prior department?

3. What are the total units to be accounted for in September?

4. What happens to the units in the beginning inventory?

5. What percent of the processing is completed on the beginning inventory?

6. How many units are started and completed during September?

7. How many units are in the ending inventory?

8. What is the EUP for September?

9. What is the total cost to be accounted for in September?

10. What is the unit processing cost?

11. What is the total cost transferred to the next department?

12. What is the total cost of the ending inventory?

13. What is the unit cost of the items in the ending inventory?

14. What are the total costs accounted for in September?

Topic 3   Problems

6-10. Prepare a cost of production report for the assembling department for the month ended August 31. The information for this report can be taken from your working papers for Topic Problems 6-4 and 6-6. Topic Problem 6-4 will provide the information you need for the quantity schedule. Topic Problem 6-6 will provide the information you need for the cost schedule of the production report. Refer to the examples of the cost of production reports illustrated in Topic 3 on pages 245 to 258 as you work through this problem.

NOTE: Save your working papers for further use with Topic Problems 6-11 and 6-12.

6-11. Answer the following questions about the cost of production report for the assembling department for August. Refer to Topic Problem 6-10.

a. What is the total number of actual units to be accounted for in August?

b. How many EUP are included in the ending inventory?

c. How many units are transferred to the next department?

d. What are the total processing costs of the units transferred to the next department?

e. What is the unit cost of the units transferred?

f. What is the total cost of the ending inventory?

6-12. Prepare a cost of production report for the assembling department for the month ended September 30. Use the information from Topic Problems 6-8 and 6-10. The Work-in-Process account for the assembling department has a balance of $30,820 on September 30. This balance includes the following amounts.

$ 940	Beginning inventory in the assembling department on September 1.		from the milling department.
$20,520	Costs for processing the 5,400 units transferred	$ 5,200	Direct labor.
		$ 4,160	Applied factory overhead.

6-13. Answer the following questions about the September cost of production report for the assembling department. Refer to Topic Problem 6-12.

a. What is the total number of actual units to be accounted for?

b. How many EUP are included in the ending inventory?

c. How many units are transferred to the next department?

d. What are the total processing costs of the units transferred to the next department?

e. What is the unit cost of the units transferred?

f. What is the total cost of the ending inventory?

The Language of Business

Here are some basic terms that make up the language of business. Do you understand the meaning of each? Can you define each term and use it in an original sentence?

process cost
  accounting system
unit cost
average costing
stores ledger card

materials requisition
predetermined
  overhead
cost of production
  report

quantity schedule
cost schedule
by-product
joint products

ending work-in-process
  inventory
equivalent units of
  production

Chapter 6   Questions

1. What are the two major cost accounting systems?
2. Explain the concept of process cost accounting.

What kinds of businesses use process cost accounting systems?

3. How is the unit cost of a product computed?
4. How many work-in-process accounts would a business with three processing departments use?
5. What kind of account is the work-in-process account? Is the account increased by debits or credits?
6. What is meant by a predetermined overhead rate? The rate is usually a percent of what production cost?
7. What kind of account is the Cost of Goods Sold account? Does this account have a debit balance or a credit balance?

8. What is meant by equivalent units of production (EUP)?
9. What is a cost of production report? Name the two parts of the report.
10. What information is provided on each part of the cost of production report?
11. What kinds of transactions are recorded in the materials requisition journal?
12. What is meant when the ending work-in-process units are reported as being 50 percent completed?

Chapter 6   Problems

Problems for Chapter 6 are given in the *Working Papers and Chapter Problems* for Part 1. If you are using the workbook, do the problems in the space provided there. Complete your assigned topic problems before answering the chapter problems.

Chapter 6   Management Cases

Bottlenecks. In a manufacturing plant, a *bottleneck* refers to any slowdown in the flow of work. A bottleneck may have any number of causes: an individual or group not working hard enough, a department not having enough employees to meet the work schedules, equipment breaking down, or an inventory not having enough goods or materials.

Bottlenecks can develop in production departments as well as in service departments, such as the factory office. Management relies on accurate accounting reports to identify these bottlenecks as well as to evaluate the efficiency of the production departments.

Case 6M-1. Joseph Herrman is president of the Moto Company. Moto is a small manufacturing business that produces mopeds (motor-assisted bicycles). With the rising price of gasoline, Moto's sales of mopeds, which use far less fuel than cars, have been rapidly increasing.

The increased demand for mopeds is also bringing about more competition from large manufacturers. Mr. Herrman is determined that the Moto Company will retain its share of the market and continue to increase in sales. He is confident that the workers at the Moto Company are as good as those at any other company. However, Mr. Herrman does have some questions about the costs of production.

A review of the accounting procedures revealed that the same work-in-process account is used for all three processing departments. All direct materials, direct labor, and factory overhead costs are charged to a single work-in-process account. When questioned about this procedure, the plant manager replied that process cost accounting is concerned only with an average cost and that the use of a single work-in-process account eliminated needless paper work.

The president now turns to you, the accountant, and asks what you think of using only one work-in-process account for three departments.
a. How would you answer the president?
b. What are the advantages of using more than one work-in-process account?
c. How do you think the supervisors in the three departments would react to the use of three work-in-process accounts?
d. How will the use of more than one work-in-process account affect the monthly cost of production reports?

Case 6M-2. A bottleneck has developed in the accounting office of the Moto Company. Specifically, the problem is concerned with computing and paying the weekly factory payroll. While the employees are paid on time, the payroll records are stacking up.

The office manager insists there is too much work for the one clerk in the payroll department. The payroll clerk must collect 300 time cards, verify the hours worked, compute the net pay, and prepare the checks for the employees. In addition to these activities, the payroll clerk must update the individual earnings records and complete several reports concerning the deductions from the employees' paychecks. The payroll clerk also keeps the payroll records for the administrative and office personnel at the factory.

The office manager has recommended two solutions to the problem. The first solution is the hiring of an additional employee in the payroll department. If the payroll department had two employees, the flow of work would not be interrupted and payroll reports and records would be kept current. The second solution involves the purchase of an electronic timekeeper and a microcomputer. With these two devices, the one payroll clerk could keep up with the amount of work involved with the payroll records.

The electronic timekeeper costs $3,000 and would require that each employee be given a plastic badge with an employee number printed in magnetic ink.

This plastic badge is permanent and would replace the weekly time cards and time clock now used by employees. The plastic badge is similar to the popular bank cards used with automated teller machines. The employee's plastic badge is inserted in the timekeeper, and the time of arrival and departure are electronically recorded. Hours worked, overtime, gross pay, and net pay are also computed automatically.

The microcomputer would cost $4,500 and would require the payroll clerk to learn a computer language. The payroll records would also have to be changed over to an electronic system. The office manager realizes that considerable time might be involved in changing to an electronic payroll accounting system and in working the "bugs" out of the new system.

a. What are some advantages of hiring the second payroll clerk? What are some disadvantages?

b. What are some advantages of purchasing the electronic equipment? What are some disadvantages?

c. Which solution do you recommend for solving the bottleneck in the payroll department? Explain.

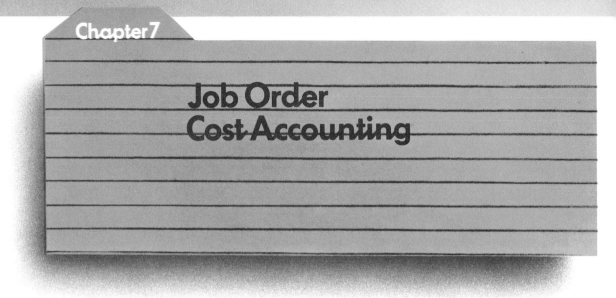

Job Order Cost Accounting

In a job order cost accounting system, cost data is gathered for each job.

A job order cost accounting system is used when there is a need to know the cost of producing specific items. The items may be made to fit the customer's requirements, and each job—or order—is kept separate. Job order cost accounting is also used when goods are produced in batches.

A process cost accounting system is used when items are produced on a continuous basis and the items are very similar to each other. When the items or the work required for each job differ greatly, the job order cost system is used.

Topic 1
The Flow of Costs

A *How do costs flow in a job order cost accounting system?* The flow of costs in a job order cost accounting system is similar to the flow of costs in a process cost accounting system. The chart on page 263 shows the flow of costs for a specific job.

The direct materials, direct labor, and factory overhead costs flow from the Materials account, the Factory Payroll account, and the Factory Overhead account. Note that there is only *one* Work-in-Process account instead of a different account for each department. The costs

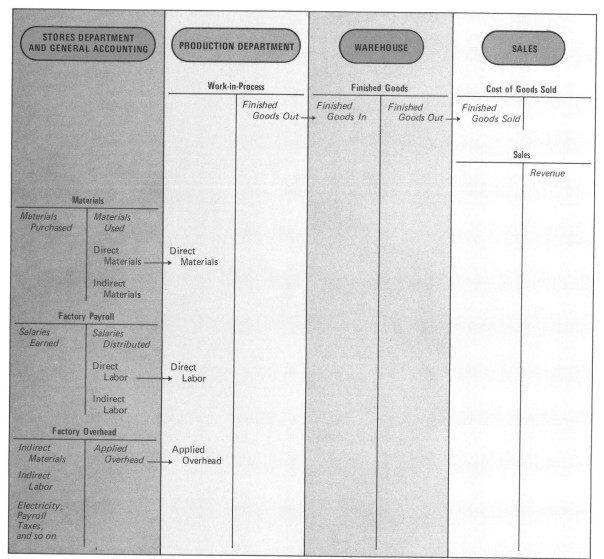

THE FLOW OF COSTS IN A JOB ORDER
COST ACCOUNTING SYSTEM

recorded in the Work-in-Process account are the total costs of direct materials, direct labor, and factory overhead for all jobs in process. Notice also that there is one Finished Goods account. When the finished goods are transferred from the production department to the warehouse, the costs of the finished goods are transferred to the Finished Goods account.

Stanley Rosenfeld/Morris Rosenfeld & Sons

Large yachts are usually custom-made. The ship-builder uses job order cost accounting. Small pleasure boats are mass-produced. The manufacturer uses process cost accounting.

Rosemount Manufacturing Company Chart of Accounts

Assets
111   Accounts Receivable
121   Materials
122   Work-in-Process
125   Finished Goods

Liabilities
211   Accounts Payable

Revenue
401   Sales

Factory Costs
501   Factory Overhead
502   Factory Payroll
511   Cost of Goods Sold

Job Cost Sheets

A record of the costs for a specific job must be kept. In a job order cost accounting system, costs are accumulated by job rather than by department. Each job is given a number when it is started. A form, called a **job (order) cost sheet,** is set up for that job. The direct materials, the direct labor costs, and the factory overhead for that specific job are entered on the job cost sheet. Thus the job cost sheet contains the total costs for completing a job.

The Boyd Chair Company, in Chapter 6, produced wooden chairs on a continuous basis. It used a process cost accounting system. The Rosemount Manufacturing Company, whose chart of accounts is shown here, produces special furniture, one job at a time, for specific customers. Thus it uses a job order cost accounting system.

The job cost sheet for Job 15 to be produced by the Rosemount Manufacturing Company is shown on the next page. For Job 15, 300 model CL-9 chairs (a special type of chair) must be manufactured for Colonial Furniture Stores. Job 15 was started on July 16.

As the job cost sheet of Job 15 shows, the top of the job cost sheet records the job number, the specific item to be manufactured, the customer's name, the quantity of items to be produced, the date the job is

JOB COST SHEET

Job No. __15__

Item __CL-9 Chairs__

Customer __Colonial Furniture Stores__

Quantity __300__

Date Started __July 16, 19—__

Date Wanted __July 24, 19—__

Date Completed ____

MATERIALS			LABOR			OVERHEAD			SUMMARY OF COSTS	
DATE	REQ. NO.	AMOUNT	DATE	COST SHEET NO.	AMOUNT	DATE	RATE	AMOUNT		
									Materials	$
									Labor	
									Overhead	
									Total	$
									No. Units	
									Unit Cost	$

Job Cost Sheet for Job 15.

started, the date the job is to be completed, and the date when the job is actually completed. The completion date is not filled in until the job is finished.

The costs for each incompleted job are recorded on an **open job order sheet.** All the open job cost sheets serve as a subsidiary ledger for the Work-in-Process account. Thus the total of the costs recorded on the individual job cost sheets must equal the costs recorded in the Work-in-Process account in the general ledger.

The cost of direct material is entered on the job cost sheet from the materials requisition forms. At the end of each payroll period, the direct labor costs are also entered on the cost sheet from the analysis of labor costs sheet. When the labor costs are entered, the factory overhead is applied to that job by using a predetermined overhead rate, as explained in Chapter 5.

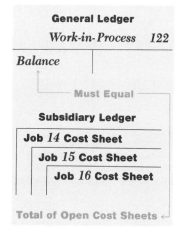

General Ledger

Work-in-Process   122

Balance

Must Equal

Subsidiary Ledger

Job *14* Cost Sheet

Job *15* Cost Sheet

Job *16* Cost Sheet

Total of Open Cost Sheets

Accounting Concept:
Job Order Cost Accounting System. A method of accumulating (gathering) costs for each job is the job order cost accounting system. Costs are accumulated for each job.

Activity A. Answer the following questions about job order cost accounting systems. Refer to the text and illustrations on pages 262 to 265.

1. How many work-in-process accounts are used in a job order cost accounting system?

2. Which form is used to accumulate costs for each job?

3. The total of all open job cost

sheets should always equal the balance in which account?

4. How many inventory accounts are included in the chart of accounts for a business using job order cost accounting? Which inventory accounts are these?

5. The Work-in-Process account is debited for the cost of certain items required in manufacturing a product. What are these items?

6. When is the Work-in-Process account credited?

7. When is the Finished Goods account debited? When is the account credited?

8. Which account is debited for the cost of products sold?

9. Which product is being manufactured in Job 15?

10. What is the name of the customer who ordered the chairs? How many chairs have been ordered?

11. When was Job 15 started?

12. When does the customer want the chairs?

Direct and Indirect Materials

| B |

Are the costs for direct and indirect materials in a job order cost accounting system recorded in the same way as in a process cost accounting system? The journal entries are the same, except only one Work-in-Process account is used in a job order cost accounting system. The major difference is that the direct material costs must also be entered on the job cost sheets for the specific jobs.

The purchase invoice is the source document for recording raw materials purchased for use in producing the furniture at Rosemount Manufacturing Company. The Materials account is debited, and the Accounts Payable account is credited. The journal entry here records the July 14 purchase of $35,000 of materials on credit from Pacific

Only one Work-in-Process account is used in a job order cost accounting system.

Entry for purchase invoice for $35,000 of lumber. Lumber received is also entered in stores ledger.

GENERAL JOURNAL					Page *1*
DATE	**ACCOUNT TITLE AND EXPLANATION**	**POST. REF.**	**DEBIT**		**CREDIT**
19— July 14	Materials	121	35,000 00		
	Accounts Payable/Pacific Foresters	211/√			35,000 00
	Purchase lumber on credit.				

General Ledger

Materials	121		Accounts Payable	211
19— July 14 J1	35,000		19— July 14 J1	35,000

Subsidiary Ledger

Pacific Foresters

19— July 14 J1	35,000

Foresters. (If the materials had been purchased for cash, the Cash account would have been credited.)

We will study the job order cost accounting system by following the steps used to complete Jobs 14, 15, and 16. We will begin with the requisition of materials for these jobs. As you read, note page 263.

Materials requisition forms are issued to move materials from the stores department to the production department. On July 16 direct and indirect materials costing $3,300 were requisitioned for Jobs 14, 15, and 16. The materials requisition form is the source document for recording the entry in the materials requisition journal.

ROSEMOUNT MANUFACTURING COMPANY

MATERIALS REQUISITION

No. **806**

Deliver to Milling Department

Date July 16, 19--

Charge: Job No. 15

Account Work-in-Process, 122

Account

Quantity	Material No.	Description	Unit Price	Amount
38	195	Plywood sheets	$10.00	$380.00
600	89	Framing slats, 8'	0.50	300.00
300	112	Supporting slats, 6'	0.40	120.00
1,250	37	Angle supports	0.08	100.00
				Total $900.00

Approved by *DRC*

Delivered by *Ron S.*

Received by *Jane C. Moss*

COPY 2 — STORES DEPARTMENT

MATERIALS REQUISITION JOURNAL   Page *1*

DATE		REQ. NO.	JOB OR DEPARTMENT	WORK-IN-PROCESS DEBIT 122	FACTORY OVERHEAD DEBIT 501	MATERIALS CREDIT 121
19—						
July	16	804	*14*	1,000 00		1,000 00
		805	*Indirect*		300 00	300 00
		806	*15*	900 00		900 00
		807	*16*	1,100 00		1,100 00
				3,000 00	300 00	3,300 00

Entry for direct and indirect materials requisitioned.

Posting would look like this if made during month. In practice, journal would not be posted until end of month.

Materials 121		*Work-in-Process* 122		*Factory Overhead* 501	
19—	19—	19—		19—	
July 14 J1 35,000	July 16 MR1 3,300	July 16 MR1 3,000		July 16 MR1 300	

The Work-in-Process account is debited for the direct materials, and the Factory Overhead account is debited for the indirect materials. The total amount is credited to the Materials account.

The amount of the direct materials must be entered not only in the materials requisition journal, but also on the cost sheet for that job.

The job cost sheets here show the entries for the direct materials to Jobs 14, 15, and 16. The total amount of materials recorded for Jobs 14, 15, and 16 equals the amount of direct materials recorded in the Work-in-Process account.

Direct materials entered on job cost sheets for Jobs 14, 15, and 16.

JOB COST SHEET

Job No. ___15___
Item ___CL-9 Chairs___   Date Started ___July 16, 19—___
Customer ___Colonial Furniture Stores___   Date Wanted ___July 24, 19—___
Quantity ___300___   Date Completed _____

MATERIALS			LABOR			OVERHEAD			SUMMARY OF COSTS	
DATE	REQ. NO.	AMOUNT	DATE	COST SHEET NO.	AMOUNT	DATE	RATE	AMOUNT		
19— July 16	806	900 00							Materials	$
									Labor	
									Overhead	___
									Total	$ ___
									No. Units	___
									Unit Cost	$ ___

Job No. 14

MATERIALS		
DATE	REQ. NO.	AMOUNT
19— July 16	804	1,000 00

Job No. 16

MATERIALS		
DATE	REQ. NO.	AMOUNT
19— July 16	807	1,100 00

Activity B. Answer the following questions about direct and indirect materials. Refer to the text and illustrations on pages 266 to 268.

1. What is the cost of the materials purchased on July 14?
2. Which journal is used to record the purchase? Which account is debited and which is credited?
3. How many jobs have been started in process during July? What are the job numbers?
4. What is the cost of the materials requisitioned for these jobs?

5. Which form is used to request the materials for the jobs?
6. Which journal is used to record the materials requested for the jobs?
7. What is the source document for recording the entry in the journal?
8. Which account is debited for the direct materials used for the jobs?
9. Which account is debited for the indirect materials used for the jobs?
10. Which account is credited for the total cost of materials used for the jobs?
11. What is the amount of direct materials requested for Job 14? Job 15? Job 16?
12. What is the number of the materials requisition form used to request the materials for Job 15?
13. Who approves the request for materials for Job 15?
14. Who receives the goods for Job 15?

Direct and Indirect Labor

C *Are the costs for direct and indirect labor and factory overhead in a job order accounting system distributed the same way as in a process cost accounting system?* The costs are distributed for job order cost accounting in much the same way. The major difference is that the costs must also be entered on the job cost sheets.

The analysis of labor costs sheet is the source document for distributing the labor costs. The analysis of labor costs sheet is prepared at the end of each pay period and is used for recording the direct and indirect labor costs in the general journal.

Prepare the labor costs sheets at the end of each pay period.

ROSEMOUNT MANUFACTURING COMPANY			
Analysis of Labor Costs			
For the Week Ended July 17, 19—			No. 29
Job or Department	Direct Labor	Indirect Labor	Total Cost
14	$ 800		$ 800
15	600		600
16	1,000		1,000
Indirect		$600	600
	$2,400	$600	$3,000

Analysis of labor costs sheet 29 for pay period ended July 17.

The Work-in-Process account is increased for direct labor, and the Factory Overhead account is increased for indirect labor. The total labor cost is credited to Factory Payroll. Note that the analysis of labor costs sheet for the week ended July 17 shows $3,000 in direct and indirect labor costs. The Work-in-Process account and the Factory Overhead account are debited. The Factory Payroll account is credited.

The increase recorded in the Work-in-Process account is also entered on the individual job cost sheets. The $2,400 direct labor cost is divided among Jobs 14, 15, and 16 on the analysis of labor costs.

Direct Labor Costs:
Job 14 . . . . $ 800
Job 15 600
Job 16 1,000
Work-in-
Process $2,400

Entry for direct and indirect labor costs for pay period ended July 17.

		GENERAL JOURNAL			Page 2
DATE		ACCOUNT TITLE AND EXPLANATION	POST. REF.	DEBIT	CREDIT
19— July	17	Work-in-Process	122	2,400 00	
		Factory Overhead	501	600 00	
		Factory Payroll	502		3,000 00
		Distribute labor costs for pay period ended July 17.			

Work-in-Process	122		Factory Overhead	501		Factory Payroll	502
19— July 16 MR1 3,000			19— July 16 MR1 300				19— July 17 J2 3,000
17 J2 2,400			17 J2 600				

JOB COST SHEET

Job No. **15**

Item **CL-9 Chairs**   Date Started **July 16, 19—**

Customer **Colonial Furniture Stores**   Date Wanted **July 24, 19—**

Quantity **300**   Date Completed _____

MATERIALS			LABOR			OVERHEAD			SUMMARY OF COSTS
DATE	REQ. NO.	AMOUNT	DATE	COST SHEET NO.	AMOUNT	DATE	RATE	AMOUNT	
19— July	16	806	900 00	19— July	17	29	600 00		Materials $
									Labor
									Overhead ____
									Total $ ____
									No. Units ____
									Unit Cost $ ____

Job cost sheet showing direct labor and factory overhead for pay period ended July 17.

The job cost sheet for Job 15 shows $600 in direct labor costs. The total labor recorded on the job cost sheets for Jobs 14, 15, and 16 must equal the amount of labor costs entered in the Work-in-Process controlling account in the general ledger.

Factory Overhead Costs

The factory overhead costs are applied to work in process by means of a predetermined overhead rate. Based on past experience, Rosemount

Manufacturing estimates its factory overhead rate at 80 percent of direct labor costs. Thus it computes the factory overhead costs by multiplying the total labor costs by the predetermined overhead rate. The July 17 entry shown here is made to record applied factory overhead for Jobs 14, 15, and 16.

	GENERAL JOURNAL			Page 3
DATE	**ACCOUNT TITLE AND EXPLANATION**	**POST. REF.**	**DEBIT**	**CREDIT**
19— July 17	Work-in-Process . . . . Factory Overhead . . . . Record overhead applied for pay period ended July 17.	122 501	1,920 00	1,920 00

Work-in-Process	122	Factory Overhead		501
19— July 16 MR1 3,000 17 J2 2,400 17 J3 1,920		19— July 16 MR1 300 17 J2 600	19— July 17 J3	1,920

The Work-in-Process account is debited for the applied factory overhead, and the Factory Overhead account is credited. The increase to the Work-in-Process account must also be allocated to the jobs on the individual job cost sheets. The overhead costs are distributed to Jobs 14, 15, and 16 as shown here. Job cost sheet for Job 15 is shown on page 272.

Activity C. Answer the following questions about direct labor, indirect labor, and factory overhead. Refer to the text and illustrations on pages 269 to 271.

1. What is the source document for recording labor costs?
2. What is the amount of direct labor used for Job 14? Job 15? Job 16?
3. What is the amount of indirect labor used for the week ended July 17?
4. What is the total labor cost for the week ended July 17?
5. Which journal is used to record the factory payroll?

6. Which account(s) is (are) debited for the factory payroll? Which account is credited?
7. What percent of direct labor is used to apply factory overhead to the jobs?
8. What amount of factory overhead is applied to Job 14? Job 15? Job 16?

Job No. 14

OVERHEAD		
DATE	**RATE**	**AMOUNT**
19— July 17	80%	640 00

Job No. 15

OVERHEAD		
DATE	**RATE**	**AMOUNT**
19— July 17	80%	480 00

Job No. 16

OVERHEAD		
DATE	**RATE**	**AMOUNT**
19— July 17	80%	800 00

Completing the Job Cost Sheet

D *How is a job cost sheet closed for a job?* When a job is completed, the finished goods are transferred from production to the warehouse. The job cost sheet is now completed for that job, and a journal

JOB COST SHEET

Job No. __15__

Item __CL-9 Chairs__   Date Started __July 16, 19—__

Customer __Colonial Furniture Stores__   Date Wanted __July 24, 19—__

Quantity __300__   Date Completed __July 24, 19—__

MATERIALS			LABOR			OVERHEAD			SUMMARY OF COSTS	
DATE	REQ. NO.	AMOUNT	DATE	COST SHEET NO.	AMOUNT	DATE	RATE	AMOUNT		
19—			19—			19—			Materials	$2,100.00
July	16	806	900 00	July	17	29	600 00	July	17	80%	480 00	Labor	2,000.00
	22	835	1,200 00		24	30	1,400 00		24	80%	1,120 00	Overhead	1,600.00
		2,100 00			2,000 00			1,600 00	Total	$5,700.00
									No. Units	300
									Unit Cost	$19.00

Job No. *14*

SUMMARY OF COSTS	
Materials	$2,300.00
Labor	2,700.00
Overhead	2,160.00
Total	$7,160.00

Job No. *16*

SUMMARY OF COSTS	
Materials	$2,600.00
Labor	3,300.00
Overhead	2,640.00
Total	$8,540.00

entry is made to record the transfer. The job cost sheet for Job 15 was closed, as shown above.

The date completed is recorded. Job 15 is completed on July 24. The direct materials must be added, and the total is entered in the Summary of Costs section of the job cost sheet. Note that additional materials for $1,200 are recorded on July 22. The direct labor and factory overhead are also added. The direct labor for the pay period ended July 24 is $1,400, and the factory overhead is $1,120 (80 percent × $1,400 = $1,120). Both entries are journalized and entered on the job cost sheet.

Factory overhead costs recorded on the job cost sheets represent estimated or applied factory overhead. The actual overhead costs are recorded as a debit to the Factory Overhead account and as credits to specific general ledger accounts, such as Payroll Taxes Expense, Depreciation Expense, Rent Expense, and Supplies Expense. The actual factory overhead costs are not known until the end of the accounting period.

Factory overhead costs may be computed in other ways than as a percent of direct labor. Other common ways of computing them are discussed in Chapter 5. These include the following: estimating direct labor hours, estimating machine hours, estimating direct materials cost, and estimating units of production. If one of these four methods is used, the factory overhead costs could be recorded when the job is completed. In this case only one entry would be made for factory overhead costs.

The cost of completing each job can be determined from the job cost sheet. The costs for materials, labor, and overhead in the Summary section are added for each job cost sheet.

The unit cost for each job can easily be computed. The total cost is divided by the number of units produced. The result is the **unit cost.** For Job 15, the total cost ($5,700) divided by the number of units (300) gives a unit cost of $19.

The total costs and unit cost for Job 15 are recorded on the job cost sheet on page 272.

Estimating Factory Overhead Costs:
- Direct labor cost
- Direct labor hours
- Machine hours
- Direct material cost
- Units of production

$$\text{Unit Cost} = \frac{\text{Total Costs}}{\text{Units Produced}}$$

$$\$19 = \frac{\$5,700}{300}$$

Finished Goods

When the job is completed, a journal entry is made to transfer the costs to the Finished Goods account. The source document for the entry is the job cost sheet.

The July 24 general journal entry here records the transfer of Job 15 to the Finished Goods account. The Finished Goods account is debited, and the Work-in-Process account is credited.

The total cost for Job 14 was $7,160, and Job 16 was $8,540. The T accounts on page 274 show the July 16, 17, 22, 24, and 31 entries to record direct materials, direct labor, factory overhead, and completed jobs.

Selling the Finished Goods. When the units of a job order are shipped to the customer, two entries are made to record the transac-

GENERAL JOURNAL				Page 5	
DATE	**ACCOUNT TITLE AND EXPLANATION**	**POST. REF.**	**DEBIT**	**CREDIT**	
19—					
July 24	Finished Goods	125	5,700 00		
	Work-in-Process.	122		5,700 00	
	Job 15 completed for				
	Colonial Furniture Stores.				
30	Finished Goods	125	7,160 00		
	Work-in-Process.	122		7,160 00	
	Job 14 completed for				
	Futuristic Designs.				
31	Finished Goods	125	8,540 00		
	Work-in-Process.	122		8,540 00	
	Job 16 completed for				
	National Brands.				

Entries to transfer completed Jobs 14, 15, and 16 from production to warehouse.

Work-in-Process		122		Finished Goods		125
19—			19—		19—	
July 16 MR1	3,000	July 24 J5	5,700	July 24 J5	5,700	
17 J2	2,400	30 J5	7,160	30 J5	7,160	
17 J3	1,920	31 J5	8,540	31 J5	8,540	
22 J4	3,200					
24 J4	3,700					
24 J4	2,960					
31 J5	800					
31 J5	1,900					
31 J5	1,520					
	21,400		21,400		21,400	

tion. A separate entry is made to record the decrease in the Finished Goods account and another to recognize the cost of goods sold. The goods for Job 15 cost $5,700 and sold for $8,000. The entries to record the transactions are shown here.

Since the sale is a credit sale, the Accounts Receivable account is debited for the amount of the sale. The Sales account is credited. If the goods were sold for cash, the debit entry would be to the Cash account.

The entry for Jobs 14 and 16 are also shown. As you have seen, each job is identifiable in each step of the manufacturing process.

SALES JOURNAL						Page 1
DATE	INVOICE NO.	ACCOUNT DEBITED	TERMS	POST. REF.	AMOUNT	
19—						
Aug. 5	101	Colonial Furniture Stores	n/30	√	8,000	00
6	102	Futuristic Designs	n/30	√	10,000	00
7	103	National Brands........................	n/30	√	12,000	00
					30,000	00

Entries for sale and decrease in cost of finished goods for Invoices 101, 102, and 103.

GENERAL JOURNAL						Page 6
DATE		ACCOUNT TITLE AND EXPLANATION	POST. REF.	DEBIT	CREDIT	
19—						
Aug.	5	Cost of Goods Sold............	511	5,700 00		
		Finished Goods	125		5,700	00
		Inv. 101 to Colonial Furniture Stores.				
	6	Cost of Goods Sold............	511	7,160 00		
		Finished Goods	125		7,160	00
		Inv. 102 to Futuristic Designs.				
	7	Cost of Goods Sold............	511	8,540 00		
		Finished Goods	125		8,540	00
		Inv. 103 to National Brands.				

General Ledger

Accounts Receivable		111
19—		
Aug. 7 S1	30,000	

Finished Goods				125
19—			19—	
July 24 J5	5,700		Aug. 5 J6	5,700
30 J5	7,160		6 J6	7,160
31 J5	8,540		7 J6	8,540
	21,400			21,400

Sales			401
		19—	
		Aug. 7 S1	30,000

Cost of Goods Sold		511
19—		
Aug. 5 J6	5,700	
6 J6	7,160	
7 J6	8,540	
	21,400	

Subsidiary Ledger

Colonial Furniture Stores	
19—	
Aug. 5	8,000

Futuristic Designs	
19—	
Aug. 6	10,000

National Brands	
19—	
Aug. 7	12,000

Note: The postings to Accounts Receivable and Sales are not normally made until the end of the month.

Activity D. Answer the following questions about completing the job cost sheet and about the entries to the Finished Goods account. Refer to the text and illustrations on pages 272 to 275.

1. When was Job 15 completed?

2. What is the total cost of Job 14? Job 15? Job 16?

3. How many units are produced on Job 15?

4. What is the unit cost of the items produced on Job 15?

5. Which account is debited in the general journal for the 300 chairs finished on Job 15? Which account is credited?

6. What is the July 31 balance of the Finished Goods account?

7. What is the July 31 balance of the Work-in-Process account?

8. Which entry is made to record

the cost of the chairs sold to Colonial Furniture Stores? Which journal is used to record the transaction?

9. Which entry is made to record the sale of the chairs to Colonial Furniture Stores? Which journal is used to record the transaction?

10. What is the total of the three sales recorded in the sales journal in August?

Topic 1   Problems

7-1. The Henderson Corporation manufactures electric clothes dryers made to the specifications of various customers. T-Mark Inc. ordered 100 dryers for installment in a special apartment building project. Complete the job cost sheet for producing these clothes dryers.

JOB COST SHEET

Job No. _70_

Item _TX4 Clothes Dryers_   Date Started _April 4, 19—_

Customer _T-Mark, Inc._   Date Wanted _April 11, 19—_

Quantity _100_   Date Completed _April 11, 19—_

MATERIALS			LABOR			OVERHEAD			SUMMARY OF COSTS
DATE	REQ. NO.	AMOUNT	DATE	COST SHEET NO.	AMOUNT	DATE	RATE	AMOUNT	
19— Apr.	4	417	9,000 00	19— Apr.	6	10	8,000 00			Materials $ Labor Overhead ___ Total $ ___ No. Units ___ Units Costs $ ___

a. Apply factory overhead to the job. Use 80 percent of the direct labor cost.

b. Complete the Summary of Costs section of the job cost sheet.

c. Which account is debited to transfer the dryers to finished goods until shipment? Which account is credited?

d. Which account is debited to record the credit sale of the dryers? Which account is credited?

e. Which account is debited to record the cost of the dryers? Which account is credited to record the decrease in finished goods?

7-2. The Morella Company manufactures lamps and other indoor and outdoor lighting fixtures. The company uses a job order cost system.

The following information and transactions apply to three orders for a special type of lamp.

a. Enter the following data on three job cost sheets.

b. Record the following transactions in a general journal or a materials requisition journal.

c. Post the transactions to the general ledger accounts and the job cost sheets.

d. Complete the Summary of Costs section of each job cost sheet.

Job Number: 21
Item: NZ-9 Lamps
Customer: Robinette Furniture
  Stores
Quantity: 250
Date Started: March 3, 19—
Date Wanted: March 10, 19—
Date Completed:
Job Number: 22
Item: NZ-9 Lamps
Customer: Davis Stores, Inc.

Quantity: 300
Date Started: March 3, 19—
Date Wanted: March 10, 19—
Date Completed:
Job Number: 23
Item: NZ-9 Lamps
Customer: Pack's Building Supply
Quantity: 200
Date Started: March 3, 19—
Date Wanted: March 10, 19—
Date Completed:

March 3 Bought materials for $11,000 on credit to use in manufacturing the lamps.

3 Recorded the following materials requisitions for the three jobs: Materials Requisition 602 for Job 21, $2,500; Materials Requisition 603 for Job 22, $3,000; Materials Requisition 604 for Job 23, $2,000; Materials Requisition 605 for indirect materials, $500.

8 Recorded labor costs for the three jobs. The analysis of labor costs sheet showed the following labor costs: Direct Labor for Job 21, $1,500; Direct Labor for Job 22, $1,800; Direct Labor for Job 23, $1,200; Indirect Labor, $900.

March 8 Recorded applied factory overhead for the work in process. Overhead is estimated as 80 percent of direct labor cost for each job.

NOTE: Save your working papers for further use in Topic Problem 7-3.

7-3. Use the sales journal and the information from Topic Problem 7-2.

a. Record the transactions given on page 278 in the appropriate journals.

b. Post the transactions to the general ledger and pencil-foot the accounts.

c. Answer the following questions for Mr. Borski, the factory manager. What is the balance of the Work-in-Process account? the Finished Goods account? the Cost of Goods Sold account?

March 10 Transferred the completed lamps to the warehouse. Use a separate entry for each of the three jobs.

12 Sold lamps to Robinette Furniture Stores on Invoice 319. The unit sales price for Job 21 was $35.

12 Sold lamps to Davis Stores, Inc. on Invoice 320. The unit sales price for Job 22 was $35.

March 12 Sold lamps to Pack's Building Supply on Invoice 321. The unit sales price for Job 23 was $35.

12 Recorded the cost of goods sold for Invoices 319, 320, and 321.

Topic 2
Financial Statements for a Manufacturing Business

Major Financial Statements for Manufacturing Business:
- Income statement
- Statement of stockholders' equity
- Balance sheet
- Schedule of cost of goods manufactured

A *What are the major financial statements for a manufacturing business?* The major financial statements for a manufacturing business include an income statement, a statement of stockholders' equity, a balance sheet, and a schedule of cost of goods manufactured. The preparation of these statements using perpetual inventory procedures is discussed in this topic. Another statement prepared by a manufacturing business is the Statement of Changes in Financial Position. This statement is discussed in Chapter 14.

Perpetual Inventory Procedures

A review of the special features of perpetual inventory procedures may be helpful at this point. These are the same procedures used in the process and job order cost accounting systems you just completed in Chapter 6 and Topic 1 of this chapter.

Materials. A Materials account is used to report the beginning balance for materials inventory. This account is debited for materials purchased and transportation costs. The account is credited for materials used, purchases returns and allowances, and purchases discounts. Daily (perpetual) balances are maintained in the Materials account and on the stores ledger cards.

Materials	
Balance Materials Purchased Transportation Costs	Materials Used Purchases Returns and Allowances Purchases Discounts

Factory Payroll. The Factory Payroll account is debited to record the total factory labor costs. The account is credited when the factory payroll is distributed to the Work-in-Process account (direct labor) and to the Factory Overhead account (indirect labor). The Factory Payroll account always has a zero balance after the factory payroll has been distributed.

Factory Payroll	
Factory Labor Costs	Factory Payroll Distributed

Factory Overhead. The Factory Overhead account is debited for indirect materials, indirect labor, and other actual factory costs, such as lighting and rent. The Factory Overhead account is credited when factory overhead is applied to work in process. The account always has a zero balance after all the overhead has been applied. Factory overhead is the control account for the factory overhead ledger.

Factory Overhead	
Indirect Materials	Overhead Applied
Indirect Labor	
Lighting	
Rent	

Work in Process. The Work-in-Process account is debited for the cost of direct materials, direct labor, and applied factory overhead. This account is credited when goods are completed and transferred to finished goods (warehouse).

Work-in-Process	
Direct Materials	Goods Completed
Direct Labor	and Transferred
Applied Factory	to Finished
Overhead	Goods

Finished Goods. The Finished Goods account is debited for all goods produced. The account is credited for the cost of goods sold. The balance of the Finished Goods account as well as the balances of the accounts in the finished goods subsidiary ledger are maintained on a daily basis.

Finished Goods	
Goods Produced	Cost of Goods
	Sold

Cost of Goods Sold. The Cost of Goods Sold account is a basic feature of accounting systems using perpetual inventory procedures. This account is debited for the cost of goods sold. It is credited at the end of the period when all the temporary accounts are closed to the Income Summary account. The Cost of Goods Sold account eliminates the need to compute cost of goods sold on the income statement. The debit balance of this account is the amount of cost of goods sold reported on the income statement.

Cost of Goods Sold	
Cost of Goods	Balance Closed to
Sold	Income Sum-
	mary

Physical Inventory. A physical inventory is taken at least once a year to verify the balances in the Materials, Work-in-Process, and Finished Goods accounts.

Worksheet. The worksheet for a manufacturing business is adapted from the worksheet for a merchandising business. In order to simplify the illustration, we have omitted the trial balance and adjustments sections. The illustration starts with the Adjusted Trial Balance section. Also, the number of accounts have been held to a minimum.

The worksheet provides data for preparing the income statement, statement of stockholders' equity, and the balance sheet. Information needed for the schedule of cost of goods manufactured is taken from ledger accounts. These statements will now be explained. (Perpetual inventory procedures are being used.)

Schedule of Cost of Goods Manufactured

The schedule of cost of goods manufactured summarizes the amount of direct materials, direct labor, and factory overhead required to produce the products during the accounting period.

A schedule of cost of goods manufactured summarizes direct materials, direct labor, and factory overhead for manufacturing goods during the accounting period.

HARRIS MANUFACTURING COMPANY
Worksheet
For the Year Ended December 31, 19—

	ADJUSTED TRIAL BALANCE		INCOME STATEMENT		STATEMENT OF STOCKHOLDERS' EQUITY		BALANCE SHEET	
	DEBIT	CREDIT	DEBIT	CREDIT	DEBIT	CREDIT	DEBIT	CREDIT
Cash	50,000						50,000	
Accounts Receivable .	41,000						41,000	
Materials Inventory .	90,000						90,000	
Work-in-Process Inv. .	130,000						130,000	
Finished Goods Inv. .	400,000						400,000	
Prepaid Insurance. . .	30,000						30,000	
Supplies on Hand . . .	2,000						2,000	
Land	100,000						100,000	
Buildings	960,000						960,000	
Accumulated Depreciation— Buildings		390,000						390,000
Office Equipment . . .	100,000						100,000	
Accumulated Depreciation— Office Equipment. .		25,000						25,000
Plant Equipment . . .	585,000						585,000	
Accumulated Depreciation— Plant Equipment . .		210,000						210,000
Loans Payable.		170,000						170,000
Accounts Payable . . .		88,500						88,500
Mortgage Payable. . .		300,000						300,000
Capital Stock		700,000				700,000		
Retained Earnings . .		476,500				476,500		
Sales		1,600,000		1,600,000				
Sales Ret. and Allow.	20,000		20,000					
Cost of Goods Sold . .	932,000		932,000					
Advertising Expense .	30,000		30,000					
Delivery Expense . . .	140,000		140,000					
Sales Salaries Expense	180,000		180,000					
Uncollectible Accounts Expense .	5,000		5,000					
Depreciation Exp.— Office Equipment. .	5,000		5,000					
Salary Expense— Administrative . . .	140,000		140,000					
Payroll Taxes Expense —Sell. and Admin.	20,000		20,000					
	3,960,000	3,960,000	1,472,000	1,600,000		1,176,500	2,488,000	1,183,500
				1,472,000				
Net Income			128,000			128,000		
						1,304,500		1,304,500
							2,488,000	2,488,000

NOTE: The cents columns have been omitted.

The schedule of cost of goods *manufactured* for a manufacturing business is similar to the schedule of cost of goods sold for a merchandising business. In a merchandising business the cost of goods *sold* is computed by using the following formula.

Schedule of cost of goods manufactured supports the income statement.

| Beginning Inventory (Merchandise Inventory) | + | Net Purchases | = | Cost of Goods Available for Sale | − | Ending Inventory (Merchandise Inventory) | = | Cost of Goods Sold |

In a manufacturing business the cost of goods manufactured is found in a similar manner, as follows.

| Beginning Inventory (Work in Process) | + | Manufacturing Costs (Direct Materials + Direct Labor + Factory Overhead) | = | Cost of Goods in Process During Period | − | Ending Inventory (Work in Process) | = | Cost of Goods Manufactured |

A schedule of cost of goods manufactured for the Harris Manufacturing Company is shown on page 282. The statement covers the year ended December 31, 19—. The procedure used to prepare the schedule of cost of goods manufactured involves the following steps:

STEP 1. *Enter the beginning inventory for work in process.* The beginning inventory is the work in process on the first day of the accounting period, in this case January 1. The amount of the beginning inventory is taken from the Work-in-Process account. The beginning inventory amount for Harris Manufacturing is $140,000.

STEP 2. *Determine the Cost of Direct Materials Used.* Begin with the balance of the Materials account at the beginning of the accounting period (January 1). This amount is obtained from the ledger account. The beginning balance of the Materials account is $100,000.

Work-in-Process				Materials		
Jan. 1 Balance	140,000	832,000	Cost Transferred to Finished Goods	Jan. 1 Balance 100,000	10,000	Purchases Returns and Allowances
				Purchases 498,000	498,000	Materials Used
Materials 498,000				Dec. 31 Balance 90,000		
Labor 180,000						
Factory Overhead 144,000						
Dec. 31 Balance 130,000						

HARRIS MANUFACTURING COMPANY
Schedule of Cost of Goods Manufactured
For the Year Ended December 31, 19—

Work-in-Process Inventory, January 1			140,000 00
Direct Materials Used:			
Materials Inventory, January 1	$100,000		
Materials Purchases—Net	488,000		
Cost of Materials Available for Use	588,000		
Less: Materials Inventory, December 31	90,000		
Cost of Materials Used		498,000 00	
Direct Labor		180,000 00	
Factory Overhead:			
Depreciation Expense—Buildings	$ 7,200		
Depreciation Expense—Plant Equipment	18,750		
Indirect Labor	30,000		
Insurance Expense	9,000		
Payroll Taxes Expense—Factory	16,700		
Plant Maintenance Expense	12,350		
Salaries—Factory Management	35,000		
Supplies Expense—Factory	3,000		
Utilities Expense—Factory	12,000		
Total Factory Overhead		144,000 00	
Total Manufacturing Costs			822,000 00
Total Work-in-Process During Period			962,000 00
Less: Work-in-Process Inventory, December 31			130,000 00
Cost of Goods Manufactured			832,000 00

Next, the purchases returns and allowances ($10,000) is subtracted from the purchases of materials ($498,000) to get the net purchases of materials ($488,000). Note that the Materials account is debited for purchases of materials and credited for purchases returns and allowances.

In the schedule, Harris Manufacturing shows that the net purchases of materials was $488,000. Thus the total cost of materials available for use during the year is $588,000 ($100,000 in materials inventory + $488,000 in net purchases of materials).

Next, the December 31 inventory of materials ($90,000) is subtracted from the cost of materials available for use ($588,000) to find the cost of direct materials actually used during the year ($498,000).

STEP 3. *Determine the cost of direct labor.* The cost of the direct labor is the $180,000 credit to the Factory Payroll account. The amount of direct labor cost can also be found on the analysis of labor cost sheets. As the Factory Payroll account shows, the total amount of factory payroll has been distributed to direct labor ($180,000) and indirect labor or factory overhead ($30,000).

Factory Payroll	
Total Payroll 210,000	180,000 Distributed as Direct Labor
	30,000 Distributed as Indirect Labor

STEP 4. *Determine the total factory overhead costs.* List the balances of the factory overhead expense accounts. The account balances are found in the factory overhead subsidiary ledger. The total of the account balances is $144,000—the total factory overhead expense for the year. Note that this is the same amount debited to the Factory Overhead account in the general ledger.

Factory Overhead			
Actual Overhead	144,000	144,000	Applied Overhead

Information From Factory Overhead Subsidiary Ledger

Depreciation Expense—Buildings	7,200
Depreciation Expense—Plant Equipment	18,750
Indirect Labor	30,000
Insurance Expense	9,000
Payroll Taxes Expense—Factory	16,700
Plant Maintenance Expense	12,350
Salaries—Factory Management	35,000
Supplies Expense—Factory	3,000
Utilities Expense—Factory	12,000
Total Factory Overhead	$144,000

STEP 5. *Determine the total manufacturing costs.* Add the costs of materials used, direct labor, and total factory overhead on the schedule. The total manufacturing costs for Harris Manufacturing is $822,000 ($498,000 + $180,000 + $144,000 = $822,000).

STEP 6. *Determine the total work in process during the period.* Add the total manufacturing costs for the period to the beginning work-in-process inventory. This amount is the total work in process during the period. For Harris Manufacturing the total work in process during the period is $962,000 ($140,000 + $822,000).

STEP 7. *Enter the ending inventory for work in process.* The ending inventory is the work in process on the last day of the accounting period, in this case December 31. The ending inventory for work in process is the balance ($130,000) in the Work-in-Process account.

Work-in-Process			
Jan. 1 Balance	140,000	832,000	Cost Trans- ferred to Finished Goods
Materials	498,000		
Labor	180,000		
Factory Over- head	144,000		
Dec. 31 Balance	130,000		

Finished Goods			
Jan. 1 Balance	500,000	932,000	Cost of Goods Sold
Cost of Goods Manufac- tured	832,000		
Dec. 31 Balance	400,000		

STEP 8. *Determine the cost of goods manufactured.* To complete the schedule of cost of goods manufactured, subtract the ending work-in-process inventory from the total work in process during the period

to find the cost of goods manufactured. For Harris Manufacturing this is $832,000 ($962,000 − $130,000).

Accounting Concept:
Cost of Goods Manufactured. A relationship exists between the cost of goods manufactured and the cost of goods sold. The cost of goods manufactured is debited to the Finished Goods account. The cost of goods sold is credited to the Finished Goods account.

Activity A-1. Determine the correct amount for each of the following items. Refer to the text and illustrations on pages 278 to 284.

1. Total of adjusted trial balance
2. Amount of net income
3. Work-in-process inventory, January 1
4. Amount of net purchases
5. Cost of materials available for use
6. Cost of materials used
7. Cost of direct labor
8. Total factory overhead
9. Total manufacturing costs
10. Total work in process during period
11. Work in process, December 31
12. Cost of goods manufactured

Activity A-2. Complete the following formula for determining the cost of goods manufactured.

Income Statement

B *How is the income statement for a manufacturing business prepared?* The income statement for a manufacturing firm is prepared in much the same way as the income statement for a merchandising business. However, the Cost of Goods Sold section differs because the merchant *purchases* products to sell. The manufacturer *makes* products to sell.

The December 31 income statement for Harris Manufacturing Company is shown on page 285. The procedure used to prepare the income statement is as follows.

STEP 1. *Determine Net Sales.* The net sales are computed the same as for a merchandising business. For Harris Manufacturing the sales returns and allowances ($20,000) are subtracted from the sales ($1,600,000) to find the net sales ($1,580,000). You will recall that information for the income statement is taken from the worksheet.

HARRIS MANUFACTURING COMPANY
Income Statement
For the Year Ended December 31, 19—

Revenue From Sales:			
Sales		1,600,000 00	
Less: Sales Returns and Allowances		20,000 00	
Net Sales		1,580,000 00	
Less: Cost of Goods Sold		932,000 00	
Gross Profit on Sales		648,000 00	
Operating Expenses:			
Selling Expenses:			
Advertising Expense	$ 30,000		
Delivery Expense	140,000		
Sales Salaries Expense	180,000		
Total Selling Expenses		350,000 00	
Administrative Expenses:			
Uncollectible Accounts Expense	5,000		
Depreciation Expense—Office			
Equipment	5,000		
Salary Expense—Administrative	140,000		
Payroll Taxes Expense—Selling and			
Administrative	20,000		
Total Administrative Expenses		170,000 00	
Total Operating Expenses			520,000 00
Net Income			128,000 00

STEP 2. *Enter the Cost of Goods Sold.* Next, the debit balance of the cost of goods sold account ($932,000) is entered on the income statement.

Cost of Goods Sold	
Dec. 31 Bal- 932,000	
ance	

STEP 3. *Find the Gross Profit on Sales.* The cost of goods sold ($932,000) is subtracted from the net sales ($1,580,000) to get the gross profit on sales ($648,000).

STEP 4. *Compute the Total Operating Expenses.* In this case the operating expenses are divided into selling expenses and administrative expenses. (Factory overhead expenses are not included since they were listed in the statement of cost of goods manufactured.) The total of the selling expenses and the administrative expenses ($350,000 + $170,000) gives the total operating expenses ($520,000).

STEP 5. *Compute the Net Income.* The total operating expenses ($520,000) are subtracted from the gross profit ($648,000) to obtain the net income ($128,000) amount.

Accounting Concept:
Income Statement for a Manufacturing Business. The manufacturing income statement reports cost of goods manufactured. The merchandising statement reports cost of goods purchased.

Activity B. Answer the following questions about the income statement for a manufacturing business. Refer to the text and illustrations on pages 284 and 285.

1. What is the amount of net sales?

2. What is the amount of cost of goods sold?

3. What is the amount of gross profits on sales?

4. What is the amount of selling expenses? administrative expenses?

5. What is the amount of total operating expenses?

Balance Sheet and Statement of Stockholders' Equity

Special Accounts on a Manufacturing Business's Balance Sheet:

- Materials account (inventory)
- Work-in-Process account (inventory)
- Finished goods (inventory)
- Plant and equipment

C *How is the balance sheet for a manufacturing firm prepared?* The balance sheet for a manufacturing firm is prepared in the same manner as the balance sheet for a merchandising business. In both instances the total assets equal the total liabilities and stockholders' (owner's) equity. However, there are special account titles that will appear only on the balance sheet for the manufacturing firm. These accounts are inventory accounts: Materials, Work-in-Process, and Finished Goods. There are also usually plant and equipment accounts. The three inventory accounts are listed as current assets. The plant and equipment accounts are listed in a separate section on the balance sheet. The balance sheet for a merchandising business includes only one inventory account—a merchandise inventory account.

The balance sheet and statement of stockholders' equity for the Harris Manufacturing Company are shown on page 287.

Closing Accounts

Close the revenue, cost, and expense accounts to Income Summary account.

The revenue, cost, and expense accounts used by manufacturing businesses are closed at the end of each accounting period. All of these accounts are closed to the Income Summary account. The Income Summary account is closed to the Retained Earnings account (the account used to report profits kept in the business).

Another part of the closing procedure is to prove the subsidiary ledgers—the stores ledger and factory overhead ledger. The stores ledger is reconciled with the balance in the Materials account. The factory overhead ledger is reconciled with the amount of applied factory overhead credited to the Factory Overhead account. Sometimes there will be a difference between the total of the subsidiary ledger and the applied factory overhead credited to the Factory Overhead account. This difference will be either *underapplied* or *overapplied* factory overhead. When this happens the difference is transferred to the Cost of Goods Sold account.

HARRIS MANUFACTURING COMPANY
Balance Sheet
December 31, 19—

ASSETS			
Current Assets:			
Cash	50,000 00		
Accounts Receivable	41,000 00		
Materials Inventory	90,000 00		
Work-in-Process Inventory	130,000 00		
Finished Goods Inventory	100,000 00		
Prepaid Insurance	30,000 00		
Supplies on Hand	2,000 00		
Total Current Assets		743,500 00	
Plant and Equipment:			
Land	100,000 00		
Buildings $960,000			
Accumulated Depreciation—Bldgs. 390,000	570,000 00		
Office Equipment $100,000			
Accumulated Depreciation—Office Eq. 25,000	75,000 00		
Plant Equipment $585,000			
Accumulated Depreciation—Plant Eq. 210,000	375,000 00		
Total Plant and Equipment		1,120,000 00	
Total Assets		1,863,000 00	
LIABILITIES			
Current Liabilities:			
Loans Payable	170,000 00		
Accounts Payable	88,500 00		
Total Current Liabilities		258,500 00	
Long-Term Liabilities:			
Mortgage Payable		300,000 00	
Total Liabilities		558,500 00	
STOCKHOLDERS' EQUITY			
Capital Stock	700,000 00		
Retained Earnings	604,500 00		
Total Stockholders' Equity		1,304,500 00	
Total Liabilities and Stockholders' Equity		1,863,000 00	

HARRIS MANUFACTURING COMPANY
Statement of Stockholders' Equity
December 31, 19—

Capital Stock		700,000 00	
Retained Earnings, January 1, 19—	476,500 00		
Plus: Net Income for the Year	128,000 00		
Retained Earnings, December 31, 19—		604,500 00	
Total Stockholders' Equity		1,304,500 00	

Activity C. Answer the following questions about the balance sheet for
Harris Manufacturing Company. Refer to the text and illustrations on
pages 286 and 287.

1. How many inventory accounts are listed as current assets?
2. What are the inventory accounts listed as current assets?
3. What is the amount of plant and equipment assets?
4. What is the amount of total assets?
5. What is the amount of current liabilities?
6. What is the amount of long-term liabilities?
7. What is the amount of retained earnings on December 31?
8. What is the amount of net income added to retained earnings?
9. What is the amount of stockholders' equity?
10. What is the amount of total liabilities and stockholders' equity?

Topic 2   Problems

7-4. Look over the items listed here. Indicate on which report each item appears. Some items may appear on more than one report. Use BS for Balance Sheet, IS for Income Statement, CGM for Cost of Goods Manufactured Schedule, and SE for Statement of Stockholders' Equity.

a. Sales Returns and Allowances
b. Retained Earnings
c. Prepaid Insurance
d. Sales Expense
e. Loans Payable
f. Factory Payroll
g. Materials Inventory
h. Utilities Expense (Factory)
i. Mortgage Payable
j. Plant Maintenance Expense
k. Work-in-Process Inventory
l. Depreciation Expense—Office Equipment
m. Depreciation Expense—Plant Equipment
n. Capital Stock
o. Sales
p. Cost of Goods Sold
q. Advertising Expense
r. Indirect Labor
s. Cost of Materials Available for Use
t. Total Work in Process During Period
u. Total Administrative Expenses
v. Total Manufacturing Costs

7-5. Prepare a schedule of cost of goods manufactured as of December 31, 19—, for the Foley Manufacturing Company. The information you need for this management report may be found in the general ledger accounts and factory ledger accounts provided here. Refer to the illustration on page 282 as you complete the schedule.

Factory Overhead Ledger Balances

Depr. Expense—Building	$ 8,000
Depr. Expense—Plant & Equipment	25,000
Indirect Labor	76,000
Insurance Expense	5,000
Payroll Taxes Expense—Factory	36,000
Plant Maintenance Expense	26,000
Salaries Expense—Management	50,000
Utilities Expense—Factory	14,000

Materials

| Jan. 1 Balance | 150,000 | 10,000 | Purchases Returns and Allowances |
| Purchases | 380,000 | 400,000 | Materials Used |

Work-in-Process

Jan. 1 Balance	200,000	915,000	Cost Transferred to Finished Goods
Material	400,000		
Labor	300,000		
Factory Overhead	240,000		

Factory Overhead

| Actual Overhead | 240,000 | 240,000 | Applied Overhead |

Factory Payroll

| Total Payroll | 376,000 | 300,000 | Direct Labor |
| | | 76,000 | Indirect Labor |

The Language of Business

Here are some basic terms that make up the language of business. Do you understand the meaning of each? Can you define each term and use it in an original sentence?

job order cost
  accounting

process cost account-
  ing system

job cost sheet
open job cost sheet

schedule of cost of
  goods manufactured

Chapter 7 Questions

1. When is a job order cost accounting system used?
2. What kinds of information are recorded on the job cost sheet?
3. Which account is debited for the purchase of materials on credit? Which account is credited?
4. Which account is debited to transfer products from work in process to the warehouse? What account is credited?
5. Which account is debited to record the cost of products sold? Which account is credited?

6. Which account is debited for the sales price of products sold on credit? Which account is credited?
7. Which are major financial statements for a manufacturing business?
8. What are the basic features of perpetual inventory procedures?
9. What is the purpose of the schedule of cost of goods manufactured?
10. List the inventory accounts usually found on the balance sheet for the manufacturing business.

Chapter 7 Problems

Problems for Chapter 7 are given in the *Working Papers and Chapter Problems* for Part 1. If you are using the workbook, do the problems in the space provided there. Complete your assigned topic problems before answering the chapter problems.

Chapter 7 Management Cases

Performance Analysis. The managers of a business must know how well they have performed their jobs. Such performance analysis is the best way to learn how to improve efficiency and profits. Sometimes the analysis of financial statements and other management reports will provide clues to past failures and future levels of operations.

Case 7M-1. The owner of the Obetz Manufacturing Company is planning a sales budget for October. Examine the income statement for September, shown on page 290, and answer the following questions. Assume that costs and expenses will remain the same. The unit sales price is $200.
a. How many units were sold during September?
b. How many additional units must be sold to break even, or make up the loss? (*HINT:* Divide the loss by the unit sales price.)

c. How many units will have to be sold during October to break even?
d. How many units will have to be sold in order to make a profit of $20,000 in October? (*HINT:* This number will be in addition to the number in Question **c.**)
e. The owner is thinking about increasing the sales price to $250. How many units would have to be sold at this new price in order for the company to break even?
f. What factors should the owner consider before increasing the sales price?

Case 7M-2. Owners and managers use many kinds of reports to evaluate the results of operations. An example of one report is the income statement prepared for Obetz Manufacturing Company (Case 7M-1). Another important report is the Schedule of Cost

OBETZ MANUFACTURING COMPANY
Income Statement
For the Month Ended September 30, 19—

Net Sales	*50,000*
Less: Cost of Goods Sold	*40,000*
Gross Profit on Sales	*10,000*
Less: Operating Expenses—	
Selling & Administrative	*30,000*
Net Income (Loss)	*(20,000)*

of Goods Manufactured. Examine the cost schedule for Obetz Manufacturing and answer the following questions.

a. What percent is the cost of materials used to the total cost of goods manufactured?

b. What percent is direct labor costs to the total cost of goods manufactured?

c. What percent is total factory overhead costs to the total cost of goods manufactured?

d. Assume that the manufacturing percentages are higher this month than for August. Can you suggest ways to reduce direct materials cost? direct labor costs? factory overhead costs?

OBETZ MANUFACTURING COMPANY
Schedule of Cost of Goods Manufactured
For the Month Ended September 30, 19—

Work-in-Process, September 1		5,000 00
Direct Materials Used:		
Materials Inventory, September 1	10,000 00	
Materials Purchase—Net	25,000 00	
Cost of Materials Available for Use	35,000 00	
Less: Materials Inventory, September 30 . . .	20,000 00	
Cost of Materials Used	15,000 00	
Direct Labor	10,000 00	
Factory Overhead	8,000 00	
Total Manufacturing Costs		33,000 00
Total Work-in-Process During Period		38,000 00
Less: Work-in-Process, September 30		8,000 00
Cost of Goods Manufactured		30,000 00

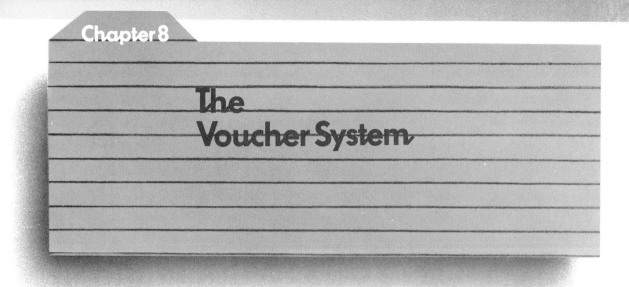

The Voucher System

All business managers are concerned about controlling business assets, especially cash. Yes, they should be concerned, especially about cash. Cash, if uncontrolled, might be stolen or mishandled. Thus many managers put more effort into protecting their cash than they do into protecting their other assets, such as supplies, inventories, equipment, and other assets. In this chapter we discuss the voucher system, one method used to control cash payments.

Topic 1
Understanding the Voucher System

A *What is a voucher system?* The **voucher system,** a system for internal control of cash payments, combines certain features of the cash payments subsystem and the purchases subsystem. Some of the features of the voucher system are as follows.

A voucher system is a system for internal control of cash payments.

• All payments of money, except small petty cash payments, must be made by check.

• Small cash payments are made through the petty cash fund.

A petty cash fund contains cash on hand to pay small amounts.

• A *voucher* must be issued by an authorized person before any check is written. Petty cash vouchers are used to authorize payments from the petty cash fund. Regular vouchers are used to authorize checks to be written. (Whenever the word **voucher** is used, it refers to an authorization for a check. A petty cash voucher is identified by the words *petty cash*.)

An authorized employee must issue a voucher before a check can be written.

- A **voucher register** is a multicolumn journal that is used instead of a purchases journal. All vouchers must be recorded in the voucher register. A voucher must be recorded before a check can be written.
- A **check register** is a multicolumn journal that is used instead of a cash payments journal. All checks must be recorded in the check register.
- A *Vouchers Payable account* is used in place of the Accounts Payable account.
- An **unpaid vouchers file** replaces the accounts payable ledger. Unpaid vouchers are filed according to due date. This eliminates the need for posting to the individual creditor's account.

The voucher system is very useful for large businesses.

The voucher system is especially useful for large businesses that have several employees who authorize cash payments. In these cases standard procedures must be established for making cash payments. The businesses that use the voucher system find that the amount of paper work involved is its major disadvantage.

Voucher Forms

A voucher may take many forms depending upon the particular needs of the business. However, several characteristics are common to most voucher forms. These characteristics are as follows.

- The voucher is usually a preprinted form.
- The voucher most often contains printed information on both sides.
- Vouchers are prenumbered consecutively.
- An individual voucher is prepared for each invoice or batch of invoices from the same creditor.
- Usually the inside of the voucher shows the preprinted voucher number, invoice date, terms, due date, supplier's name and address, invoice number, voucher details, invoice amount, and space for authorized approval.
- Usually the outside of the voucher shows the voucher number, due date, supplier's name, voucher summary, payment summary, account distribution, and space for authorized approval. The space for the voucher register page number is left blank until the voucher is recorded in the voucher register.
- The voucher form printed on both sides is folded in order to make a **jacket,** or pocket, which will hold supporting documents of the transaction, such as the invoice.

Verifying the Invoice

The use of the voucher system begins with the receipt of an invoice. Refer to the invoice on the next page for the discussion that follows.

QUALITY PLASTICS, INC.
109 Dunn Avenue
Portland, Oregon 97265

Sold To

Bundy Company
14 Crescent Road
Redlands, CA 92373

INVOICE No. **1347**

Ship To

Same

Date 3/14/--

Terms 2/10, n/30

Purchase Order No.	Date	Shipped Via	FOB	No. of Packages
103-249	3/1/--	Truck	Portland	2

QUANTITY	STOCK NUMBER	DESCRIPTION	UNIT PRICE	AMOUNT
250	K29	Calculator cases	0.40	$100.00
100	2543	Calculator cases	0.45	45.00
4,000	2433	Plastic number keys	0.03	120.00
350	307	On/Off keys	0.10	35.00
				$300.00

Approval Date	3/20/--	
Quantities Received	LFJ	
Prices Charged	CA	
Extensions and Totals	D. Adams	$300.00
Accounts Debited	Materials	$300.00
Accounts Credited	Vouchers Payable	
Voucher No.	903 *	
Date Paid	3/22/- *	

COPY 1 — CUSTOMER

*Not entered until recorded in voucher register.

The Bundy Company received Invoice 1347 from Quality Plastics, Inc., for materials it purchased to manufacture hand-held calculators. When the invoice is received, the face of the invoice is stamped with an approval stamp. The invoice is then verified regarding the quantities received, prices charged, extensions, and totals tallied. The accounts to be debited and credited are indicated, as is the date the invoice is approved. As each section is verified, the employee responsible for verification indicates approval by initialing the approval stamp. The voucher number and voucher date lines are left blank until the voucher is prepared.

Preparing the Voucher

After an invoice is approved, it is sent to the accounting department for payment. A voucher must be prepared before the accounting clerk can issue a check in payment of the invoice.

A voucher is a written authorization to make a cash payment.

In a voucher system a special form called a voucher must be completed and signed before a check can be written. The **voucher** is a written authorization, usually on a prenumbered form, to make a cash payment. Without this authorization, the accounting clerk is not allowed to issue checks for any purpose. By requiring vouchers for all major expenses, management is able to control cash payments.

In the voucher shown below, the Bundy Company must issue a check in payment of Invoice 1347. The accounting clerk fills out the information on the inside of the next available prenumbered voucher form. In this case the next voucher number is 903. The information needed to complete the inside of the voucher is found on the approved invoice that is to be paid. A voucher cannot be prepared unless an invoice has been verified and approved.

BUNDY COMPANY
14 Crescent Road
Redlands, California 92373

Voucher No. **903**

Invoice Date   March 14, 19--   Due Date   March 22, 19--

Supplier   Quality Plastics, Inc.   Terms   2/10, n/30
Address   109 Dunn Avenue
               Portland, OR 97265

Invoice No.	Voucher Details	Invoice Amount
1347	Materials purchased	300.00
		Total 300.00

Approved by _____ *MW* _____

Inside of Voucher

Next, the invoice date, the due date, and the terms are entered on the voucher. The actual due date for Voucher 903 is the last day of the discount period (March 24). However, the Bundy Company *pays its vouchers two days before the due date* in order to allow time to process the voucher and mail the check. Thus the Bundy Company pays Voucher 903 on *March* 22 so that the cash discount can be deducted.

The name and address of Quality Plastics, Inc. are also entered on the inside of the voucher. This is to indicate what the supplier's name is and where the check is being sent.

The accounting clerk then enters the invoice number, voucher details, and the invoice amount. Because the completed voucher becomes the basis for the accounting entry, an authorized employee must approve the accuracy of the transaction by signing or initialing the inside of the voucher.

A completed voucher becomes the basis for the accounting entry.

ACCOUNT DISTRIBUTION				VOUCHER		NO. **903**
Accounts Debited	**Amount**		Due Date March 22, 19--			
Materials	300	00				
Sales Supplies			Recorded on Voucher Register Page 20 *			
Advertising Expense						
Delivery Expense			Supplier Quality Plastics, Inc.			
Misc. Selling Expense						
Misc. General Expense						
Transportation In						
Factory Payroll Payable			Voucher Summary			
Factory Overhead			Amount		300	00
			Adjustment		0	00
Total Debits	300	00	Discount		6	00
			Net		294	00
Accounts Credited	**Amount**		Approved *R a*		Controller	
Vouchers Payable	300	00	Recorded *TRB*			
Employee Inc. Tax Payable						
FICA Taxes Payable			Payment Summary			
			Date March 22, 19--			
			Amount $294.00			
Total Credits	300	00	Check No. 2019			
			Approved CRT		Treasurer	
Distribution Approved *DH*			Recorded *DC*			

Outside of Voucher

*Not entered until recorded in voucher register.

The accounting clerk also uses information from the invoice to complete the outside of the voucher. The information recorded on this part of the voucher includes the due date, supplier's names, voucher summary, payment summary, and account distribution.

The account distribution section is used to indicate the accounts that are to be debited and credited. In this instance, Materials is debited for $300 and Vouchers Payable is credited for $300. (The Vouchers Payable account is used instead of the Accounts Payable account.) The accounting clerk records the voucher number and invoice date on the invoice.

After the outside of the voucher is completed, the voucher is folded so that it forms a jacket for the invoice. The invoice is then placed inside the voucher.

The accounting clerk sends the voucher jacket, with the invoice inside, to the accounting supervisor for approval. The supervisor rechecks the invoice and the voucher and then initials the voucher. The voucher is now ready to be recorded in the voucher register.

Accounting Concept:
Control—Cash Payments. Special procedures are often established to ensure accuracy, honesty, efficiency, and speed in handling and recording cash payments.

Activity A. Answer the following questions about the invoice and voucher. Refer to the text and illustrations on pages 291 to 296.

1. What is the number of the invoice to be paid?

2. What are the credit terms for the invoice?

3. What is the total amount of the invoice?

4. Who checks the extensions and totals on the invoice?

5. Who verifies the quantities received?

6. What is the name of the supplier?

7. What is the number of the voucher issued to pay the invoice?

8. What is the due date for the payment of the voucher?

9. Who approves the voucher?

10. What is the amount of the check to be written?

11. What is the number of the check issued for payment of the voucher?

12. Who is the treasurer?

13. Who records the voucher?

14. Which account is debited for the items purchased? Which account is credited?

15. Who is the controller?

16. What is the page of the voucher register on which the voucher is recorded?

17. Who checks the prices charged on the invoice?

Recording the Voucher

A voucher register replaces the purchases journal.

B *Where is the voucher recorded?* After the voucher has been completed, it is recorded in the voucher register. As you just learned, the voucher register is a special journal that takes the place of the purchases journal. The voucher register also provides special amount columns for recording costs and expenses for such items as materials, factory payroll, factory overhead, and sales supplies. General ledger debit and credit columns are also provided.

Martin Bough / Studios. Inc.

The accountant records a completed voucher in the
voucher register.

Transactions are recorded in the voucher register in the same way
that they are in any multicolumn journal. A page from the Bundy
Company's voucher register is shown on pages 298 and 299. Note that
Voucher 903 is recorded in the voucher register on March 18. Notice
that the $300 is entered in the Vouchers Payable credit column and in
the Materials debit column. Note also that vouchers are recorded in
sequence—881, 882, 883. This procedure helps to ensure that all
vouchers are entered.

The date and check number columns under the Paid columns are
not filled in when the voucher is recorded. These columns are completed when the check is written. The check to pay Voucher 903 is
written on the due date of March 22. At that time the accounting clerk
enters the date and check number in the Paid columns of the voucher
register.

When the voucher has been recorded in the voucher register, the
accounting clerk records the voucher register page number on the top
section of the outside of the voucher jacket.

Once a voucher is recorded in the voucher register, it is filed, according to due date, in the Unpaid Vouchers file. The voucher will remain
in this file until the due date recorded on the jacket.

On the due date the voucher is removed from the file and verified for
payment by a supervisor other than the employee who initialed the

VOUCHER

DATE		VOUCHER NO.	PAYEE	PAID		VOUCHERS PAYABLE CREDIT
				DATE	CHECK NO.	
19—						
Mar.	1	881	Petty Cash	3/1	1095	50 00
	2	882	A and W Supplies Co.			30 00
	2	883	Point Express	3/2	1096	21 50
	3	884	Burke Co.	See Vo.	907	2,000 00
	18	903	Quality Plastics, Inc.	3/22	2019	300 00
	22	904	Industrial Machines, Inc. . . .	3/28	2030	1,000 00
	22	905	Industrial Machines, Inc. . . .			2,300 00
	22	906	Industrial Machines, Inc. . . .			2,300 00
	23	907	Burke Co.	3/29	2072	1,500 00
	23	908	Roe Insurance	See Vo.	910	1,200 00
	24	909	Petty Cash	3/24	2085	37 40
	25	910	Roe Insurance			1,600 00
	25	911	D. O'Neill; Payroll Clerk . . .	3/25		719 50
						22,000 00
						(211)

inside of the voucher. This second supervisor indicates final approval by signing the outside of the voucher. Once this is done, a check can be issued and payment can be recorded in the voucher register and in the check register.

Recording Other Types of Transactions

A voucher must be prepared for all transactions which are to be recorded in the voucher register. The preparation of Voucher 903 for Invoice 1347 is illustrated on page 294. Procedures to record vouchers

REGISTER   Page 20

MATERIALS DEBIT	FACTORY PAYROLL DEBIT	FACTORY OVERHEAD POST. REF.	FACTORY OVERHEAD DEBIT	SALES SUPPLIES DEBIT	OTHER GENERAL LEDGER ACCOUNTS ACCOUNT TITLE	POST. REF.	DEBIT	CREDIT
					Petty Cash.....	102	50 00	
				30 00				
21 50								
2,000 00								
300 00								
					Equipment.....	165	5,600 00	
1,500 00								
		√	1,200 00					
				6 30	Advertising Exp..	612	27 10	
					Delivery Exp....	605	4 00	
		√	1,600 00					
	1,000 00				FICA Tax Payable	222		60 50
					Inc. Tax Payable	221		220 00
6,000 00	1,000 00		4,100 00	400 00			11,250 00	750 00
(121)	(502)		(501)	(141)			(—)	(—)

DISTRIBUTION OF ACCOUNTS

for other types of transactions are described here. These transactions are recorded in the voucher register shown above.

Petty Cash. Petty cash is debited and Vouchers Payable is credited (Voucher 881) to establish the petty cash fund. The petty cash fund is replenished (Voucher 909) by debiting the expense accounts involved and crediting Vouchers Payable. When a special debit column is not provided for an account, the account is debited in the General Ledger section of the voucher register.

Supplies. The purchase of sales supplies requires a debit to the Sales Supplies account and a credit to Vouchers Payable (Voucher 882).

Insurance. Insurance expense is recorded as a debit to Factory Overhead—Insurance Expense and a credit to Vouchers Payable (Voucher 908). You will recall that factory overhead is a general ledger account and is the control account for the factory overhead ledger. Insurance Expense is one of the accounts in the factory overhead ledger.

Payroll. The voucher to record the factory payroll is a debit to Factory Payroll (Voucher 911). The check is made payable to the payroll clerk, who will cash the check and distribute the payroll to the employees.

Equipment. Equipment purchased is recorded as a debit to the Equipment account and a credit to Vouchers Payable. If the equipment is purchased on the installment plan, a separate voucher is prepared for each installment payment (Vouchers 904, 905, and 906).

Notes Payable. A general journal entry is used to record notes issued in payment of vouchers. The entry is a debit to Vouchers Payable and a credit to Notes Payable.

Posting From the Voucher Register

At the end of each month the specific account columns in the voucher register are footed and the equality (balance) of the debit and credit columns is verified. The register is then totaled and ruled. The column totals are then posted to the appropriate general ledger accounts. For example, the total of the Vouchers Payable Credit column is posted to the Vouchers Payable account. The number of the account to which each column total is posted is written in parentheses under the total.

All specific account column totals are posted with the exception of the Other General Ledger Accounts columns. Each amount entered in the debit and credit columns of the Other General Ledger Accounts is posted individually to the correct account on a daily basis during the month. The account number is entered in the posting reference column of the register. Each factory overhead amount is also posted to the appropriate account in the factory overhead ledger.

Activity B. Answer the following questions about the voucher register. Refer to the text and illustrations on pages 296 to 300.

1. When is Voucher 903 recorded?
2. What is the number of the first voucher recorded for March?
3. Which account is debited for the voucher recorded on March 1? Which account is credited for the voucher recorded on March 1?
4. What is the number of the check written to pay the voucher on March 1? What is the date of the check?
5. When is Voucher 903 paid?
6. What is the number of the check written to pay Voucher 903?
7. Why is Voucher 909 prepared?
8. Why is Voucher 882 prepared?
9. What is the number of the voucher prepared for the payroll?

Which account is debited for the payroll? Which account is credited? **10.** How many vouchers are used to record the purchase of equipment? What are the numbers of the vouchers?

11. What is the total of the Vouchers Payable Credit column?
12. What is the number of the general ledger account for vouchers payable?

Paying the Voucher

C *What is the purpose of the check register?* The check register is a multicolumn journal that is used to record the payment of vouchers. The check register takes the place of the cash payments journal. The payment of Voucher 903, as shown on page 294, proceeds as follows.

A check register replaces the cash payments journal.

Voucher 903 is removed from the Unpaid Voucher file on March 22 and verified for payment. The first approval is given on the inside while the second approval is placed on the outside of the voucher. When this is done, a check is issued and payment is recorded in the check register. At this time a check is written for the amount due and then sent to Quality Plastics, Inc.

The amount of the check to pay Voucher 903 is $294. This is the amount owed to Quality Plastics after deducting the $6 purchase discount from the invoice total of $300.

The debit of $300 is entered in the Vouchers Payable Debit column of the check register. The amount of the discount is entered in the Materials (Purchases Discount) Credit column, and the amount of the check is entered in the Cash Credit column of the check register. (When perpetual inventory procedures are used, purchases discounts are recorded as credits to the Materials account.) The issue date of the check (March 22) and the check number (2019) can now be entered in the Paid section of the voucher register. This information can also be entered on the invoice and the outside of the voucher. The voucher is stamped *Paid* and is filed in the paid voucher file according to voucher number. The check register is shown on page 302.

It is important to note that the employee who records the check in the check register is usually someone other than the employee who wrote the check. This helps prevent mishandling or dishonesty, and thus allows for greater control over cash payments.

Posting From the Check Register

There are no general ledger columns in the check register, as shown on page 302, and so no entries are posted from the check register during the month. At the end of the month the specific columns are footed and the equality (balance) of the debit and credit columns is verified.

The check register has no general ledger columns.

				CHECK REGISTER			Page 23
DATE	CHECK NO.	NAME OF PAYEE	VOUCHER NO.	VOUCHERS PAYABLE DEBIT	MATERIALS (PURCHASES DISCOUNT) CREDIT	CASH CREDIT	
19—							
Mar. 1	1095	Petty Cash	881	50 00		50 00	
2	1096	Point Express	883	21 50		21 50	
22	2019	Quality Plastics, Inc.	903	300 00	6 00	294 00	
31		Totals		6,600 00	266 00	6,334 00	
				(211)	(121)	(101)	

The check register is then totaled, ruled, and posted. The account numbers are written in parentheses under the column totals as posting references.

Activity C. Answer the following questions about the check register and proof. Refer to the text and illustrations on pages 301 and 302.

1. Which check is used to pay Voucher 903?

2. Which account is debited with the payment of Voucher 903? Which accounts are credited?

3. What is the total of the Vouchers Payable Debit column?

4. What is the total of the Materials Purchases Discount Credit column?

5. What is the total of the Cash Credit column?

6. What is the posting reference for the Vouchers Payable Debit column?

Special Accounting Problems: Schedule of Vouchers Payable

D *What special accounting procedures are necessary with the voucher system?* A business that uses the voucher system will find that special procedures are needed to record purchases returns and allowances, partial payments, and to correct errors. These procedures are explained here.

Purchases Returns and Allowances. The Bundy Company sometimes finds it necessary to return inventory items to the supplier. In other instances Bundy receives an allowance (deduction) for inventory items damaged on arrival at its receiving department. Both of these situations result in a decrease in the amount owed to a creditor. These purchases returns and allowances require two entries: (1) a general journal entry to cancel the original voucher and (2) an entry to the voucher register to record a new balance for the amount owed.

For example, on March 3 Voucher 884 was recorded for an invoice from the Burke Company in the amount of $2,000 for materials inventory. This entry involved a debit to Materials and a credit to Vouchers Payable. Later it was discovered that some of the materials ($500 worth) covered by Voucher 884 were defective. Those materials were returned for credit. The return of the materials requires a general journal entry debiting Vouchers Payable for $2,000 and crediting Materials for $2,000. The entry shown here cancels Voucher 884.

		GENERAL JOURNAL			Page 39
DATE		ACCOUNT TITLE AND EXPLANATION	POST. REF.	DEBIT	CREDIT
19—					
Mar.	23	Vouchers Payable	211	2,000 00	
		Materials.	121		2,000 00
		Cancel Voucher 884 for			
		materials returned for credit.			

It should be noted that a Purchases Returns and Allowances account is not always used with the voucher system. The return of purchases is credited to the Materials account.

After this entry has been recorded and posted, the original voucher must be removed from the Unpaid Voucher File and marked *Canceled.* Another voucher (Voucher 907) for the new amount ($1,500) is prepared and recorded in the voucher register. This transaction involves a debit to Materials and a credit to Vouchers Payable, as shown at the top of pages 304 and 305.

Partial Payments. On March 22 the Bundy Company purchased a new shop machine at a cost of $5,600. The company paid $1,000 down and agreed to pay the balance in two equal installments. The installments are to be paid on April 30 and May 31. A separate voucher is prepared for each of the payments. Thus Voucher 904 is prepared for the down payment of $1,000, Voucher 905 is prepared for the April 30 installment payment of $2,300, and Voucher 906 is prepared for the May 31 installment payment of $2,300.

The entry to record the machine purchase is shown at the bottom of pages 304 and 305. Check 2030 is issued on March 28 in the amount of $1,000 to make the down payment on the machine. On April 30 the first installment (Voucher 905) is paid by using a note payable for $2,300. This entry is recorded in the general journal. On May 31 the

VOUCHER

DATE		VOUCHER NO.	PAYEE	PAID		VOUCHERS PAYABLE CREDIT
				DATE	CHECK NO.	
19—						
Mar.	3	884	Burke Co.	See Vo.	907	2,000 00
	23	907	Burke Co.	3/29	2072	1,500 00

second installment (Voucher 906) is paid by again using a note payable for $2,300.

Two entries are required to correct errors in the voucher register. **Correcting Errors.** Sometimes prior to payment, an error is discovered in a voucher that has been recorded in the voucher register. Correcting errors in the voucher register requires two entries: (1) a general journal entry to cancel the original voucher and (2) an entry to the voucher register to record a new balance for the amount owed.

For example, on March 23 Voucher 908 was recorded from an invoice sent by Roe Insurance in the amount of $1,600 for a new factory insurance policy. On March 25 the accounting supervisor noticed that the amount of the invoice was $1,600 but that the accounting clerk had posted the amount of Voucher 908 as $1,200 to the voucher register. The correction of the error required a general journal entry

VOUCHER

DATE		VOUCHER NO.	PAYEE	PAID		VOUCHERS PAYABLE CREDIT
				DATE	CHECK NO.	
19—						
Mar.	22	904	Industrial Machines, Inc...	3/28	2030	1,000 00
	22	905	Industrial Machines, Inc...	4/30	Note Pay.	2,300 00
	22	906	Industrial Machines, Inc...	5/31	Note Pay.	2,300 00

REGISTER Page 20

					OTHER GENERAL LEDGER ACCOUNTS				
MATERIALS DEBIT	FACTORY PAYROLL DEBIT	FACTORY OVERHEAD POST. REF.	FACTORY OVERHEAD DEBIT	SALES SUPPLIES DEBIT	ACCOUNT TITLE	POST. REF.	DEBIT	CREDIT	
2,000 00									
1,500 00									

debiting Vouchers Payable for $1,200 and crediting Factory Overhead—Insurance Expense for $1,200. The journal entry shown here cancels Voucher 908.

GENERAL JOURNAL Page 4

DATE	ACCOUNT TITLE AND EXPLANATION	POST. REF.	DEBIT	CREDIT
19— Mar. 25	Vouchers Payable	211	1,200 00	
	Factory Overhead/Insurance Expense..............	501/√		1,200 00
	Correct error on Voucher 908.			

REGISTER Page 20

					OTHER GENERAL LEDGER ACCOUNTS				
MATERIALS DEBIT	FACTORY PAYROLL DEBIT	FACTORY OVERHEAD POST. REF.	FACTORY OVERHEAD DEBIT	SALES SUPPLIES DEBIT	ACCOUNT TITLE	POST. REF.	DEBIT	CREDIT	
					Equipment.....	165	5,600 00		

VOUCHER

DATE	VOUCHER NO.	PAYEE	PAID DATE	PAID CHECK NO.	VOUCHERS PAYABLE CREDIT	
19—						
Mar. 23	908	Roe Insurance . . .	See Vo.	910	1,200	00
24	909	Petty Cash	3/24	2085	37	40
25	910	Roe Insurance . . .			1,600	00

Again, after the entry has been posted, the original voucher (908) is removed from the Unpaid Voucher File and marked *Canceled.* Another voucher (Voucher 910) for the correct amount of $1,600 is prepared and recorded in the voucher register. A reference to "See Voucher 910" is entered in the Paid section opposite Voucher 908.

Schedule of Unpaid Vouchers

Vouchers Payable

19—
Mar. 31 6,930 Balance

After the voucher register and the check register have been posted, a schedule of unpaid vouchers is prepared to prove the accuracy of the balance in the Vouchers Payable account. This schedule can be prepared by adding all the vouchers in the voucher register that have not been paid by March 31. Another way to prepare the schedule is by adding all the vouchers in the Unpaid Voucher File.

The total of these unpaid vouchers must equal the balance in the Vouchers Payable account. A Schedule of Unpaid Vouchers is shown here. This schedule replaces the schedule of accounts payable when a voucher system is used.

BUNDY COMPANY
Schedule of Unpaid Vouchers
March 31, 19—

Voucher	Payee	Amount
882	A and W Supplies Company	$ 30.00
905	Industrial Machines	2,300.00
906	Industrial Machines	2,300.00
910	Roe Insurance	1,600.00
927	Black Supply	700.00
	Total	$6,930.00

REGISTER

		\multicolumn{7}{c}{DISTRIBUTION OF ACCOUNTS}				
MATERIALS DEBIT	FACTORY PAYROLL DEBIT	\multicolumn{2}{c}{FACTORY OVERHEAD}	SALES SUPPLIES DEBIT	\multicolumn{4}{c}{OTHER GENERAL LEDGER ACCOUNTS}		
		POST. REF.	DEBIT		ACCOUNT TITLE	POST. REF.	DEBIT	CREDIT
		✓	1,200 00					
				6 30	Advertising Exp..	612	27 10	
					Delivery Exp....	605	4 00	
		✓	1,600 00					

Activity D. Answer the following questions about special accounting problems and the schedule of unpaid vouchers. Refer to the text and illustrations on pages 302 to 307.

1. What is the purpose of the March 23 entry in the general journal?

2. Which account is debited for the March 23 entry in the general journal? Which account is credited?

3. What is the amount of Voucher 907?

4. Which account is debited for Voucher 907? Which account is credited?

5. How many vouchers were issued to buy the equipment on March 22? Why were so many issued?

6. What is the number of the check issued for the down payment on the equipment?

7. How is Voucher 905 paid? How is Voucher 906 paid?

8. What is the purpose of the March 25 entry in the general journal?

9. What is the amount of Voucher 910?

10. Which account is debited for Voucher 910? Which account is credited?

11. Which schedule does the Schedule of Unpaid Vouchers replace when a voucher system is used?

12. What is the balance in the Vouchers Payable account?

Topic 1   Problems

8-1. You are an accounting clerk for the Apple Corporation. Part of your duties is to verify invoices and prepare vouchers for payment.

a. Verify the extensions and total on the invoice from Shumaker Manufacturing Company. After you have verified the amounts, enter your initials on the Extensions and Total line.

b. Prepare a voucher for the payment of the invoice by doing the tasks listed at the top of page 308.

• Enter the voucher number on the invoice.
• Complete the inside of the voucher. (You are to approve the voucher.)
• Complete the account distribution on the outside of the voucher. The distribution will be approved by your supervisor at a later date.
• Compute the discount and complete the summary. Leave the approval and recorded lines blank.

• The voucher will be recorded on page 14 of the voucher register. Enter the page number in the appropriate place.
• Complete the payment summary. Check 510 is to be issued for this voucher. Leave the approved and recorded lines blank.
• Fold the voucher to make a jacket and insert the invoice. The voucher is now ready for the final approvals, recording, and filing.

8-2. Listed here are statements about the voucher and the voucher system. Indicate whether each statement is true or false.

a. A voucher register is used instead of a general journal.
b. All payments of money must be made by check.
c. A Voucher Payable account is used in place of the Accounts Payable account.
d. The voucher is a preprinted form.
e. The voucher form most often contains information on both sides.
f. An unpaid voucher file replaces the accounts payable ledger.

g. Voucher forms are not prenumbered consecutively.
h. Unpaid vouchers are filed by invoice date.
i. A voucher form printed on both sides is folded in order to make a jacket which will hold supporting documents of the transaction.
j. A check register is used in addition to a cash payments journal.

The Language of Business

Here are some basic terms that make up the language of business. Do you understand the meaning of each? Can you define each term and use it in an original sentence?

voucher system
vouchers payable account

voucher
voucher register

check register
petty cash fund

unpaid vouchers file
jacket

Chapter 8   Questions

1. What are the features of a voucher system?
2. List the characteristics of most voucher forms?
3. Which journal does the voucher register replace? Why does it replace this journal?
4. Where is a voucher filed after it is recorded in the voucher register? How is it filed?
5. Which journal does the check register replace? Why does it replace this journal?

6. How many entries are required to record purchases returns and allowances in a voucher system? What are the entries?
7. How many entries are required to correct errors in a voucher system? What are the entries?
8. What is the purpose of the schedule of unpaid vouchers?

Chapter 8   Problems

Problems for Chapter 8 are given in the *Working Papers and Chapter Problems* for Part 1. If you are using the workbook, do the problems in the space provided there. Complete your assigned topic problems before answering the chapter problems.

Chapter 8   Management Cases

Evaluating Accounting Systems. Any accounting system needs evaluation to determine whether financial data is being processed efficiently, accurately, and on time. Thus each of the four components of an accounting system—procedures, equipment, forms, and people—must be evaluated on a regular basis. Other reasons for evaluating accounting systems include determining whether management is being provided with needed information and whether employees are performing their jobs according to established procedures.

Case 8M-1. Beth Chan is the owner of a company that manufactures office equipment. The company uses the following journals with its accounting system: cash receipts, cash payments, sales, purchases, and general journal. The business also uses a general ledger, an accounts receivable ledger, and an accounts payable ledger. While Ms. Chan is satisfied with most of the accounting procedures currently in use, she is concerned about the control of cash payments. Recently there have been several instances where checks have been written for the wrong amounts. In still other cases checks have been written too late to benefit from the purchases discount. To correct these problems, Ms. Chan is considering adopting the voucher system to provide additional control of cash payments. Your supervisor has asked you, the accounting clerk, to review the features of the voucher system and answer the following questions for Ms. Chan.

a. How will the voucher system correct the problem of writing checks for the wrong amount?

b. Is the voucher system likely to ensure that checks will be written during the discount period? Explain.

c. If the voucher system is adopted, what changes (if any) will be required in the journals now being used?

d. Will adopting the voucher system affect the number of ledgers now being used? Explain.

e. Would you recommend changing to the voucher system as a means of correcting the problems described by Ms. Chan? Explain.

Case 8M-2. A recent issue of one of the state's leading newspapers carried a feature story on fraud in business. The subject of the story was an employee who had stolen $80,000 from his employer over a period of five years. The employee worked in the accounting department and was responsible for writing checks, making deposits, and reconciling the bank statement. One day the employee simply wrote a check to a fictitious creditor, cashed it, and used the money to pay a personal debt. Since he was the only one who would ever see the check, the employee was confident he could repeat the procedure again and again. He was right; no one suspected anything. However, five years after he had begun this procedure of writing periodic fictitious checks, the employee became ill and had to miss work.

During the employee's absence, another accounting employee assumed the responsibility of reconciling the bank statement. By chance this second employee was also responsible for issuing purchase orders. Thus, while the bank reconciliation was being completed, a check written to the fictitious creditor turned up. Being familiar with all the creditors, the second employee was confused by the name on this check. After searching the files and finding no trace of such a creditor, the second employee informed the manager of the situation. Eventually an audit was conducted of the cash payments procedures which led to the discovery of the fraudulent activity of the first accounting employee. When confronted with the evidence of his fraud, the accounting employee shrugged and said, "You never would have caught me if I had not gotten sick."

a. Did this business follow sound procedures of internal control for protecting cash payments? Explain.

b. Assuming the voucher system was used by the business, would it have been possible for the employee to steal the $80,000? Explain.

Financial accounting provides information about the financial position and future profitability of a business. It helps answer questions such as the following.

- Will the business have enough cash to pay its debts during the next six months?
- Shall the business buy or rent a new building?
- How can funds be obtained for expansion?

Business managers must decide what type of assets they want to own. Tying up too much money in inventory is not productive. Having too little inventory available will result in sales problems. Financial accounting helps managers control financial resources.

Part 2

Introduction to Financial Accounting

Accounting begins with recording the initial transaction. The source document prepared by the salesclerk provides sales data to the seller. The source document also provides purchase data for the buyer. Transactions are recorded, classified, and reported by personnel in the accounting department.

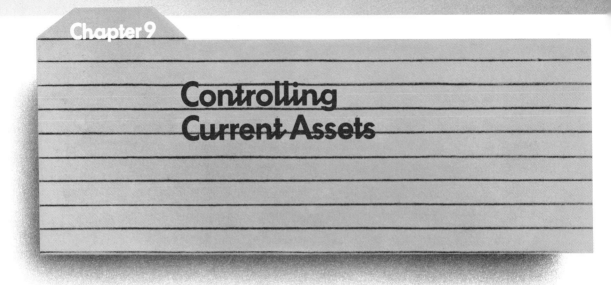

Controlling Current Assets

Assets are usually reported on the balance sheet in groups. The groups generally include current assets, plant and equipment, investments, and intangible assets. Chapter 9 focuses on current assets.

Topic 1
Accounting for Cash in Bank

A *What are examples of the asset groups?* **Current assets** include cash, assets that can or will soon be converted into cash, and assets that will be used up in a short time—usually within a year from the date of the balance sheet. Assets that are intended to produce revenue over a longer period of time are classified as **plant and equipment** or **fixed assets.** (**Natural resources**—sometimes called *wasting assets*—such as standing timber, mineral deposits, and gas and oil wells, are sometimes listed as *plant and equipment.*) Assets that a business intends to hold for longer than a year or that a business cannot quickly convert to cash are called **investments** or **other assets.** Some assets, called **intangible assets,** have no physical nature. Examples of intangible assets are patents, trademarks, and copyrights.

Current assets include cash and other assets that will be converted into cash or used within one year.

Plant and equipment is an asset used to produce revenue over a number of years.

Current Assets

The five major types of current assets are as follows.
• **Cash** includes all forms of money. This includes cash on hand, cash in the bank, cash for imprest funds, and certificates of deposit. (An

imprest cash fund is a fixed amount of cash kept on hand for making small payments, like a petty cash fund.)

• **Marketable securities** are investments that are easily sold or traded. The money can be obtained within a year of the balance sheet date. Included are stocks, bonds, and United States government bonds.

• **Short-term receivables** are accounts receivable, notes receivable, interest receivable, and other receivables collectible within one year of the balance sheet date.

• **Inventories** are items for sale, items in production, and items that will be used within the accounting period. Inventories include raw materials, work-in-process, finished goods, and merchandise inventory.

• **Prepaid expenses** are the costs of certain supplies and services that have been paid before they are used. Prepaid expenses include amounts paid for supplies, insurance, and rent.

Current assets are listed on the balance sheet according to liquidity. **Liquidity** refers to how easily an asset can be converted into cash or how quickly the asset is expected to be used. Cash is listed first on the balance sheet because it is immediately available to pay debts. The remaining current assets are measured against cash, that is, by the time required for the assets to be converted into cash.

Cash:
• Coins
• Currency
• Checks
• Money orders
• Deposits in bank
• Certificates of deposit
• Imprest cash funds

GALLO COMPANY
Balance Sheet
December 31, 19—

ASSETS			
Current Assets:			
Cash on Hand and in Banks	33,075 00		
Marketable Securities.	15,190 00		
Notes Receivable	1,500 00		
Interest Receivable	10 00		
Accounts Receivable $9,000			
Less: Allowance for			
Doubtful Accounts 900	8,100 00		
Merchandise Inventory	6,000 00		
Prepaid Insurance	450 00		
Supplies on Hand	120 00		
Total Current Assets.		64,445 00	
Plant and Equipment:			
Investments:			
Intangible Assets:			

Partial balance sheet showing assets classified by groups. Current assets are listed in order of liquidity.

Time and intent determine how an asset is classified. An asset is classified as a current asset if it can be converted into cash, sold, or used up *within one year* of the balance sheet date or during the normal operating cycle of the business. Investments either cannot be easily converted into cash within a year or are not *intended* to be converted into cash. Plant and equipment and intangible assets are intended to produce revenue over a number of years.

Accounting Principle:

Defining Current Assets. It is a generally accepted accounting principle that current assets include cash and other resources which are expected to be converted into cash, sold, or used up within one year of the balance sheet date or during the normal operations of the business, whichever is longer.

Activity A-1. Answer the following questions about current assets. Refer to the text and illustrations on pages 312 to 314.

1. What are current assets?

2. Is plant and equipment a current asset? Explain.

3. What type of current asset is cash on hand? stocks? accounts receivable? finished goods? supplies?

4. Why is cash listed first on the balance sheet?

5. How does time affect the classifying of assets?

6. How does intent affect the classifying of assets?

Activity A-2. Account titles are listed here. Classify each account title as either a current asset or not a current asset.

EXAMPLE: Accounts Receivable—Current asset

1. Cash

2. Land

3. Accounts Payable

4. Marketable Securities (not intended to be converted to cash)

5. Work-in-Process

6. Prepaid Insurance

7. Insurance Expense

8. Marketable Securities (will be converted to cash)

9. Notes Receivable

10. Delivery Equipment

11. Patent

12. Oil Well

Cash Management and Cash Controls

B *What is classified as cash?* In accounting, cash includes coins, currency, checks, money orders, deposits in banks, and certificates of deposit. In general the rule is this: Any item that a bank will accept for deposit is classified as cash.

Cash Management

The management of cash is of great concern to every business. There are several reasons for this. Cash is the most current and most liquid of all assets. Cash transactions also make up a large part of daily business activity. Most important, cash is frequently used to pay debts and

Cash management is important for every business.
Adequate procedures must be established to control
cash.

measure revenue. Thus every business needs an effective cash management plan that includes procedures to do the following.

- *Prevent theft, fraud, and misuse.* Control procedures must be followed for receiving and paying cash. The control procedures are designed to ensure accuracy, honesty, efficiency, and speed. The procedures provide for a series of "checks and balances." If employees know
that their records must agree with other records, they will be discour-
aged from misusing or stealing cash.
- *Provide accurate records of cash receipts, cash payments, and cash
balances.* Cash records are used to make many business decisions.
Thus managers need accurate records.
- *Provide enough cash to meet current debts.* An effective plan must
include forecasting (predicting) the need for cash. Management must
determine the cash inflow (receipts) and cash outflow (payments). The
purpose of cash forecasting is to determine the availability of cash for
the payment of debts.

Cash Management Plan:
- Prevent theft, fraud, and
  misuse.
- Provide accurate cash
  records.
- Provide cash for current
  debts.
- Eliminate idle cash.

• *Eliminate idle cash.* Cash that is not producing revenue is called **idle cash.** Business must have enough cash on hand to meet current debts. The rest of its cash should be earning revenue—for example, as marketable securities.

Electronic Funds Transfer (EFT). A recent development in the management of cash is the use of **electronic funds transfer (EFT).** EFT refers to procedures that allow banks to debit and credit checking accounts without needing depositors' written checks. Thus EFT speeds up the processing of cash transactions by reducing the amount of office paper work. EFT is part of a change in office procedure that is producing the "paperless" office.

One way EFT procedures may be used is in preparing the payroll. The bank electronically debits (decreases) the employer's checking account and credits (increases) each employee's checking account. Thus the employee does not receive a paycheck which must be cashed or deposited. The employee receives a voucher that shows the amount of gross earnings, the amount of each deduction, and the amount of net pay that has been automatically credited to the employee's checking account. Other applications of EFT include processing cash sales and collections on account. In each case EFT requires the cooperation of the banks, the employer, and the employees.

Procedures for Controlling Cash Receipts

Every business needs internal control over its cash. These controls provide accurate records. They also provide for the quick and efficient handling of cash and reduce the possibility of mishandling and theft.
The internal controls for recording cash receipts are as follows.
• Create source documents as soon as cash is received.
• Use prenumbered forms.
• Lock up tapes or copies.
• Prove cash frequently, usually at the end of each day.
• Deposit all cash receipts intact.
• Divide the responsibility.

Procedures for Controlling Cash Payments

The internal controls for recording cash payments are as follows.
• Verify and approve invoices.
• Pay by check.
• Use prenumbered checks.
• Cancel paid invoices.
• Prove cash frequently.
• Divide the responsibility.

TRANSACTIONS	USE FORMS	PRENUMBER FORMS	PROTECT FORMS	PROVE CASH	USE BANK ACCOUNT	DIVIDE RESPONSIBILITY
Cash Receipts	Create source documents.	Use pre-numbered forms.	Lock up tapes	Prove cash frequently.	Deposit all receipts intact.	Divide Responsibility.
	Cash Register Tapes, Sales Slips, Re-mittance Slips.	Forms are numbered when printed.	Copies are locked in forms register or cash register.	Cash proofs are prepared to verify that cash handled agrees with cash records.	All cash receipts are deposited intact.	Handling of cash is separated from recording of cash.
Cash Payments	Verify and approve invoices.	Use pre-numbered checks.	Cancel all invoices.	Prove cash frequently.	Pay by check.	Divide Responsibility.
	No invoice is paid without approval.	Every check issued or voided is accounted for.	Paid invoices are stamped "Paid."	Bank recon-cilations are prepared to verify the checkbook balance.	All payments (except petty cash) are made by check.	Handling of cash is separated from recording of cash.

INTERNAL CONTROLS FOR CASH

Activity B-1. Indicate under which internal control of cash you would find the cash procedures listed here. Mark an "X" in the correct column.

Cash Procedure	Use Forms	Use Prenumbered Forms	Protect Forms	Prove Cash	Use Bank Account	Divide Responsibility
EXAMPLE: *Create source documents.*	X					

1. Deposit all receipts intact.
2. Separate handling function from recording function.
3. Use prenumbered checks.
4. Pay by check.

5. Verify and approve invoices.
6. Cancel all invoices.
7. Lock up tapes.
8. Prove cash frequently.

Activity B-2. A number of cash items are listed here. Classify each item as cash or noncash.

EXAMPLE: Check—Cash

1. Coins
2. Postage stamps
3. Currency
4. Cash coupons that are redeemable from the manufacturer
5. Dishonored checks
6. Checks received from customers
7. Money orders
8. Cash in the bank (savings account)
9. Cash in the bank (checking)
10. Food stamps
11. Marketable securities (short-term)
12. Marketable securities (long-term)

Cash in Bank

C *How should a business safeguard its cash?* Except for small amounts for petty cash and change funds, all cash should be kept in bank accounts. A checking account should be used to pay current debts. Extra cash should be invested in marketable securities, certificates of deposit, or savings accounts to earn interest.

The Bank Statement. Three important internal controls for cash in a bank are (1) depositing all cash receipts intact, (2) making all payments, except small petty cash items, by check, and (3) using prenumbered checks. When these controls are followed, the bank statement becomes an external source of control for cash. A bank statement is shown on the next page.

A bank usually sends each depositor a bank statement once a month. However, the cash balance on the statement seldom agrees with the cash balance in the depositor's checkbook. The reasons for the differences between the bank statement balance and the checkbook balance may include the following.

Deposits in transit must be added to bank statement balance.

• *Deposits in transit.* Deposits are added to the depositor's checkbook as soon as they are mailed or placed in the bank. Some deposits may not have been received by the bank until after it has closed its records. Thus deposits in transit have been added to the checkbook by the depositor but have not been added by the bank.

Outstanding checks must be subtracted from bank statement balance.

• *Outstanding checks.* Checks are subtracted from the depositor's checkbook as soon as the checks are drawn. Some checks, however, may not have been presented to the bank for payment until after it has closed its records. Thus outstanding checks are subtracted from the checkbook by the depositor but have not been subtracted by the bank.

Service charges and fees must be subtracted from checkbook balance.

• *Service charges and fees.* Most banks charge for some of their services. These banks subtract the amounts for the service charges and fees from the depositor's account. However, a bank may not have notified

SECOND NATIONAL BANK
Rome, New York 13440

Gallo Company
1421 West James Street
Rome, NY 13440

ACCOUNT NUMBER   396-5211

PERIOD ENDING   12/31/--

Checks	Checks	Deposits	Date	Balance
			11/30	9,855.00
		1,090.00	12/3	10,945.00
50.00			12/5	10,895.00
20.00	15.00		12/8	10,860.00
2,045.00		1,100.00	12/11	9,915.00
90.00	160.00		12/14	9,665.00
1,000.00 RI			12/15	8,665.00
15.00 SC			12/15	8,650.00
		1,240.00	12/18	9,890.00
		1,400.00	12/20	11,290.00
	3,000.00	1,210.00	12/22	9,500.00
80.00			12/23	9,420.00
		2,200.00	12/24	11,620.00
1,300.00			12/24	10,320.00
70.00		190.00	12/26	10,440.00
	259.52		12/27	10,180.48
	1,180.48		12/28	9,000.00

Beginning Balance	Total Amount of Deposits and Credits	Total Amount of Checks Paid	Total Charges	Ending Balance
9,855.00	8,430.00	8,270.00	1,015.00	9,000.00

	Number of Deposits Made	Number of Checks Paid	Number of Other Charges	
	7	12	2	

Codes: CC Certified Check   OD Overdrawn
        DM Debit Memorandum   RI Returned Item
        EC Error Correction   SC Service Charge

Please examine this statement upon receipt and report at once if you find any difference. If no error is reported in ten days, the account will be considered correct. All items are subject to final payment.

Bank Statement Shows:
- **Beginning balance**
- **Deposits and credits added**
- **Checks subtracted**
- **Charges subtracted**
- **Ending balance**

the depositor until the statement was sent. Thus the service charges and fees have been subtracted by the bank but have not been subtracted from the checkbook by the depositor.

• *Dishonored checks.* Sometimes checks that have been deposited are not paid even when properly presented to the bank. A depositor's account will not agree with the bank's records if checks are dishonored,

Dishonored checks must be subtracted from checkbook balance.

because these checks have been added as deposits by the depositor, but the bank has not added them to the depositor's account.

Errors must be corrected.

- *Errors.* Sometimes the depositors or the banks make errors in keeping their records. These errors must be corrected. Some errors will correct themselves in time. Other errors, however, require the depositor or the bank to make corrections in their records. Banks should be told of any errors they have made so that they can correct them.

Verifying the Cash Balance

Before reconciling the bank statement balance, each depositor should verify that the Cash ledger account balance agrees with the checkbook balance. (When a business has several cash items, Cash in Bank may be used as the account title in the ledger.) If the balance of the Cash account and the checkbook do not agree, check that the ledger is in balance. If the ledger is in balance, the error is probably in the checkbook. Correct any errors so that the cash account balance and the checkbook balance agree.

Proving Cash—Internal Sources

Reconciling the Bank Statement

The Gallo Company has three bank accounts. For illustration purposes, however, assume that it has only one bank account.

On December 31 the Cash ledger account for the Gallo Company has a debit balance of $10,000. The checkbook balance shows the same amount. The bank statement, however, shows a balance of $9,000 on December 31.

These two amounts must be reconciled for the following reasons.

- To discover errors made in recording cash transactions.
- To provide information necessary to bring the accounting records up to date.
- To show the correct cash balance on the balance sheet.

Most bank statements have forms printed on the back for use in reconciling the bank statement. Follow these steps in preparing the bank reconciliation.

Depositor _Gallo Company_
BANK RECONCILIATION STATEMENT
December 31, 19—

| BALANCE SHOWN ON BANK STATEMENT | $9,000.00 | (1) | BALANCE SHOWN ON CHECKBOOK STUB | $10,000.00 | (6) |

Plus: Deposits in Transit

Date	Amount
12/31	$ 850 00
Total Deposits in Transit	$ 850.00 (2)

Plus: Corrections

Description	Amount
Check 880	$15 00
Total Additions	$ 15.00 (7)

| | SUBTOTAL | $9,850.00 (3) |

| | SUBTOTAL | $10,015.00 (8) |

Less: Checks Outstanding

Number	Amount
920	$600 00
935	50 00
941	200 00
Total Checks Outstanding	$ 850.00 (4)

Less: Charges, Fees, and Corrections

Description	Amount
Service Charge	$ 15 00
Returned check Thomas McElroy	1,000 00
Total Deductions	$1,015.00 (9)

| ADJUSTED BANK BALANCE | $9,000.00 (5) |

| ADJUSTED CHECKBOOK BALANCE | $9,000.00 (10) |

1 *Enter the Balance Shown on Bank Statement.*

2 *List and add Deposits in Transit.*

3 *Add Total Deposits in Transit to Balance Shown on Bank Statement to obtain the subtotal.*

4 *List and add Checks Outstanding.* (a) Sort all canceled (*Paid*) checks, stop payment orders, and voided checks in numeric order, (b) check off (✓) each of the checks on the checkbook stub, and (c) add the total checks outstanding.

5 *Subtract Total Checks Outstanding from the subtotal to obtain the Adjusted Bank Balance.*

6 *Enter the Balance Shown on Checkbook Stub.*

7 *List and add any corrections that increase the checkbook balance.* When the checks were compared with the stubs, Check 880 was issued for $80 but it was recorded on the checkbook stub as $95. Thus $15 must be added to the checkbook balance. (Check 880 was also recorded at $95 in the cash payments journal.)

8 *Add the Total Additions to the Balance Shown on Checkbook Stub.*

9 *List and total bank charges and any corrections that decrease the checkbook balance.* The bank charged $15 for checks and service charges for December. Also, a dishonored check of $1,000 from Thomas McElroy, a customer, was returned. The check was marked *NSF* (not sufficient funds).

10 *Subtract the Total Deductions from the Subtotal.*

NO._____$_____		
DATE *Dec. 31,*___19___		
TO_____		
FOR *Bank Reconciliation*		
Corrections		
	DOLLARS	CENTS
BALANCE *Plus error on check 880*	10,000	00
~~AMT. DEPOSITED~~ +	15	00
Less returned check	10,015	00
~~TOTAL~~ *Service charge*	-1,000	00
~~AMT. THIS CHECK~~ −	15	00
BALANCE	9,000	00

Latest check stub must be updated.

Entries to adjust Cash account are recorded in the general journal since cash receipts journal and cash payments journal are closed for the month.

Updating the Checkbook and Ledger

After the bank reconciliation statement has been prepared, the checkbook balance and the Cash in Bank account must be updated. Adjustments must be made for any errors and items not recorded in the depositor's records.

Any additions to and subtractions from the Balance Shown on Checkbook Stub must be recorded on the latest check stub. If an error was made on a previous check stub, a notation should be made on that stub that the error was corrected. The $15 error on Check 880 must be added. The dishonored check and service charges are subtracted.

After the checkbook has been updated, these adjustments must be journalized and posted. When the entries have been posted, the balance of the Cash ledger account will agree with the balance in the checkbook and with the Adjusted Checkbook Balance on the bank reconciliation statement.

The amount of cash on the balance sheet should be reported accurately. Thus the entry to record the adjustments to Cash should be made as of the last date of the accounting period. Since the cash receipts journal and the cash payments journal would ordinarily be ruled for the end of the month, the cash adjustment entries would be recorded in the general journal.

	GENERAL JOURNAL			Page 87
DATE	**ACCOUNT TITLE AND EXPLANATION**	**POST. REF.**	**DEBIT**	**CREDIT**
19— *Dec.* 31	Cash	101	15 00	
	Accounts Payable/Reality Corporation			15 00
	Correction of Check 880, issued as $80 but recorded as $95.			
31	Miscellaneous Expense		15 00	
	Cash	101		15 00
	Monthly service charges.			
31	Accounts Receivable/Thomas McElroy.		1,000 00	
	Cash	101		1,000 00
	Returned check of December 19.			

Cash

19—		19—	
Dec. 31 Bal. 10,000		Dec. 31 J87	15
31 J87	15	31 J87	1,000
	10,015		1,015

Bal. 9,000

The additions (deposits in transit) and subtractions (checks outstanding) on the Balance Shown on the Bank Statement do not have to be journalized. Each item will appear on the bank statement as soon as the bank processes it.

Accounting Concept:
Safeguarding Cash. A bank account safeguards cash and serves as an external record for the control of cash.

Activity C. Answer the following questions about how a business safeguards its cash. Refer to the text and illustrations on pages 318 to 323.

1. What is the Total Amount of Checks Paid on the Second National Bank statement? the Total Charges? the Ending Balance? the amount of the returned item? the number of certified checks?

2. What is the checkbook balance of cash?

3. What is the balance of cash shown on the bank statement?

4. How many checks are outstanding? What are the amounts?

5. What are the total additions to the checkbook stub balance?

6. Which customer's check is returned? Why is it returned?

7. What is the service charge?

8. What are the total additions to cash recorded on December 31? the total deductions from cash?

9. What is the Adjusted Checkbook Balance on December 31? Does the Adjusted Checkbook Balance agree with the Adjusted Bank Balance?

Using Several Bank Accounts

D *Does a business usually keep its cash all in one bank account?* No, a business often uses several bank accounts. Bank accounts may be used to help control cash or for convenience, and they may be in one bank or in several banks.

Special Bank Accounts

A **special bank account** is an account used for only one kind of cash activity, such as payroll. When a business uses special bank accounts, the main bank account is referred to as the **general bank account.** Each bank statement for each special bank account is reconciled with its own checkbook balance. Businesses having more than one store may use a special bank account for each store.

Payroll Bank Accounts. Businesses with many employees find it convenient to establish a special payroll bank account. The **payroll bank account** is used to pay employees, and only payroll checks are drawn on the account. It is not used for any other payments.

To establish the payroll bank account, a company draws a check on the general bank account and deposits it in the payroll bank account. The amount of the check is for the total net pay in the payroll register.

PAYROLL REGISTER

For the Week Beginning December 20, 19 — and Ending December 26, 19 —
Paid December 28, 19 — Check No. 942

EMPLOYEE DATA					**EARNINGS**			**DEDUCTIONS**						**NET PAY**	
NO.	NAME	MARITAL STATUS	EXEMP.	HOURS	REGULAR	OVERTIME	TOTAL	INCOME TAX	FICA TAX	INSURANCE PREMIUMS	UNION DUES	OTHER	TOTAL	AMOUNT	CK. NO.
1	Margaret Church	S	1	40	280 00		280 00	49 40	17 16		5 00		71 56	208 44	
2	Paul Royce	S	1	40	240 00		240 00	39 00	14 71		5 00		58 71	181 29	
3	Maria Valdez	S	1	40	240 00		240 00	39 00	14 71		5 00		58 71	181 29	
4	Steven Worski	M	2	40	240 00		240 00	26 40	14 71		5 00		46 11	193 89	
5	Carl Wunsch	S	1	40	240 00		240 00	39 00	14 71		5 00		58 71	181 29	
6	Rosea Young	S	1	40	320 00		320 00	61 10	19 62		5 00		85 72	234 28	
					1,560 00		1,560 00	253 90	95 62		30 00		379 52	1,180 48	

After the check for the payroll is deposited, paychecks are written for each employee. The amount for each check is taken directly from the payroll register. The paychecks are drawn against the payroll bank account.

No entry is made in the cash payments journal, since Cash was credited when the check was issued from the general bank account.

GENERAL JOURNAL
Page 94

DATE	ACCOUNT TITLE AND EXPLANATION	POST. REF.	DEBIT	CREDIT
19— Dec. 26	Salary Expense		1,560 00	
	Employee Income Taxes Payable .			253 90
	FICA Taxes Payable			95 62
	Union Dues Payable			30 00
	Salaries Payable			1,180 48
	Record weekly payroll.			

CASH PAYMENTS JOURNAL
Page 28

DATE	ACCOUNT DEBITED	EXPLANATION	CHECK NO.	POST. REF.	GENERAL LEDGER DEBIT	ACCOUNTS PAYABLE DEBIT	PURCHASES DISCOUNT CREDIT	NET CASH CREDIT
19— Dec. 28	Salaries Payable . .	Weekly payroll . . .	942		1,180 48			1,180 48

GALLO COMPANY.
1421 West James Street
Rome, New York 13440   NO. 942

PAY
TO THE
ORDER OF *Maria Valdez, Payroll Cashier* ————— $1,180 48/100

December 28, 19 —   50-218 / 213

One thousand one hundred eighty and 48/100 ————— DOLLARS

SECOND NATIONAL BANK
Rome, New York 13440

Joseph Gallo

⑃0213⑃0218⑃ 396⑃5211⑃

Check is drawn to order of person responsible.

Check is drawn for total net pay and is deposited in payroll bank account.

GALLO COMPANY —
PAYROLL ACCOUNT
1421 West James Street
Rome, New York 13440   NO. P0132

PAY
TO THE
ORDER OF *Margaret Church* ————— $208 44/100

December 28, 19 —   50-218 / 213

Two hundred eight and 44/100 ————— DOLLARS

SECOND NATIONAL BANK
Rome, New York 13440

Joseph Gallo

⑃0213⑃0218⑃ 447⑃9911⑃

Liability to employee is canceled when payroll checks are drawn.

The illustrations show how to establish and use the payroll bank account. As you study the illustrations, focus on the following items.

• Only one check is drawn against the general bank account for each pay period. Thus reconciling the Cash account with the bank statement is easier. There are no outstanding payroll checks from the general bank account. The outstanding payroll checks are reconciled with the payroll bank account statement.

• Only one ledger account is used for cash.

• The checkbook balance of the special payroll account should always be zero after all paychecks have been issued for the period. Only the total net pay is deposited in the payroll bank account. The total of the checks written is equal to the total net pay.

• The responsibility for the payroll account can be delegated to one person. There is control because another person is responsible for the general bank account.

Special General Accounts

Businesses may deposit cash in many banks. For example, a business that has stores or offices in several communities may find it convenient to use a bank close to each store or office. Using local banks also creates good relations with the community.

When several general bank accounts are used, some accountants use only one cash account in the general ledger for all bank accounts. Other accountants use separate cash ledger accounts for each bank account.

Checkbooks are treated as a subsidiary ledger.

If only one cash account is used, the cash account becomes a controlling account. The checkbooks are treated as a subsidiary ledger. The total of all the checkbook balances must equal the balance of the cash account.

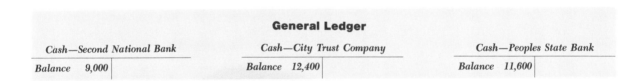

General Ledger		**Subsidiary Ledger Concept**	
Cash—General 101		*Checkbook Balances*	
Bal. 33,000		*Second National Bank*	9,000
		City Trust Company	12,400
		Peoples State Bank	11,600
			33,000

Controlling Account = Subsidiary Ledger

There is a cash ledger account for each bank account.

If a separate cash ledger account is kept for each general bank account, then each cash account must be identified by the bank account title.

General Ledger

Cash—Second National Bank	*Cash—City Trust Company*	*Cash—Peoples State Bank*
Balance 9,000	*Balance* 12,400	*Balance* 11,600

Although a business may use separate cash accounts in the general ledger, it is customary to list only the total of all the accounts on the balance sheet. The total would include all bank accounts plus the balances of any cash funds (petty cash or change fund.) The Gallo Company, for example, lists all cash on the balance sheet under the title Cash on Hand and in Banks.

GALLO COMPANY
Balance Sheet
December 31, 19—

ASSETS			
Current Assets:			
Cash on Hand and in Banks	33,075	00	

All cash accounts are
shown as one amount.

Activity D. Answer the following questions about special bank accounts. Refer to the text and illustrations on pages 323 to 327.

1. How many kinds of cash activities are in special bank accounts?

2. What entry is made to establish a payroll bank account?

3. Is the entry to establish a payroll bank account equal to the amount of the total earnings or the net pay? Explain.

4. What is the checkbook balance of the payroll bank account after all paychecks have been issued?

5. What is the amount of all checks written on the payroll bank account for the week ended December 26?

6. What is the amount of the check issued to Steven Worski?

7. What is the amount of Salaries Payable recorded in the General Journal?

8. Who is the payroll cashier?

9. How many cash accounts are used by the Gallo Company? How many bank accounts are used?

10. The checkbook balances for the three bank accounts used by the Gallo Company must equal what ledger account? What is the total of the checkbook balances? What is the general ledger account balance?

Topic 1 Problems

9-1. Look at the Current Assets section of the balance sheet illustrated here. A number of errors have been made. You are asked to prepare a revised section. Be sure to include all current assets in proper order.

Current Assets

Cash	.$ 1,050
Accounts Receivable.	4,000
Marketable Securities	2,500
Store Equipment	7,500
Petty Cash	100
Supplies on Hand	150
Prepaid Insurance	200
Notes Receivable	2,000
Insurance Expense.	50
Total Current Assets $17,550	

Additional Data

a. Included in the balance of Accounts Receivable is a $500 charge sale that cannot be collected.

b. Included in the balance of Marketable Securities is $1,000 in securities bought as a long-term investment.

c. The accountant did not take an inventory of Supplies on

Hand. The cost of Supplies on Hand is $120.

d. The balance of cash includes a dishonored check from A. Rundel for $50. The check was returned by the Second National Bank.

9-2. Before reconciling the bank statement, the payroll clerk asks your assistance. A number of possible reconciling items are listed here. Indicate for the payroll clerk how the various items are handled when reconciling the bank statement. Mark an "X" in the correct column.

Item	Added to Bank Balance	Subtracted From Bank Balance	Added to Checkbook Balance	Subtracted From Checkbook Balance	Not a Reconciling Item
EXAMPLE: *Paid* *Checks.*					X

a. Returned deposit tickets
b. Outstanding checks
c. Deposits in transit
d. Dishonored checks

e. Errors by the bank
f. Service charges
g. Errors in the checkbook

9-3. Use the data given below about Murat Publications to do the following.

a. Prepare a bank reconciliation statement as of November 30.
b. Record any corrections in the checkbook and general journal.

c. Notify the bank of any errors affecting the bank statement.

- Bank balance as shown on bank statement: $16,436.20.
- Checkbook balance: $14,441.60.
- Deposit put in night depository on last day of month: $9,105. Amount was recorded in checkbook but not shown on bank statement.
- Check 490, $36, was outstanding on the October 31 bank reconciliation and is still outstanding.
- Checks outstanding: Check 554, $3,902.50; Check 558, $6,751.20.
- Service charge: $17.10.
- Note receivable collected by the bank: $400 (debit Cash and credit Notes Receivable for $400).
- A check written for a merchandise purchase to P. Briggs for $736 (correct amount) was recorded in the checkbook and cash payments journal for $763. The check number was 556.

NOTE: Save your work for further use in Topic Problem 9-4.

9-4. After analyzing the bank statements for Murat Publications for a period of one year, you come to the conclusion that the bank balance is always similar to the Adjusted Bank Balance in Topic Problem 9-3. Also, the bank balance during the month has never gone below $10,000. Using your knowledge about idle cash, prepare a recommendation for Carmen Murat, owner of Murat Publications.

9-5. The payroll register for Murat Publications is illustrated here. Murat Publications uses a general and a payroll bank account.

a. Verify the extensions and complete the payroll register.
b. Record the payroll in the general journal.
c. Establish the payroll bank account by writing a check for the net pay on the general bank account. (Cheryl Blake is the payroll

cashier; Carmen Murat will sign the check.)
d. Record the payroll check (Check 114) in the cash payments journal.
e. Write paychecks for each employee (beginning with Check 0553).

PAYROLL REGISTER

For the Week Beginning _August 8,_ 19 — and Ending _August 15,_ 19 —

	EMPLOYEE DATA				EARNINGS			DEDUCTIONS					NET PAY		
NO.	NAME	MARITAL STATUS	EXEMP.	HOURS	REGULAR	OVERTIME	TOTAL	INCOME TAX	FICA TAX	INSURANCE PREMIUMS	UNION DUES	OTHER	TOTAL	AMOUNT	CK. NO.
	Cheryl Blake	S	1	40	340 00		340 00	64 80	20 84		5 00		90 64	249 36	
	Mark Burns	S	1	40	240 00		240 00	32 70	14 71		5 00		52 41	187 59	
	Karen Glover	S	1	40	300 00		300 00	46 90	18 39		5 00		70 29	229 71	
	Marianne Picini	M	2	40	380 00		380 00	63 40	23 29		5 00		91 69	288 31	
	Aaron Shea	S	1	40	480 00		480 00	87 60	29 42		5 00		122 02	357 98	
	Paul Schwab	S	1	40	320 00		320 00	52 00	19 62		5 00		76 62	243 38	
					2,060 00		2,060 00	347 40	126 27		30 00		503 67	1,556 33	

Topic 2
Accounting for Imprest Cash Funds

A *Is it practical to pay all amounts by check?* No, it is not. Businesses usually keep fixed amounts of cash on hand to pay small amounts. These "funds" are generally handled as imprest cash funds.

As you learned earlier, an imprest cash fund is a fixed amount of cash kept on hand for making small payments. When cash is paid out of the fund, a receipt is put into the fund to replace the cash removed. At all times the total of the receipts plus the cash left in the fund must equal the original amount of the fund.

From time to time, the cash fund is restored to its original amount. A check drawn on the general bank account is cashed, and the money is placed back in the fund. The cash in the fund is then equal to the original amount. Two imprest cash funds are discussed here: a petty cash fund and a change fund.

Petty Cash

The petty cash fund is an imprest fund. When the petty cash fund is established, a check is drawn on the general bank account. The check

To Establish Petty Cash Fund:
- Asset Petty Cash increases by $50.
- Asset Cash decreases by $50.

is made payable to the person responsible for the fund. The check is endorsed and cashed, and the money is placed in a secure place, such as a locked drawer. The entry for the check debits the Petty Cash account and credits the Cash account.

CASH PAYMENTS JOURNAL									Page *17*
DATE	ACCOUNT DEBITED	EXPLANATION	CHECK NO.	POST. REF.	GENERAL LEDGER DEBIT	ACCOUNTS PAYABLE DEBIT	PURCHASES DISCOUNT CREDIT	NET CASH CREDIT	
19— May	1	Petty Cash	Establish fund	437	102	50 00				50 00

Amount $ 2.50

PETTY CASH VOUCHER

Date *May 15, 19—*

Paid to *Office Service Center*

For *Pens*

Charge to *Office Expense*

GALLO COMPANY

Approved by   Received by

Debit Cash Short and Over account for a shortage. Credit Cash Short and Over account for an overage.

Petty cash vouchers, or receipts, are put in the fund when cash is removed. The total of the vouchers plus the cash left in the drawer must equal the amount of the petty cash fund.

In some systems, a **petty cash register** is kept. All cash put into and taken out of the fund is recorded in the petty cash register. In other systems, the petty cash vouchers are batched and kept as the day-to-day record.

When the fund gets low on cash, it must be restored to the original amount. This process is called **replenishing** the petty cash fund. To replenish the petty cash fund, a company draws a check on its general bank account. The amount of the check is equal to the total payments made from the fund. At the end of each accounting period the fund is replenished regardless of the cash left in the fund. This is done so that the payments are recorded during the accounting period in which they occur.

Sometimes the petty cashier makes mistakes in handling the cash. Thus there may be more or less cash in the drawer than there ought to be. Any **cash overages** or **cash shortages** must be recorded in the journal. A temporary owner's equity account called Cash Short and Over is used. An overage is credited to the account as revenue because it increases owner's equity. A shortage is debited to the account as an expense because it decreases owner's equity.

The Gallo Company does not use a petty cash register. Each payment must have a petty cash voucher properly signed.

The procedures followed to replenish the petty cash fund are described here.
- The vouchers are totaled.
- The fund is proved by adding the total of the vouchers to the remaining cash in the fund. The total should equal the original amount of the fund. Any excess cash is credited to the Cash Short and Over account. Any shortage is debited to the Cash Short and Over account.
- The expenses are classified according to account titles.

• A check is drawn for the total payments plus a cash shortage or for the total payments minus a cash overage.
• The vouchers are canceled so that they cannot be used again.
• The check and vouchers are submitted to an authorized individual for signature.
• After the check is signed, the vouchers are filed.
• The check is cashed, and the money is placed in the fund. Thus the amount of cash is back to the original amount.

GALLO COMPANY
Petty Cash Memorandum
May 1 to May 15, 19—

Advertising Expense	$ 8.00
Delivery Expense	22.00
Miscellaneous Expense	3.50
Office Expense	12.75
Total Disbursements	46.25
Cash on Hand	3.75
Amount of Fund	$50.00

The check to replenish the fund does not affect the Petty Cash account. The individual expense accounts are debited, and the Cash account is credited. Thus the amount of the Petty Cash account will remain the same as the original amount, unless the amount of the fund is increased or decreased.

The Petty Cash account is an asset account. The account is listed on the Current Assets section of the balance sheet, immediately after Cash.

To Replenish Petty Cash Fund:
• Expenses decrease owner's equity by $46.25.
• Asset Cash decreases by $46.25.

	CASH PAYMENTS JOURNAL							Page 14	
DATE	ACCOUNT DEBITED	EXPLANATION	CHECK NO.	POST. REF.	GENERAL LEDGER DEBIT	ACCOUNTS PAYABLE DEBIT	PURCHASES DISCOUNT CREDIT	NET CASH CREDIT	
19— May 15	Advertising Expense .	Replenish petty cash fund	450		8 00			46 25	
	Delivery Expense . . .				22 00			— 00	
	Miscellaneous Expense				3 50			— 00	
	Office Expense				12 75			— 00	

Activity A. Answer the following questions about establishing, using, and replenishing the petty cash fund. Refer to the text and illustrations on pages 329 to 331.

1. On which bank account is the check to establish the petty cash fund drawn?
2. What is the debit entry to establish the petty cash fund? the credit entry?
3. What is put in the petty cash fund when cash is removed?
4. The check to replenish the petty cash fund is equal to what amount?
5. What are the total petty cash expenditures for the period May 1 to May 15?
6. Is an overage debited or credited to Cash Short and Over?

7. Is a shortage debited or credited to Cash Short and Over?
8. Does the Gallo Company use petty cash vouchers or a petty cash register?
9. What effect does the entry to replenish the petty cash fund have on the Petty Cash account?
10. How is the Petty Cash account classified? Where is it listed on the balance sheet?
11. In which journal is the entry to replenish the petty cash fund recorded?

Change Funds

To Establish Change Fund:
- Asset Change Fund increases by $25.
- Asset Cash decreases by $25.

B *What is a change fund?* A **change fund** is a fixed amount of cash used for making change for customers. It is a second type of cash fund.

When the change fund is established, a check is drawn on the general bank account. The check is made payable to the person responsible for the fund. The check is endorsed and cashed, and the money is placed in the cash register drawer. The entry for the check debits the Change Fund account and credits the Cash account, as shown here.

		CASH PAYMENTS JOURNAL							Page 17
DATE	ACCOUNT DEBITED	EXPLANATION	CHECK NO.	POST. REF.	GENERAL LEDGER DEBIT	ACCOUNTS PAYABLE DEBIT	PURCHASES DISCOUNT CREDIT	NET CASH CREDIT	
19— May 1	Change Fund	Establish fund	438		25 00			25 00	

At the beginning of each day the change fund is placed in the cash register drawers to make change for customers. As cash sales are made, the sales clerks put the cash received into the cash register drawers. They take cash out to give the customers change.

When the cash is proved, the cash in the drawer is counted. The amount of the change fund is subtracted from the total cash in the drawer to determine the amount of the net cash handled. This amount is then checked against the cash register tape or the net cash received on the cash proof. The change fund is replenished each day from the total cash in the drawer.

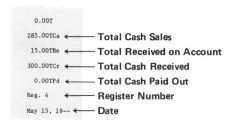

Unlike the petty cash fund, the change fund is replenished by cash from the cash drawer. It is not necessary to draw a check to replenish the change fund. The cash needed to replenish the fund comes from the cash drawer. Any shortage is taken from the cash received and is debited to the Cash Short and Over account. Any overage is credited to the Cash Short and Over account.

To replenish the change fund, no entry is necessary since exact amount is returned from cash received.

Other Imprest Funds

Other funds may be kept to pay small amounts. For example, a **sales returns and allowances fund** may be used to give refunds for sales returns and allowances.

Funds may be kept for other reasons, such as cash advances for travel and returns of bottles and cans for recycling.

Reporting Cash Funds

Good control procedures should be followed in keeping the cash funds. One employee should be responsible for the handling of the cash funds. Another employee should be responsible for drawing the checks from the general bank account. Thus there is a division of responsibility. The cash vouchers and slips should be prenumbered, and receipts should be marked *Paid*. The fund should be proved frequently.

The cash funds accounts are asset accounts. Each fund could be listed on the balance sheet directly after Cash, or the cash funds could be combined with cash on the balance sheet. In this case only one amount is shown opposite the Cash on Hand and in Bank title.

Balance sheet showing only one amount for cash in bank and cash on hand.

GALLO COMPANY
Balance Sheet
December 31, 19—

ASSETS				
Current Assets:				
Cash on Hand and in Bank	33,075	00		

Activity B. Answer the following questions about establishing, using, and replenishing change funds. Refer to the text and illustrations on pages 332 to 334.

1. What is the purpose of a change fund?

2. On which bank account is the check to establish a change fund drawn?

3. Which account is debited to establish the change fund? Which account is credited?

4. In which journal is the entry to establish the change fund recorded?

5. How often is the change fund replenished?

6. Is a check drawn to replenish the change fund? Explain.

7. What are the cash sales for May 15? the amount of the change fund? the Net Cash Handled?

8. What is the purpose of the sales returns and allowances fund?

9. How is division of responsibility accomplished when keeping cash funds?

10. What is the balance sheet balance of the Cash account when cash funds are combined with the Cash in Bank account?

Topic 2   Problems

9-6. You have been hired by the Carr Company. One of your responsibilities is handling the petty cash fund. You are asked to complete the following procedures.

a. Issue Check 550 for $30 to establish the petty cash fund on December 1. The owner, Madelyn Carr, will sign the check. (The checkbook balance is $1,040.)

b. Record the check to establish the petty cash fund in the cash payments journal.

c. Issue the following petty cash vouchers. Issue checks and record in cash payments journal.

d. On December 31 Ms. Carr informs you that you will no longer have responsibility for petty cash.

However, she asks you to make recommendations for improving control of the fund. You review the fund for the past three months and the items listed here. Use your findings to write a recommendation.

(1) Petty cash receipts have been written for amounts up to $20, even though Ms. Carr stated on June 30 that no petty cash payments should exceed $10.

(2) Some petty cash receipts have not been signed.

(3) Petty cash has been used to pay for coffee and pastries for office personnel.

(4) One person has handled all petty cash transactions, includ-

ing writing the check to replenish the fund.

(5) Small sales returns and allowances are frequently paid out of the petty cash fund.

Dec. 2 Postage due on various letters and packages, $2.70; paid to R. Johnson (Miscellaneous Expense).

2 Paid $3.50 to M. Lopez for typewriting paper and rubber bands (Office Expense).

4 Paid $10 to A. Johnson for an advertisement in the local high school yearbook (Advertising Expense).

8 Issued Check 556 to replenish petty cash. (The petty cash fund has a balance of $13.80.)

8 Recorded the check to replenish petty cash in the cash payments journal.

10 Paid $7.50 to the U-Carry Company (P. Milot) for delivery of merchandise purchases (Transportation-In).

10 After a discussion with Madelyn Carr, you de-

cided to increase the petty cash fund to $50. Issued Check 570 to increase the petty cash fund.

Dec 10 Recorded the check to increase the petty cash fund in the cash payments journal.

12 Paid $4.80 to R. Johnson for cleaning supplies (Office Expense).

13 Paid $15 to M. Keegan for an ad in the Civic Ballet program (Advertising Expense).

20 Paid $3.10 to R. Johnson for postage due (Miscellaneous Expense).

22 Paid $12.30 to the U-Carry Company (P. Milot) for delivery of merchandise purchases.

31 Replenished petty cash. Used Check 580.

31 Recorded the check to replenish petty cash in the cash payments journal.

9-7. On December 1 Carrie Coyle, owner of CC Services, asks you to do the following.

a. Establish a change fund for $30. Ms. Coyle will sign the check. Record the check (Check 551) in the cash payments journal.

b. Complete a cash proof on December 1 using the following information: cash sales, $270; received on account, $40 (from Karen James); no cash was paid out; cash in drawer, $340; change fund, $30. Record the

cash proof in the cash receipts journal.

c. Complete a cash proof on December 2 using the following information: cash sales, $265; received on account, $30 (Ray Crider); no cash was paid out; cash in drawer, $324; change fund, $30. Record the cash proof in the cash receipts journal and cash payments journal.

HINT: The net cash debit is $310 for December 1 and $295 for December 2.

Topic 3
Accounting for Marketable Securities

A *What are marketable securities?* **Marketable securities** are investments that can be quickly converted into cash. Marketable securities consist mainly of United States government bonds and of stocks (shares) and bonds issued by large corporations.

Good cash management requires that any cash not needed to meet current debts should be invested to earn revenue. Bonds produce interest revenue. Stocks produce dividend revenue when the corporations declare dividends. These items are easily converted into cash. Thus marketable securities are listed directly beneath the Cash items on the balance sheet. This means that marketable securities are viewed as being more liquid than accounts receivable or merchandise inventory.

Recording the Purchase of Marketable Securities

When the securities are acquired, the Marketable Securities account is debited for the total cost. The cost includes any commissions and any transfer taxes.

The Gallo Company purchased ten bonds for a price of $1,000 each plus a brokerage commission of $100. The entry which records the purchase of these bonds is given here. Other types of investments, such as investments in stocks, are also recorded at cost.

September 1 Gallo Company purchases ten 8 percent bonds of the Mueller Corporation for $1,000 each and pays a commission of $100.

September 2 Gallo Company purchases 100 shares of stock in the Mountain Power Company for $50 each and pays a commission of $90.

Total Cost of Bonds:

Price for bonds . . . $10,000
Plus: Brokerage
commission . . . . . +100
Total cost $10,100

Asset Marketable Securities increases by $10,100.

Asset Cash decreases by $10,100.

Total Cost of Stocks:

Price of stocks $5,000
Plus: Brokerage
commission . . . . . . +90
Total cost $5,090

Asset Marketable Securities increases by $5,090.

Asset Cash decreases by $5,090.

Accounting Principle:
Marketable Securities. The generally accepted accounting principle is that marketable securities should be recorded at cost.

		CASH PAYMENTS JOURNAL							Page 22
DATE	ACCOUNT DEBITED	EXPLANATION	CHECK NO.	POST. REF.	GENERAL LEDGER DEBIT	ACCOUNTS PAYABLE DEBIT	PURCHASES DISCOUNT CREDIT	NET CASH CREDIT	
19— Sept. 1	*Marketable Securities*	*(10 Mueller Corp. 8 percent bonds plus $100 commission*	670		10,100 00			10,100 00	
2	*Marketable Securities*	*(100 Mountain Power Co. stocks plus $90 commission*	671		5,090 00			5,090 00	

Activity A. Answer the following questions about marketable securities. Refer to the text and illustrations on pages 336 and 337.

1. Where are marketable securities listed on the balance sheet?
2. What is the price of each bond purchased by the Gallo Company?
3. What is the brokerage commission for the purchase of the bonds?
4. What is the total cost of the bonds?
5. What is the debit entry to record the purchase of Mountain Power Company stock? the credit entry?
6. What accounting principle would be violated if the Mountain Power Company stocks are recorded at $5,000?
7. What is the total cost of the Mueller Company bonds and Mountain Power Company stock?

Recording Investment Revenue

B *What types of revenue do investments provide to the investor?* Investments provide the investor with revenue in the form of interest or dividends.

Investment revenue may be received during the accounting period in which it is earned. Sometimes, however, it is earned during one accounting period but is not received until another accounting period. In this topic we will discuss revenue that has been earned and received in the same accounting period. Revenue earned in one period but received in another is discussed in Topic 4.

Recording Bond Interest

Interest represents money paid for the use of borrowed money. Investors in bonds *receive* interest because they have loaned money to the issuer of the bonds.

Interest earned and received in the same accounting period is recorded by debiting the Cash account and crediting the Interest Revenue account for the amount received. The entry to record the quarterly bond interest check from the Mueller Corporation is shown on page 338.

December 1 The Gallo Company receives a check for $200 from Mueller Corporation for quarterly bond interest.

Asset Cash increases by $200.

Revenue from interest increases owner's equity by $200.

Recording Cash Dividends

Stocks provide the investor with revenue in the form of dividends. **Dividends** represent the portion of the corporation's earnings that are distributed to stockholders. Dividends, however, are not guaranteed.

On November 15 the board of directors of Mountain Power Company declared a cash dividend of $1 for each share of outstanding common stock, payable on December 1. On December 2 the Gallo Com-

Asset Cash increases by $100. Revenue from dividends increases owner's equity by $100.

pany received a dividend check from Mountain Power for $100. The check is recorded in the cash receipts journal.

December 2 The Gallo Company receives a check for $100 from Mountain Power Company for quarterly dividend.

	CASH RECEIPTS JOURNAL							Page 27
DATE	ACCOUNT CREDITED	EXPLANATION	POST. REF.	GENERAL LEDGER CREDIT	ACCOUNTS RECEIVABLE CREDIT	SALES DISCOUNT DEBIT		NET CASH DEBIT
19—								
Dec. 1	Interest Revenue	{ Mueller Corp. { quarterly interest		200 00				200 00
2	Dividend Revenue	{ Mountain Power Co. { quarterly dividend		100 00				100 00

Reporting Interest and Dividend Revenue

Revenues earned from investments are not the normal type of transactions completed by the Gallo Company. Revenue arising from normal operations is separated from revenue arising from nonoperating transactions. As a result, special revenue accounts (Interest Revenue and Dividend Revenue) are used to record the $200 interest and $100 dividend received by the Gallo Company. These accounts are included in the Other Revenue section on the income statement.

GALLO COMPANY
Income Statement
For the Period Ending December 31, 19—

Revenue From Sales:			
Net Income From Operations.		23,350 00	
Other Revenue:			
Interest Revenue	200 00		
Dividend Revenue	100 00		
Total Other Revenue		300 00	

GALLO COMPANY
Balance Sheet
December 31, 19—

ASSETS		
Current Assets:		
Cash on Hand and in Bank.	33,075 00	
Marketable Securities.	15,190 00	

Activity B. Answer the following questions about recording investment revenue. Refer to the text and illustrations on pages 337 and 338.

1. What is the entry to record interest revenue?

2. What is the entry to record dividend revenue?

3. Is interest revenue or dividend revenue recorded on December 1? What is the amount?

4. Is interest revenue or dividend revenue recorded on December 2? What is the amount?

5. How many dollars per share dividend revenue are received from the Mountain Power Company?

6. What is the total investment revenue received on December 1 and 2?

7. In which journal is the receipt of investment revenue recorded?

8. Which income statement section lists interest and dividend revenue?

Sale of Marketable Securities

C *How is the sale of marketable securities recorded?* Securities are recorded in the accounting records at original costs. However, certain investments, such as stock investments, also have a market value that rarely is the same as the original cost. The market value of stock may vary depending on a company's earnings, the general economy, and numerous other factors. It is highly unlikely that, as time passes, the market value of a stock investment will remain the same as the original cost price. Therefore, when an investment is sold, the cash received is usually more or less than the cost price.

If the cash received is less than the amount paid for the stocks or bonds, there is a loss. If the securities are sold for more than the cost, there is a gain on the sale. Any loss or gain must be recorded.

Recording a Loss

Suppose the Gallo Company sells its Mueller Corporation bonds on April 1 for $990 each, for a total of $9,900 (10 × $990). The commission on the sale is $100. The Gallo Company receives $9,800 ($9,900 − $100). Since Gallo paid $10,100 for the bonds, there is a loss of $300 on the sale. The loss is recorded as follows.

Sale of Bonds

Price received . . .	$ 9,900
Less: Brokerage commission	−100
Total received	$ 9,800
Cost	−10,100
Loss on sale	$ 300

April 1 The Gallo Company sells 10 bonds of Mueller Corporation for $9,900 and pays a commission of $100.

The entries to record this transaction are shown on page 340. The sale of Mueller Corporation bonds at a loss requires two entries. The first is recorded in the Cash Receipts Journal to show cash received of $9,800. The dash (—) in the Posting Reference column indicates that the $9,800 is not posted to the Marketable Securities account. The second entry is recorded in the General Journal. Note the dash (—) opposite the Cash account, indicating that the $9,800 should not be posted.

CASH RECEIPTS JOURNAL								Page 41	
DATE	ACCOUNT CREDITED	EXPLANATION	POST. REF.	GENERAL LEDGER CREDIT	ACCOUNTS RECEIVABLE CREDIT	SALES DISCOUNT DEBIT	NET CASH DEBIT		
19— Apr. 1	Marketable Securities.....	Sold 10 bonds of Mueller Corp.....	—	9,800 00			9,800 00		

Asset Cash increases by $9,800.

Loss decreases owner's equity by $300.

Asset Marketable Securities decreases by $10,100.

GENERAL JOURNAL				Page 87
DATE	ACCOUNT TITLE AND EXPLANATION	POST. REF.	DEBIT	CREDIT

19—
April 1
	Cash ....
	Gains and Losses on Sale of
	   Marketable Securities ....
	Marketable Securities.........
	   Record sale of 10 Mueller Corp.
	   bonds.
		—	9,800 00
			
			300 00
				
				10,100 00

Cash			Marketable Securities			Gains and Losses on Sale of Marketable Securities	
19— Apr. 1	9,800		19— Sept. 1 10,100	19— Apr. 1 10,100		19— Apr. 1	300

The net effect of the two entries is that $9,800 was received for an investment of $10,100. The difference of $300 is a loss and is recorded in the Gains and Losses on Sale of Marketable Securities account. (The **Gains and Losses on Sale of Marketable Securities account** is an equity account and is found in the Other Revenue or Other Expense section of the income statement.) The loss is an expense because it decreases owner's equity. The loss is classified as Other Expense.

Recording a Gain

Sale of Stock:

Price received . . .	$6,000
Less: Brokerage commission	−100
Total received. . . .	$5,900
Cost	−5,090
Gain on sale.	$ 810

The Gallo Company sold its 100 shares of stock in the Mountain Power Company for $60 each. The commission on the sale is $100. The total received for the sale is $5,900 ($6,000 − $100). The cost of the stock was $5,090 including the commission. Thus the Gallo Company made a gain of $810 on the sale of the stock.

May 1 The Gallo Company sells 100 shares of Mountain Power Company for $6,000 and pays a $100 commission.

	CASH RECEIPTS JOURNAL						Page 51
DATE	ACCOUNT CREDITED	EXPLANATION	POST. REF.	GENERAL LEDGER CREDIT	ACCOUNTS RECEIVABLE CREDIT	SALES DISCOUNT DEBIT	NET CASH DEBIT
19— May 1	Marketable Securities...... Gains and Losses on Sale of Marketable Securities	Sold 100 shares of Mountain Power Co. stocks less $100 commission		5,090 00 810 00			5,900 00

Cash		Marketable Securities			Gains and Losses on Sale of Marketable Securities	
19— May 1 5,900		19— Sept. 2 5,090	19— May 1 5,090		19— Apr. 1 300	19— May 1 810

Note that $5,090 of the $5,900 is the original cost. The difference ($810) between the selling price and the original cost price is revenue and is recorded in Gains and Losses on Sale of Marketable Securities.

The current market price of stocks tends to rise and fall from day to day. When the stock is sold, the holder recognizes the loss or gain caused by this change in market price. If the stock is not sold, however, the investment recorded on the balance sheet does not reflect this change in price. The accounting principle is that the securities should be recorded at cost. However, the principle goes further by stating that securities should be shown on the balance sheet at cost or at current market value, whichever is lower.

Asset Cash increases by $5,900.
Gain increases owner's equity by $810.
Asset Marketable Securities decreases by $5,090.

GALLO COMPANY
Income Statement
For the Period Ending December 31, 19—

Revenue From Sales:			
Other Revenue:			
Interest Revenue	200 00		
Dividend Revenue	100 00		
Gains and Losses on Sales of Marketable Securities	510 00		
Total Other Revenue		810 00	

Income statement showing Gains and Losses on Sale of Marketable Securities as Other Revenue.

Activity C. Answer the following questions about the sale of marketable securities. Refer to the text and illustrations on pages 339 to 341.

1. What factors cause the market value of stock investments to vary?

2. When is there a loss on the sale of stocks or bonds? When is there a gain?

3. How much does the Gallo Company receive for each Mueller Corporation bond sold on April 1? What is the total commission? What is the total amount of cash received?

4. Is there a loss or gain on the April 1 sale? How much? How is it computed?

5. How many entries are necessary to record the sale of bonds on April 1? Which amounts are posted to the general ledger from the Cash Receipts Journal? Which amounts are posted from the General Journal?

6. What is the *net effect* on the General Ledger accounts after the sale on April 1 is recorded and posted?

7. How much does the Gallo Company receive for each share of stock sold on May 1? What is the total commission on May 1? What is the total amount of cash received?

8. Is there a gain or loss on the May 1 sale of stock? How much? How is it computed?

9. In which journal is the sale of stock on May 1 recorded? What is the entry?

10. How is Gains and Losses on Sale of Marketable Securities classified? Where is it shown on the income statement?

Topic 3   Problems

9-8. The Calumet Corporation has a policy of investing idle cash in various marketable securities. Record the following purchases of marketable securities in a cash payments journal.

a. Jan.   1 Purchased four 8 percent $1,000 bonds from the Gold Company. Fees and taxes were $125.

b. Jan.   15 Purchased 100 shares of Pride Corporation stock for $20 per share. Brokerage fees and taxes were $100.

c. March 10 Purchased 100 shares of Pride Corporation stock for $18 per share. Brokerage fees and taxes were $100.

d. March 30 Purchased 25 shares of Minex Corporation stock for $12.50 per share. Fees and taxes were $37.

NOTE: Save your work on Topic Problem 9-8 for further use in Topic Problems 9-9 and 9-11.

9-9. Record the following interest revenue and dividend revenue transactions in a cash receipts journal.

a. April 3 Received the quarterly dividend check from the Pride Corporation. The dividend was declared on March 27 at $0.25 per share and payable on March 31.

b. July 2 Received the quarterly dividend check from the Pride Corporation. The dividend was declared

on June 27 at $0.25 per share and payable on June 30.

c. July 2 Received the semiannual interest revenue check from the Gold Company. (*HINT*: 8 percent represents annual interest, and the check received on July 2 was for semi-annual interest.)

9-10. In a table similar to the one shown here, supply the missing amounts (indicated by letters in parentheses) relative to purchasing and selling marketable securities.

	Purchase of Securities				Sale of Securities			
	Price of Security	Number of Shares/Bonds	Fees and Taxes	Total Cost	Selling Price	Fees and Taxes	Cash Received	Loss or Gain on Sale
Ex.	**$ 60**	**100**	**$100**	**$6,100**	**$6,050**	**$100**	**$5,950**	**$ 150 Loss**
a.	1,000	10	100	(a)	9,800	100	9,700	(b)
b.	120	200	(c)	24,200	26,000	(d)	(e)	1,500 Gain
c.	(f)	1,200	300	(g)	(h)	200	14,900	400 Loss
d.	12.50	(i)	300	15,300	15,100	200	(j)	(k)
e.	(l)	12	200	12,200	12,400	200	(m)	(n)
f.	20,000	(o)	300	(p)	(q)	200	20,800	500 Gain
g.	3.75	2,000	75	(r)	16,000	200	(s)	(t)

9-11. In Topic Problem 9-8 you recorded the purchase of various marketable securities. Using your work from Topic Problem 9-8, record the following sales in a cash receipts journal and general journal.

a. Sept. 11 Sold 50 shares of Pride Corporation stock purchased on January 15. The sale price was $22 per share minus $100 for fees and taxes.

b. Oct. 2 Sold 125 shares of Pride Corporation stock for $18 per share. Fees and taxes were $100.

c. Oct. 15 Sold the remaining shares of Pride Corporation stock for $18.50 per share. Fees and taxes were $25. The market price of this stock was $19 on October 14.

d. Nov. 1 Sold the Minex Corporation stock for $16.50 per share. Fees and taxes were $40.

Topic 4
Accounting for Notes Receivable and Accrued Interest

A *What are receivables?* Receivables can be a variety of claims that generally result in receiving cash. Receivables include notes receivable, interest receivable, and accounts receivable.

Notes Receivable

Negotiability Requirements of a Note:
- It is written.
- It is signed by maker (Rona Underhill).
- It has an unconditional promise to pay ($2,000).
- It is payable in 90 days (September 29).
- It is payable to order of a designated payee (Gallo Company) or to bearer.

A **promissory note** is a written promise by one person (maker) to pay money to another (payee). Promissory notes are claims that a business has against the customer's assets.

Most notes are **negotiable.** That is, the note can be transferred from person to person. The **holder**—the person who legally owns (holds) a negotiable note—can sell the note or can borrow money against it.

The note here was received by the Gallo Company from Rona Underhill. This note is negotiable. It is written, signed by the maker (Rona Underhill), promises unconditionally to pay $2,000 at a definite time (September 29), and is payable to the order of the Gallo Company.

> $ 2,000.00   July 1,   19—
>
> _____Ninety days_____ after date I promise to pay to
> the order of _Gallo Company_
> _Two thousand and 00/100_ ————————————Dollars
> Payable at _Second National Bank_
> Value received _with interest at 8 percent_
> No. _12_ Due _September 29, 19—_   Rona Underhill

Recording Notes Receivable

A promissory note received from a debtor is called a **note receivable.** Most notes are short-term receivables because they are usually due within a year. Notes are usually received (1) at the time a sale is made, (2) in exchange for an account receivable, or (3) for the loan of cash.

Recording a Note Receivable at Time of Sale. The note receivable from Rona Underhill was received at the time of a sale. The entry to record the note is recorded in the general journal. The Notes Receivable account is debited, and the Sales account is credited.

July 1 Gallo Company receives a 90-day 8 percent note for $2,000 from Rona Underhill for sale of merchandise.

GENERAL JOURNAL					Page 43
DATE		ACCOUNT TITLE AND EXPLANATION	POST. REF.	DEBIT	CREDIT
19—					
July	1	Notes Receivable	121	2,000 00	
		Sales	401		2,000 00
		Received 90-day, 8 percent note from Rona Underhill.			
July	2	Notes Receivable	121	1,000 00	
		Accounts Receivable/			
		David Lee	131/ √		1,000 00
		Received 4-month, 8 percent note.			

Asset Notes Receivable increases by $2,000. Revenue from sale increases the owner's equity by $2,000.

Asset Notes Receivable increases by $1,000. Asset Accounts Receivable decreases by $1,000.

Exchanging a Note Receivable for an Account Receivable.

Customers who cannot pay their accounts receivable in the normal credit period may be asked to sign notes. For accounting purposes, one asset (a note receivable) is exchanged for another asset (an account receivable). The exchange does not affect the total current assets. The Notes Receivable account is debited, and the Accounts Receivable account is credited. The amount recorded is the **face value, or principal,** of the note, which is the amount of money the maker promises to pay. Both accounts are assets. The customer's account in the subsidiary ledger is also credited for this amount.

The note recorded in the general journal on July 2 was received in exchange for an Accounts Receivable.

July 2 Gallo Company receives a 4-month 8 percent note for $1,000 from David Lee to replace account receivable.

Notes Receivable			Sales			Accounts Receivable	
19—				19—		19—	
July 1	2,000			July 1	2,000	July 2	1,000
July 2	1,000						

Subsidiary Ledger

David Lee			
19—		19—	
May 30	1,000	July 2	1,000

Recording a Note Received for Money Loaned to Another.
Sometimes a business may loan money as an investment and may receive a negotiable note in return. This is seldom done except by businesses that make loans in the normal course of their operations. The note simply covers the loan. The account debited is usually called the **Loans Receivable account** instead of Notes Receivable.

Activity A. Answer the following questions about the nature of notes receivable and recording notes receivable. Refer to the text and illustrations on pages 344 to 346.

1. What are receivables?

2. How does a note receivable differ from an account receivable?

3. Who is the maker of a promissory note? the holder? the payee?

4. Who is the maker of the note illustrated on page 344? the holder? the payee?

5. When are notes receivable usually received?

6. What is the entry to record a notes receivable at the time of a sale? In which journal is the entry recorded?

7. What is the entry to record a notes receivable in exchange for an accounts receivable? In which journal is the exchange recorded?

8. Is the entry on July 1 to record a notes receivable at the time of a sale or to exchange a notes receivable for an accounts receivable?

9. After what period of time must David Lee pay his notes receivable?

Interest-Bearing Notes Receivable

B *Is interest received on a note receivable?* A note receivable may be issued as a non-interest-bearing note or as an interest-bearing note. On an **interest-bearing note,** interest will be paid on the money owed. Interest on a note is earned daily, but it is not recorded each day. The interest is not received until the note becomes due.

$2,000.00   July 1,   19—

Ninety days   after date I promise to pay to
the order of Gallo Company
Two thousand and 00/100 ——————————Dollars
Payable at Second National Bank
Value received with interest at 8 percent
No. 12   Due September 29, 19—   Rona Underhill

The note receivable from Rona Underhill shows that she is using Gallo Company funds for 90 days. In return, she agrees to pay the

Gallo Company $2,000 (face of the note) plus $40 interest for 90 days. The interest will be paid when the note is due.

Receiving Cash for a Note Receivable. On September 29 the Gallo Company received $2,040 from Rona Underhill for the note ($2,000) and interest ($40). The entry is recorded in the cash receipts journal. Cash is debited for the amount received ($2,040), and Notes Receivable is credited for the face amount of the note ($2,000). The interest ($40) is revenue to the Gallo Company and is credited to the Interest Revenue account.

8 percent interest on $2,000 for 90 days is $40.

$$\$2,000 \times \frac{8}{100} \times \frac{90}{360} = \$40$$

Asset Cash increases by $2,040.
Asset Notes Receivable decreases by $2,000.
Revenue from interest increases owner's equity by $40.

September 29 Gallo Company receives $2,040 from Rona Underhill in payment of note for $2,000 and interest of $40.

	CASH RECEIPTS JOURNAL							Page 45
DATE	ACCOUNT CREDITED	EXPLANATION	POST. REF.	GENERAL LEDGER CREDIT	ACCOUNTS RECEIVABLE CREDIT	SALES DISCOUNT DEBIT	NET CASH DEBIT	
19—								
Sept. 29	Notes	Rona Underhill,						
	Receivable....	July 1.........	121	2,000 00			2,040 00	
	Interest	Interest for 90						
	Revenue	days..........	491	40 00			— 00	

Cash

19—	
Sept. 29	2,040

Notes Receivable

19—		19—	
July 1	2,000	Sept. 29	2,000
July 2	1,000		

Interest Revenue

19—	
Sept. 29	40

Activity B. Answer the following questions about interest-bearing notes receivable. Refer to the text and illustrations on pages 346 and 347.
1. What is an interest-bearing note?
2. How long will Rona Underhill be using Gallo Company funds?
3. How much interest must Rona Underhill pay Gallo Company? How is the interest computed?
4. How much cash is received from Rona Underhill on September 29?
5. What portion of the cash that is received on September 29 is interest?
6. In which journal is the receipt of cash from Rona Underhill recorded? What is the entry?
7. What is the effect on total assets when the cash was received from Rona Underhill? the effect on owner's equity?

Accrued Revenue

C *How is interest on a note treated if it is not received during the accounting period in which it is earned?* Revenue that is earned during the current accounting period but will not be received until a future period is known as **accrued revenue.** Interest receivable is an example of accrued revenue. Interest earned is revenue to the holder of the note and should be recorded in the accounting period in which it is earned.

The **accrual method of accounting** requires that revenue be recorded in the period in which it is earned. It is not necessary for cash to be received. An example of accrual accounting familiar to you is the method used to record credit sales. When a credit sale is made, the asset Accounts Receivable account and the revenue Sales account are increased. Thus the revenue is recorded in the accounting period when the merchandise is sold, even though the cash may not be recorded until the next accounting period.

A second illustration of the accrual method of accounting relates to recording interest on notes receivable.

Accrued Interest Revenue and Adjusting Interest Revenue

When the cash for a note receivable is received in the same accounting period the note was issued, the cash and interest are recorded when they are received. If, however, the note is issued in one accounting period and is due in a future accounting period, interest has accumulated on the note. In this case an adjusting entry must be made at the end of the accounting period to record the interest that has been earned but not yet received. Accrued interest revenue is used to show the procedure for recording accrued revenue.

Accrued Interest Revenue. On December 1 John James gives Gallo Company a 6-month 8 percent note for $1,500 for his account.

December 1 Gallo Company receives a 6-month 8 percent note for $1,500 from John James to replace account receivable.

Asset Notes Receivable increases by $1,500. Asset Accounts Receivable decreases by $1,500.

	GENERAL JOURNAL			Page 48
DATE	**ACCOUNT TITLE AND EXPLANATION**	**POST. REF.**	**DEBIT**	**CREDIT**
19—				
Dec. 1	*Notes Receivable*	121	1,500 00	
	Accounts Receivable/John James .	131/√		1,500 00
	Received 6-month, 8 percent			
	note on account.			

The note receivable from John James is recorded at its face value ($1,500). This amount remains in the Notes Receivable account until the note is due. The entry to record this note is shown on the next page.

Interest on the note is earned daily but is not recorded each day. No interest will be received until the note is due. Thus no cash will be received until June 1. At that time interest will be received for the previous six months (from December 1 to June 1). The Gallo Company has an annual accounting period that ends on December 31. Thus the interest will be earned in two accounting periods: from December 1 to December 31 in one period and from January 1 to June 1 in another. An adjusting entry is therefore needed to reflect accurately the total assets, total revenue, and net income for the two accounting periods.

Date of Note		Due Date
Dec. 1	Dec. 31	June 1

Adjusting Interest Revenue. The interest accrued on the $1,500 note receivable from December 1 to December 31 is $10 (30 days at 8 percent). The Interest Revenue account must be credited for $10 in order to include the interest earned during the period. The $10 is also a claim against the maker of the note until the interest is paid. Thus the accrued interest of $10 is also a receivable, which is an asset.

An Interest Receivable account is used to record the interest accrued on notes receivable. This asset account is debited to show the increase in assets.

December 31 Gallo Company records $10 as interest accrued for 30 days on note receivable.

GENERAL JOURNAL					Page 48	
DATE	ACCOUNT TITLE AND EXPLANATION	POST. REF.	DEBIT		CREDIT	
19—						
Dec. 31	Interest Receivable	122	10	00		
	Interest Revenue	491			10	00
	Record interest accrued on John James's Dec. 1 note.					

8 percent interest on $1,500 for one month is $10.

$$\$1,500 \times \frac{8}{100} \times \frac{30}{360} = \$10$$

Notes Receivable	Interest Receivable	Interest Revenue
19— Dec. 1 1,500	19— Dec. 31 10	19— Dec. 31 10

Asset Interest Receivable increases by $10. Revenue from interest increases owner's equity by $10.

After the adjusting entry is posted, the three accounts related to notes receivable show the following. The Notes Receivable account shows the amount of the note receivable ($1,500). The Interest Receivable account shows the amount of the interest that has been earned but not yet received ($10). The Interest Revenue account shows the amount of the interest that has been earned during the current accounting period ($10).

When the closing entries are made, interest revenue is closed into the Income Summary account. Interest receivable is a permanent account and remains open until the accrued interest has been received.

Interest Receivable is listed immediately after Notes Receivable in the Current Assets section of the balance sheet. (Accrued revenue items are also referred to as *accrued assets.*)

Order of listing current assets on balance sheet:
* **Cash**
* **Marketable securities**
* **Notes and interest receivable**

GALLO COMPANY
Balance Sheet
December 31, 19—

ASSETS			
Current Assets:			
Cash	33,075 00		
Marketable Securities.............	15,190 00		
Notes Receivable..................	1,500 00		
Interest Receivable	10 00		

Activity C. Answer the following questions about interest receivable and accrued revenue. Refer to the text and illustrations on pages 348 to 350.

1. What is accrued revenue?

2. Is it necessary for cash to be received in order for revenue to be earned? Explain.

3. Which method of accounting records revenue in the period in which it is earned?

4. Is accrued revenue involved when a note receivable is recorded and the cash is collected in the same accounting period? Explain.

5. On which date did John James give his note to the Gallo Company? On which date is the note due?

6. What is the total interest John James must pay the Gallo Company?
7. What portion of the total interest is earned during the first accounting period? the second accounting period?
8. What type of accounting entry is necessary to record accrued interest?
9. How much accrued interest is recorded by the Gallo Company on December 31?
10. What is the entry to record accrued interest on December 31?
11. How is interest receivable classified? interest revenue?
12. Is either interest receivable or interest revenue closed on December 31? Explain.
13. How is interest receivable shown on the balance sheet?

Receiving Cash for a Note Receivable

D *How is cash recorded for accrued revenue?* When the cash for accrued revenue is received, it must be credited to the receivable account. For example, on June 1 the Gallo Company receives $1,560 from John James in payment of his note ($1,500) plus interest ($60). Of the $60 total interest received, $10 was recorded as revenue in the last accounting period. The remaining interest ($50) is revenue for the present accounting period. Thus the Interest Revenue account must be credited for $50 to record revenue for the present accounting period. The Interest Receivable account must be credited for $10 to decrease the asset that was recorded in the last accounting period.

Interest on note is $60.

$$\$1,500 \times \frac{8}{100} \times \frac{6}{12} = \$60$$

Date of Note — Dec. 1 ... Dec. 31 .... Due Date — June 1
$10 .... $50
Total Interest $60

The entry to record the receipt of cash for the note receivable and the interest covering two accounting periods is shown here. The entry is recorded in the cash receipts journal.

June 1 Gallo Company receives $1,560 from John James for a note receivable of $1,500 plus interest of $60.
    After the entry is posted, the Notes Receivable account has a zero balance, showing the note was paid. The Interest Receivable account also has a zero balance, showing the interest to be received from the previous period was received. The Interest Revenue account now shows the interest revenue earned during the current accounting period ($50).

			CASH RECEIPTS JOURNAL					Page 54
DATE	ACCOUNT CREDITED	EXPLANATION	POST. REF.	GENERAL LEDGER CREDIT	ACCOUNTS RECEIVABLE CREDIT	SALES DISCOUNT DEBIT	NET CASH DEBIT	
19—								
June 1	Notes Receivable .	John James, Dec. 1..	121	1,500 00			1,560 00	
	Interest	Interest for						
	Receivable....	one month......	122	10 00			— 00	
	Interest	Interest for						
	Revenue	five months	491	50 00			— 00	

Asset Cash increases by $1,560. Asset Notes Receivable decreases by $1,500. Asset Interest Receivable decreases by $10. Revenue from interest increases owner's equity by $67.

Cash
19—		
June 1	1,560	

Notes Receivable
19—		19—	
Dec. 1	1,500	June 1	1,500

Interest Receivable
19—		19—	
Dec. 31	10	June 1	10

Interest Revenue
		19—	
		June 1	50

Activity D. Answer the following questions about recording cash for accrued revenue. Refer to the text and illustrations on pages 351 and 352.

1. What is the entry to record payment of John James's note receivable on June 1?

2. What portion of the $1,560 decreases the asset Notes Receivable? What portion is revenue? What portion decreases the asset Interest Receivable?

3. What is the balance of the Notes Receivable, Interest Receivable, and Interest Revenue accounts after the entry on June 1 is posted?

4. The $50 balance in interest revenue is revenue for what period of time?

Accrued Bond Interest

E *What is bond interest?* Interest is money paid for the use of borrowed money. Thus investors in bonds receive interest because they have loaned money to the issuer of the bonds. Interest earned and received in the same accounting period is recorded by debiting the Cash account and crediting the Interest Revenue account for the amount received.

When a business is on the accrual basis, an adjusting entry is needed at the end of the accounting period to record any interest earned but not yet received. In Topic 3 the Gallo Company bought bonds issued by the Mueller Corporation. The interest is paid semiannually (every six months) on June 1 and December 1.

The accounting period for the Gallo Company ends on December 31. Thus an adjusting entry must be made on December 31 to record the unpaid interest from December 1 to December 31. At 8 percent per year, the interest on $10,000 would be $67 ($66.66) for 1 month. The adjusting entry would be recorded at the end of the accounting period.

Asset Interest Receivable increases by $67.
Revenue from interest increases owner's equity by $67.

December 31 Gallo Company records interest revenue of $67 accrued for 1 month on bonds.

		GENERAL JOURNAL			Page 48
DATE		ACCOUNT TITLE AND EXPLANATION	POST. REF.	DEBIT	CREDIT
19—					
Dec.	31	Interest Receivable.	122	67 00	
		Interest Revenue	491		67 00
		Record one month interest on			
		Mueller Corporation bonds.			

Marketable Securities	Interest Receivable	Interest Revenue
Bal. 15,190	19— Dec. 31 67	19— Dec. 31 67

Receiving Accrued Bond Interest

On June 1 a check for $400 is received for the interest from December 1 to May 31. The interest is recorded as follows.

June 1 Gallo Company receives a check for $400 from Mueller Corporation for semiannual bond interest.

		CASH RECEIPTS JOURNAL							Page 57
DATE		ACCOUNT CREDITED	EXPLANATION	POST. REF.	GENERAL LEDGER CREDIT	ACCOUNTS RECEIVABLE CREDIT	SALES DISCOUNT DEBIT	NET CASH DEBIT	
19—									
June	1	Interest Receivable	Semiannual interest	122	67 00			400 00	
		Interest Revenue .	from Mueller bonds	491	333 00			— 00	

Cash		Interest Receivable		Interest Revenue	
19—		19—	19—		19—
June 1 400		Dec. 31 67	June 1 67		June 1 333

Asset Cash increases by $400. Asset Interest Receivable decreases by $67. Revenue from interest increases owner's equity by $333.

The entry is journalized in the cash receipts journal. After the entry is posted, the Interest Receivable account has a zero balance because the interest earned during the previous accounting period has now been received. The Interest Revenue account shows the amount of interest that is revenue for the current accounting period.

Dividends on Stocks

Dividends on most stocks are not guaranteed. Thus the holder does not know the amount of the dividend until the board of directors of the corporation declares the dividend. As a result, dividends received on stocks are recorded when the revenue is received. Adjusting entries are generally *not* made at the end of the accounting period for dividends.

Activity E. Answer the following questions about accrued bond interest. Refer to the text and illustrations on pages 352 to 354.

1. What type of entry is necessary to record bond interest earned in one period but not yet received?
2. How much accrued interest revenue is recorded on December 31 for Mueller Corporation bonds? What is the entry?
3. Which entry records the receipt of revenue on June 1?
4. What portion of the cash received on June 1 is revenue for the period beginning on January 1? What portion relates to revenue recorded in the period that ended on December 31?
5. What is the balance of Interest Receivable after the entry on June 1 is posted?
6. By what amount do total assets increase after recording and posting the entry on June 1? By what amount does owner's equity increase?
7. Are adjusting entries generally made for stock dividends at the end of the accounting period?

Topic 4   Problems

9-12. The Sol-Dex Company received four notes receivable during the current year. Details for the four notes are shown at the top of the next page. Record each note in the general journal. Save your work for further use in Topic Problems 9-13 to 9-15.

Purpose for Note	Amount of Note	Date of Note	Interest Rate	Term of Note	Due Date	Amount of Interest
a. Note 1: Sale to P. Shimuzu	$ 600	Jan. 13	7%	90 days		
b. Note 2: Exchanged accounts receivable for P. Shirk	1,350	Sept. 10	8	6 months		
c. Note 3: Exchanged accounts receivable for Cole Brothers	1,200	Sept. 30	8	1 year		
d. Note 4: Sale to Rex Inc.	800	Dec. 1	7	90 days		

9-13. Determine the due date, interest, and amount due for each of the notes receivable in Topic Problem 9-12.
NOTE: Save your work for further use in Topic Problem 9-15.

9-14. Do the following activities.
a. Determine the accrued interest for each note in Topic Problem 9-12. The end of the accounting period is December 31.
b. Record the entries for accrued interest in the general journal, as of December 31. Use your work in instruction **a** above to determine the amount of the adjusting entries.

9-15. Record the receipt of cash for each note receivable in the cash receipts journal. Use your work from Topic Problem 9-13 to find the due dates and amounts due. (*HINT:* Consider the adjusting entries in Topic Problem 9-14 when recording your entries.)

Topic 5
Accounting for Accounts Receivable

A *What is the most common form of receivable?* In the majority of businesses, the most common receivables are accounts receivable that result from the sale of goods and services.

Accounts Receivable

Generally accounts receivable are unsecured open accounts. An **unsecured open account** is an account where the customer (debtor) does not pledge property or have a second-party guarantee payment for each sale. Once the sale is completed, the customer must pay in cash, subject to the terms of the sale. The terms can include trade discounts, cash discounts, discount periods, and credit periods.

Opening an Account. No business wants to sell to a customer who will not pay the amount owed. Thus most businesses have a credit department. The credit department determines whether a customer is a good credit risk. That is, the credit department determines whether the customer is likely to pay the bill when it comes due. Some businesses require an individual to fill out an application requesting that an account be opened in his or her name.

If the customer is a business, the credit department may request the customer's financial statements. The statements are analyzed to determine the customer's ability to meet financial obligations. The credit department also checks the customer's past record of paying bills on time.

When the account is opened, the amount of credit is usually limited. For example, Victor Franco applied to the Gallo Company for credit. The credit department approved giving him credit, but it limited to $1,200 the amount that he could owe at any one time. This amount is shown on the ledger account set up for Victor Franco.

ACCOUNTS RECEIVABLE LEDGER						
Name Victor Franco				Credit Limit $1,200		
Address 14 River Drive, Buffton, OH				Telephone 555-2213		
DATE	EXPLANATION	POST. REF.	DEBIT	CREDIT	DEBIT BALANCE	

Procedures for the Control of Credit Sales

The internal controls to follow in handling and recording sales on credit are as follows.
- Fill customer's orders promptly.
- Use prenumbered forms.
- Verify the data on the customer's order.
- Check customer's credit before shipping the merchandise.
- Divide the responsibility.
- Remove the merchandise from stock only if there is proper authorization.
- Bill customer for all merchandise shipped.
- Record all receivables from completed sales transactions.
- Issue refunds and credits only for approved returns and allowances.
- Collect all receivables as soon as possible.

Billing the Customer

In some businesses, customers are expected to pay when the invoices are issued. Other businesses might grant their customers credit terms. For example, an invoice may be issued with credit terms of 2/10, n/30. Thus the customer may deduct a *sales discount* (2%) on the amount of the sale if he or she pays within the *discount period* (10 days). Otherwise, the full amount will be due at the end of the *credit period* (30 days). In still other businesses, customers pay their accounts once a month. The customer is expected to pay the full amount due within a certain number of days, such as 10 or 30 days from the date of the statement.

Businesses with a large number of customers, such as large department stores and utility companies, find it impossible to send statements to all customers on the same day of the month. These businesses use **cycle billing** to spread the work out during the month. In cycle billing, the accounts receivable are divided into groups. The groups may be based on the alphabetic sequence of the customers' last names, the geographic locations of the customers, or the type of customer. The Gallo Company, for example, mails statements to different groups of customers at stated intervals during the month.

Cycle billing is used to spread out work during the month.

GALLO COMPANY CYCLE BILLING SCHEDULE

Last Names Beginning With	Closing Date	Billing Covers Changes and Payments for These Dates
A–E	6	7th of the month to 6th of the next month
F–J	12	13th of the month to 12th of the next month
K–O	18	19th of the month to 18th of the next month
P–S	24	25th of the month to 24th of the next month
T–Z	30	1st of the month to end of the month

Thus a statement is sent to Joan Allison on the sixth of each month. Her June statement would show all the sales and payments between May 7 and June 6.

By following this plan, the Gallo Company spreads the billing work throughout the month. It also has a smooth cash flow since the payments from the customers are due throughout the month, not all at one time.

Activity A. Answer the following questions about accounts receivable and billing customers. Refer to the text and illustrations on pages 355 to 357.

1. What is an unsecured open account?

2. What is the purpose of a credit department?

3. What might a customer be asked to complete when applying for credit?

4. What was the credit limit for Victor Gallo?

5. What is meant by the credit terms 2/10, n/30?

6. What is the last day payment can be made for a January 6 sale when the terms are n/30?

7. When would a statement from the Gallo Company be sent to John Zajac if the company used cycle billing?

Uncollectible Accounts

B *Do all customers pay their accounts?* No, some customers do not pay. Before giving credit, sellers usually check credit ratings and attempt to give credit to those customers who will probably pay their debts. Still, even though sellers carefully check, some of their customers may not pay their accounts receivable.

There are various reasons why customers do not pay their accounts. Some customers do not have enough money, some may have forgotten, and others are dissatisfied with the service or merchandise. Accounts receivable that cannot be collected are known as **uncollectible accounts** (sometimes referred to as *doubtful accounts* or *bad debts*).

An important accounting point is that the balance of the Accounts Receivable account is not the realizable value of this account. The **realizable value** of accounts receivable is the amount a business actually expects to receive from the credit customers.

When a business makes a credit sale, it assumes that the full amount will be realized. That is, it assumes that the customer will eventually pay. Thus the Accounts Receivable account is debited and the Sales account is credited for the full amount of the sale. But experience has shown that some credit sales are likely to be uncollectible. Thus the accounts receivable shown on the balance sheet must be reduced to show the amount estimated to be collectible.

SALES JOURNAL								Page 48
DATE	INVOICE NO.	ACCOUNT DEBITED	TERMS	POST. REF.	ACCOUNTS RECEIVABLE DEBIT	SALES TAX PAYABLE CREDIT	SALES CREDIT	
19X4 Dec. 1	841	Victor Franco..........	2/10, 2/30	√	500 00		500 00	
31		Accounts Receivable Debit/Sales Credit.....		131/401	9,000 00		9,000 00	

There are two methods for recording losses from uncollectible accounts. They are the direct write-off method and the allowance method. In the **direct write-off method,** an uncollectible debt loss is recorded when the customer's account is found to be uncollectible. In the **allowance method,** an estimated amount for the uncollectible debt loss is recorded in the accounting period in which the sale is made.

**Methods to Record
Losses From
Uncollectible Accounts:**
• Direct write-off method
• Allowance method

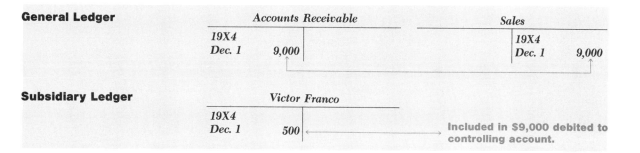

Included in $9,000 debited to controlling account.

Activity B. Answer the following questions about uncollectible accounts. Refer to the text and illustrations on pages 358 and 359.

1. What is the realizable value of accounts receivable? How does it differ from the balance of accounts receivable?

2. What are two methods for recording uncollectible accounts expense?

3. What are other names for uncollectible accounts?

4. Is a shortage of money the only reason customers do not pay their accounts? Explain.

The Direct Write-Off Method

C *How is the uncollectible account expense recorded using the direct write-off method?* In the direct write-off method, the uncollectible account expense is recorded when the customer's account is found to be uncollectible. A sale for $500 on credit to Victor Franco on December 1, 19X4, will be used to illustrate the direct write-off method.

Victor Franco did not pay his account when it became due. Many attempts to collect it failed. On September 1, 19X5, it was decided to write off the balance of the account as uncollectible. Transferring the balance of an asset account to a loss (expense) account is called **writing off an account.**

The entry to write off Mr. Franco's account consists of a credit to accounts receivable and to the customer's account in the subsidiary ledger for $500. The debit is to the Uncollectible Accounts Expense account for $500. The Uncollectible Accounts Expense account is used

Asset Accounts Receivable decreases by $500. Expense for uncollectible accounts decreases owner's equity by $500.

to record losses from uncollectible accounts. Other account titles that are used are Doubtful Accounts Expense and Bad Debts Expense.

This entry decreases Mr. Franco's account in the subsidiary ledger to zero and decreases the Accounts Receivable controlling account in the general ledger by $500. The entry also decreases owner's equity (Uncollectible Accounts Expense). Remember that owner's equity was increased when the original sale was recorded as revenue. Owner's equity is now decreased by the debit to Uncollectible Accounts Expense.

The direct write-off method is used by businesses that have few uncollectible accounts. Accountants often criticize the direct write-off method because it does not follow the principle of matching revenues and expenses in an accounting period.

	GENERAL JOURNAL			Page 56
DATE	**ACCOUNT TITLE AND EXPLANATION**	**POST. REF.**	**DEBIT**	**CREDIT**
19X5 Sept. 1	Uncollectible Accounts Expense . . . Accounts Receivable/ Victor Franco. . . . . Write off account as uncollectible.	521 131/√	500 00	500 00

General Ledger

Accounts Receivable		Uncollectible Accounts Expense
Bal. 9,000	19X5 Sept. 1 500	19X5 Sept. 1 500

Subsidiary Ledger

Victor Franco	
19X4 Dec. 1 500	19X5 Sept. 1 500

Revenue is received in one accounting period, and the uncollectible account expense is not recorded until a future period. As a result, the financial statements for two accounting periods show incorrect amounts, as shown at the top of the next page.

• *The income statements for two accounting periods are incorrect.* The net income is overstated in the accounting period in which the sale is made because the uncollectible accounts expense was omitted from the income statement. Also, the net income is understated in the accounting period in which the uncollectible accounts expense is recorded. This is a result of deducting an expense for a *prior* accounting period from the gross profit in the *current* period.

Income Statement	Balance Sheet
19X4 Uncollectible Accounts Expense not included. Net Income *overstated* by $500.	Accounts Receivable overstated by $500.
19X5 Uncollectible Accounts Expense from previous period included. Net Income *understated* by $500.	After write-off, Accounts Receivable is now shown correctly.

• *The balance sheet is incorrect until the accounts receivable is written off.* Uncollectible accounts should not be included among the assets. Thus the total assets are overstated on each balance sheet prepared prior to the write-off of the account.

To overcome these criticisms, accountants often use the allowance method to write off losses from uncollectible accounts. This method is discussed in the next learning unit.

Accounting Principle:
Matching Revenue and Expenses. The generally accepted accounting principle is that revenue must be matched with the expenses incurred in obtaining that revenue within each accounting period.

Activity C-1. Answer the following questions about the direct write-off method. Refer to the text and illustrations on pages 359 to 361.

1. When is the uncollectible accounts expense recorded in the direct write-off method?

2. What was the amount of Victor Franco's account?

3. On what date was the Victor Franco account written off?

4. What was the effect on current assets by not recording the Victor Franco account as uncollectible in 19X4? the effect on net income?

5. What is the entry to record an uncollectible account using the direct write-off method?

Activity C-2. Determine the effect on the following when the direct write-off method is used to record an uncollectible account for G. Mazur. The sale was made to G. Mazur in 19X5, and the debt was recorded as uncollectible in 19X6. Mark an "X" in the correct column.

	Understated		Overstated		No Effect	
	19X5	19X6	19X5	19X6	19X5	19X6
1. Current assets						
2. Total assets						
3. Total liabilities						
4. Owner's equity						
5. Net sales						
6. Cost of goods sold						
7. Net income						

The Allowance Method

D *How is the uncollectible accounts expense recorded using the allowance method?* The allowance method records uncollectible accounts expenses before they actually occur. To do this, it is necessary to estimate the expenses from uncollectible accounts. The estimate is then recorded in the same period as is the revenue from the sale.

In the allowance method, an adjusting entry is made at the end of each accounting period to record the estimated uncollectible accounts expenses. The adjusting entry is a debit to the Uncollectible Accounts Expense account and a credit to the Allowance for Doubtful Accounts account. *Allowance for Doubtful Accounts* is the most commonly used title for the account.

Valuation Asset Allowance for Doubtful Accounts decreases the Asset Accounts Receivable by $900. Expenses from uncollectible accounts decrease owner's equity by $900.

	GENERAL JOURNAL			Page 48
DATE	**ACCOUNT TITLE AND EXPLANATION**	**POST. REF.**	**DEBIT**	**CREDIT**
19X4 Dec. 31	Uncollectible Accounts Expense ... Allowance for Doubtful Accounts Record estimated loss.	521 132	900 00	900 00

General Ledger

Accounts Receivable	Allowance for Doubtful Accounts	Uncollectible Accounts Expense
Balance 9,000	19X4 Dec. 31 900	19X4 Dec. 31 900

Subsidiary Ledger *No Entry*

No entry is made at this time in the subsidiary ledger because there is no way of telling which customers' accounts will be uncollectible. Thus the accountant can only estimate the losses. The Accounts Receivable account cannot be credited. If it were, the controlling account would no longer agree with the subsidiary ledger. Using the Allowance for Doubtful Accounts account makes it possible to show a reduction in accounts receivable without crediting the controlling account.

Contra Accounts

A **contra account,** or valuation account, is an account used for recording deductions in the balance of another account. (The word *contra* means *contrary;* in this case it means contrary to the normal balance.) An asset contra account always has a credit balance because it represents the credit side of an asset account.

The Allowance for Doubtful Accounts account is a contra account. This contra account is used to show the estimated realizable value of the asset Accounts Receivable.

GALLO COMPANY
Balance Sheet
December 31, 19X4

ASSETS				
Current Assets:				
Cash			33,075 00	
Marketable Securities			15,190 00	
Notes Receivable			1,500 00	
Interest Receivable			10 00	
Accounts Receivable	9,000 00			
Less: Allowance for Doubtful Accounts	900 00		8,100 00	

On the balance sheet shown here, the contra account balance ($900) is subtracted from the asset account ($9,000) to show the estimated realizable value of that asset ($8,100). To help distinguish between the accounts used in the allowance method, keep the following in mind.

- Accounts Receivable shows the total amount to be received from customers according to the revenue recorded.
- Allowance for Doubtful Accounts is the estimated uncollectible portion of the accounts receivable.
- The difference between Accounts Receivable and Allowance for Doubtful Accounts is the *realizable value of the accounts receivable.*
- Uncollectible Accounts Expense is an operating expense matched against revenue for the accounting period.
- Both Accounts Receivable and Allowance for Doubtful Accounts must be shown on the balance sheet so that users have complete information.

Accounts Receivable shows total to be received from credit customers. Allowance for Doubtful Accounts shows estimated uncollectible portion. Difference between two is realizable value of accounts receivable.

Activity D. Answer the following questions about the allowance method. Refer to the text and illustrations on pages 362 and 363.

1. When is the uncollectible accounts expense recorded?

2. Through what type entry is the estimate for uncollectible accounts recorded?

3. Is an entry made in the subsidiary ledger at the time the estimate is recorded? Explain.

4. What is the effect on accounts receivable when Allowance for Doubtful Accounts is credited?

5. How is Allowance for Doubtful Accounts classified?

6. What is the amount of Uncollectible Accounts Expense? In which journal is it recorded?

Estimating Uncollectible Account Expenses

E *How are uncollectible account expenses estimated?* The amount estimated for the uncollectible accounts expenses is commonly based on the amount of sales, the amount of accounts receivable, or the age of the accounts receivable.

Percent of Net Sales. Uncollectible accounts expenses can often be related to net sales. Suppose that for the past five years the losses have been approximately 1 percent of the net sales. Then you could assume that the losses for this year would also be about 1 percent of net sales. The method is used when there are many customers and each customer owes a small but fairly equal amount.

Net Sales	$ 100,000
Percent	×0.01
Estimated Uncollectible Accounts	$1,000.00

To find the estimated amount of uncollectible accounts expense, multiply the net sales by the percent. The percent used should be based on the business's experience over the past years or on the experiences of similar businesses. In the marginal illustration 1 percent was used to obtain the amount for the uncollectible account expense.

Percent of Accounts Receivable. A second method for estimating uncollectible account expenses is to use a **percent of accounts receivable.** In the marginal illustration it was estimated that 5 percent of the accounts receivable ($9,000) would be uncollectible. Again, this was based on the past experiences of this business or of similar businesses.

Total Accounts Receivable	$ 9,000
Percent	×0.05
Estimated Uncollectible Accounts	$450.00

Percent of Aged Accounts Receivable. Another method for relating uncollectible accounts expenses to accounts receivable is the **percent of aged accounts receivable.** This method is more accurate than the first two methods because the individual accounts receivable are analyzed. Each accounts receivable is assigned to an age group according to the age of the invoice. The first step is to prepare a schedule of accounts receivable by age.

GALLO COMPANY
Schedule of Accounts Receivable by Age
December 31, 19X4

ACCOUNT WITH	BALANCE	1–30 DAYS	31–60 DAYS	61–90 DAYS	91–120 DAYS	OVER 120 DAYS
Atlas Company	100 00	100 00				
James Borski	200 00	200 00				
Cutler Signs	300 00				200 00	100 00
Victor Franco	500 00	500 00				
Mainline Corp.	1,500 00	900 00	600 00			
Glenda O'Hara, Inc.	100 00					100 00
Totals	9,000 00	6,000 00	1,000 00	900 00	600 00	500 00

The schedule of accounts receivable by age shows the name and balance of each account receivable. The balance of each account is then classified into age groups according to the number of days that the invoice has been outstanding. The ages of the accounts are determined according to the data in the accounts receivable ledger.

The procedures to follow when determining the age of an account receivable are as follows.

- Begin with the most recent unpaid invoice. Find how many days have passed since the invoice was issued.
- Analyze the next latest unpaid invoice.
- Continue until all unpaid invoices have been analyzed.
- Record the total unpaid invoices according to the various age groups.

The schedule for the Gallo Company shows the following.

The Atlas Company owes $100; the invoice was issued 1–30 days ago. A $200 sale was made to Cutler Signs 91–120 days ago, and a $100 sale was made to Cutler Signs over 120 days ago.

The loss from uncollectible accounts is estimated by taking a percentage of the total of each age group. The percentage varies from group to group, because the older the account is the less likely it is to be collected. For example, 50 percent of the accounts that are more than 120 days past due might be uncollectible, while only 1 percent of the accounts with a current balance might be uncollectible. The percentages shown in the margin are based on the past experience of the Gallo Company. The estimated uncollectible accounts expenses for the Gallo Company according to the aged accounts receivable is shown here.

Percentage of Probable Losses

1–30 Days. . . .	1 percent
31–60 Days. . . .	2
61–90 Days. . . .	.10
91–120 Days. . . .	.25
Over 120 Days. . . .	.50

Age Group (in days)	Total	Estimated Percentage	Estimated Loss
1–30	$6,000	1%	$ 60
31–60	1,000	2	20
61–90	900	10	90
91–120	600	25	150
Over 120	500	50	250
	$9,000		$570

Activity E. Answer the following questions about estimating uncollectible accounts expenses. Refer to the text and illustrations on pages 364 and 365.

1. What percentage is used to estimate the uncollectible accounts expenses when the Percent of Net Sales is used? when the Percent of Accounts Receivable is used?

2. What is the amount of accounts receivable in the Over 120 Days category on the Schedule of Accounts Receivable?

3. What portion of the Cutler Sign account is in the 31–60 Days category? the 91–120 Days category?

4. What percentage of those accounts in the Over 120 Days category are estimated as uncollectible?

5. What is the estimated loss when the Percent of Aged Accounts Receivable method is used?

Recording the Estimate for Uncollectible Accounts

[F] *When is the estimate made for uncollectible accounts expenses?* The estimate of the uncollectible accounts expenses is recorded as an adjusting entry at the end of the accounting period. The debit is to Uncollectible Accounts Expense. The expense for uncollectible accounts is an operating expense and decreases owner's equity. The credit is to the Allowance for Doubtful Accounts.

The amount for the adjusting entry depends on the method used to estimate the doubtful accounts.

In the net sales method, the amount of adjustment is the amount computed regardless of balance of Allowance for Doubtful Accounts account.

Percent of Net Sales. When the estimated uncollectible account expense is based on a percent of net sales, the adjustment is the amount computed *regardless* of any balance in the Allowance for Doubtful Accounts. Suppose the Allowance for Doubtful Accounts has a credit balance of $100, and the estimated uncollectible account loss for the current period is $1,000. The amount of the adjustment is $1,000. The new balance of the Allowance for Doubtful Accounts account will be $1,100 ($100 + $1,000).

Accounts Receivable				Allowance for Doubtful Accounts		
Balance	*9,000*				*Balance*	*100*
					19X4	
					Dec. 31	*1,000*
		Balance is $1,100				

Sales				Uncollectible Accounts Expense		
	Balance	*100,000*		*19X4*		
				Dec. 31	*1,000*	

In the percent of accounts receivable method, the balance of Allowance for Doubtful Accounts must equal estimated loss.

Percent of Accounts Receivable. In this method the balance of the Allowance for Doubtful Accounts must equal the estimated loss. Suppose the estimate for uncollectible accounts was $450. Then the account balance of Allowance for Doubtful Accounts must be $450. Thus before the adjusting entry can be made, the present balance must be considered.

Suppose the Allowance for Doubtful Accounts has a credit balance of $100. An adjusting entry for a $350 credit must then be made in order to increase the credit balance to $450.

Accounts Receivable				Allowance for Doubtful Accounts	
Balance	9,000			Balance	100
				19X4	
				Dec. 31	350

Balance
is
$450

Sales				Uncollectible Accounts Expense	
		Balance	100,000	19X4	
				Dec. 31	350

If the Allowance for Doubtful Accounts has a debit balance, the adjustment must change the debit balance to a credit balance. Suppose the Allowance for Doubtful Accounts has a debit balance of $100. The adjustment must then be for $550 ($450 + $100). After the adjustment is posted, the allowance account will have a balance of $450, the estimated doubtful account losses.

Accounts Receivable				Allowance for Doubtful Accounts	
Balance	9,000			Balance	100	19X4
					Dec. 31	550

Balance
is
$450

Sales				Uncollectible Accounts Expense	
		Balance	100,000	19X4	
				Dec. 31	550

Percent of Aged Accounts Receivable. Recording the estimate on the aged accounts receivable is the same as when the estimate is based on the percent of accounts receivable. The balance of the Allowance for Doubtful Accounts must be equal to the estimated loss. Suppose the amount of the estimated loss from uncollectible accounts is $570. If Allowance for Doubtful Accounts has a credit balance of $250, the adjusting entry must credit the account for $320.

In the aged accounts receivable method, the balance of Allowance for Doubtful Accounts account must equal estimated loss.

Accounts Receivable		Allowance for Doubtful Accounts	
Balance 9,000		Balance 250	
		19X4	
	Balance is $570	Dec. 31 320	

Sales		Uncollectible Accounts Expense	
	Balance 100,000	19X4	
		Dec. 31 320	

Activity F. Answer the following questions about recording the estimate for uncollectible accounts. Refer to the text and illustrations on pages 366 to 368.

1. What is the entry for recording the adjusting entry for uncollectible accounts?

2. Is the balance of the accounts receivable account considered when the Percent of Net Sales method is used? Explain.

3. What is the amount of the adjusting entry when the Percent of Net Sales method is used? when the Percent of Accounts Receivable method is used? when the Percent of Aged Accounts method is used?

4. How is the amount of $550 computed when the Percent of Accounts Receivable method is used? What is the balance of the Allowance for Doubtful Accounts before the adjusting entry? after the adjusting entry?

Recording Uncollectible Account Expenses

G *How are uncollectible accounts expenses recorded?* When a customer's account is found to be uncollectible, an entry is made to reduce the balance to zero. The entry consists of credits to the Accounts Receivable controlling account and to the customer's account in the subsidiary ledger. The debit is to the Allowance for Doubtful Accounts. The entry to write off Victor Franco's account using the allowance method is shown on the next page.

Note that writing off a customer's account using the allowance method does not affect the Uncollectible Accounts Expense for the accounting period. The expense was recorded in the period when the sale was made. The write-off entry now shows the part of the estimated amount that has not been paid.

	GENERAL JOURNAL			Page 56

DATE		ACCOUNT TITLE AND EXPLANATION	POST. REF.	DEBIT	CREDIT
19X5 Sept.	1	Allowance for Doubtful Accounts . .	132	500 00	
		Accounts Receivable/			
		Victor Franco.	131/√		500 00
		Write off the account			
		as uncollectible.			

GENERAL LEDGER

Accounts Receivable Account No. 131

DATE		EXPLANATION	POST. REF.	DEBIT	CREDIT	BALANCE DEBIT	BALANCE CREDIT
19X4 Dec.	31	Balance	—			9,000 00	
19X5 Sept.	1	. . . . . ., ...	J56		500 00	8,500 00	

Allowance for Doubtful Accounts Account No. 132

DATE		EXPLANATION	POST. REF.	DEBIT	CREDIT	BALANCE DEBIT	BALANCE CREDIT
19X4 Jan.	1	Balance	—				570 00
19X5 Sept.	1	Victor Franco	J56	500 00			70 00

$570 is amount of uncollectible loss estimated at the end of previous period. $70 is amount estimated after Mr. Franco's account was written off.

Uncollectible Accounts Expense Account No. 521

DATE		EXPLANATION	POST. REF.	DEBIT	CREDIT	BALANCE DEBIT	BALANCE CREDIT

Amount written off does not appear as an expense of this period. The expense was recorded at the end of the previous period.

Collection of Accounts Written Off

If an account that has been written off is later collected, the write-off entry must be reversed. If Victor Franco decides to pay his account on November 20, 19X5, two steps must be taken.

• The write-off entry must be reversed to put the uncollectible account back in the Accounts Receivable.

Customer's account in subsidiary ledger after posting write-off entry.

ACCOUNTS RECEIVABLE LEDGER

| Name | Victor Franco | | | | Credit Limit | $1,200 |
| Address | 14 River Drive, Buffton OH | | | | Telephone | 555-2213 |

DATE		EXPLANATION	POST. REF.	DEBIT	CREDIT	DEBIT BALANCE
19X4 Dec.	1	Invoice 548	548	500 00		500 00
19X5 Sept.	1	Uncollectible	J56		500 00	— 00

Entry to reinstate customer's account.

GENERAL JOURNAL   Page 59

DATE		ACCOUNT TITLE AND EXPLANATION	POST. REF.	DEBIT	CREDIT
19X5 Nov.	20	Accounts Receivable/Victor Franco .	131/√	500 00	
		Allowance for Doubtful Accounts	132		500 00
		Reverse entry of Sept. 1, 1985,			
		writing off this account,			
		which was collected in			
		full today.			

• The customer's account must be reduced in the normal manner with an entry in the cash receipts journal.

CASH RECEIPTS JOURNAL   Page 59

DATE		ACCOUNT CREDITED	EXPLANATION	POST. REF.	GENERAL LEDGER CREDIT	ACCOUNTS RECEIVABLE CREDIT	SALES DISCOUNT DEBIT	NET CASH DEBIT
19X5 Nov.	20	Victor Franco	On account	√		500 00		500 00

By reversing the original write-off entry, we obtain a complete record of all transactions affecting the customer's account in the Accounts Receivable ledger.

ACCOUNTS RECEIVABLE LEDGER

Name Victor Franco   **Credit Limit** $1,200

Address 14 River Drive, Buffton OH   **Telephone** 555-2213

DATE		EXPLANATION	POST. REF.	DEBIT	CREDIT	DEBIT BALANCE
19X4						
Dec.	1	Invoice 548	S17	500 00		500 00
19X5						
Sept.	1	Uncollectible	J56		500 00	— 00
Nov.	20	Reinstated uncollectible account.......	J59	500 00		500 00
	20	Collected in full	CR53		500 00	— 00

Activity G. Answer the following questions about recording uncollectible account expenses. Refer to the text and illustrations on pages 368 to 371.

1. What is the entry for recording the write-off of Victor Franco's account?

2. What is the effect of the write-off on the Allowance for Uncollectible Accounts account? on Accounts Receivable? on the realizable value of accounts receivable? on Uncollectible Accounts Expense?

3. What is the purpose of the first entry on November 20? the second entry?

4. What is the balance of Victor Franco's account after the entries in November are posted?

5. In which year is the sale made to Victor Franco? In which year is it collected? In which year is it written off?

Topic 5 Problems

9-16. The Pullman Appliance Company estimates its uncollectible accounts expense as a percent of net sales. The ledger on December 31 shows these account balances: Sales, $42,100; Sales Returns and Allowances, $900; and Sales Discount, $400.

a. Record the adjusting entry for the uncollectible accounts expense in the general journal. The rate used for the estimate is 1 percent of net sales. The Allowance for Doubtful Accounts has a zero balance.

b. Record the adjusting entry if Allowance for Doubtful Accounts had a credit balance of $40.

c. Record the adjusting entry if Allowance for Doubtful Accounts had a debit balance of $10.

9-17. The Bella Vita Fuel Company estimates its uncollectible accounts expense as a percent of aged accounts receivable. The ages of the accounts receivable on September 30 are grouped as follows.

Age Group	Total of Group
1–30 Days	$ 9,000
31–60 Days	5,800
61–90 Days	3,200
91–120 Days	1,600
Over 120 Days	900
	$20,500

a. Compute the estimated uncollectible accounts expense. Use the percentages shown on page 365.

b. Record the adjusting entry for uncollectible accounts expense in the general journal. The Allowance for Doubtful Accounts account has a zero balance.

c. Record the adjusting entry if Allowance for Doubtful Accounts has a credit balance of $120.

d. Record the adjusting entry if Allowance for Doubtful Accounts has a debit balance of $75.

9-18. Record the following entries in a sales journal, cash receipts journal, and general journal. All terms are 2/10, n/30.

a. June 30, 19X5. Sold merchandise for $400 on account to Maco Supply; Invoice 401.

b. July 15, 19X5. Sold merchandise for $360 on account to Ever-More Co.; Invoice 566.

c. September 8, 19X5. Sold merchandise for $35 on account to Mis-T Inc.; Invoice 666.

d. December 31, 19X5. Recorded the adjusting entry for uncollectible accounts expense. The Percent of Accounts Receivable method was used. The estimate of uncollectible accounts receivable is 8 percent, and accounts receivable has a balance of $30,000; the balance of Allowance for Doubtful Accounts is $150 (debit).

e. April 30, 19X6. Wrote off the Ever-More Co. account as uncollectible.

f. April 30, 19X6. Collected $100 from Maco Supply and wrote off the balance as uncollectible. (*HINT*: Make two entries, one in the cash receipts journal.)

g. June 15, 19X6. Collected the Ever-More Co. account in full.

h. July 1, 19X6. Wrote off the Mis-T Inc. account as uncollectible.

i. September 30, 19X6. Collected the Mis-T Inc. account in full.

Topic 6
Accounting for Merchandise Inventory and Prepaid Expenses

Merchandise inventory is the goods held for sale to customers.

A *What is merchandise inventory?* **Merchandise inventory** is the goods held for sale to customers by a merchandising business. There are two types of merchandising businesses: wholesalers and retailers. **Wholesalers** buy finished goods in large quantities from the manufacturer (producer) and sell the goods, in small quantities, to retailers. **Retailers** buy (finished) goods from wholesalers or manufacturers and sell them to consumers. **Consumers** buy and use goods.

Procedures for Controlling Merchandise Inventory

The sale of inventory is the main source of revenue for most businesses. Inventory is purchased and sold continuously. The following procedures for controlling merchandise inventory should be established.
• Needed merchandise is identified.
• Purchases are initiated by authorized personnel.
• Prenumbered forms are used.
• Responsibility is divided.
• Purchases are made from approved suppliers.
• Shipments must include the approved quantity and quality of merchandise ordered.
• Payment is made only after the quantities, quality, terms, prices, and computations on invoices are approved.
• Merchandise in stock must be verified with inventory records.
• Purchase transactions are recorded.
• Refunds or credits are obtained for purchase returns and allowances.
• Invoices are paid in time to take cash discounts.

   The controls listed above are included in four purchasing activities.
• Ordering merchandise.
• Receiving merchandise.
• Accounting for merchandise.
• Storing merchandise.

   A fifth activity—computing the cost of merchandise inventory—is important when preparing the balance sheet and income statements.

Activity A. Answer the following questions about the control of merchandise inventory. Refer to the text and illustrations on pages 372 and 373.
1. What is a retailer?
2. In which procedure for controlling merchandise inventory is payment approved?
3. In which procedure are purchases approved?
4. In which procedure are purchase transactions recorded?

Cost of Merchandise Inventory

B *How important is the cost of merchandise inventory?* The cost of merchandise inventory is extremely important. At the end of the accounting period the cost of merchandise inventory is a current asset and is used to compute Cost of Goods Sold. Thus the cost of merchandise inventory affects both the balance sheet and the income statement.

INVENTORY CARD

No. *C7-97*

Item *Circular Saws*

| Location: | Aisle *1* | | Bin *2* | |
| Maximum *22* | | | Minimum *10* | |

Date	Quant. Rec'd	Unit Cost	Quant. Sold	Balance
19— 5/12	22	18.50		22
5/15			3	19
5/30			2	17
6/1			1	16
7/1			1	15
7/15			2	13
8/1			3	10

Perpetual inventory card showing maximum and minimum stock.

Methods of Computing Cost of Merchandise Inventory:

- FIFO method
- LIFO method
- Specific identification method

Periodic Inventory Procedure

At the end of the accounting period a **physical inventory** is completed. That is, items of merchandise are counted and recorded. There are two purposes for a physical inventory: (1) to verify the perpetual inventory records and (2) to start the first step in computing the cost of merchandise inventory.

Verifying the Perpetual Inventory Records. Businesses that keep perpetual inventory records must, periodically, see if those records are accurate. To verify the perpetual inventory records, a business must take a physical inventory and compare the actual counts of the various items to the inventory cards. The perpetual inventory records must be verified at least once a year if a business is to have accurate financial statements.

Computing the Cost of Merchandise Inventory. At the end of the accounting period the accountant asks how much did the ending merchandise inventory cost? The question is asked because the cost of merchandise inventory is the amount recorded for Merchandise Inventory as a current asset and is one amount used to compute Cost of Goods Sold.

There are three different methods for computing the cost of merchandise inventory: (1) FIFO (first in, first out), (2) LIFO (last in, first out), and (3) specific identification. The three methods are discussed here. To keep the discussion simple, assume that the Gallo Company has only one inventory item. The item is purchased in varying amounts during the accounting period. Also assume that the Gallo Company began the period with 140 items and that 100 items are on hand on December 31. The beginning merchandise inventory (140 items) and purchases are illustrated here.

Purchases	Units	×	Unit Cost	=	Total
1/1 (Inventory)	140		$50		$ 7,000
2/15	250		51		12,750
3/17	249		52		12,948
6/2	241		54		13,014
8/3	200		55		11,000
9/26	250		56		14,000
11/14	236		58		13,688
12/1	100		60		6,000
					$90,400

FIFO (First In, First Out) Method

The **FIFO method** is one method of finding the cost of merchandise inventory. In the FIFO method the cost of the most recent purchases are used for the merchandise inventory cost. Thus the cost of the most recent purchases are carried to the next period as a current asset. The beginning inventory and the first purchases are part of Cost of Goods Sold and are matched against revenue on the income statement.

FIFO (FIRST-IN, FIRST-OUT)

Purchases	Units	×	Unit Cost	=	Total
1/1 (Inventory)	140		$50		$ 7,000
2/15	250		51		12,750
3/17	249		52		12,948
6/2	241		54		13,014
8/3	200		55		11,000
9/26	250		56		14,000
11/14	236		58		13,688
12/1	100		60		6,000
					90,400

Early purchases are part of Cost of Goods Sold ($84,400).

Recent purchases are Merchandise Inventory (100 × $60 = $6,000).

In the illustration the accountant refers to the purchases invoices and finds the cost of the last 100 items purchased. The last 100 items are purchased on December 1, at a unit price of $60. Thus the asset value for merchandise inventory on December 31 is $6,000 ($60 × 100). The remainder of the $90,400 ($84,400) is cost of goods sold and is matched against revenue.

The FIFO method of finding the cost of merchandise inventory is logical. It assumes that the flow of costs is the same as the flow of merchandise. Just as the first merchandise purchased is the first sold, the first costs are matched against revenue. The most recent costs are the asset value.

The FIFO method assumes flow of costs equals that of merchandise.

Activity B. Answer the following questions about the cost of merchandise inventory. Refer to the text and illustrations on pages 373 to 375.

1. How does the cost of merchandise inventory affect the balance sheet? the income statement?

2. What is a physical inventory?

3. How many purchases of merchandise are shown on the illustration above?

4. How many items are on hand on January 1? on December 31?

5. Why must the perpetual inventory records be verified?

6. Which portion of the $90,400 becomes Cost of Goods Sold?

7. Which portion of the $90,400 becomes merchandise inventory?

8. How is the $6,000 cost for merchandise inventory computed?

LIFO (Last In, First Out) Method

C *What is the LIFO method?* The **LIFO method** of finding the cost of merchandise inventory assumes that the first costs of merchandise are current assets. The most recent costs are Cost of Goods Sold.

These must be matched against revenue. To compute the merchandise inventory, the accountant asks what the cost was of the first 100 items. In our illustration the first 100 items cost $5,000 (100 × $50). Thus the asset value for merchandise inventory is $5,000. All other costs ($85,400) are Cost of Goods Sold and are matched against revenue.

LIFO (LAST IN, FIRST OUT)

Early purchases are Merchandise Inventory (100 × $50 = $5,000).

Recent purchases are Cost of Goods Sold ($90,400 − 5,000 = $85,400).

Purchases	Units	×	Unit Cost	=	Total
1/1 (Inventory)	140		$50		$ 7,000
2/15	250		51		12,750
3/17	249		52		12,948
6/2	241		54		13,014
8/3	200		55		11,000
9/26	250		56		14,000
11/14	236		58		13,688
12/1	100		60		6,000
					90,400

The LIFO method matches the most recent costs against current revenues.

The LIFO method of computing the cost of merchandise inventory is supported by many accountants because it matches the most recent costs against current revenues. You should also recognize that the LIFO method shows an asset value for merchandise inventory that relates to the first purchases rather than to recent purchases. Thus the merchandise on hand is valued at the oldest invoice prices.

Specific Identification Method

The specific identification method is used when few items of expensive merchandise are sold.

The **specific identification method** is one in which the cost of items in the merchandise inventory is related to particular purchases. The cost of the merchandise inventory for the Gallo Company is $5,580, assuming that the 100 items in inventory were purchased as illustrated below.

The specific identification method of computing the cost of merchandise inventory is used primarily when a company sells relatively few items of expensive merchandise.

SPECIFIC IDENTIFICATION

Purchase	Units	×	Unit Cost	=	Total
2/15	20		$51		$1,020
6/2	40		54		2,160
12/1	40		60		2,400
					5,580

Activity C. Answer the following questions about the cost of merchandise inventory. Refer to the text and illustrations on pages 375 and 376.

1. What is the cost of merchandise inventory using the LIFO method? How is the cost determined?

2. What portion of the $90,400 is Cost of Goods Sold using the LIFO method?

3. How does the specific identifica-tion method differ from the LIFO method?

4. What is the cost of merchandise inventory using the specific identifi-cation method? How is it com-puted?

Comparing Merchandise Inventory Methods

D *What is the effect of the methods for computing the cost of mer-chandise inventory?* The three methods for computing the cost of merchandise inventory produce different inventory values. The cost of merchandise inventory is a current asset and is also used to compute Cost of Goods Sold. Thus a change in the cost of merchandise inven-tory affects both the balance sheet and the income statement. The changes in Cost of Goods Sold and current assets that result from our illustrations are shown here.

		FIFO	LIFO	Specific Identification
Merchandise Inventory, January 1		$ 7,000	$ 7,000	$ 7,000
Net Purchases		83,400	83,400	83,400
Cost of Goods Available for Sale		90,400	90,400	90,400
Merchandise Inventory, December 31		6,000	5,000	5,580
Cost of Goods Sold		$84,400	$85,400	$84,920
Total Current Assets for Each Method:				
Current Assets				
Cash		$33,075	$33,075	$33,075
Marketable Securities		15,190	15,190	15,190
Notes Receivable		1,500	1,500	1,500
Interest Receivable		10	10	10
Accounts Receivable	$9,000			
Less: Allowance for Doubtful Accounts	900	8,100	8,100	8,100
Merchandise Inventory		6,000	5,000	5,580
Prepaid Insurance		450	450	450
Supplies on Hand		120	120	120
Total Current Assets		$64,445	$63,445	$64,025

It should be noted that the change in Cost of Goods Sold as shown above will also change gross profit. Also, a change in gross profit affects net income. Thus businesses very carefully study the possible effect on net income when adopting (choosing) a method to compute merchan-dise inventory.

Activity D. Answer the following questions about comparing inventory methods. Refer to the text and illustrations on page 377.

1. What is Cost of Goods Sold using the FIFO method? the LIFO method? the specific identification method?

2. What causes the Total Current Assets to change?

Prepaid Expenses

E *What are prepaid expenses?* **Prepaid expenses** are the costs of items and services bought for use in operating the business but are not used at the end of the accounting period. Prepaid expenses are current assets because they will normally be used or consumed in one year. Examples of prepaid expenses are supplies, prepaid insurance, and prepaid rent.

When a prepaid expense is bought, an asset account is debited and cash or accounts payable is credited. For instance, the purchase of a two-year fire insurance policy by the Gallo Company for $600 is illustrated here.

CASH PAYMENTS JOURNAL							Page 18
DATE	ACCOUNT CREDITED	EXPLANATION	POST. REF.	GENERAL LEDGER DEBIT	ACCOUNTS PAYABLE DEBIT	PURCHASES DISCOUNT CREDIT	NET CASH CREDIT
19—							
June 30	Prepaid Insurance....	Two-year fire policy ..	146	600 00			600 00

As you view the above transaction, keep in mind that the Gallo Company now has two years of protection. It *owns* the right to have its property protected in case of fire. Thus the $600 is an asset. (The $600 would be classified as a current asset even though the life is longer than one year.)

Adjusting Prepaid Expenses. At the end of the accounting period the Gallo Company must analyze each prepaid expense to find out which portion is still a current asset and which portion is an expense. The portion of the prepaid expense that has been consumed or expired is an expense of doing business and must be matched against revenues.

Life of policy:	24 months (2 years)
Expired on December 31:	6 months
Cost of Policy:	$600

$$\frac{6 \text{ months}}{24 \text{ months}} \times \$600 = \$150 \quad \text{Insurance Expense (expense)}$$

$$\frac{18 \text{ months}}{24 \text{ months}} \times \$600 = \$450 \qquad \text{Prepaid Insurance}$$
$$\text{(asset)}$$

The accountant for the Gallo Company finds that the fire insurance policy has been in effect six months, from June 30 to December 31. Thus six months of the premium cost of $600 expired. To record the expired premium cost, the accountant makes an adjusting entry for $150.

Prepaid Insurance				Insurance Expense	
June 30	600	Dec. 31	150	Dec. 31	150

Adjusting Entry

The above transaction indicates the following. One-fourth of the premium cost ($150) is an expense and is matched against revenue. Three-fourths of the premium cost ($450) is a current asset and will be matched against future revenues.

The accountant for the Gallo Company will now find out what portion of the other prepaid expenses are still current assets and what portion are expenses. Similar adjusting entries will be made so that current assets and operating expenses are shown at proper amounts.

Activity E. Answer the following questions about prepaid expenses. Refer to the text and illustrations on pages 378 and 379.

1. What does the two-year fire insurance policy cost Gallo Company?
2. What portion of the cost of the policy is an expense in the accounting period ended December 31?
3. What is the prepaid expense for Prepaid Insurance on January 1?
4. How many months of protection are left on January 1?
5. What would be the effect on net income if the adjusting entry for prepaid insurance is not made on December 31? the effect on current assets?

Topic 6 Problems

9-19. The Shimizu Company has only two items in its merchandise inventory. Using the information given at the top of page 380, compute the cost of merchandise inventory by the (a) FIFO method, (b) LIFO method, and (c) specific identification method.
Additional information: Of the 32 units of Model M. Motors, 16 were purchased on November 16 and 16 on July 12. Of the 5 units of Model

Item: Model M. Motors			Item: Model P. Motors		
Purchases	Units	Unit Price	Purchases	Units	Unit Price
January 1	26	$32.50	January 1	3	$152.00
February 15	20	35.00	March 6	6	152.00
May 6	30	35.00	May 6	6	155.00
July 12	30	36.25	July 18	6	159.00
September 28	30	36.25	September 13	3	165.00
November 16	30	37.00	November 30	1	170.00
Physical count of Model M. Motors on December 31: 32 items.			Physical count of Model P. Motors on December 31: 5 items.		

P. Motors, 1 was purchased on November 30, 3 on September 13, and 1 on July 18.

NOTE: Save your work for further use in Topic Problems 9-20 and 9-21.

9-20. Using the following information and the information in Topic Problem 9-19, prepare the Cost of Goods Sold section for an income statement. Use each method for computing the cost of merchandise inventory.

The beginning inventory was $1,301; purchases, $8,496; transportation, $330; and purchases returns and allowances, $125.
NOTE: Save your work for further use in Topic Problem 9-21.

9-21. Refer to your work in Topic Problems 9-19 and 9-20 and answer the following questions.

a. Would the LIFO or FIFO method of computing the cost of merchandise inventory show the smallest gross profit in a period of rising prices?

b. Would the LIFO or FIFO method show the largest gross profit in a period of rising prices?

c. Which method (LIFO or FIFO) shows an asset value more nearly approximating current costs for inventory?

d. Which method (LIFO or FIFO) shows a more conservative (smaller) asset value?

The Language of Business

Here are some basic terms that make up the language of business. Do you understand the meaning of each? Can you define each term and use it in an original sentence?

current assets	natural resources	intangible assets	imprest cash fund
plant and equipment	investments	cash	marketable securities

short-term receivables	sales returns and	interest-bearing note	valuation account
inventories	allowances fund	accrued revenue	asset valuation account
prepaid expenses	interest	accrual method of	percent of accounts
liquidity	Gains and Losses on	accounting	receivable method
cash management plan	Sale of Marketable	interest receivable	percent of aged
idle cash	Securities account	unsecured open	accounts receivable
EFT	promissory note	account	method
special bank account	negotiable	uncollectible account	merchandise inventory
general bank account	holder	realizable value of	wholesaler
payroll bank account	maker	accounts receivable	retailer
petty cash register	payee	direct write-off method	physical inventory
replenishing petty cash	bearer	allowance method	FIFO method
cash overage	note receivable	writing off an account	LIFO method
cash shortage	face value	uncollectible accounts	specific identification
change fund	principal	expense	method
consumer	Loans Receivable account	contra account	prepaid expense

Chapter 9 Questions

1. What are the five major types of current assets?
2. What are the purposes for the procedures in an effective cash management plan?
3. How does a bank account serve as a safeguard for cash?
4. What is a special bank account?
5. Why does a business invest in marketable securities?
6. What is the effect on total assets of *not* recording accrued interest? on total revenue? on owner's equity?
7. Does the "matching principle" tend to support the use of the direct write-off method or the allowance method for recording uncollectible accounts expense?
8. What is the effect on total expenses when writing off an uncollectible account using the allowance method?
9. Does the LIFO or FIFO method for computing the cost of merchandise inventory produce higher net income in a period of rising prices? Explain.
10. What is the effect on total expenses when prepaid expenses are not adjusted? on owner's equity? on net income? on total assets?

Chapter 9 Problems

Problems for Chapter 9 are given in the *Working Papers and Chapter Problems* for Part 2. If you are using the workbook, do the problems in the space provided there. Complete your assigned topic problems before answering the chapter problems.

Chapter 9 Management Cases

Internal Control. A good accounting system includes controls to insure accuracy, honesty, efficiency, and speed. There are times when individuals attempt to use the absence of controls for personal gain.

Case 9M-1. Stan Larsen was employed as a full-charge bookkeeper for the MacDade Company. To pay off some large personal debts, Mr. Larsen began to steal cash from MacDade, using the following plan. Mr. Larsen charged credit sales to fictitious customers. That is, instead of charging the real customer's account, he charged a fictitious customer. When the real customers paid their accounts, Mr. Larsen would keep the cash or checks and leave the fictitious customer's accounts as accounts receivable. At the end of the accounting period, the independent auditors mailed account statements to each of MacDade's customers and soon discovered Mr. Larsen's dishonesty. Specifically, the real customers questioned their accounts because the statements did not show any purchases or payments. The statements sent to fictitious customers came back marked *Addressee Unknown.*

What recommendations for improving the control of cash and accounts receivable can you make to the management of MacDade Company?

Merchandise Inventory. The cost of ending inventory is very important because it affects both current assets and the cost of goods sold. A difficult problem that many businesses face is what to include in the ending inventory; that is, what items are counted and what items are priced.

Case 9M-2. You have been hired to work in a local department store. One of your first duties is counting and pricing the merchandise inventory. You have determined the value of merchandise inventory to be $8,900. However, a number of items concern you. How should you handle the following? Should each be a part of merchandise inventory? What is the revised merchandise inventory value?

a. Merchandise sold but held as a favor to the customer while a new storage area is being built. Cost: $1,200.

b. Pocket novels on display as part of a *consignment purchase.* Cost: $150. (You might have to do independent research on the nature of consigned merchandise.)

c. Merchandise on the delivery truck that has been ordered by customers. Cost: $250.

d. Merchandise that cost $600 has been ruined by a water leak.

e. The merchandise inventory includes Davy Crockett hats that cost $100 and have not been sold for two years.

Accounting for Plant and Equipment, Intangible Assets, and Natural Resources

The generally accepted accounting principle (GAAP) is that assets should be shown in at least two categories—current assets and plant and equipment. In Chapter 9 you learned about current assets. In this chapter you will learn that there are different kinds of plant and equipment. This chapter also focuses on intangible assets and natural resources.

Topic 1
Cost and Depreciation of Plant and Equipment

A *What is plant and equipment?* **Plant and equipment** is an asset that has physical form and long life, produces revenue, and is not intended for resale. Examples of plant and equipment are office equipment, delivery equipment, machinery, furniture, fixtures, buildings, and land.

Recording Plant and Equipment

The amount recorded in the accounting records when plant and equipment is purchased includes *all costs necessary to obtain the equipment and place it in service.* The breakdown of the costs for a used delivery truck is illustrated in the margin. The accounting entry is recorded as shown on page 384.

Plant and Equipment Assets:
- Have physical form.
- Have long life.
- Produce revenue.
- Are not intended for re-sale.

Cost of Delivery Truck:

Selling price	$3,800
Sales tax	150
New tires	300
Paint	150
Cost of delivery truck	$4,400

CASH PAYMENTS JOURNAL									Page *12*
DATE	ACCOUNT DEBITED	EXPLANATION	CHECK NO.	POST. REF.	GENERAL LEDGER DEBIT	ACCOUNTS PAYABLE DEBIT	PURCHASES DISCOUNT CREDIT		NET CASH CREDIT
19— *Apr.* 1	*Delivery Equipment*	*Used truck*	*146*	*155*	*4,400 00*				*4,400 00*

The entry to record the purchase of a delivery truck includes a debit to Delivery Equipment and a credit to Cash. Delivery Equipment is a plant and equipment asset. The amount recorded includes *all* costs necessary to put the truck into service. Thus expenditures in addition to the selling price are included in the cost.

Depreciation

Plant and equipment assets produce revenue. You know from your earlier studies that all expenses must be matched against revenue. Thus a portion of the cost of plant and equipment, which is an expense, must be matched against revenue. The procedure used to allocate (distribute) the cost of plant and equipment over the asset's life is known as **depreciation.**

To understand depreciation, look again at the entry shown above to record the purchase of a delivery truck. The entire cost is recorded as an asset. The truck will be used to produce revenue over a number of accounting periods. As the truck produces revenue, a portion of the cost of the truck should be matched against that revenue as an expense.

Land is assumed to have unlimited useful life.

Allocating the Cost of Plant and Equipment. Most plant and equipment assets have a limited useful life. That is, plant and equipment assets produce revenue over a limited number of accounting periods. The one exception is land, which is said to have unlimited useful life. The useful lives of other plant and equipment assets are limited because of the gradual effects of wear and tear, **obsolescence** (the process of becoming out of date), or **inadequacy** (insufficient in capacity or use because more efficient equipment is needed). Thus a part of the cost of plant and equipment should be charged as an expense to each accounting period in which the asset is used.

The cost of the delivery equipment discussed above is $4,400. It is estimated that the delivery equipment has a useful life of 4 years. In effect, the Gallo Company has purchased for $4,400 the use of the delivery equipment for 4 years. A portion of the $4,400 should be matched against revenue as service is received from the equipment.

The accountant for the Gallo Company must now decide what portion of the asset cost is matched against revenue each accounting period. The Internal Revenue Service allows businesses to choose from several methods.

Two basic depreciation methods—straight-line and accelerated—are discussed later in this topic.

Accounting Principle:
Depreciation. The generally accepted accounting principle is that depreciation is a process of allocating (distributing) the cost of a plant and equipment asset over its expected useful life. Depreciation is a process of allocation, not of valuation.

Accounting Principle:
Matching. The generally accepted accounting principle is that revenue must be matched against expenses in obtaining that revenue.

Activity A-1. Answer the following questions about the cost and depreciation of plant and equipment. Refer to the text and illustrations on pages 383 to 385.

1. What is the cost of the delivery truck?

2. Why is the delivery truck classified as plant and equipment?

3. What accounting entries are needed to record the purchase of the delivery truck?

4. Which journal is used to record the purchase of the delivery truck?

Activity A-2. A number of items relative to the cost of a delivery truck are listed here. Indicate if an item should be included or not included as part of the cost of Delivery Equipment.
EXAMPLE: Outside mirror—$60—included.

1. Gasoline—$14

2. Inspection sticker—$14

3. Invoice price—$5,000

4. Sales tax—$300

5. Driver training program—$300

6. License fee for driver—$10

7. New tires—$300

8. Speeding ticket issued when delivering truck—$50

9. Insurance—$310

Depreciation Methods

B *What methods are used to compute depreciation?* The accountant for the Gallo Company has the choice of a number of methods for computing depreciation. Two basic methods—the straight-line method and the accelerated method—are explained here. Other methods of depreciation are explained in more advanced accounting courses.

Two Methods of Depreciation:
• Straight-line method
• Accelerated method

Straight-Line Depreciation. In the **straight-line method** of depreciation, an equal amount (a "straight line") of depreciation is recorded each year. The assumption is that an equal amount of the cost of the asset is being used each year. To compute depreciation using the straight-line method, the accountant must estimate the useful life and disposal value of the asset. **Disposal value** is the value of the asset at the end of its useful life. The estimates of the useful life and disposal value are needed because depreciation of plant and equipment is computed in advance. The accountant records the depreciation of plant and equipment at the end of each accounting period.

**Factors Needed to
Compute Depreciation:**
• Cost
• Useful life (estimated)
• Disposal value (estimated)

To estimate the depreciation of plant and equipment, the accountant needs three amounts: (1) the cost, (2) the years of estimated useful life, and (3) the disposal value. Accountants may use guidelines published by the Internal Revenue Service to estimate the useful life.

The delivery truck purchased for $4,400 is used to show how the annual depreciation of plant and equipment is computed. Assume the truck has an estimated useful life of 4 years and an estimated disposal value of $400. Annual Depreciation is computed as follows.

Cost	− Disposal Value =	Total Depreciation
$4,400	− $400 =	$4,000
Total Depreciation	÷ Years of Use =	Annual Depreciation
$4,000	÷ 4 =	$1,000
Annual Depreciation ÷	12	= Monthly Depreciation
$1,000	÷ 12	= $83.33

STEP 1. Subtract the estimated disposal value from the cost to obtain the total depreciation.
STEP 2. Divide the total depreciation by the estimated years of useful life to obtain the annual depreciation.
STEP 3. To compute depreciation for less than a year, find the annual depreciation and divide that amount by the part of the year considered. Monthly depreciation is computed by dividing annual depreciation by 12.

After the truck has been used for 4 years, it will have an estimated disposal value of $400. In effect, the business has purchased 4 years' use of the truck at a total cost of $4,000. The $4,000 that is depreciation should be distributed over the useful life of the truck. Thus the truck has an annual depreciation of $1,000 ($4,000 ÷ 4), or a monthly depreciation of $83.33 ($1,000 ÷ 12).

**DEPRECIATION OF DELIVERY TRUCK DURING
FOUR-YEAR USEFUL LIFE: COST, $4,400**

Year 1	Year 2	Year 3	Year 4	Disposal Value
$1,000	$1,000	$1,000	$1,000	$400

Activity B-1. Answer the following questions about the straight-line method for computing depreciation. Refer to the text and illustrations on pages 385 and 386.

1. What is the cost of the delivery truck? its useful life? its disposal value?

2. What is the total depreciation over the useful life of the truck?

3. How much depreciation is there for the first year of useful life? the second year? the third year? the fourth year?

Activity B-2. Compute the amount of straight-line annual and monthly depreciation for each of the following pieces of equipment.

Cost of Equipment	Useful Life (Years)	Disposal Value	Amount of Annual Depreciation	Amount of Monthly Depreciation
1. $4,950	6	$ 150		
2. 9,100	10	1,100		
3. 596	3	50		
4. 6,800	6	500		

Accelerated Depreciation

|C| *What is accelerated depreciation?* Businesses that use the straight-line method assume that the revenue produced by the asset is similar over the useful life. Also, the straight-line method is simple and easy to compute. However, many companies feel that certain assets produce more revenue when they are first purchased, and thus a greater portion of the asset cost should be matched against revenue in its early life. For these businesses, accelerated methods for computing depreciation are used.

Accelerated depreciation is a method that matches more expense against revenue in the asset's early life. Two accelerated methods for computing depreciation—sum-of-the-years'-digits and declining-balance—are discussed here.

Sum-of-the-Years'-Digits Method. The **sum-of-the-years'-digits method** matches a larger portion of the asset cost against revenue in the asset's early life than does the straight-line method.

Annual depreciation in the sum-of-the-years'-digits method is computed as follows.

STEP 1. *Subtract the disposal value from the asset cost to find the total amount to be depreciated (depreciable value).*

STEP 2. *Convert each year of useful life to a fraction of the total. The denominator (bottom half of the fraction) is the sum of the years of*

Two Accelerated Depreciation Methods:
- Sum-of-the-years'-digits method
- Declining balance method

Asset cost	$4,400
Less: Disposal value	−400
Depreciable value (total depreciation)	$4,000

Denominator = Sum of the years' digits

Numerator = Life at beginning of year

useful life. The numerator (top half of the fraction) changes each year and is the number of years of useful life at the beginning of that year. If the asset has an estimated useful life of 4 years, the denominator would always be 10 (4 + 3 + 2 + 1). The numerator would be 4 for the first year, 3 for the second, and so on.

STEP 3. *Multiply the depreciable value (cost-disposal value) by the fraction for each year.* The annual depreciation for an asset having a cost of $4,400, 4 years of useful life, and a $400 disposal value is shown here.

SUM-OF-THE-YEARS'-DIGITS METHOD

Year	Remaining Life (Years)	Depreciable Value		Annual Depreciation
1	4	4/10 × $4,000	=	$1,600
2	3	3/10 × 4,000	=	1,200
3	2	2/10 × 4,000	=	800
4	1	1/10 × 4,000	=	400
10				$4,000 (Total Depreciation)

Declining-Balance Method. Like the sum-of-the-years'-digits method, the **declining-balance method** matches a larger portion of the asset's cost against revenue in the asset's early life than does the straight-line method. Annual depreciation is computed by multiplying the book value of the asset by the adjusted annual depreciation rate. **Book value** is the asset cost minus the accumulated depreciation. The adjusted annual depreciation rate is normally twice the straight-line rate. The procedure for computing depreciation by the declining-balance method is shown here.

STEP 1. *Find the annual depreciation rate as in the straight-line method.* For example, an asset with a 4-year life would have an annual depreciation rate of 25 percent (100 percent ÷ 4).

STEP 2. *Double the annual depreciation rate to arrive at an adjusted annual depreciation rate.* Thus a 25 percent straight-line rate would be a 50 percent adjusted rate (25 percent × 2).

STEP 3. *Multiply the book value at the end of each year by the adjusted depreciation rate.* The disposal value is *not* considered when using the declining-balance method because the asset would never be entirely depreciated.

Depreciation is computed here using the declining-balance method for delivery equipment that has a 4-year useful life, an original cost of $4,400, and a $400 disposal value.

DECLINING-BALANCE METHOD

Year	Depreciation Rate	×	Book Value	=	Depreciation	Accumulated Depreciation
1	50%	×	$4,400	=	$2,200	$2,200
2	50	×	2,200	=	1,100	3,300
3	50	×	1,100	=	550	3,850
4	50	×	550	=	150*	4,000

*Note that the depreciation for the fourth year is only $150. In the declining-balance method, depreciation is not taken *below* the disposal value ($400).

Comparing Depreciation Methods

When comparing the straight-line and accelerated methods of depreciation, note the following. The accelerated methods match a larger portion of the asset cost against revenue in the asset's early life. An advantage of using the accelerated method is that federal income taxes would be lower in the asset's early life because expenses are higher. An advantage of using the straight-line method is that it is easier to compute and matches the same expense against revenue each year.

Asset Cost: $4,400   Life: 4 years   Disposal Value: $400

		Accelerated Methods	
Year	Straight-Line Method	Sum-of-the-Years'-Digits Method	Declining-Balance Method
1	$1,000	$1,600	$2,200
2	1,000	1,200	1,100
3	1,000	800	550
4	1,000	400	150

Annual Depreciation

A business can choose the depreciation method it wishes to use. Classes of plant and equipment can be depreciated using different methods. If the revenue produced by a building is similar over the life of a building, a business might choose the straight-line method. However, if a delivery truck is expected to produce declining amounts of revenue over its useful life, the business might choose an accelerated method for depreciating delivery equipment. The depreciation method used for a particular class of plant and equipment cannot be changed unless permission is obtained from the Internal Revenue Service.

Activity C-1. Answer the following questions about the sum-of-the-years'-digits method for computing depreciation. Refer to the text and illustrations on pages 387 and 388.

1. What is the denominator in the fraction used to compute depreciation? How is it computed?
2. What is the depreciation in the first year? in the fourth year?

3. What is the numerator in the fraction in the first year? in the fourth year? How were the numerators found?

Activity C-2. Answer the following questions about the declining-balance method for computing depreciation. Refer to the text and illustrations on pages 388 and 389.

1. What is the straight-line percent rate? What is the adjusted rate? How is the adjusted rate computed?
2. What is the depreciation in the first year? in the fourth year?

3. Why is the depreciation only $150 for the fourth year?
4. What is the disposal value after taking depreciation for the fourth year?

Activity C-3. Answer the following questions about comparing depreciation methods. Refer to the text and illustrations on page 389.

1. Does the straight-line or accelerated method result in larger depreciation in the asset's early life? in the asset's later life?

2. Which method—straight-line or accelerated—would give smaller net incomes in the asset's early life? in the asset's later life?

Recording Depreciation

D *How is estimated depreciation recorded?* Estimated depreciation is recorded as an adjusting entry at the end of each accounting period. Adjusting entries are made for all plant and equipment accounts except land. The adjusting entry includes a debit to an expense account (Depreciation Expense) and a credit to an asset contra account (Accumulated Depreciation). Separate expense and contra accounts are kept in the ledger for each type of plant and equipment: delivery equipment, office equipment, buildings, and so on.

Depreciation is not recorded for land.

The plant and equipment account is not credited because the amount of the depreciation is only an estimate. Furthermore, if the plant and equipment account were credited, it would appear as though the business had disposed of part of the plant and equipment. Two accounts are used: the plant and equipment account shows the original cost of the asset, and the accumulated depreciation account shows the depreciation recorded up to that time. The difference between the balance of the plant and equipment account and the balance of the accumulated depreciation account is the book value of plant and equipment. As stated earlier, the book value is that portion of the asset cost that has not been depreciated.

Accumulated depreciation includes the total amount of recorded depreciation.

The adjusting entry to record the first year's depreciation on office equipment that cost $3,000, with an estimated 6-year useful life and no disposal value, is illustrated here. It is assumed the equipment was purchased on January 1.

Depreciation for First Year

Office Equipment 151		Accumulated Depreciation— Office Equipment 152		Depreciation Expense— Office Equipment 512	
19X4			19X4		19X4
Jan. 1 3,000			Dec. 31 500		Dec. 31 500

The Depreciation Expense—Office Equipment account shows the amount of depreciation ($500) for the accounting period. It is an expense account and is debited to record the decrease in owner's equity. At the end of the accounting period, it is closed with the other expense accounts into the Income Summary account.

The Office Equipment account shows the original cost of the plant and equipment ($3,000) and is not affected by the adjusting entry. The Accumulated Depreciation—Office Equipment account shows the total amount of depreciation that has been estimated and recorded for the first year ($500).

At the end of the second year, an adjusting entry is made to record the second year's depreciation. Office Equipment and the related accounts would appear as shown here.

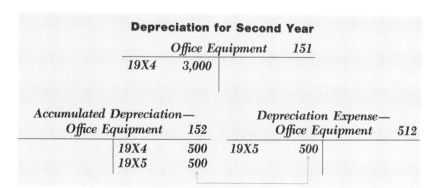

Depreciation for Second Year

Office Equipment 151	
19X4 3,000	

Accumulated Depreciation— Office Equipment 152		Depreciation Expense— Office Equipment 512	
	19X4 500	19X5 500	
	19X5 500		

The Office Equipment account still shows the cost of the equipment ($3,000). The Accumulated Depreciation—Office Equipment account now has a balance of $1,000 ($500 + $500). The Depreciation Expense—Office Equipment account shows the expense recorded for the second year ($500). The book value is now $2,000 ($3,000 − $1,000).

If these entries are made for each year, at the end of the fifth year the accounts will appear as shown at the top of page 392.

Gallo Company Chart of Accounts

Plant and Equipment
151 Office Equipment
152 Accumulated Depreciation—Office Equipment
153 Furniture and Fixtures
154 Accumulated Depreciation—Furniture and Fixtures
155 Delivery Equipment
156 Accumulated Depreciation—Delivery Equipment
157 Building
158 Accumulated Depreciation—Building
159 Land

Costs and Expenses
512 Depreciation Expense—Office Equipment
513 Depreciation Expense—Furniture and Fixtures
514 Depreciation Expense—Delivery Equipment
515 Depreciation Expense—Building

Book Value at End of Second Year:

Office Equipment	$3,000
Less: Accumulated Depreciation	1,000
Book Value	$2,000

	Depreciation for Fifth Year		
	Accumulated Depreciation—		*Depreciation Expense—*
Office Equipment 151	*Office Equipment 152*		*Office Equipment 512*
19X4 3,000	19X4 500	19X8 500
	19X5 500	
	19X6 500	
	19X7 500	
	19X8 500	

The illustration shows the recording of estimated depreciation for Office Equipment. Recording depreciation for other plant and equipment assets would be similar. Also, the straight-line method for computing depreciation is illustrated. Recording depreciation for the accelerated method would be similar, although the amounts would change.

Activity D. Answer the following questions about recording depreciation. Refer to the text and illustrations on pages 390 to 392.

1. What is the book value of Office Equipment at the end of the third year?

2. How is Accumulated Depreciation—Office Equipment classified on the balance sheet? Explain.

3. Which entry is made in the general journal to record depreciation?

4. What depreciation method is used for the Office Equipment?

5. What effect will the annual depreciation have on the net income of the company?

6. What is the balance of the Office Equipment account at the end of the second year?

7. How much depreciation was recorded on Office Equipment on December 31, 19X5?

Topic 1 Problems

10-1. For each of the following transactions, indicate which journal would be used to record each entry and which accounts would be debited and credited.

Transaction	Journal	Account(s) Debited	Account(s) Credited
EXAMPLE: Purchased factory machine on credit.	*General Journal*	*Factory Equipment*	*Accounts Payable*
a. Purchased office machine for cash.			
b. Recorded straight-line depreciation on factory machine.			
c. Recorded accumulated depreciation on office machine.			
d. Closed the depreciation expense account at the end of the year.			

10-2. The Mogul Company purchased a high-speed drill on January 10, using Check 517.

a. Determine the cost of the equipment, assuming the following.

  (1) Invoice price, $1,250.
  (2) Sales tax, 6%.
  (3) Shipping, $120.
  (4) Insurance during shipping, $50.
  (5) Installation costs, $50.

b. Record the cost of the drill in a cash payments journal. (Use Equipment as your account title and only one entry, even though several checks might be drawn.)

c. Is the high-speed drill a plant and equipment asset that will depreciate? Explain.

d. Which factors might affect the life of the drill?

10-3. Compute the first year's annual depreciation for the plant and equipment assets here. Use the straight-line, declining-balance, and sum-of-the-years'-digits methods for each asset.

Asset	Cost	Disposal Value	Estimated Useful Life (in years)	Straight-Line Method	Declining-Balance Method	Sum-of-the-Years'-Digits Method
					Annual Depreciation	
EX. Automobile	$ 6,500	$ 500	5	$1,200	$2,600	$2,000
a. Building	71,000	8,000	20*			
b. Furniture	12,000	1,000	10			
c. Machinery	34,000	3,000	10			
d. Truck	9,800	800	4			

*Denominator is 210.

10-4. Compute the first two years' annual depreciation for the plant and equipment listed here. Use the straight-line, declining-balance, and the sum-of-the-years'-digits methods for each asset.

	Total Cost	Estimated Life	Disposal Value	Straight-Line Year 1	Straight-Line Year 2	Declining-Balance Year 1	Declining-Balance Year 2	Sum-of-the-Years'-Digits Year 1	Sum-of-the-Years'-Digits Year 2
						Annual Depreciation			
a. Delivery truck	$5,100	4 years	$300						
b. Typewriter	340	5 years	40						
c. Coal conveyor	8,000	5 years	500						
d. Boiler	9,600	10 years	100						

NOTE: Save your work for further use in Topic Problem 10-5.

10-5. Use your work for Topic Problem 10-4 to record the annual depreciation expense for the first two years of useful life for each piece of plant and equipment. (December 31 is the end of the accounting period.) Use the sum-of-the-years'-digits amounts for your entries.

Topic 2
Disposing of Plant and Equipment

A *How does a company dispose of plant and equipment?* When no longer useful, plant and equipment is sold, traded, or discarded. A business may dispose of an asset because repairs are costly, the asset is no longer needed, or more efficient equipment is necessary.

Discarding and Selling Plant and Equipment

Discarding or Selling Plant and Equipment:
• Update depreciation.
• Compute book value.
• Compute loss or gain.
• Record disposal.

There are times when a business discards or sells plant and equipment. When plant and equipment is *discarded,* no cash is received. When plant and equipment is *sold,* cash is received. The accounting procedures for discarding or selling plant and equipment are similar and are discussed here. Assume that an asset that cost $550, with a five-year life and $50 disposal value, is sold. Accumulated depreciation has a balance of $400 as of the end of the last accounting period, December 31. Assume also that the asset is sold for $25 on July 1.

	GENERAL JOURNAL			Page 4	
DATE	**ACCOUNT TITLE AND EXPLANATION**	**POST. REF.**	**DEBIT**	**CREDIT**	
19X4					
July 1	Depreciation Expense—				
	Office Equipment	512	50 00		
	Accumulated Depreciation—				
	Office Equipment	152		50 00	
	Recorded six months'				
	depreciation.				

Office Equipment 151		Accumulated Depreciation— Office Equipment 152		Depreciation Expense 512	
19X0			19X3	19X4	
Jan. 1 550			Dec. 31 400	July 1 50	
			19X4		
			July 1 50		

STEP 1. *Compute and record depreciation for the current accounting period.* The accountant first records depreciation from the end of the last accounting period to the date of disposal—January 1 to July 1. The entry is recorded in the general journal, shown on page 394, and posted to the proper accounts. (Annual depreciation is $100.)

STEP 2. *Determine book value.* The book value ($100) is computed by subtracting accumulated depreciation from the asset cost.

STEP 3. *Determine loss or gain.* Loss or gain is computed by subtracting the cash received from the book value. In our illustration, $25 is received and the loss is $75. If cash received is less than the book value, a loss is recorded. If cash is greater than the book value, a gain is recorded.

STEP 4. *Record disposal of plant and equipment.* Two entries are made to record the disposal. The first entry records the cash received. The second entry removes the asset cost and accumulated depreciation from the accounting records and records the loss on disposal.

Book Value:

Asset cost	$550
Less: Accumulated Depreciation . .	−450
Book value	$100
Book value	$100
Less: Cash received . .	−25
Loss on disposal	$ 75

It is not possible to record the sale of office equipment in one journal. First, the cash received is recorded in the cash receipts journal. The dash (—) for the Office Equipment entry indicates that the amount will not be posted to the Office Equipment account. Second, the entire transaction is recorded in the general journal. However, the dash (—) opposite Cash in the general journal indicates that the amount will not be posted to the Cash account.

CASH RECEIPTS JOURNAL Page *13*

DATE	ACCOUNT CREDITED	EXPLANATION	POST. REF.	GENERAL LEDGER CREDIT	ACCOUNTS RECEIVABLE CREDIT	SALES DISCOUNT DEBIT	NET CASH DEBIT
19X4							
July 1	*Office Equipment .*	*Sold Equipment . . . .*	—	25 00			25 00

GENERAL JOURNAL Page *4*

DATE	ACCOUNT TITLE AND EXPLANATION	POST. REF.	DEBIT	CREDIT
19X4				
July 1	*Cash . . . .*	—	25 00	
	Accumulated Depreciation—			
	Office Equipment	152	450 00	
	Gains and Losses on Disposal of			
	Plant and Equipment	592	75 00	
	Office Equipment	151		550 00
	Sold typewriter.			

	Cash	101		Office Equipment	151
19X4			19X0		19X4
July 1	25		Jan. 1	550	July 1	550

	Accumulated Depreciation— Office Equipment	152		Gains and Losses on Disposal of Plant and Equipment	592
19X4		19X0		19X4	
July 1	450	Dec. 31	100	July 1	75
		19X1			
		Dec. 31	100		
		19X2			
		Dec. 31	100		
		19X3			
		Dec. 31	100		
		19X4			
		July 1	50		

The journal entries to record the disposal of plant and equipment accomplish the following. First, cash is recorded, and the accounts associated with the plant and equipment asset are removed from the accounting records. That is, both the original cost of the equipment and the accumulated depreciation are removed. Second, the Gains and Losses on Disposal of Plant and Equipment is recorded. This account is shown on the income statement under Other Expenses.

The Gains and Losses on Disposal of Plant and Equipment account requires some explanation. A business allocates the cost of plant and equipment to expense over the useful life of the asset. The annual depreciation charges are, at best, estimates, because the useful life and disposal values are estimates. The only time the accountant knows the accuracy of the estimates is at the time of disposal. In the illustration above, the accountant recorded as a loss the expense that was not recorded over the asset's useful life.

If the Gallo Company had not received anything for the asset, the loss would have been $100 (book value). If, however, $125 had been received, the Gallo Company would have a gain of $25 that will be shown on the income statement under Other Revenue. The cash received would have been more than the book value, and the sale would be recorded as shown on page 397.

Gains and Losses on Disposal of Plant and Equipment:
• Losses are expenses.
• Gains are revenue.

Cash		101
19X4		
July 1	125	

Office Equipment		151
19X0		19X4
Jan. 2	550	July 1 550

Accumulated Depreciation— Office Equipment		152
19X4		19X0
July 1	450	Jan. 1 100
		19X1
		Jan. 1 100
		19X2
		Jan. 1 100
		19X3
		Jan. 1 100
		19X4
		July 1 50

Gains and Losses on Disposal of Plant and Equipment		592
		19X4
		July 1 25

Activity A-1. Answer the following questions about disposing of plant and equipment. Refer to the text and illustrations on pages 394 to 397.

1. What is the amount of depreciation expense recorded on July 1?

2. What is the July 1 balance in the Accumulated Depreciation— Office Equipment account?

3. What is the balance in the Office Equipment account?

4. How much cash is received for the disposal of office equipment?

5. What is the book value of the Office Equipment?

6. Is there a gain or loss in the disposal of the office equipment? How much?

7. Which journals are used to record the disposal of office equipment?

Activity A-2. Rearrange the steps followed in discarding or selling plant and equipment in the correct sequence.

Record current depreciation.
Determine gain or loss on disposal
   of plant and equipment.
Record disposal of plant and equipment.
Determine book value.

Trading Plant and Equipment

B *What are the accounting procedures for trading plant and equipment?* Plant and equipment is often traded for newer and more efficient models. That is, the old asset is exchanged, along with an amount of cash or credit, for a new asset of the same type. The old asset and the accumulated depreciation must be removed from the accounting records, and the amount of cash (or credit) and the new asset must be recorded.

New Asset Cost:

Book value of old asset	+	Cash (or Credit)	=	Cost of new asset

Internal Revenue Service regulations require that no gain or loss be recorded when trading plant and equipment. The new asset has a cost, for accounting purposes, of the book value of the old asset plus the cash (or credit) paid by the purchaser. To illustrate, assume that on May 3 the Gallo Company purchases a new delivery truck for $10,000 cash and a trade of the old truck. The old truck has an original cost of $6,600. The accumulated depreciation on January 1 is $3,500. The annual depreciation rate is 25 percent, with a disposal value of $600. To record the purchase, the accountant must complete the following steps.

DEPRECIATION FROM JANUARY 1 TO MAY 3 (4 MONTHS)

Cost	$6,600
Disposal Value	600
Depreciable Value	$6,000

$$\frac{\text{Depreciable Value}}{\text{Useful Life}} \quad \frac{\$6,000}{4} = \$1,500 \text{ Annual Depreciation}$$

Annual Depreciation $1,500 \times \frac{4}{12} = \$500$ Jan. 1–May 3 Depreciation

---

GENERAL JOURNAL					Page 7
DATE	ACCOUNT TITLE AND EXPLANATION	POST. REF.	DEBIT	CREDIT	
19X4					
May 3	Depreciation Expense— Delivery Equipment	514	500 00		
	Accumulated Depreciation— Delivery Equipment	156		500 00	
	Four months' depreciation.				

Accumulated Depreciation— Delivery Equipment		514		Depreciation Expense— Delivery Equipment		156
	19X4			*19X4*		
	Jan. 1	*3,500*		*May 3*	*500*	
	May 3	*500*				

STEP 1. *Compute and record depreciation for the current accounting period.* Four months' depreciation, from January 1 to May 3, is $500 in the straight-line method.

STEP 2. *Compute the book value of the old (traded) asset.* The book value of the old (traded) asset is found by subtracting the accumulated depreciation at disposal from the original cost of the old truck; in our example, the book value at disposal is $2,600 ($6,600 − $4,000).

STEP 3. *Compute the cost to be recorded for the new asset.* The book value of the old asset plus the cash paid equals the cost of the new asset, in this case $12,600 ($2,600 + $10,000).

The cost of the new truck recorded on the books may be more or less than its cash value. For example, although the truck will be recorded at a cost of $12,600, it may have a cash value of $11,000 or some other value. The new truck will be depreciated based on its recorded cost. For accounting purposes, any gain or loss at the time of the trade is not recorded. Gains or losses are included in the recorded cost of the new asset. A loss is shown as an increased cost for the new asset and increased depreciation expense over the asset's useful life. Similarly, any gain on the trade will be shown as a decreased cost for the new asset and decreased depreciation expense over the asset's useful life.

STEP 4. *Record the new asset.* Two sets of entries are required. One complete entry is made in the general journal. It consists of a debit to Delivery Equipment for the cost of the new asset ($12,600), a debit to the Accumulated Depreciation account for the amount of accumulated depreciation on the old truck ($4,000), a credit to Delivery Equipment for the cost of the old truck ($6,600), and a credit to Cash for the amount paid ($10,000). The second entry is made in the cash payments journal. It consists of a debit to Delivery Equipment and a credit to Cash for the amount paid ($10,000). To avoid double postings, the accountant places a dash in the Posting Reference column of the general journal opposite Cash and in the Posting Reference column of the cash payments journal opposite Delivery Equipment.

Accumulated Depreciation:

January 1	$3,500
January 1 to May 3	+500
Accumulated depreciation	$4,000

Trading Plant and Equipment:
- Update depreciation.
- Compute book value.
- Add book value to cash (or credit) paid.
- Record trade.

Losses or gains on trading plant and equipment are shown in the cost of the new asset.

		GENERAL JOURNAL				Page 13

DATE		ACCOUNT TITLE AND EXPLANATION	POST. REF.	DEBIT	CREDIT
19X4					
May	3	Delivery Equipment	155	12,600 00	
		Accumulated Depreciation—Delivery Equipment	156	4,000 00	
		Delivery Equipment	155		6,600 00
		Cash	—		10,000 00
		Traded delivery truck.			

			CASH PAYMENTS JOURNAL						Page 10

DATE		ACCOUNT CREDITED	EXPLANATION	POST. REF.	GENERAL LEDGER DEBIT	ACCOUNTS PAYABLE DEBIT	PURCHASES DISCOUNT CREDIT	NET CASH CREDIT
19X4								
May	3	Delivery Equipment . . .	To purchase new truck .	—	10,000 00			10,000 00

	Delivery Equipment		155		Accumulated Depreciation— Delivery Equipment 156				Cash		101
19X1 Sept. 1	6,600	19X4 May 3	6,600	19X4 May 3	4,000	19X3 Jan. 1	3,500		19X4 May 3	10,000	
19X4 May 3	12,600					19X4 May 3	500				

Activity B-1. Answer the following questions about trading plant and equipment. Refer to the text and illustrations on pages 397 to 400.

1. What asset is traded on May 3?

2. What is the depreciation expense for the current accounting period?

3. What is paid for the new asset?

4. What amount is debited to the asset account?

5. What is the difference between the amount debited to the asset account and the amount of cash paid?

6. What journals are used to record the trade-in of the asset?

Activity B-2. Rearrange the following accounting procedures for trading plant and equipment in the correct order.

Determine book value.

Record current depreciation.

Record new asset.

Determine cost of new asset.

Discarding Plant and Equipment Assets

C *What are the accounting procedures for discarding plant and equipment?* Plant and equipment assets that are no longer useful or needed and that cannot be sold or traded are discarded. Assume that office equipment with an original cost of $1,800 and an accumulated depreciation of $1,800 is declared worthless. Since the asset is fully depreciated, there is no book value. The following entry is made on July 1 in the general journal to record that the asset is discarded.

GENERAL JOURNAL					Page 15
DATE		ACCOUNT TITLE AND EXPLANATION	POST. REF.	DEBIT	CREDIT
19— July	1	Accumulated Depreciation— Office Equipment	152	1,800 00	
		Office Equipment.	151		1,800 00
		Record disposal.			

In this example, the asset is fully depreciated and has no book value ($1,800 − $1,800 = $0). Assets may also be discarded before they are fully depreciated. In such cases an entry is needed to record depreciation since the end of the previous accounting period.

Assume that the accumulated depreciation account has a credit balance of $1,440. If the asset's useful life is estimated to be 10 years, the annual depreciation is $180 ($1,800 ÷ 10). Depreciation computed for 6 months, from January 1 to July 1, will be $90 (6/12 × $180). The book value of the asset is now $270 ($1,800 − $1,530). Thus a loss equal to the book value must be shown on the accounting records. The entries needed to record depreciation for 6 months and to discard the asset are shown here.

	GENERAL JOURNAL			Page 16
DATE	**ACCOUNT TITLE AND EXPLANATION**	**POST. REF.**	**DEBIT**	**CREDIT**
19— July 1	*Depreciation Expense— Office Equipment*	512	90 00	
	Accumulated Depreciation— Office Equipment.	152		90 00
	Record depreciation for Jan. 1–July 1.			
19— July 1	*Gains and Losses on Disposal of Plant and Equipment*	592	270 00	
	Accumulated Depreciation— Office Equipment	152	1,530 00	
	Office Equipment.	151		1,800 00
	Record disposal of office equipment.			

Companies may continue to use a fully depreciated asset as long as it is needed and of value. The asset will continue to be shown on the balance sheet. However, depreciation will not be computed or recorded after the accumulated depreciation equals the depreciable cost of the asset.

Activity C. Answer the following questions about discarding plant and equipment. Refer to the text and illustrations on pages 400 and 401.

1. What is the amount of loss on discarding a fully depreciated asset?

2. How many years of depreciation (assuming straight-line depreciation) are recorded on the asset that has an accumulated depreciation of $1,440?

3. How is a loss computed on an asset that is discarded before it is fully depreciated?

Subsidiary Ledger for Plant and Equipment

D *What is the plant and equipment ledger?* Information for the depreciation adjustments is found in the plant and equipment ledger. The **plant and equipment ledger** is a subsidiary ledger that contains details of the plant and equipment accounts found in the general ledger. Thus each plant and equipment account in the general ledger is a controlling account. For example, the Delivery Equipment account in the general ledger might represent various pieces of delivery equipment.

Information about each item of plant and equipment may be found on a computer printout or on a card similar to the **plant and equipment record** illustrated here. As you review the plant and equipment record, note the following.

② Controlling Account in General Ledger

③ Depreciation Information

PLANT AND EQUIPMENT RECORD

Item ① *Filing Cabinet*   **General Ledger Account** *Office Equipment*

Serial No *E—8764*   **Purchased From** *Omaha Office Sales*

Description *Allied Four Drawer*   **Location** *Accounting Department*

Cost When Acquired *$140*   **Age When Acquired** *New*

Estimated Life *6 yrs.*   **Estimated Disposal or Trade-In Value** *$20*   **Annual Depreciation** *$20*

DATE			EXPLANATION	PLANT EQUIPMENT ACCOUNTS			ACCUMULATED DEPRECIATION			BOOK VALUE
MO.	DAY	YR.		DEBIT	CREDIT	BALANCE	DEBIT	CREDIT	BALANCE	
1	2	X9	Purchased	140 00		140 00				140 00
12	31	X9						20 00	20 00	120 00
12	31	X0						20 00	40 00	100 00
12	31	X1						20 00	60 00	80 00
12	31	X2						20 00	80 00	60 00
12	31	X3						20 00	100 00	40 00
12	31	X4						20 00	120 00	20 00
1	2	X5	Sold		140 00	— 00	120 00		— 00	— 00

Sold, Traded, or Scrapped to: *Joanne Herring 1/2/X5*   **Amount Received: $22**

⑤

Entries Affecting Plant and Equipment Account in General Ledger [Original Cost]

Entries Affecting Contra Account in General Ledger [Expired Cost]

Balance of Plant and Equipment Account Minus Accumulated Depreciation [Current Unexpired Cost or Book Value]

④

1 The item of plant and equipment is a filing cabinet.
2 The general ledger controlling account is Office Equipment.
3 The information needed to prepare the depreciation adjusting

entry—original cost, useful life, and disposal value—is found on the card.

4 Accumulated depreciation and book value are posted each time depreciation is recorded in the general ledger.

5 When the filing cabinet is sold, the plant and equipment asset is credited for $140 and accumulated depreciation is debited for $120. The entry leaves the plant and equipment record with a zero balance. The plant and equipment record will now be removed from the plant and equipment ledger.

To prove the plant and equipment accounts (such as Office Equipment), the accountant totals the balance of the Plant and Equipment Account section on each card for that asset. The total of all the balances must equal the balance of the Plant and Equipment account in the general ledger. The contra account is proved by adding the balance of the Accumulated Depreciation on each card. The total of all the balances must equal the balance of the contra account in the general ledger. The book value on all the cards is equal to the difference between the balance of the asset account and the balance of the contra account.

When plant and equipment accounts are verified, general ledger accounts must equal total of plant and equipment record cards.

Activity D. Answer the following questions about the plant and equipment record. Refer to the text and illustrations on pages 402 and 403.

1. What is the purpose of the plant and equipment record?

2. How can the cards be used to prove the balance of the office equipment account?

3. Which piece of equipment is shown on the plant and equipment record?

4. What happens to the filing cabinet?

5. How much is received for the filing cabinet?

Topic 2 Problems

10-6. The Bender Corporation decides to sell or discard several of its plant and equipment assets. Use the list here to compute the book value and amount of gain or loss on disposal of the assets.

Asset	Cost	Accumulated Depreciation At Time of Disposal	Method of Disposal	Book Value	Gain (or Loss)
EXAMPLE: Building	**$48,600**	**$44,000**	**sold for $5,000**	**$4,600**	**$400**
a. Lathe machine	2,875	2,400	sold for $300		
b. Paper cutter	49	49	sold for $17		
c. Postal scale	75	60	discarded		
d. Truck	6,200	6,130	sold for $300		
e. Truck	5,800	5,400	sold for $250		
f. Typewriter	450	450	discarded as worthless		

10-7. Use a general journal, a cash receipts journal, cash payment journals, and T accounts to record the following transactions relating to the disposal of plant and equipment assets. (*HINT:* Post depreciation expense for each asset.) The accumulated depreciation accounts were posted on December 31, the end of the last accounting period. Use the straight-line method of depreciation.

Feb. 3 The company had an old typewriter that had cost $325, had an estimated useful life of 5 years, had a disposal value of $25, and had an accumulated depreciation of $275. The old typewriter and $420 cash was exchanged for a new typewriter. (Issued Check 565.)

March 10 An old truck with an estimated life of 3 years that had cost $5,000, had a disposal value of $200, and had accumulated depreciation of $4,200 was traded in for a new truck. In addition to the old truck, $5,400 cash was required. (Issued Check 590.)

April 28 An old typewriter that had cost $360, had no disposal value, had an estimated life of 5 years, and had accumulated depreciation of $288 was sold for $20.

Aug. 4 A duplicating machine that had cost $460, had a disposal value of $40, had an estimated life of 7 years, and had accumulated depreciation of $385 was discarded as worthless.

10-8. On June 15 the Blanda Company trades an old office machine for a newer electronic model. The cost of the old machine is $2,800, and the accumulated depreciation is $2,400. The new machine costs $12,000. The Blanda Company is allowed a $700 trade-in allowance. (Use Check 714.) The old machine was fully depreciated.

a. What is the book value of the old office machine?

b. Does the Blanda Company realize a gain or a loss on the trade of the machine?

c. Is the gain or loss actually recorded?

d. Record the journal entry for the trade of the office machine.

10-9. On September 1 the Gobel Company receives $220 for an old delivery truck. The original cost of the truck is $4,800, and the accumulated depreciation is $4,700. The old truck was fully depreciated.

a. What is the book value of the delivery truck?

b. Does the Gobel Company realize a gain or a loss?

c. Make the necessary entries to record the disposal of the delivery truck.

Topic 3
Accounting for Intangible Assets and Natural Resources

A *What are intangible assets?* Intangible assets are not easy to classify. It is easier to see why Cash is classified as a current asset and why Office Equipment is classified plant and equipment.

Intangible assets are assets that are not physical, have long life, and provide a business with rights, privileges, or competitive advantages. Examples include patents, copyrights, trademarks, leaseholds, goodwill, and franchises.

Two intangible assets—patents and leaseholds—are used to illustrate our definition. They are two of a wide variety of assets included in the intangible category. A discussion of other intangible assets is included in more advanced accounting courses.

Intangible Assets:
• Nonphysical
• Produce revenue
• Not intended for resale
• Long life

Intangible Assets:
• Patents
• Copyrights
• Trademarks
• Leaseholds
• Goodwill
• Franchises

Patents. A **patent** is an exclusive right granted by the federal government to manufacture, sell, use, and profit from an invention. Patents are granted for 17 years. Remember the definition of intangible assets given above and compare the characteristics of a patent against it. A patent is a right and, therefore, has no physical substance. A patent has a long life: 17 years. And a patent provides the developing or purchasing company with an advantage. No one else may use, sell, market, or benefit from the purchasing or developing company's invention.

Leaseholds. Companies often sign property leases for 20 or 30 years or more. In some long-term leases, advance payments are required that apply to future years. The payments provide the leaseholder with the right to use property. Again recall the definition of intangible assets to see how a leasehold fits. Leaseholds relate to future years—beyond one accounting period. In a period of rising prices, a lease signed for 5 or 10 years is extremely valuable and may provide the leaseholder with an advantage over competition.

Leaseholds provide the right to and use of leased property.

Cost and Amortization of Intangible Assets

Intangible assets are recorded at cost. For a patent, the cost includes development costs, research costs, lawyer's fees, and so on. The cost of a trademark would include all the costs necessary to register the trademark.

Intangible assets that are obtained without cost are not recorded in the accounting records. An example of an intangible asset that does not always require an expenditure is a franchise.

Intangible assets that are purchased are recorded in the accounting records at cost.

Recording Amortization

Amortization is the allocation of the cost of intangible assets to expense over the asset's useful life.

The cost of an intangible asset must be matched against the revenue produced by that asset. The procedure for allocating the cost of an intangible asset to expense over the asset's useful life is known as **amortization.**

Intangible assets must have a fixed or determinable useful life to be amortized.

To amortize an intangible asset, the asset's cost must be known. Second, the asset's life must be *fixed or determinable.* This is sometimes difficult, for certain intangible assets do not have a fixed or determinable life. **Organization costs** are the costs that are necessary to form a corporation, such as attorney's fees and incorporation fees. Another example of an intangible asset would be certain franchises. (Not all franchises are intangible assets because not all franchises are awarded for a specified time period.)

Annual amortization

$$\text{Cost of intangible asset} \div \text{Useful life}$$

$$\$3,000 = \$51,000 \div 17 \text{ years}$$

When an intangible asset has a fixed or determinable useful life, the annual amortization is computed by dividing the asset cost by the useful life. For instance, the annual amortization expense would be $3,000 for a patent costing $51,000 and having a useful life of 17 years. The adjusting entry to record amortization is made in the general journal. After the amortization for 19X4 has been recorded, the accounts would appear as follows.

	Patents	162		Amortization Expense—Patents	531
19X2		*19X2*		*19X4*	
June 30	*51,000*	*Dec. 31* *1,500*		*Dec. 31* *3,000*	
		19X3			
		Dec. 31 *3,000*			
		19X4			
		Dec. 31 *3,000*			

Adjusting entry for annual amortization expense:
Debit: Amortization Expense
Credit: Intangible Asset

Note that the entry to record the annual amortization of an intangible asset includes a debit to the Amortization Expense—Patents account. Amortization Expense is an operating expense and is closed to the Income Summary account.

Activity A-1. Answer the following questions about intangible assets. Refer to the text and illustrations on pages 405 and 406.

1. What is amortization? Which accounts are used to record amortization?

2. What is the June 30, 19X3, balance of the Patents account?

3. What credits have been made to the Patents account since 19X2?

4. What is the amount of amortization expense recorded in 19X4?

Activity A-2. Decide which of the following accounts can be classified as intangible assets.

EXAMPLE: Electronic calculator—No

1. Accounts Payable
2. Jane Bettis, Capital
3. Patents
4. Cash
5. Trademarks
6. Franchises
7. Office Supplies
8. Leaseholds
9. Copyrights
10. Goodwill
11. Notes Receivable
12. Mortgage Payable
13. Accounts Receivable
14. Rent Expense

Accounting for Natural Resources

B *What are natural resources?* **Natural resources**—sometimes called *wasting assets*—are assets that are held in their natural state until the product is removed. Examples of natural resources are mining property, timber tracts, and oil and gas wells. Eventually ore will be removed from the mines, lumber from the timber, and petroleum from oil wells.

Courtesy International Harvester

As units of the natural resource are removed, a proportion of the cost of the natural resource is depleted.

Cost of Natural Resources

The primary costs of natural resources are those related to the original purchase. Included would be the original cost of the property, legal fees, and survey costs.

Depletion of Natural Resources

Depletion relates to the use of a natural resource.

Depletion is the term used to describe the allocation of the cost of natural resources to expense. To understand depletion, view the cost of a natural resource as the purchase of units of some item. The purchase of a coal mine is really the purchase of tons of coal in the ground. A tract of timber is viewed as purchasing units of lumber. And the purchase of property for drilling oil or gas wells is viewed as the purchase of barrels of oil.

As units of a natural resource are removed from the earth, a proportion of the cost of the natural resource is transferred to expense.

Assume that a quarry is purchased for $32,000. It is estimated that 8,000 tons of stone are in the ground. Each ton of stone is viewed as having a cost of $4 ($32,000 ÷ 8,000). Annual depletion charges can now be related to the number of units (tons) consumed or converted to inventory.

$$1,000 \text{ tons} \times \$4 \text{ a ton} = \$4000 \text{ annual depletion expense}$$

Recording Depletion. If 1,000 tons of stone are mined and sold during the accounting period, the depletion expense will be $4,000 (1,000 × $4). Annual depletion would be recorded first on the worksheet as an adjusting entry. The general journal entry for annual depletion is found here.

		GENERAL JOURNAL			Page *21*
DATE		**ACCOUNT TITLE AND EXPLANATION**	**POST. REF.**	**DEBIT**	**CREDIT**
19—					
Dec.	*31*	*Depletion Expense—Stone Quarry* . .		*4,000 00*	
		Accumulated Depletion—			
		Stone Quarry			*4,000 00*
		Record depletion of			
		Stone Quarry.			

Depletion Expense is an operating expense and is closed to the Income Summary account. Accumulated Depletion is a contra asset account used to compute the unexpired cost of the Stone Quarry (asset) account.

The method used for recording depletion expenses for other types of natural resources is similar to the method used in the illustration. That is, depletion expenses are closely associated with the number of units consumed or converted to inventory. Special accounting problems related to the exploration and development costs associated with oil and gas properties are included in more advanced accounting courses.

Activity B-1. Answer the following questions about accounting for natural resources. Refer to the text and illustrations on pages 407 to 409.

1. What items are included in the cost of natural resources?
2. How is the cost of natural resources allocated to expense?
3. What is the depletion expense for each ton of stone? How is it computed?
4. What is the annual depletion expense? How is it computed?

5. What is the entry to record depletion expense?
6. What kind of entry is used to record depletion expense?
7. What kind of account is Accumulated Depletion?

Activity B-2. Decide which of the following assets can be classified as natural resources.

EXAMPLE: Gas—YES

1. Supplies
2. Oil
3. Accounts Receivable
4. Iron Ore
5. Cash

6. Coal
7. Trucks
8. Timber
9. Equipment

Topic 3   Problems

10-10. Various asset characteristics are listed here. Relate the asset characteristic to an asset classification, as shown in the example. Write an "X" in the appropriate column.

Characteristic	Not Applicable	Plant and Equipment	Intangible Asset	Natural Resources
EXAMPLE: Long life.		X	X	X

a. Produces revenue.
b. Physical substance.
c. Consumed within the accounting period or one year.
d. Not purchased for resale.
e. Converted to cash within one year or the accounting cycle.

f. Grants rights.
g. Purchased for resale.
h. Provides competitive advantages.
i. Depreciates.
j. Amortized.
k. Depletes.

10-11. The Conwell and Beasley Company purchases the following intangible assets on January 1 of the current year. Record the adjustments that are required on December 31 to amortize the assets in general journal.

Asset	Cost	Useful Life
a. Copyright	$36,000	8 years
b. Patents	34,000	17 years
c. Trademarks	10,000	5 years

10-12. For each transaction listed here, indicate the journal that would be used to record the transaction and the account that would be debited and credited.

Transaction	Journal	Account(s) Debited	Account(s) Credited
EXAMPLE: *Recorded amortization of organization costs*	*General Journal*	*Amortization Expense— Organization Costs*	*Organization Costs*

a. Recorded amortization of patent
b. Paid legal fees to organize the business
c. Signed a lease for building
d. Recorded depletion of coal reserves

e. Paid fee for copyright of printed material
f. Recorded depletion of timber supply

10-13. Compute the annual depletion expense for each of the following natural resources.

a. A coal mine was purchased for $300,000 with an estimated reserve of 60,000 tons of coal. During the current accounting period, 10,000 tons were mined.
b. An oil well was purchased for $800,000 with an estimated reserve of 400,000 barrels of oil. During the current accounting period, 100,000 barrels of oil were recovered.

NOTE: Save your work for further use in Topic Problem 10-14.

10-14. Record the annual depletion expenses that you computed above (in Topic Problem 10-13) in a general journal, as of December 31.

The Language of Business

Here are some basic terms that make up the language of business. Do you understand the meaning of each? Can you define each term and use it in an original sentence?

plant and equipment	accelerated	depreciation expense	intangible assets
assets	depreciation	accumulated	patent
depreciation	sum-of-the-years'-digits	depreciation	amortization
obsolescence	method	plant and equipment	natural resources
inadequacy	declining balance	ledger	depletion
straight-line method	method	plant and equipment	
disposal value	book value	record	

Chapter 10   Questions

1. What is plant and equipment?
2. What items are included in the cost of plant and equipment?
3. What are three methods for computing depreciation?
4. How is book value determined?
5. What can be done with items of plant and equipment that are no longer useful?
6. Are gains and losses recorded for plant and equipment items traded for newer plant and equipment? Why or why not?

7. What is the effect on owner's equity if no adjustment is recorded for depreciation?
8. Can the account Office Equipment be a controlling account? When?
9. Why is the amount of depreciation credited to a contra account?
10. What is included in the cost of an intangible asset?

Chapter 10   Problems

Problems for Chapter 10 are given in the *Working Papers and Chapter Problems* for Part 2. If you are using the workbook, do the problems in the space provided there. Complete your assigned topic problems before answering the chapter problems.

Chapter 10   Management Cases

Accelerated Depreciation. The reasons for choosing an accelerated depreciation method will vary from business to business. One business may choose an accelerated method because of the matching principle and another to obtain an income tax advantage. Net income for similar businesses will differ depending on the method chosen for computing depreciation.

Two management cases follow. The first case places you in a position where you must understand the effect on net income of two methods of computing depreciation from the viewpoint of someone purchasing a business. The second management case asks you to respond to a phrase frequently used in relation to accelerated depreciation.

Case 10M-1. Eva Butler and Bob Kelly are interested in purchasing one of two businesses. Each business is similar, with the exception of the method used to compute depreciation on equipment purchased 3 years ago. The equipment at both businesses has an original cost of $65,000, a 10-year useful life, and a $10,000 scrap value. One of the businesses, Cutchins Inc. uses straight-line depreciation; the other, McCann Products, uses the sum-of-the-years'-digits method (the denominator of the fraction is 55).

Ms. Butler and Mr. Kelly are considering purchasing Cutchins Inc. because of net income figures shown here.

Year	Cutchins Inc. (Net Income)	McCann Products (Net Income)
1	$28,500	$27,000
2	34,000	32,800
3	36,000	35,000

a. What additional data can you provide Ms. Butler and Mr. Kelly concerning the reported net incomes?

You might want to compute revised net incomes for the three years.

b. Would your additional data encourage you to recommend the purchase of one business over the other?

c. Using the information provided above, why might the cash position for McCann Products be stronger than Cutchins Inc.?

Case 10M-2. The professional accountant for Marjory Company recommended that the company use an accelerated depreciation method, rather than the straight-line method. The reason for the recommendation was that accelerated methods provide interest-free working capital in the early life of plant and equipment. What do you think the accountant meant by the "interest-free working capital" statement? (You might want to refer to Chapter 14 to find out what is meant by working capital.)

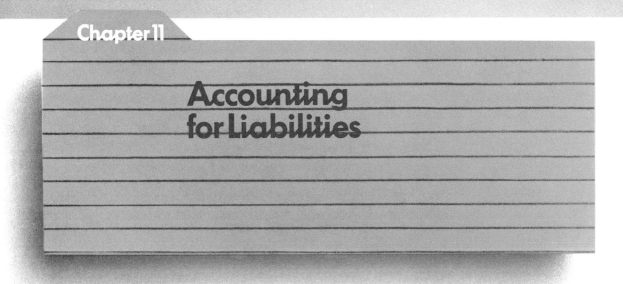

Accounting for Liabilities

The decisions and procedures for accounting for liabilities are not the same as those for accounting for assets. Chapters 9 and 10 describe many decisions and procedures related to the accounting for assets. But there are also decisions and procedures that must be considered before incurring liabilities. The decisions and procedures related to liabilities are presented in this chapter.

Topic 1
The Nature of Liabilities

A *What are liabilities?* **Liabilities** are debts that must be paid. Liabilities are also claims against assets. *Total liabilities* are the claims creditors have against assets. **Owner's equity** is also a claim against assets. The claims of creditors plus the claims of owners equals the total claims against assets in any business. Thus, in this sense, creditors and owners are very similar. The relationship between owners and creditors is summarized in the following accounting equation.

Liabilities are a first claim against assets.

Owner's equity is a second claim against assets.

$$\text{Assets} \quad = \quad \begin{array}{c} \text{Liabilities} \\ \text{(Claims of Creditors)} \end{array} \quad + \quad \begin{array}{c} \text{Owner's Equity} \\ \text{(Claims of Owners)} \end{array}$$

Incurring Liabilities

Liabilities are incurred when goods and services are purchased on credit, money is borrowed, payment is received before services are performed, or taxes are levied. Why do businesses incur liabilities? Is

Liabilities are incurred out of necessity and sound business practice.

there any advantage in doing so? The answers depend on two factors: necessity and sound business practice.

Sometimes it is necessary to incur liabilities. For example, it is customary for sales taxes to be collected and payroll taxes withheld but not paid immediately. An arrangement may be made for having merchandise delivered with full or partial payment made at a later date. Or a business may not have the money to make immediate payment. In this case it may be given credit to continue operations. The business incurs this liability in the form of credit with the expectation that the assets or services received will produce revenue. In time, the revenue will result in sufficient cash receipts to pay the liability.

It is often sound business practice to incur liabilities. Suppose a business needs to expand a building to increase productivity and increase revenue. The owner may not want to pay for the improvement in full immediately. Several options are available. The money for the expansion can be borrowed. The withdrawal of earnings by the owner can be delayed. Or the owner can contribute personal funds.

Each of these methods has advantages. Only one—the borrowing of money—results in a liability. The other two methods change the owner's equity. When money is borrowed, the control of a business is not changed. The owner still controls the business. The interest charged for borrowing money, however, is another cost of doing business.

Management may decide to borrow money for expansion for another reason. Borrowing money allows management to practice trading on the equity. **Trading on the equity** refers to a situation where the equity (cash) of creditors is used to increase the equity of owners.

Activity A. Answer the following questions about incurring liabilities. Refer to the text on pages 413 and 414.

1. Which two groups have a claim against assets?
2. Give three examples in which liabilities are incurred.
3. How can sound business practice increase liabilities?
4. Name two ways that a company might obtain cash.
5. Is the control of the business changed when money is borrowed? Explain.
6. What is the meaning of trading on the equity?

Classifying Liabilities

B *How are liabilities classified?* Liabilities are classified as current liabilities or long-term liabilities. Current liabilities are discussed first.

Current liabilities are debts payable in one year.

Current liabilities are debts that are payable within one year. Also the payment of a current liability will normally require the use of a current asset. The use of current assets to pay or satisfy current liabilities means that the two classifications are closely related. Current liabilities include the following.

- **Accounts payable** include payables for merchandise purchases and payables for utilities or other services.
- **Accruals** include obligations related to the current accounting period that have been incurred but not paid. Some examples of accruals are liabilities for salaries, wages, commissions, interest, and taxes that have been incurred but not paid.
- **Deferrals** include payments received before goods have been delivered or services performed.

Each of the above categories will be discussed in the following topics.

Accounting Principle:
Classifying Liabilities. The generally accepted accounting principle is that liabilities reported on the balance sheet should be classified into at least two groups: current liabilities and long-term liabilities.

Accounting Principle:
Current Liabilities. The generally accepted accounting principle is that current liabilities should include items payable within one year or at the end of the operating cycle used in the classification of current assets. Accounts should be shown separately for notes payable to banks, notes payable to others, and accounts payable.

Activity B. Answer the following questions about classifying liabilities. Refer to the text on pages 414 and 415.

1. Name two ways in which liabilities can be classified.

2. When are current liabilities payable, and what does the payment require?

3. Should current liabilities be listed separately? Explain.

4. Name the three categories of current liabilities.

5. Give an example of each category of current liabilities.

Topic 1 Problems

11-1. Which of the following accounts can be classified as a current liability? Answer *Yes* or *No* as appropriate.

EXAMPLE: Commissions—No

a. Cash Short and Over
b. Mortgage Payable
c. Notes Receivable
d. Accounts Payable
e. Salaries Payable

f. Notes Payable
g. FICA Taxes Payable
h. Trade Discounts
i. Accumulated Depreciation
j. Sales Taxes Payable

11-2. Account titles and account balances are listed here. Use your knowledge of current liabilities to determine the total current liabilities.

a. Salaries Payable, $300
b. Accumulated Depreciation, $5,000
c. Sales Taxes Payable, $300
d. Salary Expense, $7,000
e. Mortgage Payable, $5,000
f. Accounts Payable, $2,050

g. FICA Taxes Payable, $100
h. Union Dues Payable, $200
i. Allowance for Doubtful Accounts, $700
j. Paul Mazur, Capital, $5,000
k. Sales, $9,000

11-3. Cora Craig owns CC Regal. Ms. Craig wants to expand the business and estimates that she will need $5,000. The money can be borrowed on a one-year promissory note at 14 percent interest. It is estimated that the $5,000 will result in increased sales of $17,000. However, the cost of goods and operating expenses are expected to be 92 percent of the increased sales.

a. What is the interest for the note for one year?
b. By what amount does borrowing the money increase owner's equity after the first year?
c. How much cash must be paid

when the note comes due after one year?
d. What other methods of obtaining cash to expand the business might Ms. Craig consider?

Topic 2
Accounting for Accounts Payable

A *What kinds of debts are most accounts payable?* Accounts payable most often refers to debts related to purchasing merchandise. The usual source document for recording this liability is an invoice. Two methods for recording the liability for accounts payable are the gross method and the net method. The illustrations shown on page 417 demonstrate the gross method for recording a liability for accounts payable.

Accounting for Accounts Payable:
• Gross Method
• Net Method

Gross Method

In the gross method, invoices are recorded at gross amounts.

In the **gross method** for recording accounts payable, invoices are recorded at gross amounts. The gross method is illustrated here. Assume that merchandise is purchased on April 1 with terms 2/10, n/30. Payment is made on April 10, within the discount period. Note that on April 1 the purchase is recorded at the gross amount ($1,000). The $1,000 debt is paid on April 10 with $980 cash by taking advantage of the $20 purchases discount.

Gross Method:
Purchases	$1,000
Payment	$ 980
Discount	$ 20

Customer Order No.	Order Date	Our Order No.	Customer No.	Territory	Salesclerk	Invoice No.	Invoice Date
278	3/27/19--	2722	807-B	1	Jones	1111	4/1/19--

SOLD TO   Gallo Company
1421 West James Street
Rome, NY 13440

SHIP TO   Same

Shipped Via	Terms	All claims must be reported within 10 days of receipt of goods.		
Truck	2/10, n/30			
QUANTITY	CODE NO.	DESCRIPTION	UNIT PRICE	AMOUNT
20	77	CF-7 Circular saws	50.00	1,000.00

PURCHASES JOURNAL   Page *1*

DATE	ACCOUNT CREDITED	INVOICE NO.	INVOICE DATE	TERMS	POST. REF.	AMOUNT
19— April 11	Apex Supply Company	1111	4/1/—	2/10, n/30	√	1,000 00

CASH PAYMENTS JOURNAL   Page *1*

DATE	ACCOUNT DEBITED	EXPLANATION	CHECK NO.	POST. REF.	GENERAL LEDGER DEBIT	ACCOUNTS PAYABLE DEBIT	PURCHASES DISCOUNT CREDIT	NET CASH CREDIT
19— April 10	Purchases Discount	Invoice 1111, 4/1/—	126	502		1,000 00	20 00	980 00

General Ledger

Cash

	Apr. 10 980

Purchases

Apr. 1 1,000	

Accounts Payable

Apr. 10 1,000	Apr. 1 1,000
payment	purchase

Subsidiary Ledger

Apex Supply

Apr. 10 1,000	Apr. 1 1,000

Purchase Discount

	Apr. 10 20

Activity A. Answer the following questions about the gross method for recording accounts payable. Refer to the text and illustrations on pages 416 and 417.

1. What is the amount of purchase made on April 1?

2. Which account is debited for the April 1 purchase? credited? For what amount?

3. When is the purchase discount recorded?

4. How much cash is required to pay the April 1 invoice?

5. What accounts are debited on April 10? credited?

Net Method

B *What is the net method for recording accounts payable?* The **net method** records the purchase and accounts payable at the net amount. The net amount is the gross amount of the invoice ($1,000) minus the allowable discount ($20). The net method for recording the purchase on April 1 is illustrated here.

April 1 Bought merchandise from Apex Supply for $1,000 on account; terms 2/10, n/30.

PURCHASES JOURNAL						Page 1
DATE	ACCOUNT CREDITED	INVOICE NO.	INVOICE DATE	TERMS	POST. REF.	AMOUNT
19— Apr. 1	Apex Supply Company	1111	4/1	2/10, n/30	√	980 00

General Ledger

Purchases			Accounts Payable	
Apr. 1	980		Apr. 1	980

purchase

Subsidiary Ledger

	Apex Supply	
	Apr. 1	980

Net Method:

Gross Amount of Invoice	. . . .	$1,000
Less Discount	. . . . .	−20
Net Amount	. . . . . .	$ 980

Note that in the net method, only the net amount to be paid is recorded. The payment of the liability on April 10 is illustrated at the top of the next page.

April 10 Paid the Apex Supply for purchase of April 1.

	CASH PAYMENTS JOURNAL							Page 3
DATE	ACCOUNT DEBITED	EXPLANATION	CHECK NO.	POST. REF.	GENERAL LEDGER DEBIT	ACCOUNTS PAYABLE DEBIT	NET CASH CREDIT	
19— Apr. 10	Apex Supply Company . . .	Inv. 1111 . .	126	√		980 00	980 00	

General Ledger

Cash	Accounts Payable	Purchases
Apr. 10 980	Apr. 10 980 | Apr. 1 980	Apr. 1 980
payment	*purchase*	

	Apex Supply	
Subsidiary Ledger	Apr. 10 980 | Apr. 1 980	

In the net method illustrated above, the invoice ($980) is recorded on April 1 and paid on April 10. But what happens when the invoice is not paid within the discount period (April 1–10)? The answer is illustrated here.

April 15 Paid Apex Supply for purchase of April 1.

	CASH PAYMENTS JOURNAL							Page 3
DATE	ACCOUNT DEBITED	EXPLANATION	CHECK NO.	POST. REF.	GENERAL LEDGER DEBIT	ACCOUNTS PAYABLE DEBIT	NET CASH CREDIT	
19— Apr. 15	Purchase Discounts Lost . .	Inv. 1111 . .	126	505	20 00	980 00	1,000 00	

General Ledger

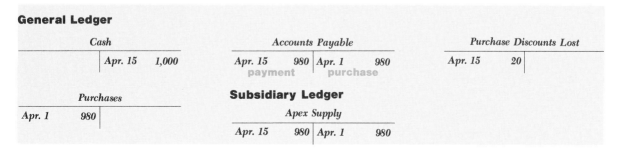

Cash	Accounts Payable	Purchase Discounts Lost
Apr. 15 1,000	Apr. 15 980 | Apr. 1 980	Apr. 15 20
	payment *purchase*	

Purchases	**Subsidiary Ledger**	
Apr. 1 980	Apex Supply	
	Apr. 15 980 | Apr. 1 980	

Discounts not taken are debited to Purchase Discounts Lost, an operating expense.

The gross amount of the invoice ($1,000) must be paid when payments are not made in the discount period. Thus $1,000 must be paid for the Accounts Payable ($980), recorded on April 1. The difference ($20) between what is recorded on April 1 ($980) and paid on April 15 ($1,000) is an expense. *Purchases Discounts Lost* is the expense account to record discounts not taken.

Recording accounts payable by the net method focuses on purchase discounts not taken. Purchase discounts not taken are seen by management as balances in the Purchase Discounts Lost account.

Differences Between the Gross and Net Methods

A comparison of the gross method and the net method for recording accounts payable reveals several differences.

Gross Method	*Net Method*
• Shows discounts *taken*.	• Shows discounts *lost*.
• Requires a Purchases Discount account.	• Does not require Purchases Discount account.
• Does not require a Purchase Discounts Lost account.	• Requires a Purchases Discounts Lost account.
• Requires routine accounting for discounts.	• Eliminates routine accounting for discounts.
• Purchases shown at gross amount.	• Purchases shown at net amount.

Activity B-1. Answer the following questions about the net method for recording accounts payable. Refer to the text and illustrations on pages 418 to 420.

1. What is the total amount of merchandise purchased on April 1?
2. Which account is debited for merchandise purchased? Which account is credited? What is the amount of the debit and credit?
3. Which journal is used to record the purchase of merchandise? What is the amount of the purchase entered in this journal?
4. What entry is made to record the payment for the merchandise on April 10?
5. Which journal is used to record the payment? What account is debited? Which account is credited?

Activity B-2. Answer the following questions about purchases discounts lost. Refer to the text and illustrations on pages 419 and 420.

1. What is the purpose of the April 15 entry?
2. Which account(s) is (are) debited? Which account(s) is (are) credited?
3. Which journal is used to record the payment of the purchase invoice?
4. Why is $20 entered in the general ledger debit column?

5. What kind of account is Purchases Discounts Lost?

6. What amount was credited to cash? Why?

7. What does the net method highlight?

Topic 2   Problems

11-4. Record the following transactions in the appropriate journals. Use the gross method for recording accounts payable.

Sept. **3** Bought merchandise from Best Supply for $630 on credit; terms 2/10, n/30; Invoice 1009, dated September 1.

7 Bought merchandise from Rocco, Inc., for $710 on credit; terms 1/10, n/30; Invoice M310, dated September 5.

9 Bought merchandise for $525; Invoice 216C, Check 518.

13 Paid Invoice 1009 and took discount of 2 percent; Check 520.

14 Bought merchandise from Morren Company for $1,130 on credit; terms n/30; Invoice 742, dated September 12.

Sept. **15** Bought merchandise from DiSalvo and Son for $439 on credit; terms 2/10, n/30; Invoice 1110, dated September 13.

17 Paid Invoice M310 and took the 1 percent discount; Check 530.

23 Paid Invoice 742, Check 540.

27 Paid Invoice 1110, Check 548.

11-5. Record the transactions in Topic Problem 11-4 using the net method for recording accounts payable.

Topic 3
Accounting for Accrued and Deferred Liabilities

Accrued Liabilities

A *What are accrued liabilities?* **Accrued liabilities** are current liabilities incurred during the accounting period but not paid and recorded. For example, interest on a loan is charged for each day the borrower uses the money. The borrower, however, does not pay the interest each day, nor is interest recorded each day. The interest will not be recorded and paid until the due date of the loan. Thus an adjusting entry is necessary to record the accrued liability (interest payable)

Accrued liabilities are liabilities incurred but not recorded and paid.

and accrued expense (interest expense) for the current accounting period.

Accrued Interest. Assume that on December 1, 19X4, the Gallo Company issues the Macar Company a 90-day 9 percent promissory note for $2,000 in payment of its account. The transaction is recorded in the general journal.

$2,000.00	December 1, 19X4

Ninety days after date *I* promise to pay to the order of *Macar Company*

Two thousand and 00/100 ————————— Dollars

Payable at *Park Bank*

Value received *with interest at 9 percent*

No. ———— Due *March 1, 19X5*   *The Gallo Company*

COMPUTING THE DUE DATE

December	31 Days	
	−1	
	30 Days	
January	31	
February	28	
March	1	(Due Date)
	90 Days	

Maturity
Value = Principal + Interest
$2,045 = $2,000 + $45

Interest
= Principal × Rate × Time
$45 = $2,000 × $\frac{9}{100}$ × $\frac{90}{360}$
Total Interest $45

The interest on the note accrues (adds up) day by day over the 90-day period. The interest is not paid or recorded each day. When the note becomes due on March 1, 19X5, a total of $2,045 is paid: $2,000 for the note and $45 for the interest. However, not all of the interest relates to the 19X5 accounting period. The first 30 days' interest (from December 1 to December 31) relates to the 19X4 accounting period.

	GENERAL JOURNAL			Page 2
DATE	**ACCOUNT TITLE AND EXPLANATION**	**POST. REF.**	**DEBIT**	**CREDIT**
19X4				
Dec. 1	*Accounts Payable/Macar Company* .	*211/√*	*2,000 00*	
	Notes Payable	*201*		*2,000 00*
	Gave 90-day, 9 percent note.			

If interest is not recorded for 30 days in 19X4, both liabilities and expenses will be understated. Thus net income and owner's equity will be overstated. An adjusting entry is necessary to make the financial statements accurate. The adjusting entry records liabilities and expenses incurred but not yet paid.

The interest that accrues on the $2,000 note payable during the last 30 days of 19X4 is $15. The Interest Expense account is debited for $15 to record the accrued interest. This reflects the actual interest expense ($15) for 19X4. The $15 is not paid in cash until March 1, 19X5. Thus the $15 is interest owed and a liability. The amount must also be credited to the liability account Interest Payable.

Interest for 30 Days:

$$\$15 = \$2,000 \times \tfrac{9}{100} \times \tfrac{30}{360}$$

December 31, 19X4 The Gallo Company recorded interest expense of $15 accrued for 30 days on a Macar Company note payable.

		GENERAL JOURNAL			Page 5
DATE		**ACCOUNT TITLE AND EXPLANATION**	**POST. REF.**	**DEBIT**	**CREDIT**
19X4					
Dec.	31	Interest Expense.............	591	15 00	
		Interest Payable	202		15 00
		Record accrued interest on			
		Macar note.			

Notes Payable 201	Interest Payable 202	Interest Expense 591
Dec. 1 2,000	Dec. 31 15	Dec. 31 15

After the adjusting entry is posted, the Notes Payable account shows the amount of the note ($2,000), the Interest Payable account shows the liability for accrued interest ($15), and the Interest Expense account shows the interest expense incurred during the accounting period ($15).

After the closing entries are made, Interest Expense is closed. Interest Payable remains open until the liability is paid.

Paying the Interest. On March 1, 19X5, the Gallo Company pays $2,045 to the payee: $2,000 to pay the note and $45 to pay the total interest. Of the total interest, $15 (the amount from December 1 to

Dec. 1 Dec. 31 March 1

|———————|———————|

19X4 19X5

December 31) is recorded as expense in the previous accounting period (19X4). The remainder of the interest ($30) is an expense of the 19X5 accounting period. Thus the Interest Expense account is debited for $30 to record the interest expense for 19X5. Also, the Interest Payable account is debited for $15 to decrease the liability recorded in the previous period (19X4).

March 1, 19X5 The Gallo Company paid $2,045 to the Macar Company for a promissory note of $2,000 and interest of $45 for 90 days.

		CASH PAYMENTS JOURNAL							Page 5
DATE	ACCOUNT DEBITED	EXPLANATION	CHECK NO.	POST. REF.	GENERAL LEDGER DEBIT	ACCOUNTS PAYABLE DEBIT	PURCHASES DISCOUNT CREDIT	NET CASH CREDIT	
19X5									
Mar. 1	Notes Payable	Note dated 12/1/—.	143	201	2,000 00			2,045 00	
	Interest Payable . . .	Int. for 30 days . . .	—	202	15 00			—	
	Interest Expense. . . .	Int. for 60 days . . .	—	591	30 00			—	

After the entry is posted, the liability accounts for Notes Payable and Interest Payable have zero balances. Interest Expense shows the amount of interest for the current period.

Notes Payable	201		Interest Payable	202
19X5	19X4		19X5	19X4
Mar. 1 2,000	Dec. 1 2,000		Mar. 1 15	Dec. 31 15

Interest Expense	591		Cash	101
19X5				19X5
Mar. 1 30				Mar. 1 2,045

Payment of Interest-Bearing Note

Activity A-1. Answer the following questions about accrued interest. Refer to the text and illustrations on pages 421 to 424.

1. What is the amount of the Gallo Company note issued on December 1?
2. Is this an interest-bearing note? If so, what is the rate of interest?
3. What is the term (number of days) of the note?

4. Will this note reach maturity during the 19X4 accounting period or in the 19X5 accounting period?
5. How much interest must be paid on the note at maturity? What is the maturity value of the note?

6. Does this note require an adjusting entry on December 31? If so, give the accrued interest amount.

7. Which account is debited in the adjusting entry? Which account is credited?

Activity A-2. Determine the amount of accrued interest on each of the following notes payable as of December 31.

1. $5,000: 9 percent, 60 days, dated December 3.

2. $6,150: 8 percent, 30 days, dated December 21.

3. $475: 8½ percent, 90 days, dated November 30.

Accrued Salaries

B *What are accrued salaries?* **Accrued salaries** are a liability and an expense incurred in the current accounting period but not paid until the next period. For example, employees earn salaries day to day. However, salaries are not recorded and paid until the end of the pay period. If the end of the pay period and the end of the accounting period are not the same, accrued salaries must be recorded.

The Gallo Company has a pay period ending on Friday. The end of the current accounting period ends on Monday. Thus an adjusting entry for accrued salaries for one day (Monday) in the current accounting period must be recorded. The salaries earned but not paid for Monday, December 31, are $120.

The adjusting entry includes a debit to Salaries Expense to record the expense and a credit to Salaries Payable to record the liability.

The Salaries Expense account is closed into the Income Summary account through the closing entries. The Salaries Payable account remains open until the liability is paid.

December

S M T W T F S
30 31
                          19X4

January

S M T W T F S
   1 2 3 4 5
                          19X5

Accrued Salaries Adjusting Entry
Debit: Salaries Expense
Credit: Salaries Payable

	GENERAL JOURNAL			Page 7
DATE	**ACCOUNT TITLE AND EXPLANATION**	**POST. REF.**	**DEBIT**	**CREDIT**
19X4				
Dec. 31	*Salaries Expense*	525	120 00	
	Salaries Payable	235		120 00
	Record accrued salaries.			

Salaries Payable	235		*Salaries Expense*	525
	19X4		*19X4*	
	Dec. 31 120		*Dec. 31* 120	

Recording Accrued Salaries

Paying Salaries. The salaries are paid on January 4 of the next accounting period. The Salaries Payable account is debited for $120 to record the decrease in the liability recorded in the previous period (for the salaries earned on December 31). The Salaries Expense account is debited to record the salary expense ($480) for the new accounting period (the salaries earned on January 1–4). The employees' withholding taxes and cash are credited to record payment of the payroll.

	GENERAL JOURNAL				Page 1
DATE	ACCOUNT TITLE AND EXPLANATION	POST. REF.	DEBIT	CREDIT	
19X5					
Jan. 4	Salaries Expense	525	480 00		
	Salaries Payable	235	120 00		
	Employee Income Taxes Payable .	231		108 00	
	FICA Taxes Payable	232		36 78	
	Cash	—		455 22	
	Record weekly payroll.				

Cash 101		Emp. Inc. Taxes Payable 231		FICA Taxes Payable 232
19X5 Jan. 4 455.22		19X5 Jan. 4 108.00		19X5 Jan. 4 36.78

Salaries Payable 235		Salaries Expense 525
19X5 Jan. 4 120.00 | 19X4 Dec. 31 120.00		19X5 Jan. 4 480.00

Paying Accrued Salaries

Cash is posted from the cash payments journal.

Activity B. Answer the following questions about recording and paying accrued salaries. Refer to the text and illustrations on pages 425 and 426.

1. What is the amount of accrued salaries on December 31?

2. Which account is debited for accrued salaries? Which account is credited?

3. Are either of these accounts closed on December 31? If so, which one?

4. When will the accrued salaries be paid?

5. Which account(s) is (are) debited to record the January 4 payroll? Which account(s) is (are) credited?

6. What is the purpose of the $120 debit to Salaries Payable?

7. What amount of the salaries paid on January 4 is an expense for 19X5?

Deferred Revenue

C *What is deferred revenue?* Revenue received before it is earned is **deferred revenue.** The term **deferred** means that the recording of revenue is postponed until it is earned. Until the revenue is earned, the amount received is recorded as a liability in the accounting records.

The current liabilities studied to this point have been satisfied (paid) with cash. Accounts payable were paid in cash, the notes payable and interest payable were paid in cash, and so on. Now we discuss current liabilities satisfied by providing a service or product. Examples of this are as follows.

• An owner of an office building receives rent four months in advance from a tenant.
• A magazine publisher receives payment for a two-year subscription in advance.
• An insurance company requires the policyholder to pay the premiums on an insurance policy months or years in advance.
• A company receives partial payment for work to be completed in the future.

The examples above have one thing in common: Revenue is received before it is earned.

Recording Deferred Revenue. The procedure to record deferred revenue can best be explained by an example. Assume that the Gallo Company permits the Price Mart to install a billboard on its property. On August 1, 19X4, the Price Mart pays $720 for one year's rental in advance for the use of the land. The Gallo Company has received the money and must rent the property for the entire year.

The $720 received for the rent is recorded in the cash receipts journal. The cash account is debited for $720. The $720 is credited to Unearned Rental Revenue, a liability account. The term *unearned* is used because the Gallo Company has received the rent but has not earned the revenue. The entry to record the receipt of deferred revenue is shown here.

To Record Deferred Rental Revenue:
Debit: Cash
Credit: Unearned Rental Revenue.

				CASH RECEIPTS JOURNAL				Page 7
DATE	ACCOUNT CREDITED	EXPLANATION	POST. REF.	GENERAL LEDGER CREDIT	ACCOUNTS RECEIVABLE CREDIT	SALES DISCOUNT DEBIT	NET CASH DEBIT	
19X4 Aug. 1	Unearned Rental Revenue	Price Mart, one year rent	241	720 00			720 00	

Cash	101	Unearned Rental Revenue	241
19X4 Aug. 1 720		19X4 Aug. 1 CR72 720	

Adjusting Deferred Revenue. At the end of the accounting period, an adjusting entry is needed to transfer unearned revenue from the liability account to a revenue account. If the adjusting entry is not made, the liabilities for the current accounting period will be over- stated and revenue will be understated. Also, owner's equity will be understated.

On December 31, 19X4, the Gallo Company has earned 5 months' rent (August through December). The rent for 1 year is $720. The rent for 1 month is $60 ($720 ÷ 12). The revenue earned for 5 months is $300 ($60 × 5). The adjusting entry is found here.

December 31, 19X4 The Gallo Company recorded $300 of deferred rental revenue as rent earned for 5 months.

	GENERAL JOURNAL			Page _1_
DATE	**ACCOUNT TITLE AND EXPLANATION**	**POST. REF.**	**DEBIT**	**CREDIT**
19X4 Dec. 31	Unearned Rental Revenue	241	300 00	
	Rental Revenue	493		300 00
	Record rental revenue.			

Unearned Rental Revenue	241	Rental Revenue	493
19X4 Dec. 31 300	19X4 Aug. 1 720		19X4 Dec. 31 300

Adjusting Entry for Deferred Revenue

Note that the adjusting entry includes a debit to the Unearned Rental Revenue liability account and a credit to the Rental Revenue account. The debit reduces the liability, and the credit shows the por- tion of the total rent ($720) that has been earned ($300) in 19X4.

After the adjusting entry is posted, the Unearned Rental Revenue account shows the amount of deferred revenue ($420) that has not yet been earned. The Rental Revenue account shows the amount of revenue earned during the current accounting period ($300). Rental Revenue is closed into the Income Summary account. Unearned Rental Revenue is a liability account and remains open until all the deferred revenue has been earned.

Activity C. Answer the following questions about recording and adjusting deferred revenue. Refer to the text and illustrations on pages 427 to 429.

1. How much billboard rent does the Price Mart pay to the Gallo Company on August 1?
2. What period of time does this rent payment cover?
3. Which entry is made to record the receipt of the rent payment? Which journal is used to record this entry?

4. Is part of this rent payment unearned on December 31? If so, how much?
5. Is an adjusting entry made on December 31? If so, which account is debited? Which account is credited?

Topic 3   Problems

11-6. Record the following transactions in the appropriate journals.

Nov. 23 Issued a 30-day 8 percent note payable to the Wendy Company for an account payable for $525.
Dec. 1 Received $900 in advance for 3 months' rental on unused warehouse space.
     11 Issued a 60-day 8½ percent note payable to David Miller for purchases on credit for $820.
     23 Paid the note owed to the Wendy Company (Check 115).
     31 Recorded the accrued in-

terest owed on the note given to David Miller.
Dec. 31 Recorded accrued salaries of $329.
     31 Recorded adjusting entry for unearned rental income.
Jan. 4 Paid the weekly payroll of $1,200. The payroll taxes withheld were $73.56, and the employees' income taxes were $216 (Check 217).
Feb. 9 Paid the note issued to David Miller (Check 230).

11-7. The Xeno Company completed the transactions found here. Record the adjusting entries, payments for notes payable, and the January payroll, assuming all entries are made on the proper dates.

Additional Information

FICA taxes are $91.95; union dues are $60; and employee's income taxes are $270.

July 31 Issued a 1-year 9 percent note payable to Phillips Tile Company for an account payable for $600.

Aug. 15 Issued a 4-month 9 percent note payable to Creative Paper for merchandise purchased for $400 on credit.

Dec. 1 Received $1,200 in advance for 1 years' rental on unused warehouse space from Beltway Tire Company.

Dec. 16 Issued a 90-day 10 percent note payable to Longhorn Motors for a used pickup truck for $600.

31 Recorded 2 days' accrued salaries for the weekly payroll. (Weekly payroll is $1,500, and the end of the pay period is January 4.)

Topic 4
Accounting for Long-Term Liabilities

The Nature of Long-Term Liabilities

Examples of Long-Term Liabilities:
- mortgages on land
- mortgages on buildings
- bonds to finance major expansions

A *What is a long-term liability?* A **long-term liability** is a debt that is not due within a year. Examples are mortgages on land and buildings, and bonds issued to finance major expansions. Mortgages and bonds create long-term debts that must be paid, along with interest payments.

A review of a balance sheet for the Gallo Company shows that various kinds of liabilities were incurred. For instance, merchandise was purchased on open account. A short-term promissory note was exchanged for an account payable. And liabilities were incurred for accrued salaries and interest. Each of the above is a current liability.

The balance sheet for the Gallo Company also lists Mortgage Payable, a long-term liability. In Topic 4 the focus is on the accounting for such long-term liabilities as mortgages and bonds.

Mortgages. A **mortgage** is a long-term debt in which the borrower signs a note agreeing to pay the **face value** (amount of money maker promises to pay) of the note plus interest to the payee over 20 or 30 years or more. The borrower ''pledges'' land and buildings (real estate) as security for the note.

Bonds. **Bonds** are long-term debts for which the issuing company receives cash in return for a promise to pay the face or par value of the bond over an extended time period. The **par value** of the bond is the amount that must be paid at the maturity date.

Bonds mature (become payable) over 5, 10, or 20 years or more. Bonds are also negotiable. Thus bonds can pass freely from person to person by endorsement.

Michael Weisbrot

A long-term liability, such as a mortgage for a house, is paid over a long period of time along with the interest.

Most bonds are issued (sold) at a par value of $1,000. The bonds of large corporations are bought and sold on the securities exchanges, such as the New York Stock Exchange, American Stock Exchange, Pacific Stock Exchange, and Chicago Board Options Trade.

The **market value** is the price investors are willing to pay for a bond. The market value may be more or less than the face value and is stated in percentage form. If a bond is selling for $1,000, it is quoted on the exchange at 100. If it is selling at $1,030, it is quoted at 103. And if it is selling for $970, it is quoted at 97.

Bonds have many characteristics. The characteristics are found by reading the bond indenture. A **bond indenture** is the written agreement, passed between the issuing company and the bondholder or investor, that describes the bond's characteristics.

Secured Bonds. Bonds that are protected by a mortgage on real estate are called **secured bonds.** The security is often identified by statements such as *First Mortgage, 15 percent, 19X7 bonds.*

Unsecured Bonds. Bonds that are not protected by a mortgage are called **unsecured** or **debenture bonds.** Such bonds are, in effect, only a promise to pay. The value depends on the credit of the company issuing them.

Types of Bonds:
- Secured bonds
- Unsecured bonds
- Registered bonds
- Serial bonds
- Fixed maturity bonds

Registered Bonds. When the name of a bondholder is registered with the issuing company, the bond is called a **registered bond.** Interest is then paid by check to the bondholder. A record showing the names and addresses of all bondholders is kept by the issuing corporation or its agent. When registered bonds are transferred, the company must be notified so that the new bondholder can receive the interest payment.

Serial Bonds. Bonds that mature at different times are known as **serial bonds.** For example, a $200,000 issue of 20-year serial bonds may be arranged so that bonds amounting to $10,000 mature at the end of each year of the 20-year period.

Fixed Maturity Bonds. Bonds that have a single maturity date are known as **fixed maturity bonds.** Thus a $200,000 issue of 20-year fixed maturity bonds would all be payable on the same date.

Activity A. Which of the following accounts can be classified as a long-term liability? Answer *Yes* or *No* as appropriate. Refer to the text and illustrations on pages 430 to 432.
EXAMPLE: Salaries Payable—No
1. Mortgage Payable
2. Secured Bonds (due in ten years)
3. Common Stock
4. Payments due on merchandise purchased
5. Serial Bonds (due over the next ten years)
6. Accounts Payable
7. Preferred Stock
8. Unsecured Bonds (due in four years)
9. Interest Payable

Accounting for Mortgages

B *What are the accounting procedures for recording and paying mortgages?* The amount of the note issued when obtaining a mortgage is credited to Mortgage Payable, a long-term liability. The recording of a mortgage payable for the original purchase of the Gallo Company's land and building is found here. It is necessary to record the entry in both the cash payments journal and general journal.

CASH PAYMENTS JOURNAL Page *21*

DATE		ACCOUNT DEBITED	EXPLANATION	CHECK NO.	POST. REF.	GENERAL LEDGER DEBIT	ACCOUNTS PAYABLE DEBIT	PURCHASES DISCOUNT CREDIT	NET CASH CREDIT
19—									
Jan.	31	Building	Purchased real estate	101	—	38,400 00			38,400 00

GENERAL JOURNAL					Page 6
DATE	ACCOUNT TITLE AND EXPLANATION	POST. REF.	DEBIT	CREDIT	

DATE		ACCOUNT TITLE AND EXPLANATION	POST. REF.	DEBIT	CREDIT
19—					
Jan.	31	Building	157	70,000 00	
		Land	159	21,900 00	
		Mortgage Payable	252		53,500 00
		Cash	—		38,400 00
		Purchased real estate.			

The assets Land and Building are recorded separately because the building depreciates and the land does not. A cash payment of $38,400 is made. And a long-term liability, Mortgage Payable, is incurred for the remainder of the purchase price ($53,500). (In practice, the mortgage company would forward $53,500 directly to the seller.)

The mortgage note requires that the $53,500 plus 8 percent interest be paid over a 20-year period. Monthly payments are $401.25. Each payment includes interest on the unpaid balance of the mortgage note and a reduction of the Mortgage Payable liability account. A schedule for three monthly payments is illustrated here. The schedule shows how the amounts of interest and the mortgage payable change over the life of the mortgage. The date of purchase is January 31, 19—.

	Monthly Payment	Interest for One Month At 8 Percent of Unpaid Balance	Reduction in Long-Term Liability	Mortgage Payable (Principal of Note)
Principal Balance				$53,500.00
Payment on Feb. 28	$401.25	$356.66	$44.59	53,455.41
Payment on March 31	401.25	356.37	44.88	53,410.53
Payment on April 30	401.25	356.07	45.18	53,365.35

Supplied with a schedule like the one shown above or with similar information, the accountant can now record the monthly mortgage payments.

As the unpaid principal of the mortgage note decreases, the portion of each payment applied to interest and mortgage payable changes. As the principal decreases, the amount of interest decreases. More of the payment is used to reduce the liability.

		CASH PAYMENTS JOURNAL					Page 23	
DATE	**ACCOUNT DEBITED**	**EXPLANATION**	**CHECK NO.**	**POST. REF.**	**GENERAL LEDGER DEBIT**		**NET CASH CREDIT**	
19— Feb. 28	*Interest Expense . . .* *Mortgage Payable . .*	{*Monthly mortgages* {*payment*	116	591 252	356 66 44 59		401 25	} First Monthly Payment
19— Mar. 31	*Interest Expense . . .* *Mortgage Payable . .*	{*Monthly mortgages* {*payment*	172	591 252	356 37 44 88		401 25	} Second Monthly Payment

Activity B. Answer the following questions about accounting for mortgages. Refer to the text and illustrations on pages 432 to 434.

1. What is the cost of the building?

2. What is the cost of the land?

3. What is the cash payment on these assets?

4. How is the balance to be paid? What is the balance amount?

5. Which journals are used to record the purchase of the two assets?

6. Which accounts are debited? Which accounts are credited?

7. What is the monthly payment on the mortgage?

8. What is the interest rate on the mortgage?

9. What is the balance owed on the mortgage on April 30?

Accounting for a Bond Issue

C *What are the management decisions related to issuing bonds?* A bond issue involves the need for large sums of capital (money). Before issuing bonds, management will consider many factors. Some are described here.

Equity Capital Versus Debt Capital. Large businesses needing to increase their capital must decide what the source of new capital will be. There are two sources available: equity capital or debt capital. **Equity capital** arises by reinvesting net income or from investments by owners. Thus, because the business uses its already existing funds, equity capital might be viewed as self-financing. **Debt capital,** however, is obtained by borrowing from outside the business. Debt capital arises through the sale of bonds.

Two sources of new capital are equity capital and debt capital.

The management decisions concerning debt capital as a source of new money focus on the following concerns.

• *A bond issue is a debt to the issuing company.* Thus creditors' claims against assets are increased.

• *A bond issue requires regular interest payments over a long time period.* The interest payments may cause a serious drain on cash, particularly when added to the cash demands for daily operations.

• *The bond issue must be repaid at some future date.* The payment of bonds requires a large cash outlay that must be added to cash needs for interest payments and daily operations.

Underwriter's Fees. A company does not usually sell its own bonds. Instead, the bonds are placed with an underwriter, such as a bank, trust company, or brokerage firm. An **underwriter** is a company that purchases the bonds at a set price. The underwriter then sells individual bonds to the public at a slightly higher price. By selling to an underwriter, the issuing company receives cash on a specified date. However, there is a reduced amount of cash received by the issuing company. The reduction in cash received must be considered in advance.

Setting Interest Rates. Setting the interest rate is a problem for companies selling bonds.

The interest on bonds must be paid over a long time period. Thus management will attempt to set the interest rate as low as possible. On the other hand, purchasers of bonds seek both security and maximum return on their investments. They will attempt to set the interest rate as high as possible. Thus there is often a difference between the interest rate set by management and the rate investors are willing to accept. The rate of interest set by management is known as the **contract interest rate.** The rate of interest investors are willing to accept is known as the **effective interest rate.** When there is a difference between the two rates, it may be necessary for bonds to be sold at more or less than the par value.

Debt Capital:
• Increases creditors' claims
• Requires interest payments
• Must be repaid

Activity C. Answer the following questions on equity capital and debt capital. Classify the following items as equity capital (E), debt capital (D), or neither equity nor debt capital (N). Refer to the text and illustrations from pages 434 and 435.

EXAMPLE: Bank loan—D

1. Profits retained in the business
2. Mortgages
3. Debenture bonds
4. Notes receivable
5. Withdrawal by owner
6. Accounts receivable
7. Serial bonds
8. Investment by owners
9. Machinery
10. Accrued salaries payable

Accounting for Bonds Sold at Par Value

D *What accounting entries are necessary for bonds sold at par value?* The accounting entries for bonds sold at par value include recording the bond issue, semiannual interest payments, and the bond retirement.

Par Value		Number of Bonds		Bond Issue
$1,000	×	100	=	$100,000

Recording the Bond Issue. Assume the Pine-Gold Company issues 20-year 10 percent bonds for $100,000. Thus 100 bonds are issued for $1,000 each. The entry to record the issue is a debit to Cash and a credit to Bonds Payable, a long-term liability.

	CASH RECEIPTS JOURNAL						Page 35

DATE	ACCOUNT CREDITED	EXPLANATION	POST. REF.	GENERAL LEDGER CREDIT	ACCOUNTS RECEIVABLE CREDIT	SALES DISCOUNT DEBIT	NET CASH DEBIT
19— July 1	Bonds Payable . . .	20-year, 10 percent issue.	253	100,000 00			100,000 00

Recording Interest Payments. Interest on the Pine-Gold bonds is paid semiannually. Semiannual interest on the Pine-Gold bonds is $5,000. The interest payment is recorded in the cash payments journal.

	CASH PAYMENTS JOURNAL							Page 37

DATE	ACCOUNT DEBITED	EXPLANATION	CHECK NO.	POST. REF.	GENERAL LEDGER DEBIT	ACCOUNTS PAYABLE DEBIT	PURCHASES DISCOUNT CREDIT	NET CASH CREDIT
19— Dec. 31	Interest Expense. . .	Semiannual interest	217	591	5,000 00			5,000 00

The debit to Interest Expense is an operating expense. The Pine-Gold Company must pay interest to bondholders for use of the bondholders' capital (money). The actual payment of cash to the bondholders depends on the bond indenture. If the bonds are registered, the $5,000 could be placed in a special checking account. Checks would be drawn and mailed to individual bondholders. Or interest could be paid at the Pine-Gold Company's bank. In this case the $5,000 would be sent to the bank. The bank would then make payments to the bondholders.

Recording the Bond Retirement. A corporation may establish a bond sinking fund. The **bond sinking fund** is a fund used to assure the investors that the bond issue will be paid when due. The corporation pays an amount of money into the sinking fund each year. The

Bond Sinking Fund is an asset account. The cash in the Bond Sinking Fund is normally invested. Thus the Bond Sinking Fund account is classified in the asset category Investments. After 20 years, the bond issue will reach maturity and be retired or canceled.

The Pine-Gold Company will pay approximately $5,000 for each of the 20 years. At the maturity date in 20 years, the fund will have $100,000 ($5,000 × 20). This is the amount of cash needed to pay the bonds.

The cash placed in the fund over a 20-year period earns interest because it is reinvested. Thus Pine-Gold actually pays less than $5,000 into the fund each year. The accumulated interest plus the total cash paid into the fund must equal $100,000 at the maturity date of the bonds (20 years after issue date).

The bond sinking fund is usually established with a *trustee*. The **trustee** is an outside agent, such as a bank or agent handling the bond issue.

The entry to record the deposit to the bond sinking fund is recorded in the cash payments journal. The entry is made annually. The entry is a debit to the Bond Sinking Fund and a credit to Cash.

CASH PAYMENTS JOURNAL Page 40

DATE		ACCOUNT DEBITED	EXPLANATION	CHECK NO.	POST. REF.	GENERAL LEDGER DEBIT	ACCOUNTS PAYABLE DEBIT	PURCHASES DISCOUNT CREDIT	NET CASH CREDIT
19— July	1	Bond Sinking Fund	Annual deposit . . .	723	145	5,000 00			5,000 00

Activity D. Answer the following questions about bonds sold at par value and bond sinking funds. Refer to the text and illustrations on pages 435 to 437.

1. How many bonds are sold by the Pine-Gold Company on July 1?

2. What is the interest rate on the bonds?

3. What is the par value (amount) of each bond?

4. How much does the Pine-Gold Company receive for each bond?

5. What is the total amount of bonds sold?

6. Which journal is used to record the sale of the bonds? Which account is debited? credited? For what amount?

7. What is the amount of annual interest due on these bonds? What is the amount of the semiannual interest?

8. Which journal is used to record the semiannual interest payments? What account is debited? credited?

9. What is a bond sinking fund?

10. Describe the entry to record the deposit to the bond sinking fund.

Bond   Contract   Annual
Issue   × Rate   = Interest

$100,000 × 0.10   = $10,000

Semiannual Interest

$10,000 ÷ $\frac{6}{12}$ = $5,000

Number of   Dollar value
bonds issued = of bond issue
                 par value

100 = $\frac{\$100,000}{\$1,000}$

Discount   Par value   Cash
for each = for each   Received
bond   bond   − for each
                         bond

$20 = $1,000 − $980

Total   Discount   Number
         = for each × of bonds
discount   bond   issued

$2,000 = $20 × 100

$100,000 par value
− 2,000 discount
$ 98,000 cash received

Date of   Date of
issue   Payment
  ↓   ↓
       20 years
|_____|
$98,000 $100,000
Received   Paid

Accounting for Bonds Sold at a Discount

 *Why are bonds sold at a discount?* A bond issue sold at less than par value is said to be sold at a **discount.** Sometimes buyers are not willing to buy bonds at their par value. For example, a company offering bonds may not have a top rating, and so investors may think that the company will be unable to pay its debts.

The Pine-Gold Company offers the $100,000 bond issue at 10 percent. Thus the company is willing to borrow $100,000 and pay $10,000 ($100,000 × 0.10) per year for the use of investors' money. If investors are not willing to purchase the bonds at 100 percent of par value, the company must withdraw the issue or sell it at less than par value. If the best price obtainable for the bonds is 98 percent of par ($980 for each $1,000 bond), the discount is $20 per bond, or $2,000 for the entire issue. (100 × $20)

By issuing the bonds at 98, the company obtains $98,000. That is, it obtains the par value of the bonds ($100,000) minus the discount ($2,000). The company must pay the creditors (investors) $100,000 at the date of maturity. Thus $98,000 is received, and 20 years later $100,000 is paid. For accounting purposes, the discount becomes an expense of doing business over the life of the bond issue. On the date of the issue, the discount is debited to a contra liability account entitled Bond Discount. The accounting entry to record the sale of bonds at a discount is illustrated here.

July 1 Sold $100,000 of Pine-Gold Company 20-year 10 percent bonds at 98.

	GENERAL JOURNAL			Page 12

DATE	ACCOUNT TITLE AND EXPLANATION	POST. REF.	DEBIT	CREDIT
19—				
July 1	Cash	—	98,000 00	
	Bond Discount	254	2,000 00	
	Bonds Payable	253		100,000 00
	Sold bonds at 98.			

	CASH RECEIPTS JOURNAL						Page 38

DATE	ACCOUNT CREDITED	EXPLANATION	POST. REF.	GENERAL LEDGER CREDIT	ACCOUNTS RECEIVABLE CREDIT	SALES DISCOUNT DEBIT	NET CASH DEBIT
19—							
July 1	Bonds Payable . . .		—	98,000 00			98,000 00

As you analyze the entries, focus on the following points.
- *The par value of the bond issue ($100,000) is credited to Bonds Payable, the long-term liability.* This must be paid in cash at maturity.
- *The discount is debited to Bond Discount, a contra liability account.* A **contra account** is used to record deductions in the balance of another account. Bond Discount is used to reduce the balance of Bonds Payable to its carrying value of $98,000. **Carrying value** is the difference between the balances of Bonds Payable and Bond Discount.
- *The dash (—) on the Bonds Payable line in the cash receipts journal and on the Cash line in the general journal indicates that the amounts are not posted.*

Bond Discount and Annual Interest Charges. The annual interest expense for bonds sold at par value is the contract interest. When bonds are sold at a discount, the annual interest expense is the contract interest *plus* a portion of the bond discount.

In our illustration, the annual interest payment is $10,000. To obtain the annual interest expense for the Pine-Gold Company, we must add $\frac{1}{20}$ of the bond discount each year to $10,000. The annual interest expense is thus $10,100. It is made up of two elements: the $10,000 interest payment plus $100 for the bond discount.

Two accounting entries are necessary to record the semiannual interest payment. The first records the semiannual interest payment. The second records the semiannual transfer of Bond Discount to expense.

December 31 Pine-Gold Company recorded the semiannual interest payment.

$$\frac{\text{Carrying}}{\text{value}} = \frac{\text{Bonds}}{\text{payable}} - \frac{\text{Bond}}{\text{discount}}$$

$$\$98,000 = \$100,000 - \$2,000$$

Annual Interest Expense:
Bonds sold at a discount

$$\frac{\text{Annual}}{\text{interest}} = \frac{\text{Contract}}{\text{interest}} + \frac{\text{Portion}}{\text{of bond}}_{\text{discount}}$$

$$\$10,000 = \$10,000 + \$100$$

$$\frac{\text{Contract}}{\text{interest}} = \frac{\text{Par}}{\text{value}} \times \frac{\text{Contract}}{\text{interest}}_{\text{rate}}$$

$$\$10,100 = \$100,000 \times \frac{10}{100}$$

$$\frac{\text{Portion of}}{\text{bond}}_{\text{discount}} = \frac{\text{Bond}}{\text{discount}}_{\text{Life of}}^{\text{bond issue}}$$

$$\$100 = \frac{\$2,000}{20 \text{ years}}$$

		CASH PAYMENTS JOURNAL							Page 45
DATE	ACCOUNT DEBITED	EXPLANATION	CHECK NO.	POST. REF.	GENERAL LEDGER DEBIT	ACCOUNTS PAYABLE DEBIT	PURCHASES DISCOUNT CREDIT	NET CASH CREDIT
19— Dec. 31	Interest Expense....	Semiannual interest	470	591	5,000 00				5,000 00

	GENERAL JOURNAL		Page 15	
DATE	ACCOUNT TITLE AND EXPLANATION	POST. REF.	DEBIT	CREDIT
19— Dec. 31	Interest Expense. . . . . Bond Discount . . . . Recorded semiannual transfer of bond discount.	591 254	50 00	50 00

Cash		101		Bonds Payable		253
	Dec. 31	5,000			July 1	100,000

Bond Discount			254		Interest Expense		591
July 1	2,000	Dec. 31	50	Dec. 31	5,000		
				Dec. 31	50		

Record Semiannual Interest Payment on Bonds Sold at a Discount

The entry to record semiannual interest includes two elements: the semiannual interest payment and one-half of the annual transfer of Bond Discount. Also, the decrease in the Bond Discount account increases the carrying value of the bonds.

INCREASE IN CARRYING VALUE OF BONDS

Before Semiannual Interest Payment

Bonds Payable	253		Bond Discount	254			Carrying Value
	100,000	+		2,000		=	$98,000

After Semiannual Interest Payment

Bonds Payable	253		Bond Discount	254			Carrying Value
	100,000	+		2,000	50	=	$98,050

Accounting Concept:
Annual interest expense is greater than contract interest expense when bonds are sold at a discount.

Activity E. Answer the following questions about bonds sold at a discount. Refer to the text and illustrations on pages 438 to 440.

1. How many bonds are sold by the Pine-Gold Company on July 1?
2. What is the interest rate on these bonds?
3. What is the par value (amount) of each bond?
4. How much does the Pine-Gold Company receive for each bond sold?
5. What is the total par value of the bonds sold? What is the total amount of money received for the bonds?
6. What is the difference between the par value of each bond and the amount of cash received for each bond called?
7. Which journals are used to record the sale of bonds at a discount?
8. Which accounts are debited and which are credited for the bond sale? For what amounts?
9. What is the amount of semiannual interest expense? Which journal is used to record the interest payment? Which account is debited? credited?

10. What is the purpose of the December 31 entry recorded in the general journal?

11. Which account is debited in the general journal? credited? For what amount?

Accounting for Bonds Sold at a Premium

F *Why are bonds sold at a premium?* Bonds sold for more than 100 percent of par value are said to be sold at a **premium.** A premium arises when the effective interest rate in the marketplace is greater than the contract interest rate. Let's change our illustration and assume that the bonds are sold at 102, or $1,020 for each bond. The entry to record the sale appears as follows.

$$\frac{\text{Premium}}{\text{for each}} = \frac{\text{Cash}}{\text{received}} - \frac{\text{Par}}{\text{value}}$$
$$\text{bond} \qquad \text{bond}$$

$$\$20 = \$1,020 - \$1,000$$

$$\frac{\text{Total}}{\text{premium}} = \frac{\text{Premium}}{\text{for each}} \times \frac{\text{Number}}{\text{of bonds}}$$
$$\text{bond} \qquad \text{issued}$$

$$\$2,000 = \$20 \times 100$$

July 1 Sold $100,000 of Pine-Gold Company 20-year 10 percent bonds at 102.

		CASH RECEIPTS JOURNAL						Page 39
DATE	ACCOUNT CREDITED	EXPLANATION	POST. REF.	GENERAL LEDGER CREDIT	ACCOUNTS RECEIVABLE CREDIT	SALES DISCOUNT DEBIT	NET CASH DEBIT
19— July 1	Bonds Payable ... Bond Premium ...	{Sold 20-year, 10% bonds at 102	253 259	100,000 00 2,000 00			102,000 00

Cash	101		Bonds Payable	253		Bond Premium	259
July 1	102,000			July 1	100,000		July 1	2,000

Record Bonds Sold at a Premium

As you analyze the above transaction, note that $102,000 is received and $100,000 is to be repaid 20 years later. Why are creditors willing to pay $102,000 and receive $100,000? The answer is that investors are willing to pay a premium because the contract interest rate is apparently higher than the effective interest rate.

How should the $2,000 bond premium be viewed? The answer is that the Bond Premium is a long-term liability closely associated with Bonds Payable. Investors give the company $2,000 of the interest they will receive over 20 years. The $2,000 interest advance is a liability that is returned to investors in semiannual interest payments.

How is the carrying value computed for bonds sold at a premium? The answer is that *carrying value* is the sum of bonds payable plus the premium. In our illustration, the carrying value is $102,000.

$$\frac{\text{Carrying}}{\text{value}} = \frac{\text{Bonds}}{\text{payable}} + \frac{\text{Bond}}{\text{premium}}$$

$$\$102,000 = \$100,000 + \$2,000$$

Annual Interest Expense: Bonds Sold at a Premium

$$\text{Annual interest expense} = \text{Contract interest} - \text{Portion of bond premium}$$

$$\$9,900 = \$10,000 - \$100$$

$$\text{Portion of bond premium} = \frac{\text{Bond premium}}{\text{Life of bond}}$$

$$\$100 = \frac{\$2,000}{20 \text{ years}}$$

Bond Premium and Annual Interest Charges. The annual interest expense for bonds sold at a premium is the contract interest minus a ratable portion of the bond premium.

In our illustration, the contract interest is $10,000. To obtain the annual interest expense, we must deduct $\frac{1}{20}$ of the bond premium from $10,000 ($9,900 = $10,000 − $100).

The company must pay bond interest semiannually. The following accounting entry is necessary to record the semiannual interest payment.

December 31 Recorded the semiannual interest payment.

			CASH PAYMENTS JOURNAL							Page 47
DATE	ACCOUNT DEBITED	EXPLANATION	CHECK NO.	POST. REF.	GENERAL LEDGER DEBIT	ACCOUNTS PAYABLE DEBIT	PURCHASES DISCOUNT CREDIT			NET CASH CREDIT
19— Dec. 31	Interest Expense.... Bond Premium	Semiannual interest payment	167	591 259	4,950 00 50 00					5,000 00

Cash			101		Bonds Payable		253
	Dec. 31	5,000				July 1	100,000

Bond Premium			259		Interest Expense		591
Dec. 31	50	July 1	2,000	Dec. 31	4,950		

Record Semiannual Interest Payment on Bonds Sold at a Premium

The entry to record semiannual interest includes two elements: the semiannual interest payment ($5,000) minus one-half of the annual transfer of Bond Premium ($50). Also, the decrease in the Bond Premium account decreases the carrying value of the bonds.

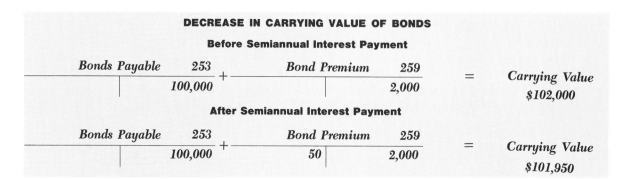

DECREASE IN CARRYING VALUE OF BONDS

Before Semiannual Interest Payment

Bonds Payable	253		Bond Premium	259		Carrying Value
	100,000	+		2,000	=	$102,000

After Semiannual Interest Payment

Bonds Payable	253		Bond Premium	259		Carrying Value
	100,000	+	50	2,000	=	$101,950

Activity F. Answer the following questions about bonds sold at a premium. Refer to the text and illustrations on pages 441 and 442.

1. How many bonds are sold by the Pine-Gold Company on July 1?

2. What is the interest rate on these bonds?

3. What is the face value (amount) of each bond?

4. How much does the Pine-Gold Company receive for each bond?

5. What is the total face value of the bonds sold? What is the total amount of money received for the bonds?

6. What is the difference between the face value of each bond and the amount of cash received for each bond called?

7. Which journal is used to record the sale of these bonds at a premium?

8. Which accounts are debited? credited? For what amounts?

9. What is the amount of semiannual interest? Which journal is used to record the interest payment? What account is debited? credited?

Topic 4   Problems

11-8. Record the following transactions in the appropriate journal for the Kelley Company.

Jan. 1 Sold $50,000 of 20-year 9 percent bonds at face value. Interest payment dates are July 1 and December 31.

July 1 Paid semiannual interest payment on bonds sold on January 1 (Check 117).

1 Sold $100,000 of 20-year 8 percent bonds at 98. Interest is payable on July 1 and December 31, each year.

Aug. 1 Bought a $50,000 building by making a $20,000 down payment and signing a mortgage for the balance (Check 130). (An independent appraiser indicates that the land is worth $10,000.)

Sept. 1 Made a $450 payment on the mortgage; interest $200, principal $250 (Check 180).

Oct. 1 Sold $50,000 of 20-year $9\frac{1}{2}$ percent bonds at 101. Interest is payable on April 1 and October 1, each year.

1 Made a $450 payment on the mortgage; interest $249.50, principal, $200.50 (Check 210).

Nov. 1 Made a $450 payment on the mortgage; interest $249.00, principal, $201 (Check 230).

Dec. 1 Made a $450 payment on the mortgage; interest $248.50, principal $201.50 (Check 265).

31 Paid interest on bonds sold on January 1 (Check 280).

31 Paid interest on bonds sold on July 1 (Check 281).

31 Recorded accrued interest on bonds sold on October 1.

**Worksheet Sections for
Single Proprietorship:**
- Unadjusted Trial Balance
- Adjustments
- Adjusted Trial Balance
- Income Statement
- Balance Sheet

Topic 5
General Accounting Subsystem for a Single Proprietorship

A *What are the sections of a worksheet for a single proprietorship?*
The sections of a worksheet for a single proprietorship are the Unadjusted Trial Balance, Adjustments, Adjusted Trial Balance, Income Statement, and Balance Sheet. The discussion in this topic focuses on how the new accounting content comes together in the general accounting subsystem. You will learn about the worksheet, financial statements, and adjusting and closing entries for a single proprietorship.

Worksheet for a Single Proprietorship

The worksheet for the Gallo Company, prepared as of December 31, is shown on pages 446 and 447. The worksheet indicates the accounting period, lists account titles and account numbers, and includes five additional sections.

Unadjusted Trial Balance Section. The amounts found in the Unadjusted Trial Balance section are taken directly from the general ledger, as of December 31.

Adjustments Section. The purpose of the Adjustments section is to bring each account up to date. Thus the accountant carefully analyzes each account on the Unadjusted Trial Balance to see if it is current. When an account balance is not current, the proper increase or decrease is made.
- *Adjustments to Current Assets.* The Adjustments section enables the accountant to bring various accounts up to date. Thus the adjustments labeled (a) to (e) bring current assets and various other accounts up to date. For example, the (a) adjustment increases the current asset Interest Receivable and increases the revenue account Interest Revenue by $77. The $77 is accrued interest for the Notes Receivable ($10) and bonds held as Marketable Securities ($67). The (b) adjustment increases the contra asset Allowance for Doubtful Accounts and increases the expense account Uncollectible Accounts Expense by $800. The $800 is the estimate for uncollectible accounts.
- *Adjustments to Plant and Equipment.* The adjustments labeled (f) to (i) record depreciation for the current accounting period. For example, adjustment (f) increases the contra asset account Accumulated Depreciation—Office Equipment and increases the expense account Depreciation Expense—Office Equipment by $500. Adjustments (g) to (i) are similar to the Office Equipment adjustment.

- *Adjustments to Current Liabilities.* Adjustments (j) to (l) bring the balance of current liability accounts up to date. Adjustments (j) and (k) are examples of accrued liabilities and accrued expenses. That is, each records liabilities and expenses that have been *incurred but not recorded.* Adjustment (j) increases Interest Expense and the current liability Interest Payable by $15. The $15 is accrued interest on the Notes Payable for one month. The (k) adjustment records accrued salaries.

The (l) adjustment affects a current liability and is an example of deferred revenue. That is, it adjusts revenue that has been *received but not earned.* The (l) adjustment decreases the current liability Unearned Rental Revenue and increases the revenue account Rental Revenue by $300.

Adjusted Trial Balance Section. The amounts in the Adjusted Trial Balance section are found by combining amounts in the Unadjusted Trial Balance and Adjustments sections. After the accountant combines all amounts, the Adjusted Trial Balance section is footed to determine if the debit and credit columns are equal.

Income Statement and Balance Sheet Sections. The amounts in the Income Statement and Balance Sheet sections are found by analyzing the Adjusted Trial Balance columns. That is, the accountant analyzes each account on the Adjusted Trial Balance and determines if it is an Income Statement or Balance Sheet account. The accountant then extends the amount to the proper debit or credit column.

Determining the Net Income or Net Loss

After each amount has been transferred to the Income Statement or Balance Sheet section, the four money columns are totaled. The amounts are not equal, because the business has earned either a Net Income or a Net Loss.

Net Income. If the total of the Income Statement credit column is greater than the debit column, a net income has been earned. In our illustration, the Gallo Company earns a net income of $40,082. That is, as a result of business activity, there is a net increase in owner's equity.

The amount of the net income is computed by placing the total of the Income Statement debit column ($232,195) beneath the credit column ($272,277). The net income (the difference between the debit and credit columns) is then moved beneath the credit column of the Balance Sheet section. This is done to show that a net income increases owner's equity and owner's equity increases on the credit side. Finally,

INCOME STATEMENT		BALANCE SHEET	
DEBIT	CREDIT	DEBIT	CREDIT
232,195	272,277	187,312	147,230
	232,195		
	40,082		40,082
		187,312	187,312

COMPUTING NET INCOME ON THE WORKSHEET

GALLO COMPANY
Worksheet
For the Year Ended December 31, 19—

#	ACCOUNT TITLE	ACCT. NO.	UNADJUSTED TRIAL BALANCE DEBIT	UNADJUSTED TRIAL BALANCE CREDIT	ADJUSTMENTS DEBIT	ADJUSTMENTS CREDIT	ADJUSTED TRIAL BALANCE DEBIT	ADJUSTED TRIAL BALANCE CREDIT	INCOME STATEMENT DEBIT	INCOME STATEMENT CREDIT	BALANCE SHEET DEBIT	BALANCE SHEET CREDIT	#
1	Cash	101	33,000				33,000				33,000		1
2	Petty Cash	102	50				50				50		2
3	Change Fund	103	25				25				25		3
4	Marketable Securities	111	15,190				15,190				15,190		4
5	Notes Receivable	121	1,500				1,500				1,500		5
6	Interest Receivable	122			(a) 77		77				77		6
7	Accounts Receivable	131	9,000				9,000				9,000		7
8	Allowance for Doubtful Accounts	132		100		(b) 800		900				900	8
9	Merchandise Inventory	141	7,000			(c) 2,000	5,000				5,000		9
10	Prepaid Insurance	142	600			(d) 150	450				450		10
11	Supplies on Hand	143	400			(e) 280	120				120		11
12	Office Equipment	151	3,000				3,000				3,000		12
13	Acc. Depr.—Office Equipment	152		500		(f) 500		1,000				1,000	13
14	Furniture and Fixtures	153	4,000				4,000				4,000		14
15	Acc. Depr.—Furniture and Fixtures	154		900		(g) 300		1,200				1,200	15
16	Delivery Equipment	155	6,000				6,000				6,000		16
17	Acc. Depr.—Delivery Equipment	156		2,100		(h) 1,400		3,500				3,500	17
18	Building	157	70,000				70,000				70,000		18
19	Acc. Depr.—Building	158		10,500		(i) 1,250		11,750				11,750	19
20	Land	159	21,900				21,900				21,900		20
21	Notes Payable	201		2,000				2,000				2,000	21
22	Interest Payable	202		—		(j) 15		15				15	22
23	Accounts Payable	211		6,380				6,380				6,380	23
24	Sales Taxes Payable	221		210				210				210	24
25	Employees Income Taxes Payable	231		1,000				1,000				1,000	25
26	FICA Taxes Payable	232		340				340				340	26
27	Federal Unemployment Taxes Payable	233		120				120				120	27
28	State Unemployment Taxes Payable	234		230				230				230	28
29	Salaries Payable	235		—		(k) 120		120				120	29
30	Union Dues Payable	236		150				150				150	30
31	Unearned Rental Revenue	241		720	(l) 300			420				420	31
32	Mortgage Payable	252		38,500				38,500				38,500	32
33	Ralph Gallo, Capital	301		79,395				79,395				79,395	33
34	Ralph Gallo, Drawing	302	18,000				18,000				18,000		34
35	Income Summary	303			(c) 2,000		2,000		2,000				35
36	Sales	401		267,000				267,000		267,000			36
37	Sales Returns and Allowances	402	7,600				7,600		7,600				37
38	Sales Discounts	403	2,300				2,300		2,300				38
39	Interest Revenue	491		200		(a) 77		277		277			39
40	Dividend Revenue	492		100				100		100			40
41	Rental Revenue	493			(l) 300			300		300			41
42	Purchases	501	165,450				165,450		165,450				42
43	Purchases Discounts	502		1,620				1,620		1,620			43
44	Transportation In	503	3,600				3,600		3,600				44
45	Purchases Returns and Allowances	504		2,280				2,280		2,280			45
46	Advertising Expense	511	6,000				6,000		6,000				46
47	Cash Short and Over	512	30				30		30				47
48	Delivery Expense	513	1,800				1,800		1,800				48
49	Depr. Exp.—Delivery Equipment	514	—		(h) 1,400		1,400		1,400				49
50	Depr. Exp.—Furniture and Fixtures	515	—		(g) 300		300		300				50
51	Depr. Exp.—Office Equipment	516	—		(f) 500		500		500				51
52	Dept. Exp.—Building	517	—		(i) 1,250		1,250		1,250				52
53	Insurance Expense	521	—		(d) 150		150		150				53
54	Miscellaneous Expense	522	230				230		230				54
55	Office Expense	523	1,200				1,200		1,200				55
56	Payroll Taxes Expense	524	2,250				2,250		2,250				56
57	Salaries Expense	525	27,335		(k) 120		27,455		27,455				57
58	Supplies Expense	526			(e) 280		280		280				58
59	Uncollectible Accounts Expense	527	—		(b) 800		800		800				59
60	Utilities Expense	528	4,600				4,600		4,600				60
61	Interest Expense	591	2,685		(j) 15		2,700		2,700				61
62	Gains and Losses on Disp. of P. & E.	592	300				300		300				62
63	Gains and Losses on Sales of M. S.	593		700				700		700			63
64			415,045	415,045	7,192	7,192	419,507	419,507	232,195	272,277	187,312	147,230	64
									→ 232,195				
65	Net Income								40,082 →			→ 40,082	65
66											187,312	187,312	66

Explanations for adjustments
(a) *One-month interest ($10) on note from J. James and one-month interest ($67) on Mueller Co. bonds.*
(b) *Increased allowance to 10% of accounts receivable.*
(c) *Reduced merchandise inventory to $5,000.*
(d) *Recorded six months expired insurance on a two-year policy.*
(e) *Recorded supplies used.*
(f)-(i) *Recorded one year's depreciation.*
(j) *Recorded one-month's interest on Macar Co. note payable.*
(k) *Recorded one day's accrued salaries for Monday, December 31.*
(l) *Recorded five months' revenue on land rented to Price Mart.*

the debit and credit columns of the Balance Sheet section are added to show that total debits and credits are equal.

Net Loss. A net loss is computed as follows. First, the total of the Income Statement credit column is placed under the debit column and subtracted. The difference is the net loss. Second, the net loss is moved to the Balance Sheet debit column to show a decrease in owner's equity. This is done because owner's equity is decreased on the debit side. Third, the net loss is added to the total of the debit column. The Balance Sheet debit and credit columns should now be equal ($150,000).

INCOME STATEMENT		BALANCE SHEET	
DEBIT	CREDIT	DEBIT	CREDIT
100,000	90,000	140,000	150,000
90,000			
10,000		10,000	
		150,000	150,000

COMPUTING NET LOSS
ON THE WORKSHEET

Activity A. Answer the following questions about the worksheet for a single proprietorship. Refer to the text and illustrations on pages 444 to 447.

1. How many money columns are contained in the worksheet? Name each column.
2. What is the total of the Unadjusted Trial Balance columns?
3. How many adjustments are recorded?
4. What is the purpose of the (g) adjustment? the (c) adjustment?
5. Does the Gallo Company earn a net income or a net loss? What is the amount?
6. How is each amount on the Adjusted Trial Balance computed?

7. Where does the accountant get the amounts for the Unadjusted Trial Balance section?
8. Why is the net income moved to the Balance Sheet credit column?
9. How is a net loss computed?
10. What is the Interest Revenue for the year? the total Salaries Expenses? the Interest Payable?
11. What is the balance of Merchandise Inventory on December 31? the balance of Allowance for Doubtful Accounts?

Financial Statements for a Single Proprietorship

B *Which financial statements are prepared for a single proprietorship?* Financial statements provide users with information about the results of operations and the status of assets, liabilities, and owner's equity. In addition, financial statements are the basis for making management decisions. The Gallo Company prepares an income state-ment, balance sheet, and a statement of owner's equity. The informa-tion to prepare each statement is found on the worksheet. (In Chapter 14, you will learn about two additional statements prepared by many businesses—the statement of changes in financial position and the cash-flow statement.)

Income Statement Sections for Merchandising Business:
- Revenue From Sales
- Cost of Goods Sold
- Operating Expenses
- Net Income From Opera-tions
- Other Revenue and Ex-pense
- Net Income (Net Loss)

Income Statement and Schedule of Cost of Goods Sold. The **income statement** provides users with detailed information about the business operations. The income statement shows revenue, costs, expenses, and net income or net loss for the accounting period. The income statement for a merchandising business usually contains the following sections: Revenue From Sales, Cost of Goods Sold, Operating Expenses, Net Income From Operations, Other Revenue and Expenses, and Net Income or Loss. The Income Statement for the Gallo Company is found on the next page and is used to illustrate each section.

1 *Revenue From Sales.* Net sales for the Gallo Company are $257,100. The net sales are computed by subtracting Sales Returns and Allow-ances and Sales Discount From Sales.

2 *Cost of Goods Sold.* The total cost of goods sold is shown on the income statement ($167,150). The detail of the total is shown on the Schedule of Cost of Goods Sold illustrated below. A **schedule of cost of goods sold** shows the computation of the cost of goods sold during the accounting period. Notice that the January 1 Merchandise Inven-tory is added to the Net Purchases. The result is cost of goods available for sale, the dollar value of goods that could have been sold. However, the December 31 Merchandise Inventory ($5,000) must be subtracted and carried forward as an asset to the next accounting period. Some companies will show the entire Cost of Goods Sold computation on the income statement. However, the trend is to put computations in sched-ules, and thus remove much detail.

GALLO COMPANY
Schedule of Cost of Goods Sold
For the Year Ended December 31, 19—

Merchandise Inventory, January 1			7,000 00
Purchases	165,450 00		
Add: Transportation In	3,600 00		
Cost of Delivered Goods	169,050 00		
Less: Purchases Returns and Allowances . $1,620.00			
Purchases Discounts 2,280.00	3,900 00		
Net Purchases			165,150 00
Cost of Goods Available for Sale			172,150 00
Less: Merchandise Inventory, December 31			5,000 00
Cost of Goods Sold			167,150 00

GALLO COMPANY
Income Statement
For the Year Ended December 31, 19—

①	**Revenue From Sales:**			
	Sales		267,000 00	
	Less: Sales Returns and Allowances . . $7,600.00			
	Sales Discount 2,300.00		9,900 00	
	Net Sales			257,100 00
②	Cost of Goods Sold *(see schedule)*			167,150 00
	Gross Profit on Sales			89,950 00
③	**Operating Expenses:**			
	Advertising Expense		6,000 00	
	Cash Short and Over		30 00	
	Delivery Expense		1,800 00	
	Depreciation Expense: Office Equipment		500 00	
	Depreciation Expense: Furniture and Fixtures . .		300 00	
	Depreciation Expense: Delivery Equipment		1,400 00	
	Depreciation Expense: Building		1,250 00	
	Insurance Expense		150 00	
	Miscellaneous Expense		230 00	
	Office Expense		1,200 00	
	Payroll Taxes Expense		2,250 00	
	Salaries Expense		27,455 00	
	Supplies Expense		280 00	
	Uncollectible Accounts Expense		800 00	
	Utilities Expense		4,600 00	
	Total Operating Expenses			48,245 00
④	Net Income From Operations			41,705 00
⑤	**Other Revenue:**			
	Interest Revenue . . . . $ 277.00			
	Dividend Revenue 100.00			
	Rental Revenue 300.00			
	Gains and Losses on Sales			
	of Marketable Securities 700.00			
	Total Other Revenue		1,377 00	
⑤	**Other Expenses:**			
	Interest Expense $2,700.00			
	Gains and Losses on Disposal			
	of Plant and Equip. 300.00			
	Total Other Expense		3,000 00	
	Net Other Expense			1,623 00
⑥	Net Income			40,082 00

3 *Operating Expenses.* The Operating Expenses section includes all expenses incurred in normal business activity. Thus expenses not normally incurred by the Gallo Company, such as Interest Expense, are not included as operating expenses.

4 *Net Income From Operations.* The Operating Expenses ($48,245) are subtracted from Gross Profit on Sales ($89,950). The difference is the Net Income from Operations ($41,705).

5 *Other Revenue and Expenses.* The Gallo Company earns revenue in transactions with its customers and incurs various expenses to earn that revenue. Other (miscellaneous) sources of revenue and expenses not due to normal operations are shown at the bottom of the income statement. Other revenue and expense items are separated from normal operations items to provide users with a clear picture of business activity. The results of operations are shown without effects of "other" items. As you review the Other Revenue and Other Expenses sections, notice that there are four sources of Other Revenue that total $1,377 and two sources of Other Expenses that total $3,000. The difference ($1,623) is labeled Net Other Expense.

6 *Net Income.* The Net Income for the Gallo Company is $40,082. That is, the net increase in owner's equity from operations and other sources of revenue and expense is $40,082.

Balance Sheet. A **balance sheet** shows assets, liabilities, and owner's equity on a specific date. The balance sheet on the next page is classified. That is, there are sections for Current Assets, Plant and Equipment, Current Liabilities, and Long-Term Liabilities. The balance sheet also illustrates the GAAP that both assets and liabilities should be classified in at least two groups: current and long-term.

As you review the balance sheet, note the following. First, the realizable value of accounts receivable ($8,100) is listed with Current Assets. The general ledger balance for Accounts Receivable is $9,000 and for Allowance for Doubtful Accounts is $900. Second, there are three amounts shown for each item of plant and equipment: the original cost, the accumulated depreciation, and the book value. For example, the original cost of Office Equipment is $3,000, the accumulated depreciation is $1,000, and the book value is $2,000.

Statement of Owner's Equity. A **statement of owner's equity** shows changes in owner's equity during the accounting period. The statement of owner's equity is prepared to show investments and withdrawals for the period, as well as net income and net loss. Some companies will include the computation of capital on the balance sheet. Here the trend is to place detail in separate statements or schedules.

GALLO COMPANY
Statement of Owner's Equity
For the Year Ended December 31, 19—

Capital, January 1		79,395 00
Net Income for the Year	40,082 00	
Less: Withdrawals	18,000 00	
Increase in Capital		22,082 00
Capital, December 31		101,477 00

GALLO COMPANY
Balance Sheet
December 31, 19—

ASSETS			
Current Assets:			
Cash on Hand and in Bank		33,075 00	
Marketable Securities		15,190 00	
Notes Receivable		1,500 00	
Interest Receivable		77 00	
Accounts Receivable . . . . $ 9,000.00			
Less: Allowance for			
Doubtful Accounts 900.00		8,100 00	
Merchandise Inventory		5,000 00	
Prepaid Insurance		450 00	
Supplies on Hand		120 00	
Total Current Assets			63,512 00
Plant and Equipment:			
Office Equipment . . . . $ 3,000.00			
Less: Accumulated Depreciation . . 1,000.00		2,000 00	
Furniture and Fixtures . . . . $ 4,000.00			
Less: Accumulated Depreciation . . 1,200.00		2,800 00	
Delivery Equipment . . . . $ 6,000.00			
Less: Accumulated Depreciation . . 3,500.00		2,500 00	
Building $70,000.00			
Less: Accumulated Depreciation . . 11,750.00		58,250 00	
Land		21,900 00	
Total Plant and Equipment			87,450 00
Total Assets			150,962 00
LIABILITIES			
Current Liabilities:			
Notes Payable		2,000 00	
Interest Payable		15 00	
Accounts Payable		6,380 00	
Sales Taxes Payable		210 00	
Employees Income Taxes Payable		1,000 00	
FICA Taxes Payable		340 00	
Federal Unemployment Taxes Payable		120 00	
State Unemployment Taxes Payable		230 00	
Salaries Payable		120 00	
Union Dues Payable		150 00	
Unearned Rental Revenue		420 00	
Total Current Liabilities			10,985 00
Long-Term Liabilities:			
Mortgage Payable			38,500 00
Total Liabilities			49,485 00
OWNER'S EQUITY			
Ralph Gallo, Capital			101,477 00
Total Liabilities and Owner's Equity			150,962 00

The statement of owner's equity illustrated on page 450 indicates that Gallo began the year with capital of $79,395. During the year, there are no investments, $18,000 is withdrawn, and the net income is $40,082. It also shows that Gallo capital is $101,477 on December 31. The $101,477 is transferred directly to the balance sheet and is included as the capital on December 31, under Owner's Equity.

Activity B-1. Answer the following questions on preparing the Income Statement and Schedule of Cost of Goods Sold. Refer to the text and illustrations on pages 447 to 450.

1. What is the gross revenue from sales? the net income?

2. Does the Income Statement show the detail of Cost of Goods Sold? Explain.

3. What are the net purchases? How are they computed?

4. What are the total Operating Expenses?

5. What are the total Depreciation Expenses?

6. Is the Net Income from Operations increased or decreased by Other Revenue and Expense? By how much?

7. Is the ending inventory more or less than the beginning inventory? By how much?

Activity B-2. Answer the following questions about preparing a balance sheet and statement of owner's equity. Refer to the text and illustrations on pages 450 to 452.

1. By what amount does Gallo's capital increase for the year?

2. How much does Mr. Gallo withdraw per month? for the year?

3. What are the total Current Assets? total Plant and Equipment? total Current Liabilities?

4. What is the book value of Plant and Equipment?

5. What is the book value of Furniture and Fixtures?

Adjusting and Closing Entries

C *What entries are necessary at the end of the accounting period for a single proprietorship?* A single proprietorship must (1) record and post adjusting entries to update the ledger and (2) record and post closing entries to transfer the results of all business activity to owner's equity.

Adjusting Entries. **Adjusting entries** are entries that bring ledger accounts up to date. The accountant recorded adjusting entries (a) to (l) on the worksheet. Now the accountant must prepare a journal entry that, when posted, will bring the ledger accounts up to date. The journal entry that the accountant prepared for the Gallo Company is found on the next page.

GENERAL JOURNAL   Page 76

DATE		ACCOUNT TITLE AND EXPLANATION	POST. REF.	DEBIT	CREDIT
19—					
Dec.	31	Interest Receivable	122	77 00	
		Interest Revenue	491		77 00
		Adjust interest earned.			
	31	Uncollectible Accounts Expense . . .	527	800 00	
		Allowance for Doubtful Accounts	132		800 00
		Adjust for estimated uncollectible accounts.			
	31	Income Summary	303	2,000 00	
		Merchandise Inventory	141		2,000 00
		Adjust merchandise inventory.			
	31	Insurance Expense	521	150 00	
		Prepaid Insurance	142		150 00
		Record expired insurance.			
	31	Supplies Expense	526	280 00	
		Supplies on Hand	143		280 00
		Record supplies used.			
	31	Depreciation Expense—Office Equipment	514	500 00	
		Accumulated Depreciation— Office Equipment	152		500 00
		Record one year's depreciation.			
	31	Depreciation Expense—Furniture and Fixtures	515	300 00	
		Accumulated Depreciation— Furniture and Fixtures	154		300 00
		Record one year's depreciation.			
	31	Depreciation Expense—Delivery Equipment	516	1,400 00	
		Accumulated Depreciation— Delivery Equipment	156		1,400 00
		Record one year's depreciation.			
	31	Depreciation Expense—Building . . .	517	1,250 00	
		Accumulated Depreciation— Building	158		1,250 00
		Record one year's depreciation.			
	31	Interest Expense	591	15 00	
		Interest Payable	202		15 00
		Record one month's interest on Macar note.			
	31	Salaries Expense	525	120 00	
		Salaries Payable	235		120 00
		Record one day's accrued salaries.			
	31	Unearned Rental Revenue	241	300 00	
		Rental Revenue	493		300 00
		Record five months' rental revenue.			

After the entry is posted, each general ledger account will have the same balance, as shown in the Income Statement and Balance Sheet sections of the worksheet.

Closing Entries. **Closing entries** are entries made to prepare accounts for accumulation of data for the next accounting period. After the adjusting entries are posted, the asset and liability accounts have up-to-date balances. However, the Capital account is not up to date. Why? Because the results of operations are still shown as balances in the various revenue, cost, and expense accounts. Refer to the general journal on the next page as you read the explanations below.

The purpose of the closing entries is to transfer the balances of the temporary owner's equity accounts—Revenue, Cost, Expense, Drawing, and Summary—to the Capital account. The four closing entries are described here.

1 Close the Revenue and Cost accounts in the Credit column on the Income Statement section of the worksheet to the Income Summary account.

2 Close all accounts (except Income Summary) in the Debit column of the Income Statement section of the worksheet to the Income Summary account. The Income Summary account now contains the results of business activity. That is, the balance is now the Net Income or Net Loss for the accounting period.

3 Close the Income Summary account to the Capital account. This entry transfers the Net Income or Net Loss to Capital, the permanent owner's equity account.

4 Close the Drawing account to the Capital account. The owner makes withdrawals during the accounting period against expected net income. In our illustration, Mr. Gallo withdrew $18,000 against expected net income.

The Drawing account is closed to the Capital account so that withdrawals can be offset against net income. In our illustration, the withdrawals of $18,000 are offset against net income of $40,082. The difference ($22,082) is the net incease in capital for the accounting period.

Postclosing Trial Balance. After the adjusting and closing entries are recorded and posted, a postclosing trial balance is prepared. The **postclosing trial balance** is a listing prepared after the ledger has been closed. It verifies that the debit and credit balances for the asset, liability, and capital accounts are equal. When verified, the accounting records are then ready for the next period's accounting entries.

GENERAL JOURNAL Page 77

DATE		ACCOUNT TITLE AND EXPLANATION	POST. REF.	DEBIT	CREDIT
19—					
Dec.	31	Sales	401	267,000 00	
		Interest Revenue	491	277 00	
		Dividend Revenue	492	100 00	
		Purchases Discounts	502	1,620 00	
		Purchases Returns and Allowances	504	2,280 00	
		Gains and Losses on Sales of Marketable			
		Securities	593	700 00	
		Rental Revenue	493	300 00	
		Income Summary	303		272,277 00
		Close accounts with credit balances.			
		Income Summary	303	230,195 00	
		Sales Returns and Allowances	402		7,600 00
		Sales Discount	403		2,300 00
		Purchases	501		165,450 00
		Transportation In	503		3,600 00
		Advertising Expense	511		6,000 00
		Cash Short and Over	512		30 00
		Delivery Expense—Office Equipment	513		1,800 00
		Depreciation Expense—Office			
		Equipment.	514		500 00
		Depreciation Expense—Furniture and			
		Fixtures	515		300 00
		Depreciation Expense—Delivery			
		Equipment.	516		1,400 00
		Depreciation Expenses—Building	517		1,250 00
		Insurance Expense	521		150 00
		Miscellaneous Expense	522		230 00
		Office Expense	523		1,200 00
		Payroll Taxes Expense	524		2,250 00
		Salaries Expense	525		27,455 00
		Supplies Expense	526		280 00
		Uncollectible Accounts Expense	527		800 00
		Utilities Expense	528		4,600 00
		Interest Expense	591		2,700 00
		Gains and Losses on Disposal of Plant			
		and Equipment	592		300 00
		Close accounts with debit balances.			
	31	Income Summary	303	40,082 00	
		Ralph Gallo, Capital	301		40,082 00
		Transfer net income.			
	31	Ralph Gallo, Capital	301	18,000 00	
		Ralph Gallo, Drawing	302		18,000 00
		Transfer drawing.			

GALLO COMPANY
Postclosing Trial Balance
December 31, 19___

ACCOUNT TITLE	ACCT. NO.	DEBIT	CREDIT
Cash	101	33,000 00	
Petty Cash	102	50 00	
Change Fund	103	25 00	
Marketable Securities	111	15,190 00	
Notes Receivable	121	1,500 00	
Interest Receivable	122	77 00	
Accounts Receivable	131	9,000 00	
Allowance for Doubtful Accounts	132		900 00
Merchandise Inventory	141	5,000 00	
Prepaid Insurance	142	450 00	
Supplies on Hand	143	120 00	
Office Equipment	151	3,000 00	
Accumulated Depreciation—Office Equipment	152		1,000 00
Furniture and Fixtures	153	4,000 00	
Accumulated Depreciation—Furniture and Fixtures	154		1,200 00
Delivery Equipment	155	6,000 00	
Accumulated Depreciation—Delivery Equipment	156		3,500 00
Building	157	70,000 00	
Accumulated Depreciation—Building	158		11,750 00
Land	159	21,900 00	
Notes Payable	201		2,000 00
Interest Payable	202		15 00
Accounts Payable	211		6,380 00
Sales Taxes Payable	221		210 00
Employees Income Taxes Payable	231		1,000 00
FICA Taxes Payable	232		340 00
Federal Unemployment Taxes Payable	233		120 00
State Unemployment Taxes Payable	234		230 00
Salaries Payable	235		120 00
Union Dues Payable	236		150 00
Unearned Rental Revenue	241		420 00
Mortgage Payable	252		38,500 00
Ralph Gallo, Capital	301		101,477 00
		169,312 00	169,312 00

Activity C. Answer the following questions about adjusting and closing entries. Refer to the text and illustrations on pages 452 to 456.

1. What is the purpose of the adjusting entries?

2. Where does the accountant get the information for the adjusting entries?

3. In which journals are the adjusting entries recorded?

4. How many adjusting entries are recorded on December 31?

5. What is the purpose of the closing entries?

6. What is the source of the closing entries?

7. How many closing entries are recorded on December 31?

8. What is the amount transferred to Income Summary by the first closing entry? the second closing entry?

9. What is the purpose of the third closing entry?

10. What is the net increase in capital for Gallo for the year?

11. What is the purpose of the postclosing trial balance?

Contingent Liabilities

D *What is a contingent liability?* A **contingent liability** is a possible liability that may become a real liability, *depending on a related future event.* For example, suppose a company is involved in a lawsuit at the end of the accounting period. If the company loses the lawsuit, the loss could affect the company's entire financial status. Thus the possible lawsuit liability should be made known to users of the company's financial statements.

Contingent liabilities are not real liabilities, and thus are not included on the balance sheet as part of Total Liabilities. Contingent liabilities are reported as a footnote to the balance sheet or in notes attached to the financial statements.

Accounting Concept:
Reporting Contingent Liabilities. Contingent liabilities of importance should be reported.

Activity D. Decide which of the following are contingent liabilities. Write *Yes* or *No* after the item, as appropriate.
EXAMPLE: Lawsuit liability—Yes.

1. Mortgage Payable

2. Lawsuit pending

3. Discounted note

4. Accounts Payable

Topic 5   Problems

11-9. Unadjusted account balances for the Trim-Jean Company, as of December 31, 19X1, are listed here. Use the account balances and additional information found on page 458 to prepare a worksheet for the year ended December 31, 19X1.

Account Number	Account Title	Balance
101	Cash	$ 9,600
111	Marketable Securities	10,000
121	Notes Receivable	1,200
122	Interest Receivable	—
131	Accounts Receivable	5,600
132	Allowance for Doubtful Accounts	50 (Cr)
141	Merchandise Inventory	7,600
142	Prepaid Insurance	500
143	Supplies on Hand	150
151	Office Equipment	2,500
152	Accumulated Depreciation—Office Equipment	1,000
153	Building	25,000
154	Accumulated Depreciation—Building	13,000
155	Land	15,000
201	Notes Payable	4,000
211	Accounts Payable	6,300
231	Payroll Taxes Payable	400
235	Salaries Payable	—
241	Unearned Rental Revenue	500
252	Mortgage Payable	15,000
301	Carla Martin, Capital	42,280
302	Carla Martin, Drawing	12,000
399	Income Summary	—
401	Sales	98,000
402	Sales Returns and Allowances	3,200
403	Sales Discount	100
491	Interest Revenue	30
493	Rental Revenue	—
501	Purchases	53,500
502	Transportation In	270
503	Purchases Discounts	520
504	Purchases Returns and Allowances	600
511	Advertising Expense	6,000
514	Depreciation Expense—Office Equipment	—
515	Depreciation Expense—Building	—
521	Insurance Expense	—
522	Payroll Taxes Expense	1,600
525	Salaries Expense	21,700
526	Supplies Expense	—
528	Utilities Expense	4,300
591	Interest Expense	1,560
592	Gains and Losses on Disposal of Plant and Equipment	300 (Dr)

Additional Information

a. The Marketable Securities pay 9 percent interest. The interest is paid semiannually, and was last paid on November 1.

b. Paul Exner signed a 60-day, 9-percent note for $1,200, receivable on December 1.

c. Estimated uncollectible accounts are 1 percent of gross sales.

d. A physical inventory was taken on December 31 and priced. The cost value of the inventory is $6,000.

e. The Prepaid Insurance is a five-year policy purchased on January 1 of the current year.
f. The supplies inventory on December 31 is $100.
g. Depreciation on the office equipment is 20 percent a year of the original cost.
h. Depreciation on the building is $2\frac{1}{2}$ percent a year of the original cost.

i. The note payable is a 6-month 8 percent note signed on October 2.
j. The Kring Company paid $500 in advance on July 1 to rent unused office space for one year.
k. The weekly payroll is $420. Two days' salaries are accrued on December 31.
l. There were no additional investments.

NOTE: Save your work for further use in Topic Problems 11-10 and 11-11.

11-10. Use your work from Topic Problem 11-9 and prepare a Schedule of Cost of Goods Sold, an Income Statement, a Statement of Owner's Equity, and a classified Balance Sheet.

11-11. Use your work from Topic Problem 11-9 and prepare adjusting and closing entries. Place account numbers in the Posting Reference columns of your entries, but do not post to ledger accounts.

The Language of Business

Here are some basic terms that make up the language of business. Do you understand the meaning of each? Can you define each term and use it in an original sentence?

liabilities	face value	debt capital	income statement
owner's equity	bonds	underwriter	schedule of cost of
trading on the equity	par value	contract interest rate	goods sold
current liabilities	market value	effective interest rate	balance sheet
gross method	bond indenture	bond sinking fund	statement of owner's
net method	secured bonds	trustee	equity
accrued liabilities	unsecured bonds	discount	adjusting entries
accrued salaries	registered bonds	contra account	closing entries
deferred revenue	serial bonds	carrying value	postclosing trial
long-term liabilities	fixed maturity bonds	premium	balance
mortgage	equity capital	worksheet	contingent liabilities

Chapter 11   Questions

1. Total assets must be equal to which two sets of claims?

2. What is the difference between current liabilities and long-term liabilities?

3. What is the difference between the gross method and net method for recording accounts payable?

4. What accrued liabilities must be recorded?

5. Name and define two sources of deferred revenue.

6. Why would the par value and market value of bonds differ?

7. What is the difference between equity capital and debt capital?

8. Explain the difference between bonds sold at premium and bonds sold at a discount.

9. What is meant by a contingent liability?

10. Which financial statements are prepared for a single proprietorship?

Chapter 11   Problems

Problems for Chapter 11 are given in the *Working Papers and Chapter Problems* for Part 2. If you are using the workbook, do the problems in the space provided there. Complete your assigned topic problems before answering the chapter problems.

Chapter 11   Management Cases

Management Information. The output from an accounting system can be used for two purposes. First, accounting data can be used to assess past performance. That is, management can judge current performance by comparing it to that of prior accounting periods or that found in similar businesses. A second important use of accounting information is to determine how to change or modify accounting procedures in the future.

The two management cases that follow ask you to use accounting information as the basis for modifying accounting procedures. Remember that your decisions are only as good as your information. If the information provided is poor, then your decisions, like the decisions of managers, will also be poor.

Case 11M-1. The owner of Micro-Technics asks you for some advice. A comparison of this year's income statement with the statement for last year reveals the following. Purchases totaled $200,000 this year and $180,000 last year. In addition, Purchases Discounts were $1,200 this year and $1,500 last year. Since Micro-Technics is using the same suppliers, the owner would like to know the following.

a. Is there a change in the rate of purchases discounts?

b. Are there alternative methods for recording accounts payable that might provide better information about taking purchases discounts?

c. What changes in the present system would be necessary to switch to an alternative system?

Case 11M-2. After inspecting the accounting records for Micro-Technics, you conclude that the accounting clerk in charge fails to take many purchases discounts. When you ask why the discount is often not taken, the accounting clerk responds that terms such as 2/10, n/30 allow for only a 2 percent discount and the owner is better off leaving the money in the bank where it earns 8 percent. Do you agree with the accounting clerk's thinking?

In addition to the above, you also notice that the accounting clerk does take some discounts even though the discount period has expired. When questioned why a 2 percent discount is sometimes taken after 10 days, the clerk replies, "If they want our business, they had better let us take the discount even though payment is late." What is your opinion concerning the accounting clerk's response?

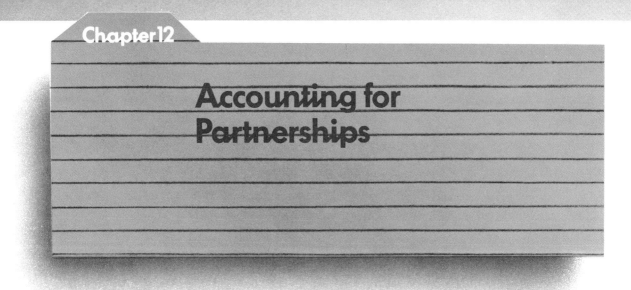

Accounting for Partnerships

The four major forms of business ownership are the single proprietorship, the cooperative, the partnership, and the corporation. Many of the businesses you learned about in your previous study of accounting were single proprietorships. The single proprietorship, you will recall, is a business owned by one person. The **cooperative** is a special form of corporation that is owned by its customers. In this chapter you will learn about the accounting procedures for a partnership. The accounting procedures for a corporation are discussed in Chapter 13.

Approximate Number of Businesses in the United States	
Single Proprietorships	9,400,000
Cooperatives	50,000
Partnerships	950,000
Corporations	1,700,000
	12,100,000

Topic 1
The Partnership

A *What is a partnership?* The Uniform Partnership Act defines a **partnership** as "an association of two or more persons to carry on, as co-owners, a business for profit." Many types of businesses are organized as partnerships—small merchandising businesses, certified public accounting firms, medical clinics, and engineering firms. People who form partnerships agree to combine resources and abilities in specific ways to form a business.

A partnership is an association of two or more persons to carry on, as co-owners, a business for profit.

   The terms of co-ownership are called the **partnership agreement** or *contract.* When the partnership agreement is written, it may be called the **articles of partnership.** Partnership agreements should be in writing to prevent legal misunderstandings or conflicts. An example

ARTICLES OF PARTNERSHIP

This agreement made the first day of January 19--, between Elaine Ortiz and David McCarthy, both of Omaha, Nebraska:

WITNESSETH:

FIRST, the said parties have this day formed a partnership to conduct a farm supply business in the city of Omaha under the firm name of the Farm Supply Store. The said business is to begin on the first day of July 19--, and is to continue indefinitely from the date hereof, unless sooner dissolved by consent.

SECOND, the investments shall be as follows: Elaine Ortiz shall invest assets valued at $110,000. The partnership shall assume accounts payable incurred by Elaine Ortiz for $10,000. The net investment by Elaine Ortiz is $100,000. David McCarthy shall invest cash of $50,000.

THIRD, David McCarthy may withdraw $1,000 a month in anticipation of net income; Elaine Ortiz may withdraw $800 a month.

FOURTH, net income or net loss shall be divided equally.

FIFTH, David McCarthy is to be the manager of the business. He is to devote full time to the interests of the business and shall not engage in any other business enterprise. Elaine Ortiz is to devote one-half time to the business. In the event of disagreement regarding the management of the business, Elaine Ortiz shall make the final decision.

SIXTH, neither partner shall, for the benefit of any third party, endorse any notes or negotiable paper, become surety or guarantor, or become otherwise liable for the benefit of any third party without the assent in writing of the other partner.

SEVENTH, full and complete set of double-entry accounting records shall be kept, which shall be open for inspection by the partners at all times. Said records shall be closed and net income determined at the end of each calendar year. The accounting records are to be audited by a CPA firm each year.

EIGHTH, upon dissolution, the net assets of the business shall be distributed in accordance with the equity of each partner as shown by the capital accounts.

NINTH, this agreement may be altered or modified by mutual agreement of the partners, in writing.

In witness whereof, the parties have hereunto set their hands and affixed their seals the day and year first above written.

In the presence of

Janet M. Damien

JANET M. DAMIEN
NOTARY PUBLIC, State of Nebraska
Number 2711391
Qualified in Douglas County
Commission Expires December 31, 19--

(Seal)

Arthur Boswick

ARTHUR BOSWICK
NOTARY PUBLIC, State of Nebraska
Number 2541698
Qualified in Douglas County
Commission Expires June 31, 19--

(Seal)

of articles of partnership is shown here. Notice that this agreement includes the following information.

Jane Hamilton-Merritt

Two or more people can form a partnership. Each shares their talents, skills, and resources to operate the partnership.

- Names of the partners
- Name, location, and nature of the business
- Starting date and length of the agreement
- Capital investments
- Limitation on withdrawal of investments
- Division of income and losses
- Duties and obligations of partners
- Accounting procedures
- Dissolution procedures

Advantages of Partnerships

The single proprietorship is the easiest form of business to organize and operate. With this form of business, one person makes the final decisions and enjoys the net income (profits) of the business. However, the partnership form of business also offers some unique advantages. Among them are the following.

Ease of Organizing. A partnership is easy to organize. It may be formed as a result of an oral agreement. However, the partnership agreement should be in writing and prepared with the aid of a lawyer.

Advantages of Partnerships:
- Ease of organizing
- Ease of managing
- Pooling of talents and skills
- Pooling of resources
- Better credit rating
- Personal incentive

Ease of Managing. The partnership is easy to manage because it is not taxed as a business. Instead, the partners report their shares of the net income on their individual tax returns. The partnership itself files only an information return.

Pooling of Talents and Skills. When a partnership is formed, each partner may bring special management talents and skills to the business.

Pooling of Resources. People forming a partnership combine their cash and other assets to provide more resources for the business.

Better Credit Rating. A partnership should have a better credit rating as a result of the pooling of resources.

Personal Incentive. The number of partners in a business can increase. Thus capable employees may work harder in hopes of being offered a share of the partnership.

Disadvantages of Partnerships

Disadvantages of Partnerships:
- Unlimited liability
- Limited resources
- Limited life
- Divided authority
- Mutual agency

The partnership also has some disadvantages as a form of business. Among them are the following.

Unlimited Liability. Each partner has **unlimited liability** for the debts of the business. This means that if the assets of the partnership are not great enough to pay the creditors, each partner may be required to use personal assets to cover the liabilities. Furthermore, if one partner has no personal assets, the other partner(s) must pay *all* the debts of the partnership.

Limited Resources. The assets of a partnership are limited to the resources and credit ratings of the partners.

Limited Life. Partnerships have **limited life;** that is, a partnership is legally ended when any partner withdraws from the business or dies. However, the remaining partners may continue the business under a new partnership agreement.

Divided Authority. The authority to make business decisions is divided among the partners. This agreement may result in disagreement over business policies.

Mutual Agency. **Mutual agency** means that the acts of one partner are legally binding on the other partner(s). In other words, the business is liable for any contracts or agreements entered into by any one partner.

Accounting Concept:
Partnerships. The partnership form of business ownership allows people to combine capital and abilities in a business venture.

Accounting Concept:
Contributions by Partners. Contributions made by partners become partnership resources and are no longer identified with individual partners.

Activity A-1. Answer the following questions about the articles of partnership. Refer to the text and illustrations on pages 461 to 465.

1. What is the name of the business described in the articles of partnership?
2. How many partners does the business have?
3. What is the amount of the net investment made by each partner?
4. How much time will each partner devote to the business?
5. Who will manage the business?
6. Which partner will make the final decision in the event of disagreements?
7. Who will audit the accounting records?
8. How much is each partner allowed to withdraw from the business each month?

Activity A-2. Classify each of the following features as either an advantage or a disadvantage of the partnership form of business.
EXAMPLE: Easy to organize—Advantage

a. Unlimited liability
b. Pooling of resources
c. Personal incentive
d. Pooling of talents and skills
e. Limited life
f. Divided authority
g. Limited resources
h. Better credit rating
i. Mutual agency

Starting a Partnership

B *How is the investment of each partner determined?* The partnership agreement states the amount and kind of investment to be made by each partner. For instance, suppose that Elaine Ortiz and David McCarthy decide to form a partnership. Ms. Ortiz is already operating the Farm Supply Store, a supply store for wheat growers in Nebraska. Mr. McCarthy is a recent college graduate with a degree in business administration.

The partners agree that Ms. Ortiz's investment will consist of the net assets (assets minus liabilities) of $100,000 listed on the balance sheet for the Farm Supply Store. Mr. McCarthy, on the other hand, will invest $50,000 cash that he has inherited from a trust fund. It is further agreed that Mr. McCarthy will devote full time to the management of the partnership while Ms. Ortiz will work only half-time. The two partners also agree to divide the net income (or net loss) equally since Mr. McCarthy is investing more time in the business.

The two partners could have chosen another way to divide the net income. These other methods are discussed in Topic 2.

FARM SUPPLY STORE Balance Sheet June 30, 19—			
ASSETS			
Current Assets:			
Cash	10,000 00		
Merchandise Inventory	70,000 00		
Total Current Assets		80,000 00	
Equipment:			
Store Equipment	40,000 00		
Accumulated Depreciation	10,000 00		
Total Equipment		30,000 00	
Total Assets		110,000 00	
LIABILITIES			
Current Liabilities:			
Accounts Payable		10,000 00	
OWNER'S EQUITY			
Elaine Ortiz, Capital	100,000 00		
Total Owner's Equity		100,000 00	
Total Liabilities and Owner's Equity		110,000 00	

Recording the Investments. The entries to record the initial investments by the partners are illustrated on the next page. The information for the investment by Elaine Ortiz is taken from the June 30 balance sheet for the Farm Supply Store, shown above.

The partners agree to accept all the items on the balance sheet at the values listed. The source document for David McCarthy's investment is the cashier's check made payable to the Farm Supply Store.

After recording the investments, the partners decide to rent a desk-type microcomputer. The microcomputer will be used to maintain the general journal, the general ledger, and accounts payable. Other decisions made are as follows.
• The partnership will continue to use the same name for the business.
• The business will begin making sales on credit.
• The general ledger will include separate capital accounts and drawing accounts for each partner.

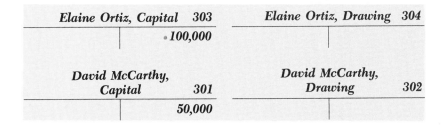

DAVID McCARTHY
240 Ellison Avenue
Omaha, Nebraska 68110

NO. 13

June 30 19 —   23-45/100

PAY TO THE ORDER OF Farm Supply Store ———— $ 50,000 00/100

Fifty thousand and ——————— 00/100 DOLLARS

ALLIANCE NATIONAL BANK
Omaha, Nebraska

David McCarthy

⑆0110⑈0045⑆ 000⑈0430⑈

GENERAL JOURNAL — Page 12

DATE		ACCOUNT TITLE AND EXPLANATION	POST. REF.	DEBIT	CREDIT
19— July	1	Cash	—	10,000 00	
		Merchandise Inventory	104	70,000 00	
		Store Equipment	151	40,000 00	
		Accumulated Depreciation—Store Equipment	152		10,000 00
		Accounts Payable	201		10,000 00
		Elaine Ortiz, Capital	303		100,000 00
		Record investment by Elaine Ortiz.			
	1	Cash	—	50,000 00	
		David McCarthy, Capital	301		50,000 00
		Record investment by David McCarthy.			

CASH RECEIPTS JOURNAL — Page 1

DATE		ACCOUNT CREDITED	EXPLANATION	POST. REF.	GENERAL LEDGER CREDIT	ACCOUNTS RECEIVABLE CREDIT	SALES DISCOUNT DEBIT	NET CASH DEBIT
19— July	1	Elaine Ortiz, Capital	Record investment.	—	10,000 00			10,000 00
		David McCarthy, Capital		—	50,000 00			50,000 00

Elaine Ortiz, Capital 303	Elaine Ortiz, Drawing 304
100,000	

David McCarthy, Capital 301	David McCarthy, Drawing 302
50,000	

• Part of the cash will be used to remodel the store and expand the inventory.

• Mr. McCarthy will be permitted to withdraw $1,000 a month from the business while Ms. Ortiz will be allowed to withdraw $800 a month. Each withdrawal will be debited to the partner's drawing account and credited to the cash account. Each partner's share of net income in excess of allowed withdrawals is to remain in the business.

A beginning balance sheet for the partnership is prepared to reflect the investment made by each partner. The assets listed on the balance sheet are the combined investments by the two partners. For instance, the $60,000 cash balance is the June 30 balance of $10,000 plus the $50,000 investment by Mr. McCarthy.

FARM SUPPLY STORE
Balance Sheet
July 1, 19—

ASSETS			
Current Assets:			
Cash	60,000 00		
Merchandise Inventory	70,000 00		
Total Current Assets		130,000 00	
Equipment:			
Store Equipment	40,000 00		
Accumulated Depreciation	10,000 00		
Total Equipment		30,000 00	
Total Assets		160,000 00	
LIABILITIES			
Current Liabilities:			
Accounts Payable		10,000 00	
PARTNERS' EQUITY			
David McCarthy, Capital	50,000 00		
Elaine Ortiz, Capital	100,000 00		
Total Partners' Equity		150,000 00	
Total Liabilities and Partners' Equity		160,000 00	

Notice too that owner's equity is now called partners' equity. It should also be noted that the balance of the David McCarthy, Capital account is $50,000 and the balance of the Elaine Ortiz, Capital account is $100,000 ($110,000 assets invested less $10,000 accounts payable assumed by the partnership).

Activity B. Answer the following questions about starting a partnership. Refer to the text and illustrations on pages 465 to 468.

1. What is the amount of investment credited to Elaine Ortiz, Capital account?

2. What are the assets Elaine Ortiz is contributing to the partnership? What is their total value?

3. Is the partnership accepting any of Elaine Ortiz's prior liabilities? If so, what is the amount of the liabilities accepted?

4. How much is David McCarthy investing in the partnership? What asset(s) is he contributing?

5. Which journals are used to record the investments of the partners?

6. What is the source of information for recording the investments by Elaine Ortiz?

7. What is the source document for recording the investment by David McCarthy?

8. What is the amount of the total assets of the partnership on July 1?

9. What is the amount of the liabilities of the partnership on July 1?

10. What is the total of partners' equity on July 1?

Topic 1   Problems

12-1. On July 1, 19—, Tom Bates and Kim Cohen decide to form a partnership to perform landscaping services. Ms. Cohen will invest $25,000 cash in the business. Mr. Bates has been operating his own business and will invest the net assets of his single proprietorship in the partnership. The partners agree to accept the assets at the values listed here. The partnership will also assume the accounts payable of the single proprietorship. The account balances of Mr. Bates's proprietorship are as follows.

Cash . . . .$ 4,000   Supplies on Hand 1,000
Store Equipment 20,000   Accounts Payable. 10,000
Merchandise Inventory 35,000

The partners agree that Mr. Bates will receive two-thirds of the net income (or net loss) and Ms. Cohen will receive the other one-third.

a. Record the investment by Tom Bates.

b. Record the investment by Kim Cohen.

c. What is the total partners' equity?

NOTE: Save your working papers for further use in Topic Problem 12-3.

12-2. Charles Price and you decide to go into business as partners. During a planning session, the two of you decide that Mr. Price will be the manager and will devote full time to the business. Complete the articles of partnership.

Topic 2
Partnerships and the General Accounting Subsystem

A *What kinds of information are processed through the general accounting subsystem?* Information needed for the end-of-period adjustments and financial statements is processed through the general accounting subsystem. The financial statements are prepared from the worksheet, and the end-of-period adjustments are recorded in the general journal. Since this information will be used to make business decisions, the general accounting subsystem must rely on internal controls to ensure the accuracy, honesty, efficiency, and quick preparation of all reports.

Financial Statements

The financial statements prepared for a partnership include an income statement, statement of partners' equity, and balance sheet. The data for these statements is taken from the worksheet for the partnership.

The Worksheet. The partial worksheet for the Farm Supply Store is an example of a worksheet for a partnership.

FARM SUPPLY STORE
Partial Worksheet
For Six Months Ended December 31, 19—

	ACCOUNT TITLE	ACCT. NO.	ADJUSTED TRIAL BALANCE		INCOME STATEMENT		STATEMENT OF PARTNERS' EQUITY		BALANCE SHEET		
			DEBIT	CREDIT	DEBIT	CREDIT	DEBIT	CREDIT	DEBIT	CREDIT	
1	Cash	101	25,000						25,000		1
2	Accounts Receivable	111	5,000						5,000		2
3	Allowance for Doubtful Accounts	112		100						100	3
30	David McCarthy, Capital	301		50,000				50,000			30
31	David McCarthy, Drawing	302	6,000				6,000				31
32	Elaine Ortiz, Capital	303		100,000				100,000			32
33	Elaine Ortiz, Drawing	304	4,800				4,800				33
34	Sales	401									34
51					208,500	223,500	10,800	150,000	184,000	30,000	51
52						208,500					52
53	Net Income				15,000			15,000			53
54								165,000			54
55								10,800			55
56	Total Partners' Equity							154,200		154,200	56
57									184,200	184,200	57

Notice on this worksheet that an Income Statement section, a Statement of Partners' Equity section, and a Balance Sheet section are included. Also, the December 31 balances in the two capital accounts and drawing accounts are shown in the Statement of Partners' Equity section. The other accounts on a partnership worksheet are the same as those found on a worksheet for a single proprietorship.

The worksheet is completed as follows.

1 The total of the Debit column in the Income Statement section is subtracted from the total of the Credit column to get the net income of $15,000 ($153,500 − $138,500).

2 The net income is then added to the total of the Credit column in the Statement of Partners' Equity section for a total of $165,000 ($15,000 + $150,000).

3 The total of the Debit column in the Statement of Partners' Equity section is subtracted from the Credit column to determine total partners' equity of $154,200 ($165,000 − $10,800).

4 The total partners' equity is then added to the Credit column of the Balance Sheet section to balance the last two columns on the worksheet ($154,200 + $30,000 = $184,200).

Income Statement. The income statement for a partnership is prepared in much the same way as other income statements you have prepared for merchandising businesses.

FARM SUPPLY STORE
Income Statement
For Six Months Ended December 31, 19—

(1)	**Revenue From Sales:**		
	Sales	151,000 00	
	Less: Sales Returns and Allowances	1,500 00	
	Net Sales		150,000 00
(2)	Less: Cost of Goods Sold (See schedule)*		114,000 00
(3)	Gross Profit		36,000 00
(4)	Total Operating Expenses:		21,000 00
(5)	Net Income		15,000 00
(6)	**Distribution of Net Income:**		
	David McCarthy	7,500 00	
	Elaine Ortiz	7,500 00	
	Net Income Allocated		15,000 00

*Schedule not shown here.

The sections on the income statement for the Farm Supply Store are (1) Revenue From Sales, (2) Cost of Goods Sold, (3) Gross Profit, (4) Total Operating Expenses, (5) Net Income, and (6) Distribution of Net Income.

The Distribution of Net Income section shows how the net income is divided between David McCarthy and Elaine Ortiz. The source of information for the first five sections is the Income Statement section of the worksheet. The basis for dividing net income is described in the fourth section of the articles of partnership. The partners of the Farm Supply Store agree to divide net income (or net loss) equally. Thus Mr. McCarthy and Ms. Ortiz will each receive $7,500 as an increase to their investment.

Methods for Dividing Net Income:
- Equally
- Fixed ratio
- Ratio based on investments
- Interest allowances on investments
- Salary allowances for partners
- Combination of salary and interest allowances

Other methods for dividing net income include the use of (1) a fixed ratio, such as 3:2 or 2:1, (2) a ratio based on the partners' investment, (3) interest allowances on partners' investments, (4) salary allowances for partners, and (5) a combination of salary and interest allowances for partners. These various methods allow for differences in the amount of investments and for differences in time devoted to the business.

Some partnerships may not have a written agreement. In these instances the net income (or net loss) is divided equally.

Statement of Partners' Equity. The statement of partners' equity summarizes the changes in the capital account for each partner. The statement for the Farm Supply Store shows the July 1 capital balances for the two partners as well as the total capital. The statement also shows each partner's share of net income ($7,500 each) as computed on the income statement. Other information included on the statement are the withdrawals by the partners and the December 31 capital balances.

FARM SUPPLY STORE
Statement of Partners' Equity
For Six Months Ended December 31, 19—

	DAVID MC CARTHY, CAPITAL	ELAINE ORTIZ, CAPITAL	TOTAL
Partners' Equity, July 1	50,000 00	100,000 00	150,000 00
Plus: Net Income	7,500 00	7,500 00	15,000 00
Totals	57,500 00	107,500 00	165,000 00
Less: Withdrawals	6,000 00	4,800 00	10,800 00
Partners' Equity, December 31	51,500 00	102,700 00	154,200 00

You will recall that David McCarthy has been allowed to withdraw $1,000 per month from the partnership since July 1 in return for managing the business and that the partnership has been in operation for six months. Thus the amount of withdrawals for David McCarthy is $6,000—the balance in his drawing account. Elaine Ortiz has been allowed to withdraw $800 per month since July 1. Thus the balance in her drawing account is $4,800 ($800 × 6). The beginning capital account and the December 31 drawing account balances are taken from the Partners' Equity section of the worksheet.

Balance Sheet. The balance sheet for a partnership has a section for partners' equity. This section replaces the Owner's Equity section found on the balance sheet for a single proprietorship. Other than this difference, the balance sheets for the partnership and single proprietorship are the same. Thus the balance sheet for the Farm Supply Store shows total assets of $184,200, total liabilities of $30,000, and total partners' equity of $154,200. The data for the balance sheet is taken from the Partners' Equity section and the Balance Sheet section of the worksheet.

FARM SUPPLY STORE
Balance Sheet
December 31, 19—

ASSETS			
Current Assets:			
Cash			25,000 00
Accounts Receivable	5,000 00		
Allowance for Doubtful Accounts	100 00		4,900 00
Total Assets			184,200 00
LIABILITIES			
Total Current Liabilities			30,000 00
PARTNERS' EQUITY			
David McCarthy, Capital			51,500 00
Elaine Ortiz, Capital			102,700 00
Total Partners' Equity			154,200 00
Total Liabilities and Partners' Equity			184,200 00

Accounting Concept:
Financial Statements. An income statement summarizes the revenues and expenses for a period of time. A balance sheet summarizes an accounting equation on a given date.

Accounting Concept:
Statement of Partners' Equity. Changes that occur in partners' equity during an accounting period are summarized in a report called the statement of partners' equity. Changes in partners' equity may result from earning a net income (net loss) as well as from other increases and decreases in the partners' investments.

Activity A. Answer the following questions about the worksheet and financial statements for the partnership. Refer to the text and illustrations on pages 470 to 473.

1. What are the four sections shown on the partial worksheet for the Farm Supply Store?

2. Which account balances are found in the Partners' Equity section?

3. What is the amount of net income shown on the worksheet?

4. What is the total partners' equity shown on the worksheet?

5. What are the six sections on the income statement for a partnership?

6. How much of the net income is distributed to David McCarthy? to Elaine Ortiz?

7. How much has Elaine Ortiz withdrawn from the partnership as of December 31?

8. What is the December 31 equity for David McCarthy? for Elaine Ortiz?

9. What is the amount of total assets as of December 31? What is the amount of total liabilities?

10. What is the amount of total partners' equity reported on the December 31 balance sheet? on the statement of partners' equity?

End-of-Period Adjustments

Partnerships must adjust and close their accounts at the end of an accounting period.

B *Do partnerships record adjusting and closing entries?* Like any other business, a partnership must adjust and close accounts at the end of each accounting period. Adjusting entries for a partnership are the same as those for the single proprietorship. The closing entries, on the other hand, are somewhat different in that there are two or more owners.

Closing Entries

A partnership, such as the Farm Supply Store, makes four closing entries during each accounting period. The data for the closing entries is taken from the worksheet. The four entries are as follows. (Refer to the general journal on the next page.)

1 *Close the revenue and cost accounts in the credit column of the Income Statement section of the worksheet.* These balances are transferred to the Income Summary account. This is done by debiting each account for the account balance and crediting the Income Summary account for the total of the balances.

2 *Close all the accounts in the debit column of the Income Statement section of the worksheet.* These balances are also transferred to the Income Summary account. This is done by debiting the Income Summary account for the total of the account balances and by crediting each account for the account balance.

3 *Close the Income Summary account.* The balance in this account is the amount of net income for the period. Thus the Income Summary

account is debited for the account balance, and the partners' capital accounts are credited. The amount of credit to each partner's capital account is determined by the provision for distributing net income. The Income Summary account balance ($15,000) for the Farm Supply Store is transferred by crediting each partner's capital account for $7,500.

CLOSING ENTRIES

GENERAL JOURNAL

Page 6

DATE		ACCOUNT TITLE AND EXPLANATION	POST. REF.	DEBIT	CREDIT
19—					
Dec.	31	Sales	401	152,500 00	
		Purchase Returns and Allowances	503	1,000 00	
		Purchase Discounts	504	70,000 00	
		Income Summary	399		223,500 00
		To close accounts with credit balances.			
Dec.	31	Income Summary	399	208,500 00	
		Sales Returns and Allowances	402		1,500 00
		Purchases	501		126,000 00
		Transportation In	502		400 00
		Cash Short and Over	511		10 00
		Depreciation Expense	512		5,000 00
		Delivery Expense	513		150 00
		Insurance Expense	514		190 00
		Miscellaneous Expense	515		400 00
		Payroll Taxes Expense	516		850 00
		Rent Expense	517		5,000 00
		Salaries Expense	518		7,600 00
		Supplies Expense	519		600 00
		Utilities Expense	520		800 00
		To close accounts with debit balances.			60,000 00
Dec.	31	Income Summary	399	15,000 00	
		David McCarthy, Capital	301		7,500 00
		Elaine Ortiz, Capital	303		7,500 00
		To transfer net income.			
Dec.	31	David McCarthy, Capital	301	6,000 00	
		Elaine Ortiz, Capital	303	4,800 00	
		David McCarthy, Drawing	302		6,000 00
		Elaine Ortiz, Drawing	304		4,800 00
		To close drawing accounts.			

4 *Close the drawing accounts.* The Farm Supply Store uses two drawing accounts—one for each partner. The debit balance of each drawing account is transferred to the respective partner's capital account.

Activity B. Answer the following questions about adjusting and closing entries for a partnership. Refer to the text and illustrations on pages 474 and 475.

1. Are the adjusting entries recorded by a partnership the same type as those recorded by a single proprietorship?

2. How are the closing entries for a partnership different from those recorded by a single proprietorship?

3. How many closing entries are recorded by a partnership?

4. What account is credited in order to transfer the balances found in the credit column of the Income Statement section of the worksheet?

5. What account is debited in order to transfer the balances found in the debit column of the Income Statement section of the worksheet?

6. What accounts are credited in order to transfer the balance ($15,000) from the Income Summary account?

7. What is the purpose of the last closing entry?

Topic 2   Problems

12-3. Assume that the first year's net income for the partnership in Topic Problem 12-1 is $33,000.

a. How much of the net income belongs to Mr. Bates? to Ms. Cohen?

b. Record the entry to distribute the net income to the partners.

c. Mr. Bates withdrew $10,000 during the year and Ms. Cohen withdrew $8,000. What is the amount of each partner's equity at the end of the first year?

12-4. Karl Slattery and Norm Wyman are owners of K-N Enterprises. The partners agree to share net income or net loss equally. The balances in the drawing accounts and income statement accounts for K-N Enterprises for June 30 are listed on page 477.

a. Record the four entries necessary to close the books for K-N Enterprises.

b. What is the amount of net income for the period ended June 30?

Topic 3
Special Accounting Procedures

A *What are some of the special accounting procedures for partnerships?* Special accounting procedures for partnerships include the admission of a new partner, withdrawal of a partner, distribution of a net loss, and liquidation of a partnership. These procedures are discussed in the following pages.

K-N ENTERPRISES
Partial Worksheet
For Six Months Ended June 30, 19—

ACCOUNT TITLE	INCOME STATEMENT DEBIT	INCOME STATEMENT CREDIT
Karl Slattery, Drawing	5,200	
Norm Wyman, Drawing	4,300	
Sales		80,000
Sales Ret. and Allow.	800	
Purchases.	50,000	
Purchases Ret. and Allow.		650
Purchases Discounts		400
Transportation In	300	
Cash Short and Over	5	
Delivery Expense	145	
Miscellaneous Expense	40	
Payroll Taxes Expense.	750	
Salaries Expense	8,000	
Utilities Expense.	600	
Supplies Expense.	400	
Insurance Expense	270	
Income Summary*	5,000	

Balance of Income Summary after adjusting Merchandise Inventory.

Admitting a New Partner

A partnership can admit new partners after the business has been formed. There are many reasons for admitting new partners. If a partner wants to retire or withdraw from the business, he or she can be replaced. Or talented and valued employees can be retained by offering them the incentive of becoming a partner. Also, new talent can be attracted to a business by expanding the number of partners.

These procedures must be followed to admit a new partner.

• The existing partners must agree to admit the new partner. The admission of a new partner formally ends one partnership agreement and begins another.

• A journal entry must be made to record the investment by the new partner.

• The partnership agreement must be changed to include the terms of the new partnership. These terms would include the duties of each partner, the amount of investment by the new partner, and the distribution of net income.

Methods for Forming a New Partnership:

- With no increase in partnership capital.
- With an increase in partnership capital.
- With a bonus to the new partner.
- With a bonus to the old partners.
- With recognition of goodwill.

There are several ways to set up the financial structure of a new partnership. Among them are the following.
- No increase in partnership equity.
- An increase in partnership equity.
- A bonus to the new partner.
- A bonus to the old partners.
- The recognition of goodwill. (**Goodwill** is an intangible asset that may represent the value of the partnership's good reputation or its advantageous location.)

Only the first method will be discussed here—admitting a new partner with no increase in partnership equity.

Assume that the two partners of the Farm Supply Store agree to admit Joel Blackburn as a third partner. The two partners also agree that Mr. Blackburn will be admitted by purchasing one-half of the December 31 balance ($102,700) in the capital account of Elaine Ortiz. In this instance the total capital of the partnership will not increase. Instead, one-half of Elaine Ortiz's capital will be transferred to a capital account for Joel Blackburn. The entry to admit the new partner involves a debit of $51,350 ($102,700 $\times \frac{1}{2}$) to the Elaine Ortiz, Capital account and a credit of $51,350 to the Joel Blackburn, Capital account.

GENERAL JOURNAL					Page *6*
DATE	**ACCOUNT TITLE AND EXPLANATION**		**POST. REF.**	**DEBIT**	**CREDIT**
19—					
Jan.	*1*	*Elaine Ortiz, Capital*	303	51,350 00	
		Joel Blackburn, Capital	305		51,350 00

Partners' Equity Before New Partner Admitted		Partners' Equity After New Partner Admitted	
David McCarthy	$ 51,500	David McCarthy	$ 51,500
Elaine Ortiz	102,700	Elaine Ortiz	51,350
		Joel Blackburn	51,350
Total	$154,200	Total	$154,200

Notice that the partnership does not receive any cash from Joel Blackburn. The $51,350 cash goes to Elaine Ortiz as a personal receipt of money in exchange for one-half of her partnership interest. Thus the total partners' equity after Joel Blackburn becomes a partner is the same as it was when there were only two partners.

Again, admitting Mr. Blackburn as a partner means that a new partnership agreement must be drawn up.

Withdrawal of a Partner

A partnership may lose a partner for any number of reasons: a partner may want to retire or withdraw for personal reasons, or a partner may die. Whatever the reason, the withdrawal of a partner dissolves the partnership. The remaining partners may buy the investment of the outgoing partner and continue operating the business. However, the withdrawal of a partner also means that a new partnership agreement must be drawn up for the business.

Distributing a Net Loss

The possibility of incurring a net loss is one of the risks of going into business. When this happens the Income Summary account will have a debit balance after the Revenue, Cost, and Expense account balances have been transferred to the Income Summary account. A net loss results in a decrease in the partners' capital accounts.

Assume that the Farm Supply Store has a net loss of $21,000. The new partnership agreement for Farm Supply calls for equal distribution of net income or net loss. Thus the entry to distribute the $21,000 loss requires a debit of $7,000 to each partner's capital account and a credit of $21,000 to the Income Summary account. Remember that a third partner has been added to the business. Thus the $21,000 loss is divided three ways, as shown here.

GENERAL JOURNAL				Page 6	
DATE	**ACCOUNT TITLE AND EXPLANATION**	**POST. REF.**	**DEBIT**	**CREDIT**	
19—					
Dec. 31	David McCarthy, Capital	301	7,000 00		
	Elaine Ortiz, Capital	303	7,000 00		
	Joel Blackburn, Capital	305	7,000 00		
	Income Summary	399		21,000 00	
	To distribute net loss.				

Liquidating a Partnership

Sometimes a partnership actually goes out of business. When this happens, the assets are liquidated (sold), creditors are paid, and the balance of cash is distributed to the partners. Accounting for a liquidation is a complex procedure that is covered in more advanced accounting courses.

Activity A. Answer the following questions about admitting a new partner and other partnership procedures. Refer to the text and illustrations on pages 476 to 479.

1. What steps must be followed when admitting a new partner?

2. What is the name of the new partner admitted to the Farm Supply Store?

3. What account is debited when the new partner is admitted? What account is credited?

4. What is the amount of the investment for the new partner?

5. Does the total partners' equity increase as a result of admitting the new partner?

6. Does the partnership receive the cash invested by the new partner?

7. What is the amount of equity for each of the three partners after the investment is recorded?

8. Does the withdrawal of a partner dissolve the partnership? Does a new partnership agreement have to be drawn up?

9. Which accounts are debited to record the $21,000 loss incurred by the Farm Supply Store? Which account is credited?

10. What happens to the assets of a partnership when the business is liquidated?

Topic 3 Problems

12-5. Edward Tracy and May Cottrell are partners in a law firm. Mr. Tracy's December 31 capital account balance is $90,000. Ms. Cottrell's capital account balance is $75,000. Mr. Tracy and Ms. Cottrell agree to admit Mel David to the law firm on January 1. Mr. David will purchase one-third of each partner's investment.

a. Record the entry to admit Mel David to the law firm.

b. What was the total partners' equity before Mr. David was admitted to the law firm? after Mr. David was admitted?

12-6. The Home Repair Shop had a net loss of $10,000 for the year ended December 31, 19—. The two owners, Susan Clay and Mike Grubb, agreed that net income and net loss would be divided equally. Record the entry to distribute the loss.

The Language of Business

Here are some basic terms that make up the language of business. Do you understand the meaning of each? Can you define each term and use it in an original sentence?

cooperative	partnership agreement	unlimited liability	mutual agency
partnership	articles of partnership	limited life	goodwill

Chapter 12   Questions

1. What are some types of businesses that are formed as partnerships?

2. What are the advantages of the partnership form of business ownership? What are the disadvantages?

3. Why is it important to have the partnership agreement in writing?

4. What are some of the points that should be covered in a written partnership agreement?

5. What financial statements are usually prepared by partnerships? What information is found on each statement?

6. Suggest a method for distributing the net income earned by a partnership.

7. Describe the closing entries made by a partnership.

8. What steps should be followed in admitting a new partner to the partnership? Suggest a method for admitting the new partner.

Chapter 12   Problems

Problems for Chapter 12 are given in the Working *Papers and Chapter Problems* for Part 2. If you are using the workbook, do the problems in the space provided there. Complete your assigned topic problems before answering the chapter problems.

Chapter 12   Management Cases

Business Organization. Next to the single proprietorship, the partnership is the easiest form of business to organize. Specifically, a partnership can result from a simple oral agreement between two or more people. However, the ease of forming a partnership does not mean that careful planning and organizing are not necessary. For instance, the duties and responsibilities of each partner must be carefully considered. Equipment also must be purchased, and business procedures must be developed.

Case 12M-1. William and Carl Able decide to form a partnership to transport small packages from suburban industrial parks to a nearby air freight company. William has operated a similar business for two years, and he contributes $12,000 to the partnership. Carl recently graduated as a business major from the local community college. Carl's contribution is $3,500 cash. Each partner agrees to work full time, either picking up and delivering freight or soliciting new business. The partners do not consider it necessary to formalize their agreement in writing, since they are brothers.

For the first year of operation, the net income is $36,000. The partners feel the net income is adequate for the first year. However, the partners do have some minor arguments. Carl has assumed, in addition to his daily duties, the role of accountant, which means spending an additional 12 hours at work per week. Thus Carl feels he has earned a larger share of the net income. William does not agree. He feels that the partnership was successful because of his capital and his knowledge of the business. In other words, William wants the larger share of the net income.

a. Describe the mistakes you feel the brothers have made in starting this partnership.

b. Suggest how the net income should be distributed.

Case 12M-2. Five engineers decide to form a consulting firm specializing in designing water-treatment plants. Each partner plans to invest an equal amount of money to start the business. During a planning session, the engineers discuss two possible organization plans.

In the first plan, one partner would be president of the firm. The other four partners would be vice presidents. Each vice president would be responsible for specific duties. The president would make the final decision regarding business operations.

In the second plan, an executive council would make all policies and major decisions. The council would be composed of the five partners. Under this second plan, each of the five partners would be a vice president. The partners have not decided which organization plan to accept.

a. Can you identify the advantages and disadvantages of each plan as a working agreement for the five partners?

b. Which plan would you recommend for the partnership? Explain.

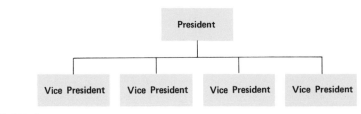

PLAN 1

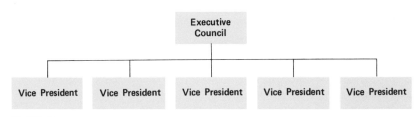

PLAN 2

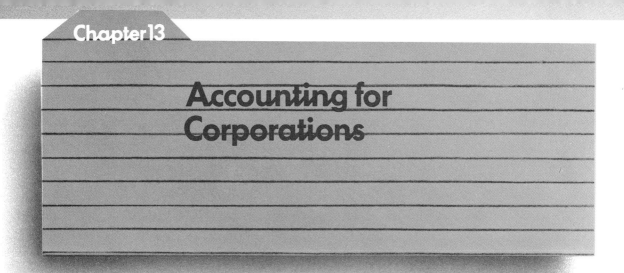

Accounting for Corporations

Of the three forms of business ownership—single proprietorships, partnerships, and corporations—corporations do the largest volume of business. Even though there are six times as many single proprietorships and partnerships, corporations still provide customers with far more goods and services. Corporations also employ more people and, as a result, provide more job opportunities in almost all areas of related employment. You have already learned about the accounting procedures for the single proprietorship and the partnership. In this chapter you will learn about the accounting procedures for a corporation.

Approximate Number of Businesses in the United States:

Single proprietorships	9,400,000
Cooperatives	50,000
Partnerships	950,000
Corporations	1,700,000
TOTAL	12,100,000

Topic 1
The Corporation

A *What is a corporation?* A **corporation** is a business that is granted the right to act as a person. These rights are provided under state law and allow the corporation to buy, own, and sell property; borrow money; and take court action in its own name.

Forming a Corporation

People who want to form a corporation must file an application with the proper state official, usually the secretary of state. This application

Examples of Corporations:
- J.C. Penney
- RCA
- IBM
- Western Airlines
- AT&T
- *Washington Post*

includes the **articles of incorporation,** which describe the terms and conditions for operating the corporation. Once the application has been approved, the articles of incorporation become the corporation's **charter.**

The articles of incorporation include (1) the name of the business, (2) the purpose of the business, (3) the amount of authorized stock, (4) the kinds of authorized stock, (5) the par value of stock, (6) the address of the corporation's main office, (7) the names and addresses of the first board of directors, and (8) the names and addresses of the incorporators. The articles of incorporation are signed by the incorporators and witnessed by a notary public. **Incorporators** are the people forming the corporation. A **notary public** is a public officer authorized to certify documents.

The articles of incorporation of the Transy Corporation are shown on page 485. Notice that the Transy Corporation is permitted to sell 4,000 shares of preferred stock and 4,000 shares of common stock. These shares represent the amount of the corporation's **authorized stock.** As stock is sold, the authorized stock will become **issued stock outstanding.**

The first board of directors of the Transy Corporation consists of three people. These individuals serve as directors for three years and will be responsible for the corporation's general supervision. The three directors will elect a chairperson from among themselves to schedule, plan, and conduct board meetings. One of the first things the board of directors will do is appoint officers to manage the corporation on a day-to-day basis.

Articles of Incorporation Include:
- Corporation's name.
- Corporation's purpose.
- Amount of authorized stock.
- Kinds of authorized stock.
- Names and addresses of individuals making up first board of directors.
- Incorporators' names and addresses.

Owners of Corporations

Stockholders may be individuals, other businesses, or investment clubs.

The owners of a corporation are variously called **stockholders,** *shareholders,* or *investors.* Stockholders may be individuals, other businesses, or investment clubs. An **investment club** consists of individuals who pool their money to purchase the stocks and bonds of corporations and agencies. Income from these purchases, or investments, is divided among the members of the club. A person or group becomes a stockholder by simply purchasing one or more shares of the corporation's authorized stock. Thus a share of stock represents part ownership in the corporation.

When a corporation sells stock, the owner is given a receipt called a **stock certificate.** The stock certificate shown on page 486 is issued to Paul McNulty, who purchased 500 shares of Transy Corporation stock. Notice that the par value of each share of stock purchased is $100. **Par value** is the amount printed on the face of the stock certificate and is

ARTICLES OF INCORPORATION
FOR
TRANSY CORPORATION

The incorporators of the Transy Corporation file the following articles of incorporation in accordance with the laws of the State of Alabama.

ARTICLE 1 – NAME
The name of the corporation is Transy Corporation.

ARTICLE 2 – PURPOSE
The purpose or purposes for which the corporation is organized are the purchase and sale of merchandise-household appliances.

ARTICLE 3 – AUTHORIZED STOCK
The corporation shall have authority to issue four thousand (4,000) shares of common stock with the par value of one hundred dollars ($100) each. The corporation shall also have the authority to issue four thousand (4,000) shares of preferred stock with the par value of one hundred dollars ($100) each.

ARTICLE 4 – ADDRESS OF CORPORATION
The address of the corporation's initial registered office is 172 Upton Street, Mobile, Alabama 36621, and the name of the corporation's initial registered agent is Carl A. Goldman.

ARTICLE 5 – LIFE OF CORPORATION
This corporation shall have continuous life beginning with the approval of these articles.

ARTICLE 6 – BOARD OF DIRECTORS
The number of directors constituting the Board of Directors shall never be less than three (3). The names and addresses of the first directors are as follows:

Mark Thompson
1500 Carmine Road
Mobile, Alabama 36621

Paul McNulty
2217 Mingold Place
Mobile, Alabama 36627

Greg Dawson
817 Paris Pike
Mobile, Alabama 36604

ARTICLE 7 – INCORPORATORS
The names and addresses of the incorporators are as follows:

Mark Thompson
1500 Carmine Road
Mobile, Alabama 36621

Paul McNulty
2217 Mingold Place
Mobile, Alabama 36627

Greg Dawson
817 Paris Pike
Mobile, Alabama 36604

ARTICLE 8 – AMENDMENTS
These articles of incorporation may be amended as prescribed by the laws of the State of Alabama and with the permission of the stockholders.

Signed and Witnesses:

Mark Thompson
Incorporator

Paul McNulty
Incorporator

Greg Dawson
Incorporator

Arlene J. Bergette
Notary Public

ARLENE J. BERGETTE
NOTARY PUBLIC, State of Alabama
Number N077
Qualified in Mobile County
Commission Expires September 1, 19—

(SEAL)

ARLENE J. BERGETTE
NOTARY
PUBLIC
STATE OF ALABAMA

A statement of stockholders' equity shows changes in stockholders' equity during the accounting period.

used in preparing the statement of stockholders' equity. The **statement of stockholders' equity** is a document showing changes in stockholders' equity during the accounting period.

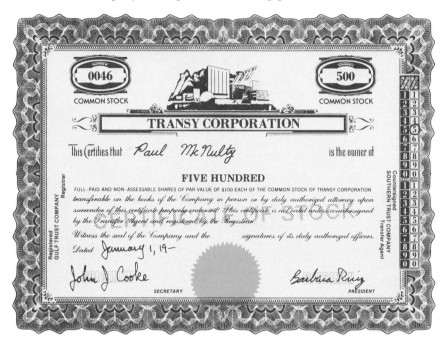

Par value of stock should not be confused with the market value of stock. A corporation may use any amount as the par value of its stock—$1, $25, or $100, for example. Once the par value has been determined, the amount will usually remain the same. **Market value,** on the other hand, is the amount investors are willing to pay for a share of stock. Market value may change every day as a result of the supply and demand for the stock.

Some corporations issue stock without a par value printed on it so that people will not confuse par value with market value. Stock that is issued without a par value is called **no-par stock.**

Stockholders' Rights Include:

- Voting for board of directors.
- Sharing in earnings of business in the form of dividends.
- Sharing in assets if the corporation goes out of business.
- Maintaining percentage of ownership.

Rights of Stockholders. As owners, the stockholders have certain rights in the corporation. These rights are as follows.

● *Stockholders usually have the right to vote at the annual stockholders' meeting.* They may exercise their votes by attending the stockholders' meetings, or they may **vote by proxy** (vote by mail). Stockholders usually have one vote for each share of stock owned.

● *Stockholders have the right to share in the earnings of the business.* Earnings that are distributed to the stockholders are called **dividends.**

● *Stockholders have the right to share in the assets if the corporation goes out of business.* When a corporation goes out of business, its assets are sold. Its creditors are paid first, and any money that remains is then distributed to the stockholders. Stockholders may receive more or less than the amount they paid for their shares of stock.

• *Stockholders have the right to maintain their percentage of ownership in the corporation.* This right is called the **preemptive right** and works as follows. Assume Paul McNulty owns 25 percent (500 shares) of the 2,000 shares of common stock outstanding in the Transy Corporation. Now assume that the board of directors decides to issue an additional 1,000 shares of stock for the purpose of raising more money. The sale of an additional 1,000 shares of stock will raise the number of outstanding shares to 3,000 (2,000 + 1,000). A 25 percent ownership will now be equal to 750 (3,000 × 25 percent) shares. Thus, under the preemptive right, Paul McNulty will be allowed to purchase 250 (750 − 500) additional shares to maintain his 25 percent ownership in the Transy Corporation. Mr. McNulty can choose not to buy any more stock, in which case his percentage of ownership will decrease to $16\frac{2}{3}$ percent (500 ÷ 3,000 shares).

Shares now owned:

$$0.25 \times \underset{\text{shares}}{2000} = \underset{\text{shares}}{500}$$

Additional shares needed:

$$\underset{\text{shares}}{750} - \underset{\text{shares}}{500} = \underset{\substack{\text{additional} \\ \text{shares} \\ \text{needed}}}{250}$$

Classifying Corporations

Corporations may be classified as either domestic or foreign. A state will classify a corporation as **domestic** if it is formed in that state. The same state will classify another corporation as **foreign** if it is formed in another state. For example, the Transy Corporation was formed in

Types of Corporations:
• Domestic
• Foreign
• Public
• Private

Stockbrokers buy and sell stock ownership through an organized market or exchange, such as the New York Stock Exchange.

Alabama and operates businesses in Alabama as well as Mississippi. According to the classification method described here, the Transy Corporation is a domestic corporation in Alabama but a foreign corporation in Mississippi. A corporation's classification (domestic or foreign) in a state will affect the amount of taxes it pays in that state. State taxes on domestic corporations are usually lower than state taxes on foreign corporations. Thus many corporations move their home offices to another state to take advantage of lower taxes.

Corporations may also be classified as public or private. **Public corporations** are government agencies formed to provide a service or to protect the public. An example of a public corporation is the U.S. Food and Drug Administration. **Private corporations,** on the other hand, may be classified as either profit or nonprofit. Examples of profit corporations are businesses such as General Motors and Texas Instruments. Examples of nonprofit organizations are state universities and the Girl Scouts of the USA.

The word *nonprofit* may be misleading. While nonprofit organizations may be formed primarily to provide a service, they too must earn enough money to pay obligations and improve services. Public corporations and nonprofit corporations do not sell stocks.

Accounting Concept:
Corporation. A corporation is a business that is granted the rights of an individual. Thus a corporation is allowed to buy, own, and sell property; borrow money; and take court action in its own name.

Activity A. Answer the following questions about the articles of incorporation and stock certificates. Refer to the text and illustrations on pages 483 to 488.

1. What is the address of the Transy Corporation's main office?
2. What kinds of products does the Transy Corporation sell?
3. How many people are involved in forming the Transy Corporation? What term is used to describe the people who form a corporation?
4. In which state was the Transy Corporation formed?
5. What is a stock certificate?
6. How many shares of stock is the Transy Corporation authorized to sell?
7. How many shares were purchased by Paul McNulty on January 1?
8. What is the number of the certificate issued to Paul McNulty?
9. What is the par value of the stock purchased by Paul McNulty?
10. What type of stock did Paul McNulty buy?

Features of a Corporation

B *How does the corporation differ from other forms of business ownership?* The corporation has several distinguishing features.

These features may be better understood when discussed as advantages or disadvantages of corporations.

Advantages of Corporations

Corporations have certain advantages over the single proprietorships and partnerships. These advantages have made the corporation a popular form of business ownership for both large and small businesses.

Limited Liability. Stockholders of a corporation can lose *at most* the amount they paid for their shares of stock. Thus stockholders have **limited liability** and cannot be held responsible for the debts of the corporation. Recall that owners in single proprietorships and partnerships can lose even their personal assets if their businesses fail.

More Resources. While one corporation may have as few as three stockholders, another corporation may have hundreds or thousands of stockholders. Thus the sale of stock makes it possible for large segments of the population to pool resources to form a corporation. This pooling of resources makes it easier for the corporation to purchase the necessary equipment or inventories for the operation of a successful business. Furthermore, a person with small amounts of money to invest can purchase stocks in a corporation. Thus more people are able to invest their money.

Continuous Life. A corporation has **continuous life.** This means it is not affected by the actions of individual stockholders. For example, the life of a corporation is not ended if a stockholder withdraws or dies.

Ease of Transferring Ownership. Stockholders in a corporation may easily sell part or all of their shares of stock. The sale may be handled by the stockholder or with the help of a special agent, called a stockbroker. **Stockbrokers** sell (transfer) stock ownership for corporations. Usually the sale is made through an organized market or exchange. Stock exchanges are usually regional. Two examples of exchanges for buying and selling stocks are the New York Stock Exchange and the Salt Lake City Stock Exchange. Stocks that are not sold on any of the stock exchanges are referred to as being sold over-the-counter or over-the-telephone.

Professional Management. The stockholders elect a board of directors to supervise the corporation and select professional managers to fill key positions. Thus the same people who invest in a corporation do not necessarily run its day-to-day operations. The stockholders do not have to rely on their own management talents. Managers who are

Advantages of Corporations:
- Limited liability.
- More resources.
- Continuous life.
- Ease of transferring ownership.
- Professional management.
- Centralized authority.

Examples of Stock Markets:
- New York Stock Exchange
- Salt Lake City Stock Exchange
- Chicago Board Options Trade
- Pacific Stock Exchange
- American Stock Exchange

skilled in running businesses are hired. The organization chart here shows some of the key positions in the Transy Corporation.

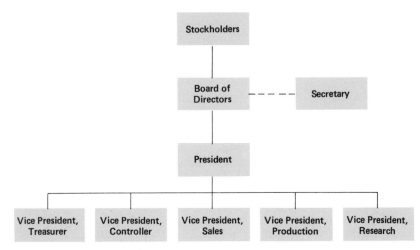

TRANSY CORPORATION

The president of the Transy Corporation is the top administrative officer and is responsible for the overall management of the business. The duties of the vice presidents of the Transy Corporation include the following.

- Treasurer—manages investments
- Controller—manages accounting staff
- Sales—manages sales representatives
- Production—manages manufacturing departments
- Research—manages consumer research projects and product development

The secretary to the board of directors is the president's executive secretary. The secretary's duties include taking minutes at the board meetings and stockholders' meetings. A permanent record of these minutes is kept in the **minutes book.**

In some corporations, the duties of the president and chairperson of the board may be combined to form a position called the **chief executive officer.** The chief executive officer may be a position above the president, or it may replace the position of the president.

Centralized Authority. The authority to make day-to-day operating decisions rests with the president and other officers of the corporation. The president reports the results of operations to the board of directors.

Disadvantages of Corporations

Corporations also have features that are disadvantages. These disadvantages should be considered before organizing a corporation.

Double Taxation. In the eyes of the law, the corporation is an individual. Thus the corporation has to file a tax return and pay taxes on its net income. Part or all of the remaining net income may then be paid as dividends to stockholders. **Dividends** are the part of the net income that is distributed to the stockholders. These dividends are then taxed a second time as personal income to the stockholders. Recall that single proprietorships and partnerships do not pay income taxes.

More Regulations. Corporations are subject to regulation by such federal agencies as the Securities and Exchange Commission (SEC) and the Internal Revenue Service (IRS). The SEC is a regulatory body of the federal government. It oversees the operation of the stock markets and regulates public corporations. The SEC requires corporations listed on the organized stock exchanges to provide detailed financial information to the general public and investors. This information is often provided in the corporation's annual report. An annual report includes a balance sheet, income statement, and statement of changes in financial position. The annual report also describes accounting procedures used during the accounting period. The IRS is the taxing body of the federal government. It administers the tax laws and is the government's tax collector. The IRS, through its tax regulations, often influences the method used in accounting for items such as uncollectible accounts and depreciation.

Complicated and Costly to Organize. Individuals who want to form a corporation must file an application with the appropriate state official, who in this case is the secretary of state. The application must include the articles of incorporation, must be signed by at least three people, and must be filed through the appropriate state agency. Those signing the application are called **incorporators.** The processing of the application usually involves legal fees and other costs. For instance, the Transy Corporation paid $550 to obtain its charter.

Disadvantages of Corporations:
- Double taxation.
- More regulations.
- Complicated and costly to organize.

Activity B. Classify each of the following features as either an advantage or a disadvantage of the corporate form of business ownership.
EXAMPLE: More resources—Advantage

1. Double taxation
2. Limited liability
3. More regulations
4. Complex and costly to organize

5. Professional management
6. Ease of transferring ownership
7. Centralized authority
8. Continuous life

Selling Stock

A corporation can sell both preferred and common stock.

C *Can a corporation sell more than one type of stock?* Yes, corporations usually sell both preferred and common stocks. The authority to sell stock is granted with the charter obtained from the state. The charter also specifies the types of stock to be sold, the par value of each type of stock, and the number of shares that can be sold. A corporation authorized to sell only one type of stock will be permitted to sell common stock.

The total amount of all stock sold by a corporation is called **capital stock.** The amount received from the sale of stock is called **paid-in capital,** or *contributed capital.*

Types of Stock

Dividends must be paid on preferred stock before being paid on common stock.

Preferred Stock. Preferred stock is the type of stock that has a first choice to the net income (profits) and the assets of the corporation. Having first choice to the profits of the corporation means that dividends must be paid on preferred stock before dividends can be paid on common stock. The amount of dividend paid on preferred stock is determined by the dividend rate printed on the stock certificate.

Having first choice to assets is an important feature of preferred stock when a corporation goes out of business. In this instance the assets of the corporation will be sold, and all amounts owed to creditors will be paid. The remaining money will then be distributed to the preferred stockholders (owners of preferred stock) and finally to common stockholders. The maximum amount that will be paid to the preferred stockholders is the amount that was paid for the preferred stock.

Common Stock. Common stock is the type of stock that gives the stockholders voting rights. Thus common stockholders (owners of common stock) elect the board of directors and vote on major issues affecting the corporation. Common stockholders are also entitled to all dividends remaining after preferred dividends have been paid. If the corporation goes out of business, common stockholders will be entitled to all money remaining *after* the creditors and preferred stockholders have been paid. Depending on the amount of money remaining, common stockholders may receive more or less than the amount of money they paid for the common stock.

Preferred Stock Sold at Par. On July 7 the Transy Corporation sold 50 shares of preferred stock at their par value of $100. This transaction is recorded as a debit of $5,000 (50 × $100) to the Cash account

**Transy Corporation
Chart of Accounts**

Intangible Assets
144　Organization Costs

Current Liabilities
218　Dividends Payable—
　　　Preferred
219　Dividends Payable—
　　　Common
226　Income Tax Payable

Stockholder's Equity
301　Capital Stock—Pre-
　　　ferred
302　Capital Stock—Com-
　　　mon
303　Retained Earnings
304　Premium On Preferred
　　　Stock
305　Discount on Common
　　　Stock

Operating Expenses
517　Income Tax Expense

Other Expenses
624　Organization Expense

and as a credit of $5,000 to Capital Stock—Preferred account. The sale of the preferred stock is recorded in the cash receipts journal.

					GENERAL LEDGER CREDIT	ACCOUNTS RECEIVABLE CREDIT	SALES DISCOUNT DEBIT	NET CASH DEBIT
CASH RECEIPTS JOURNAL								Page 7
DATE	ACCOUNT CREDITED	EXPLANATION	POST. REF.					
19—								
July 7	Capital Stock— Preferred.	To record the sale of preferred stock	301		5,000 00			5,000 00
8	Capital Stock— Common	To record the sale of common stock . . .	302		10,000 00			10,000 00

The Capital Stock—Preferred account is a stockholders' equity account and has a credit balance. The Capital Stock—Preferred account is reported on the statement of stockholders' equity as part of paid-in capital.

Common Stock Sold at Par. On July 8 the Transy Corporation sells 100 shares of common stock at their par value of $100. This transaction is recorded as a debit of $10,000 (100 × $100) to the Cash account and as a credit of $10,000 to Capital Stock—Common account. The sale of common stock is also recorded in the cash receipts journal.

Capital Stock— Preferred	301	Capital Stock— Common	302	Cash	101
	July 7 5,000		July 8 10,000	July 31 15,000	

The Capital Stock—Common account is a stockholders' equity account and has a credit balance. The Capital Stock—Common account is also reported on the statement of stockholders' equity as part of paid in capital.

Premiums and Discounts

The selling price of stock is not always the same as the par value of the stock. For instance, a stock that has a market value higher than its par value will probably sell at a **premium.** On the other hand, stock that has a market value less than its par value will probably sell at a **discount.**

Stocks not sold at par value are sold either at a premium or at a discount.

Stock Sold at a Premium. The Western Corporation sells a share of preferred stock with a par value of $100 for $110 on April 4. The entry to record this sale requires a debit of $110 to the Cash account, a credit of $100 to the Capital Stock—Preferred account, and a credit of $10 to the Premium on Preferred Stock account. This entry is recorded in the cash receipts journal as shown here.

		CASH RECEIPTS JOURNAL						Page 10
DATE	ACCOUNT CREDITED	EXPLANATION	POST. REF.	GENERAL LEDGER CREDIT	ACCOUNTS RECEIVABLE CREDIT	SALES DISCOUNT DEBIT	NET CASH DEBIT	
19— Apr. 4	Capital Stock— Preferred . . . . . . Premium on Preferred Stock . .	To record sale of stock at premium .	301 304	100 00 10 00			110 00	

The Premium on Preferred Stock account is a stockholders' equity account and has a credit balance. The account is shown on the statement of stockholders' equity as an addition to Capital Stock—Preferred.

Stock Sold at a Discount. The Wright Corporation sells a share of common stock with a par value of $50 for $45 on April 6. The entry to record this sale requires a debit of $45 to the Cash account, a debit of $5 to the Discount on Common Stock account, and a credit of $50 to

		CASH RECEIPTS JOURNAL						Page 10
DATE	ACCOUNT CREDITED	EXPLANATION	POST. REF.	GENERAL LEDGER CREDIT	ACCOUNTS RECEIVABLE CREDIT	SALES DISCOUNT DEBIT	NET CASH DEBIT	
19— Apr. 6	Capital Stock— Common	To record sale of stock at discount . .	—	45 00			45 00	

	GENERAL JOURNAL			Page 14
DATE	ACCOUNT TITLE AND EXPLANATION	POST. REF.	DEBIT	CREDIT
19— Apr. 6	Cash . . . . Discount on Common Stock . . . . . . Capital Stock—Common . . . . To record sale of stock at discount.	— 305 302	45 00 5 00	50 00

the Capital Stock—Common account. The entry is recorded in both the cash receipts journal and the general journal as shown on page 494.

The Discount on Common Stock account is a stockholders' equity account and has a debit balance. The account is shown on the statement of stockholders' equity as a deduction from the Capital Stock—Common account. Thus the Discount on Common Stock account is a contra stockholders' equity account.

Stock Splits

The stocks of popular corporations often sell at prices far above their par values. For instance, a share of common stock with a par value of $100 may sell for $370 on the market. When this happens, the price of the stock is too expensive for many people to purchase. To reduce the price of the stock, the corporation may declare a stock split. A **stock split** consists of increasing the number of outstanding stocks and reducing the par value of each stock in proportion to the number of stocks issued. Thus a stock split causes a reduction in the par value of the stock.

The par value of the stock can be split in any number of ways—2 for 1, 3 for 1, and so forth. A 2 for 1 split would result in each share of $100 par value stock being replaced with two shares of $50 par value stock. Thus a person owning 15 shares of $100 par stock would receive 30 shares of $50 par stock in the event of a 2 for 1 stock split. A stock split also results in a decline in the selling price (market value) of each share of stock, making it possible for more people to buy the stock. A stock split does not require a journal entry. However, a memorandum entry should be recorded in the general journal stating that the board of directors voted to split the stock in a 2 to 1 ratio.

Corporations use stock splits to reduce the price of the stock.

Stockholders' Record

The Transy Corporation issues a stock certificate to each person buying either preferred or common stock. These certificates are prenumbered and are kept in a **stock certificate book.** Often, the treasurer of the corporation issues the stock certificates and also keeps a record of the stocks owned by each stockholder. The record of stocks owned by each stockholder is called the **stockholders' ledger.**

Activity C. Answer the following questions about selling stock. Refer to the text and illustrations on pages 492 to 495.

1. Which account is debited for the sale of preferred stock on July 7? Which account is credited? Does this stock sell at par?

2. Which account is debited for the sale of common stock on July 8? Which account is credited? Does this stock sell at par?

3. Which account is debited to record the sale of preferred stock on April 4? Which account(s) is (are) credited? Does this stock sell for a premium or a discount?

4. Which account(s) is (are) debited to record the sale of common stock on April 6? Which account is credited? Does this stock sell for a premium or a discount?

5. How many journal entries are needed to record stock sold for a premium? for a discount?

6. What is the stock certificate book?

7. What is the stockholders' ledger?

8. Why would an investor want to buy preferred stock?

9. What is a major advantage of buying common stock?

Dividends

D *Can stockholders withdraw money from the business?* No, there is no drawing account for stockholders of a corporation. Thus stockholders cannot withdraw cash or any other asset from the corporation. Stockholders can receive cash from the corporation only when part of the earnings (net income) of the corporation are distributed in the form of dividends. The earnings of the corporation are reported in the Retained Earnings account. The Retained Earnings account is a stockholders' equity account and normally has a credit balance.

Declaring Dividends

Three dates are involved when earnings are distributed to stockholders. These dates are the date of declaration, date of record, and date of payment. The **date of declaration** is the date on which dividends are declared by the board of directors. Dividends cannot be paid unless the board of directors declares (votes) to pay dividends. The **date of record** is the date on which the stockholders' ledger is closed. People owning stock on this date are called **stockholders of record** and will receive the dividends that have been declared by the board of directors. The **date of payment** is the date on which the dividends are paid to the stockholders of record.

The board of directors of the Transy Corporation declares a $20,000 dividend on August 1. The dividends are to be paid on September 1 to stockholders of record as of August 15. The exact amount of dividends to be paid to preferred stockholders and common stockholders is determined by the number of shares of each type of stock outstanding.

The Transy Corporation has 1,000 shares of 6 percent preferred stock outstanding and 2,000 shares of common stock outstanding. Each share of preferred stock has a $100 par value. The amount of dividends to be paid on each type of stock is computed using the following procedure (it is not necessary to know the par value of common stock when computing dividends).

Preferred Stock

STEP 1. *Multiply the par value of a share of preferred stock ($100) by the dividend rate (6 percent).* Thus each share of preferred stock will receive a $6 ($100 × 0.06) dividend.

STEP 2. *Multiply the dividend per share of preferred stock ($6) by the number of shares of preferred stock outstanding (1,000).* This amount is the total dividend to be paid on preferred stock, which in this case is $6,000 ($6 × 1,000 shares).

Common Stock

STEP 3. *Subtract the total dividend to be paid on preferred stock ($6,000) from the total dividend declared ($20,000) by the board of directors.* The difference is the total amount available for common stock dividends, in this case $14,000 ($20,000 − $6,000).

STEP 4. *Divide the total amount available ($14,000) for the common stock dividend by the number of shares of common stock outstanding (2,000).* This amount is the dividend per share of common stock, in this case $7 ($14,000 ÷ 2,000).

Thus the dividend will be divided between preferred stockholders and common stockholders as follows: $6,000 for preferred stockholders and $14,000 for common stockholders. Stockholders of preferred stock will receive $6 for each share they own, and stockholders of common stock will receive $7 for each share.

Recording Dividends

The declaration of the dividend is recorded in the general journal. The entry involves a debit of $20,000 to the Retained Earnings account, a credit of $6,000 to the Dividends Payable—Preferred account, and a credit of $14,000 to the Dividends Payable—Common account.

		GENERAL JOURNAL			Page *13*
DATE		**ACCOUNT TITLE AND EXPLANATION**	**POST. REF.**	**DEBIT**	**CREDIT**
19—					
Aug.	*1*	*Retained Earnings*	303	*20,000 00*	
		Dividends Payable—Preferred . . .	218		*6,000 00*
		Dividends Payable—Common . . .	219		*14,000 00*
		To record the declaration of			
		dividends.			

The Retained Earnings account is debited because total stockholders' equity is reduced by the declaration of dividends. The Dividends

Payable—Preferred account and Dividends Payable—Common account are credited to record a current liability.

Retained Earnings 303	Dividends Payable— Preferred 218	Dividends Payable— Common 219
Aug. 1 20,000	Aug. 1 6,000	Aug. 1 14,000

Paying Dividends

The dividends declared on August 1, the date of declaration, are paid on September 1, the date of payment. The dividends are paid to the stockholders listed in the stockholders' ledger as of August 15, the date of record. The entry to pay the dividends is recorded in the cash payments journal. The Dividends Payable—Preferred account is debited for $6,000, the Dividends Payable—Common account is debited for $14,000, and the Cash account is credited for $20,000.

CASH PAYMENTS JOURNAL									Page 9
DATE	ACCOUNT DEBITED	EXPLANATION	CHECK NO.	POST. REF.	GENERAL LEDGER DEBIT	ACCOUNTS PAYABLE DEBIT	PURCHASES DISCOUNT CREDIT	NET CASH CREDIT	
19— Sept. 1	Dividends Payable— Preferred	Pay dividends	409	218	6,000 00			20,000 00	
	Dividends Payable— Common		410	219	14,000 00			—	

Dividends Payable— Preferred 218	Cash 101	Dividends Payable— Common 219
Sept. 1 6,000	Sept. 1 20,000	Sept. 1 14,000

Other Types of Dividends

Dividends on Cumulative Preferred Stock. Preferred stock on which dividends accumulate is called **cumulative preferred stock.** Generally, if dividends are not declared, stockholders are not entitled to any dividends for that year. However, dividends on cumulative preferred stock will accumulate each year that dividends are not declared. For example, stockholders of 6 percent cumulative preferred stock

Stockholders are not entitled to dividends if they are not declared by the board of directors.

with a value of $100 would be entitled to a $6 dividend on each share each year. If dividends are declared for the first time in 3 years, stockholders of cumulative preferred stock would receive $18 ($6 × 3) for each share. All dividends on cumulative preferred stock must be paid before any dividend can be paid on common stock.

Stock Dividends. A **stock dividend** is a dividend paid in shares of stock instead of cash. A stock dividend allows a corporation to keep its cash in the business as well as pay a dividend. Assume you own 100 shares of common stock in the Western Corporation at the time the board of directors declares a 10 percent stock dividend. In this instance you would receive an additional 10 shares (100 × 10 percent) of stock as a dividend.

Dividends on Participating Preferred Stock. Preferred stock that has the right to share in the excess profits of the corporation is called **participating preferred stock.** Assume the Portland Corporation has 1,000 shares of $100 par value 6 percent participating preferred stock outstanding and 2,000 shares of $100 par value common stock outstanding. A $30,000 dividend would be distributed using the following procedure:

STEP 1. *Compute dividend on preferred stock per share.* $100 par value × 6 percent = $6 a share.

STEP 2. *Compute total 6 percent dividend on preferred stock.* 1,000 shares × $6 a share = $6,000.

STEP 3. *Compute 6 percent dividend on common stock for each share.* $100 par value × 6 percent = $6 a share.

STEP 4. *Compute total 6 percent dividend on common stock.* 2,000 shares × $6 a share = $12,000.

STEP 5. *Compute total 6 percent dividend on preferred and common stock.* $6,000 + $12,000 = $18,000.

STEP 6. *Compute excess dividend.* $30,000 (total dividend) − $18,000 (6 percent dividend) = $12,000 (excess dividend).

STEP 7. *Divide excess dividend ($12,000) in proportion to the number of shares of common and preferred stock outstanding.*

$$\text{Shares of Preferred Stock Outstanding} + \text{Shares of Common Stock Outstanding} = \text{Total Shares of Stock Outstanding}$$

$$1,000 + 2,000 = 3,000$$

$$\frac{\text{Shares of Preferred Stock}}{\text{Total Shares of Stock}} = \frac{\text{Portion of Excess}}{\text{for Preferred Stock}}$$

$$\frac{1,000}{3,000} = \frac{1}{3}$$

$$\frac{\text{Shares of Common Stock}}{\text{Total Shares of Stock}} = \text{Proportion of Excess for Common Stock}$$

$$\frac{2,000}{3,000} = \frac{2}{3}$$

$$\frac{\text{Portion of Excess}}{\text{for Preferred Stock}} \times \text{Excess Dividends} = \text{Dividends to Preferred Stock}$$

$$\frac{1}{3} \times \$12,000 = \$4,000$$

$$\frac{\text{Portion of Excess}}{\text{for Common Stock}} \times \text{Excess Dividends} = \text{Dividends to Common Stock}$$

$$\frac{2}{3} \times \$12,000 = \$8,000$$

STEP 8. *Determine total dividend to be paid to each type of stock.*
Preferred: Percent Dividend on Preferred Stock + Excess Dividends = Total Dividend to Be Paid

$$\$6,000 \text{ (6 percent dividend)} + \$4,000 = \$10,000$$

Common: Percent Dividend on Common Stock + Excess Dividends = Total Dividend to Be Paid

$$\$12,000 \text{ (6 percent dividend)} + \$8,000 = \$20,000$$

The dividends paid on each share of preferred stock would be $10 ($10,000 ÷ 1,000 shares). The dividend paid on each share of common stock would alsc be $10 ($20,000 ÷ 2,000 shares).

Activity D. Answer the following questions about dividends paid by the Transy Corporation. Refer to the text and illustrations on pages 496 to 500.

1. Which journal is used to record the dividend declared by the Transy Corporation?
2. Which account is debited when the dividend is declared? Which account is credited?
3. What is the total amount of dividend declared?
4. What is the amount of preferred stock dividend a share?

5. What is the amount of common stock dividend a share?
6. Which journal is used to record the payment of the dividend?
7. Which account(s) is (are) debited when the dividend is paid? Which account is credited?
8. What is the importance of the date of declaration? date of record? date of payment?

Topic 1   Problems

13-1. Complete the following form. For each product listed, identify a brand (or make) of that product and the name of the corporation making the brand. You may want to examine advertisements in magazines and newspapers and product packages for some of your examples.

Product	Brand (or Make)	Corporation
EXAMPLE: Soft drink	*Coke*	*Coca-Cola Company*

a. Toothpaste
b. Tea
c. Radio
d. Ballpoint pen
e. Stereo
f. Car
g. Detergent

h. Jeans
i. Shoes
j. Candy
k. Soup
l. Peanut butter
m. Television
n. Gasoline

13-2. Record the following stock transactions for the Pieratt Corporation.

May 3 Sold 500 shares of $100, 5 percent preferred stock.

May 4 Sold 400 shares of $100 common stock.

13-3. Record the following stock transactions for the Bremmer Corporation.

March 14 Sold 50 shares of $100 par value preferred stock for $95 a share.

March 18 Sold 100 shares of $50 par value common stock for $75 a share.

13-4. On June 1 the Pieratt Corporation had 3,000 shares of $100, 5 percent preferred stock outstanding. The company also had 5,000 shares of $100 common stock outstanding. On June 2 the board of directors declared a $25,000 dividend. The dividend was paid on July 1.

a. How much is the dividend on one share of preferred stock?
b. What is the total dividend on preferred stock?
c. What is the total dividend on common stock?

d. How much is the dividend on one share of common stock?
e. Record the declaration of the dividend.
f. Record the payment of the dividend.

Topic 2
Corporations and the General Accounting System

A *Does a corporation process data through the general accounting subsystem?* Yes, the corporation, like all businesses, must make end-of-period adjustments and prepare financial statements. The data for these adjustments and financial statements are processed through the general accounting subsystem.

The major financial statements for a corporation include an income statement, a statement of stockholders' equity, and a balance sheet. These three financial statements are discussed in this topic. A fourth statement, the statement of changes in financial position, is discussed in Chapter 14.

Financial Statements for Corporations:
• Income statement
• Statement of stockholders' equity
• Balance sheet

Worksheet

The source document for preparing the end-of-period adjustments and the financial statements is the worksheet. The worksheet for the corporation provides the information for two adjustments that are not made by any other forms of businesses. These adjustments are for organization costs and federal income tax.

Organization Costs	144
550	

Cash	101
	550

Organization Costs. Three years ago, when the Transy Corporation was formed, $550 was paid for legal fees and other organization costs. The payment of these fees resulted in a debit of $550 to the Organization Costs account and a credit of $550 to the Cash account. Generally, organization costs are allocated over the first 5 years of a corporation's life. Thus an adjusting entry for organization costs is required at the end of each of these years. The amount of organization costs allocated to each of the 5 years is $110 ($550 ÷ 5). Each year an adjusting entry is recorded as a debit to the Organization Expense account and as a credit to the Organization Costs account. Thus the balance in the Organization Costs account at the end of 3 years is $220.

Organization Costs		144
550	110	Year 1
	110	2
	110	3

Organization Expense	624
Year 3 110	

		UNADJUSTED TRIAL BALANCE		ADJUSTMENTS		ADJUSTED TRIAL BALANCE	
	ACCOUNT TITLE	DEBIT	CREDIT	DEBIT	CREDIT	DEBIT	CREDIT
1							
3							
4	Organization Costs	330			110	220	
25	Organization Expense . . .			110		110	
26							

The balance of the Organization Expense account ($110) appears on the income statement under other expenses. The balance of the Organization Costs account ($220) appears on the balance sheet as an intangible asset. An intangible asset is one that cannot be seen or touched and has no physical characteristics.

Income Taxes. A corporation must file a federal income tax return just as any person earning income must. The tax rates for a corporation, at time of publication, are as follows.

Corporations must file an income tax return for earned income.

- 17 percent on the first $25,000 of income
- 20 percent on $25,000–$50,000 of income
- 30 percent on $50,000–$75,000 of income
- 40 percent on $75,000–$100,000 of income
- 46 percent on income over $100,000

The federal income tax for the Transy Corporation is computed using the following procedure. Refer to the worksheet on page 504.
STEP 1. *The amount of net income is determined by pencil footing the Income Statement section on the worksheet.* This was done by footing the Income Statement columns on the worksheet. The total of the debit column is $1,520,000, and the total of the credit column is $1,575,000. Net income is found by subtracting the total of the debit column from the total of the credit column. The difference is $55,000 ($1,575,000 − $1,520,000), the amount of net income before tax.
STEP 2. *The income tax on $55,000 net income is computed using the tax rates for a corporation.* Thus the Transy Corporation owes $10,750 for federal income tax.

Computing Federal Income Taxes:

$25,000	×	17%	=	$4,250
25,000	×	20	=	5,000
5,000	×	30	=	1,500
				$10,750

ACCOUNT TITLE	ADJUSTMENTS	
	DEBIT	CREDIT
1		
45		
46		
47 Income Tax Expense	10,750	
48 Income Tax Payable		10,750
49		

The $10,750 is entered in the Adjustments section of the worksheet as a debit to Income Tax Expense and as a credit to Income Tax Payable. After the Adjustments section is totaled, the amounts are recorded on the Adjusted Trial Balance section. The Income Tax Expense ($10,750) is also recorded on the Income Statement section as a debit. The Income Tax Payable ($10,750) is also extended to the Balance Sheet section as a credit. The amount of federal income taxes owed is credited to the Income Tax Payable account because the taxes are not paid until the next accounting period.

Completing the Worksheet. After the income taxes are computed, the worksheet for the Transy Corporation is completed as follows.

TRANSY CORPORATION
Worksheet
For the Year Ended December 31, 19—

ACCOUNT TITLE	ACCT. NO.	ADJUSTED TRIAL BALANCE		INCOME STATEMENT		STATEMENT OF STOCKHOLDERS' EQUITY		BALANCE SHEET	
		DEBIT	CREDIT	DEBIT	CREDIT	DEBIT	CREDIT	DEBIT	CREDIT
Cash	101	35,000						35,000	
Accounts Receivable	111	50,000						50,000	
Allowance for Doubtful Accounts	112		900						900
Marketable Securities	113	60,000						60,000	
Organization Costs	144	220						220	
Salaries Payable	225		3,000						3,000
Bonds Payable	235		100,000						100,000
Capital Stock, Preferred	301		100,000				100,000		
Capital Stock, Common	302		200,000				200,000		
Retained Earnings	303		100,000				100,000		
Sales	401		1,550,000		1,550,000				
Organization Expense		110		110					
				1,520,000	1,575,000				
Income Tax Expense	517	10,750		10,750					
Income Tax Payable	226		10,750						10,750
①		2,325,000	2,325,000	1,530,750	1,575,000		400,000	737,450	293,200
②					→1,530,750	③			
Net Income After Income Tax					44,250		→44,250	④	
							444,250		→444,250
⑤								737,450	737,450

1 The sections of the worksheet are totaled. The total of the debit column of the Income Statement section ($1,530,750) now includes the Income Tax Expense of $10,750. The amount of the credit column remains at $1,575,000, the amount of the pencil footing.

2 The total of the debit column in the Income Statement section is subtracted from the total of the credit column. The difference is the amount of net income after taxes, in this case $44,250 ($1,575,000 − $1,530,750).

3 The net income after taxes is added to the credit column in the Statement of Stockholders' Equity section, totaling $444,250 ($400,000 + $44,250).

4 The total of the credit column in the Statement of Stockholders' Equity section is added to the credit column in the Balance Sheet section. The final total of the credit column in the Balance Sheet section is $737,450 ($293,200 + $444,250).

5 The sections of the worksheet are ruled.

Activity A. Answer the following questions about the worksheet for the Transy Corporation. Refer to the text and illustrations on pages 502 to 505.

1. What is the balance of the Organization Costs account at the end of three years?

2. What is the amount of income tax expense for the year?

3. What is the amount of net income after taxes?

4. What is the total of the Stock-holders' Equity section of the work-sheet?

5. What is the final total of the credit column in the balance sheet section?

6. What is the amount of Retained Earnings? Capital Stock—Preferred? Capital Stock—Common?

Income Statement

B *What are the major sections of an income statement for a corpo-ration?* The income statement for a corporation has the following sections: (1) Revenue From Sales, (2) Cost of Goods Sold, (3) Gross Profit, (4) Operating Expenses, (5) Net Income From Operations, (6) Other Revenue, (7) Other Expenses, (8) Net Income Before Income Tax, (9) Net Income After Income Tax, and (10) Earnings on Each Share of Common Stock.

The Income Statement section of the worksheet is the source docu-ment for preparing the income statement. As you study the income statement for the Transy Corporation, shown on page 506, examine carefully sections 5 through 10.

Net Income From Operations. The amount the Transy Corporation earned from buying and selling merchandise and home appliances is $59,900.

Other Revenue. The Transy Corporation has interest revenue of $210 from investments. This revenue is kept separate from revenue from sales.

Other Expenses. Two accounts are reported as other expenses. These accounts are Interest Expense and Organization Expense. Inter-

TRANSY CORPORATION
Income Statement
For Year Ended December 31, 19—

(1) Revenue From Sales:			
Sales	1,550,000 00		
Less: Sales Returns and Allowances	10,000 00		
Net Sales		1,540,000 00	
(2) Cost of Goods Sold (see schedule)*		850,000 00	
(3) Gross Profit		690,000 00	
(4) Operating Expenses:			
Total Operating Expenses		630,100 00	
(5) Net Income From Operations:		59,900 00	
(6) Other Revenue:			
Interest Revenue	210 00		
(7) Other Expenses:			
Interest Expense	$5,000.00		
Organization Expense	110.00		
Total Other Expense	5,110 00		
Net Other Expense		4,900 00	
(8) Net Income Before Income Tax		55,000 00	
Less: Income Tax Expense		10,750 00	
(9) Net Income After Income Tax		44,250 00	
(10) Earnings on Each Share of Common Stock			19 13

*Schedule is not shown.

est Expense of $5,000 is the amount paid on bonds payable. An organization expense of $110 is the amount of organization costs allocated to this year's operations.

Net Income Before Income Tax. The Transy Corporation has a taxable income of $55,000.

Net Income After Income Tax. The amount of tax on $55,000 net income is computed using the tax rates for corporations. The income tax is subtracted from the net income to get $44,250 ($55,000 − $10,750) net income after tax.

Earnings on Each Share. Large corporations are required to show earnings on each share of common stock. The earnings on each share of common stock is $19.13. The earnings on each share is computed by following this procedure.
STEP 1. *The number of shares of preferred stock and common stock outstanding is determined.* The Transy Corporation has sold 1,000 shares of 6 percent preferred stock and 2,000 shares of common stock.
STEP 2. *The amount of dividends on preferred stock is determined.* This is the amount that must be paid to preferred stockholders before

the common stockholders can receive a distribution. The preferred stock dividend is $6,000 (1,000 shares × $6 per share).

STEP 3. *The $6,000 preferred dividend is subtracted from the $44,250 income after tax.* The difference, $38,250 ($44,250 − $6,000), is the amount available for common stock dividends.

STEP 4. *The $38,250 is divided by the 2,000 shares of common stock outstanding.* Thus each share of common stock earns $19.13 ($38,250 ÷ 2,000) this year.

Accounting Concept:
Financial Statement. An income statement summarizes the revenues and expenses for a period of time. A balance sheet summarizes an accounting equation on a given date.

Activity B. Answer the following questions about the income statement. Refer to the text and illustrations on pages 505 to 507.

1. What are the ten sections of the income statement for a corporation?

2. What is the December 31 net sales for the Transy Corporation?

3. What is the Net Income From Operations?

4. What is the total of Other Expenses on the Income Statement?

5. What is the Net Income Before Income Tax?

6. What is the Net Income After Income Tax?

7. How much does each share of common stock earn during the year?

Statement of Stockholders' Equity

C *What is the statement of stockholders' equity?* **The statement of stockholders' equity** summarizes the changes in the amount of the owners' investment. The two sections of the statement of stockholders' equity are Paid-In Capital and Retained Earnings. Let's examine the statement of stockholders' equity for the Transy Corporation, shown on page 508.

The Paid-In Capital section shows that $100,000 was paid in for the sale of preferred stock and $200,000 was paid in for the sale of common stock. This statement also shows the number of shares of stock authorized, the number of shares issued, and the par value for each type of stock. The rate on preferred stock is also shown.

The Retained Earnings section shows the January 1 balance of Retained Earnings ($120,000). The January 1 balance represents the amount of net income from previous years kept in the business. The January 1 balance for Retained Earnings is increased by the $44,250 net income after taxes and decreased by the $20,000 paid in dividends. The total of Paid-In Capital ($300,000) and the December 31 balance for Retained Earnings ($144,250) are added together to find Total

Two Sections of the Statement of Stockholders' Equity:
• Paid-In Capital
• Retained Earnings

TRANSY CORPORATION
Statement of Stockholders' Equity
For Year Ended December 31, 19—

Paid-In Capital:			
Preferred Stock, 6 percent, $100 par value, 4,000 shares authorized, 1,000 shares issued ($100 × 1,000)			100,000 00
Common Stock, $100 par value, 4,000 shares authorized, 2,000 shares issued ($100 × 2,000)			200,000 00
Total Paid-In Capital			300,000 00
Retained Earnings:			
January 1 Balance		120,000 00*	
Plus: Net Income After Income Tax . . $44,250.00			
Less: Dividends° 20,000.00			
Net Increase		24,250 00	
December 31 Balance			144,250 00
Total Stockholders' Equity			444,250 00

* Taken from Retained Earnings account.

Stockholders' Equity. The total of stockholders' equity, $444,250 ($300,000 + $144,250), will appear on the balance sheet for the Transy Corporation.

Accounting Concept:
Statement of Stockholders' Equity. Changes that occur in stockholders' equity during an accounting period are summarized in a report called the statement of stockholders' equity. Changes in stockholders' equity may result from earning a net income (net loss) as well as from the sale of capital stock.

Accounting Concept:
Stockholders' Equity. Stockholders' equity is classified by source: stockholders' equity that is paid in by stockholders, and stockholders' equity resulting from net income retained in the business.

Activity C. Answer the following questions about the statement of stockholders' equity. Refer to the text and illustrations on pages 507 and 508.

1. What are the two sections of the statement of stockholders' equity?
2. How many shares of preferred stock is the Transy Corporation authorized to issue?

3. How many shares of common stock is the Transy Corporation authorized to issue?
4. What is the dollar amount of the preferred stock outstanding on

December 31? What is the dollar amount of common stock outstanding on December 31?

5. What is the January 1 balance in Retained Earnings? What is the December 31 balance?

6. What is the net increase in Retained Earnings during the year?

7. What is the total stockholders' equity on December 31?

Balance Sheet and End-of-Period Entries

D *Does the balance sheet for a corporation differ from the balance sheet for other forms of businesses?* Yes, there are three basic differences. First, the balance sheet for a corporation may include an intangible asset account called Organization Costs and a current liability account called Income Tax Payable. Second, the corporation may show long-term liabilities in the form of Bonds Payable. Third, the owner's equity section is called stockholders' equity. The Balance Sheet section of the worksheet provides the information for the balance sheet. A partial balance sheet for the Transy Corporation is illustrated here.

TRANSY CORPORATION
Balance Sheet
December 31, 19—

ASSETS			
Current Assets			
Cash			35,000 00
Marketable Securities			60,000 00
Accounts Receivable	50,000 00		
Less: Allowance for Doubtful Accounts	900 00		49,100 00
Intangible Assets			
Organization Costs			220 00
Total Assets			737,450 00
LIABILITIES			
Current Liabilities			
Income Tax Payable			10,750 00
Long-Term Liabilities			
Bonds Payable			100,000 00
Total Liabilities			293,200 00
STOCKHOLDERS' EQUITY			
Total Stockholders' Equity (see Statement)			444,250 00
Total Liabilities and Stockholders' Equity			737,450 00

Adjusting Entries. The adjusting entries for a corporation are recorded in the general journal at the end of each accounting period. Adjusting entries recorded by a corporation are similar to adjusting entries made by any other form of business. However, corporations are required to make adjustments for organization costs and to record the federal income tax. The adjusting entries made by the Transy Corporation for organization costs and federal income tax are shown here. Data for adjusting entries is found in the Adjustment section of the worksheet.

	GENERAL JOURNAL			Page *14*	
DATE	**ACCOUNT TITLE AND EXPLANATION**	**POST. REF.**	**DEBIT**	**CREDIT**	
19—					
Dec. 31	*Organization Expense*	*624*	*110 00*		
	Organization Costs	*144*		*110 00*	
	To amortize organization costs.				
31	*Income Tax Expense*	*517*	*10,750 00*		
	Income Tax Payable	*226*		*10,750 00*	
	To record income taxes payable.				

Closing Entries. Three closing entries are recorded to close the books of the Transy Corporation. The information for the closing entries is taken from the Income Statement section of the worksheet.

The first closing entry is a debit to all of the accounts with balances in the credit column of the Income Statement section. The total of these account balances ($1,575,000) is recorded as a credit to the Income Summary account.

The second closing entry is a debit to the Income Summary account for the total of the debit column ($1,530,750) of the Income Statement section. The entry also requires a credit to each account with a balance in the debit column.

The third closing entry is a debit to the Income Summary account for the amount of net income ($44,250). The Retained Earnings account is credited for the $44,250. These entries are shown on the next page.

Other Accounting Procedures. Other accounting procedures for corporations include donated capital, book value of common stock, treasury stock, stated value, Subchapter S corporation, and stock subscriptions. These procedures are described here.

Donated Capital. **Donated capital** refers to assets given to the corporation. The Donated Capital account has a credit balance and is shown

GENERAL JOURNAL				Page 17	
DATE		**ACCOUNT TITLE AND EXPLANATION**	**POST. REF.**	**DEBIT**	**CREDIT**
19—					
Dec.	31	Sales	401	1,550,000 00	
		Purchases Returns and Allowances	503	20,000 00	
		Purchases Discount	504	5,000 00	
		Income Summary	399		1,575,000 00
		To close accounts with credit balances.			
Dec.	31	Income Summary	399	1,530,750 00	
		Sales Returns and Allowances	402		10,000 00
		Organization Expense	624		110 00
		Income Tax Expense	517		10,750 00
		All Other Accounts	—		1,509,890 00
		To close accounts with debit balances.			
Dec.	31	Income Summary	399	44,250 00	
		Retained Earnings	303		44,250 00
		To record net income.			

as an addition to stockholders' equity. The Donated Capital account appears on the statement of stockholders' equity.

Book Value of Common Stock. The **book value of common stock** is the amount of assets held for each share of common stock outstanding. Book value of common stock for the Transy Corporation is computed as follows.

STEP 1: *Total Assets — Total Liabilities = Net Assets.*

$$\$737,450 - \$293,200 = \$444,250.$$

STEP 2. *Net Assets — Preferred Stock Outstanding = Remaining Assets for Common Stock.*

$$\$444,250 - \$100,000 = \$344,250.$$

STEP 3. *Remaining Assets for Common Stock ÷ Shares of Common Stock Outstanding = Book Value of Common Stock.*

$$\$344,250 \div 2,000 = \$172.13.$$

Treasury Stock. **Treasury stock** is stock that has been sold and then bought back by a corporation. A corporation may buy its own shares of stock to provide a stock bonus to top executives. Dividends are not paid on treasury stock since it is no longer outstanding. Treasury stock is reported as a deduction from Paid-In Capital on the statement of stockholders' equity.

Stated Value. Corporations issuing no-par stock may give the stock a stated value. A **stated value** is similar to par value. Stock with stated value does not sell at a premium or discount.

Subchapter S Corporation. Small corporations may elect to file income tax returns as **Subchapter S corporations.** A corporation deciding to file in this way will be taxed as a partnership. This can result in the corporation paying taxes at lower rates.

Stock Subscriptions. Some corporations sell stock subscriptions. This arrangement allows investors to subscribe to stock and pay for it in installments. Stocks bought by subscription are not issued until the corporation collects the full amount of the sales price.

Activity D. Answer the following questions about the balance sheet, adjusting entries, and other accounting procedures. Refer to text and illustrations on pages 509 and 512.

1. How is the Organization Costs account classified on the balance sheet for the Transy Corporation?
2. What are total assets on December 31?
3. What is the amount of Bonds Payable reported on the December 31 balance sheet?
4. What is the total stockholders' equity for the Transy Corporation on December 31?
5. What is the total liabilities and stockholders' equity?

6. What is the adjusting entry for amortizing organization costs?
7. What is the adjusting entry for recording income tax for the Transy Corporation?
8. How many closing entries are recorded for the Transy Corporation?
9. Explain the following terms: Subchapter S corporation, donated capital, treasury stock, book value of common stock, and stated value.

Topic 2   Problems

13-5. The Saturn Corporation reported $65,000 net income before income tax for the year ended December 31. Saturn had 2,000 shares of $100, 7 percent, preferred stock and 3,000 shares of common stock outstanding.

a. Compute the federal income tax for the Saturn Company.

b. Compute the earnings per share for common stock.

NOTE: Save your working papers for further use in Topic Problem 13-6.

13-6. The Saturn Corporation was formed four years ago at a cost of $600. Use this information and the information from Topic Problem 13-5 to do the following.

a. Compute the amount of organization expenses for the year ended December 31.
b. Record the adjusting entry for amortizing organization cost.

c. Record the adjusting entry for the federal income tax for the year.

13-7. The accounts in the Income Statement section of the worksheet are below. Use them to record the closing entries on December 31.

ACCOUNT TITLE	DEBIT	CREDIT
Sales		390,000 00
Sales Returns and Allowances	3,000 00	
Purchases	220,000 00	
Transportation In	420 00	
Purchases Returns and Allowances		2,500 00
Purchases Discount		1,500 00
Salaries Expense	140,000 00	
Utilities Expense	2,000 00	
Rent Expense	3,600 00	
Miscellaneous Expense	240 00	
Supplies Expense	2,200 00	
Payroll Tax Expense	1,500 00	
Cash Short and Over	20 00	
Organization Expense	100 00	
Income Tax Expense	5,301 00	
Depreciation Expense	4,000 00	
Uncollectible Accounts Expense	550 00	
Income Summary °		10,000 00

*After adjusting Merchandise Inventory account.

13-8. Compute the book value for each share of common stock. See below.

Total Liabilities . . . .$250,000   Shares of Common Stock
Total Assets 950,000   Outstanding 3,000
Preferred Stock 100,000

The Language of Business

Here are some basic terms that make up the language of business. Do you understand the meaning of each? Can you define each term and use it in an original sentence?

corporation
articles of
  incorporation
charter
incorporators
notary public
authorized stock
issued stock
  outstanding
stockholders
investment club
stock certificate
par value
statement of
  stockholders' equity

market value
no-par stock
vote by proxy
preemptive right
domestic corporation
foreign corporation
public corporation
private corporation
limited liability
continuous life
stockbroker
minutes book
chief executive officer
dividend
capital stock

paid-in capital
preferred stock
common stock
premium
discount
stock split
stock certificate book
stockholders' ledger
date of declaration
date of record
stockholders of record
date of payment
cumulative preferred
  stock
stock dividend

participating preferred
  stock
donated capital
book value of common
  stock
Treasury stock
stated value
Subchapter S
  corporation

Chapter 13 Questions

1. What rights do stockholders usually have in a corporation?

2. What are the advantages of the corporation form of ownership? the disadvantages?

3. What is the difference between common stock and preferred stock?

4. What major financial statements are prepared by a corporation? What information is found on each statement?

5. How are earnings per share on common stock computed?

6. Over how many years are organization costs usually allocated?

7. What account is debited to amortize organization costs? What account is credited?

8. What is the difference between a domestic corporation and a foreign corporation?

9. What is the difference between a public corporation and a private corporation?

10. What are two types of private corporations? Give examples of each.

Chapter 13 Problems

Problems for Chapter 13 are given in the *Working Papers and Chapter Problems* for Part 2. If you are using the workbook, do the problems in the space provided there. Complete your assigned topic problems before answering the chapter problems.

Chapter 13 Management Cases

Corporate Ownership. The owners of a corporation are usually separated from the daily management of the business. Thus the owners must rely on financial statements to evaluate the results of operations. Common stockholders can exercise some control over company policies by voting at stockholders' meetings.

Case 13M-1. The stockholders' equity sections of the balance sheets for the Morella Company and Carte Company are shown at the right. The total assets and liabilities of the two businesses are the same. The companies are competitors, and they were started at the same time. Study the information provided and answer the following questions.

a. Which business is probably able to pay the larger dividend? Explain.

b. Assume you have the chance to invest in either company. Which company's stock would you purchase? What type of stock would you purchase? Explain.

	Morella	Carte
Paid-In Capital:		
Preferred Stock	$ 25,000	$ 50,000
Common Stock	50,000	50,000
Total Paid-In Capital	$ 75,000	$100,000
Retained Earnings	75,000	50,000
Total Stockholders' Equity	$150,000	$150,000

Case 13M-2. John Krom owns 600 of the 2,000 outstanding shares of common stock in Nu-Penn Manufacturing Company. Mr. Krom is upset with various company policies, such as the salaries paid to officers and the company's stand on installation of antipollution devices.

a. What percentage of the outstanding stock is owned by John Krom?

b. How might John Krom proceed to have company policies changed?

NOTE: If you are using the *Working Papers and Chapter Problems for Part 2*, complete Project 2.

Interpreting Financial Information

The information shown on a financial statement is used by different groups. Managers inside the business as well as people outside the business use the information on the financial statements. Managers use the data to make decisions regarding running the business. Outsiders—such as creditors, investors, and the government—use the data to make decisions about the business.

Some of the information is useful to all groups. However, each group emphasizes different aspects of the statements. For example, managers use the information to operate the business effectively. Creditors want to make sure that the business can repay its debts. Investors, on the other hand, want to make sure that the business has adequate earnings to protect their investment. The government uses the data for various reports and for taxing purposes.

This chapter presents an overview of how various people analyze (examine) and interpret (explain) financial statements. You will find that a vast amount of useful information can be obtained from a financial statement, if you just know how to approach it. While the examples and illustrations pertain to a corporation, the financial analyses can be used to analyze single proprietorships and partnerships.

Topic 1
Comparison and Trend Analysis

A *How do trends and changes affect the analysis of financial information?* A **trend** is an indication of how a business is operating.

Managers use comparative financial statements to identify trends and changes in their business activities over
several accounting periods.

A **change** occurs when a pattern of activities different from the usual
one takes place.

Managers try to identify trends and changes in their business activities so that they can estimate what will happen. For example, while it
is important to know that sales are rising, it is more important to know
that profits are not falling. It is also important to know if a particular
sales figure is higher or lower than past years' figures. Thus the most
efficient means of obtaining trend and change information is by using
comparative financial statements.

Comparative Financial Statements

A comparative financial
statement shows information
for two or more accounting
periods.

Comparative financial statements present financial information
for two or more accounting periods. This allows someone to view the
trends and changes of the financial position over time. The number of
years used for comparison varies. However, trends are easier to see if
viewed over longer periods of time.

A comparative income statement and a comparative statement of
stockholders' equity for the Lorenzen Company are shown on the next
page. Both statements are presented in a highly condensed form.

LORENZEN COMPANY
Comparative Income Statement (Condensed)
For the Years Ended December 31, 19X2, 19X3, and 19X4

	19X4	19X3	19X2
Net Sales	210,000 00	150,000 00	140,000 00
Cost of Goods Sold	126,000 00	97,500 00	98,000 00
Gross Profit on Sales	84,000 00	52,500 00	42,000 00
Total Operating Expenses	63,800 00	34,500 00	27,500 00
Net Income Before Income Taxes	20,200 00	18,000 00	14,500 00
Provision for Income Taxes . . .	3,400 00	3,000 00	2,500 00
Net Income After Income Taxes	16,800 00	15,000 00	12,000 00

LORENZEN COMPANY
Comparative Statement of Stockholders' Equity
For the Years Ended December 31, 19X2, 19X3, and 19X4

	19X4	19X3	19X2
Capital Stock, January 1	80,000 00	80,000 00	80,000 00
Capital Stock Issued	20,000 00	— 00	— 00
Capital Stock, December 31 . . .	100,000 00	80,000 00	80,000 00
Retained Earnings, January 1	44,000 00	30,200 00	19,800 00
Net Income After Income Taxes	16,800 00	15,000 00	12,000 00
Total	60,800 00	45,200 00	31,800 00
Less Dividends Paid	4,000 00	1,200 00	1,600 00
Retained Earnings, December 31	56,800 00	44,000 00	30,200 00
Total Stockholders' Equity, Dec. 31	156,800 00	124,000 00	110,200 00

Comparing the results of one accounting period with the results of one or more prior periods is called **trend analysis.** A trend analysis can be done for any item on the financial statements. For example, a trend analysis can be made of the net sales for 19X2, 19X3, and 19X4. The dollar amounts used in the trend analysis are $140,000, $150,000, and $210,000.

TREND ANALYSIS (DOLLAR AMOUNTS)

	19X4	19X3	19X2
Net Sales	$210,000	$150,000	$140,000
Amount of Increase	60,000	10,000	—

Line Graphs

Comparative data is frequently shown visually on a graph. Often, it is easier for people to interpret data by looking at a graph than by looking at numbers alone. The graph shown below is called a **line graph** because it uses a line to show the changes and relationships from year to year. The line graph shows the trend of the assets, liabilities, and stockholders' equity for three years: 19X2, 19X3, and 19X4. The amounts are shown in thousands of dollars.

   The comparative balance sheet on the next page shows the amounts for these three elements. The graph helps display the changes that have taken place over the three years.

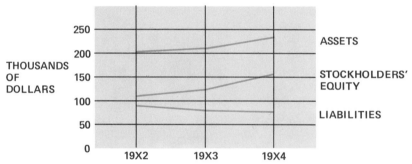

LINE GRAPH OF ASSETS, LIABILITIES, AND STOCK-
HOLDERS' EQUITY FOR THREE YEARS IN DOLLARS.

Activity A. Answer the following questions about comparative financial statements. Give answers for each of the three years: 19X2, 19X3, and 19X4. Refer to the text and illustrations on pages 515 to 518.

1. What time period is covered by the comparative income statements?

2. What are the total current assets?

3. What are the total current liabilities?

4. What are the amounts of dividends declared?

5. What are the total operating expenses?

6. What is the net income before income taxes?

7. What is the provision for income taxes?

8. What is the net income after income taxes?

9. If there were changes in individual assets, which would be more useful—the line graph or the comparative balance sheets?

LORENZEN COMPANY
Comparative Balance Sheet
December 31, 19X2, 19X3, and 19X4

	19X4		19X3		19X2	
ASSETS						
Current Assets:						
Cash	12,000	00	8,000	00	6,500	00
Marketable Securities	14,000	00	10,500	00	11,000	00
Notes Receivable	6,000	00	—	00	—	00
Accounts Receivable (net) . . .	24,000	00	18,000	00	17,000	00
Merchandise Inventory	28,000	00	23,600	00	23,500	00
Prepaid Insurance	2,000	00	2,000	00	1,500	00
Supplies on Hand.	1,000	00	400	00	500	00
Total Current Assets	87,000	00	62,500	00	60,000	00
Investments:						
Marketable Securities	15,000	00	15,000	00	10,000	00
Plant and Equipment:						
Land	37,600	00	37,600	00	37,600	00
Building.	127,000	00	107,000	00	100,000	00
Less: Accumulated						
Depreciation	(38,800	00)	(27,100	00)	(17,400	00)
Total Plant and Equipment	125,800	00	117,500	00	120,200	00
Intangible Assets:						
Patent (net)	8,000	00	9,000	00	10,000	00
Total Assets	235,800	00	204,000	00	200,200	00
LIABILITIES						
Current Liabilities:						
Interest Payable	2,500	00	2,000	00	2,100	00
Accounts Payable	16,500	00	14,000	00	16,900	00
Federal Income Taxes						
Payable	7,000	00	7,000	00	9,000	00
Payroll Taxes Payable	3,000	00	2,000	00	2,000	00
Total Current Liabilities	29,000	00	25,000	00	30,000	00
Long-Term Liabilities:						
Mortgage Payable	50,000	00	55,000	00	60,000	00
Total Liabilities	79,000	00	80,000	00	90,000	00
STOCKHOLDERS' EQUITY						
Capital Stock	100,000	00	80,000	00	80,000	00
Retained Earnings	56,800	00	44,000	00	30,200	00
Total Stockholders'						
Equity	156,800	00	124,000	00	110,200	00
Total Liabilities and						
Stockholders' Equity	235,800	00	204,000	00	200,200	00
Shares Outstanding	2,000		1,600		1,600	

Trend Percentage Analysis

B *Are trends always shown in dollar amounts?* No, dollar changes can be misleading and are often not as useful as percentage changes. The simplest form of percentage analysis is computed by (1) subtracting the dollar amount of the previous year from the comparison year amount and (2) dividing this difference by the previous year amount. A table giving the yearly percentage changes and the dollar changes for the net sales of the Lorenzen Company for 19X2, 19X3, and 19X4 is shown here. The most current year is shown first on the table.

1. Comparison Year
   − Previous Year
   ──────────────
   Increase (or Decrease)

2. $\dfrac{\text{Difference}}{\text{Previous}} = \begin{array}{c}\text{Percent}\\\text{Increase}\end{array}$
   Year (or Decrease)

TREND ANALYSIS
(DOLLAR AMOUNTS AND PERCENTS)

	19X4	19X3	19X2
Net Sales	$210,000	$150,000	$140,000
Amount of Increase	60,000	10,000	—
Percent Increase	40%	7.1%	—

This type of analysis is useful for a year-to-year comparison; here it shows a trend over a three-year period. For example, between 19X3 and 19X4 the net sales increased $60,000 (from $150,000 to $210,000), compared to an increase of $10,000 from 19X2 to 19X3 (from $140,000 to $150,000). The increase in net sales from 19X2 to 19X3 was only 7.1 percent. However, the increase in net sales between 19X3 and 19X4 was 40 percent.

Percentage changes may be more useful than dollar amount changes, but percentages should not be used in isolation. Using both dollar changes and percentage changes presents a clearer financial picture.

Trend percentages indicate increases, decreases, and the rate of the upward and downward movements. However, the percentages do not show if the trend is favorable. To be meaningful, one trend must be compared with other related trends.

The person analyzing the statements must know what to look for and how to evaluate each relationship. For example, an experienced analyst would relate the changes in the merchandise inventory to the changes in sales volume. The analyst would also relate changes in accounts receivable to the changes in sales. A 40 percent increase in inventory and no change in sales volume may indicate that too much money is being invested in inventory compared with the change in sales volume.

TREND ANALYSIS FOR THE YEARS 19X2, 19X3, AND 19X4

For Net Sales, Merchandise Inventory, and Accounts Receivable

	19X4	19X3	19X2
Net Sales:	$210,000	$150,000	$140,000
Dollar Changes	+60,000	+10,000	—
Percent Changes	+40%	+7.1%	—
Merchandise Inventory	$ 28,000	$ 23,600	$ 23,500
Dollar Changes	+4,400	+100	—
Percent Changes	+18.6%	+0.4%	—
Accounts Receivable	$ 24,000	$ 18,000	$ 17,000
Dollar Changes	+6,000	+1,000	—
Percent Changes	+33.3%	+5.9%	—

The comparative financial statements show that changes have occurred from year to year, but they do not indicate the size and causes of the changes. The accountant may use vertical and horizontal analyses, often included on comparative financial statements, to find this information. Vertical and horizontal analyses are discussed below.

Activity B. Compute the yearly percentage increases or decreases for the following items. Refer to the text and illustrations on pages 520 to 521.

	Year 5	Year 4	Year 3	Year 2	Year 1
1. Current assets	$62,000	$50,000	$40,000	$32,000	$25,000
2. Current liabilities	18,000	15,000	12,000	6,000	5,000

3. Which year shows the largest increase in current assets? Which year shows the largest increase in current liabilities?

Vertical Analysis

C *What is vertical analysis?* **Vertical analysis** is used to find the percentage relationship of one item on a financial statement to the total that includes that item. For instance, each item on the income statement may be expressed as a percentage of net sales. Note that each item is divided by the base amount, representing 100 percent, to find the component percentage. This type of analysis is also known as **component percentage analysis.**

The comparative financial statements for the Lorenzen Company on pages 522 and 523 show component percentage analysis. Note that a base amount must be selected for each statement. Financial statements

$$\frac{\text{Component}}{\text{Percentage}} = \frac{\text{Item Amount}}{\text{Base Amount}}$$

are sometimes shown in percentages only. These statements are referred to as **common-size statements.**

Comparative Income Statements. The comparative income statement for the Lorenzen Company shows each item as a percent of Net Sales. Thus Cost of Goods Sold is 60 percent of Net Sales in 19X4, compared to 65 percent in 19X3.

LORENZEN COMPANY
Comparative Income Statement (Condensed)
For the Years Ended December 31, 19X3 and 19X4

	19X4		19X3	
	AMOUNT	PERCENT	AMOUNT	PERCENT
Net Sales*	210,000 00	100.0%	150,000 00	100.0%
Cost of Goods Sold.....	126,000 00	60.0	97,500 00	65.0
Gross Profit on Sales....	84,000 00	40.0%	52,500 00	35.0%
Total Operating Expenses	63,800 00	30.4	34,500 00	23.0
Net Income Before Income Taxes	20,200 00	9.6%	18,000 00	12.0%
Provision for Income Taxes	3,400 00	1.6	3,000 00	2.0
Net Income After Income Taxes	16,800 00	8.0%	15,000 00	10.0%

*Base amounts.

As you view the comparative income statement, certain changes are evident. The Cost of Goods Sold is a smaller percentage of Net Sales in 19X4 (60 percent) than in 19X3 (65 percent). Why? Perhaps buying procedures were improved in 19X4, or procedures to control the theft or misuse of merchandise were started. What the comparative income statement *does* tell us is that the gross profit on sales is a greater percentage in 19X4 (40 percent) than in 19X3 (35 percent). As you examine the statements, you will also see that the operating expenses percentage increased in 19X4.

Comparative Statement of Stockholders' Equity. This statement shows the relationship between capital stock and retained earnings at the end of the accounting period. As you can see in the statement shown at the top of the next page, retained earnings represent 35.5 percent of the total stockholders' equity in 19X3. In 19X4 this percentage increases to 36.2 percent. Thus, even though additional capital stock is issued, the percent of capital stock decreases.

Comparative Balance Sheet. The various assets on the comparative balance sheet are stated as percentages of total assets. The liability items and stockholders' equity items are given as percentages of Total

LORENZEN COMPANY
Comparative Statement of Stockholders' Equity (Condensed)
For the Years Ended December 31, 19X3 and 19X4

	19X4		19X3	
	AMOUNT	PERCENT	AMOUNT	PERCENT
Capital Stock, December 31........	100,000 00	63.8%	80,000 00	64.5%
Retained Earnings, December 31........	56,800 00	36.2%	44,000 00	35.5%
Total Stockholders' Equity, December 31°.	156,800 00	100.0%	124,000 00	100.0%

*Base amounts.

Liabilities and Stockholders' Equity. Therefore Current Assets is 30.6 percent of Total Assets in 19X3. Investments is 7.4 percent, Plant and Equipment is 57.6 percent, and Intangible Assets is 4.4 percent. In each case the total assets are the base.

LORENZEN COMPANY
Comparative Balance Sheet (Condensed)
December 31, 19X3 and 19X4

	19X4		19X3	
	AMOUNT	PERCENT	AMOUNT	PERCENT
ASSETS				
Current Assets	87,000 00	36.9 %	62,500 00	30.6 %
Investments	15,000 00	6.4	15,000 00	7.4
Plant and Equipment ...	125,800 00	53.3	117,500 00	57.6
Intangible Assets	8,000 00	3.4	9,000 00	4.4
Total Assets°	235,800 00	100.00%	204,000 00	100.00%
LIABILITIES				
Current Liabilities	29,000 00	12.3 %	25,000 00	12.2 %
Long-Term Liabilities ...	50,000 00	21.2	55,000 00	27.0
Total Liabilities	79,000 00	33.5 %	80,000 00	39.2 %
STOCKHOLDERS' EQUITY				
Capital Stock	100,000 00	42.4 %	80,000 00	39.2 %
Retained Earnings	56,800 00	24.1	44,000 00	21.6
Total Stockholders' Equity..........	156,800 00	66.5 %	124,000 00	60.8 %
Total Liabilities and Stockholders' Equity °	235,800 00	100.00%	204,000 00	100.00%

*Base amounts.

As you examine the comparative balance sheet, note that the composition of assets is changing from year to year. Current Assets is 30.6 percent of Total Assets in 19X3, but it increases to 36.9 percent in 19X4. Plant and Equipment decreases as a percent of Total Assets (from 57.6 percent in 19X3 to 53.3 percent in 19X4).

The analysis also shows the relationship between the creditors (liabilities) and the owners (stockholders' equity). In 19X3 the creditors supply 39.2 percent of the resources and the owners supply 60.8 percent. In 19X4, however, the owners supply 66.5 percent, compared to 33.5 percent supplied by the creditors. Thus the owners' claim against the assets of the business increases.

Circle Graphs

A line graph was used earlier in this chapter to show the changes and the relationship among assets, liabilities, and stockholders' equity for three years. Another type of graph used in business is a circle graph. The **circle graph,** commonly called a *pie chart*, is a circle divided into parts to show the relationship among the items and the total. The following circle graph shows the relationship of net sales to cost of goods sold, operating expenses, and net income before taxes for 19X4.

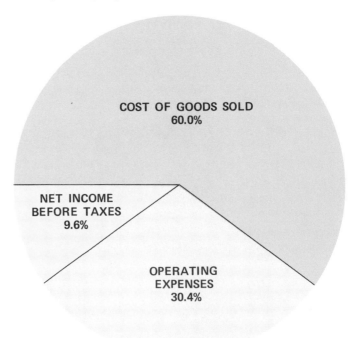

LORENZEN COMPANY
For the Year Ended December 31, 19X4

The comparative income statement below shows all the items as a percentage of net sales. The cost of goods sold in 19X4 is 60.0 percent; operating expenses are 30.4 percent; and net income before taxes is 9.6 percent. The circle graph helps display the impact that each item has on the sales revenue during the period.

Activity C. Answer the following questions about comparative financial statements. Refer to the text and illustrations on pages 521 to 525.

1. Which item is the largest percent of Total Assets for 19X3? 19X4?

2. What portion of Total Liabilities and Stockholders' Equity is represented by creditors (Total Liabilities) for 19X3? 19X4?

3. What appears to be the reason for the change in percentages listed in Question 2 above?

4. Why is the Net Income of $15,000 in 19X3 shown as 10 percent, whereas the Net Income of $16,800 in 19X4 is shown as only 8 percent?

5. Can you say that Cash increases by 6.3 percent (36.9 percent minus 30.6 percent)?

6. Would you rather have the 10 percent Net Income for 19X3 or the 8 percent Net Income for 19X4? Why?

7. What portion of the total stockholders' equity is represented by the capital stock for 19X3? 19X4?

Horizontal Analysis

D *What is horizontal analysis?* The analysis of similar items of financial information across two or more accounting periods is called **horizontal analysis.** For example, Cash on the Lorenzen Company balance sheet illustrates horizontal analysis for 19X3 and 19X4.

Cash increases from $8,000 in 19X3 to $12,000 in 19X4. This is an increase of $4,000, or 50 percent. The change in Cash is expressed as both a dollar amount (absolute change) and a percentage (relative change). The $4,000 increase takes on more importance when you

| | 19X4 | 19X3 | Increase/Decrease | |
			Amount	Percent
Current Assets:				
Cash	$12,000	$8,000	$4,000	50.0%

realize that it is a 50 percent increase. Note that the **base year** is the earlier period. Thus 19X3 is the base year used to compute the change.

Horizontal analysis can be completed for all three years (19X2, 19X3, and 19X4). The three-year illustration follows.

| | 19X4 | 19X3 | 19X2 | Increase/Decrease | | | |
| | | | | 19X3–19X4 | | 19X2–19X3 | |
				Amount	Percent	Amount	Percent
Current Assets:							
Cash	$12,000	$8,000	$6,500	$4,000	50.0%	$1,500	23.1%

With 19X2 as the base year, the increase in cash from 19X2 to 19X3 is $1,500 ($6,500 to $8,000), or 23.1 percent. Using 19X3 as the base year, the increase in cash from 19X3 to 19X4 is $4,000, or 50 percent.

Comparative financial statements, including horizontal analysis, for the Lorenzen Company for 19X3 and 19X4 are shown below and on page 527. As you study the illustrations, remember that the percentages relate only to one particular item on the statements. For example, the 50 percent change in cash relates only to cash. It does not relate to the 150 percent change in supplies or to any other changes.

LORENZEN COMPANY
Comparative Income Statement (Condensed)
For the Years Ended December 31, 19X3 and 19X4

| | 19X4 | 19X3 | INCREASE/DECREASE | |
			DOLLARS	PERCENT
Net Sales	210,000 00	150,000 00	60,000 00	40.0%
Cost of Goods Sold.	126,000 00	97,500 00	28,500 00	29.2
Gross Profit on Sales.	84,000 00	52,500 00	31,500 00	60.0
Total Operating Expenses	63,800 00	34,500 00	29,300 00	84.9
Net Income Before Income Taxes	20,200 00	18,000 00	2,200 00	12.2
Provision for Income Taxes	3,400 00	3,000 00	400 00	13.3
Net Income After Income Taxes .	16,800 00	15,000 00	1,800 00	12.0%

LORENZEN COMPANY
Comparative Statement of Stockholders' Equity
For the Years Ended December 31, 19X3 and 19X4

| | 19X4 | 19X3 | INCREASE/DECREASE | |
			DOLLARS	PERCENT
Capital Stock, January 1	80,000 00	80,000 00		
Capital Stock Issued	20,000 00	— 00		
Capital Stock, December 31	100,000 00	80,000 00	20,000 00	25.0%
Retained Earnings, January 1 . .	44,000 00	30,200 00	13,800 00	45.7
Net Income After Income Taxes .	16,800 00	15,000 00	1,800 00	12.0
Total	60,800 00	45,200 00	15,600 00	34.5
Less Dividends Declared	4,000 00	1,200 00	2,800 00	233.3
Retained Earnings, December 31 .	56,800 00	44,000 00	12,800 00	29.1%
Total Stockholder's Equity, December 31	156,800 00	124,000 00	32,800 00	26.5%

LORENZEN COMPANY
Comparative Balance Sheet
For the Years Ended December 31, 19X3 and 19X4

	19X4	19X3	INCREASE/DECREASE DOLLARS	INCREASE/DECREASE PERCENT
ASSETS				
Current Assets:				
Cash	12,000 00	8,000 00	4,000 00	50.0%
Marketable Securities	14,000 00	10,500 00	3,500 00	33.3
Notes Receivable	6,000 00	— 00	6,000 00	—
Accounts Receivable (net) . . .	24,000 00	18,000 00	6,000 00	33.3
Merchandise Inventory	28,000 00	23,600 00	4,400 00	18.6
Prepaid Insurance	2,000 00	2,000 00	— 00	0.0
Supplies	1,000 00	400 00	600 00	150.0
Total Current Assets	87,000 00	62,500 00	24,500 00	39.2%
Investments:				
Marketable Securities	15,000 00	15,000 00	— 00	0.0%
Plant and Equipment:				
Land	37,600 00	37,600 00	— 00	0.0%
Building	127,000 00	107,000 00	20,000 00	18.7
Less: Accumulated				
Depreciation	(38,800 00)	(27,100 00)	11,700 00	43.2
Total Plant and Equipment .	125,800 00	117,500 00	8,300 00	7.1%
Intangible Assets:				
Patent (net)	8,000 00	9,000 00	(1,000 00)	(11.1%)
Total Assets	235,800 00	204,000 00	31,800 00	15.6%
LIABILITIES				
Current Liabilities				
Interest Payable	2,500 00	2,000 00	500 00	25.0%
Accounts Payable	16,500 00	14,000 00	2,500 00	17.9
Federal Income Taxes Payable .	7,000 00	7,000 00	— 00	—
Payroll Taxes Payable	3,000 00	2,000 00	1,000 00	50.0
Total Current Liabilities . . .	29,000 00	25,000 00	4,000 00	16.0%
Long-Term Liabilities:				
Mortgage Payable	50,000 00	55,000 00	(5,000 00)	(9.1%)
Total Liabilities	79,000 00	80,000 00	(1,000 00)	(1.3%)
STOCKHOLDERS' EQUITY				
Capital Stock	100,000 00	80,000 00	20,000 00	25.0%
Retained Earnings	56,800 00	44,000 00	12,800 00	29.1
Total Stockholders' Equity . . .	156,800 00	124,000 00	32,800 00	26.5
Total Liabilities and				
Stockholders' Equity	235,800 00	204,000 00	31,800 00	15.6
Shares Outstanding	2,000	1,600	400	25.0%

The comparative income statement shows a sales increase of 40 percent from 19X3 to 19X4. Yet the cost of goods sold increases only 29.2 percent. This shows that sales are increasing at a greater rate than the cost of goods.

Horizontal analysis can be used to study trends on a balance sheet and an income statement.

Bar Graphs

A pie graph was used in the previous learning unit to show the relationship among the items that make up sales revenue. Earlier a line graph was used to show the trend of assets, liabilities, and stockholders' equity for three years. Another type of graph is the bar graph. The **bar graph** is so named because bars are used to show the relationship between amounts.

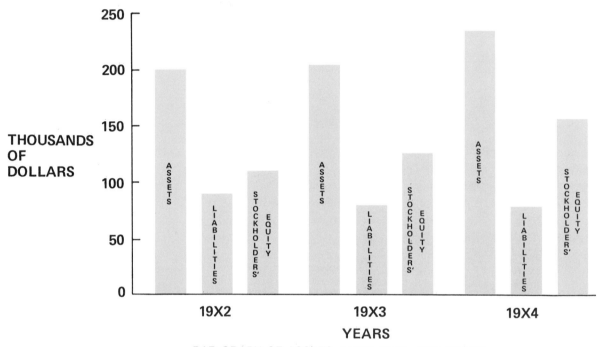

BAR GRAPH OF ASSETS, LIABILITIES, AND STOCK-HOLDERS' EQUITY FOR THREE YEARS IN DOLLARS

A bar graph is used here to show the trends and relationships among the total assets, total liabilities, and total stockholders' equity for the years 19X2, 19X3, and 19X4. This plots the same data shown in the line graph on page 519, but it does give a different appearance.

Activity D. Answer the following questions about comparative financial statements. Refer to the text and illustrations on pages 525 to 528.

1. By how much does Marketable Securities increase? By what percent?

2. What current asset has the largest percent increase?

3. What current asset has the largest dollar increase?

4. What does the (11.1) in the percent column opposite Patents indicate?

5. By looking at the amount of Retained Earnings, can you tell what caused the increase in this account? If not, where would you look?
6. Which income statement element—Net Sales, Cost of Goods Sold, Operating Expenses, or

Income Taxes—is increasing at the fastest rate?
7. Which income statement element—Net Sales, Cost of Goods Sold, Operating Expenses, or Income Taxes—is showing the largest dollar increase?

Topic 1 Problems

14-1. Listed here are nine characteristics of analyzing information. Indicate whether the characteristic describes horizontal analysis or vertical analysis.

a. Deals with two or more accounting periods.
b. Relates all equity items to Total Liabilities and Stockholders' Equity.
c. Percents relate to only one item and not to other items.
d. Indicates that the composition of balance sheet categories is changing.

e. Identifies the sources of financing for one date.
f. Uses dollar amount increases or decreases.
g. Deals with only one accounting period.
h. Uses a base year in making comparisons.
i. Percents are not compared with other accounting periods.

14-2. Financial information taken from the financial statements for the Pride Corporation for 19X3 and 19X4 is shown here. Complete the schedule by filling in the missing information.

			Increase/Decrease	
Item	**19X4**	**19X3**	**Dollars**	**Percent**
a. Cash	$ 14,000	$ 12,000	$_____	_____%
b. Supplies on Hand	14,000	_____	3,000	_____
c. Accounts Payable	_____	26,000	2,000	_____
d. Common Stock	320,000	300,000	_____	_____
e. Retained Earnings	70,000	50,000	20,000	_____
f. Net Sales	_____	300,000	60,000	20
g. Cost of Goods Sold	160,000	150,000	_____	_____
h. Net Income	_____	30,000	10,000	$33\frac{1}{3}$

14-3. Comparative financial information for Maxwell Inc. is illustrated on pages 530 and 531.
a. Complete the horizontal analysis for 19X2 and 19X3, and the horizontal analysis for 19X3 and 19X4. When comparing 19X2 with 19X3, remember that 19X2 is the base year; when comparing 19X3 with 19X4, remember that 19X3 is the base year.

MAXWELL INC.
Comparative Balance Sheet
For the Years Ended December 31, 19X2, 19X3, and 19X4

	19X4	19X3	19X2
ASSETS			
Current Assets:			
Cash	3,000 00	10,000 00	9,750 00
Marketable Securities.	19,800 00	16,500 00	16,500 00
Notes Receivable	600 00	800 00	500 00
Accounts Receivable (net) .	23,800 00	32,300 00	25,500 00
Merchandise Inventory . . .	45,800 00	44,600 00	35,250 00
Prepaid Insurance	2,000 00	1,900 00	1,750 00
Supplies on Hand	1,000 00	900 00	750 00
Total Current Assets. . . .	96,000 00	107,000 00	90,000 00
Investments:			
Marketable Securities	19,000 00	16,000 00	15,000 00
Plant and Equipment:			
Machinery (Various Assets)	247,680 00	247,680 00	206,400 00
Less: Accumulated			
Depreciation	60,540 00	45,320 00	26,100 00
Total Plant and			
Equipment	187,140 00	202,360 00	180,300 00
Intangible Assets:			
Patent (net)	13,000 00	14,000 00	15,000 00
Total Assets	315,140 00	339,360 00	300,300 00
LIABILITIES			
Current Liabilities:			
Interest Payable	2,800 00	3,600 00	3,000 00
Accounts Payable	31,500 00	30,420 00	25,350 00
Federal Income Taxes			
Payable.	2,000 00	16,200 00	13,500 00
Payroll Taxes Payable	3,700 00	3,780 00	3,150 00
Total Current Liabilities	40,000 00	54,000 00	45,000 00
Long-Term Liabilities:			
Mortgage Payable	80,000 00	85,000 00	90,000 00
Total Liabilities.	120,000 00	139,000 00	135,000 00
STOCKHOLDERS' EQUITY			
Capital Stock	147,000 00	147,000 00	120,000 00
Retained Earnings	48,140 00	53,360 00	45,300 00
Total Stockholders'			
Equity.	195,140 00	200,360 00	165,300 00
Total Liabilities and			
Stockholder's Equity	315,140 00	339,360 00	300,300 00

MAXWELL INC.
Comparative Income Statement (Condensed)
For the Years Ended December 31, 19X2, 19X3, and 19X4

	19X4	19X3	19X2
Net Sales	224,000 00	252,000 00	210,000 00
Cost of Goods Sold	165,000 00	176,400 00	147,000 00
Gross Profit on Sales	59,000 00	75,600 00	63,000 00
Total Operating Expenses . . .	54,200 00	49,100 00	41,300 00
Net Income Before Income Taxes	4,800 00	26,500 00	21,700 00
Provision for Income Taxes . .	800 00	4,900 00	3,700 00
Net Income After Income Taxes	4,000 00	21,600 00	18,00 00

b. Which item shows the largest percent increase for 19X2 to 19X3? the largest decrease?
c. Which item shows the largest percent increase for 19X3 to 19X4? the largest decrease?
d. Which income statement element appears to be contributing most to the decrease in net income from 19X3 to 19X4?

e. Which current liability appears to be contributing most to the decrease in Total Current Liabilities from 19X3 to 19X4?
f. Which item shows the greatest percent change for 19X3 to 19X4? What is the percent?
g. What appears to be happening with the composition of current assets?

NOTE: Save your working papers for further use in Topic Problems 14-4, 14-9, 14-13, and 14-17 to 14-19.

14-4. Refer to the comparative financial information for Maxwell Inc. from Topic Problem 14-3 to complete the following items.
a. Complete a vertical analysis for both 19X3 and 19X4. Compute each liability and stockholder equity item as a percent of Total Liabilities and Stockholders' Equity.

b. Which element represents the largest percent of Total Assets for 19X3?

c. What portion of Total Liabilities and Stockholders' Equity is represented by creditors (Total Liabilities) for 19X3? 19X4?

d. What appears to be contributing to the change in percents you listed in Question c above?

Topic 2
Ratios That Measure Current Position

A *Do all analyses involve trends over years?* No, many analyses involve relationships between two amounts for one accounting period. For example, analysts might want to compare the debts owed with the business's ability to pay the debts.

The numeric relationship of one amount to another amount is called a **ratio**. A ratio may be expressed as a number, a percentage, or a fraction. For example, if sales are $500,000 and net income is $50,000, the ratio can be expressed as follows.

A ratio may be a number, percentage, or fraction.

$$\text{Sales} \div \text{Net Income} = \text{Numeric Ratio}$$
$$\$500,000 \div \$50,000 = 10$$

You can say that the ratio of sales to net income is 10 to 1, often written 10:1. A ratio can also be expressed as a percent.

$$\text{Net Income} \div \text{Sales} = \text{Percentage Ratio}$$
$$\$50,000 \div \$500,000 = 0.10, \text{ or } 10\%$$

In this case you say that net income is 10 percent of sales. Also, ratios may be expressed as fractions.

$$\text{Net Income} \div \text{Sales} = \text{Fractional Ratio}$$
$$\$50,000 \div \$500,000 = \tfrac{1}{10}$$

This ratio states that net income is one-tenth of sales.

One problem when interpreting financial information is deciding what ratio is satisfactory for a given business. For example, is a 10 percent net income on sales satisfactory for the Lorenzen Company? The Carol Corporation considers a 5 percent net income on sales acceptable. The difference between the ratios that two businesses might find acceptable is found by looking at financial characteristics of the businesses.

Accountants look to different sources to compare ratios. Some sources they use are:

• The results of previous accounting periods.

• The results of similar businesses in the same industry.

• The results found in published government or investment guides.

In this topic we will look at various ratios accountants compute for their businesses. These ratios can then be compared with any of the preceding sources.

Current Ratio

For accounting purposes, **working capital** is the difference between current assets and current liabilities. For instance, if a company has current assets of $100,000 and current liabilities of $60,000, the working capital is $40,000 ($100,000 − $60,000).

A company obtains an idea of its ability to pay current debts by computing working capital. If there are more current assets than current liabilities, the company will be able to pay current debts and is described as **solvent.** If there are more current liabilities than current assets, the company will not be able to pay current debts and is described as **insolvent.**

Computing working capital is one measure used to find debt-paying ability. Working capital can be further interpreted if more information is desired.

The **current ratio,** or *working capital ratio,* is the numeric relationship between current assets and current liabilities.

The current ratio shows the number of dollars of current assets available for each dollar of current liabilities. The current ratio is found by dividing the total current assets by the total current liabilities. The current ratio computed for the Lorenzen Company appears here.

$$\frac{\text{Current Assets}}{\text{Current Liabilities}} = \text{Current Ratio}$$

$$\frac{\$87,000}{\$29,000} = 3 = 3:1$$

The current ratio for the Lorenzen Company would be expressed as 3:1, meaning that the business owns $3 of current assets for each $1 of current liabilities. You can see that Lorenzen Company is in a better position to pay current debts than a company that would have a ratio of 1.39:1 ($1.39 to $1).

The higher the current ratio, the more favorable is the financial position of the business. A current ratio of 2:1 has been generally accepted as a satisfactory ratio. But this varies from business to business. Some businesses require a larger amount of working capital. Heavy machinery manufacturers may require a current ratio as high as 5:1.

Computing working capital helps a company determine its solvency or insolvency.

The higher a business's current ratio, the more favorable is its financial position.

Accounting Concept:
Working Capital. Working capital is one indicator of a business's ability to pay its current liabilities. Working capital is the difference between current assets and current liabilities.

Activity A-1. Compute the working capital and current ratios for the following businesses. Refer to the text on pages 532 to 534.

1. Current assets, $800,000; current liabilities, $400,000.

2. Current assets, $250,000; current liabilities, $100,000.

3. Current assets, $50,000; current liabilities, $40,000.

4. Current assets, $24,000; current liabilities, $6,000.

5. Current assets, $20,000; current liabilities, $25,000.

Activity A-2. Listed here are the account balances from the Xena Corporation's financial statements.

Cash, $8,000
Accounts Receivable (net), $18,000
Sales, $210,000
Mortgage Payable, $40,000
Accounts Payable, $7,000
Merchandise Inventory, $20,000
Prepaid Insurance, $1,000

FICA Taxes Payable, $1,000
Marketable Securities, $2,000
Investments, $12,000
Supplies, $1,000
Employee Income Taxes Payable, $8,000

1. Indicate which accounts are used to compute working capital.
2. Compute the amount of the working capital.

3. Compute the current ratio for Xena Corporation.

Quick Assets Ratio

B *Does the current ratio show whether or not a company can meet sudden demands for payment?* No, individuals concerned with a company's ability to "quickly" pay current debts often compute the quick ratio. The **quick assets ratio,** also called the *acid test ratio,* is found by dividing the quick assets by the total current liabilities. **Quick assets** are current assets that are easily convertible to cash. Thus current assets like cash, accounts receivable, short-term notes receivable, and short-term investments in marketable securities are quick assets because they are readily available for paying current liabilities. Current assets like merchandise inventory, supplies, and prepaid insurance are not easily convertible to cash since they would have to be sold before cash is available.

The computation of the quick assets ratio is illustrated here.

Examples of Quick Assets:
- Cash
- Accounts receivable
- Short-term notes receivable
- Short-term marketable securities

$$\frac{\text{Quick Assets}}{\text{Current Liabilities}} = \text{Quick Assets (Acid Test) Ratio}$$

LORENZEN COMPANY
Balance Sheet
December 31, 19X4

Current Assets:			Quick Assets	
Cash	12,000	00	$12,000	00
Marketable Securities	14,000	00	14,000	00
Notes Receivable . . .	6,000	00	6,000	00
Accounts Receivable				
(net)	24,000	00	24,000	00
Merchandise Inventory	28,000	00	$56,000	00
Prepaid Insurance . .	2,000	00		
Supplies on Hand. . .	1,000	00		
Total Current Assets	87,000	00		

$$\frac{\$56,000}{\$29,000} = 1.93$$

On December 31, 19X4, the Lorenzen Company has a quick assets ratio of 1.93:1, meaning it owns $1.93 of quick assets for each $1 of current liabilities. A quick assets ratio of 1:1 is generally considered satisfactory. However, the quick ratio for a particular business must be evaluated in light of the type of business analyzed.

Activity B-1. Answer the following questions on quick ratios. Refer to the text and illustration on pages 534 and 535.

1. What are the total current assets?

2. What are the total quick assets?

3. What assets make up the quick assets?

4. What is the quick assets ratio?

5. Why is Merchandise Inventory not included as a quick asset?

Activity B-2. The current assets for the Rosen Corporation include the following: Cash, $11,000; Accounts Receivable, $13,000; Merchandise Inventory, $14,000; Supplies, $4,000; Prepaid Expenses, $1,000. Current liabilities are $16,000. Compute the quick ratio.

Activity B-3. The 19X2, 19X3, and 19X4 comparative balance sheet for the Lorenzen Company is given on page 519.

1. Compute the working capital for each of the years.

2. Compute the current ratio for each of the years.

3. Compute the quick assets ratio for each of the years.

4. From the Lorenzen Company's point of view, in which year or years was the current ratio most favorable? the quick assets ratio?

5. Are your answers in Question 4 the same for the current ratio and the quick assets ratio? Explain why they are or are not.

Accounts Receivable Turnover

C *Are there ratios that tell if customers are paying their accounts promptly?* Yes, accounts receivable turnover gives this information.

Accounts receivable turnover is used to find the number of times the average amount of accounts receivable is collected and replaced during an accounting period. To compute the accounts receivable turnover, the accountant divides the sales for the accounting period by the average amounts of accounts receivable. The 19X4 accounts receivable turnover for the Lorenzen Company is illustrated here. Notice that information is obtained from the balance sheets for 19X3 and 19X4 and the income statement for 19X4.

$$\frac{\text{Beginning Accounts Receivable} + \text{Ending Accounts Receivable}}{2} = \text{Average Accounts Receivable}$$

$$\frac{\text{Sales}}{\text{Average Accounts Receivable}} = \text{Accounts Receivable Turnover}$$

$$\frac{\$18,000 \ (19X3) + \$24,000 \ (19X4) = \$42,000}{2} = \$21,000$$

$$\frac{\$210,000}{21,000} = 10$$

In the illustration, Sales ($210,000) is obtained from the income statement prepared on December 31, 19X4. The accounts receivable balances are obtained from the balance sheets prepared on December 31, 19X3, and December 31, 19X4. The average accounts receivable is found by adding the beginning balance of Accounts Receivable ($18,000 on December 31, 19X3) to the ending balance ($24,000 on December 31, 19X4) and dividing by 2. Some businesses will use the accounts receivable balances for each month of the accounting period to eliminate seasonal differences in amounts owed by customers.

The accounts receivable turnover for the Lorenzen Company is 10. At the beginning of 19X4, the balance of accounts receivable is $18,000. During the period, charge sales increase accounts receivable. Also during the period, cash received from charge customers decreases accounts receivable. These transactions leave a $24,000 balance in accounts receivable on December 31, 19X4. Thus the average balance of accounts receivable turns over, or is collected and replaced, with charge sales 10 times during the year.

Computing the collection period for accounts receivable is another aspect of accounts receivable turnover. The **collection period** is the average length of time it takes to collect the accounts receivable. The collection period is found by dividing the number of days in the accounting period by the turnover rate.

For the Lorenzen Company, the customers are paying their accounts in 37 (36.5) days.

$$\text{Collection Period} = \frac{\text{Number of Days in Accounting Period}}{\text{Turnover Rate}}$$

$$\frac{\text{Days in Accounting Period}}{\text{Accounts Receivable Turnover}} = \text{Collection Period}$$

$$\frac{365 \text{ Days}}{10} = 36.5 \text{ Days} = 37 \text{ Days}$$

If we assume that the Lorenzen Company's credit policy is 60 days, the analysis here shows that the customers are paying on time. The average customer pays within 37 days.

Here is a schedule for the Lorenzen Company that includes accounts receivable turnover information for 19X3 and 19X4. As this illustration shows, the customers are paying their accounts sooner in 19X4 than in 19X3. This is a good position for the Lorenzen Company to be in.

COMPARATIVE ACCOUNTS RECEIVABLE TURNOVER RATES AND COLLECTION PERIODS FOR 19X3 AND 19X4

	19X4	19X3
A. Net Sales	$210,000	$150,000
Accounts Receivable:		
Beginning of Year	$ 18,000	$ 17,000
End of Year	24,000	18,000
B. Beginning and Ending Balances	$ 42,000	$ 35,000
C. Average Accounts Receivable $\left(\frac{B}{2}\right)$	$ 21,000	$ 17,500
Accounts Receivable Turnover $\left(\frac{A}{C}\right)$	10.0	8.6
Collection Period $\left(\frac{365 \text{ Days}}{\text{Turnover}}\right)$	37 Days	42 Days

The Lorenzen Company has working capital invested in accounts receivable for a shorter time in 19X4 (37 days) than in 19X3 (42 days). Customers are paying within the 60-day period set by management.

This discussion assumed that all sales were credit sales. In practice, cash sales could be subtracted from net sales to find charge sales.

Activity C-1. Answer the following questions about accounts receivable turnover and the collection period of accounts receivable. Refer to the text and illustrations on pages 536 and 537.

1. What are the net sales for 19X4?
2. How is the average accounts receivable for 19X4 computed?
3. What is the accounts receivable turnover for 19X3? 19X4?
4. What is the collection period in 19X3? 19X4?
5. How are the collection periods computed for 19X4?

6. What does an accounts receivable turnover ratio of 8.6 for 19X3 mean?
7. What does a collection period of 42 days for 19X3 mean?
8. Is the collection period better in 19X3 or in 19X4?

Activity C-2. Marcus Inc. has an annual accounting period. Compute the collection periods for the following accounts receivable turnover.

1. 10.0
2. 5.0
3. 6.0

4. 7.0
5. 8.5

Merchandise Inventory Turnover

D *Are there ratios that tell how long it takes to sell merchandise?* Yes, the merchandise inventory turnover provides this information. Merchandise inventory is the heart of a merchandising business. If customers are to be satisfied, the proper *kinds* and *quality* of merchandise must be available.

It must also be recognized that merchandise inventory represents certain costs to the business. Merchandise must be stored and insured. It must be protected against theft or damage. The cost of merchandise represents money that could be used for other purposes. Thus it is important for a company to know how much time merchandise remains as inventory. An important first step is computing merchandise inventory turnover.

Merchandise inventory turnover is the ratio between the cost of goods sold and the average inventory balance. The ratio can be viewed as a "turnover" or as "days' supply of inventory." The turnover view indicates the number of times the dollar value of inventory is sold and replaced. The days' supply view indicates the average number of days merchandise stays in the inventory until it is sold. Merchandise inventory turnover is used to find the relationship between merchandise in inventory and the merchandise sold.

Merchandise inventory turnover is computed by dividing the Cost of Goods Sold by the average merchandise inventory. The computation of merchandise inventory turnover for the Lorenzen Company is shown at the top of the next page. The procedure is similar to that discussed for finding the average accounts receivable.

$$\frac{\text{Beginning Merchandise Inventory} + \text{Ending Merchandise Inventory}}{2} = \frac{\text{Average}}{\text{Merchandise Inventory}}$$

$$\frac{\text{Cost of Goods Sold}}{\text{Average Merchandise Inventory}} = \frac{\text{Merchandise}}{\text{Inventory Turnover}}$$

$$\frac{\$23{,}600 \ (19\text{X}3) + \$28{,}000 \ (19\text{X}4)}{2} = \$25{,}800$$

$$\frac{\$126{,}000}{\$25{,}800} = 4.9$$

The Cost of Goods Sold ($126,000) is found on the income statement for 19X4. An average of the balances of the merchandise inventory is used to eliminate seasonal differences. The average merchandise inventory ($25,800) is found by adding the beginning inventory ($23,600 as of December 31, 19X3) and ending inventory ($28,000 as of December 31, 19X4) and dividing by 2.

A merchandise inventory turnover of 4.9 means that the Lorenzen Company sells, on the average, the *dollar amount* of its merchandise inventory 4.9 times during 19X4. Note the emphasis on the words *dollar amount.* It is the $25,800 average merchandise inventory that turns over 4.9 times—not every item of inventory. It may be that some inventory items turn over more than 4.9 times and some turn over less than 4.9 times. The perpetual inventory cards or the actual inventory must be reviewed to see how particular items are selling.

The merchandise analysis can be taken one more step. If sales are made from merchandise inventory, then how many days' supply of sales, on the average, does the Lorenzen Company have in inventory? The **days' supply in inventory** is the average length of time merchandise stays in inventory until it is sold.

> A higher merchandise inventory turnover rate means merchandise is being sold faster.

$$\frac{\text{Days in Accounting Period}}{\text{Merchandise Inventory Turnover}} = \text{Days' Supply in Inventory}$$

$$\frac{365}{4.9} = 74 \text{ Days}$$

To find the days' supply of merchandise in inventory, divide the number of days in the accounting period (365) by the inventory turnover rate. Dividing 4.9 into an accounting period of 365 days gives an average inventory covering 74 days' sales. You could also look at the 74 days' sales in inventory this way: A merchandise inventory turnover of

$$\frac{\text{Days'}}{\text{Supply in}} = \frac{\text{Number of Days in Accounting Period}}{\text{Inventory Turnover Rate}}$$

4.9 means that it takes 74 days to sell the average dollar amount of merchandise inventory. Or, in other words, merchandise sits on the shelf 74 days (on the average) before it is sold.

The merchandise inventory turnover for 19X4 can be compared with turnovers for other years. A comparison with the 19X3 merchandise inventory turnover is shown here.

COMPARATIVE MERCHANDISE INVENTORY TURNOVER RATES AND DAYS' SUPPLY IN INVENTORY FOR 19X3 AND 19X4

	19X4	19X3
A. Cost of Goods Sold	$126,000	$97,500
Merchandise Inventory:		
Beginning of Year	$ 23,600	$23,500
End of Year	28,000	23,600
B. Beginning and Ending Inventory	$ 51,600	$47,100
C. Average Merchandise Inventory $\left(\dfrac{B}{2}\right)$	$ 25,800	$23,550
Merchandise Inventory Turnover $\left(\dfrac{A}{C}\right)$	4.9	4.1
Days' Supply in Inventory $\left(\dfrac{365}{\text{Turnover}}\right)$	74 Days	89 Days

As this analysis shows, the Lorenzen Company has its working capital invested in merchandise inventory for a shorter period of time in 19X4 (74 days) than in 19X3 (89 days). Merchandise is turning over faster, thus reducing the chance that it will become obsolete.

Operating Cycles

Businesses that sell merchandise on account are concerned with the length of the **operating cycle.** That is, they are concerned with the amount of time it takes to purchase merchandise, convert the merchandise to accounts receivable through sales, and then convert the accounts receivable to cash. For the Lorenzen Company, for example, the operating cycles for 19X3 and 19X4 are 131 days and 111 days, respectively. The operating cycle is found by adding the days' supply in inventory to the average number of days for the collection period.

COMPARATIVE OPERATING CYCLES FOR 19X3 AND 19X4

	19X4	19X3
Days' Supply in Inventory	74 Days	89 Days
Plus: Collection Period	37	42
Operating Cycle	111 Days	131 Days

Let's look at the operating cycle for 19X4. The Lorenzen Company buys merchandise and keeps the merchandise in inventory for an average of 74 days. After the merchandise is sold, it takes, on the average, 37 days to collect the accounts receivable. Thus it takes 101 days before there is cash to make new purchases, pay expenses, and the like.

What is the significance of the fact that the operating cycle is shorter in 19X4 (101 days) than in 19X3 (131 days)? The shorter operating cycle means that cash is available at a faster rate to reinvest in merchandise, take advantage of discounts, pay salaries, and so on. That is, cash is available to meet the needs of operating the business. Many businesses fail because cash is tied up too long in merchandise inventory and accounts receivable.

RATIOS THAT MEASURE CURRENT POSITION

Ratio	Formula	What It Indicates
Current (or working capital) Ratio	$= \dfrac{\text{Current Assets}}{\text{Current Liabilities}}$	Indicates ability to pay current liabilities from current assets.
Quick (or acid test) Ratio	$= \dfrac{\text{Quick Assets}}{\text{Current Liabilities}}$	Indicates ability to pay sudden demands from liquid assets.

Accounts Receivable Turnover

Average Accounts Receivable	$= \dfrac{\substack{\text{Beginning} \\ \text{Accounts} \\ \text{Receivable}} + \substack{\text{Ending} \\ \text{Accounts} \\ \text{Receivable}}}{2}$	Indicates average dollar amount of accounts receivable uncollected.
Accounts Receivable Turnover Rate	$= \dfrac{\text{Net Sales}}{\text{Average Accounts Receivable}}$	Indicates efficiency of collecting from customers.
Collection Period	$= \dfrac{\text{Days in Accounting Period}}{\text{Accounts Receivable Turnover}}$	Indicates number of days it takes to collect the average accounts receivable.

Merchandise Inventory Turnover

Average Inventory	$= \dfrac{\substack{\text{Beginning} \\ \text{Merchandise} \\ \text{Inventory}} + \substack{\text{Ending} \\ \text{Merchandise} \\ \text{Inventory}}}{2}$	Indicates average dollar cost of goods in inventory.
Merchandise Inventory Turnover Rate	$= \dfrac{\text{Cost of Goods Sold}}{\text{Average Merchandise Inventory}}$	Indicates number of times average inventory was sold during the period.
Days Supply in Inventory	$= \dfrac{\text{Days in Accounting Period}}{\text{Inventory Turnover}}$	Indicates the number of days the average merchandise stays in inventory.
Operating Cycle	$= \substack{\text{Days Supply in Inventory} \\ + \text{ Collection Period}}$	Indicates time between purchase of inventory items and their conversion into cash.

Activity D-1. Answer the following questions about merchandise inventory turnover computations. Refer to the text and illustrations on pages 538 to 540.

1. What is the Cost of Goods Sold in 19X4?

2. How is the average merchandise inventory computed for 19X3? 19X4?

3. What is the merchandise inventory turnover for 19X3? 19X4?

4. What is the days' supply in inventory for 19X3? 19X4?

5. How is the days' supply in inventory for 19X4 computed?

6. Is the merchandise inventory turnover better in 19X3 or in 19X4?

7. Is the days' supply in inventory better in 19X3 or in 19X4?

Activity D-2. Answer the following questions about the comparative operating cycles. Refer to the text and illustrations on pages 540 and 541.

1. What is the operating cycle for 19X3? 19X4?

2. How is the operating cycle computed for 19X3? 19X4?

3. Is the operating cycle better in 19X3 or in 19X4?

Activity D-3. Answer the following questions on the 19X2, 19X3, and 19X4 comparative statements of the Lorenzen Company. Refer to the text and illustrations on pages 517 to 519.

1. Compute the accounts receivable turnover rate for 19X2. (*HINT*: The beginning accounts receivable is $18,000. This is not shown on the statements.)

2. Compute the collection period for 19X2.

3. Compute the merchandise inventory turnover rate for 19X2. (*HINT*: The beginning merchandise inventory is $25,500; this is not shown on the statements.)

4. Compute the days' supply in inventory for 19X2.

5. Compute the operating cycle for 19X2.

6. In which year(s) is the accounts receivable ratio most favorable? the merchandise inventory ratio?

7. In which year(s) is the operating cycle most favorable? Why?

Topic 2   Problems

14-5. Information taken from the accounting records of Badey Inc. is shown here. Provide the missing data.

Working Capital	=	Current Assets	−	Current Liabilities	Current Ratio
a. $40,000	=	$120,000	−	$80,000	_____
b. 50,000	=	150,000	−	_____	_____
c. _____	=	87,500	−	40,000	_____
d. 48,000	=	_____	−	96,000	_____
e. _____	=	98,000	−	_____	2:1

14-6. Account balances taken from the Xena Corporation's financial statements are listed here. (In Activity A-2 you computed the working capital and current ratio.)

Cash, $8,000

Accounts Receivable (net), $18,000

Net Sales, $210,000

Mortgage Payable, $40,000

Accounts Payable, $7,000

Merchandise Inventory, $20,000

Prepaid Insurance, $1,000

FICA Taxes Payable, $1,000

Marketable Securities, $2,000

Investments, $12,000

Supplies, $1,000

Employees' Payroll Taxes Payable, $8,000

a. Indicate which accounts are used to compute the amount of the quick assets.

b. Compute the quick assets ratio.

14-7. Various financial data for Janeway Inc. is given here.

December 31	Accounts Receivable	Net Sales
19X2	$27,000	$ —
19X3	18,000	202,500
19X4	38,000	168,000
19X5	60,000	245,000

a. Compute the accounts receivable turnover for 19X3, 19X4, and 19X5.

b. Compute the average length of

the collection period for 19X3, 19X4, and 19X5.

c. Does a trend seem to be developing? Can you explain why?

14-8. Additional financial information for Janeway Inc. is provided here.

December 31	Merchandise Inventory	Cost of Goods Sold
19X2	$40,000	$ —
19X3	35,000	150,000
19X4	50,000	233,750
19X5	50,000	250,000

a. Compute the merchandise inventory turnover for 19X3, 19X4, and 19X5.

b. Compute the average days'

supply for 19X3, 19X4, and 19X5.

c. Does a trend seem to be developing? Can you explain why?

14-9. Use the comparative financial information for Maxwell Inc. in Topic Problem 14-3 to do the following for 19X2, 19X3, and 19X4.

a. Compute the working capital.

b. Compute the current ratios.

c. Compute the quick assets ratios.

d. Indicate which accounts are used to compute the quick asset ratios.

e. Compute the accounts receivable turnover rates. (The beginning accounts receivable for 19X2 is $27,500.)

f. Compute the collection periods.

g. Compute the merchandise inventory turnover rates. (The beginning merchandise inventory for 19X2 was $33,500.)

h. Compute the days' supply in inventory.

i. Compute the operating cycles.

Topic 3
Ratios of Equity Position and Operating Results

Owners and creditors have equity in a business.

A *What groups have equity in a business?* There are two equity groups in a business: owners and creditors. Each group has *equity* in the assets of the business. That is, each has claims against the assets. The balance sheet reports the claims of the creditors (liabilities) and the claims of the owners (stockholders' equity). Ratios that measure equity position are used to show the proportion of total assets supplied by the owners and the creditors.

Ratios That Measure Equity Position

Two ratios used to measure equity position are the creditors' equity ratio to total assets and the owner's equity ratio to total assets.

Creditors' Equity Ratio. The **creditors' equity ratio** shows the proportion of total assets provided by the creditors. The ratio is computed by dividing the total liabilities by total assets. The ratio for the Lorenzen Company for 19X4 is illustrated here.

$$\frac{\text{Total Liabilities}}{\text{Total Assets}} = \text{Creditors' Equity Ratio}$$

$$\frac{\$79,000}{\$235,800} = 33.5\%$$

Owner's Equity Ratio. The **owner's equity ratio** shows the proportion of assets provided by the owners. The ratio is computed by dividing the total owner's equity by the total assets. The equity ratio for the Lorenzen Company in 19X4 is illustrated here.

$$\frac{\text{Total Owner's Equity}}{\text{Total Assets}} = \text{Owner's Equity Ratio}$$

$$\frac{\$156,800}{\$235,800} = 66.5\%$$

The data to compute the creditors' equity and the owner's equity ratio is taken from the Lorenzen Company balance sheet. The creditors' equity ratio tells you that creditors have a 33.5 percent interest in the total assets. The owner's equity ratio tells you that stockholders have a 66.5 percent interest in total assets. These two percentages equal 100 percent (33.5 percent + 66.5 percent) of the total assets. A low creditors' equity ratio means that the majority of the resources to operate the business have been contributed by stockholders.

$$\frac{\text{Total}}{\text{Assets}} = \frac{\text{Creditor's}}{\text{Equity}}$$
$$100\% = 33.5\%$$
$$+ \frac{\text{Owner's}}{\text{Equity}}$$
$$+ 66.5\%$$

RATIOS THAT MEASURE EQUITY POSITION

Ratio	Formula	What It Indicates
Creditors' Equity to Total Assets	$\dfrac{\text{Total Liabilities}}{\text{Total Assets}}$	Proportion of assets provided by the creditors.
Owner's Equity to Total Assets	$\dfrac{\text{Owner's Equity}}{\text{Total Assets}}$	Proportion of assets provided by the owner.

Activity A-1. Answer the following questions on ratios that measure equity position. Refer to the text and illustration on pages 544 and 545.

1. What is the creditors' equity ratio for 19X4?

2. How is the creditors' equity ratio computed?

3. What is the owner's equity ratio for 19X4?

4. How is the owner's equity ratio computed?

Activity A-2. Compute the creditors' equity ratio and the owner's equity ratio for each of the following cases.

Total Assets	Total Liabilities	Total Owner's Equity
1. $35,000	$ 7,000	$ 28,000
2. 8,500	3,400	5,100
3. 84,000	29,400	
4. 66,000		44,000
5. _____	75,000	125,000

Ratios That Measure Operating Results

B *Are ratios used only to measure current position and equity position?* No, a business may also use ratios to determine its ability to earn a satisfactory net income and return on investment. The following ratios relate to measuring the results from operations.

Return on Total Assets Ratio. The Lorenzen Company earns a net income by putting assets to work. A return on total assets ratio is computed to show how effectively the assets are being used. The **return on assets ratio** is computed by dividing net income after income taxes by the total assets. The computation for the Lorenzen Company in 19X4 is illustrated here.

$$\frac{\text{Net Income After Income Taxes}}{\text{Total Assets}} = \text{Return on Total Assets}$$

$$\frac{\$16,800}{\$235,800} = 7.1\%$$

The net income ($16,800) and total assets ($235,800) are taken from the Lorenzen Company financial statements. In this case the Lorenzen Company earns 7.1 cents for each $1 in assets.

Assets ———— *Produce* ————→ *Revenue*

Less: Cost of Doing Business

Return ———— *Net Income*

To interpret whether this return is sufficient, the company must compare this return with other possible returns. For example, if the company could earn more with the $235,800 invested in a bank savings account, then the company is not investing the money wisely.

Many financial analysts will add interest expense back to net income before computing the return on assets. They reason that interest paid when purchasing assets should not be included when finding the return on assets.

Return on Stockholders' Equity Ratio. Perhaps the most important relationship for owners and investors is the return on stockholders' equity. The **return on stockholders' equity** is found by dividing net income after income taxes by total stockholders' equity. The resulting percentage is an indicator of profitability for those investing in a particular business. The 19X4 return on stockholders' equity for the Lorenzen Company is illustrated here.

$$\frac{\text{Net Income After Income Taxes}}{\text{Stockholders' Equity}} = \text{Return on Stockholders' Equity}$$

$$\frac{\$16,800}{\$156,800} = 10.7\%$$

The net income ($16,800) is obtained from the income statement for 19X4, and the total stockholders' equity ($156,800) is obtained from the balance sheet. The return on stockholders' equity is viewed as follows. Stockholders, investing capital stock plus past earnings of

$156,800 in the Lorenzen Company, earn 10.7 percent on their invest-
ment for 19X4. When considering investment (or continued ownership) in a particular company, investors compare the return on stockholders' equity with other investment choices.

Assets ———————— Produce ———→ Revenue

Less: Cost of Doing Business

Stockholders'
Equity ←———————— Return ———— Net Income

Activity B-1. Answer the following questions about the ratios for return on total assets and return on stockholders' equity. Refer to the text
and illustrations on pages 545 to 547.

1. What is the return on assets for
19X4?

2. How is the return on assets computed?

3. What is the return on stockholders' equity for 19X4?

4. How is the return on stockholders' equity computed?

5. What does a 10.7 percent return
on stockholders' equity mean?

Activity B-2. Determine the return on total assets in each of the following situations.

Total Assets	Net Income
1. $ 200,000	$ 25,000
2. 1,000,000	150,000
3. 500,000	30,000

Activity B-3. Determine the return on stockholders' equity in each of
the following situations.

Stockholders' Equity	Net Income
1. $ 500,000	$ 50,000
2. 600,000	50,000
3. 1,000,000	120,000

Return on Net Sales Ratio

C *Is net income also measured against sales?* Yes, the return on net sales, sometimes referred to as profit margin, is widely used as a measure of profitability. The rate of **return on net sales** is found by dividing net income after income taxes by net sales.

The 19X4 rate of return on net sales for the Lorenzen Company is shown here.

$$\frac{\text{Net Income After Income Taxes}}{\text{Net Sales}} = \text{Return on Net Sales}$$

$$\frac{\$16,800}{\$210,000} = 8\%$$

Both the net income and the net sales come from the income statement. The rate of return of 8 percent indicates the net profitability for each dollar of sales. Thus the Lorenzen Company earns 8 cents for each $1 in sales.

It is important to remember that one important factor is missing from this formula: investments. The return on net sales does not take into consideration the amount of money that must be invested to earn the sales. As a result, the return on net sales rate is usually considered along with the rate of return on assets or on stockholders' equity.

$$\text{Earnings on Each Share of Common Stock} = \frac{\text{Net Income After Taxes}}{\text{Number of Shares of Common Stock Outstanding}}$$

Earnings on Each Share. Stockholders are also interested in the earnings on each share of stock in the company. The **earnings on each share** of stock indicates the net income, or profit, earned on each share of common stock. The earnings on each share of common stock is found by dividing the net income after income taxes by the number of shares of common stock outstanding. Assume there are 2,000 common shares outstanding and no preferred stock. The earnings on each share for 19X4 is computed as follows.

$$\frac{\text{Net Income After Income Taxes}}{\text{Number of Common Shares}} = \text{Earnings on Each Share}$$

$$\frac{\$16,800}{2,000} = \$8.40$$

Thus the earnings on each share of common stock for the Lorenzen Company in 19X4 is $8.40. This amount is used to show the ability of the company to pay dividends and to grow by reinvesting its own money.

Internal and External Comparisons. The previous discussions have related to a business making internal comparisons. This type of information is useful. However, **internal comparisons** involve only the business's present or prior performance. Managers usually like to know also how their business is doing compared with similar businesses. The Lorenzen Company, for example, is one of many businesses that make up a particular industry. There might be dozens or hundreds of similar businesses, each attempting to earn a net income. External comparisons are often made to see how one business compares with other businesses in the same industry. An **external comparison** is a comparison made with similar businesses. An external comparison might highlight areas or activities that need attention, and thus assist in making important business decisions.

Information for making external comparisons is available from various sources. Owners and managers of similar businesses may speak to one another informally. People in similar businesses might form regional associations and meet on a regular basis. Trade journals published by particular industries sometimes include summary financial information. Also, independent organizations like Dun & Bradstreet, Inc., publish trend and outlook information that is useful for making comparisons.

RATIOS THAT MEASURE OPERATING RESULTS

Ratio	Formula	What It Indicates
Return on Investment:		
Return on Total Assets	$= \dfrac{\text{Net Income After Taxes}}{\text{Total Assets}}$	Rate earned on all resources used: those supplied by the creditors and by the owners.
Return on Stockholders' Equity	$= \dfrac{\text{Net Income After Taxes}}{\text{Stockholders' Equity}}$	Rate earned by resources supplied by owners.
Return on Net Sales	$= \dfrac{\text{Net Income After Taxes}}{\text{Net Sales}}$	Net income on each dollar of sales.
Earnings on Each Share	$= \dfrac{\text{Net Income After Taxes for All Common Stocks}}{\text{Common Stocks Outstanding}}$	Profit earned on each share of common stock.

Activity C-1. Answer the following questions about the ratio for return on net sales and earnings per share. Refer to the text and illustrations on pages 548 and 549.

1. What is the return on net sales for 19X4?

2. How is the return on net sales computed?

3. What does an 8 percent return on net sales mean?

4. What are the earnings on each share for 19X4?

5. How are the earnings on each share computed?

6. What does an earnings of $8.40 on each share mean?

Activity C-2. Certain information from the financial statements of the Clover Leaf Farm Corporation is given here. Use this information to compute the return on net sales and earnings on each share.

	Net Sales	Net Income After Income Taxes	Number of Common Shares
1.	$ 410,000	$ 82,000	1,000
2.	1,500,000	120,000	20,000
3.	24,000	1,200	600
4.	86,000	10,320	25,800

Topic 3   Problems

14-10. Given here is certain financial statement information. Use this information to compute creditors' equity ratio and owner's equity ratio.

	Current Liabilities	Long-Term Liabilities	Total Liabilities	Retained Earnings	Capital Stock	Total Stockholders' Equity	Total Liabilities and Stockholders' Equity
a.	$20,000	$35,000	$ 55,000	$55,000	$110,000	$165,000	$220,000
b.	40,000	_____	100,000	80,000	_____	300,000	_____
c.	30,000	_____	_____	70,000	_____	420,000	500,000

14-11. Given here is certain financial statement information. Use this information to compute return on total assets ratio, return on stockholders' equity ratio, return on net sales ratio, and earnings on each share.

	Current Assets	All Other Assets	Total Assets	Net Sales	Net Income Before Taxes	Net Income After Taxes	Number of Common Shares	Stockholders' Equity
a.	$100,000	$120,000	$220,000	$ 200,000	$ 24,000	$ 20,000	2,000	$180,000
b.	130,000	270,000	400,000	500,000	49,000	40,000	2,000	300,000
c.	200,000	500,000	700,000	1,000,000	200,000	150,000	100,000	450,000

14-12. The 19X2, 19X3, and 19X4 comparative statements for the Lorenzen Company are given on pages 517 to 519. Use these statements to compute the following items for 19X2 and 19X3. Then compare your results with those given in the text for 19X4.

a. Compute the creditors' equity ratio. In which year is the ratio most favorable?

b. Compute the owner's equity ratio. In which year is the ratio most favorable?

c. Compute the return on total assets ratio. In which year is the ratio most favorable?

d. Compute the return on stockholders' equity ratio. In which year is the ratio most favorable?

e. Compute the return on net sales ratio. In which year is the ratio most favorable?

f. Compute the earnings on each share. In which year are the earnings most favorable?

14-13. Refer to the comparative financial statements for Maxwell Inc. in Topic Problem 14-3. Then compute the following items for 19X2, 19X3, and 19X4.

a. Creditors' equity ratio
b. Owner's equity ratio
c. Return on total assets ratio
d. Return on stockholders' equity ratio
e. Return on net sales

f. Earnings on each share (*HINT*: Common stock outstanding is 5,000 shares in 19X2, 7,700 shares in 19X3, and 7,700 shares in 19X4.)

14-14. How does Maxwell Inc. compare with similar businesses, assuming it sells lumber and building materials? Use the information from Topic Problems 14-9 and 14-13 to do the following.

• Provide the ratios for Maxwell Inc.

• Refer to the average ratios for lumber and building materials com-

panies. Compute the differences between the ratios for Maxwell Inc. and the average ratios.

	Average Ratio	Maxwell Inc.	Difference
a. Creditors' equity ratio	28.0%	_____	_____
b. Return on net sales	2.1%	_____	_____
c. Owner's equity ratio	70.0%	_____	_____
d. Collection period	54 days	_____	_____

Topic 4
Interpreting Changes in Financial Position

A *Are ratios used to interpret the changes in the financial position of a business?* No, ratios give a relationship between two things.

Nonchange Statement:
• Balance sheet

Change Statements:
• Income statement
• Statement of stockholders' equity
• Statement of changes in financial position

Ratios do not describe the changes in the asset, liability, and owner's equity accounts during the accounting period. These changes are shown in the statement of changes in financial position, the fourth major report.

The balance sheet shows the company's financial resources and the sources of those resources on a specific date. The balance sheet is not designed to show changes in assets and liabilities. It is, therefore, what is called a **nonchange statement.**

The income statement, on the other hand, is a **change statement.** It reports the changes in retained earnings caused by a net income or net loss *during* the accounting period. The income statement also provides the details of what makes up the net income or net loss.

The statement of stockholders' equity is also a change statement. It reports the changes to stockholders' equity caused by changes in retained earnings and investment *during* the accounting period.

As you can see, the change statements (the income statement and the statement of stockholders' equity) do not report the changes in assets and liabilities. As a result, the statement of changes in financial position is usually prepared. *Part A* of the statement is shown below. *Part B* is shown on the next page.

LORENZEN COMPANY
Statement of Changes in Financial Position
For the Year Ended December 31, 19X4

Part A: Sources and Uses of Working Capital			
Sources of Working Capital:			
From Current Operations:			
Net Income	16,800 00		
Add Expenses Not Affecting Working Capital:			
Depreciation	11,700 00		
Amortization	1,000 00		
Total Working Capital Provided by Operations		29,500 00	
From Sale of Capital Stock		20,000 00	
Total Sources of Working Capital		49,500 00	
Uses of Working Capital:			
Addition to Building	20,000 00		
Payments on Long-Term Mortgage	5,000 00		
Declaration and Payment of Cash Dividends	4,000 00		
Total Uses of Working Capital		29,000 00	
Net Increase in Working Capital		20,500 00	

LORENZEN COMPANY
Statement of Changes in Financial Position (Continued)
For the Year Ended December 31, 19X4

Part B: Changes in Working Capital Accounts

	19X4	19X3	INCREASE/ DECREASE
Current Assets:			
Cash	12,000 00	8,000 00	4,000 00
Marketable Securities	14,000 00	10,500 00	3,500 00
Notes Receivable	6,000 00	— 00	6,000 00
Accounts Receivable (net) . . .	24,000 00	18,000 00	6,000 00
Merchandise Inventory	28,000 00	23,600 00	4,400 00
Prepaid Insurance	2,000 00	2,000 00	— 00
Supplies on Hand	1,000 00	400 00	600 00
Total Current Assets	87,000 00	62,500 00	24,500 00
Current Liabilities:			
Interest Payable	2,500 00	2,000 00	500 00
Accounts Payable	16,500 00	14,000 00	2,500 00
Federal Income Taxes			
Payable	7,000 00	7,000 00	— 00
Payroll Taxes Payable	3,000 00	2,000 00	1,000 00
Total Current Liabilities .	29,000 00	25,000 00	4,000 00
Working Capital	58,000 00	37,500 00	
Net Increase in Working Capital			20,500 00

Statement of Changes in Financial Position

The **statement of changes in financial position** summarizes the changes that occur in the working capital accounts for an accounting period. The statement of changes in financial position for the Lorenzen Company for the year ended December 31, 19X4, is illustrated on pages 552 and 553. The statement of changes in financial position is sometimes called a *statement of sources and applications of funds.*

The statement is divided into two parts. Part A shows the sources and uses of working capital, and Part B shows the changes in working capital accounts.

Part A contains three major sections: Sources of Working Capital, Uses of Working Capital, and Net Increase (or Net Decrease) in Working Capital.

A statement of changes in financial position explains the changes in working capital in an accounting period.

Sections of Statement of Changes in Financial Position:
Part A: Sources and Uses of Working Capital
- Sources of Working Capital
- Uses of Working Capital
- Net Increase (Net Decrease) in Working Capital
Part B: Changes in Working Capital Accounts
- Current Assets
- Current Liabilities
- Net Increase (Net Decrease) in Working Capital

A transaction that increases the amount of working capital is called a **source of working capital.** An example of a source of working capital is the sale of merchandise for more than it cost. The increase in cash or receivables is greater than the decrease in merchandise inventory.

A transaction that decreases the amount of working capital is known as a **use of working capital.** An example of a use of working capital is the payment of a long-term liability. The use of cash decreases current assets. Current liabilities are unaffected.

If more working capital is supplied than used during an accounting period, there is a **net increase in working capital.** If more working capital is used than supplied during the period, there is a **net decrease in working capital.**

Part B simply shows the listing of each current asset and current liability account. The beginning balance, ending balance, and amount of increase or decrease are shown for each account. These items are taken from the comparative balance sheet.

A statement of changes in financial position explains the increase or decrease in working capital.

The purpose of the statement of changes in financial position is to explain the increase or decrease in working capital.

Transactions That Affect Working Capital

Working capital, as you recall, is the difference between the total current assets and the total current liabilities.

LORENZEN COMPANY
Computation of Net Increase in Working Capital
For the Year Ended December 31, 19X4

	19X4	19X3	Increase/ Decrease
Current Assets	$87,000	$62,500	$24,500
Less: Current Liabilities	29,000	25,000	4,000
Net Increase in Working Capital	$58,000	$37,500	$20,500

Some transactions that affect current assets and current liabilities include the following.
- Purchasing merchandise on credit.
- Selling merchandise on credit.
- Incurring and paying expenses.
- Receiving cash on account.
- Paying cash on a long-term mortgage payable.

- Paying an accounts payable.
- Buying plant and equipment.
- Paying cash dividends to stockholders.

This list shows that transactions affecting working capital also affect plant and equipment, long-term liabilities, revenue, costs, or expenses. Thus changes in working capital also cause changes in other asset, liability, and stockholders' equity accounts that determine financial position. The information showing changes in working capital and financial position is important, because it shows if a change in working capital is due to the normal operations of the business or if the change is a result of operations other than normal. Selling stock, borrowing money, and selling plant and equipment all provide working capital that does not come from normal operations.

Activity A-1. Answer the following questions about the changes in working capital for the Lorenzen Company. Refer to the text and illustrations on pages 551 to 555.

1. What is the working capital for 19X3? for 19X4?

in working capital from 19X3 to 19X4? How much?

2. Is there an increase or decrease

Activity A-2. Answer the following questions about the statement of changes in financial position. Refer to the illustration on pages 552 and 553.

1. What period of time is covered by the statement?
2. How much working capital is provided by current operations?
3. What are the total uses of working capital?

4. What is the net increase in working capital? Does this amount agree with the amount obtained from the balance sheet?

Steps in Preparing the Statement

B *Does the statement of changes in financial position show what makes up working capital?* No, the statement of changes in financial position describes *what caused* the changes in working capital. It does *not* show *what makes up* working capital. The items making up working capital (current assets and current liabilities) are found in the balance sheet.

Four basic steps are followed to prepare a statement of changes in financial position.

STEP 1. *Compute the net increase or decrease in working capital.*

STEP 2. *Determine which transactions caused the net increase or decrease in working capital.*

STEP 3. *Assemble and classify the changes in working capital as either sources or uses of working capital.*
STEP 4. *Prepare the statement of changes in financial position.*

STEP 1. Compute the Net Increase or Decrease in Working Capital

The net increase or decrease in working capital is computed by finding the difference between the amounts of working capital for the periods considered. As illustrated here, the working capital for the Lorenzen Company increases $20,500 from 19X3 to 19X4.

LORENZEN COMPANY			
Computation of Net Increase In Working Capital			
For the Year Ended December 31, 19X4			
	19X4	*19X3*	*Increase/ Decrease*
Current Assets	$87,000	$62,500	$24,500
Less: Current Liabilities	29,000	25,000	4,000
Net Increase in Working Capital	$58,000	$37,500	$20,500

STEP 2. Determine Which Transactions Caused the Increase or Decrease in Working Capital

In Step 1 the net increase or decrease in working capital is found. The next step determines which transactions *cause* the increase or decrease. For our discussion, *all* business transactions can fall into one of three categories. Only one category *causes* a change in working capital. Each category is described here.

• *Transactions that affect only current assets or current liabilities.* Many business transactions affect only current assets or current liabilities. Examples of these transactions include collecting an accounts receivable, paying a current liability, borrowing on a short-term note payable, or purchasing supplies. Each of these transactions causes changes within current assets or current liabilities, but none causes a change in working capital. For instance, collecting an accounts receivable increases cash and decreases accounts receivable with no change in working capital.

Working capital is *not* changed by transactions that affect only current assets or current liabilities.

• *Transactions that affect only noncurrent accounts.* Certain transactions do not affect current assets or current liabilities. Thus they do not affect working capital. All balance sheet accounts not classified as current accounts are called **noncurrent accounts.** An example of a

Working capital is *not* changed by transactions that affect only noncurrent accounts.

transaction that affects only noncurrent accounts is the recording of depreciation. Plant and Equipment decreases, and the expense decreases owner's equity.

- *Transactions that affect either a current asset and a noncurrent account or a current liability and a noncurrent account.* Transactions that cause increases or decreases in working capital are those that affect both current and noncurrent accounts. For example, recording the sale of merchandise increases the current asset Cash or Accounts Receivable and increases the revenue Sales. The payment of rent decreases the current asset Cash and increases the expense Rent Expense. The purchase of a building for cash decreases the current asset Cash and increases Plant and Equipment. Payment on a bond decreases Cash and decreases the long-term liability Bonds Payable. And the declaration of a cash dividend increases current liabilities and decreases Retained Earnings. The most common transactions that affect both current and noncurrent accounts are those completed during normal business operations.

> Working capital *is* changed by transactions that affect noncurrent accounts and current assets or noncurrent accounts and current liabilities.

The transactions that affect working capital are classified as sources of working capital or as uses of working capital.

Sources of Working Capital. Transactions that increase working capital are *sources* of working capital. The most common source of working capital is net income. A business has a net income when the gain from the increase in current assets from revenue transactions is greater than the combined loss from the decrease in current assets and the increase in current liabilities from expense and cost transactions. Sources of working capital *not* from current operations include receipts from the sale of plant and equipment, the issuance of long-term liabilities, and the sale of capital stock.

> Net income is the most common source of working capital.

Uses of Working Capital. Transactions that decrease working capital are *uses* of working capital. Common uses of working capital include the purchase of plant and equipment or intangible assets, the payment of long-term liabilities, and the payment of cash dividends.

The comparative balance sheet for the Lorenzen Company, illustrated on page 558, show that the following noncurrent accounts increase or decrease during 19X4.

- *Plant and Equipment—Building* increases by $20,000.
- *Plant and Equipment—Accumulated Depreciation* increases by $11,700.
- *Intangible Assets—Patent* decreases by $1,000.
- *Long-term Liabilities—Mortgage Payable* decreases by $5,000.
- *Stockholders' Equity—Capital Stock* increases by $20,000.
- *Stockholders' Equity—Retained Earnings* increases by $12,800.

LORENZEN COMPANY
Comparative Balance Sheet
For the Years Ended December 31, 19X3 and 19X4

	19X4	19X3	INCREASE/DECREASE	
			DOLLARS	PERCENT
ASSETS				
Current Assets:				
Cash	12,000 00	8,000 00	4,000 00	50.0%
Marketable Securities	14,000 00	10,500 00	3,500 00	33.3
Notes Receivable	6,000 00	— 00	6,000 00	—
Accounts Receivable (net)	24,000 00	18,000 00	6,000 00	33.3
Merchandise Inventory	28,000 00	23,600 00	4,400 00	18.6
Prepaid Insurance	2,000 00	2,000 00	— 00	0.0
Supplies on Hand	1,000 00	400 00	600 00	150.0
Total Current Assets	87,000 00	62,500 00	24,500 00	39.2%
Investments:				
Marketable Securities	15,000 00	15,000 00	— 00	0.0%
Plant and Equipment:				
Land	37,600 00	37,600 00	— 00	0.0%
Building	127,000 00	107,000 00	20,000 00	18.7%
Less: Accumulated				
Depreciation	(38,800 00)	(27,100 00)	11,700 00	43.2%
Total Plant and Equipment . .	125,800 00	117,500 00	8,300 00	7.1%
Intangible Assets:				
Patent (net)	8,000 00	9,000 00	(1,000 00)	(11.1%)
Total Assets	235,800 00	204,000 00	31,800 00	15.6%
LIABILITIES				
Current Liabilities:				
Interest Payable	2,500 00	2,000 00	500 00	25.0%
Accounts Payable	16,500 00	14,000 00	2,500 00	17.9
Federal Income Taxes Payable . .	7,000 00	7,000 00	— 00	—
Payroll Taxes Payable	3,000 00	2,000 00	1,000 00	50.0
Total Current Liabilities	29,000 00	25,000 00	4,000 00	16.0%
Long-Term Liabilities:				
Mortgage Payable	50,000 00	55,000 00	(5,000 00)	(9.1%)
Total Liabilities	79,000 00	80,000 00	(1,000 00)	(1.3%)
STOCKHOLDERS' EQUITY				
Capital Stock	100,000 00	80,000 00	20,000 00	25.0
Retained Earnings	56,800 00	44,000 00	12,800 00	29.1
Total Stockholders' Equity . . .	156,800 00	124,000 00	32,800 00	26.5
Total Liabilities & Stockholders'				
Equity	235,800 00	204,000 00	31,800 00	15.6%
Shares Outstanding	2,000 00	1,600 00	400 00	25.0%

    The condensed income statement for the Lorenzen Company shows that net income for the accounting period is $16,800.

LORENZEN COMPANY
Income Statement (Condensed)
For the Year Ended December 31, 19X4

Net Sales	210,000	00		
Cost of Goods Sold.	126,000	00		
Gross Profit on Sales.			84,000	00
Total Operating Expenses			63,800	00
Net Income Before Income Taxes			20,200	00
Provision for Income Taxes			3,400	00
Net Income After Income Taxes			16,800	00

Activity B. Answer the following questions about the comparative balance sheet and the income statement. Refer to the text and illustrations on pages 555 to 559.

1. What is the change in current assets? Does this affect working capital? How?
2. What is the change in current liabilities? Does this affect working capital? How?
3. What is the amount of the increase or decrease in working capital?
4. How much does Plant and Equipment increase?
5. How much does intangible assets increase or decrease?
6. How much does long-term liabilities increase or decrease?
7. How much does stockholders' equity increase or decrease?
8. How much is the cost of goods sold?
9. How much are the total operating expenses?
10. What is the net income before income taxes? after income taxes?

STEP 3. Assemble and Classify Changes in Working Capital

C *Once you know which noncurrent accounts change, can the statement of changes in financial position be prepared?* No, you only know which noncurrent accounts change. You must now look in the general ledger to determine the reasons for each change. The next step, therefore, is to assemble and classify the changes in noncurrent accounts so that the statement of changes in financial position can be prepared.

The general ledger for the Lorenzen Company reveals the following reasons for the changes in its noncurrent accounts during 19X4.

Changes in Noncurrent Assets

- A $20,000 addition is made to the Building (Plant and Equipment).
- The $11,700 increase in the accumulated depreciation account is due to annual depreciation charges.
- The $1,000 reduction in the Patent account is due to the annual amortization charge.

Changes in Noncurrent Liabilities

- Payments are made on the Mortgage Payable account for $5,000.

Changes in Stockholders' Equity

- Capital Stock is increased through a sale of capital stock for $20,000.
- Retained earnings is increased by net income of $16,800.
- Retained earnings are decreased by declaring and paying cash dividends of $4,000.

With the above information, we can now classify the changes as either a *source* or *use* of working capital. To assist in classifying the changes, a new type of worksheet is used. The worksheet to develop statement of changes in financial position is illustrated on page 561.

The worksheet has four money columns. The amounts for the first money column are the balances at the beginning of the accounting period. The amounts in the last money column are the balances at the end of the period. Amounts for both columns are taken from the comparative balance sheets.

The two middle money columns are used to explain the changes between the beginning and ending balances for each account listed.

The worksheet has six side headings divided into two sections. The Balance Sheet Accounts section is the upper part. This part involves the accounts (1) Working Capital, (2) Noncurrent Accounts with Debit Balances, and (3) Noncurrent Accounts with Credit Balances.

The lower section, Changes in Working Capital, shows the effect of each transaction on working capital. It lists (4) Sources of Working Capital, (5) Uses of Working Capital, (6) and the Increase (or Decrease) in Working Capital.

The worksheet is completed as follows.

- *The beginning account balances are entered as debits or credits in the first column.*
- *The ending account balances are then entered in the last column.* The beginning and ending account balances are shown in the worksheet shown on the next page.
- *After the balances are recorded, the differences between the amounts are computed and explained.* These are the changes that occur during

Side Headings of Worksheet:
Balance Sheet Accounts Section:
- Working Capital
- Noncurrent Accounts With Debit Balances
- Noncurrent Accounts With Credit Balances

Changes in Working Capital Section:
- Sources of Working Capital
- Uses of Working Capital
- Net Increase (Net Decrease) in Working Capital

LORENZEN COMPANY
Worksheet to Develop Statement of Changes in Financial Position
For the Year Ended December 31, 19X4

	ACCOUNT BALANCES DEC. 31, 19X3	ANALYSIS OF TRANSACTIONS FOR 19X4		ACCOUNT BALANCES DEC. 31, 19X4
		DEBIT	CREDIT	
Balance Sheet Accounts				
① Working Capital	37,500 00			58,000 00
② Noncurrent Accounts With Debit Balances:				
Investments	15,000 00			15,000 00
Plant and Equipment				
(Various Assets)	144,600 00			164,600 00
Patent	9,000 00			8,000 00
Total	206,100 00			245,600 00
③ Noncurrent Accounts With Credit Balances:				
Accumulated Depreciation				
(Various Accounts)	27,100 00			38,800 00
Mortgage Payable	55,000 00			50,000 00
Capital Stock	80,000 00			100,000 00
Retained Earnings	44,000 00			56,800 00
Total	206,100 00			245,600 00
Changes in Working Capital				
④ Sources of Working Capital . .				
⑤ Uses of Working Capital . . .				
⑥ Increase (or Decrease) in Working Capital				

the accounting period. The analysis is done according to the side headings, and amounts are entered in the Analysis of Transactions columns. The changes are illustrated on page 562.

Remember that each transaction is analyzed in the middle columns. Each transaction consists of a debit and a credit. An entry is made in the upper section—Balance Sheet Accounts—and in the lower section—Changes in Working Capital. In the upper section of the worksheet, the accounts are debited or credited as they were in the original transactions. In the lower section, the debits and credits are entered according to how they affect working capital. Working capital is an asset. It is increased by debits and is decreased by credits.

As you read the discussion, follow along by finding the entries in the worksheet. The debit and credit entries are identified by letters, beginning with (a).

(a) The Net Income of $16,800 increases working capital. This is a source of working capital. Thus Net Income is debited in the Changes

LORENZEN COMPANY
Worksheet to Develop Statement of Changes in Financial Position
For the Year Ended December 31, 19X4

	ACCOUNT BALANCES DEC. 31, 19X3	ANALYSIS OF TRANSACTIONS FOR 19X4 DEBIT	ANALYSIS OF TRANSACTIONS FOR 19X4 CREDIT	ACCOUNT BALANCES DEC. 31, 19X4
Balance Sheet Accounts				
① Working Capital	37,500 00	(h) 20,500 00		58,000 00
② Noncurrent Accounts With Debit Balances:				
Investments	15,000 00			15,000 00
Plant and Equipment (Various Assets)	144,600 00	(d) 20,000 00		164,600 00
Patent	9,000 00		(c) 1,000 00	8,000 00
Total	206,100 00			245,600 00
③ Noncurrent Accounts With Credit Balances:				
Accumulated Depreciation (Various Accounts)	27,000 00		(b) 11,700 00	38,800 00
Mortgage Payable	55,000 00	(e) 5,000 00		50,000 00
Capital Stock	80,000 00		(f) 20,000 00	100,000 00
Retained Earnings	44,000 00	(g) 4,000 00	(a) 16,800 00	56,800 00
Total	206,100 00	(x) 49,500 00	(x) 49,500 00	245,600 00
Changes in Working Capital				
④ Sources of Working Capital:				
Net Income From Operations . .		(a) 16,800 00		
Depreciation Expense		(b) 11,700 00		
Amortization Expense		(c) 1,000 00		
Sale of Capital Stock		(f) 20,000 00		
⑤ Uses of Working Capital:				
Addition to Building			(d) 20,000 00	
Payments on Mortgage Payable .			(e) 5,000 00	
Dividends Declared and Paid . .			(g) 4,000 00	
Subtotal		49,500 00	29,000 00	
⑥ Increase (or Decrease) in Working Capital			(h) 20,500 00	
Total		(x) 49,500 00	(x) 49,500 00	

Explanations for adjustments:

(a) Net Income of $16,800 is transferred to Retained Earnings as a source of working capital from operations.

(b) Depreciation of $11,700 is added to Net Income to obtain the source of working capital from operations.

(c) Amortization of $1,000 is added to Net Income to obtain the source of working capital from operations.

(d) An addition to the building requires a $20,000 use of working capital.

(e) Payments on the mortgage require a $5,000 use of working capital.

(f) Sale of capital stock provides a $20,000 source of working capital.

(g) Paying cash dividends requires a $4,000 use of working capital.

(h) Increase in working capital is $20,500.

in Working Capital section since working capital is increased by debits. Retained Earnings also increases. Thus Retained Earnings is credited in the Balance Sheet Accounts section.

Debit Sources of Working Capital (Net Income) $16,800
Credit Retained Earnings $16,800

(b) Depreciation of $11,700 is deducted as an expense in obtaining net income. However, depreciation does not affect current assets or current liabilities. Therefore, the depreciation is added back to net income. The entry is a debit to depreciation as an increase (source) in working capital and a credit to accumulated depreciation in the Balance Sheet Accounts section.

Debit Sources of Working Capital
           (Depreciation Expense) $11,700
Credit Accumulated Depreciation $11,700

Note that the entry to the asset account is the same as the original entry to record the depreciation. The offsetting debit or credit is shown as either an increase or decrease to working capital.

(c) Amortization, like depreciation, does not affect current assets or current liabilities. Yet it is deducted as an expense to obtain net income. The amount is added back as a source of working capital. The entry increases working capital and shows the decrease in the asset Patent account.

Debit Sources of Working Capital
           (Amortization Expense) $1,000
Credit Patents $1,000

(d) An addition to the building is made for $20,000. This caused a decrease in working capital. This entry is entered as a credit to show a use of working capital. The debit is an increase to Plant and Equipment in the Balance Sheet Account section.

Debit Plant and Equipment $20,000
Credit Uses of Working Capital
           (Addition to Building) $20,000

(e) The $5,000 payment on the Mortgage Payable uses working capital to reduce a noncurrent liability. This is a use of working capital. Thus the working capital is credited. Mortgage Payable is debited in the Balance Sheet Accounts section.

Debit Mortgage Payable $5,000
Credit Uses of Working Capital
           (Payment on Mortgage Payable) $5,000

(f) The sale of capital stock for $20,000 is entered as a source of working capital in the Changes in Working Capital section. Thus the $20,000 is debited in the bottom section. The Capital Stock account is credited in the Balance Sheet Accounts section to show the increase in the stockholders' equity.

Debit	Sources of Working Capital	
	(Sale of Capital Stock)	$20,000
Credit	Capital Stock	$20,000

(g) Cash dividends declared on capital stock reduce working capital and stockholders' equity. When cash dividends are declared, a current liability is created. Thus working capital is reduced. As a result, the analysis contains a credit to Uses of Working Capital in the Changes section. Retained Earnings is debited in the Balance Sheet Accounts section.

Debit	Retained Earnings	$4,000
Credit	Uses of Working Capital	
	(Cash Dividend Declared)	$4,000

(h) After all changes in noncurrent accounts are analyzed, the debits and credits in the Changes in Working Capital section are totaled. The debits (sources) are $49,500 and the credits (uses) are $29,000.

The next step is to enter the increase in working capital for the year, $20,500, as a debit to working capital in the Balance Sheet Accounts section. The credit for $20,500 is entered as an increase in working capital in the Changes section.

(x) The worksheet is now checked for accuracy. Add the debits and credits in the upper section. These amounts should be equal ($49,500). If they are not equal, then the error must be found before going on. The lower section is then checked for accuracy. The totals of these amounts should be the same as the totals for the upper section, since each entry affects an item in the upper section and in the lower section.

The following explanations review the entries that are made on the worksheet. Refer to the worksheet side headings as you read the explanations.

1 *Working Capital.* The Working Capital line summarizes current asset and current liability information for 19X3 and 19X4. The December 31, 19X3, working capital is $37,500. The December 31, 19X4, working capital is $58,000. The $20,500 debit (h) on the Working Capital line is the increase in this item from December 31, 19X3, to December 31, 19X4. The $20,500 is debited because working capital increases. If working capital had decreased, the amount would have been placed in the credit column.

2 *Noncurrent Accounts With Debit Balances.* The heading Noncurrent Accounts With Debit Balances contains all noncurrent balance sheet accounts with debit balances for December 31, 19X3, and December 31, 19X4. The $20,000 debit (d) on the Plant and Equipment line shows an addition to the Building account. The $1,000 credit (c) on the Patent account line shows the annual amortization charge which decreases the account.

3 *Noncurrent Accounts With Credit Balances.* The heading Noncurrent Accounts With Credit Balances contains all noncurrent balance sheet accounts with credit balances for December 31, 19X3, and December 31, 19X4. The credit (b) on the Accumulated Depreciation line shows annual depreciation and increases the balance by $11,700. The $5,000 debit (e) on the Mortgage Payable line shows total mortgage payments made during the year.

The $20,000 credit (f) on the Capital Stock line shows an addition to this account from the sale of capital stock. The $4,000 debit (g) on the Retained Earnings line shows a reduction due to a cash dividend paid. The $16,800 credit (a) on the Retained Earnings line shows an increase from net income.

4 *Sources of Working Capital.* The first heading in the lower section, Sources of Working Capital, summarizes increases in working capital. Observe that the sources of working capital are shown under Analysis of Transactions for 19X4 in the debit column. Also, each transaction has a letter which matches with a letter in the top section of the worksheet. The reason for the debit entries is that a source of working capital is really an increase in current assets. Increases in any asset are shown with a debit. The purpose for matching entries is to identify each source of working capital with a change in a noncurrent account.

Depreciation (b) and amortization (c) are added to net income (a). The result is $29,500 working capital provided by operations. The following discussion explains why the addition is necessary.

The most common source of working capital is net income, resulting when revenues are larger than expenses and costs. That is, a net income results when the gain from the increase in current assets through revenue transactions exceeds the combined loss from the decrease in current assets and the increase in current liabilities through expense and cost transactions. The explanation describing how net income affects working capital is complete, with one exception. There are expense transactions that decrease net income but do not affect working capital. These items are depreciation and amortization transactions.

All revenue, expense, and cost transactions except the depreciation and amortization transactions affect a working capital account. That is, they affect cash, receivables, or payables. To find the net income on the income statement, the accountant subtracts all expenses, including

All revenue, expense, and cost transactions except depreciation and amortization transactions affect working capital.

depreciation expense and amortization expense, from Gross Profit on Sales. Depreciation and amortization expenses are added back to net income to determine the effect of operations on working capital.

The last source of working capital is a $20,000 sale of capital stock (f). The transaction increases cash by $20,000 and increases Capital Stock by the same amount.

5 *Uses of Working Capital.* The heading Uses of Working Capital summarizes decreases in working capital. Uses of working capital are shown under the credit column because each is a decrease in the current asset or current liability. Again, each use of working capital is matched with a letter in the top section of the worksheet. The purpose for the matching is to identify each use of working capital with a change in a noncurrent account. The Lorenzen Company has three uses of working capital, described here.

During 19X4, the Lorenzen Company completes a $20,000 addition to the building. The addition (d) is paid for in cash and is a $20,000 use of working capital.

During 19X4, the Lorenzen Company makes $5,000 payments on the mortgage. The payments (e) are made in cash and represent $5,000 use of working capital.

During 19X4, the Lorenzen Company declares and pays cash dividends of $4,000. The dividend (g) is a $4,000 use of working capital.

6 *Net increase in working capital.* The total sources of working capital are $49,500 and the total uses are $29,000. The difference between the total sources and uses of working capital is $20,500 (h) and is the net increase in working capital for 19X4. The $20,500 is also the difference between our working capital on December 31, 19X3 ($37,500), and our working capital on December 31, 19X4 ($58,000).

Accountants should leave an audit trail so that someone else can tell what has been done.

It is important for accountants to leave an audit trail. That is, it is important to complete the accounting work so that someone else can tell what has been done. The trail is in the Explanation section and describes each source and use of working capital.

Activity C. Answer the following questions on developing the statement of changes in financial position. Refer to the text and worksheet on pages 559 to 566.

1. What does the (h) $20,500 on the Working Capital line represent?
2. Does the (d) $20,000 on the Plant and Equipment line represent a source or use of working capital?
3. What are the total sources of working capital? the total uses?

4. What is the largest use of working capital?
5. What is the largest source of working capital?
6. Does capital stock increase or decrease for the year? How much?

7. What causes the change in retained earnings?

8. What is the increase in working capital?

STEP 4. Prepare a Statement of Changes in Financial Position

D *What is the source of information used to prepare the statement of changes in financial position?* All the information necessary to prepare the statement of changes in financial position, illustrated below and on page 568, is taken directly from the worksheet. Note that the total working capital provided by operations includes net income, depreciation expense, and amortization expense. In addition to the $29,500 obtained from current operations, $20,000 is obtained from the sale of capital stock.

The statement of changes in financial position provides the owners, management, and other interested parties with a formal statement that assists them in making decisions about the business. They can now answer the question: What causes the change in working capital?

LORENZEN COMPANY			
Statement of Changes in Financial Position			
For the Year Ended December 31, 19X4			
Part A: Sources and Uses of Working Capital			
Sources of Working Capital:			
From Current Operations:			
Net Income	16,800 00		
Add Expenses Not Affecting Working Capital:			
Depreciation	11,700 00		
Amortization	1,000 00		
Total Working Capital Provided by Operations		29,500 00	
From Sale of Capital Stock		20,000 00	
Total Sources of Working Capital		49,500 00	
Uses of Working Capital:			
Addition to Building	20,000 00		
Payments on Long-Term Mortgage	5,000 00		
Declaration and Payment of Cash Dividends	4,000 00		
Total Uses of Working Capital		29,000 00	
Net Increase in Working Capital		20,500 00	

Working capital came from these sources.

Working capital was used for these purposes.

Working capital increased by this amount.

LORENZEN COMPANY
Statement of Changes in Financial Position (Continued)
For the Year Ended December 31, 19X4

Part B: Changes in Working Capital Accounts

	19X4	19X3	INCREASE/DECREASE
Current Assets:			
Cash	12,000 00	8,000 00	4,000 00
Marketable Securities.	14,000 00	10,500 00	3,500 00
Notes Receivable	6,000 00	— 00	6,000 00
Accounts Receivable (net) .	24,000 00	18,000 00	6,000 00
Merchandise Inventory . . .	28,000 00	23,600 00	4,400 00
Prepaid Insurance	2,000 00	2,000 00	— 00
Supplies on Hand	1,000 00	400 00	600 00
Total Current Assets. . . .	87,000 00	62,500 00	24,500 00
Current Liabilities:			
Interest Payable	2,500 00	2,000 00	500 00
Accounts Payable	16,500 00	14,000 00	2,500 00
Federal Income Taxes			
Payable.	7,000 00	7,000 00	— 00
Payroll Taxes Payable	3,000 00	2,000 00	1,000 00
Total Current Liabilities .	29,000 00	25,000 00	4,000 00
Working Capital.	58,000 00	37,500 00	
Net Increase in Working *Capital*.			20,500 00

Amount must agree with total in Part A.

Activity D. Answer the following questions about the statement of changes in financial position. Refer to the text and illustration on pages 567 and 568.

1. How much working capital is provided by operations?
2. Which source of working capital does not come from operations?
3. What use of working capital affects a noncurrent asset? noncurrent liability? stockholders' equity?
4. What is the total working capital from all sources?
5. How much cash is distributed to the owners?
6. How much does working capital increase?
7. Which current asset(s) has (have) the greatest amount of increase? the least?
8. Which current liability has the greatest increase? the least?

Topic 4   Problems

14-15. Financial information from the accounting records of Corey-Dirk Corporation is shown at the top of the next page. Determine the change in working capital from 19X2 to 19X3 and from 19X3 to 19X4.

Year	Current Assets	Current Liabilities
19X2	$30,000	$20,000
19X3	32,500	17,500
19X4	40,000	16,000

14-16. Transactions completed by Corey-Dirk Corporation are listed here. Identify each transaction as a source of working capital, a use of working capital, or a transaction that does not affect working capital.

a. Purchased merchandise for cash

b. Sold merchandise on credit

c. Issued a note payable

d. Purchased supplies on credit

e. Recorded depreciation

f. Paid income taxes that had been recorded as a current liability

g. Replaced an account payable with a note payable

h. Recorded a sales return

14-17. Answer the following questions by referring to the Maxwell Inc. worksheet for statement of changes in financial position for the year 19X3. (**NOTE:** The explanations to the worksheet are not shown.)

MAXWELL INC.
Worksheet to Develop Statement of Changes in Financial Position
For the Year Ended December 31, 19X3

	ACCOUNT BALANCES DEC. 31, 19X2	ANALYSIS OF TRANSACTIONS FOR 19X3 DEBIT	ANALYSIS OF TRANSACTIONS FOR 19X3 CREDIT	ACCOUNT BALANCES DEC. 31, 19X3
Balance Sheet Accounts				
1. Working Capital	45,000 00	① 8,000 00		53,000 00
2. Noncurrent Accounts With Debit Balances:				
Investments	15,000 00	⑩ 1,000 00		16,000 00
Machinery	206,400 00	⑥ 41,280 00		247,680 00
Patent	15,000 00		ⓒ 1,000 00	14,000 00
Total	281,400 00			330,680 00
3. Noncurrent Accounts With Credit Balances:				
Accumulated Depreciation	26,100 00		⑧ 19,220 00	45,320 00
Mortgage Payable	90,000 00	⑨ 5,000 00		85,000 00
Capital Stock	120,000 00		⑭ 27,000 00	147,000 00
Retained Earnings	45,300 00	⑨ 13,540 00	ⓐ 21,600 00	53,360 00
Total	281,400 00	Ⓧ 68,820 00	Ⓧ 68,820 00	330,680 00
Changes in Working Capital				
4. Sources of Working Capital:				
Net Income from Operations		ⓐ 21,600 00		
Depreciation Expense		⑧ 19,220 00		
Amortization Expense		ⓒ 1,000 00		
Sale of Capital Stock		⑭ 27,000 00		
5. Uses of Working Capital:				
Bought Investments			⑩ 1,000 00	
Bought Equipment			⑥ 41,280 00	
Payments on Mortgage Payable			⑨ 5,000 00	
Dividend Declared and Paid			⑨ 13,540 00	
Subtotal		68,820 00	60,820 00	
6. Increase in Working Capital			① 8,000 00	
Total		Ⓧ 68,820 00	Ⓧ 68,820 00	

a. What does the (D) 1,000 on the Investments line represent?
b. Does Patent increase or decrease during 19X3?
c. What are the total sources of working capital?

d. What are the total uses of working capital?
e. What is the cost of machinery purchased during 19X3?

NOTE: Save your working papers for further use in Topic Problem 14-18.

14-18. Prepare a statement of changes in financial position for 19X3 for Maxwell Inc. Use your work from Topic Problems 14-3 and 14-17 for the necessary information.

14-19. Use the comparative income statement and balance sheet for Maxwell Inc., that were given in Topic Problem 14-3 to do the following.
a. Compute the net increase or decrease in working capital for the year ended 19X4.
b. Prepare a worksheet to develop a statement of changes in financial position for 19X4.

(*HINT:* A cash dividend of $9,220 is declared and paid in 19X4.)
c. Prepare a statement of changes in financial position for the year ended 19X4.

Topic 5
Interpreting Changes in Cash Flow

A *Does the statement of changes in financial position give the sources and uses of cash?* No, the statement of changes in financial position focuses on the sources and uses of current assets and current liabilities, that is, of working capital. In addition to having information about working capital, many managers also find it valuable to have information on the "flow" of one particular current asset: cash.

Cash Flow

On December 31, 19X3, the Lorenzen Company has a cash balance of $8,000. On December 31, 19X4, the cash balance is $12,000, an increase of $4,000 for the year. Refer to the comparative balance sheet on the next page.

Knowing about this increase in cash is important to management. However, knowing that there is a $4,000 increase in cash for the year represents only a small portion of a much larger picture. Cash flows

LORENZEN COMPANY
Comparative Balance Sheet
For the Years Ended December 31, 19X3 and 19X4

	19X4	19X3	INCREASE/DECREASE DOLLARS	INCREASE/DECREASE PERCENT
ASSETS				
Current Assets:				
Cash	12,000 00	8,000 00	4,000 00	50.0%
Marketable Securities	14,000 00	10,500 00	3,500 00	33.3
Notes Receivable	6,000 00	— 00	6,000 00	—
Accounts Receivable (net) . . .	24,000 00	18,000 00	6,000 00	33.3
Merchandise Inventory	28,000 00	23,600 00	4,400 00	18.6
Prepaid Insurance	2,000 00	2,000 00	— 00	0.0
Supplies on Hand	1,000 00	400 00	600 00	150.0
Total Current Assets	87,000 00	62,500 00	24,500 00	39.2%
Investments:				
Common Stock	15,000 00	15,000 00	— 00	0.0%
Plant and Equipment:				
Land	37,600 00	37,600 00	— 00	0.0%
Building	127,000 00	107,000 00	20,000 00	18.7
Less: Accumulated				
Depreciation	(38,800 00)	(27,100 00)	11,700 00	43.2
Total Plant and Equipment .	125,800 00	117,500 00	8,300 00	7.1%
Intangible Assets:				
Patent (net).	8,000 00	9,000 00	(1,000 00)	(11.1%)
Total Assets	235,800 00	204,000 00	31,800 00	15.6%
LIABILITIES				
Current Liabilities:				
Interest Payable	2,500 00	2,000 00	500 00	25.0%
Accounts Payable	16,500 00	14,000 00	2,500 00	17.9
Federal Income Taxes Payable .	7,000 00	7,000 00	— 00	—
Payroll Taxes Payable	3,000 00	2,000 00	1,000 00	50.0
Total Current Liabilities . . .	29,000 00	25,000 00	4,000 00	16.0%
Long-Term Liabilities:				
Mortgage Payable	50,000 00	55,000 00	(5,000 00)	(9.1%)
Total Liabilities	79,000 00	80,000 00	(1,000 00)	(1.3%)
STOCKHOLDERS' EQUITY				
Capital Stock	100,000 00	80,000 00	20,000 00	25.0%
Retained Earnings	56,800 00	44,000 00	12,800 00	29.1
Total Stockholders' Equity . .	156,800 00	124,000 00	32,800 00	26.5
Total Liabilities & Stockholders'				
Equity	235,800 00	204,000 00	31,800 00	15.6
Shares Outstanding	2,000 00	1,600 00	400 00	25.0%

into and out of the company daily. During 19X4, there had to be sufficient cash to pay operating expenses, make mortgage payments, and pay dividends. Thus, because of the multiple sources and uses of cash, the Lorenzen Company needs to determine where its cash *comes from* and *how it is spent.* **Cash flow** is the difference between cash receipts and cash payments for a period of time. Cash flow information enables management to plan better for the future of the company. A cash flow statement is prepared in order to provide this information.

Cash-Flow Statement

A **cash-flow statement** is a summary of cash receipts (the sources of cash) and cash payments (the uses of cash) for an accounting period. The cash-flow statement is similar to the statement of changes in financial position, but it explains the flow of cash rather than working capital.

LORENZEN COMPANY
Cash-Flow Statement
For the Year Ended December 31, 19X4

Part A: Sources and Uses of Cash			
Sources of Cash:			
From Current Operations..............	16,500 00		
From Sale of Capital Stock	20,000 00		
Total Sources of Cash..............		36,500 00	
Uses of Cash:			
Purchase of Marketable Securities	3,500 00		
Addition to Building................	20,000 00		
Payments on Mortgage	5,000 00		
Payment of Cash Dividends...........	4,000 00		
Total Uses of Cash..............		32,500 00	
Net Increase in Cash		4,000 00	
Part B: Changes in the Cash Account			
Cash Balance, December 31, 19X4.........	12,000 00		
Cash Balance, December 31, 19X3.........	8,000 00		
Net Increase in Cash		4,000 00	

Sections of Cash Flow Statement:
Part A: Sources and Uses of Cash
• Sources of Cash
• Uses of Cash
• Net Increase (Net Decrease) in Cash
Part B: Changes in the Cash Account
• Beginning Cash Balance
• Ending Cash Balance
• Net Increase (Net Decrease) in Cash

The cash-flow statement is divided into two parts. Part A shows the sources and uses of cash, and Part B shows the changes in the Cash account during the accounting period.

Part A contains three major sections: Sources of Cash, Uses of Cash, and Net Increase (or Decrease) in Cash during the accounting period.

A transaction that increases the amount of cash is called a **source of cash.** A transaction that decreases the amount of cash is called a **use**

of cash. If more cash is supplied than used during the accounting period, there is a **net increase in cash.** If more cash is used than supplied, there is a **net decrease in cash.**

The purpose of the cash-flow statement is to explain the net increase or net decrease in cash during the accounting period.

Activity A. Answer the following questions about the cash-flow statement for the Lorenzen Company. Refer to the text and illustrations on pages 570 to 573.

1. What period of time is covered by the statement?

2. How much cash is supplied by current operations?

3. What are the total sources of cash?

4. What are the total uses of cash?

5. What is the net increase (or decrease) in cash? Does this amount agree with the amount shown in Part B?

Steps in Preparing the Cash-Flow Statement

B *Is the cash-flow statement prepared in the same way as the statement of changes in financial position?* The procedure is similar, but the transactions are analyzed as they affect cash instead of working capital. Specifically, a cash-flow statement is prepared by completing the following three steps.

STEP 1. *Determine the effect of operating transactions on cash flow.*

STEP 2. *Determine the effect of nonoperating transactions on cash flow.*

STEP 3. *Prepare the cash flow statement.*

STEP 1. Determining The Effect of Operating Transactions on Cash Flow

The most common types of transactions that result in sources and uses of cash are **operating transactions,** that is, transactions that affect revenue, cost, and expense accounts. Thus the income statement, which has the results of operations, is the starting point in preparing a cash-flow statement.

The condensed income statement for the Lorenzen Company for the year ended December 31, 19X4, is illustrated at the top of page 574.

Several questions arise when the income statement is reviewed. Is cash received for all sales? Is cash paid for all purchases? Is cash paid for all expenses? The answer to these questions is no. The Lorenzen

LORENZEN COMPANY
Income Statement
For the Year Ended December 31, 19X4

Revenue From Sales:			
Net Sales			210,000 00
Cost of Goods Sold:			
Merchandise Inventory, January 1	23,600 00		
Net Purchases	130,400 00		
Cost of Goods Available for Sale	154,000 00		
Less: Merchandise Inventory, Dec. 31	28,000 00		
Cost of Goods Sold			126,000 00
Gross Profit on Sales			84,000 00
Operating Expenses:			
Total Operating Expenses			63,800 00
Net Income Before Income Taxes			20,200 00
Provision for Income Taxes			3,400 00
Net Income After Income Taxes			16,800 00

Company, like most others, maintains its accounting records on the accrual basis.

In the **accrual basis of accounting,** revenue is recorded when it is earned and expenses are recorded when they are incurred. The accrual basis of accounting means that revenue is recorded when a sale is made regardless of when cash is received. In addition, expenses and costs are recorded regardless of when cash is paid. Thus the revenue, cost, and expense amounts on the income statement may not represent the actual cash receipts and cash payments. In order to prepare the cash-flow statement, the accountant must convert the operating amounts on the income statement from the accrual basis to the cash basis.

In the **cash basis of accounting,** revenue is recorded when it is received and expenses are recorded when they are paid. Certain information is needed from the balance sheet as well as from the income statement. The operating transactions that affect cash are now identified. Look at the computations at the top of the next page.

Cash Receipts From Sales. Sales are made on either a cash basis or credit basis. Thus the cash actually received from sales during the year must be computed. On December 31, 19X3, customers owed $18,000, the balance of Accounts Receivable (since Notes Receivable had a zero balance). During 19X4, Sales of $210,000 were made to customers (see the income statement above). Thus $228,000 ($18,000 + $210,000) is the most cash that could have been collected

$ 18,000	Accounts Receivable, December 31, 19X3
+135,000	Sales, 19X4
$153,000	
−30,000	Accounts Receivable and Notes Receivable, December 31, 19X4
$123,000	Cash Received From Customers

from customers. Since the balance of Accounts Receivable and Notes Receivable on December 31, 19X4, is $30,000 ($24,000 + $6,000), the Lorenzen Company did not collect $228,000 during 19X4. The actual cash received was $198,000 ($18,000 + $210,000 − $30,000).

$ 18,000	Accounts Receivable, December 31, 19X3
+210,000	Add: Sales During 19X4
$228,000	Total Cash to Be Collected
−30,000	Less: Accounts Receivable and Notes Receivable, December 31, 19X4
$198,000	Total Cash Received From Sales
$210,000	Net Sales
−12,000	Less: Increase in Accounts Receivable and Notes Receivable
$198,000	Total Cash Received From Sales

The method by which sales made on the accrual basis are converted to a cash basis indicates that the relationship between the two figures depends upon the beginning and ending balances of Accounts Receivable and Notes Receivable.

$$\text{Net Sales (Accrual Basis)} \quad \begin{matrix} + \text{A Decrease in Receivables} \\ or \\ - \text{An Increase in Receivables} \end{matrix} \quad = \quad \text{Total Cash Received From Sales}$$

In making income statement changes, a worksheet to convert revenue and expenses from an accrual basis to a cash basis is used. The $12,000 increase in receivables is labeled (a).

LORENZEN COMPANY
Worksheet to Convert Income Statement From
Accrual Basis to Cash Basis
For the Year Ended December 31, 19X4

	ACCRUAL BASIS	ANALYSIS OF TRANSACTIONS		CASH BASIS
		ADD	DEDUCT	
Revenue From Sales:				
Net Sales	210,000 00			
Less: Increase in Receivables . . .			(a) 12,000 00	198,000 00
Cost of Goods Sold:				
Merchandise Inventory,				
January 1 . . . . $ 23,600				
Net Purchases 130,400				
Cost of Goods Available				
for Sale 154,000				
Less Merchandise				
Inventory, Dec. 31 . . . 28,000				
Cost of Goods Sold	126,000 00			
Less: Increase in Payables			(b) 2,500 00	
Add: Increase in Inventory		(c) 4,400 00		127,900 00
Gross Profit on Sales	84,000 00			70,100 00
Operating Expenses and Income Taxes:				
Operating Expenses $63,800				
Income Taxes 3,400				
Total Operating Expenses &				
Income Taxes	67,200 00			
Add: Increase in Prepaid Expenses		(d) 600 00		
Deduct: Increase in Accrued				
Expenses			(e) 1,500 00	
Depreciation Expense . .			(f) 11,700 00	
Amortization Expense . .			(f) 1,000 00	53,600 00
Net Income After Income Taxes	16,800 00			
Cash Flow From Operations				16,500 00
Explanation for adjustments				
(a) Increase in Accounts Receivable				
and Notes Receivable				
(b) Increase in Accounts Payable				
(c) Increase in Merchandise				
Inventory				
(d) Increase in Supplies				
(e) Increase in Interest Payable,				
Federal Income Taxes Payable,				
and Payroll Taxes Payable				
(f) Increase in Depreciation and				
Amortization Expense				

Sources of Cash {
Uses of Cash {
Uses of Cash {

Cash Paid for Cost of Goods Sold. The income statement for the Lorenzen Company shows cost of goods sold of $126,000. However, the $126,000 is not the amount of cash paid for the goods sold. To convert the cost of goods sold from the accrual basis to the cash basis, the actual cash paid for purchases and the change in merchandise inventory balances must be computed.

Cash Paid for Purchases. The income statement shows net purchases of $130,400. However, this $130,400 does not represent the cash paid for purchases, since the purchase of merchandise and the payment for purchases take place at different times.

In order to determine how much actual cash was paid for purchases, the Accounts Payable and Net Purchases balances must be considered. For example, on December 31, 19X3, the Lorenzen Company owed creditors $14,000, the balance of Accounts Payable. During 19X4, additional merchandise was purchased for $130,400. Thus the Lorenzen Company could have paid accounts payable of $144,400 ($14,000 + $130,400). But the Lorenzen Company did not pay all of its creditors (there is still a balance of $16,500 in Accounts Payable on December 31, 19X4). Thus the actual cash paid for purchases was $127,900 ($14,000 + $130,400 − $16,500).

$ 14,000	Accounts Payable, December 31, 19X3
+130,400	Add: Net Purchases During 19X4
$144,400	Total Cash to Be Paid
−16,500	Less: Accounts Payable and Notes Payable, December 31, 19X4
$127,900	Total Cash Paid for Purchases
$130,400	Net Purchases
−2,500	Less: Increase in Payables
$127,900	Total Cash Paid for Purchases

The explanation here indicates that the relationship between cash paid for purchases and Net Purchases on the income statement depends on the beginning and ending balances of Accounts Payable.

$$
\begin{array}{c}
\text{Net Purchases} \\
\text{(Accrual Basis)}
\end{array}
\begin{array}{c}
+ \\
-
\end{array}
\begin{array}{c}
\text{A Decrease} \\
\text{in Payables} \\
or \\
\text{An Increase} \\
\text{in Payables}
\end{array}
=
\begin{array}{c}
\text{Total Cash} \\
\text{Paid for} \\
\text{Purchases}
\end{array}
$$

Changes in Merchandise Inventory Balances. Merchandise inventory increased by $4,400 from December 31, 19X3, to December 31, 19X4. The beginning inventory was $23,600, and the ending inventory was $28,000. The $4,400 increase in inventory came from the Net Purchases, since goods apparently were purchased but not sold. Now the $4,400 must be added to the Cost of Goods Sold because the beginning inventory and ending inventory balances are different, not because cash was paid.

$28,000	Merchandise Inventory, December 31, 19X4
−23,600	Less: Merchandise Inventory, December 31, 19X3
$ 4,400	Increase in Merchandise Inventory
$23,600	Merchandise Inventory, December 31, 19X3
+4,400	Add: Increase in Merchandise Inventory
$28,000	Merchandise Increase, December 31, 19X4

On the worksheet to convert the income statement from accrual basis to cash basis, the $2,500 increase in Accounts Payable is labeled (b) and the $4,400 increase in Merchandise Inventory is labeled (c).

$$\text{Cost of Goods Sold} + \text{An Increase in Inventory} = \begin{array}{c}\text{Total Cash}\\\text{Paid for}\\\text{Goods Sold}\end{array}$$

$126,000	Cost of Goods Sold (Accrual Basis)
−2,500	Less: Increase in Accounts Payable
$123,500	
+4,400	Add: Increase in Merchandise Inventory
$127,900	Cash Paid for Goods Sold

Cash Paid for Expenses. The income statement for the Lorenzen Company shows that the Operating Expenses and Income Taxes total $67,200 ($63,800 + $3,400). However, because not all expenses shown on the income statement are matched by cash payments, the $67,200 does not represent actual cash paid out for expenses. Again, this is due to the accrual basis of accounting.

Expenses are recorded when salaries, utilities, repairs, and similar items are paid. Also, expenses are recorded at the close of the accounting period when various adjustments are recorded. Included are adjustments for depreciation, prepaid expenses, and accrued items such as salaries. Thus expenses arise from paying with cash, writing off prepaid expenses, and incurring accrued expenses. Expenses arising through cash payments during the accounting period do not require an

Expenses incurred and paid represent cash payments.

adjustment. However, prepaid expenses and accrued expenses (liabilities) do require adjustments, because cash is not paid for these expenses during this accounting period.

Prepaid Expenses. The Lorenzen Company has two prepaid expenses: Prepaid Insurance and Supplies. During the accounting period, the balance of Supplies (a prepaid expense) increased by $600. Prepaid Insurance, another prepaid expense, had the same balance at the beginning and at the end of the period. Prepaid expenses arose through cash payments being made during 19X4 but the actual expense not being recorded until 19X5.

Since prepaid expenses were $600 more in 19X4 than in 19X3, the $600 increase in prepaid expenses must be added to Operating Expenses and Income Taxes to convert this amount to a cash basis. Remember that cash was actually paid in 19X4 for the prepaid expenses.

Expenses paid but not incurred represent cash payments.

On the worksheet to convert the income statement from accrual basis to cash basis, the $600 increase in prepaid expenses is labeled (d).

$3,000	Prepaid Insurance and Supplies, December 31, 19X4
−2,400	Less: Prepaid Insurance and Supplies, December 31, 19X3
$ 600	Increase in Prepaid Expenses

Accrued Expenses. Consider the effect of accrued expenses (liabilities) on Operating Expenses and Income Taxes. Accrued expenses are recorded by debiting an expense and crediting a liability at the end of an accounting period. The liability is not paid until the next accounting period. Thus the cash paid for salaries, interest, and other expenses requiring accrual entries is probably different than the income statement amounts for these items.

Expenses incurred but not paid do not represent cash payments.

On December 31, 19X4, the Lorenzen Company has three accrued liabilities totaling $12,500. These accrued liabilities are the total of Federal Income Taxes Payable, Payroll Taxes Payable, and Interest Payable ($7,000 + $3,000 + $2,500). Each of these accounts originated from an accrual entry that included debits to expense accounts. During 19X4, the cash payments for accrued liabilities was $11,000— the balances of Interest Payable ($2,000), Federal Income Taxes Payable ($7,000), and Payroll Taxes Payable ($2,000), on December 31, 19X3. Thus the accrued liabilities for 19X4 ($12,500) exceeded payments made for 19X3 accruals ($11,000) by $1,500. The $1,500 increased expenses but did not require cash payments. To convert Operating Expenses and Income Taxes from the accrual basis to the cash

basis, the $1,500 must be deducted from the total Operating Expenses
and Income Taxes of $67,200. (See entry e.)

Accrued Expenses (Liabilities)	
$12,500	Accrued Expenses Incurred in 19X4 to Be Paid in 19X5
−11,000	Less: Accrued Expenses Incurred in 19X3 but Paid in 19X4
$ 1,500	More Accrued Expenses Incurred in 19X4 Than Were Paid
$12,500	Accrued Expenses, December 31, 19X4
−1,500	Less: Increase in Accrued Expenses
$11,000	Total Cash Paid for Accrued Expenses

Depreciation and amortization increase operating expenses but do not require cash payments.

Depreciation and Amortization. The final adjustment to convert
Operating Expenses and Income Taxes to the cash basis includes consideration of depreciation and amortization. The adjustment for depreciation and amortization, recorded at the end of the accounting period,
increased the Lorenzen Company expenses but had no effect on cash.
Thus it is necessary to deduct the depreciation ($11,700) and amorti-
zation ($1,000) from Operating Expenses and Income Taxes to convert
to the cash basis. This is because an increase in Operating Expenses
and Income Taxes caused by depreciation ($11,700) and amortization
($1,000) does not require a cash payment during the period. Thus both
depreciation and amortization must be deducted to arrive at the cash
paid for expenses. The entries are identified as (f) on the worksheet.

The explanations above indicate that the relationship between the
income statement amounts and the cash paid for Operating Expenses
and Income Taxes depends upon the beginning and ending balances
of prepaid expenses, accrued liabilities, and depreciation and amortization.

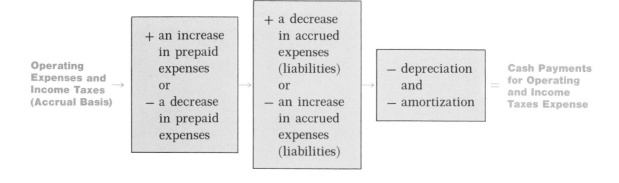

The actual cash flow from operations can be determined by following the conversion of the income statement from an accrual basis to a cash basis.

Sales yielded $198,000 as a source of cash. The Cost of Goods Sold required a $127,900 use of cash, and Operating Expenses and Income Taxes required a $53,600 use of cash. The difference between the total sources and uses of cash was $16,500, and this difference is labeled Cash Flow From Operations. That is, operations provided a net $16,500 source of cash.

Sources of Cash:			
Net Sales			198,000 00
Uses of Cash:			
Cost of Goods Sold	127,900 00		
Operating Expenses and Income Taxes	53,600 00		
Total Uses of Cash			181,500 00
Cash Flow From Operations			16,500 00

CASH FLOW FROM OPERATING TRANSACTIONS

Activity B. Answer the following questions about the worksheet to convert the income statement from accrual basis to cash basis. Refer to the text and illustrations on pages 573 to 581.

1. What does the (a) $12,000 deduction from Net Sales represent?

2. How much cash is received from Net Sales?

3. What does the (b) $2,500 deduction from Cost of Goods Sold represent?

4. What does the (c) $4,400 increase to Cost of Goods Sold represent?

5. What is the amount of change in prepaid expenses during the year?

6. Does the change in prepaid expenses increase or decrease the operating expenses converted to the cash basis?

7. Why are the accrued expenses (e) deducted from total operating expenses and income taxes? Why are the depreciation and amortization expenses (f) deducted from the total operating expenses and income taxes?

8. What is the amount of cash flow from operations for 19X4?

STEP 2. Determining the Effect of Nonoperating Transactions on Cash Flow

C *Are operating transactions the only transactions that affect cash flow?* No; the majority of transactions affecting cash flow are operating transactions, but there are also nonoperating transactions that may also affect cash.

Each nonoperating source or use of cash is found on the Lorenzen Company balance sheet. But one must look in the ledger to see whether the transactions affect cash. The transactions involving cash received and cash paid by the Lorenzen Company during 19X4 are given here.

Cash Received From Sale of Capital Stock. During 19X4, the Lorenzen Company sold $20,000 of capital stock. The sale represented a $20,000 source of cash and increased capital stock by the same amount.

Cash Paid for Marketable Securities. Marketable securities were acquired for $3,500. This increased marketable securities by $3,500 and representd a use of cash for the same amount.

Cash Paid for Addition to Building. During 19X4, the Lorenzen Company completed a $20,000 addition to its existing building. The addition was paid for in cash and represented a $20,000 use of cash.

Cash Payments on Mortgage. During 19X4, the Lorenzen Company paid $5,000 in mortgage payments. The payments were made in cash and represented a $5,000 use of cash.

Cash Paid for Dividends. During 19X4, the Lorenzen Company declared and paid $4,000 for cash dividends. The dividends represented a $4,000 use of cash.

Nonoperating transactions must now be classified as either sources or uses of cash.

Sources of Cash:			
Sale of Capital Stock			*20,000 00*
Uses of Cash:			
Purchase of Marketable Securities	*3,500 00*		
Addition to Building	*20,000 00*		
Payments on Mortgage	*5,000 00*		
Cash Dividends	*4,000 00*		
Total Uses of Cash			*32,500 00*
Cash Flow From Nonoperating Transactions			*(12,500 00)*

CASH FLOW FROM NONOPERATING TRANSACTIONS

STEP 3. Preparing the Cash-Flow Statement

The cash-flow statement for the Lorenzen Company is presented on the next page. The operating and nonoperating transactions are listed as either sources or uses of cash. This was determined by subtracting the uses of cash ($32,500) from the sources of cash ($36,500). At the bot-

tom of the cash-flow statement, the difference between the cash balance on December 31, 19X3, and December 31, 19X4, is given as
$4,000. This figure verifies the accuracy of the arithmetic.

LORENZEN COMPANY
Cash-Flow Statement
For the Year Ended December 31, 19X4

Part A: Sources and Uses of Cash			
Sources of Cash:			
From Current Operations.............		16,500 00	Cash came
From Sale of Capital Stock		20,000 00	from these sources.
Total Sources of Cash..............		36,500 00	
Uses of Cash:			
Purchase of Marketable Securities	3,500 00		
Addition to Building................	20,000 00		Cash was used for
Payments on Mortgage	5,000 00		these purposes.
Payment of Cash Dividends...........	4,000 00		
Total Uses of Cash................		32,500 00	Cash increased by
Net Increase in Cash During the Year		4,000 00	this amount.
Part B: Changes in the Cash Account			
Cash Balance, December 31, 19X4.........	12,000 00		
Cash Balance, December 31, 19X3.........	8,000 00		
Increase in Cash During the Year		4,000 00	Amount must agree with Total in Part A.

Activity C. Answer the following questions about the cash-flow statement. Refer to the text and illustrations on pages 581 to 583.

1. What are the two sources and
amount of each source of cash for
19X4?
2. What is the total sources of
cash?
3. What are the four uses of cash
during 19X4?
4. How much cash was used to
purchase marketable securities during 19X4?
5. How much cash was used for
cash dividends?

6. What was the total uses of cash?
7. Did cash increase or decrease
during 19X4? By how much?
8. What was the December 31,
19X3, cash balance? What was the
December 31, 19X4, cash balance?
9. What is the difference between
the 19X4 and 19X3 cash balances?
10. Is the amount of difference in
Question 9 the same as the net increase in cash during the year?

Topic 5   Problems

14-20. Use the following information to compute the total cash the
Maxwell Company received from sales in 19X4.

Net Sales for 19X4 are $224,000.

Accounts Receivable for 19X3 are $32,300 and for 19X4 are $23,800.

Notes Receivable for 19X3 are $800 and for 19X4 are $600.

14-21. Financial information from the income statement and balance sheet for the Maxwell Company is presented here. Use the following information to compute the total cash paid for purchases during 19X4.

Net Purchases for 19X4 are $150,000.

Accounts Payable for 19X3 are $30,420 and for 19X4 are $31,500.

14-22. Information on accrued expenses for the Sims Company is given here. Use the following information to compute the total cash paid for accrued expenses.

Accrued expenses on December 31, 19X3, are $13,000.

Accrued expenses on December 31, 19X4, are $14,500.

14-23. A partial cash-flow statement for the Nivens Company is presented here. Use the information given to complete the statement.

NIVENS COMPANY
Cash-Flow Statement
For the Year Ended December 31, 19X4

Part A: Sources and Uses of Cash			
Sources of Cash:			
From Current Operations..............	48,500 00		
From Sale of Capital Stock			
Total Sources of Cash...............			69,500 00
Uses of Cash:			
Purchase of Marketable Securities	2,000 00		
Addition to Building.................	45,000 00		
Payments on Mortgage	10,000 00		
Payment of Cash Dividends...........			
Total Uses of Cash................			65,000 00
Net Increase in Cash During the Year			
Part B: Changes in the Cash Account			
Cash Balance, December 31, 19X4.........			
Cash Balance, December 31, 19X3.........	15,000 00		
Increase in Cash During the Year			4,500 00

The Language of Business

Here are some basic terms that make up the language of business. Do you understand the meaning of each? Can you define each term and use it in an original sentence?

trend	ratio	owner's equity ratio	net increase in
change	working capital	return on total assets	working capital
comparative financial	solvent	ratio	net decrease in
statements	insolvent	return on stockholders'	working capital
trend analysis	current ratio	equity	noncurrent accounts
line graph	quick assets ratio	return on net sales	cash flow
percentage analysis	quick assets	earnings on each share	cash-flow statement
vertical analysis	accounts receivable	internal comparisons	source of cash
component percentage	turnover	external comparisons	use of cash
analysis	collection period	nonchange statement	net increase in cash
common-size	merchandise inventory	change statement	net decrease in cash
statements	turnover	statement of changes	operating transactions
circle graph	days' supply in	in financial position	accrual basis of
horizontal analysis	inventory	sources of working	accounting
base year	operating cycle	capital	cash basis of
bar graph	creditors' equity ratio	uses of working capital	accounting

Chapter 14   Questions

1. Why are comparative financial statements prepared?

2. What is the purpose of horizontal analysis? vertical analysis?

3. Why are ratio analyses used?

4. Which ratios are used mainly by creditors? by owners?

5. What current assets are normally included as quick assets?

6. How does a company determine what caused changes in working capital?

7. What types of transactions cause changes in working capital?

8. How can a business determine if customers are paying promptly?

9. What is the value of making external comparisons?

10. Which item on the income statement is used as the basis for all percent computations? Why?

Chapter 14   Problems

Problems for Chapter 14 are given in the *Working Papers and Chapter Problems* for Part 2. If you are using the workbook, do the problems in the space provided there. Complete your assigned topic problems before answering the chapter problems.

Chapter 14   Management Cases

Replacement Cost Accounting. Some accountants propose changes to accounting procedures that would have an effect on financial data. One such proposal is to use replacement-cost accounting for plant and equipment assets. Instead of being carried at the original cost price, plant and equipment assets would be carried at their replacement costs, that is, at a "value" that approximates the cost to "replace" the items of plant and equipment with similar assets. The intent of replacement-cost accounting is to take into consideration the impact of inflation on *both* the cost of assets and the annual depreciation charges on them. Thus annual depreciation charges would be based on replacement costs (that include the effects of inflation) and not on original costs.

Case 14M-1. Using the above information and your knowledge of accounting, discuss the impact of replacement-cost accounting on financial data and the interpretation of financial data.

a. What effect would replacement-cost accounting have on net income?

b. What would the difficulty be of determining replacement costs?

c. Why is the use of original costs for computing annual depreciation said to inflate net income?

d. How would replacement-cost accounting affect income tax liabilities?

e. What points—for or against—replacement-cost accounting do you think are important to consider?

NOTE: Entries in boldface type refer to accounting concepts or principles.

A Accelerated depreciation, 387–389; *def.*, 387
book value and, 388
compared with straight-line, 389
declining-balance, 388–389
sum-of-the-year's-digits, 387–388
Accounting department, 115–116
Accounting systems (*see* Centralized accounting system; Decentralized accounting system)
Accounts payable, 416–421; *def.*, 415
as current liability, 415
purchases discounts lost and, 420
recording
differences between gross and net methods, 420–421
gross method for, 416–418; *illus.*, 417
net method for, 418–420; *illus.*, 418, 419
Accounts receivable, 355–372; *def.*, 355–356
billing the customer, 357
control of credit sales and, 356
exchanging notes receivable for, 345
installment, 134, 141–143
opening an account, 356
realizable value of, 358
reporting, 135
uncollectible (*see* Uncollectible accounts)
as unsecured open accounts, 355–356
Accounts receivable ledger, 12; *illus.*, 356
Accounts receivable turnover, 536–538
Accrual basis of accounting, *def.*, 348, 574
change to cash basis, 575–581
Accrued interest expense, 422–425; *illus.*, 422, 423
paying the interest, 423, 425; *illus.*, 424

Accrued interest revenue, 348–351; *def.*, 348
adjusting interest revenue, 349–350
on bonds, 352–354
recording cash and, 351–352
stock dividends, 354
Accrued liabilities, 421–426; *def.*, 415, 421
as current liability, 415
interest, 422–425; *illus.*, 422, 423
paying, 423–425; *illus.*, 424
salaries, 425–426; *illus.*, 425
paying, 426; *illus.*, 426
Accrued revenue, *def.*, 348
Accrued salaries, 425–426; *def.*, 425; *illus.*, 425
paying, 426; *illus.*, 426
Actual factory overhead, *def.*, 195
accounting for, 198–200
allocating costs to departments, 201–203
comparing applied with, 201
Adjusting entries
for corporations, 510; *illus.*, 510
for single proprietorship, 452–454; *illus.*, 453
Advertising expense, 59–61
net sales method of allocation of, 59
time/space method of allocation of, 59–61
Allowance for doubtful accounts, 362; *def.*, 146
as contra account, 363
Analysis of labor costs report, *def.*, 187; *illus.*, 188
Applied factory overhead, *def.*, 195
accounting for, 198–200
comparing actual with, 201
computing, 194–198
direct labor cost method, 195–196
direct labor hours method, 196
direct materials cost method, 197

Applied factory overhead, computing (*continued*)
machine hours method, 196–197
units of production method, 197–198
Articles of incorporation, 484; *illus.*, 485
Articles of partnership, 461–463; *illus.*, 462
Asset accounts, home office, 90
Assets, 313 (*see also specific types of assets*)
claims against (*see* Liabilities; Owner's equity)
depreciation of (*see* Depreciation)
Auditor, 90
Authorized stock, 484
Automated inventory, 46–47; *illus.*, 47
Average costing, *def.*, 212

B Bad debts (*see* Uncollectible accounts)
Balance sheet, *def.*, 450
chain store, 98; *illus.*, 98
combined, 109–111; *def.*, 107; *illus.*, 110
worksheet for, 109–110; *illus.*, 109
comparative, 522–524; *illus.*, 523 (*see also* Comparison and trend analysis)
contra accounts and, 363
for corporations, 509; *illus.*, 509
financial accounting and, 3
home office, 102–103; *illus.*, 102
liquidity and, 313; *illus.*, 313
for a manufacturing business, 286; *illus.*, 287
as nonchange statement, 552
for partnership, 473; *illus.*, 468, 473
for sole proprietorship, 450; *illus.*, 451
writing off an account on, 361
Bank accounts, 323–327
general, 323
payroll, 323–325
special, 323–327
special general, 326–327
Bank statement, 318–323; *illus.*, 319
deposits in transit and, 318
dishonored checks and, 319–320
errors and, 320
outstanding checks and, 318
reconciling, 320–321; *illus.*, 321
service charges and fees and, 318–319
updating the checkbook and ledger and, 322–323
verifying the cash balance and, 320
Bar code, 14, 117; *illus.*, 14
Bar graphs, 528

Beginning work-in-process inventory
cost of production reports and, 254–257
cost schedule and, 256–257
quantity schedule and, 254–256
report balances and, 257
equivalent units of production and, 235, 239
computing, 239–240
Bill of materials, *def.*, 174–175; *illus.*, 175
Bin tag, *def.*, 178
Bond indenture, *def.*, 431
Bond interest (*see also* Interest, bond issue)
accrued, 352–354
receiving, 353–354
recording, 337
Bond sinking fund, *def.*, 436–437
trustee of, 437
Bonds, 430–442; *def.*, 430
debenture, 431
fixed maturity, 432
issue of, 434–435
contract interest rate and, 435
debt capital and, 434–435
effective interest rate and, 435
equity capital and, 434
underwriter's fees and, 435
as long-term liability, 430
market value of, 431
maturity of, 430
par value of, 430–431
registered, 432
secured, 431
serial, 432
sold at a discount, 438–441
carrying value and, 439
contra account and, 439
interest charges and, 439–440
sold at par value, 435–437
bond issue and, 436
bond retirement and, 436–437
interest payments and, 436
sinking fund and, 436–437
trustee and, 437
sold at a premium, 441–443
carrying value and, 441
interest charges and, 442
unsecured, 431
Book value, *def.*, 388
of common stock, 511
Bookkeeper, full-charge, *def.*, 90
Bottom line, *def.*, 81
By-product, *def.*, 257

C Capital
debt, 434–435; *def.*, 434
donated, 510–511
equity, *def.*, 434
working, *def.*, 533
Capital stock, 492
Carrying charge, *def.*, 131

Carrying value
of discounted bonds, *def.*, 439
of premium bonds, *def.*, 441
Cash, *def.*, 312–313
control of, 296 (*see also* Voucher system)
procedures for, 316–317
idle, 316
imprest account (*see* Imprest cash funds)
management of, 314–316
procedures for, 315–316
payments, 316–317; *illus.*, 317
petty, 329–332
receipts, 316; *illus.*, 317
received from installments, 138–139
receiving, for a note receivable, 351–352
safeguarding, 323
transfers of, 92–93
electronic, 316
Cash in bank, 312–329
bank statement and, 318–323
reconciling, 320–321
updating the checkbook and ledger and, 322–323
verifying the cash balance and, 320
special bank accounts, 323–327
general bank account, 323
payroll bank account, 323–325
special general accounts, 326–327
Cash basis of accounting, *def.*, 574
change from accrual basis, 575–581
Cash flow, 570–572; *def.*, 572
interpreting changes in, 570–586
net decrease in cash and, 573
net increase in cash and, 573
source of cash and, 572
use of cash and, 572–573
Cash-flow statement, 572–586; *def.*, 572; *illus.*, 572
steps in preparing, 573–584
nonoperating transactions and, 581–582
operating transactions and, 573–581
Cash on delivery (*see entries beginning with term:* COD)
Cash payments journal, *illus.*, 33
Cash payments request, 86; *illus.*, 87
Cash proof, 12, 14, 15
Cash proof form, 16; *illus.*, 16
Cash receipts journal, 12; *illus.*, 16
cash proof and, 16
cash received from installments and, 138–139
Cash receipts journal by departments, 16–17; *def.*, 16; *illus.*, 17
posting from, 19, 21
proof of, *illus.*, 21
Cash receipts summary, 85–86; *illus.*, 86

Cash registers, 11, 12
audit tape of, 12, 14, 15
cash sales and, 14
credit sales and, 12
electronic, 14; *def.*, 117
Cash sales, 11, 12
accounting for, 134
journalizing by department, 15–18
originating by department, 14
processing, *illus.*, 12
returns and allowances on, 23
Cash short and over, 62
Centralized accounting system, 84–88; *def.*, 84
general accounting and, 87–88
payroll and, 87, 88
purchases and cash payments and, 86–87
sales and cash receipts and, 85–86
Chain store
accounts, 91–92
cost of goods sold, 92
owner's equity, 91
closing entries for, 103–105
computer processing at
of purchases and cash payments, 119–120
of sales and cash receipts, 117
financial statements, 96–99
balance sheet, 98
income statement, 96–98
schedule of cost of goods sold, 96–97
Change, *def.*, 516
Change funds, 332–333; *def.*, 332
Change statement, *def.*, 552
Charge account sales, 134 (*see also* Credit sales)
Chart of accounts, *illus.*, 22
Charter, corporate, 484
Check register, 121; *def.*, 292; *illus.*, 121
posting from, 301–302
purpose of, 301
Check stub, 33; *illus.*, 33
Chief executive officer, 490
Circle graphs, 524–525
Closing entries
chain store, 103–105; *illus.*, 104
for corporations, 510; *illus.*, 511
home office, 105; *illus.*, 106
for a manufacturing business, 286
for a partnership, 474–476; *illus.*, 475
for a single proprietorship, 454; *illus.*, 455
COD receivable account, *def.*, 152
COD sales, 150–158; *def.*, 150
accounting for, 151–152
recording
delivered by the seller, 152–154
delivered by a transportation service, 154–156
payments for deliveries of COD goods, 156

COD sales, recording (*continued*)
  returns on COD sales, 156–157
  shipping charge and, 152
  transportation expense on returned
    COD goods account and, 157
  transportation on sales account
    and, 152
COD sales account, *def.*, 152
Coding, 14; *illus.*, 14
  bar code, 14, 117
Combination journal, 12
Combined financial statements,
  107–111; *def.*, 107, **111**
  balance sheet, 109–111; *def.*, 107;
    illus., 110
    worksheet for, 109–110; *illus.*,
      109
  income statement, 107–108; *def.*,
    107; *illus.*, 108
    worksheet for, 107–108; *illus.*,
      108
  schedule of cost of goods sold,
    illus., 109
  statement of owner's equity, *illus.*,
    111
Common-size statements, 522
Common stock, 492
  book value of, 511
  declaring dividends for, 497
  sold at par, 493
Comparison and trend analysis,
  515–532
  bar graphs and, 528
  change and, 516
  circle graphs and, 524–525
  comparative balance sheet,
    522–524
  comparative income statements,
    522
  comparative statement of
    stockholders' equity, 522
  component percentage analysis, 521
  horizontal analysis and, 525–527
  line graphs and, 518–519
  trend and, 515
  trend analysis and, 517
  trend percentage analysis, 520–521
  vertical analysis and, 521–525
Component percentage analysis,
  521–525
Computers, *def.*, 115
  application of (*see* Multistore
    businesses, computer
    application for)
Conditional sales contract, 131
Contingent liability, *def.*, 457
Continuous life, *def.*, 489
Contra account, 362–363
  for bonds sold at a discount, 439
Contract interest rate, *def.*, 435
Conversion costs, *def.*, 169
Corporations, 483–514; *def.*, 483,
  488
  adjusting entries, 510; *illus.*, 510
  advantages of, 489–490

Corporations (*continued*)
  articles of incorporation and, 484;
    illus., 485
  charter of, 484
  closing entries, 510; *illus.*, 511
  disadvantages of, 491
  domestic, 487–488
  financial statements for, 505–509
    balance sheet, 509; *illus.*, 509
    income statement, 505–507;
      illus., 506
    statement of stockholders' equity,
      507–509; *illus.*, 508
  foreign, 487–488
  forming, 483–484
  other accounting procedures,
    510–512
    book value of common stock,
      511
    donated capital, 510–511
    stated value of stock, 511
    stock subscription, 512
    Subchapter S corporations, 512
    treasury stock, 511
  owners of, 484–487
    rights of, 486–487
  private, 488
  public, 488
  stock of (*see* Stocks)
  worksheet for, 502–505; *illus.*,
    504
    completing, 504–505
    income taxes and, 503–504
    organization costs and, 502–503
Cost accountants, *def.*, 169–180
Cost accounting, *def.*, 167
  automated procedures for, 205
  conversion costs and, 169
  direct labor and, 168
  direct materials and, 168
  elements of, 168–169
  factory overhead and, 168–169
  indirect labor and, 168
  indirect materials and, 168
  manufacturing supplies and, 168
  prime costs and, 169
  systems of, 169–170 (*see also* Job
    order cost accounting; Process
    cost accounting system)
Cost center, *def.*, 5
Cost clerks, *def.*, 169, 170
**Cost of goods manufactured, 169,
  284**
  computation of, 281
  schedule of, 279–284
Cost of goods sold, *def.*, 3
  chain store accounts, 92
  computation of, 281
  home office accounts, 91
  perpetual inventory procedures
    and, 279
  recording, 232
  reporting, 3–4
  schedule of (*see* Schedule of cost of
    goods sold)

Cost of production reports (actual
  example of), 245–259; *def.*, 245,
  250; *illus.*, 246–247
  beginning work-in-process
    inventory, 254–257
    cost schedule and, 256–257
    quantity schedule and, 254–256
    report balances and, 257
  by-products and, 257
  cost schedule, 245, 247–250
  ending work-in-process inventory,
    251–254
    cost schedule and, 253–254
    quantity schedule and, 252–253
  joint products and, 258
  quantity schedule, 245, 247
Cost schedule, 247–250; *def.*, 245;
  illus., 246–247
  beginning work-in-process inventory
    and, 256–257
  ending work-in-process inventory
    and, 253–254
Credit card fee expense account, *def.*,
  162
Credit card sales, 158–162
  processing, 158–161
    checking customer's credit, 160
    obtaining payment from the
      bank, 160–161
    preparing source documents,
      159–160
    recording, 161–162
Credit card sales account, *def.*, 162
Credit memorandum, 23; *illus.*, 23
Credit policies, 130–131
  opening an account and, 356
Credit sales, 12, 134
  billing the customer for, 357
  control of, 356
  imprinting devices and, 12
  journalizing by department, 18–19
  originating by department, 14–15
  processing, *illus.*, 13
  returns and allowances on, 22–24
Creditors' equity ratio, 544
Cumulative preferred stock, 498–499
Current assets, 312–314; *def.*, 312,
  314 (*see also specific current
  assets*)
  current liabilities and, 414–415
Current liabilities, *def.*, 414–415,
  415
  current assets and, 414–415
  examples of, 415
Current position, ratios that measure
  532–544
  accounts receivable turnover,
    536–538
  current ratio, 533–534
  merchandise inventory turnover,
    538–540
  operating cycles, 540–541
  quick assets ratio, 534–535
Current ratio, 533–534
Cycle billing, *def.*, 357

D Data collector, 117
Data processing
cash registers and, 11
for multistore businesses (*see*
Multistore businesses,
computer application for)
Day's supply in inventory, 539–540
Debenture bonds, *def.*, 431
Debt capital, 434–435; *def.*, 434
Decentralized accounting system,
89–114, *def.*, 84
chain store accounts, 91–92
cost of goods sold account, 92
owner's equity account, 91
chain store closing entries,
103–105
chain store financial statements,
96–99
balance sheet, 98
income statement, 96–98
schedule of cost of goods sold,
96–97
combined financial statements,
107–111
balance sheet, 107, 109–111
income statement, 107–108
full-charge bookkeeper and, 90
home office accounts, 90–91
asset accounts, 90
cost of goods sold accounts, 91
owner's equity account, 91
revenue accounts, 90–91
home office closing entries, 105,
106
home office financial statements,
99–103
balance sheet, 102–103
income statement, 100–102
net income of each store and,
99–100
schedule of cost of goods sold,
100, 101
statement of owner's equity,
102–103
internal transactions and, 92–95
examples of, 92
transfers of cash, 92–93
transfers of merchandise, 93–95
Declining-balance method of
depreciation, 388–389; *def.*, 388
compared with other methods, 389
Deferred revenue, 427–429; *def.*,
415, 427
adjusting, 428–429; *illus.*, 428
recording, 427; *illus.*, 427, 428
Delivery expense, 62–63
Departmental accounts, 9
Departmental gross profit, 50
Departmental journals, 22, 38
Departmental net income, 58–59
Departmental net loss, 58–59
Departmentalized accounting systems,
4
Depletion of natural resources,
408–409

Depreciation, 384–394; *def.*, 64,
384, **385**
accelerated, 387–389
declining-balance, 388–389
sum-of-the-year's-digits, 387–388
book value and, 388
comparing methods of, 389–390
disposal value and, 386
inadequacy and, 384
obsolescence and, 384
recording estimated, 390–392
straight-line, 385–387
Depreciation expense, 64
Determinable life of an asset, 406
Direct expense, *def.*, 58
Direct labor, *def.*, 168
job order cost accounting and,
269–270
process cost accounting and
assembling department, 224
finishing department, 228
milling department, 218–219
Direct labor cost method of setting
overhead rates, 195–196
Direct labor hours method of setting
overhead rates, 196
Direct materials, *def.*, 168
job order cost accounting and,
266–269
process cost accounting and
assembling department, 223–224
finishing department, 227–228
milling department, 217–218
source documents for recording,
216–217
Direct materials cost method of
setting overhead rates, 197
Discounted bonds, 438–441; *def.*,
438; *illus.*, 438
annual interest charges for,
439–440, **440,** *illus.*, 439,
440
carrying value and, 439
contra account and, 439
Discounted stocks, 493–495
Disposal value of an asset, *def.*, 386
Dividends, 354
date of declaration and, 496
date of payment and, 496
date of record and, 496
declaring, 496–497
other types of
on cumulative preferred stock,
498–499
on participating preferred stock,
499–500
stock dividends, 499
paying, 498
recording, 337–338, 497–498
stockholders of record and, 496
stockholders' rights to, 486
Domestic corporation, 487–488
Donated capital, 510–511
Doubtful accounts expense (*see*
Uncollectible accounts)

Down payment, *def.*, 131
journalizing, 136, 138

E Effective interest rate,
def., 435
Electronic cash register, 14; *def.*, 117
Electronic funds transfer (EFT), *def.*,
316
Employee earnings records, *def.*, 186
Ending work-in-process inventory,
236–237; *def.*, 235–236
computing, 239–240
cost of production reports and,
251–254
cost schedule and, 253–254
quantity schedule and, 252–253
Equipment used method of allocating
expenses, 64–65
depreciation expense and, 64
insurance expense and, 65
Equity, *def.*, 544
ratios that measure, 544–547
Equity capital, *def.*, 434
Equity position ratios, 544–545
Equivalent units of production
(actual example of), 235–245;
def., 236
allocating process costs and,
237–239
beginning work-in-process inventory
and, 235, 239
computing, 239–241
ending work-in-process inventory
and, 235–237
Expenses, *def.*, 3
allocating, 57–58 (*see also*
Operations, summarizing and
analyzing the results of)
cash short and over, 62
comparing, 77–78
delivery, 62–63
depreciation, 64
direct, 58
indirect, 58
insurance, 65
matching revenue and, 361
operating, 57
rent, 66
reporting, 3–4
salaries, 67
supplies, 63
uncollectible accounts, 61–62
utilities, 66

F Face value, *def.*, 430
Factory burden (*see*
Factory overhead)
Factory labor costs, 185–193
accounting for, 189–191
controlling, 191
determining, 186–187
payroll procedures and, 185–186
perpetual inventory procedures
and, 278

Factory overhead, 168–169, 193–210;
  def., 168
  actual, 195
    accounting for, 198–200
    allocating costs to departments,
      201–203
    comparing applied with, 201
  applied (*see* Applied factory
    overhead)
  fixed overhead costs, 195
  job order cost accounting and,
    270–271
  overapplied, 201
  perpetual inventory procedures
    and, 279
  predetermined overhead rate, 220
  process cost accounting and
    assembling department, 224
    finishing department, 228
    milling department, 219–220
  underapplied, 201
  variable overhead costs, 194–195
Factory overhead account, *def.,* 182
  imbalance in, 201
Factory overhead ledger, *def.,* 198–199
FIFO (first in, first out) method of
  valuing inventory, 374–375
Finance charge, *def.,* 131
Finance charges account, 134
Financial position, interpreting
  changes in, 551–570
Financial statements, *def.,* **473**
  (*see also under* Corporations;
    Manufacturing businesses;
    Partnership; Single
    proprietorship; *specific
    statements*)
  chain store, 96–99
  combined (*see* Combined financial
    statements)
  comparative, 516–517 (*see also*
    Comparison and trend analysis)
  computerized, 124; *illus.,* 125
  home office, 99–103
Finished goods, sale of
  job order cost accounting and,
    273–275
  process cost accounting and,
    231–235
    gross profit on sales and, 233
    recording the cost of goods sold
      and, 232
    recording the sale and, 232
Finished goods account, *def.,* 171
  perpetual inventory procedures
    and, 279
Fixed assets (*see* Plant and
  equipment)
Fixed life of an asset, 406
Fixed maturity bonds, *def.,* 432
Fixed overhead costs, *def.,* 195
Flow of cash (*see* Cash flow)
Flow of costs (process cost
  accounting), 204–205, 211–235;
  illus., 204, 213–215 (*see also* Job

Flow of costs (*continued*)
  order cost accounting, flow of
    costs)
  assembling department costs,
    223–227
    factory overhead, 224
    labor, 224
    materials, 223–224
    work in process, 225–226
  finishing department costs, 227–231
    factory overhead, 228
    labor, 228
    materials, 227–228
    work in process, 229–231
  flowchart of, 212–213; *illus.,*
    213–215
  milling department costs, 217–223
    factory overhead, 219–220
    labor, 218–219
    materials, 217–218
    work in process, 220–221
  raw materials cost, 216–217
  selling the finished goods, 231–235
    gross profit on sales, 233
    recording the cost of goods sold,
      232
    recording the sale, 232
  unit costs and, 212
Flow of work, 212–213, **214**
  control of, 198
Foreign corporation, 487–488
Forms registers, 11
Franchises, 405, 406
Full-charge bookkeeper, *def.,* 90

G Gains and losses on sale
    of marketable
  securities account,
  def., 340
General accounting and centralized
  accounting systems, 87–88
General bank account, *def.,* 323
Goodwill, *def.,* 478
Gross earnings, *def.,* 185, **187**
Gross profit
  by departments, 49–54
    income statement and, 53–54
    preparing a statement of, 50
    profit centers and, 49, 51
  on sales, 4, 233

H Home office
    accounts (*see* Decentralized
    accounting system, home office
    accounts)
  closing entries, 105, 106
  computerized processing at
    of purchases and cash payments,
      120–121
    of sales and cash receipts,117–119
  financial statements (*see
    Decentralized accounting
    system, home office financial
    statements*)

Horizontal analysis, 525–527; *def.,*
  525
Hourly-rate pay plan, *def.,* 185

I Idle cash, *def.,* 316
    Imprest cash funds,
  329–335; *def.,* 313
  change funds, 332–333
  petty cash, 329–332
    cash overages or shortages and,
      330
    petty cash register and, 330
    petty cash vouchers and, 330
    replenishing, 330–331
  reporting, 333–334
  sales returns and allowances fund,
    333
Imprinting devices, 11, 12
Income statement(s), *def.,* 448;
  illus., 8
  chain store, 96–98; *illus.,* 97
  as change statement, 552
  combined, 107–108; *def.,* 107;
    illus., 108
    worksheet for, 107–108; *illus.,*
      108
  comparative, 76, 522; *illus.,* 76,
    522 (*see also* Comparison and
    trend analysis)
  computerized, 124; *illus.,* 125
  for corporations, 505–507; *illus.,*
    506
  home office, 100–102; *illus.,* 100
  interpreting a series, 76–79; *illus.,*
    76
  managerial accounting and, 3, 9
  for a manufacturing business,
    284–286; *illus.,* 285
  for a partnership, 471–472; *illus.,*
    471
  for sole proprietorship, 448–450;
    illus., 449
  statement of gross profit by
    departments and, 53–54; *illus.,*
    54
  writing off an account on, 360
Income statement analysis sheet,
  illus., 80
**Income statement by
  departments,** 4, 72–80; *def.,*
  75; *illus.,* 73
  interpreting, 74–75
  a series of, 76–79
  preparing, 72
Incorporators, 484
Indirect expense, *def.,* 58
Indirect labor, *def.,* 168
  job order cost accounting and,
    269–270
  process cost accounting and
    assembling department, 224
    finishing department, 228
    milling department, 218–219
Indirect manufacturing costs (*see*
  Factory overhead)

Indirect materials, *def.,* 168
  job order cost accounting and,
    266–269
  process cost accounting and
    assembling department, 223–224
    finishing department, 227–228
    milling department, 217–218
Insolvency, *def.,* 533
Installment accounts receivable, *def.,*
  134
  controlling, 141–142
  reporting, 142–143
Installment accounts receivable
  ledger, posting to, 139–141;
    illus., 140
Installment contract, *def.,* 131; *illus.,*
  132
Installment sales, 130–150; *def.,* 131
  accounting for, 133–136
  advantages of, 132, 133
  disadvantages of, 133
  down payment and, 131
  features of, 131
  finance charge and, 131
  financing, 147–148
  installment accounts receivable
    and, 134
    controlling, 141–142
    reporting, 142–143
  installment contract and, 131, 132
  installments and, 131
  insurance and, 135
  journalizing, 136–139
    cash received from installments,
      138–139
    down payments, 136, 138
    installment sales, 136, 137
  ownership of goods and, 131
  posting to the installment accounts
    receivable ledger and, 139–141
  reporting, 142
  repossessions and, 143–147
  time period of, 131
Installment sales account, 134
Installments, *def.,* 131
Insurance expense, 65
  voucher system and, 300
Insurance payable account, *def.,* 135
Intangible assets, 405–407; *def.,* 405
  amortization of, 406
  cost of, 405, 406
  examples of, 405
  franchises, 405, 406
  leaseholds, 405
  life of, 406
  patents, 405
Interest
  bond
    accrued, 352–354
      receiving, 353–354
      recording, 337
  bond issue
    contract rates, 435
    effective rates, 435
    setting rates, 435

Interest, bond issue (*continued*)
    sold at a discount, 439–440
    sold at par value, 436
    sold at a premium, 442
  revenue
    accrued, 348–349
    adjusting, 349–350
    recording, 337–339
Interest receivable account, 349–350;
  def., 349
Internal transactions of multistore
  businesses, 92–95
  examples of, 92
  transfers of cash, 92–93
  transfers of merchandise, 93–95
Inventory, *def.,* 313
  bill of materials and, 174–175
  computing merchandise, 44–47
    automated inventory, 46–47
    periodic inventory procedure,
      45–46
    perpetual inventory procedure,
      45
  as current asset (*see* Merchandise
    inventory)
  merchandise (*see* Merchandise
    inventory)
  perpetual inventory procedure (*see*
    Perpetual inventory procedure)
  perpetual inventory records and,
    177
    kinds of, 178
  physical, 45, 180–181, 279
  purchase order and, 175–176
  purchase requisition and, 174
  reorder point and, 173–174
  reorder quantity and, 173–174
  stores department and, 172
  verifying materials, 180–181
Inventory tag, *def.,* 178; *illus.,* 178
  issuing materials and, 180
Investment club, *def.,* 484
Investments, *def.,* 312
Invoices, 32; *illus.,* 32
Issued stock outstanding, 484

 Job cost sheets, *def.,*
  264–265; *illus.,* 265
  completing, 272–273
  open, 265
Job order cost accounting,
  262–290; *def.,* 170, **265**
  financial statements and (*see*
    Manufacturing businesses,
    financial statements for)
  flow of costs, 262–278; *illus.,* 279
    [*see also* Flow of costs (process
    cost accounting)]
    direct and indirect labor and,
      269–270
    direct and indirect materials and,
      266–269
    factory overhead costs and,
      270–271

Job order cost accounting, flow of
  costs (*continued*)
    finished goods and, 273–275
    job cost sheets and, 264–265,
      272–273
Joint products, *def.,* 258
Journalizing installment sales,
  136–139
  cash received from installments,
    138–139
  down payments, 136, 138
Journalizing purchases by
  department, 33–36
  for cash, 33
  on credit, 33–34
  for purchases returns and
    allowances, 38–39
Journalizing sales by department,
  15–19
  cash sales, 15–18
  credit sales, 18–19
  sales returns and allowances,
    22–26
    on cash sales, 23
    on credit sales, 23–24
    posting from, 24–25

K Key-to-cassette device,
  def., 119

L Labor costs
    analysis of, 187, 188
  direct (*see* Direct labor)
  factory, 185–193
  indirect (*see* Indirect labor)
Leaseholds, 405
Liabilities, 413–460; *def.,* 413
  accounts payable, 416–421
    gross method for recording,
      416–418, 420–421
    net method for recording,
      418–421
    purchases discounts lost and, 420
  accrued, 421–426
    interest, 422–425
    salaries, 425–426
  classifying, 414–415, **415**
  contingent, 457
  current, 414–415, **415**
  deferred revenue, 427–429
    adjusting, 428–429
    recording, 427–428
  incurring, 413–414
  limited, 489
  long-term
    bonds (*see* Bonds)
    mortgages, 430, 432–434
  owner's equity and, 413
  single proprietorship and (*see*
    Single proprietorship)
  total, 413
  trading on the equity and, 414
  unlimited, 464

LIFO (last in, first out) method of valuing inventory, 375–376
Limited liability, *def.*, 489
Limited life, *def.*, 464
Line graph, *def.*, 518; *illus.*, 519
Liquidity, *def.*, 313
Loans receivable account, *def.*, 346
Long-term liabilities
  bonds (*see* Bonds)
  mortgages, 430, 432–434
Loss on repossessed merchandise account, *def.*, 145

M Machine hours method of setting overhead rates, 196–197
Managerial accounting, 2–4, 7–11; *def.*, 4
  characteristics of, 7
  cost of goods sold and, 3
  elements of, 3–4
  expense and, 3
  gross profit by departments and, 49–54
    income statement and, 53–54
    preparing a statement of, 50
    profit centers and, 49, 51
  income statement and, 3
  information provided by, 2
  for manufacturing businesses (*see* Cost accounting)
  for merchandising businesses (*see* Merchandising businesses)
  objectives of, 4
  recording data and (*see* Recording purchases data by departments; Recording sales data by departments)
  revenues and, 3
  sales departments and, 3–4
Manufacturing businesses, *def.*, 167
  accounting for (*see* Cost accounting)
  accounts in, 170–171
  acquisition and control of materials and (*see* Materials)
  factory labor costs and, 185–193
  factory overhead costs and (*see* Factory overhead)
  financial statements for, 278–288
    balance sheet, 286
    closing accounts, 286–288
    income statement, 284–286
    perpetual inventory procedures, 278–279
    schedule of cost of goods manufactured, 279–284
    statement of owner's equity, 286
  organization of, 171–172
  production department and, 172
  service department and, 172
  stores department and, 172
Manufacturing overhead (*see* Factory overhead)

Manufacturing process, 167–173; *def.*, 167
  completing the, 203–205
    automated cost accounting procedures and, 205
    flow of costs and, 204–205
  cost accounting and, 168–169 (*see also* Cost accounting)
Manufacturing supplies, *def.*, 168
Market value
  of bonds, 431
  of stocks, 486
Marketable securities, 336–343; *def.*, 313, 336, **336**
  recording investment revenue, 337–339
    bond interest, 337
    interest and dividend revenue, 338
    stock dividends, 337–338
  recording the purchase of, 336–337
  recording sale of, 339–341
    at a gain, 340–341
    at a loss, 339–340
Mass-produced goods, *def.*, 170
Matching revenue and expense, *def.*, **361, 385**
Materials
  accounting for, 182
  direct (*see* Direct materials)
  indirect (*see* Indirect materials)
  issuing, 179–180
  perpetual inventory procedures and, 278
  purchasing, 173–176
    bill of materials and, 175
    purchase order and, 175–176
    purchase requisition and, 174
    reorder point and, 173–174
    reorder quantity and, 173–174
  raw (*see* Direct materials)
  storing, 177–179
    inventory tag and, 178
    perpetual inventory records and, 177
    receiving report and, 177
    stores ledger and, 178
  verifying inventory and, 180–181
Materials account, *def.*, 171
Materials requisition, *def.*, 179–180; *illus.*, 180
Materials requisitions journal, 218; *def.*, 182; *illus.*, 218
Merchandise, transfers of, 93–94
Merchandise inventory, 372–382; *def.*, 372
  computing the cost of, 374
    comparing the methods of, 377–378
    FIFO method, 374–375
    LIFO method, 375–376
    specific identification method, 376
  periodic inventory procedure and, 374

Merchandise inventory (*continued*)
  physical inventory, 374
  procedures for controlling, 373
  retailers and, 373
  verifying the perpetual inventory records and, 374
  wholesalers and, 372–373
Merchandise inventory turnover, 538–540
Merchandising businesses
  managerial accounting for, 2–56 (*see also* COD sales; Credit card sales; Installment sales; Multistore businesses; Operations, summarizing and analyzing the results of)
  organization of, 4–7
    advantages of departmental, 6–7
    ownership and, 5
    types of departments and, 6
    units of operation and, 5–6
  recording data by departments and (*see* Recording purchases data by departments; Recording sales data by departments)
  retailers, 373
  wholesalers, 372–373
Minutes book, 490
Monthly reports, computerized, 123–124
Mortgages, *def.*, 430
  accounting for, 432–434; *illus.*, 432–434
  face value of, 430
Multistore businesses, 83–129; *def.*, 83
  accounting systems of, 83–114
    centralized (*see* Centralized accounting system)
    decentralized (*see* Decentralized accounting system)
    subsystems of, 84
    types of, 84
  computer application for, 115–129
    accounting system and, 115–116
    division of work in, *illus.*, 115
    financial statements and, 124, 125
    merchandising procedures and, 116
    monthly reports and, 123–124
    processing purchases and cash payments, 119–121
    processing sales and cash receipts, 116–119
    weekly reports and, 122–123
Mutual agency, *def.*, 464

N Natural resources, 407–409; *def.*, 312, 407
cost of, 408
depletion of, 408
  recording, 408–409

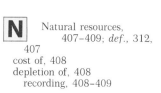

Negotiable notes, *def.*, 344
Net income, 4
  comparing, 76–77
  single proprietorship worksheet
    and, 445, 447; *illus.*, 447
Net loss, 447; *illus.*, 447
  distributing, 479
Net pay, *def.*, 185–186
Net sales, comparing, 77
Net sales method of allocating
    expenses, 59–64
  advertising expense and, 59–61
  cash short and over and, 62
  computation of, *illus.*, 59
  delivery expense and, 62–63
  supplies expense and, 63
  time/space method and, 59–61
  uncollectible accounts expense and,
    61–62
No-par stock, 486
Nonchange statement, *def.*, 552
Noncurrent accounts, 556–557
Nonoperating transactions, 581–582
Notary public, 484
Notes receivable, 344–347
  holder of, 344
  interest-bearing, 346–347
    receiving cash for, 347
  negotiability and, 344
  promissory note, 344
  receiving cash for, 351–352
  recording, 344–346
    exchanging a note receivable for
      an account receivable, 345
    for money loaned to another, 346
    at time of sale, 344–345

Open job order sheet, 265
Operating cycles, 540–541
Operating expenses, *def.*, 57
  direct, 58
  indirect, 58
Operating results ratios, 545–551
  summary of, 549
Operating transactions, 573–581
Operations, summarizing and
    analyzing the results of, 57–82
  **income statement by
    departments** and, 72–80;
    def., **75**
    interpreting, 74–75
    preparing, 72
    interpreting a series of income
      statements and, 76–79; *illus.*,
      76
  methods for allocating expenses to
    departments, 57–72
    advertising expense and, 59–61
    cash short and, 62
    delivery expense and, 62–63
    depreciation expense and, 64
    by equipment used method,
      64–65
    insurance expense and, 65

Operations, methods for allocating
    expenses to departments
    (*continued*)
    by net sales method, 59–64
    payroll taxes expense and, 68
    rent expense and, 66
    salaries expense and, 67
    by salaries method, 67–68
    by space occupied method, 66–67
    supplies expense and, 63–64
    types of operating expenses and,
      58–59
    uncollectible accounts expense
      and, 61–62
    utilities expense and, 66–67
  worksheet for, 69, 70
Optical scanners, 11
Other assets, *def.*, 312
Overhead (*see* Factory overhead)
Owner's equity, *def.*, 413
  statement of (*see* Statement of
    owner's equity)
  trading on the equity and, 414
Owner's equity account, 91
Owner's equity ratio, 544–545
Ownership of businesses, 5

Paid-in capital, 492
Paid-out slip, 23;
  illus., 23
"Paperless" office, 316
Par value, *def.*, 430
  bonds sold at (*see* Bonds, sold at
    par value)
  of stocks, 484, 486
Partial payments and voucher system,
    303–304
Participating preferred stock,
    499–500
Partnership, 461–482; *def.*, 461,
    464
  adjusting entries, 452–454, 474;
    illus., 453
  advantages of, 463–464
  articles of, 461–463
  closing entries, 474–476; *illus.*, 475
  contributions by partners, 464
  disadvantages of, 464
  financial statements for, 470–474
    balance sheet, 473; *illus.*, 473
    income statement, 471–472;
      illus., 471
    statement of partner's equity,
      472–473; *illus.*, 472
    worksheet, 470–471; *illus.*, 470
  special accounting procedures,
    476–480
    admitting a new partner,
      477–479; *illus.*, 478
    distributing a net loss, 479
    goodwill and, 478
    liquidating a partnership,
      479–480
    withdrawal of a partner, 479

Partnership (*continued*)
  starting a, 465–469
    balance sheet and, *illus.*, 468
    recording investments, 466–468;
      illus., 467
Patents, 405
Payroll
  centralized accounting systems and,
    87, 88
  perpetual inventory procedures
    and, 278
  procedures in a factory, 185–186
  taxes, 68, 186, 189–191
  voucher system and, 300
Payroll bank accounts, 323–325
Payroll journal, 186; *illus.*, 187
Payroll register, *def.*, 186
Payroll taxes expense, 68
Periodic inventory procedures, 45–46;
    def., 45; *illus.*, 46
  computing the cost of merchandise
    inventory and, 374
  verifying perpetual inventory
    records and, 374
Perpetual inventory procedure, *def.*,
    45; *illus.*, 45
  cost of goods sold and, 279
  factory overhead and, 279
  factory payroll and, 278
  finished goods and, 279
  materials and, 278
  physical inventory and, 279
  work in process and, 279
  worksheet and, 279, 280
Perpetual inventory records, *def.*, 177
  inventory tag and, 178
  stores ledger and, 178
  verifying, 374
Petty cash, 329–332
  cash overages or shortages and, 330
  replenishing, 330–331
Petty cash register, 330
Petty cash voucher, 291, 299, 330
Physical inventory, 180–181; *def.*, 45
  perpetual inventory and, 279
  verifying, 374
Pie chart, 524–525
Piece-rate pay plan, *def.*, 185
Plant and equipment, 383–404; *def.*,
    312, 383
  allocating the cost of, 384–385
  depreciation of (*see* Depreciation)
  disposing of, 394–401
    discarding, 400–401
    selling, 394–397
    trading, 397–400
  purchase of, 383–384
  subsidiary ledger for, 402–403
Plant and equipment ledger, *def.*, 402
Plant and equipment record, *illus.*, 402
Postclosing trial balance, 454; *illus.*,
    456
Posting
  from cash receipts journal by
    departments, 19, 21

Posting *(continued)*
  to the installment accounts
      receivable ledger, 139–141
  from sales journal by departments,
      19–20
  from sales returns and allowances
      journal by deparments, 24–25
Predetermined overhead rate, *def.*,
    220
Preemptive right, *def.*, 487
Preferred stock, 492
  cumulative, 498–499
  declaring dividends for, 497
  participating, 499–500
  sold at par, 492–493
Premium bonds, 441–443; *def.*, 441;
    illus., 441
  carrying value and, 441
  interest charges and, 442; *illus.*,
      442
Premium stocks, 493, 494
Prepaid expenses, 378–379; *def.*,
    313, 378
  adjusting, 378–379
Prime costs of manufacturing, *def.*,
    169
Private corporations, *def.*, 488
Process cost accounting system,
    def., 170, 211, **214** (*see also* Cost
    of production reports; Equivalent
    units of production; Flow of
    costs)
  computing unit costs and, 212
Processing costs, allocating,
    237–238
Production department, *def.*, 172
Profit, gross
  by departments, 49–54
  on sales, 4, 233
Profit center, *def.*, 49, **51**
Promissory note, *def.*, 344
Proprietorship (*see* Single
    proprietorship)
Public corporations, *def.*, 488
Purchase discounts, 41–42
Purchase order, *def.*, 175–176; *illus.*,
    176
Purchase requisition, *def.*, 174; *illus.*,
    174
Purchases, 33–34
Purchases and cash payments
  centralized accounting systems and,
      86–87
  computerized processing of
      at chain store, 119–120
      at home office, 120–121
Purchases discounts lost, 420
Purchases journal by departments,
    33–34; *illus.*, 34–35
  posting from, 36–38
  proof of, *illus.*, 36
Purchases returns and allowances
  journal of, 39–40; *illus.*, 39
  proof of, *illus.*, 40
  voucher system and, 302–303

 Quantity schedule, 247;
      def., 245; *illus.*, 246
  beginning work-in-process inventory
      and, 254–256
  ending work-in-process inventory
      and, 252–253
Quick assets, *def.*, 534
Quick assets ratio, 534–535

R Ratios, 532–551;
      def., 532
  current position (*see* Current
      position, ratios that measure)
  equity position, 544–545
  operating results, 545–547
  return on net sales, 548–549
Raw materials (*see* Direct materials)
Receiving report, *def.*, 177; *illus.*,
    177
Recording purchases data by
    departments, 30–49
  automated methods of, 44
  computing inventory by
      departments, 44–47
      automated inventory, 46–47
      periodic inventory procedure,
          45–46
      perpetual inventory procedure,
          45
  determining net purchases by
      departments, 42–43
  journalizing by departments,
      33–36
  originating purchases data by
      departments, 32
  posting by departments
      purchases journal and, 36–38
      purchases returns and allowances
          and, 40
  processing purchases data, 30–32
      controlling purchases, 32
      forms and procedures and, 31
      people and, 31–32
  purchase discounts, 41–42
  time-saving manual methods of,
      43–44
  transportation charges, 42
Recording sales data by departments,
    11–30
  automated methods of, 27–28
  journalizing by departments, 15–19
      cash sales, 15–18
      credit sales, 18–19
      sales returns and allowances,
          22–26
  originating sales data by
      departments, 13–15
      cash sales, 14
      coding and, 14
      credit sales, 14–15
      sales slips and, 14–15
  posting by departments, 19–22
      cash receipts journal and, 19, 21
      sales journal and, 19–20

Recording sales data by departments
    (continued)
  processing sales data, 11–13
      controlling sales and, 13
      equipment and, 11–12
      forms and procedures and, 12
      people and, 12–13
  time-saving manual methods of, 27
Registered bonds, *def.*, 432
Rent expense, 66
Reorder point, *def.*, 173–174
Reorder quantity, *def.*, 173–174
Reporting receivables, 135
Reports for management,
    computerized, 122–124; *illus.*,
    123
Repossessed merchandise purchases
    account, 144
Repossessed merchandise sales
    account, *def.*, 147
Repossessions
  recording, 143–146
  selling repossessed merchandise,
      146–147
Responsibility accounting, *def.*, 55
Retailers, *def.*, 373
Retained earnings account, 496
Return on net sales ratio, 548–550
  earnings on each share and, 548
  external comparisons and, 549
  internal comparisons and, 548–549
Return on stockholders' equity ratio,
    546–547
Return on total assets ratio, 545–546
Revenue accounts, home office, 90–91
Revenues, *def.*, 3
  matching expenses and, **361**
  reporting, 3–4

S Salaries expense, 67
      accrued, 425–426;
      illus., 425
  paying, 426; *illus.*, 426
Salaries method of allocating
    expenses, 67–68
  payroll taxes expense and, 68
  salaries expense and, 67
Salary pay plan, *def.*, 185
Sales
  cash (*see* Cash sales)
  COD (*see* COD sales)
  comparing net, 77
  controlling, 13
  credit (*see* Credit sales)
  credit card (*see* Credit card sales)
  determining net, by departments,
      24–25
  of finished goods (*see* Finished
      goods, sale of)
  gross profit on, 4, 233
  installment (*see* Installment sales)
  originating data by departments,
      13–15
  processing data, 11–13

Sales (*continued*)
  recording (*see* Recording sales data by departments)
Sales and cash receipts
  centralized accounting systems and, 85–86
  computerized processing of, 116–119
    at chain store, 117
    at home office, 117–119
Sales data, recording of (*see* Recording sales data by departments)
Sales department, *def.*, 6
Sales journal, 12
  installment sales and, 136
Sales journal by departments, 18–19; *def.*, 18; *illus.*, 19
  posting from, 19–20
  proof of, *illus.*, 20
Sales returns and allowances by departments, 22–24
  on cash sales, 23
  on credit sales, 23–24
Sales returns and allowances fund, *def.*, 333
Sales returns and allowances journal by departments, *illus.*, 24
  credit sales and, 22–24
  posting from, 24–26
    determining net sales by departments and, 24–26
  proof of, *illus.*, 24
Sales slip, 12; *illus.*, 15, 18
  journalizing credit sales and, 18
  originating sales data and, 14–15
Salesclerk productivity, comparing, 78
Schedule of cost of goods sold, *def.*, 448
  chain store, 96–97
  combined, *illus.*, 109
  home office, 100, 101
  for single proprietorship, 448; *illus.*, 448
Schedule of cost of goods sold by departments, *def.*, 30; *illus.*, 30
Schedule of unpaid vouchers, 306–307
Schedule of vouchers payable, 302–306
Secured bonds, *def.*, 431
Serial bonds, *def.*, 432
Service businesses, 3
Service department, *def.*, 172
Shipping charge, *def.*, 152
Short-term receivables, *def.*, 313 (*see also* Accounts receivable; Accrued interest revenue; Notes receivable)
Single proprietorship, 444–457
  adjusting entries, 452–454; *illus.*, 453
  closing entries, 454; *illus.*, 455

Single proprietorship (*continued*)
  contingent liabilities, 457
  financial statements for, 447–452
    balance sheet, 450; *illus.*, 450
    income statement, 448–450; *illus.*, 449
    schedule of cost of goods sold, 448; *illus.*, 448
    statement of owner's equity, 450, 452; *illus.*, 450
    postclosing trial balance, 454; *illus.*, 456
    worksheet for, 444–447; *illus.*, 446–447
      adjusted trial balance section, 445
      adjustments section, 444–445
      balance sheet section, 445
      income statement section, 445
      net income and, 445–447; *illus.*, 447
      net loss and, 447; *illus.*, 447
      unadjusted trial balance section, 444
Sinking fund, bond, *def.*, 436–437
  trustee of, 437
Solvency, *def.*, 533
Space occupied method of allocating expenses, 66–67
  rent expense and, 66
  utilities expense and, 66
Special bank account, 323–327; *def.*, 323
Special general bank accounts, 326–327
Special journals, 26
Specific identification method of valuing inventory, 376
Stated value of stock, 511
Statement of changes in financial position, 551–570; *def.*, 553; *illus.*, 552
  steps in preparing, 555–568
  transactions that affect working capital and, 554–555
Statement of gross profit by departments, *def.*, 50
Statement of owner's equity, *def.*, 450
  combined, *illus.*, 111
  home office, 102–103; *illus.*, 102
  for a manufacturing business, 286; *illus.*, 287
  for sole proprietorship, 450, 452; *illus.*, 450
Statement of partner's equity, 472–473; *def.*, **473**; *illus.*, 472
Statement of stockholders' equity, 486, 507–509; *def.*, **508**; *illus.*, 508
  as change statement, 552
  comparative, 522; *illus.*, 523 (*see also* Comparison and trend analysis)

Statements, financial, *def.*, **473**
  (*see also* Corporations; Manufacturing businesses; Partnership; Single proprietorship; *specific statements*)
Stock certificate, 484; *illus.*, 486
Stock certificate book, 495
Stock dividends, 499
Stock subscription, 512
Stockbroker, 489
Stockholders, 484–487
  features of a corporation and, 488–491
  record of stocks owned by, 495
  rights of, 486–487
  statement of equity of, 486, 507–509
Stockholders' equity, 508
  return on, 546–547
Stockholders' ledger, 495
Stockholders of record, 496
Stocks, 492–500
  authorized, 484
  capital, 492
  common (*see* Common stock)
  cumulative preferred, 498–499
  dividends of (*see* Dividends)
  issued stock outstanding, 484
  market value of, 486
  no-par, 486, 511
  paid-in capital and, 492
  par value of, 484, 486
  participating preferred, 499–500
  preferred, 492
    sold at par, 492–493
    sold at a discount, 493–495
    sold at a premium, 493–494
    stated value of, 511
    stock splits, 495
    stockholders' records, 495
    treasury, 511
Stores department, *def.*, 172
Stores ledger, *def.*, 178; *illus.*, 178
Stores ledger card, 216–217
Straight-line method of depreciation, *def.*, 385–386
  compared to accelerated method, 389–390
Subchapter S corporations, 512
Sum-of-the-year's-digits method of depreciation, 387–388; *def.*, 387
  compared with other methods, 389
Supplies expense, 63
  voucher system and, 299
Supportive department, *def.*, 6
  comparing expenses for, 78–79

T Tag printer, *def.*, 120
  Tag reader, 14; *def.*, 117
Taxes
  corporate, 491, 503–504
  double, 491
  payroll, 186, 189–191

Time cards, *def.*, 185
Time clocks, *def.*, 185
Time/space method of allocating
  advertising expenses, 59–61
Time ticket, 185; *def.*, 186–187;
  illus., 187
Total liabilities, *def.*, 413
Trading on the equity, *def.*, 414
Transportation expense on returned
  COD goods account, *def.*, 157;
  illus., 157
Transportation on sales account, *def.*,
  152
Treasury stock, 511
Trend, *def.*, 515
Trend analysis, *def.*, 517; *illus.*, 518
  (*see also* Comparison and trend
  analysis)
Trend percentage analysis, 520–521
Trustee, *def.*, 437

U Uncollectible accounts,
  358–372; *def.*, 358
  allowance method of recording,
    362–363; *def.*, 359
  collection of, 370–371
  contra accounts and, 362–363
  direct write-off method of
    recording, 359–361; *def.*, 359
    balance sheet and, 361
    income statement and, 360
  as doubtful accounts expense,
    61–62
  estimating expenses for, 364–366
    percent of accounts receivable,
      364
    percent of aged accounts
      receivable, 364–365
    percent of net sales, 364
  realizable value of accounts
    receivable and, 358
  recording the estimate for,
    366–368
    percent of accounts receivable,
      366–367
    percent of aged accounts
      receivable, 367–368

Uncollectible accounts, recording the
  estimate for (*continued*)
    percent of net sales, 366
  recording expenses, 368–371
Underwriter, *def.*, 435
Underwriter's fees, 435
Unit cost, *def.*, 212
Unit of operation, 5–6; *def.*, 5
Units of production method of setting
  overhead rates, 197–198
Unlimited liabilitiy, *def.*, 464
Unpaid vouchers file, *def.*, 292
  schedule of, 306–307
Unsecured bonds, *def.*, 431
Unsecured open account, *def.*,
  355–356
Utilities expense, 66

V Variable overhead costs,
  def., 194–195
Vertical analysis, 521–525; *def.*, 521
Vote by proxy, 486
Voucher, *def.*, 291, 294
Voucher jacket, *def.*, 292
Voucher payable account, *def.*, 292
  schedule of, 302–306
Voucher payroll checks, *def.*, 186
Voucher register, *def.*, 182, 292
  posting from, 300–301
Voucher system, 291–309; *def.*, 291
  features of, 291–292
  paying the voucher, 301
  posting
    from the check register, 301–302
    from the voucher register,
      300–301
  preparing the voucher, 294–296
  recording, 296–298
  recording the types of transactions
    298–300
    equipment, 300
    insurance, 300
    notes payable, 300
    payroll, 300
    petty cash, 299
    supplies, 299
  schedule of unpaid vouchers,
    306–307

Voucher system (*continued*)
  schedule of vouchers payable,
    302–306
  special accounting problems and,
    302–306
    correcting errors, 304–306
    partial payments, 303–304
    purchases returns and
      allowances, 302–303
  verifying the invoice, 292–294
  voucher forms, 292

W Weekly reports,
  computerized,
  122–123; *illus.*, 123
Wholesalers, *def.*, 372–373
Work-in-process account, *def.*, 171
  perpetual inventory procedures
    and, 279
  process cost accounting and
    assembling department, 225–226
    finishing department, 229–231
    milling department, 220–221
Work-in-process inventory (*see*
  Beginning work-in-process
  inventory; Ending
  work-in-process inventory)
Working capital, *def.*, 533, **534**
  net decrease in, 554
  net increase in, 554
  source of, 554
  statement of changes in financial
    position and, 551–570
  transactions that affect, 554–555
  use of, 554
Working capital ratio, 533
Worksheet
  for combined financial statements,
    107–110; *illus.*, 108, 109
  for corporations, 502–505; *illus.*,
    504
  for partnership, 470–471; *illus.*,
    470
  for single proprietorship, 444–447;
    illus., 446–447
Writing off an account, *def.*, 359
  reversal of, 370–371